Riccardo Freda

ALSO BY ROBERTO CURTI
AND FROM McFARLAND

Italian Gothic Horror Films, 1970–1979 (2017)
Tonino Valerii: The Films (2016)
Italian Gothic Horror Films, 1957–1969 (2015)
Italian Crime Filmography, 1968–1980 (2013)

Riccardo Freda

The Life and Works of a Born Filmmaker

ROBERTO CURTI

McFarland & Company, Inc., Publishers
Jefferson, North Carolina

LIBRARY OF CONGRESS CATALOGUING-IN-PUBLICATION DATA

Names: Curti, Roberto, 1971– author.
Title: Riccardo Freda : the life and works of a born filmmaker / Roberto Curti.
Description: Jefferson, North Carolina : McFarland & Company, Inc., Publishers, 2017. | Includes bibliographical references and index.
Identifiers: LCCN 2017006357 | ISBN 9781476669700 (softcover : acid free paper) ∞
Subjects: LCSH: Freda, Riccardo. | Motion picture producers and directors—Italy—Biography.
Classification: LCC PN1998.3.F7454 C87 2017 | DDC 791.4302/33092 [B] —dc23
LC record available at https://lccn.loc.gov/2017006357

BRITISH LIBRARY CATALOGUING DATA ARE AVAILABLE

ISBN (print) 978-1-4766-6970-0
ISBN (ebook) 978-1-4766-2838-7

© 2017 Roberto Curti. All rights reserved

No part of this book may be reproduced or transmitted in any form or by any means, electronic or mechanical, including photocopying or recording, or by any information storage and retrieval system, without permission in writing from the publisher.

Front cover fogli manifesto for *Il conte Ugolino*, 1949

Printed in the United States of America

McFarland & Company, Inc., Publishers
Box 611, Jefferson, North Carolina 28640
www.mcfarlandpub.com

A Nicola,
il mio più caro amico.
In memoriam.

Acknowledgments

First and foremost, my most sincere gratitude goes to Jacqueline and Guislaine Freda, who were willing to discuss their father's life and career and provided invaluable information. Thanks also to Enzo Boetani, Stephen Forsyth, Ernesto Gastaldi, Brett Halsey, Alfredo Leone, Michael Maien and Stefano Patrizi, who kindly agreed to discuss their work with Freda; the renowned Italian film critics and historians Paolo Mereghetti and Roberto Poppi, who kindly helped me gather precious production information; Trinidad Del Rio and Eduardo Sastre at the Filmoteca Española in Madrid, who gracefully helped my research on the director; Alessio Di Rocco and Stefano Raffaele, who provided ministerial papers for some of Freda's unfilmed projects; Gianni Vitale, who kindly shared his memories about the period Freda spent in Padua, teaching at the Promovies film school; Fábio Vellozo (Cinemateca do MAM in Rio de Janeiro) and Marco Antonio Santos Freitas, for their help on Freda's Brazilian period; Brazilian film critic and historian João Carlos Rodrigues, who kindly sent me a copy of Freda's elusive *Um caçula do barulho*; fellow McFarland author David C. Tucker, who thoroughly proofread the manuscript; Steve Fenton, who helped polishing the images; Uwe Hüber, who kindly helped me contact Michael Maien and Erwin C. Dietrich and provided further useful information on Freda's German films.

I am also deeply grateful to the following, who in one way or the other provided vital contribution to this book: Lucas Balbo, Ron Campbell, Davide Cavaciocchi, Francesco Cesari, Luigi Cozzi, Sergio Donati, Adv. Paolo Dondina, Sir Christopher Frayling, Marcello Garofalo, Troy Howarth, Peter Jilmstad, Frank Lafond, Emanuele Leotta, Stefano Loparco, Antonio Marchesani, Domenico Monetti, Alain Petit, Alberto Pezzotta, Pietro Reggiani, Steven Smith, Pete Tombs, Gary Vanisian. And, last but not least, Carme Tierz and Antonio José Navarro, for being such wonderful friends, and my beloved wife Cristina, for every single moment spent together.

Table of Contents

Acknowledgments — vi
Introduction — 1

1. A Portrait of the Filmmaker as a Young Man — 13
2. Learning the Craft — 20
3. Filming During Wartime — 31
4. Adventure, Italian-style — 45
5. Brazil … and Back — 65
6. Under the Sign of Melodrama — 84
7. Historia Magistra Vitae — 99
8. Diving into Genres — 126
9. Exploring the Myth — 147
10. Intermezzo—A Director for Hire — 168
11. The Gothic Years — 177
12. In Exile — 206
13. A Sort of Homecoming — 230
14. The Twilight Years — 259

Epilogue — 279
Filmography — 289
Chapter Notes — 331
Essential Bibliography — 351
Index — 353

Introduction

Either one is born a director or he'll never become one.[1]

"I believe I was born to be a film director," Riccardo Freda wrote in his autobiography, *Divoratori di celluloide*. He was right. In the history of Italian cinema, Freda has been one of the few authentic natural born filmmakers, in the purest sense of the word. He often had to deal with low budgets, bad screenplays and lousy actors, and more than once he simply did not care about any of these, because he could make movies as easy as he could breathe. "Give me one week, and I'll make you an Antonioni film. Do you want to take the bet?" he once facetiously challenged (or maybe not) his interviewer, a young Bertrand Tavernier.[2]

The assertion is significant from a number of perspectives. First, it stresses Freda's speed: he could indeed knock out a movie in two weeks, if he wanted to. And he did. There are several well-known anecdotes, and the director himself often delighted in touting his ability to wrap up a picture in a short shooting period, while at the same time underlining his technical skills. Freda would halt at nothing to make a film—going so far as replacing his leading actor with a double, if necessity called. "The ideal would be to put the reel of film in the camera, call 'Action' and never stop!"[3]

Second, the Antonioni reference. The aforementioned interview dated from 1963, at a time where Antonioni was at his commercial and critical peak, after such works as *L'avventura* (1960) and *L'eclisse* (a.k.a. *Eclipse*, 1962). Dismissing his work so sharply was gutsy. Freda's tastes were quite clear from his own works, and he was usually very vocal about them. He was also adamant when it came to mentioning what directors and films he did *not* like. His gargantuan self esteem was paired with a scarce consideration toward many of his peers, both behind and in front of the camera. It was part of his temper, so notoriously choleric that his attitude during filming sometimes led to heated arguments and his walking off the set.

Third, the bet. Freda loved to bet, in cinema and in life. He liked gambling, expensive houses, fancy cars and works of art, and courting beautiful women. He was very rich at a certain point in his life. To paraphrase a famous George Best quote, he spent a lot of money on gambling, ladies and fast cars—the rest, he just squandered. He was very self-conscious and cynical about such an attitude: "It's my worst films that bring me the most of my royalties," he said.[4]

For these and other reasons, Riccardo Freda was a paradox. Or, to quote his friend, colleague and collaborator Yves Boisset, he was "one of the great mysteries in cinema history."[5] As technically proficient as anyone, he made a number of quite good films and some extraordinary ones, with several box-office hits and very few flops. But he was never considered an *auteur* in his home country until his later years. Italian critics barely recognized the spectacular and technical values of his works, and dismissed them as mere entertainment for the masses. Needless to say, the lack of feeling was reciprocated. As he put it himself, he was too American for the Italians, and too Italian to make movies in America.[6]

Freda's collaborators and those who worked in the business had quite a different opinion of him as a director.

> Freda made beautiful period films which, among other things, were appreciated in the right measure in France whereas not so much over here. I have been a good friend of his and held him in esteem. I can just say that Freda's fault was not to have Visconti's luck. He was very intelligent, and very good, with an enormous sensibility; unfortunately he lacked that bit of luck you always need in life. The fact that he did not reach Visconti's level depends only from this specific deficiency.[7]

These words came from Goffredo Lombardo, the head of Titanus, one of Italy's greatest film companies, and the producer of Visconti's *Rocco e i suoi fratelli* (a.k.a. *Rocco and His Brothers*, 1960) and *Il gattopardo* (a.k.a. *The Leopard*, 1963).

French film critic Jacques Lourcelles synthesized Freda's nature by pointing out the director's "duplicitous tendency toward enthusiasm on one hand, and his cynicism and disenchanted sneer on the other."[8] An unlikely balance of opposites that allowed him on the one hand to dream and make movies based on adventure and spectacle that would give Italian cinema that sense of greatness it lacked, and on the other brought him not only to darker territories such as the horror film, but also characterized his time-saving methods, work-for-hire choices and ultimately his downward spiral in the Italian film industry.

So, if Riccardo Freda was born to be a filmmaker, chances are that he was not born in the right country—which might seem a contradiction since he was actually born in Egypt, to a wealthy Italian family. And his Egyptian childhood years were actually more formative for his vision of cinema than his apprenticeship in the Italian film business. In Egypt, as a child, he learned to love movies, watching them in theaters packed full with people of all social classes, and witnessing the absolute enthusiasm and participation of the filmgoers, who lived each film as a cathartic physical experience, as if the story was really happening before their eyes. That shaped his will to make movies that would thrill the audience. "I don't care about cold films, literary films, films that lack participation, films that do not take the audience into account. Those I wanted to make are films that the crowd takes part in, films that are able to arouse it."[9]

Which he did.

"Righteous characters are sad"[10]

When he wrote the first complete retrospective essay on the director, in the Spring 1963 issue of the magazine *Présence du cinéma*, Jacques Lourcelles chose the title "Un homme seul." A man alone. That's what Freda was, indeed. He was alone in waving the flag of a spectacle-based, artistically self-confident popular cinema (which is something very different from the low-budget genre flicks that caught on by the late '50s), and he was alone in the later phases of his career, when his approach to the genres and filmmaking became more sparse and idiosyncratic. He was alone compared to the majority of his colleagues, as he bluntly refused the Italian way of being everybody's friend, and on the contrary consistently spat acid on those filmmakers whose work and attitude he just could not stand.

In Italy, Freda had to fight to shape a vision which no one else seemed to share, the idea of a cinema which would rival Hollywood's. A man with "an anticonformist vocation of researcher, of pioneer, of conqueror," as Jean-Marie Sabatier put it,[11] who made swashbucklers at a time when filmmakers explored the misery of post-war Italy through the lens of Neorealism, and who rediscovered the epicness of the sword-and-sandal genre while his peers were busy making harmless comedies about "bread, love and dreams," to quote the title of Luigi Comencini's *Pane, amore e fantasia* (1953). Last but not least, he invented the Italian horror film out of the blue with

Riccardo Freda on the set of *I Vampiri*.

I vampiri (1957), paving the way to the works of Bava, Ferroni, Margheriti, Argento and unleashing the darker, hidden side of Italian cinema.

Had he been born in the United States, Freda would have found a proper environment for his films. The French critics, the first to praise his work, labeled him "the European Raoul Walsh,"[12] and he was adamant in stating that, to him, there would be no competition between Walsh and Ingmar Bergman: the former breathed cinema, the latter did not.[13] Still, and herein lies yet another paradox, for all its limitations, working in the Italian film industry allowed Freda a freedom that he would not have had overseas, where his unbridled creativity and brilliancy at troubleshooting would be crushed by the suffocating gears of the U.S. studio system. The director himself was well aware of it, and he was just as sharp-tongued about the American filmmakers he had worked with, underlining their shortcomings and incapability of "seeing" a scene. Presumptuous? Certainly. Harsh? No doubt about it. Sincere? Absolutely. As Italian film historian Stefano Della Casa pointed out, "such an uneasy character, a genius so deeply convinced of his own idea of filmmaking and so unwilling to maintain good neighborly relations could only be seen as an foreign object, if not even as an enemy, by critics who were deeply conditioned by the Neorealist experience."[14]

Freda was a man alone in life as well, from what we can gather. Not a lonely man, but a loner: his friendships, selected and cultivated, were usually outside the shallow and hypocritical film business. Of all the producers he worked with, he had kind words for Riccardo Gualino and Ermanno Donati: with the latter, he used to pal around outside the set as well, despite the many arguments they had during their collaboration, whereas Gualino—the head of the powerful Lux Film—was another rare bird, one of the few cultured figures in the film industry, an intellectual with whom he could discuss literature and art. For the rest, rather than waste time with his peers, he would more gladly spend it in the company of his beloved dogs and horses.

Even more significant are Freda's longtime friendships with two outsiders such as Panfilo Gentile (1889–1971) and Leo Longanesi (1905–1957). Gentile, a philosopher, journalist and politician, was always a fervent opponent of mass regimes, starting with Fascism. His book *Democrazie mafiose* argued that all democracies are basically Mafia, since they are ruled by demagogic élites that captivate the masses only to tenaciously preserve the power for their own profit. A loner as well, indeed.

Longanesi, on the other hand, was a born contrarian: a brilliant journalist, painter and drawing artist whose nonconformity had gained him hatred from each and every political faction. Despite being a Fascist sympathizer, he used to poke fun at Mussolini and his dictatorship in the satirical magazine *L'italiano*. "Totalitarian regimes do not allow jokes but they have the involuntary merit of arousing them. During the big liberal black-outs, the spirit, the taste of comedy, the irony languish. Satire is much more effective when it is directed against intolerant regimes,"[15] he wrote. After the fall of Fascism, Longanesi was recruited by the Allied troops to make Anti-fascist propaganda on the radio program *Stella bianca*, together with Freda, scriptwriter Stefano Vanzina (better known as Steno) and writer-cum-director Mario Soldati, but his disillusionment was soon evident: "Italy is a democracy in which a third of the citizens regret the past dictatorship, the other third await the Soviet era and the remaining ones are willing to adapt to the next Democratic Christian regime," he quipped. His criticism toward the flooding conformism culminated in the creation of the controversial magazine *Il Borghese*, in 1950, whose habit of criticizing both the left and the right soon had Longanesi surrounded by enemies, even—or rather, especially—among friends.

In many ways, Freda was just like Longanesi. He could be so sharp with words as to destroy somebody with a one-line epigram, and would pay no special favors to anyone. And, like Longanesi, he would eventually find himself isolated, within a film industry where his character, work, opinions, and skills as a filmmaker had been barely tolerated when he was commercially successful, then were merely exploited and eventually ignored, in the declining part of his career ... and of Italian genre cinema as well.

Above all, Riccardo Freda was an individualist, like the heroes in his favorite films. He looked at politics and organized religion, the foundation of organized societies, with barely dissimulated annoyance. Rather than give himself up into the arms of a political leader or a deity, he'd rather give a chance to the unpredictable, and therefore more respectable, unknown forces of magic. This reflected in his vision of movie heroes. "The banal man, the everyday man, I'm not the least bit interested in them. I'm cynical about that. I don't care about them in real life either. I'm interested in heroes.... I'm interested in the space explorer, not in the guy who built the starship on which the former travels."[16]

Freda's love for heroics on screen can as well be seen as the counterpart of his disillusionment, if not utter disdain, toward human nature in real life. Even though his view on the Fascist regime is debatable at times, as he lived through it from a privileged position, it contains sharp-as-nails observations. One of his favorite targets was Nicola De Pirro, the General Manager of Cinematography in the post–World War II years, who had been a Fascist hierarch during the regime—the kind of obtuse-minded, grey bureaucrat who represented the qualities Freda despised so much. The tragicomic traits of Fascism, the intellectuals' submission to the dictatorship and their opportunism in shedding skin and changing sides whenever the wind blew in one direction or another, all but heightened his basic contempt toward society as opposed to the single man's will. This is patent in his films, centered on solitary figures who fight social order and the authority with all their will, or take on heroic challenges, counting solely on their will: take Prince Dubrovsky (*Aquila nera*, 1946; *La vendetta di Aquila Nera*, 1951), Casanova (*Il cavaliere misterioso*, 1948), Count Ugolino della Gherardesca (*Il conte Ugolino*, 1949), D'Artagnan's son Raoul (*Il figlio di d'Artagnan*, 1950), Spartacus the gladiator (*Spartaco*, 1953), Jason (*I giganti della Tessaglia*, 1960), Maciste (*Maciste alla corte del Gran Khan*, 1961; *Maciste all'inferno*, 1962), Benvenuto Cellini (*Il magnifico avventuriero*, 1963). Even characters that belong to a different context, such as Jean Valjean (*I miserabili*, 1948) and Roger Laroque (*Roger la Honte*, 1966), are reshaped accordingly.

But in Freda's cinema there is also room for unforgettable female portraits, such as the eponymous heroines in *Teodora* (1954) and *Beatrice Cenci* (1956), two of his very best efforts. Freda loved women very much and had a troubled personal life. "Women took my fortune and my illusions," he once admitted. A bitterly ironic passage in his memoir recounts when the director came back to Rome after the end of the war, in 1945, only to find his house at Trinità dei Monti occupied by Yugoslavian soldiers, and discovering that his wife Angiola Dondina had become the lover of the platoon's commander. They never divorced, though, and after Dondina's untimely death Freda was officially a widower. The great love of his life was actress Gianna Maria Canale, much younger than him and possibly the most beautiful woman in Italian cinema of the 1950s. They were a couple for a decade, and worked together in 12 films, from *Il cavaliere misterioso* to *I vampiri*. The split with Canale was quite painful, according to those who knew the director.[17] Later on Freda met a younger woman, Silvana Merli (1939–2000), with whom he moved to France in 1963. She gave him two daughters: Jacqueline, born in 1963, and Guislaine, born in 1965. Silvana—whom he eventually married in 1996—was a key presence in his life, albeit an often overlooked one, and had a significant impact on his profession. Freda himself never talked about it, and it is thanks to the recollections of Jacqueline and Guislaine Freda that the curtain on an obscure period in the director's career, between the gory Gothic horror *Estratto dagli archivi segreti della polizia di una capitale europea* (1972) and the swan song *Murder Obsession* (1981) can be finally raised. More on that later.

Divoratori di celluloide opens with an enigmatic, tragic and ultimately unforgettable episode which blends in equal parts cynicism, romanticism, and an inner core of fatalism—plus a taste for the detail that only a real aesthete could have. The director notices a beautiful young girl buying a rose, only one single scarlet rose, in Rome's via Veneto. She turns to him; their eyes meet. Not a word is spoken. Irresistibly attracted to the woman, but at the same time too timid to attempt an approach, Freda begins to follow her. She turns back again and smiles at him "with the same smile, a bit Leonardo-like," before crossing the road and disappearing behind the door of a boardinghouse. He is baffled: was that smile an erotic invitation? An act of coquetry? A self-pleased statement? The next day, Freda reads in the newspaper that the girl committed suicide, throwing herself from her room's window with the rose in her hands. She had been promised a role in exchange for sexual favors by a film director who then went back on his word. Freda concludes: "Had I addressed to her, had I distracted her, had I promised too a role, keeping my word as I have always done, maybe that beautiful girl would not have died in that dark courtyard, with a rose not so boldly red amid so much blood."[18]

Whether the result of memory or invention, the anecdote conveys perfectly Freda's world view, and at the same time it has all the traits of his best work. It functions at a purely visual level, with its colorful details (the red rose, like the one Klaus Kinski squeezes in his hands in *A doppia faccia*, 1969), the reference to Renaissance art (the smile that recalls Leonardo Da Vinci's paintings), the element of mystery, the Grand-Guignol, and the fatal twist ending. And it also conveys a vision of woman as a mysterious, ever-changing universe, impossible to decipher and yet irresistible—and at the same time doomed to abuse and desecration on the part of the stronger sex.

"Cinema is action, emotion, tension, velocity"[19]

Jacques Lourcelles labeled Freda "one of the great aesthetes in the history of cinema,"[20] and fellow director Vittorio Cottafavi called him "a master of the image, a remarkable painter."[21] It would take just a passing look at the opening of *Beatrice Cenci* or the climactic scenes in *Teodora* to second those statements. His artistic sensibility and his apprenticeship as a sculptor were vital in forming his style as a filmmaker. He used to reiterate that there is only one camera angle, one set-up for each scene, and a natural born director *has* to know it. Leonardo knew it when he painted *The Last Supper*, as did John Ford when he shot *My Darling Clementine* (1946). Therefore, to Freda, film is essentially a visual art. "The picture is mute and visual. Sound, which in fact was stitched to it much later, must be a complement, albeit at times an extraordinary one, yet always secondary to the power of the image."[22] Which partly explains why he never cared much about the dialogue, even when he was making a film based on a Shakespeare play, and preferred to use sound and music as a nuance to best highlight the visual canvas.

Such a vision is also inherently coherent with Freda's view of the world. Like his heroes, a filmmaker is ultimately a man alone, in victory and in defeat. To him, the only thing that prevented cinema from being a complete art form was collaboration, whereas a sculptor, or a painter, is alone throughout all the creation phases: in his ideal view, the director alone would have to take up all the artistic duties, including scriptwriting, lighting, editing.

> What art there can be when a movie is the product of more brains—when there are brains—and it is a strange mixture of ideas, musical notes, lights and shadows, and therefore the work of many individuals, sometimes very different in culture, taste, artistic sensibility, social background?[23]

One of the most beautiful scenes in Freda's *oeuvre* is the ending of *Il magnifico avventuriero*, where Benvenuto Cellini is in the throes of a creative bout while making his most famous statue, the Perseus with the Head of Medusa. Here, the identification between the director and the protagonist is complete: Cellini's artistic feat is equated in all respects to a heroic act, and his creative fury is the same that most likely pervaded Freda while piling up shot after shot, in a feverish trance. If in *Pierrot le Fou* (1965) Godard had Samuel Fuller say that film is like a battleground, to Freda it was like a rough block of marble waiting to be shaped into form—as fast as possible. "The faster you go, the closer you follow inspiration. Cinema is action for a filmmaker as well."[24]

To Freda, cinema was all about challenge and discovery. Challenge, as seen earlier, was first and foremost in the act of making a motion picture itself. He considered cinema as the most challenging form of spectacle, because it had the means to portray what others could not. "The ideal would be ... to film the Bible, for instance The Creation. The world takes shape, life appears, the huge prehistoric animals. All that you can't express with another form of spectacle," he explained. "Because you can paint the Creation, but the result will be a motionless canvas. Stravinsky did something similar with music, with *The Rite of Spring*, which is an extraordinary musical piece, but lacks the image. With literature, it is the same. So, all this, all you can't express with another art form, to me is the ideal cinema."[25] What is more, his favorite stories were centered on a challenge that Freda's heroes would face—against a sworn enemy, a collective plot, or even a supernatural menace. His films were themselves an act of challenge, a gauntlet to the dominant Neorealist vision he so utterly despised. And he maintained such a vision throughout his life.[26]

Discovery, in Freda's films, similarly pertains to the visuals and the narrative alike. The director's favorite stylistic device, the sideways tracking shot, is essential to understand such a notion. To him, such a movement is "the instrument to discover, one after another, things, objects or people, placed in a way as to surprise, affect or move the viewer."[27] Visual discovery was the basic means to convey a sense of wonder in the audience and create a compelling, dynamic spectacle:

> The secret of movies is the progressive disclosure of the *décor*, of the world surrounding the characters. The image must be a continuous surprise for the eyes. The camera must never reveal a scene all of a sudden in its entirety, but have the viewers find out about it slowly, and progressively uncover its beauty.[28]

Discovery is also a vital element to the story itself, as the cinematic narrative must follow a linear process of discovering. Will Dubrovsky beat his enemy? Will Valjean escape his sworn enemy Javert? Will Casanova defeat the conspiracy against his country and save his brother? Will Maciste rescue the poor girl who is about to be burnt at the stake as a witch? Will Cynthia escape her diabolical husband, Dr. Hichcock? To put it shortly, Freda's cinema is, as Lourcelles put it, "naturally spectacular," since "every human relationship in it is solved in spatial terms."[29]

At first, such a process is charged with a positive meaning. Challenge and discovery take the form of journeys in space and time (*I miserabili*'s spawning narrative arc encompasses more than two decades) and culminate in a satisfactory denouement: order is reestablished and life can start again on a new beginning, in a circular process that often finds its visual representation in a symmetrical camera movement: take the opening and ending of the Neapolitan melodrama *Vedi Napoli e poi muori* (1952). The narratives are a recurring pattern, like a still life or Christ's deposition from the cross for a painter. Psychologies are minimal, and must be so, because, in the director's own words, "The audience does not give a damn about the villain's childhood negative experiences. They simply want film characters to be clearly divided, with the hero on one side and the scoundrel on the other."[30] Still, such a faith in the classical rules of narration is continually undermined by Freda's own pessimism: Casanova succeeds, but we see him leave alone, mournful after the death of his beloved (*Il cavaliere misterioso*); Valjean saves his daughter's reputation, but is treacherously killed in the process (*I miserabili*); Count Ugolino's name is cleared too late, after he has succumbed to a horrible and fatal punishment (*Il conte Ugolino*)…

Similarly, Freda's own challenge was doomed to defeat. Even though *Aquila nera* topped the box-office in 1946 and the director's following works were produced by the prestigious Lux Film, he never managed to fully achieved what he hoped for. The ever-changing texture and landscape of popular cinema proved too unstable: a few years after the period adventure drama craze, audiences were crowding to see tearjerking melodramas set in the present day. Freda obliged with variable results, the best being the *film noir*-tinged *Il tradimento (Passato che uccide)* (1951), and again in the early 1950s he seemed to find his ideal environment in the *peplum*, with such ambitious productions as *Spartaco* and *Teodora*. But the undercurrents of the national film industry were in turmoil, and by the end of the 1950s he had adapted once and for good to genre filmmaking—this time without any hope of topping the box-office, but struggling in the realm of the ever-growing flood of B-pictures that were being churned out in Cinecittà at breakneck pace.

"I keep trying to make … very imaginative films, and nothing else"[31]

From the mid–1950s onwards, Freda's filmography became bleaker and bleaker. The stories were more intimate, and touched such scabrous topics as incest (*Beatrice Cenci*), vampirism (*I vampiri*), and necrophilia (*L'orribile segreto del Dr. Hichcock*). The "very human sadism" which, according to his colleague Vittorio Cottafavi,[32] imbued his films, came to the fore. The dark side of the human condition took center stage, more prominently in his outstanding Gothic diptych formed by *L'orribile segreto del Dr. Hichcock* (1962) and *Lo spettro* (1963), but it crept under the surface of apparently more amiable works such as *Caccia all'uomo* (1961).

Partly, it was the logical consequence of the changing nature of genre cinema, which was accommodating a more complex spectrum of elements, with an emphasis on violence, morbidity, eroticism. But there was more. Freda's attitude toward filmmaking grew more and more disillusioned. The turning point is perhaps *Beatrice Cenci*, his most ambitious film to date and possibly his masterpiece, whose disappointing box-office performance resulted in the director descending into the realm of B-cinema and trying his hand at various genres: sword-and-sandal, horror, Western, crime films and *gialli*. Significantly, after *Beatrice Cenci* Freda helmed two low-budget films under tight if not difficult production circumstances. And it matters little that *I vampiri* was one of his most impressive efforts while his next movie *Agguato a Tangeri* (1957) was one of the least interesting: the feeling that both pictures exude is that, while the Italian film industry was experiencing the first taste of the commercially fruitful genre production which would characterize the following decade, Freda—who had paved the way with his work in popular cinema—hardly managed to grasp the bandwagon.

Even though *I vampiri* did start the Gothic horror thread, its nondescript box-office gross proved another disappointment, while Freda's take on science fiction with *Caltiki il mostro immortale* (1959) led to one of his walk-offs, with Mario Bava taking over the directorial duties. The director returned to horror a few years later, this time when the Gothic was an established commercial reality, and found it a fertile terrain to explore themes that were closer to his world view compared to the sunnier *peplum* and adventure films—so much so that in the mid–1960s he often declared horror to be his favorite genre, after the fading of the old-school swashbucklers. If *L'orribile segreto del Dr. Hichcock* is perhaps his more striking-looking Gothic film, *Lo spettro* is the most personal and fully coherent, a *huis clos* drama which proves that, if he wanted, Freda could indeed make an intimate film of sorts—if not the kind one would expect from Antonioni or Bergman. *Lo spettro* contains the core of Freda's vision—one would call it nihilistic. As a character says at the end, "The Devil is a very real person," a line that fits perfectly the human monsters the director had portrayed over the years and would continue to feature in his later films.

Still, the growing slapdashness, the increasingly low budgets, the flood of cookie-cutter sub-products that, in his view, were just badly made copies of the kind of films he always strived for, made him more and more disinterested and lazy. Once, he was the only one. Now, he was one of the many. It mattered little that he was better than most. By this time, Freda had realized that he could put his skills to better use and make more money by directing one single scene than a whole movie. Such a presumptuous detachment concealed another challenge: to rub shoulders with the American filmmakers who had created the kind of films he loved, and show them he could make them even better—and relish in the type of scenes he loved most: battles, rides on horseback, arena fights. Freda's work as second unit or action director on *peplum* and period adventure films between 1958 and 1963 shows not only his growing disinterest in the so-called human factor, but also the radicalization of his view of motion picture as spectacle.

Significantly, one of the works in which he took more pride, among those he made in the 1960s, was *Romeo e Giulietta* (1964), Shakespeare's tragedy reread as a swashbuckler/Western crossover of sorts, with little regard for the precision of the acting (a sacrilege for scholars of the Bard's *oeuvre*) but an amazing capacity to reinvent the original material, and turn it into something else—not necessarily better, but more cinematically engrossing, at least in the way Freda intended movies. It was the kind of products he used to make for Riccardo Gualino's Lux Films, when he was Italian cinema's top grossing director, whereas now he was drifting among Italy, Spain and France, docking his boat whenever he would find a project in line with his style, even if this meant having to deal with all sorts of compromises—bad scripts, lousy actors, laughable budgets. Meanwhile, the French critics discovered his work and greeted him as an *auteur*. France, to Freda, was an illusory *buen retiro*, where he attempted to revive the type of cinema he mastered, the period drama and adventure stories, with such films as *Les deux orphelines* (1965) or the excellent *Roger La Honte*, before giving up to the flood: such is the case of the two James Bond–type films that he directed for producer Robert De Nesle, *Coplan FX 18 casse tout* (1965) and *Coplan ouvre le feu à Mexico* (1967), the latter marking the end of his French period.

The last part of Freda's career can be summarized under the heading of disenchantment and disinterest. After his return to Italy he helmed six films in fifteen years, which were far from his best efforts, such as the unpleasant *giallo L'iguana dalla lingua di fuoco* (1971) and the Gothic horror pics *Estratto dagli archivi segreti della polizia di una capitale europea* and *Murder Obsession*. And yet, today these are among his best known works, due to their adhering to genres that are more popular among the younger generations of cinephiles, their overreliance on blood and gore and their distribution on home video.

In this sense, Freda's critical evaluation has been somewhat unbalanced and leads to the umpteenth paradox. Italian critics started praising his movies in the early to mid–1970s, and film festivals hosted retrospectives on his work in the 1980s and 1990s.

Meanwhile, abroad, many horror cinema scholars who did not know (or bother to search) his work outside the genre attempted to sum up his career based on a handful of films alone, and nurtured the misleading concept of Freda being basically a horror film director, a sort of mentor to Mario Bava—which, in a career spanning five decades and with only a handful of titles that fall into the realm of the horror film, is quite limiting and short-sighted.[33]

What is more, the director's later films were mostly far from his best work. In no small part, this might be due to the director's trenchant vision of post–1968 cinema:

> Today, everything is easier and settled. The photography, even in color, is not an issue anymore, and as for the story itself, the more it is messed up and ungrammatical, the more chances it has to be praised by the critics. I am certain that if the slow-motion, the zoom, the flashback, the light-in-camera were prohibited, we would witness a real hecatomb of filmmakers![34]

He obliged to the ongoing trends, but his heart was far from it, and even if he hadn't expressed it explicitly, it would have been evident just the same. Compare *L'iguana dalla lingua di fuoco* with, say, Mario Bava's *5 bambole per la luna d'agosto* (a.k.a. *Five Dolls for an August Moon*, 1970). Two movies made in the same period, and which their makers did not care the least bit about: Bava used to maintain that his film, a *Ten Little Indians* ripoff, was his very worst effort, whereas Freda adopted yet another pseudonym for the occasion, the *una tantum* Willy Pareto. Nevertheless, even at a first glance, these two films couldn't be more different from one another. Whereas Freda openly treated the material with contempt, resorting to gleefully ugly shock effects and putting aside any attempt at style, Bava dealt with the bad screenplay he had been given in the same way Benvenuto Cellini would have done with a rough block of argyle, resorting to zooms, weird angles, psychedelic focus/out-of-focus passages and an array of assorted visual tricks to squeeze life out of it, if only for a brief sequence. This sums up two different ways of moviemaking even more than a thousand words. As Sabatier noted,

> Freda does not care about the "second degree," the detachment and the irony. Contrarily to the major part of his colleagues ... he deeply believes in what he does and—whether it be *peplum*, melodrama or horror—he keeps a total sincerity, playing the game up to the very end.[35]

Therefore, when such conviction cracks, so does the final result.

It would be tempting, and foolishly romantic, to depict Freda's detachment from cinema in his later years as an act of aristocratic self-imposed exile like that of *I vampiri*'s Duchess Du Grand in her castle, surrounded by the memories of a past glorious age—or, perhaps even more fittingly, like the characters in *Lo spettro* and *Murder Obsession*, who end their days in a darkened, solitary tomb, similar to dying animals. Such a reading could even be used for the disastrous attempt at returning behind the camera with the ill-fated *La fille de d'Artagnan* (a.k.a. *Revenge of the Musketeers*, 1994) and in the octagenarian director's uncompromising refusal to mend fences with his leading actress, Sophie Marceau—the last bout of suicidal arrogance on the part of a filmmaker who, even when he had to accept his oncoming fate, chose to do it his own way. But it did not go like that.

Even though partly imposed by the economic and productive contingencies that gradually drained the national film industry of its blood with even more precision than Dr. Du Grand's transfusions, Freda's protracted absence from the set was mainly due to harsh family issues. Cinema, with which he had been growing increasingly disenchanted anyway, eventually became a collateral damage—especially after the failure to mount the one project he truly cared about, the World War I epic *Francesco Baracca*. Freda never mentioned such issues, and no trace of it can be found either in his memoir, interviews or books on his career. He never asked for comprehension, let alone compassion. His daughter Jacqueline called him a stoic, and that is the most appropriate word.

"Instead, here I am, 'derelict and abandoned,' like the title of a bad 19th century novel or a good film based on it." To dissipate the gloomy air that hung over the last pages of *Divoratori di celluloide*, the director chose to end his memoir with a humorous quip which nevertheless contained a painful truth. At 72, he portrayed himself as "a modest retired man, ignored by all, who is sitting like that Chinese on a river's edge, looking at his enemies' bodies carried away by the swirling waters of death. One by one, everyone goes…. Shivering, I think: when will my turn be?"[36]

An eerie image, indeed, and one destined to remain fixed in time for almost two decades, until his death in 1999. But one that somehow concealed the truth: it sounded as if Riccardo Freda had cut himself away from the world, whereas in fact, as Jacqueline puts it, "It was life that cut him away from it."[37]

1

A Portrait of the Filmmaker as a Young Man

An Italian in Egypt

The most powerful, populous and influential of Arabic nations, Egypt had a key economic position in the Mediterranean basin. The opening of the Suez canal in 1869, which granted a direct access to the Indian Ocean, with the understandable advantages for commercial shipments to and from the Orient, had proven a gargantuan effort on the part of the ambitious Khedive Isma'il Pasha, whose dreams of modernizing and reforming the country left Egypt in deep debt to the European nations. This led to the Khedive selling the canal to the British in 1875, and to the subsequent intervention of foreign powers to restore credit: the so-called *"Caisse de la Dette."* Foreign control resulted in a period of political turmoil, with the Urabi Revolt and the deposition of Isma'il on the part of the Ottoman Sultan (under pressure from the French and the British), and led to the installment of the "veiled protectorate" in 1882.

Under the military control of the British, the Egyptian territory developed a strong multicultural presence, which included Italians as well. One such was Vittorio Freda, formerly a modest bank clerk of Campanian roots (he was born in Acerno, near Salerno) who, despite his humble origins, had managed to become a bank president and gathered a remarkable fortune. Vittorio had married Emma, a good-looking young woman whose dreams to become an opera singer had collapsed against her parents' prejudices: in a male-oriented society such as late 1800s Italy, singers were considered little better than prostitutes. Eventually Emma had to give up her aspirations, and dedicated herself to raising a family. The Fredas moved to Egypt in 1905: an agency of Banco di Roma opened in Alexandria, to support the interests of the Italian cotton importers, and Vittorio was called on to be its president. Riccardo was born there, in Alexandria—whose modern part was built by Italian architects in early 1900, and looked very much like Italian cities such as Torino—on February 24, 1909, one of ten siblings—seven males and three females.

Freda's recollections of his early childhood in Egypt, in a huge villa complete with servants and a chauffeur, were nothing short of fairytale-like. And the figure of Vittorio stood out as nothing short of heroic, so much so that one has the impression that, even more than on those heroes he had read about in books or admired on the silver screen, Freda's film characters were modeled first and foremost upon him. Riccardo spoke of his father with open admiration, calling him a revolutionary, a free thinker, and a man ahead of his time, and praising his stern moral fiber. Vittorio was a self-made man, who climbed the social ladder via his capabilities and force of will, and yet being part of the bourgeoisie did not prevent him from remaining faithful to his ideas. He was a severe man—the director liked to recall how no one in the family could stand Vittorio's stare—who just could not tolerate injustice. He utterly despised the British' racist attitude toward the Egyptians, who were treated as inferiors, and believed in the indigenous population's right to regain their independence. As Freda would point out, "He fought for a principle against contempt, segregation and colonialism," by donating large sums to the insurrectional movement and becoming a covert financer of the 1915 Arab revolution. Actually, it is more likely that Vittorio Freda financed the revolutionaries not out of personal convictions, but on behalf of Italian interests in the country.

The anecdotes Freda told about his father are surrounded by a literary aura that makes them look suspiciously like excerpts from the adventure books that Riccardo devoured as a kid. Such as, for instance, the image of the two wooden chests filled with gifts that the Arabs delivered to the Freda mansion every Christmas, out of gratitude … making Vittorio angry since he did not want any gifts. Another episode had him hide in the house and cure a wounded fugitive Australian, chased by the Arabs, even though the injured man had taken sides with the English enemy … only to ask him to leave, to avoid having his daughter fall in love with him. Last but not least, Vittorio Freda used to give great parties for his Arab friends to celebrate the end of the *ramadan*, the Arab month of purifying fasting: "For us children, it was a real dream. Incense, dances, silver tableware and fires in the night … the Arabs chanted and danced amid Gargantuan plates."[1] An image that predates the many fascinating and luxurious feast scenes in the director's filmography, from *Aquila nera* to *Spartaco*, from *Beatrice Cenci* to *Agi Murad—Il diavolo bianco* (1959).

If his father instilled in Riccardo the admiration for strong-willed, antagonistic and heroic figures, his mother was responsible for the child's lifelong passion. Emma's frustrated artistic velleities and romantic sensibility resulted in an insatiable love for cinema. Each day, she got in the car and told the chauffeur to take her to the movies: she would watch two or three films in a row. And she dragged little Riccardo—who did not attend school, but studied at home with a preceptor, as did the members of the city's wealthiest families—with her. "We went to a theater, watched a movie, got out, and went to another one. Certainly, according to the dictates of psychoanalysis, this caused in me the wish to reproduce the films I was watching, without a precise idea on how to do it."[2]

Freda's childhood memories were populated by fragments of early silent films, seen in crowded Egyptian theaters. "The movie houses … were divided in three parts. The lucky Europeans were sitting in the first rows, the Europeans of a more modest social class occupied the second rows, and finally, behind a wooden balustrade, there were the Arabs. And they were the show within the show.…"[3] Serials were in vogue, and audiences followed with astonishing involvement the adventures of such heroines as Pearl White, who at the end of each installment was about to be submitted to all sorts of horrible tortures by bandits, in typical cliffhanger style.

> For the Egyptians and the Europeans, Pearl White was almost a goddess. When the lights turned on, the Egyptians were like mad. They gesticulated, shouted and cursed the brigands, shaking their fists in the air. For a kid, it was an incredible sight. I very quickly realized the magical impact of cinema on the audience.[4]

Besides his parents and siblings, two more individuals were part of Riccardo's enlarged family: his father's brothers were staying at the villa, and were quite peculiar types too. One, Federico, was a doctor, who perfected a collyrium that made him rich, but wasted all his money gambling at the local casinos. The other uncle was the family's black sheep, an idler with an acute aversion to any activity vaguely resembling a job: when Emma asked him to watch one of the kids, as soon as he was alone he would just drop the child and go out the window. Again, as with other episodes of his childhood, the director's recollections look more like footage from an imaginary movie, this time a Mack Sennett one-reel, with even more unlikely developments: the black sheep uncle moved to Sicily, became a priest, seduced all the most beautiful women in his parish and eventually had to marry one whom he got pregnant. According to Freda, after shedding his cassock to the winds, he relocated in Philadelphia and became a millionaire.

Riccardo's early life in Egypt shaped his temper, his beliefs and his worldview as well. He grew up in a state of enviable freedom of mind, untouched by the Italian mores and way of life, including Catholicism; he claimed he was not baptized, and was given total freedom of choice once he became of age—unlike his siblings, he never obliged. Living in a wealthy family allowed him to savor a lifestyle that was closer to that of the 19th century aristocracy, and was gradually getting lost in the Western world. However, the time eventually came for little Riccardo to return to the land of his ancestors.

The exact date of Freda's arrival in Italy varies according to the different sources: in early interviews, he mentioned that his family moved from Egypt at the outbreak of World War I, and speaking with Éric Poindron, he said that his departure, aboard a boat named *Esperia*, took place in 1914, when he was five.[5] On the other hand, Freda's youngest daughter Guislaine, basing on her aunt's recollection, dates her father's arrival in Italy to the time when he was about fourteen years old, that is 1923. Whatever the date, the reason for the Fredas moving to Italy was strictly family business. Among other qualities that his son envied him, Vittorio Freda was, in Riccardo's words, "an incorrigible seducer." Even though he was the father of ten children, he fell in love with Emma's sister, Paolina, which led to a fatal decision. He took his family to Milan, bought a huge villa for his wife and children in Viale Monterosa, and left to the United States (namely, Cincinnati) with Paolina, who gave him ten more children. Vittorio showed up in Milan only once, a few years later, to pay a visit to Emma and the kids. His appearance before the mansion was so unexpected that a couple of children, Riccardo included, locked themselves in the bathroom out of fright. However, since it was the day of the races, eventually all the family went to the San Siro racetrack: horses were a common passion which would become very important in Riccardo's life as well.

Vittorio Freda died at the age of 52. He had ultimately become a stranger, an almost mythical and distant figure, not unlike those heroes that his son used to read about in books.

Daydreaming in Milan

Once in Italy, young Riccardo was forced to conform to the rules—starting with enrolling in school, which he hated. Still, Egypt was something he could not forget, so much so that he claimed that he and his brothers sometimes still talked in Arab just for the fun of it. And he maintained his steady diet from the Egyptian days: books and movies.

Reading was an absorbing activity: Riccardo used to isolate himself under a tree in some quiet spot of the villa's park, and get lost in the adventures of Dumas' musketeers or Emilio Salgari's corsairs. He also loved Hugo's *Les Misérables* and *Notre Dame de Paris* and the great Russian novelists such as Tolstoy and Pushkin, but above all he had a passion for the works of Alexandre Dumas, *père*, from *The Three Musketeers* to *The Count of Monte Cristo*, from *The Tower of Nesle* to *Ascanio*.

Moviegoing was an equally strong habit, as Riccardo regularly accompanied his mother—or, as she was known among her acquaintances, "*Madame Pellicola*" (Madame Film). "My mom and I went to the movies like others go to church,"[6] he commented, speaking of which, "given Italians' illiteracy, whenever a caption appeared on screen, the whole audience read it out loud, in unison. It seemed like being in church, or at the oratory...."[7] Emma Freda liked sentimental films, those starring Lillian Gish, Mary Pickford, Pola Negri or Italian divas such as Lyda Borelli and Francesca Bertini, whereas Riccardo's favorites were the adventure films—Douglas Fairbanks' *The Mark of Zorro* and *Robin Hood*, Valentino's *The Eagle*, as well as early Westerns. At a young age he discovered the greats: Lang, Murnau, Griffith ("To me, Griffith was like Dumas in literature"), Vidor, and Von Stroheim—whom he later met and befriended in Marrakech, during the making of *Alerte au sud* (a.k.a. *Alert in the South*, 1953, Jean-Devaivre, co-starring Gianna Maria Canale). He was also remarkably impressed by Giovanni Pastrone's *Cabiria* (1914), with its technical innovations and its inventive special effects and *maquettes*.

Riccardo's favorite theater was the Cinema Silenzioso in Milan, where all the motion pictures starring popular comedians such as Charlie Chaplin and Buster Keaton were screened. A pianist was there to accompany the films, but each time he hit a note or two, the roars from the audience forced him to stop. Some time later he would give it another try, with the same result. The episode taught Riccardo that "music shall never supplant the image nor "fabricate" the emotion. Emotion is what's on the screen, music isn't but a dynamic complement to the show."[8] Freda witnessed another ill-fated experimentation involving sound effects at another theater, the Dal Verme. The owner attempted to achieve a kind of sonorization *ante litteram*, by installing huge naphta engines beneath the screen which were ignited during the famous scene of the parting of the troops in King Vidor's *The Big Parade* (1925): soon the place was filled with smelly gas, making the air unbreathable and causing an uproar in the room.

Another episode which Freda claimed to have witnessed as a kid, and which left a vivid memory in him, was when he had the chance to watch the shooting of a motion picture right in the park of the family villa. A coach with a woman on it would drive past the gate, a solitary man would then sneak in and approach the house of his beloved; then he would lean against a tree and press a hand against his chest, as if his heart could not stand the pain. From behind his bedroom's window, Riccardo could see the scene in its making: despite the actor's none-too-subtle mimicry, the director was not satisfied, and take after take he kept asking him for more, yelling and yelling like mad to achieve the desired effect from the unfortunate thespian. Even though, as other flashes from Freda's past, the scene sounds like a fabrication of sorts, it functions as a key to read some of the director's peculiar views on cinema, such as his disdain for actors and his view (and embodiment) of the director as an absolute monarch, with the power of life and death over his cast and crew. More than anything else, the experience served as an early advice: movies are made of illusion and simulation, nothing else. "And I thought to myself: what bullshit cinema is!"[9]

Ars Gratia Artis

Riccardo's elder brother had become an important engineer; another was one of Milan's most distinguished lawyers. He was expected to take an equally prestigious path. "Like all those students who don't want to study, I chose law school," he quipped. It took him just one lesson to decide he wasn't made to become a barrister. Instead, he wanted to be an artist. For one year, he was an apprentice at the workshop of Attilio Prendoni, a renowned sculptor who specialized in modeling horse figures, and who would eventually lose all his money in gambling, in San Remo. After learning the rudiments of drawing and modeling with Prendoni, Freda entered the workshop of the illustrious Adolfo Wildt, to learn marble sculpting. He loved to recall that his first work as a sculptor was a marble egg, an image of simplicity that hid a tremendous effort behind it; then came reproductions of famous works, including Michelangelo's *Pietà*.

Freda's apprenticeship with Wildt would not last long, though. At the age of 23, he married a girl by the name of Angiola Dondina, and the couple moved into a small apartment in via Monforte, in the palace owned by the Visconti family. The descendant of a wealthy Milanese lineage, and the sister of an eminent lawyer, Dondina had aspirations to be a painter and convinced Riccardo to pursue an artistic career, renouncing a job as an archivist at the Milan township. It was Angiola who introduced him to the renowned Barbaroux Gallery. Starting in the 1920s, alongside public spaces that hosted exhibitions and performances, Milan saw the birth of several private galleries that played a vital role in the orientation, taste, and formation of many artists, and pushed forward the evolution of the key Italian artistic movements of the era. Vittorio Barbaroux was possibly the country's most important patron, who gave work, nourishment and accommodation to a number of young painters and sculptors, including soon-to-be-famous names such as Aligi Sassu and Giacomo Manzù.

Riccardo and Angiola did not live the bohemian life, though. Unlike many of his peers he had a day job, giving Latin and art lessons, which allowed him to have his daily bread on his table, even though the butter was often missing. The renowned Silvio Vigezzi, director of Milan's contemporary art gallery, organized Freda's first exhibition, but none of his early works seem to have survived, not even in photographs. Freda claimed they all got lost during the war. The only testimony to his skills are the sculptures he would create for his own movies, such as the colossus on *I giganti della Tessaglia* and the Buddhas in *Maciste alla corte del Gran Khan*.

Even though his position in the art world was to remain marginal, during his days as a sculptor Freda got to meet a number of important personalities, and became close friends with the great sculptor Arturo Martini. In the meantime, he also moonlighted as art critic for the Fascist journal *L'Ardito d'Italia*, "The Magazine of the Italian Assault Troops," edited by the prince Valerio Pignatelli. "I did not care about the mag's opinions," Freda would later comment: "I took advantage to stick up for the young artists and notably Modigliani, for whom I had the greatest admiration."[10] As it would happen often in his career, he seemed to thoroughly enjoy his status as a contrarian, going so far as recounting with visible satisfaction the effects of his counter-current criticism on the artistic status quo, which resulted in heated phone calls at the magazine's headquarters.

Even though he never was a left-wing person, Freda did not enroll in the Fascist Party. Like many artists and intellectuals during the regime, he tried to cope with Fascism by carefully moving within its bureaucratic mesh while dealing with the inner obtuseness of many hierarchs, and sneering at his peers' awe, concealed under a façade of moral pride. He often recalled sarcastically when, in Milan, he had been part of the group of artists who founded the "*Accademia di Sant'Ambrogio*" (Academy of St. Ambrogio). The Academy was a movement that comprised many of the period's most celebrated names in the artistic *milieu*—Achille Funi, Mario Sironi, Felice Casorati, Giò Ponti ...—and its statute was firmly critical of the regime's attitude toward art. Its manifesto was published in the newspaper *L'Ambrosiano*. The next day a telegram from Rome was delivered to the Academy's headquarters, consisting of three words: "*Sciogliere immediatamente Accademia*" ("Disband Academy immediately"). Its members duly obliged with their tail between their legs. Their artistic rebellion against the regime had lasted only one day.

On the Way to Cinecittà

In 1933, the 24-year-old Riccardo Freda left Milan for Rome, following the advice of his friend, the well-known painter Esodo Pratelli, who had been summoned to the Capital to work at the Under-Secretariat for Press and Propaganda, headed by Mussolini's son-in-law, Galeazzo Ciano. Perhaps Freda's inner pragmatism had convinced him that there was no artistic future for him in sight. After all, his friendship with Arturo Martini made him realize that great artists are destined not to be recognized, and that talent alone does not pay: Martini, perhaps the greatest sculptor of his era, had become so disillusioned that in 1945, two years before his untimely death, he published an essay against his own métier, *Scultura, lingua morta* (Sculpture, a dead language). Freda always believed in predestination, and was a self-professed fatalist. Therefore, one could say that cinema was written in his future even before he knew it, and the circumstances that led him to take his first steps in the movie business are odd to say the least: the director himself labeled them as "resembling a complicated chess match."[11]

Founded in 1934 on behalf of Galeazzo Ciano, the "*Direzione Generale per la Cinematografia*" (General Direction of Cinematography) constituted an attempt on the part of Fascism to install a thorough control over the national film industry, and shape its output according to the propaganda needs of the regime. Ciano appointed Luigi Freddi, a former Futurist, then the editor and special correspondent of the newspaper founded by Mussolini himself, *Il Popolo d'Italia*, as General Director. "This young man had all the qualities that the Duce lacked: he was a womanizer, drank only champagne and always won at poker. I am certain that Mussolini secretly admired him," Freda recalled.[12] On his part, he obviously did, as Freddi's lifestyle would become his own for the best part of his life. During the highs and lows of his film career, Freda always treated himself to the very best—women, cars, houses, the good life—, to the point of accepting a white Rolls Royce as payment for making a Western he did not care the least bit about, as Yves Boisset recalled.[13]

When Ciano entrusted Freddi as General Director, the latter gathered a small group of people to write down the organization's statute. He asked his friend Esodo Pratelli to give him a hand, and the artist called aboard two more friends: another painter, Guglielmo Usellini, and Riccardo Freda. The gathering of two painters and a sculptor—admittedly quite an unusual aggregation for such a job—to write down the statute resulted in a linguistic misunderstanding that plagued Freda for a lifetime: many journalists, historians and even his own biographers wrote that he had sculpted the *statues* at the General Direction of Cinematography.[14]

In writing the statute, Freddi (who had met D. W. Griffith during a trip to the States, where he became interested in the production aspects of moviemaking) and his acolytes took inspiration from the Russian film industry. "Our production does not bother to define and create an Italian type of film, to look for a peculiar originality, a seal of nobleness, a sure warranty of success," the journalist wrote to Mussolini, thus listing the basic idea that Italian films would have to convey: the aesthetic and ethical education of the masses, the conveyance of the ideas and principles of the Italian nation, the demonstration of its people's intellectual, moral, artistic, and political potential.[15] Therefore, through the General Direction of Cinematography, the Fascist State would intervene directly in national film production, focusing on its regulation on all fronts, from the economic facilities to a strict censorial activity that contemplated the prior reading of the scripts and demanded that each completed motion picture be submitted to a board of censors. The rule book to which the board conformed its actions (instituted in 1923) would remain operative until 1962, when the new law on censorship was passed—which speaks volumes about the way censorship operated long after the fall of the regime in the post–World War II years.[16]

In Freda's opinion, however, Mussolini basically just wanted Italian cinema to be a showcase for the regime, an idea best embodied by *Scipione l'Africano* (a.k.a. *Scipio Africanus: The Defeat of Hannibal*, 1937, Carmine Gallone), the big-budget *peplum* on the Ancient Roman general who defeated Hannibal's army, which portrayed Rome's ancient glory with patent references to the present. Similarly, Freddi's idea was to develop the Italian film industry without turning it into a propaganda machine the way Goebbels had done in Germany, as proven by an ill-fated project that should have involved the director of the legendary *Cabiria*, Giovanni Pastrone.

> Before the shooting of *Scipione l'Africano*, which had to be the glory of Fascism, Freddi had thought of Pastrone to make a film. It was a symbolic enterprise, because Pastrone has made Italian cinema shine before the whole world. We had proposed him to adapt a baroque Polish novel [possibly *The Manuscript Found in Saragossa* by Jan Potocki].... No one has heard of this project because it aborted. Pastrone was old and disillusioned. After one month, Freddi gave up to this project of prestige. And me, without ever having to decide anything, I seconded and followed Freddi in my new career.[17]

In Rome, for a while, Freda immersed himself in the realm of bureaucracy. Despite not being enrolled in the Fascist party, he had a vantage position at the Office of Tourism, where he took care of propaganda and advertising until 1937, a year that marked a turning point for Italian cinema and for his own career in it. The regime's reshaping and boosting of the national film industry—under the slogan "*Il cinema è l'arma più forte*" ("Cinema is the strongest weapon")—also included the opening of Rome's Centro Sperimentale di Cinematografia (Experimental Film Center, the State's official film school which, despite what some sources claim, Freda never attended[18]); the Venice Festival becoming an annual event, with the Coppa Mussolini (Mussolini Cup) being awarded to the best Italian film as well as to the best foreign one; the incorporation of the educational Istituto Luce (founded in 1924) under the Ministry for Popular Culture and Propaganda (MinCulPop); and the creation of Enic—Ente Nazionale per le Industrie Cinematografiche (National Entity for Film Industries). Then, in April 1937, came the opening of Cinecittà—the largest film studio in the country, a real "city of cinema" risen just outside Rome. That same year, Riccardo Freda had his first experience in filmmaking. Perhaps it was indeed written in destiny.

2

Learning the Craft

Abandon All Hope Ye Who Enter Here: The Early Comedies

Freda's first steps in the movie business were the result of his acquaintance with Raffaele Colamonici, one of those larger-than-life characters who were often to be found within the Italian film industry. A former actor under the alias Guido Di San Giusto (later Guido Saint-Just), Colamonici had eventually become a production manager: according to Freda, he was a real *guappo*, that is affiliated with the Camorra.[1] Which, considering that most Italian producers acted as filibusters when it came to collecting money for a movie (or not paying creditors their due), could even be true after all.

Colamonici entrusted Freda with his first scriptwriting job, the adaptation of a 1936 play by Athos Setti: also known as *La fortuna si diverte* (Luck Has Fun), it would become a *pièce de résistance* in Eduardo De Filippo's repertory, under the title *Sogno di una notte di mezza sbornia* (A Middrunkenness Night's Dream, turned into a film in 1959). The result was a very simple and unpretentious flick, *Lasciate ogni speranza* (Abandon All Hope, 1937), directed by Gennaro Righelli, the first in a series of "small comedies without any importance,"[2] as Freda would later dismiss them, on which he worked, that nevertheless were very popular back then. He and Colamonici would team up together again in the late 1940s on *Il conte Ugolino*—curiously, a film based on Dante's *Inferno*, which the title of Righelli's comedy evokes ("Abandon all hope, ye who enter here!" is the inscription at the entrance of Hell in Dante's poem), the swashbuckler *Il figlio di d'Artagnan* and the World War I drama *La leggenda del Piave* (1952).

Freda claimed to have scripted *Lasciate ogni speranza* with his friend Edoardo Antonelli (1910–1986), whose name is not mentioned in the credits. Antonelli, who regularly employed the alias Edoardo Anton, had been Freda's classmate at the lyceum, and one of the causes of the latter's growing interest in magic and the supernatural, which can be detected in this film as well. Starring the popular stage actor Antonio Gandusio (1873–1951) and the Italian-Argentinian beauty María Denis (1916–2004),[3] *Lasciate ogni speranza* centers on destiny and predestination, a recurring theme in Freda's subsequent work. When the numbers he played at a lottery following a nightmare (which depicted the exact time of his death) prove to be winning, the protagonist starts fearing that the dreamed events will become real, giving way to a series of mildly comical events and misunderstandings. Interestingly, Freda reprised the idea of the opening nightmare in his third feature film, *Tutta la città canta* (1945).

As for the director, the Neapolitan Gennaro Righelli (1886–1949), a veteran filmmaker who had been making movies since the early days of silent cinema, Freda recalled that he lived alone at the Hotel Majestic in Rome, in a room literally clouded with cigarette smoke, where the scriptwriting meetings took place.

> Righelli belonged to that group of directors who became popular after World War I (Genina, Gallone, Camerini…), and he had very precise and somewhat dated ideas on filmmaking. For instance, he rejected American-style screenplays and required the so-called "dicing." What does it mean? Simple. A man and a woman are talking, then there is a cut and we see him taking the train to Paris, and the dialogue will later explain this fact: that's an American-style script. The dicing consists in depicting their encounter, their goodbye and then the man leaving to the train station. According to Righelli, the audience could understand only this second solution, otherwise they would be lost. These directors had an analytical mentality and refused modern editing (for instance, Godard would have caused them an apoplectic fit).[4]

The second of the six films Freda wrote for the prolific Righelli (who directed no less than 20 flicks over a six year period in the mid–1930s) was again a comedy of errors. *Fuochi d'artificio* (Fireworks, 1938) was based on a stage play centered around an old-hat premise which Freda reprised in *Tutta la città canta*. He despised this kind of fatuous, vapid comedy, and his contribution was, as in other similar occurrences, a mere work-for-hire job. Critics were not kind either, and compared unfavorably the result with its source: "Too bad that the film is not enough fireworks, that is it somewhat lacks those sparkling, crackling, brilliant qualities … the acting is resolute and rickety, which (strangely) in movies is often the result of haste."[5]

L'allegro cantante (The Merry Singer, 1938)—not to be confused with the movie of the same name directed in Germany the following year by Carmine Gallone—was also based on a play (by Luigi Chiarelli, who co-write the script with Freda and Righelli) and featured the recurring elements of the comedies made in Italy during that period, the so-called "*Telefoni bianchi*,"[6] such as the high society setting, and the overly optimistic feeling that makes the story more similar to a modern fairytale, as any attempt at realism is carefully bypassed. Nevertheless, the result lacks the qualities of others and livelier *telefoni bianchi* films, such as those directed by Mario Camerini. The young protagonist (Giovanni Manurita) was a singer, allowing for the inclusion of a couple of song numbers (*Canta che ti passa* and *Presentimento*), while the comic relief was provided by the De Rege brothers, who also played supporting roles in *Lasciate ogni speranza*. Guido and Giorgio De Rege were the typical vaudeville comic duo, with the elder (Guido) playing the stooge and the younger (Giorgio) acting as the funny man. Their comedy leaned on verbal wordplay that often veered on the absurd, with Giorgio specializing as a stuttering type. Their popularity came to an abrupt halt during the war: Guido de Rege died in early 1945, near the end of the conflict, and Giorgio replaced him with Carlo Dapporto; however, the second De Rege brother also met an untimely death a few years later, in 1948, while performing on stage. Their repertoire was picked up in the 1950s on television by Carlo Campanini and Walter Chiari, who reprised the De Rege's comic leitmotif, the phrase "*Vieni avanti, cretino!*" ("Come forward, you idiot!").[7] Righelli's assistant director was Filippo Walter Ratti, who would then embark on a nondescript directorial career on his own and whose path again crossed Freda's over thirty years later, on the ill-fated *Estratto dagli archivi segreti della polizia di una capitale europea*.

Freda recalled an anecdote about the film which spoke volumes about the amateurishness with which the Cinecittà crews and technicians were moving their early steps. For a scene which borrowed from a classic moment in Charlie Chaplin's *The Circus* (1928), Giorgio De Rege had to perform a gag that required him to be locked inside a cage with a lion: the animal would be kept separated from the actor by an invisible glass panel in the middle of the cage. The crystal was, according to the special effects technician, "bulletproof." However, De Rege was not at all convinced about the trick, and demanded that a rehearsal be made with the lion alone. Righelli obliged. As soon as the animal entered the cage, he approached the glass, sniffed it ... and broke it into pieces by simply leaning its paw on it.[8]

Next came *La voce senza volto* (The Faceless Voice, 1939), yet another *telefoni bianchi* comedy focused on a poor but very talented young singer (a character that Freda would recycle in his second film as a director, *Non canto più*, 1945) which took place in the movie business, just like a number of other works of the era—*La signora di tutti* (1934, Max Ophüls), *Inventiamo l'amore* (1938, Camillo Mastrocinque), *Due milioni per un sorriso* (1939, Carlo Borghesio, Mario Soldati), *Dora Nelson* (1940, Mario Soldati). A reviewer of the period commented that "the story, which looks like so many others, becomes interesting because of the environment in which it takes place, the film world filled with hysterical divas, big-bellied superstars and neurasthenic directors...."[9] There are curious similarities with *Singin' in the Rain* (1952), starting with the idea of the unknown singer's voice replacing the titular one; however, the self-reflexive scenery here seems mostly an excuse to display the modernity and efficiency of the Cinecittà studios, inaugurated in April 1937. Righelli's camera explores the sets, corridors and cafeteria, all swarming with extras, with plenty of serpentine long takes and tracking shots, exuding a visible relish in showing off the marvels of a seemingly top-notch film industry intent on fabricating lavish musicals for the masses (as opposed to period films: "We don't like that type of movies," one character says—a line perhaps coming from Freda's sharp pen). As customary with Italian films of the era, *La voce senza volto* paints an optimistic picture of Italy as an ideal country where everybody is happy and smiling: "Everyone here sings," comments the caretaker in the shipyard where Gino works, and a scene shows the workers leaving the site on their bikes, all singing in unison with the protagonist. Despite Righelli's pride in showing the wonders of Cinecittà, the scene is filmed via a crude back projection.

The script was co-written by Freda and Corrado D'Errico (1902–1941), a former critic and correspondent for the LUCE newsreels, who also directed a dozen movies before his untimely death, including a couple of posthumous swashbucklers adapted from Emilio Salgari novels, *Capitan Tempesta* (1942, completed by Umberto Scarpelli) and *Il leone di Damasco* (1942, completed by Enrico Guazzoni), which displayed all the shortcomings of Italian adventure films of the period, such as the blatant Fascist propaganda applied to genre cinema and the slapdash dueling scenes, only slightly camouflaged by Massimo Terzano's expert cinematography.

As in *L'allegro cantante*, the lead is played by Giovanni Manurita (1895–1984), a very popular tenor who embarked on a brief movie career: *La voce senza volto* (in which he sings the number *Ultimo bolero*) was his third and last film. He is surrounded by a number of very good voice actors (such as Carlo Romano and Romolo Costa) in supporting roles. Due to soundtrack damage, the circulating Italian print is a hodgepodge, as the original dubbing is often replaced with recently redubbed scenes that feature debatably modernized dialogue: it is very unlikely that in 1939 a German character would be heard uttering the word "*Scheisse*" (shit) on film, let alone an Italian one.

Freda's fifth stint as a scriptwriter for Gennaro Righelli, *Il barone di Corbò* (The Baron of Corbò, 1939), was a forgettable farce, based on the 1929 stage play of the same name by Luigi Antonelli, Edoardo's father. The starting point—in a villa in the countryside, a man and his family are terrorized by the news of lunatics escaped from a nearby hospital, and start suspecting that one of their guests, the alleged "Baron of Corbò," is one of them—draws from the typical "old dark house" comedy-horror films and stage plays, and the idea of the lunatics passing themselves off as doctors was likely inspired by Edgar Allan Poe's *The System of Doctor Tarr and Professor Feather*, to spice up the predictable game of misunderstandings, fake identities and unfunny gags. Righelli's direction does not do much to overcome the overall staginess, and the characters are hopelessly dull, with the exception of Armando Migliari, as a would-be unfaithful husband oppressed by his wife and three daughters, whose secret rendezvous with his mistress is ruined by a series of unfortunate circumstances.

Around the same period, Freda did uncredited work as film doctor on *Fascino* (Fascination, 1939), the only movie role of Italian soprano singer Iva Pacetti, a monumental-looking lady who was very popular in Italy and abroad at that time. He told Giuseppe Tornatore:

> The film had been financed by ... the owner of a big hotel in Rome and the lover of this elephantine woman.... This film was horrendous and at a certain point they asked me if I could [sort it out]? "The only way to sort it out is to throw it down the toilet," I said, "but seeing that you insist, I could give you some advice, but I'm not filming anything." There's only one scene worthy of this name and that's the fire scene, that's come out pretty well. I said: "Use the fire scene at least three times during the film." "And how on earth are we going to do that?" "Well, I mean, let's say the film starts with the fire scene, the public's curiosity is already aroused. Then, later on one of the characters remembers ... the fire! And at the end, again ... the fire!" ... It was still a load of shit, but in the end it managed to get released because of the fire scene."[10]

Young Adventurers

Freda's first important scriptwriting credit, *Piccoli naufraghi* (Shipwrecked Boys, 1939) was one of the ten motion pictures announced right after the proclamation of the Fascist colonial empire, on March 9, 1936, following the end of the Second Italo-Ethiopian War. In spite of the blatant propaganda undertones, and a view of adolescence in tune with Fascism's emphasis on team spirit and physical fitness, director Flavio Calzavara's film debut was a peculiar work in the national production of the period, being one of the first movies centered almost exclusively on children—although not the very first as Freda claimed, since in 1935 an adaptation of Ferenc Molnar's classic novel *The Boys of via Paal* had been helmed by Alberto Mondadori and Mario Monicelli. However, due to its exotic setting and unusual story—a group of kids embark clandestinely on a boat and shipwreck on a desert island, which turns out to be the lair of a gang of arms smugglers—*Piccoli naufraghi* has the feel of Freda's beloved popular adventure novels for children. "I like the company of kids very much," enthused the notoriously misanthropic filmmaker,

> and I used to follow their adventures through Mark Twain or Dickens, Stevenson, as well as Collodi and Pinocchio ... furthermore, American cinema loved to put kids on scene.... I have always loved smart kids and those who had the taste of adventure as well as of danger: Huckleberry Finn, the intrepid Oliver Twist ... but I could not transpose them into Italian cinema.[11]

One wonders what an Italian version of *The Adventures of Huckleberry Finn* or an adaptation of Dickens' masterpiece might have been in Freda's hands.

As opposed to his often poor opinion of grown-up actors, Freda always claimed that he was much more at ease directing children, whose frankness and spontaneity allowed him to achieve convincing results with minimal advice on his part. However, the dozen of teens co-starring in *Piccoli naufraghi* are all rather clumsy-looking, acting-wise, and despite several amusing bits the film itself suffers from a rather schematic script. At one point, when conflict ensues between the two factions of the young shipwrecked, it almost seems that *Piccoli naufraghi* is turning into something predating *Lord of the Flies*, but the impression is soon to be contradicted. The appearance of the arms smugglers pushes the story closer to Robert Luis Stevenson's *Treasure Island*, while keeping in with the regime's need for propaganda: the villains deal with the Negus, Ethiopia's monarch. The film's best qualities pertain to its fascinating exteriors, filmed at the Isola of Giglio, off the coast of Tuscany.

Whether Freda actually had a hand in the direction is unclear, as he contradicted himself on several occasions: he claimed he did collaborate with Calzavara when interviewed by Stefano Della Casa,[12] and mentioned the fact in passing in his memoir as well,[13] but vehemently denied this (and even his participation as co-scriptwriter) with Éric Poindron.[14] However, he temporarily acted as cameraman and had a vital role in allowing Aldo Tonti (the still photographer on the set) to make his film debut after the director of photography Arturo Gallea fell ill. As Tonti recalled, "My debut scene as operator-in-chief was quite a complex take: a very long dolly shot.... I rehearsed the camera movement, placed the lights and mirrors, then shot the scene without hesitation. The director looked as he was about to boggle. After the first take, he asked me how the scene had turned out. "Excellent!" I said. Since he was used at shooting five or six takes for each scene, my "Excellent" sounded to him like a true challenge ... seeing that I showed no sign of wanting to do other takes.... Calzavara curtly ordered to stop shooting.... The footage I shot left toward Rome. Forty-eight hours later the developed film was back on the island together with a projector, so that the result of that job that I prematurely labeled as excellent would be screened to the director. And excellent it was indeed."[15]

On *Piccoli naufraghi*, Freda even made one of his rare appearances as an actor, under the a.k.a. Riccardo Santelmi, and for once without his inseparable glasses, in a small supporting role. Amusingly, for a man who claimed that he "always hated every kind of school, under any form,"[16] he played the boys' benevolent and inspirational Latin professor, Giannini, who embarks on a liner to Oceania to meet a sad destiny. "I was asked to play other acting roles," he proudly boasted, "and even in a film alongside Doris Duranti![17] It was in this period that I thought it would be better to leave administration aside and move on to filmmaking practice." Freda's claims seem to be the product of his imperishable self-esteem, though, as he has very little screen time in the movie: almost all his lines are declaimed off-screen, and even his death scene takes place accordingly, suggesting that perhaps Calzavara was not too convinced of his acting chops. Freda also took care of the editing, together with Ferdinando Maria Poggioli, one of the most brilliant and underrated directors in Italian cinema, and the author of such minor masterpieces as *Gelosia* (1942) and *Il cappello da prete* (1944). The Italian title was changed to *Piccoli Avventurieri* (Little Adventurers) from the original *Piccoli naufraghi* (Shipwrecked Boys) for the film's ethnic language-house release in the United States. A copy is kept at the Library of Congress Film Study Center in Culpeper, Virginia.

Of Knights, Duchesses and Fallen Stars...

Coming after a string of nondescript comedies and farces, *Il cavaliere di San Marco* (a.k.a. *The Knight of San Marco*, 1939) was a change of pace for Gennaro Righelli: a period drama which was certainly more in tune with Freda's sensibility and taste, since the plot had all the typical staples of the swashbuckling films he admired so much. Its rereading of the Italian *Risorgimento* (Resurgence), the period that led to the unification of the country in 1861, is an attempt at portraying Italian history in an interesting light, more akin to popular novels than to Alessandro Blasetti's exemplary *1860* (1934). Freda—who co-scripted it with Alessandro De Stefani, Gherardo Gherardi, Edoardo Anton and future film director Renato Castellani—would recycle several plot points in his later films: the inn scene, with the encounter between the protagonist and the woman who turns out to be in cahoots with the enemy, predates *Don Cesare di Bazan* (1942), whereas the theme of hero's brother being unjustly imprisoned will return in *Il cavaliere misterioso*; last but not least, the elusive "Knight of San Marco," the mysterious head of the patriots, hints at such legendary popular heroes as Black Eagle. However, the results are so stagey and talky that they perfectly sum up the dusty approach to the adventure genre from which Freda would sweep away with his debut. Reviewers were not kind either: "What a haughtiness and pomposity in this adventure film, and what stuffed characters, what silly puppets! ... When Italian cinema attempts to be magnificent, serious trouble ensues. Behind those fake golden frames one can feel the phoniness and the ostentatious from a mile away."[18]

Freda's next assignment as a scriptwriter, *In campagna è caduta una stella* (a.k.a. *In the Country Fell a Star*, 1939), marked the directorial debut of the renowned Neapolitan stage actor Eduardo (here credited as "Edoardo") De Filippo. Eduardo was also the producer, together with his brother Peppino, who had written the 1932 play on which the film was based. Besides helping him adapt the play for the screen, Freda would also have to act as a technical supervisor to the direction, since De Filippo had no filmmaking experience whatsoever: in fact, Freda is credited as "collaborator to the director." However, after some time spent working together on the screenplay, his relationship with Eduardo deteriorated during the shooting, since the egocentric De Filippo stubbornly refused each and every word of advice his collaborator would give him.

Eduardo also had a tormented working relationship with his brother Peppino, who co-starred in the film, and often treated him in a rough manner—so much so that Peppino often broke out in tears while confiding Freda his frustration for his brother's attitude, as they drove back home together from the set. Over the years the De Filippo brothers went separate ways. Eduardo would be celebrated as one of Italy's greatest stage actors and playwrights, and often appeared in films, most memorably in Vittorio De Sica's *L'oro di Napoli* (*The Gold of Naples*, 1954). He also directed a number of critically acclaimed pictures (such as 1950s *Napoli milionaria* and 1954's *Questi fantasmi*). On the other hand, Peppino would become one of Totò's recurrent partners on screen.

In addition to the De Filippo brothers, the female lead was played by the Canadian-born Rosina Lawrence—best known for her role as Mary Roberts in the Laurel & Hardy vehicle *Way Out West* (1937)—who had been sent to Italy by producer Hal Roach, for a movie adaptation of *Rigoletto* that did not materialize. Shooting took place at Tirrenia Studios, during a troubled period: news came that the war was about to start, which sent Lawrence into panic. She often burst into fits of crying for fear of being stuck in Italy because of the ongoing conflict. Filming was briefly interrupted in August 1939 and resumed a few weeks later, with makeshift means; meanwhile the actress had returned overseas. *In campagna è caduta una stella* was released in Naples, De Filippo's hometown, in November 1939, whereas it was distributed in the rest of Italy in the spring of 1940, to tepid reviews: "The De Filippo brothers have never been employed cinematically as they deserved: however, after this first sample, I think they will better put themselves in the hands of people of the movie business," one critic wrote.[19] The film was not released in the United States until 1950. By then, Lawrence had long retired acting: De Filippo's had been her final film.

Freda returned to scripting comedies with *La granduchessa si diverte* (The Grand Duchess Has Fun, 1940). A tale in the vein of Viennese operettas and Lubitsch's films, and with nods to the Billy Wilder-scripted *Ihre Hoheit befiehit* (a.k.a. *Her Grace Commands*, 1931, Hanns Schwarz), it was set in an imaginary Mitteleuropean state and based on an identity swap that owed to Mark Twain's *The Prince and the Pauper* and Anthony Hope's *The Prisoner of Zenda*. It was Giacomo Gentilomo's third feature film. Gentilomo (1909–2001) went on to a respected career within the realm of popular cinema, from melodrama (*La cieca di Sorrento*, a.k.a. *The Blind Woman of Sorrento*, 1952) to peplum (*Maciste contro il vampiro*, a.k.a. *Goliath and the Vampires*, 1961). After giving up directing, he focused on painting, with remarkable results.

Besides the typical game of misunderstandings, *La granduchessa si diverte* features a number of humorous sideswipes to the regime—such as the caricatured bureaucrats or the grand duchess' habit of addressing her interlocutors with "*voi*" (a rule imposed by the regime to fight "bourgeois servilism"[20])—which may well be the result of the uncredited contribution to the script on the part of the young Mario Monicelli, who was also the assistant director.[21] He and Freda would team up again several years later, for some of the director's most interesting films.

Compared to Gentilomo's sprightly effort, *Cento lettere d'amore* (One Hundred Love Letters, 1940, Max Neufeld) marked for Freda a return to the routine, nondescript comedies he had been involved in so far. In the hands of a director like Max Ophüls, the story—one hundred compromising love letters sent by a married woman to her lover are found by her husband's secretary, whose wife in turn believes the missives were addressed to her spouse, leading to a series of misunderstandings—would have sparkled, whereas Neufeld turned it into the umpteenth light farce, populated with vapid characters. Freda's comment on the Austrian-born director—70 films directed between 1919 and 1957—was curt: "Neufeld was an unpleasant man and he didn't understand a thing about cinema."[22]

Notte di fortuna (Lucky Night, 1941, Raffaello Matarazzo) was, after *Quei due* (1935, Gennaro Righelli), Peppino De Filippo's attempt at a comic career of his own, detached from his brother Eduardo's overwhelming shadow. The story was far from original, and openly drew from French and American models, but for the first time it allowed Peppino to let his comic skills loose. In the film, he plays a pharmacist's clerk who wins a huge sum of money at the San Remo casino with the help of a mysterious woman, but then loses all at the very last gamble. Back in his village, however, everyone thinks he has become a billionaire.... The theme of the man gambling all his money in San Remo was not new to Freda, whose early sculptor master Attilio Prendoni had lost all his fortune at the green table. He himself would be a passionate gambler throughout his life.

The film marked Freda's first collaboration with Raffaello Matarazzo, one of the unsung masters of Italian popular cinema, who literally started a new trend after the success of his melodrama *Catene* (1949) paved the way for a whole season of tearjerking dramas. Freda was good friends with Matarazzo, and often praised his merits as a filmmaker, even at a time where the latter's work had been long reviled by the critics, and forgotten by the public. Matarazzo's death in 1966 came after the director had fallen into a commercial oblivion, as his later films were badly distributed and turned out as box-office flops: it was only a decade later that the critics started a critical reappraisal of his work. In many ways, and despite having set out a commercially fruitful trend such as the melodrama, Matarazzo was a man alone in post-war Italian cinema, just like Freda. However, even though he was quite at ease with comedies as well, *Notte di fortuna* was not one of the director's more memorable efforts. The story had been tampered by censors (originally, it was to be set in Montecarlo, where the protagonist would take his employer's wife), and according to Peppino De Filippo, Matarazzo even walked off the set at one point: the movie was finished by the director of photography Ugo Lombardi, who in turn was replaced as d.o.p. by the great Václav Vích.

Despite its amiable quality, *Notte di fortuna* was rather tepidly received by the critics.

> A little farce, rather naively conceived.... Peppino De Filippo does his best and is often funny, but he would have been much more than that, had he put aside certain ill-fated Charlot-like references, and stuck to that homely, countrylike realism which, at least in the movies, is his true path. Matarazzo directs haphazardly, making do within the limits of a rushed production.[23]

In the meantime, Italy had entered World War II on Germany's side against the "plutocratic and reactionary democracies of the West." On June 10, 1940, on the balcony of Piazza Venezia in Rome, Mussolini announced the news to the population, in a short and emotional speech. "The hour, marked by fate, has come," the Duce declared, wrongly believing that the conflict would end soon, allowing him to take part in the peace negotiations as a winner. This did not seem to affect the movie industry: Cinecittà was still churning out films that mostly seemed blissfully detached from their time.

The Elica Film Years

A vital moment in Freda's career came when the 31-year-old scriptwriter got in touch with two Southern gentlemen, Francesco Curato and a partner of his by the name of Carbone, who had been convinced to try their hand at producing a film on the great Italian painter Michelangelo Merisi da Caravaggio (1578–1610) by a certain Renato Angiolillo. Needless to say, the inexperienced beginners had seen the expense account rise higher and higher, as the budget kept swelling like a soufflé. When he met the pair of aspiring producers, Freda asked them *carte blanche*: he was well aware of the way the film's executive producer was inflating the costs for his own personal advantage, and his remedies were drastic. "I took the helm of that boat that was leaking from all sides, and applied a strict administrative supervision: the effect was that all, and I mean all the people in the production crew, from Angiolillo to the last production secretary, left on the spot since they found it unbearable that someone would question their honesty."[24]

Shot in 1940 and released early the following year, *Caravaggio, il pittore maledetto* was the first fruit of the production company Elica Film, and perhaps the closest to Freda's idea of filmmaking, as it told the troubled life of Caravaggio as a lurid adventure drama. It was one of several pictures made in those years about famous painters of the past, whose lives were the basis for dramatic or adventurous stories: examples were *Un'avventura di Salvator Rosa* (a.k.a. *An Adventure of Salvator Rosa*, 1939, Alessandro Blasetti) and *La fornarina* (1944, Enrico Guazzoni), as well as *Il bravo di Venezia* (1941, Carlo Campogalliani), which featured scenes in the workshop of Paolo Veronese. Freda and his fellow scriptwriters were not shy when it came to fleshing out Caravaggio's life with a little bit of historical fabrication: for one thing, the painter was never appointed a Knight of Malta as the film shows.

Caravaggio was played by Amedeo Nazzari, who later starred in the director's 1951 melodrama *Il tradimento (Passato che uccide)*. Freda had a taste of the actor's vain and spoiled behavior on set. Nazzari, then Italy's most popular thespian, was flabbergasted by the fact that in the film Caravaggio did not embrace and kiss any woman—something which, he feared, would put his career at risk. The female lead was Clara Calamai, one of the great divas of the Fascist regime: the next year she would cause a controversy by briefly exposing her breast—the first nude scene in an Italian film—in Alessandro Blasetti's *La cena delle beffe* (a.k.a. *The Jester's Supper*, 1942), and then would play alongside Massimo Girotti in Luchino Visconti's masterpiece *Ossessione* (a.k.a. *Obsession*, 1943). Over thirty years later she would turn up again in yet another unforgettable role, in Dario Argento's *Profondo rosso* (a.k.a. *Deep Red*, 1975).

In the opening titles of *Caravaggio, il pittore maledetto*, Freda receives a special credit, which states that he "has collaborated to the making of the film." Indeed, his involvement was on various fronts. Besides acting as executive producer, he worked on the art direction, and created a *maquette* of the port of Ostia, replete with docks, galleons and goods. Freda later claimed: "I gave Alessandrini a very precise outline of work and he, despite such authoritarianism, was always a good friend."[25] Goffredo Alessandrini (1904–1978), then Anna Magnani's partner, was an offbeat character. Born in Egypt, like Freda, after working with Alessandro Blasetti he became a popular director of *telefoni bianchi* comedies and then of propaganda war dramas such as *Cavalleria* (1936), *Luciano Serra Pilota* (1938, starring Nazzari) and *Abuna Messias* (1942). His post–World War II output was equally interesting, with such works as *L'ebreo errante* (1947, based on Eugène Sue's novel and starring Vittorio Gassman) and *Camicie rosse* (1952), on Italian Resurgence.

Freda's efforts were such that not only *Caravaggio, il pittore maledetto* was completed on schedule, but it was also a good commercial success and saved Elica Films from bankruptcy. The critics were also unusually kind for a film of this type:

> Scriptwriters and writers haven't always seen the true dramatic line of this character, and here and there have impoverished him with useless or scarcely significant episodes; however, the film is staged with great wealth of resources, and it is exquisitely made, especially in the indoor scenes. Alessandrini has framed these scenes ... with results that one would often be tempted to call Caravaggio-like.[26]

After *Caravaggio*, Freda took part (uncredited) as production supervisor on other titles financed by Elica Film: *Dove andiamo signora?* (1942, Gian Maria Cominetti), *Musica proibita* (1942, Carlo Campogalliani) and possibly the Italian-Spanish co-production *Buongiorno, Madrid!* a.k.a. *Madrid de mis sueños* (1942, Gian Maria Cominetti, Max Neufeld), although he later denied having taken part in the latter.[27] However, the best film he collaborated to during this period was Raffaello Matarazzo's *L'avventuriera del piano di sopra* (The Adventuress Upstairs, 1941), a lively screwball comedy shot during the spring and summer 1941 at SAFA studios, which allowed the young Vittorio De Sica one of his best starring roles of the period as a man who is married to a very jealous

Left to right: Clara Calamai, Carlo Campanini and Vittorio De Sica in a set still from *L'avventuriera del piano di sopra* (1941, Raffaello Matarazzo).

woman, and whose quiet life is upset after the meeting with his mysterious upstairs neighbor, played by the ravishing Clara Calamai, which gives way to a series of misconceptions. According to Freda, *L'avventuriera del piano di sopra* was Matarazzo's first truly personal work, and further proof of his eclecticism.

Despite being credited with scriptwriting duties, Freda later denied having had a hand in the script, which was solely the work of Matarazzo and Edoardo Antonelli. He simply took care of the art direction and the editing, besides handling the production duties on the part of Elica Film, and was proud of the result, "one of the wildest of the period, it featured a forbidden situation such as adultery which was not allowed and which passed the censors probably because it was just hinted at." Freda refers to the ending, where, after all the misunderstandings have settled Fabrizio (De Sica) says "Now we are neighbors. We'll come upstairs…" and Bianca Maria (Calamai) replies, "And we'll come downstairs," hinting at a transgressive *ménage à quatre*. To Freda, *L'avventuriera del piano di sopra* "was the proof that Matarazzo was really a complete filmmaker, who could make all kinds of films and not just melodramas."[28] With his typical sharp tongue, he also delighted in recounting that Mario Soldati's future wife Jucci Kellerman was then his mistress, and that he provided her a small role in the film.

As with *Caravaggio*, the impressive sets were the work of Veniero Colasanti, the son of the renowned art critic Arduino Colasanti: the Colasanti family was closely tied to the

Fascist hierarchs, which helped Veniero find his way in the movie biz. Over the years he would become one of Italy's best art directors and costume designers, and gained an Academy Award nomination for his work on *El Cid* (1961).

The basic plot for *L'avventuriera del piano di sopra* was reused twice: Matarazzo himself, after moving to Spain from 1943 to 1945, recycled it for the stage play *Una mujer entre los brazos* (1945), and Freda himself submitted the story to Alberto Sordi: the resulting remake, *Buonanotte ... avvocato!* (1955), starring Sordi and directed by Giorgio Bianchi, credited Matarazzo for the story, while the screenplay was rewritten by Sordi, Ruggero Maccari, Ettore Scola, Giovanni Grimaldi and Felice Zappulla.

After five years dabbling as a scriptwriter and an already consistent (if hardly memorable) string of collaborations, it was time for Riccardo Freda to make his official film debut. The circumstances were hardly favorable, as Italy was experiencing the harsh reality of a war that was proving to be quite different from the blitzkrieg that Mussolini had imagined.

3

Filming During Wartime

Don Cesare di Bazan

When he was given the opportunity to make his debut as a director, Riccardo Freda was already a well-respected and wealthy scriptwriter. "I told myself why not, didn't jump for joy. The future proved I was right,"[1] he later claimed. Even though a war was raging, the movie industry seemed to have been only slightly affected by it. Propaganda was secondary compared to what happened in other countries, and the films dealing with the ongoing conflict were few and far between: war movies started appearing later on, when Italy was already experiencing tough times in the battlefield. Because of their relative freedom and independence from the regime, most filmmakers were able to move in different directions.

For his feature film debut, Freda took inspiration from the literary passions of his youth. Even though the credits for *Don Cesare di Bazan* list it as based on the French comic *opéra Don César de Bazan* by Adolphe d'Ennery and Philippe Dumanoir—virtually unknown in Italy, despite having been adapted for the screen a number of times in the past since the early silent era[2]—the script actually drew back to Victor Hugo's drama *Ruy Blas*, which had in turn inspired d'Ennery and Dumanoir's work. As a fan of historical and adventure films since an early age, and a devoted reader of Dumas' *oeuvre*, Freda chose to heighten the swashbuckling aspect, albeit throwing in a bit of Shakespeare for good measure, when Don Cesare's attendant mockingly recites him a line from *Romeo and Juliet*. Set in late 17th century, the film centers on the titular hero, a Spanish Count who casually uncovers a conspiracy against the king of Spain, but is framed by the conspirators and sentenced to death, only to escape from jail and triumphantly return to save the king's life. Freda and his collaborators kept only a few basic elements from the original play—Don Cesare being imprisoned after a duel, his marriage in prison with a beautiful woman whose face he does not even get to see, and a young boy's trick to save him from the firing squad—and threw the rest away, concocting a new story altogether.

Freda collaborated on the script with two prestigious names, the Sicilian writer Vitaliano Brancati, in his first effort as a scriptwriter, and Cesare Zavattini. Brancati (1907–1954) would go on and write a number of excellent novels set about the mores (mostly sexual) of his region, including *Don Giovanni in Sicilia* (*Don Juan in Sicily*), brought to the screen by Alberto Lattuada in 1967, *Il bell'Antonio* (*Beautiful Antonio*) made into a film in 1959 by Mauro Bolognini, and the posthumous *Paolo il caldo* (*Paolo Unbound*), which was adapted into a box office hit by Marco Vicario in 1973. Brancati's works often caused controversy, and his scripts and stage plays were sometimes heavily censored: a case in point was the writer's vitriolic take on the Fascist regime *Anni difficili* (1948, Luigi Zampa), based on his own novel. A former journalist and satirical author, Zavattini (1902–1989) would soon become one of the founding fathers of Neorealism due to his collaborations with Vittorio De Sica, which included *Sciuscià* (a.k.a. *Shoeshine*, 1946), *Ladri di biciclette* (a.k.a. *The Bicycle Thief*, 1948) and *Miracolo a Milano* (a.k.a. *Miracle in Milan*, 1951).

Even though he held Zavattini in high esteem, Freda would always be very critical toward Neorealism over the years, and pointed out the writer's substantial detachment from the genre he was always associated with.

> The funny thing is that Zavattini was a fan of this type of films [such as *Don Cesare di Bazan*]. That is to say, if he had to go to the movies, he'd never go and see a Zavattini-penned film, he would watch *Zorro* instead. When this chance came, he took it with frank enthusiasm, without that snobbish attitude like, well, I don't care about it since I'm doing it for the money.[3]

Later on, Freda and Zavattini worked together on another script, the sadly never made *Orlando furioso* (The Frenzy of Orlando), based on Ludovico Ariosto's epic poem.

Italian poster for *Don Cesare di Bazan* (1942).

The third credited scriptwriter was the renowned Sergio Amidei, but Freda denied that he had any involvement in the making of the film. On the other hand Amidei, when interviewed by film historian Francesco Savio, claimed to have written the script for director Mario Bonnard.[4] Still, several sources indicate the participation of the essayist and literary critic Giacomo Debenedetti, who, being a Jew, did not officially feature among the scriptwriting credits due to Fascism's racial laws; during that period, Amidei often figured as a front for him.

Don Cesare di Bazan has its share of nods to the regime. Significantly, Spain—where a similar Fascist regime ruled, led by General Francisco Franco with the consent of the Church—is described in terms that could well be applied to Fascist Italy. It is labeled as "powerful," his soldiers returning home "full of glory," whereas the enemy—that is, France—is called "envious" and depicted as scheming and duplicitous. Another important value is national unity: Don Cesare fights against the separatists who are attempting to divide Catalonia from the "motherland." This was not uncommon in adventure films of the period, such as *La figlia del Corsaro Verde* (1940, Enrico Guazzoni) or D'Errico's *Capitan Tempesta*, where the period setting was often a pretext for blatant propaganda messages. Still, the opening line functions mostly as decoy, as overall the film proves positively devoid of explicit patriotic innuendo.

Freda immediately established himself as an assured, if often choleric, filmmaker. His innovative and refreshing approach is evident from the very opening, set inside a crowded tavern in Barcelona. After a brief lateral tracking shot to the left which effectively sketches the ambience, populated with gallant knights and beautiful women of dubious virtue, a cross-dissolve cuts to a quartet of players—the closest to the camera being only a synecdoche, his hands playing the guitar; then, a remarkable, much longer tracking shot to the opposite direction follows a beautiful female flamenco dancer who advances in time with the music across the tavern, gaily avoiding the many customers who try to grab her. The camera moves like a living presence, passing behind groups of people while exquisitely crossing the whole environment, and the scene is choreographed like a fresco, with different depths of field and a keen eye on composition and the movement of extras.

The tracking shot will become one of Freda's signature techniques, allowing him to put minimal budgets to best use and enhance the spectacular values of his films by highlighting movement and dynamism, while at the same time emphasizing the scene's emotional value. Freda cuts to the woman jumping on the table, while still dancing, then to Don Cesare, surrounded by two ladies. Then, the editing gets tighter, with no less than 15 shots in 25 seconds, as the protagonist and his friends look dazzled by the music and inebriated by wine as well as by the sight of the glamorous dancer, applauding and beating their hands in time with the music. When the number ends, Don Cesare welcomes the dancer in his arms. More wine is brought to the table, and someone proposes a toast "to the most heroic soldier in Spain." Don Cesare corrects him: "No—to all the women in Spain. To the passionate ones in Sevilla, the suave in Toledo, the sweetest in Malaga … and to all of you, the oh-so-unfaithful in Barcelona!" he concludes, before passionately kissing her. In just a couple of minutes, Freda portrayed the filmic universe he loved and whose memory he perpetrated throughout most of his work: music, entertainment, beautiful women, gallant adventurers who love them as much as they love their sword. And, to quote one line in the film, "to beauty and heroes everything is due."

Compared with the adventure epics made in Italy in the early 1940s, *Don Cesare di Bazan* immediately displays a more energetic approach, which reflected the director's idea of film as pure spectacle. The camera moves restlessly—mostly with sideways tracking shots, preferring the use of long takes to a succession of still plans—and the style is patently influenced by such great filmmakers as D. W. Griffith, F. W. Murnau, Fritz Lang and John Ford; the latter's influence is evident in the shots of the musicians, with light-and-shadows touches that in turn hint at Ford's own interpretation of Expressionism. The modernity of the style is evident in the adoption of many different points of view throughout a scene, as in the remarkable sequence that follows Don Cesare's introduction, the meeting of the conspirators in the tavern's canteen, where the director brings an outstanding rhythm to a dense, information-ridden dialogue scene. Another example is the scene in which the wagons with the gunpowder are traveling through the countryside, drawn by oxen: it almost looks as if it was taken from a Hollywood Western, with plenty of cross-dissolves and an airy use of exteriors (including the falls at Monte Gelato, near Rome) as opposed to the heavily contrasted studio-bound scenes.

Freda's reliance on American-style film techniques at times proved challenging for his collaborators, who were sticking to a more cautious approach to filmmaking. When he illustrated to his director of photography Mario Craveri his intention to make an axial cut from a medium shot to a close-up—a rather common occurrence in Hollywood pics—Craveri considered it nothing short of heresy. "When I told him that the Americans used to do that, he rolled his eyes and merely whispered: 'Oh, the Americans, that's another thing....'"[5] Moral of the story: Freda had to wait two or three more films before he could finally make an axial cut.

The debuting director also refused to oblige to a common unwritten rule in Italian cinema, that is lighting the actors' face as well as putting a backlight behind them so that they would always be surrounded by what looked like a luminous aura: instead, he demanded a less artificial, more subdued lighting. Given that at that time, due to the American Majors' embargo toward the Fascist regime,[6] no one had seen the more recent Hollywood productions such as *Stagecoach* (1939, John Ford) and *Citizen Kane* (1941, Orson Welles), Freda's attitude was even more disruptive within the static and conservative Italian cinema of the period.

For the climax Freda injected a comedy note which also functioned as an ironic self-reference to his own somewhat innovative approach, as Don Cesare and his acolytes sneak into the Count's castle (where the conspirators are planning to dispatch the king) by posing as an itinerant stage company, that is to put on stage the *Don Juan*. The rehearsal and stage play scenes offer some amusing gags, as Don Cesare's valet Sancho flatly refuses to play a woman's role ("That would be an offense, to me and to art!") and the chief comedian sighs in desperation, "But then who is Don Juan going to seduce?," to which Don Cesare indifferently replies: "Let's just start, in any case we won't get to the end of the play!" Later on, as the actor playing Don Juan refuses to bow down in front of someone (actually out of fear that his tight scene costume might rip up), a member of the audience comments that he is a "modern, new Don Juan," to which another adds: "With this modernity craze of this new century, who knows where we will end!"

Don Cesare di Bazan was entirely filmed at the Pisorno studios in Tirrenia, the oldest in the country. The director's knowledge of figurative arts is well in evidence, as the movie reeks with visual references that make it one of the most luxurious-looking films of the period. For one thing, there are nods to the great 17th century Spanish painter Diego Velázquez: the depiction of King Philip IV and his court—complete with a dwarf with a dog on the leash—looks like the characters were lifted off one of his masterpieces, such as *Las Meninas*; incidentally, Freda managed to include Velázquez in a scene, played by film producer Ermanno Donati. On the other hand, the set pieces, by Gastone Medin (Harriet White's husband, and one of Italian cinema's greatest production designers), recall the etchings of the 18th century incisor Giovanni Battista Piranesi, whose "Imaginary Prisons" proved a great influence on Romanticism and Surrealism. Freda claimed he personally designed some sets: "There is a sequence, set at night, on a harbor where Don Cesare punctures the barrels of powder. I made the *maquette* myself: the pontoon, the galleons, the fog—it's a rather short scene but very effective."[7]

Still, *Don Cesare di Bazan* remains a rather stale-looking film, mostly because of the overly stilted dialogue as well as of Gino Cervi's somewhat flawed casting as the titular swashbuckler. The lead was practically imposed on the director—an understandable commercial move, since Cervi was then perhaps Italy's biggest star, having appeared in such box-office hits as Alessandro Blasetti's *Un'avventura di Salvator Rosa*, where he played the 17th century baroque painter-cum-adventurer, and *La corona di ferro* (1941). Still, to Freda he was not fit for the role: despite his assured, flamboyant performance, Cervi's portly appearance (not to mention his frightening wig) severely diminishes Don Cesare's charisma. For the action scenes, such as the hero jumping on tables and the like, the crew had to make do with hidden trampolines, and partially succeeded in suggesting an air of agility.[8]

The other characters are a bit by-the-numbers. As the villain, the Neapolitan Enrico Glori (real name Enrico Musy)—who the previous year had played Don Rodrigo in Mario Camerini's *I promessi sposi* (*The Spirit and the Flesh*, 1941, based on Alessandro Manzoni's novel *The Betrothed*)—is a bit too mannered: his cold posture, tiny mustache and goatee and affected manners sound a tad wooden, even though Freda attempts a few understated humorous bits, such as in the scene where the effeminate Ambassador is seen doing his ablutions, coquettishly applying perfume on his face and lip balm over his lips before another conspirator, the decidedly more rude-looking Don José. As the love interest—Renèè, the woman who Don Cesare is forced to marry in prison, not knowing she is one of the conspirators—the German-born Anneliese Uhlig's ravishing beauty somehow makes up for Renèè's blandly sketched inner turmoil. Even though her character is not among the most memorable of Freda's career, the director staged an impressive romantic scene between Renèè and Don Cesare, in which the man slyly replaces the blade she is handling out of defense with a rose: the stiletto falls onto the floor over the woman's long skirt while the two kiss passionately.

For the comedy relief, the film mostly relies on Paolo Stoppa, as Don Cesare's valet Sancho, who dreams of being an actor and playing Hamlet. One of the great thesps of Italian stage, Stoppa was a chameleon-like presence in Italian cinema of the period, often playing supporting parts that went from drama to broad comedy, and even adventure (such as the rebel peasant in *Un'avventura di Salvator Rosa*). Further proof of Stoppa's eclecticism is his starring role as the bizarre comic character Signor Bonaventura (Mister Goodluck) in Sergio Tofano's fairytale *Cenerentola e il signor Bonaventura* (a.k.a. *Princess Cinderella*, 1941), adapted from Tofano's own strip. On the other hand, the imposing Enzo Biliotti, as King Philip IV, was often employed in similar commanding roles: that same year he played Napoleon III in Flavio Calzavara's historical drama *La contessa Castiglione* (a.k.a. *The Countess of Castiglione*, 1942). Freda's love for juvenile adventure can also be found in the lively portrayal of the soldier kid whom Cesare rescues from punishment and who in turn will save the Count's life.

The critics welcomed the film rather positively, noting that the director displayed "the technical, spectacular and narrative ease of a veteran" and praising the "lively and elegant care for details."[9] The most important positive review was penned by Leo Longanesi, the renowned satirical author who was one of the regime's most influential voices. He and Freda would soon become close friends, under adventurous circumstances. However, the director was so critical toward his feature film debut that he would remake it twenty years later, with *Le sette spade del vendicatore* (1962). Freda believed *Don Cesare di Bazan* had not aged well: he labeled the action sequences as unconvincing, and the story as a bit too simplistic. This last observation was not completely off-mark, though: the Ambassador's plan, which has Don Cesare marry Renèè just before execution so that she can inherit his title and castle, and therefore invite King Philip to the manor where he will be killed by the conspirators, is far-fetched and contrived. Here, it is evident how Freda cared more about the visuals and the overall concept of the two newlyweds who do not even get to see each other, as the wedding takes place with both of them segregated and separated by a thick, dense grid. The result is among the most beautiful-looking scenes in the picture.

As for the action bits, the climactic fight atop the castle may not be up to the rest of the film, indeed: besides being staged a bit perfunctorily, it suffers from a not-too-convincing set as well as from an euphemistic depiction of violence which makes it less convincing and barbaric than it is supposed to be. Still, it features suitably dramatic lighting, with Don Cesare's gigantic shadow towering over the wily Ambassador and bouts of lighting that intermittently punctuate the action. When Renéè shows up near the end of the duel, a quick tracking shot onwards to her face highlights her desperate scream, warning her beloved Don Cesare of impending danger (his wounded enemy is about to hit him in the back) and saving his life: the unexpectedly abrupt camera movement has a neat dramatic effect that predates the use of zoom in years to come and, despite the imperfect focusing, shows how the debuting director was already in full grasp of the medium. A similar insistence on a woman's desperate cry for maximum climactic effect will return in some of Freda's future works, such as *Il conte Ugolino* as well as his last picture, *Murder Obsession*. Elsewhere, he occasionally exceeds in underlining a visual effect: an example is Bazan's off-screen murder of the treacherous Prime Minister, as the camera didactically advances toward a court edict where the line can be read, "thus Justice strikes the guilty ruthlessly, relentlessly, very firmly."

All in all, *Don Cesare di Bazan* is a worthy introduction to Freda's *oeuvre*: a flawed yet incredibly vital, sprightly feature which nevertheless—when compared with the growing pains of Italian cinema, that would result in Luchino Visconti's *Ossessione* and lead to the post-war season of Neorealism—feels strangely timeless, a quality that will mark most of the director's work, making him a unique figure within the national film industry. What is more, it includes a line which perfectly summarizes Freda's vision of cinema as well as of life. "What thing in the world is more beautiful than illusion?"

Non canto più

Freda's sophomore directorial effort was a definite change of pace from *Don Cesare di Bazan*. Even though he claimed that the then-General Director of Cinematography, Eitel Monaco, personally wrote him a letter to praise his first picture, Freda maintained that his subsequent projects were rejected by the censors, starting with a movie on the boxing world titled *L'atleta di cristallo* (The Crystal Athlete).

> I was going to make a film about ... the behind-the-scenes, the skullduggery ... after months of discussions, it was rejected because they told me that you can't show that prizefighting takes place in a corrupted setting. After that one ... there was another project, which was also rejected for similar reasons. The motivation, generally, was that I was too American-oriented a filmmaker, you understand? That is, my type of films, according to them, was not Italian.[10]

Therefore, Freda was forced to accept whatever came handy; besides, being a film director, he could use long licences and avoid leaving for the front. There came *Non canto più*. The director recalled:

> The genesis of this film is rather amusing. One day I met Leo Longanesi and Mario Pannunzio, a journalist, a distinguished writer and a politician, at Rome's Imperiale theater. The owner was a certain Vassarotti, who was also a mythomaniac and an illitterate producer. That day, he told us about his next film, a big project with American stars. We listened to that daydreamer with mockery and affection. He thought of Gary Cooper and Ingrid Bergman for his movie. And if Bergman was not available, then he would settle on Garbo. Next day, the project followed its course, with Gary Cooper being replaced by some unknown, nondescript Italian thesp.... According to him, I would direct a film starring Gary Cooper, and found myself with Enzo Fiermonte, the contender for the world boxing championship and a pathetic actor.[11]

A former middleweight champion, Fiermonte (1908–1993) had abandoned boxing in 1934, and—after a brief stint at car racing—started his film career in 1941 with Piero Ballerini's boxing drama *L'ultimo combattimento*. Among other things, he was cast in Guido Brignone's version of *Beatrice Cenci*, but one of his most important roles was as the titular bandit in Luigi Zampa's *Fra' Diavolo* (1942). Freda's film was his first attempt at comedy. For the singing parts, Fiermonte was supposed to be dubbed by the popular tenor Beniamino Gigli, but eventually the makers opted for a German opera singer in Rome, who was much cheaper to work with.[12]

Freda wrote *Non canto più* with his friend Stefano Vanzina (better known as Steno) and Vittorio Metz, and shot it at Titanus Studios in Rome. After graduating at the Academy of Fine Arts, Vanzina (1915–1988) enrolled at Rome's Centro Sperimentale di Cinematografia, and at the same time he started collaborating as a drawing artist with a number of satirical magazines, such as *Tribuna Illustrata* and the famous *Marc'Aurelio*, where he worked alongside Marcello Marchesi and Metz (both popular playwrights and screenplayers) as well as with the young Federico Fellini. Steno's next step was scriptwriting: he took part in a huge number of films, and eventually made his debut behind the camera co-directing with Mario Monicelli *Al diavolo la celebrità* (a.k.a. *Fame and the Devil*, 1949). Steno would go on to become one of Italy's most important comedy filmmakers.

The plot of *Non canto più* revolves around a talented young singer named Giulio (Fiermonte) and a scheming theatrical agent (Paola Borboni), who, unbeknownst to him, concocts a complex scheme involving the theft of a valuable necklace in order to launch his career. The simulated theft puts in motion a series of events that lead Giulio to be arrested and undergo a series of misadventures, before the expected happy ending.

The opening scene, as usually with Freda, sets the tone and is remarkably well-staged. After a couple of establishing exterior shots of a seemingly American city, we are led inside a theatrical agency where a varied crowd can be observed: a juggler nonchalantly playing his game with a pair of oranges with just one hand, the other firmly in his pocket; a pair of identically-dressed twins; several model types reading fashion magazines; a woman raising over a table what at first appears to be a kid and is then revealed as a cigar-smoking midget; and an incredibly thin, semi-naked man who wears a turban, accompanied by a typical Indian melody. It is an impressive opening, and overall Freda's direction is never dull: here and there, he manages to set up a number of interesting shots, including a musical number played by a quartet of *mariachi* players that visually recall the flamenco quartet in *Don Cesare di Bazan*.

Despite the story being so puerile that even in its day it might have sounded preposterous, Freda and his scriptwriters come up with a variety of visual gags and surreal ideas—possibly drawing from Steno and Metz's experience at *Marc'Aurelio*—which subtly poke fun at the authorities and law enforcement, portrayed as ineffectual and dumb: the best one has the police forcing suspects to sing so as to compare their voice to Giulio's, thus giving literal meaning to a typical slang expression. Another amusing bit has a pair of doctors apparently performing a difficult surgery who are revealed to be veterinarians intent on operating on a bull. On the other hand, the climax is an ingenious tour de force in pure screwball comedy fashion, with misunderstandings galore and all the main characters converging behind a theater's stage while frantically attempting to get rid of the stolen necklace, which pops up in the most unexpected places. Overall, the mere existence of *Non canto più* should be enough to wipe away superficial observations about the lack of humor in Freda's filmography.

The characterizations owe a lot to the Italian *telefoni bianchi* films, but with the injection of a sharp subversive vein: the main example is the ruthless impresario Greta Arden, who is so money-minded that, when presented with a poster announcing "Juanito, the Mad Singer" whose drawing does not resemble the singer at all, instead of having the poster replaced she asks Juanito to change his looks via plastic surgery instead. Speaking of the protagonist's vocal qualities, she claims: "He does not have a throat, but a checking account!" to which Giulio will later add, "You're not a woman, you're an accounting log!"

The restrictions imposed by the Fascist regime make for a few unintended chuckles: even though the setting is—rather unlikely—Mexico, all the names are Italianized due to Fascism's strict rules about films set abroad, while Guadalajara is misspelled as "Guadalaiana." Despite the overall light tone, political correctness is not 100 percent guaranteed: a cringe-inducing moment has the hero passingly remarking that he "hates niggers."

The cast is a mixed bunch. Enzo Fiermonte is a hopelessly dull lead with no flair for comedy. After a brief shot at celebrity, he was soon relegated to secondary roles in post-war years: one of his most memorable appearances is in Roger Corman's *The Secret Invasion* (1964), as the Italian general that must be rescued from a Yugoslavian prison during World War II. In the 1950s Freda concocted a scenario for his omnibus project *Il dito di Dio* (God's Finger), which was partly inspired by Fiermonte's childhood during the early days of Fascism and his career as a prizefighter, but the film never got made. German actress Vera Bergman, who enjoyed a brief popularity in Italy after appearing in Vittorio De Sica's *Maddalena ... zero in condotta* (a.k.a. *Maddalena, Zero for Conduct*, 1940), is more lively as the love interest, Lisa, while Paola Borboni (1900–1995), one of Italy's most enduring actresses, with a career spanning nine decades, from 1916 to her death, is perfect as the greedy agent. Arturo Bragaglia (the brother of director Carlo Ludovico Bragaglia, who worked frequently with Totò, and of the great stage director Anton Giulio Bragaglia) plays the film's funniest character, a corpulent Commissioner who dresses like the Mexican bandits in Western flicks. All the scenes featuring him and Lisa's veterinarian fiancé (played by comedian Virgilio Riento) are consistently amusing, and hint at what a much better film *Non canto più* might have been, had Freda and his acolytes got rid of the romantic plot and piled on the comedy.

Even though it was filmed in 1943, *Non canto più* was shelved for two years because of the troubled situation following the fall of Fascism, Mussolini's arrest and the armistice. It was eventually submitted to the board of censors only on December 26, 1944, and received a Visa in March 1945, several months after the liberation of Rome. It was finally distributed in September 1945.

The troubled days of Summer 1943, when Italy was about to collapse under the fall of the Fascist regime, also saw the making of a project on which Freda had worked as a scriptwriter, *L'abito nero da sposa* (The Black Wedding Dress), based on *The Cardinal* by Louis N. Parker, a dusty stage play which had some notoriety in Italy (and had been blacklisted by the Church), set in 16th century Florence, about the innocent Giuliano de' Medici being unjustly accused of murder, and his brother, Cardinal Giovanni, unmasking the real culprit. It was originally to be directed by the debuting Mario Pannunzio, who then backed out. Luigi Zampa, who was in the army and about to leave for the Russian front, was given a 60-day permit to direct the film. Even though *L'abito nero da sposa* is far from his best work, it probably saved his life. On September the 8th, 1943, during principal shooting, General Badoglio signed the armistice and joined the Allies as cobelligerent. Filming was interrupted and resumed after the arrival of the American troops in Rome, in June 1944. *L'abito nero da sposa* was eventually released in May 1945, right after the end of the war.

Zampa was trenchant about his early films, this included: "I prefer not to remember [them]. They taught me how to move the camera and direct the actors. But I never tried to watch them again, there is nothing inside them. They were just spectacles."[13] On the other hand, the critics panned *L'abito nero da sposa*. "Amidst pompous sets, wigs and fake beards, our actors ... bear these archaic make-ups with dignified easiness.... Hopefully this film will forever end the cycle of Italian-made costume dramas—just for good!"[14] a reviewer sharply wrote. And indeed there is very little to salvage in this static drama, despite the names involved. Freda collaborated with the prestigious Ennio Flaiano (Fellini's *La dolce vita*, 1960) and his friend Leo Longanesi, but the trio did very little to inject some life into the overly theatrical proceedings. The result had all the flaws of the period films made in Italy during the decade—exceedingly talky, turgid and ultimately dull as hell—with few points of interest. Zampa also included a rather risqué bit, in which a group of young girls who are taking a bath are abducted by soldiers, signaling the possibility that a more explicit version might have been intended for the foreign markets—something that would definitely happen with Freda's own *Aquila nera*. Perhaps Freda was mostly interested in the vague crime story elements, with the character of the cardinal (played with hammy self-indulgence by Fosco Giachetti) turning out to be a detective of sorts, but ultimately there is very little in *L'abito nero da sposa* that anticipates his future work, if not by contrast. And this becomes evident when comparing Zampa's film with his own debut, *Don Cesare di Bazan*.

Tutta la città canta

Freda's third feature film as a director was yet another a musical comedy, the kind of light-hearted entertainment that was being produced during the regime's last days. Once again the inspiration was Hollywood: the idea was to put together a "revue" film comprising the period's major singers and movie stars, along the vein of *The Hollywood Revue of 1929* (1929, Charles F. Reisner). Interestingly, the main focus was jazz music, a very delicate topic during Fascism: despite the regime's strong Anti-Americanism, jazz became more and more popular in the country, so much so that one of the Duce's sons, Romano, was an accomplished jazz pianist; he would often work in the movies, scoring such titles as Umberto Lenzi's *Kriminal* (1966). On January 14, 1935, Louis Armstrong performed a show in Turin, and soon a number of jazz clubs opened in the major cities, followed between 1937 and 1941 by the first Italian music labels that specialized in the genre. However, a 1936 law imposed to translate in Italian all the English terms in the songs, as well as the artists' names: Armstrong became "Luigi Braccioforte" while Benny Goodman was baptized "Beniamino Buonomo"—that is, the literal translation of their names. Nevertheless, as late as 1938 jazz was still enjoying an enormous popularity in the country: every night at 8:40 the national broadcasting radio service EIAR featured a jazz music quartet. Then, after the 1938 racial laws, Jazz was labeled as "Negroid music" and banished from the radio. After Italy entered the war in June 1940, night clubs were closed and American music was utterly forbidden, forcing record label executives and musicians to camouflage their American sources under Italian titles and names.

For his film, Freda gathered an impressive group of players, led by Nino Taranto (1907–1986), a crackerjack Neapolitan stage and radio comedian who in the following years would often pair up with Totò, and act in about a hundred films up to 1971. Natalino Otto (1912–1969) was a jazz singer who had often performed on American radio in the 1930s, and whose repertoire included Italianized versions of U.S. jazz standards such as *Saint Louis Blues* or *Mr. Paganini*: his popularity in Italy was amazing, considering that he had been banned from the radio by the regime, due to his "barbaric Negro anti-music." Singer-actress Vivi Gioi (1914–1975) had became a recurring presence in the *telefoni bianchi* films, but her 1943 interpretation of the song *Lili Marleen* was censored because of its allegedly pacifist message, which was accused of "depressing the soldiers' morale." Last but not least, the three Bonos brothers (Gianni, 1907–1956; Vittorio, 1908–1956; and Luigi, 1910–2000) were a trio of fantasists who specialized in a wacky comic routine somehow reminiscent of the Marx Brothers' antics, but with a certain circus-like flair.

During the scriptwriting phase, Freda met a young satirical cartoonist who would become Italy's greatest film director: the then 23-year-old Federico Fellini, who at that time was still a contributor to the satirical magazines *Bertoldo* and *Marc'Aurelio*. Freda recalled his contribution to the film:

> Vittorio Metz introduced him to me.... Fellini took part, so to speak, to two or three meetings. He listened heedlessly, while scribbling on sheet after sheet of paper with a pen. Those were neither suggestions nor notes: Federico just kept drawing, and he drew huge naked women, real giantesses. I think paroxysmally fat women were one of his hidden obsessions. Then, probably rightly so, he disappeared.[15]

Fellini and Freda met again several times over the years, and the latter's judgment on the creator of *La dolce vita* was—as it often happened—harsh to the point of insult. "Up until the end, when we bumped on each other somewhere, he used to call me "my little Riccardino," which embarrassed me. I met him some time later, strangely enough, in a night club. I was with [Gianna Maria] Canale, he was with his wife, Giulietta Masina, who had that unmistakable, really unpleasant voice. I remember that he offered to produce my next film: it was probably because of Canale, who was absolutely ravishing, that such an idea came to him. Then we never met again, except fleetingly. Once, casually, in a Parisian street. He hugged me with his usual hypocritical and insincere affection, then never again. I called him on the phone a couple of times, and he refused to speak to me."[16]

As Freda recalled, recording the music for the film had to be done in a very discreet way. "We recorded the music at Fono Roma, the biggest studio in town, whose technicians took us for revolutionaries. On the street outside I had placed some watchmen who had to warn us of the arrival of Blackshirts. And in a few seconds we would replace *Louisiana Blues* with a Neapolitan song," he recalled amusedly.[17]

Principal shooting started in 1943 at the Pisorno studios in Tirrenia—with Freda's wife Angiola (credited as Angela Freda) credited as assistant director and costume designer—under the title *6 × 8 / 48* (based on one of the musical numbers) and came to a halt after a couple of weeks, as the events of the war were rapidly escalating. Italy was on its knees, after the fall of Tunis in May, the bombings on Rome and the landing of the Allies in Sicily, and both the king and the Fascist hierarchs were looking for an exit strategy: change the government, get out of the war and get rid of the alliance with Germany as soon as possible. On July 25, the Grand Council of Fascism saw the passing of a vote of no confidence against Benito Mussolini, marking the *de facto* end of the 21-year-old regime. Mussolini was arrested by order of King Vittorio Emanuele III and 46 days later, on September 8, Italy signed the Armistice with the Allies. The belief that such a move would mark the end of the war soon proved illusory: confusion ensued, as the majority of the Italian Army had not been informed about the armistice and no orders had been issued about the line of conduct to be taken in the face of the German armed forces. The Nazi troops were still occupying the Northern and Central regions of the country, and checked the Allies for over a year, while Mussolini and his most faithful hierarchs, rescued by the Germans, founded the short-lived Italian Social Republic in Northern Italy, based in Salò. A cruel conflict ensued between German and RSI troops on one hand and the Italian resistance movement on the other.

After the Armistice, the film industry virtually stopped dead in its tracks. Cinecittà was gravely damaged by the Allied bombings and ransacked by the German troops. A production center named Cinevillaggio was created by the RSI between Venice, Turin and Montecatini Terme, with the aim of shooting propaganda films: a small number of actors and directors adhered to it, including regime stars such as Osvaldo Valenti and Luisa Ferida and filmmakers Giorgio Ferroni, Carmine Gallone and Francesco De Robertis. It produced 16 films in a couple of years. The majority chose to make themselves unavailable. Freda and his friends Steno, Leo Longanesi and Enzo Fiermonte fled from Rome and headed to Naples, following a winding route in the countryside to avoid the Germans.

The recollection of that fortuitous escape occupies some of the most intense pages in Freda's memoir *Divoratori di celluloide*: besides the occasional amusing anecdote—such as the director and his acolytes posing as allied officers and introducing themselves as Captain Warner, Colonel Metro, Lieutenant Erkaio (that is, RKO…) and Captain Universal—the book paints a vivid picture of the chaotic, desperate situation that the Italian people were experiencing in those days. At the end of their adventurous journey, Freda, Steno and Longanesi took refuge at Torella dei Lombardi, near Avellino, at Dino De Laurentiis' house, where they joined Mario Soldati, who had also fled from the Capital, and then moved to Sorrento, Capri and Naples. There, Freda and Longanesi were destined to the Centro Italiano di Propaganda (Italian Propaganda Center) and worked on a daily radio broadcast called *Stella bianca* (White Star), which consisted of comedy sketches, anti–Fascist satire and classical music. They also concocted a comic magazine, *L'Adolfo*, which told Mussolini's life as a *feuilleton* spoof, with drawings by Longanesi himself, and which lasted only one issue. Freda then left for Bari, where he worked for the O.S.S. He returned to his house at Trinità dei Monti in Rome right after the liberation.

Production for *6 × 8 / 48* was resumed only in the late Spring of 1945, but the director had to deal with the fact that most of the cast was not available, while the female star Vivi Gioi had put on weight. In a move that he would repeat quite a few times in the future, he simply chose to go along, replacing actors with doubles and making ample use of quick cutting and camera movements so as for the audience not to notice. The film was finally submitted to the board of censors in July 1945 and was released theatrically the following month as *Tutta la città canta*[18]—a title that hinted at *The Whole Town's Talking* (1935), in a further nod to the director's love for John Ford—to little commercial success. By then, jazz was no longer a "hot" topic: it had became legal once again and did not have the same forbidden taste as just a couple of years earlier.

Tutta la città canta opens in an off-putting way, with a brief 30-second fragment that displays Freda's technique and influences and at the same time announces the free-spirited, even anarchic mood that imbues the film. The setting is a prison, filled with oblique shadows, Expressionist-like camera angles and ominous lighting. An off-screen voice announces "It's about eight!" while an ugly man in a top hat stands next to a switch: he is an executioner, waiting for the hour to come to administer capital punishment. An inmate in a horizontal-striped prison uniform is being tied to an electric chair by two guards, while a stern-looking man (the prison warden) is watching a clock on the wall as the fatal hour approaches. A quick montage follows: a close-up of the anguished prisoner; the executioner (whose angular face vividly resembles a skull) with his hand about to push the switch; the prison warden; the clock; and again the prisoner, whose face is lit by an intermittent light-and-shadow effect. The clock strikes eight, the warden nods, the switch is turned on, the camera rapidly advances as the condemned shakes on the chair … under an incongruous bout of water. It turns out that it was only a dream. The inmate is actually the protagonist, Orazio, who is being awakened in a decidedly rough manner—by way of a watering can—by his two hag-like aunts: it's eight o' clock, he must wake up…

It is yet another impressive beginning, which gives a good idea of the ingenious screenplay that Freda and his co-writers concocted. The director's description of the film as being some sort of companion to Hollywood's revue films is diminishing: even though it features several musical numbers, *Tutta la città canta* is first and foremost a comedy, with a wide variety of gags. The feeble red thread—the ongoing misunderstanding between Orazio, who believes he has inherited a goldmine (whereas he has actually been bequeathed a stage company named Gold Mine!), his greedy relatives and the company members, who in turn believe he is a millionaire—is revived with a wild amount of gags, which vary from wordplay to surreal bravado, and which are seemingly in tone with the comic magazines of the period, such as the renowned weekly *Bertoldo*, published between 1936 and 1943, which featured such collaborators as Fellini and Vittorio Metz, plus Cesare Zavattini as the editor-in-chief. One gag at the beginning has Orazio—who is being mercilessly exploited by his aunts, Cinderella-style—act as a "human floor polisher," rubbing the floor with his hands while his hulking cousin holds him by the legs; when his aunt complains that she can't find the cat, he objects: "I'm not eating any mice then!"

Taranto, an exceptionally gifted comic actor, gives a commanding performance which requires him as many physical feats as singing skills, in pure vaudeville spirit. In a number of occasions—such as Orazio's arrival at a luxury hotel after learning about his heritage, appropriately dressed as a miner and carrying a pickaxe, or the amusing scene where he unwittingly wears a "musical jacket" in front of the whole school—his antics distinctly recall Totò, not only because of Taranto's passing resemblance to the great Neapolitan comedian, but also because of their common roots in vaudeville. That said, many of the film's gags rely on the shoulders of the "3 Bonos," whose approach to physical and verbal comedy may be not to everyone's taste. The bad-toothed brothers are oblivious to the meaning of the word "subtlety," and yet Freda somehow manages to keep them on a leash, basically by keeping a spirited pace throughout. An example is the silent sequence where the three obnoxious comedians wreak havoc at a public bath and go around painting people's faces, trimming their beards and cutting their mustaches (a bizarre way indeed to convince the victims to gather at their theater, pay the ticket and punish the responsible ... that is, the unaware Orazio). Here, Freda employs weird angles galore so as to heighten the scene's dreamlike absurdity.

Overall, the mise-en-scène is suitably dynamic, with the director's beloved sideways tracking shots helping define the characters' comic function as well as building up a gag through their movements within the shot, as in the scene where the company members are preparing lunch in their crowded dressing room; another of Freda's formal traits is the tracking shot forwards or backwards, which is put to good use during a musical number featuring Natalino Otto and the "3 Bonos"; what is more, an impressively whirling shot follows Taranto's frantic run up a set of stairs, pursued by his furious aunts, with the camera mounted on a crane and making a 360 degree turn while ascending. However, Freda's claims that he had to replace the actors with doubles on many scenes for the additional shooting seem to be an exaggeration: only sporadically, as in the final number, one has the impression that the long shots feature different performers.

Despite its zaniness being all over the place, *Tutta la città canta* conveys a distinct anarchic spirit which is aimed at precise targets. Orazio's aunts are the quintessence of petit-bourgeoisie's craving for wealth and respectability, paired with the will to appear much more refined and elegant than they are: as soon as they learn about Orazio's heritage, the two women move to a palace ridden with art objects, and blather about having bought a painting by "Raffaello Da Vinci" (Freda will poke fun at the general public's ignorance about art in his second Coplan film as well). Even more caustic is the script's take on authority, represented by the duplicitous and scheming principal of the school where Orazio is employed, the "Institute of Severity and Culture."

The authors' vision of school as a grey, joyless place and their rebellious satire on it is evident from the beginning—two students are even named after Marchesi and Steno ("You're a small kid but you talk too much!" Orazio warns the latter)—and climaxes in a delicious musical number where multiplication tables become the lyrics for the song "6 × 6," sung by Natalino Otto in schoolboy uniform. What is more, Fascism's cult of physical shape is openly ridiculed: "It doesn't matter that the body be sane. My grandpa, even though he was very healthy, was a complete idiot," bursts out the General Inspector, who seems to have inherited quite a bit from his grandfather. As Steno later observed,

> working on these films was some kind of a release. I don't want to say that we stirred up a revolt, but we were content with working on topics that were extraneous to the regime. Perhaps it was also a way to put our heads underground, like ostriches, but at least it was an attempt to make a discourse that would not compromise us on a political plan.[19]

Freda had no kind words for *Tutta la città canta*, going so far as calling it "a terrible turnip of a film" and maintaining (in his conversation with Éric Poindron) that he would give two million *lire* to the viewer who would spot all the "52 technical errors" in the picture. However, he admitted that "the attempt at jazz was amusing. It was a '*spaghetti musical*.'"[20] The film was restored by the Cineteca of Milan and screened at the 2010 Venice Festival.

The hectic days after the liberation saw Freda return to work, although briefly, on a bland comedy starring baritone Tito Gobbi, *07... tassì* (07... Taxi, 1945). He never mentioned his uncredited contribution to the film; however, according to some sources, he seemingly worked on it not only as editor but also as a director, albeit for a minimal period. The production started with scenarist Marcello Pagliero (one of Italy's very best scriptwriters, in Freda's opinion, in his debut behind the camera) under precarious conditions: actress Germana Paolieri recalled shooting had often to be stopped because of blackouts and bombings. It was halted after the 1943 armistice, briefly resumed by Freda and eventually finished by Alberto D'Aversa after the liberation of Rome. D'Aversa (1920–1969) directed another film in Italy, *Una voce nel tuo cuore* (1949, starring Vittorio Gassman) before moving to South America in 1950. According to film historian Aldo Bernardini, *07... tassì* was "the only movie made in Rome after the Capital's liberation which managed to be released before the end of 1944,"[21] while other sources date the release to late 1945 or early 1946. A reviewer, panning the film, wrote: "The posters don't carry the director's name, and we, understanding the reasons of such discretion, will keep it a secret."[22]

4

Adventure, Italian-style

Aquila nera

Following a forced period of inactivity right after the end of the war, which even pushed him to sell rare books in order to make ends meet as all his projects seemed to fall under a bad sign, in 1946 Freda could finally return to filmmaking. This time, though, after two musical comedies which he could hardly care less about, he was allowed to put together a period adventure film. The timing could not have been worse: with the end of the conflict, Italian directors were developing a new, groundbreaking way of filmmaking, which took inspiration from the harsh, dramatic reality of a country in ruins, and told stories of ordinary people and their ordinary lives.

Freda could never stand Neorealism. To him, it represented the opposite of the type of cinema that he learned to love as a child and would always pursue as a filmmaker throughout his career. "Whereas Fascist cinematic Italy was tied to the umbilical cord of the *telefoni bianchi*, in a squalid line of insipid comedies and homemade dramas, post-Liberation Italy was submerged by films that exalted local markets and bicycle thieves," he contemptuously wrote in his memoir.[1]

Freda's judgments seem ill-fated at best, and his obstinacy in denying the importance and skills of such directors as Rossellini and De Sica seems hardly justifiable at all. And yet, it is clear that he spoke from the heart. His background led him to the firm conviction that realism is the worst possible form of artistic expression, since "art in general is the metamorphosis of the real as seen through the prism of the author's fantasy."[2] One example he used to make was the decadence of realist painting, the *trompe-l'oeil*, which strived to create the optical illusion of objects really existing: after a period of popularity, it was wiped away by Impressionism, which changed the story of painting for good with its revolutionary conception of light, paving the way to such movements as Fauvism, Cubism and so on, each farther and farther from realism.

To Riccardo Freda, cinema was not to be the equivalent of *trompe l'oeil*—quite the opposite. That is why he dismissed Neorealism as a despicable aberration: paying the ticket and sitting in a dark theater to watch something that was the equivalent of life outside, in the real world, was useless, even stupid. Cinema is all about dreams, for moviegoers and filmmakers alike, and Freda's dream was to build an Italian popular cinema that would rival with Hollywood's greats: engrossing stories, charismatic heroes, glamorous women, intrigue and duels, betrayals and recognitions, deaths and salvations, bold romanticism and turgid melodrama—in a word, spectacle. And *Aquila nera* was the ideal material for all this.

Gino Cervi (left) and Rossano Brazzi in *Aquila nera* (1946).

Alexander Pushkin's unfinished novel *Dubrovsky* (written in 1832 and published in 1841, four years after Pushkin's death; the title was chosen by the publisher) had already been brought to the silver screen, and quite impressively, during the silent era. Clarence Brown's *The Eagle* (1925) had been one of Rudolph Valentino's most popular exploits as the Russian nobleman Vladimir Dubrovsky, who becomes a masked outlaw in order to take revenge on the man who killed his father and stole his land, but falls for the latter's beautiful and innocent daughter. A second version, unreleased in Italy, had been filmed in Russia in 1936: *Dubrovskiy*, directed by Alexsandr Ivanovsky and starring Boris Livanov.

A passionate lover of Russian literature, Freda had always been fascinated by Pushkin's adventurous figure, and was quite familiar with his novel as well as with the Valentino movie, which he claimed to have seen no less than twenty times as a young kid. However, the project was met with diffidence to say the least.

> My film went beyond verism or what the producers were willing to accept, and it consisted of totally different elements. The idea of *Aquila nera*, especially since it was set in Russia, was considered some kind of madness. They could not imagine how our *ciociari* [the inhabitants of the South-East Lazio countryside] could play Cossacks. On the other hand, I saw and conceived cinema only this way. So I insisted, and because of a series of circumstances I met a producer who now is long gone and, I'm sorry to say that, was the most disqualified of all those in activity at that time: his name was Angioletti.... Well, for one of those weird occurrences, he immediately realized the story's potential and gave me *carte blanche*.[3]

Having already written a script which had ended up in a drawer, this time Freda worked with his friend Steno and a 31-year-old scriptwriter who would become one of Italian cinema's greatest directors: Mario Monicelli. The teaming proved fruitful, and Monicelli and Steno became close friends: they worked together for many years, until they eventually pursued separate careers. Freda did not have kind words for Monicelli, claiming that, as soon as he got famous, his former collaborator regularly avoided him. Such distance was likely augmented by their different political views, with Monicelli proudly claiming himself a communist throughout his life—a vision poles apart from Freda's; what is more, the director never appreciated the so-called *commedia all'italiana*, which had in Monicelli one of its strongest representatives, together with Dino Risi. Still, traces of Freda's cinema can be found in some of Monicelli's own films, despite their apparent gap—compare, for instance, the battle scenes in *La leggenda del Piave* with those in Monicelli's World War I fresco *La grande guerra* (a.k.a. *The Great War*, 1959).

The trio's working method was extremely democratic. "After reading the text, we compared our points of view, each of us wrote his own version [of the scene] and compared them. Each and every observation was taken into account and each of us had his own independence."[4] The result was impressive, and displayed the writers' attention to characters and details. For one thing, the script cleverly splits the villain into three, for better dramatic effect. The first, and least, is the slimy President of Court who settles in Dubrovsky's palace and orders the servants to cancel every trace of its previous inhabitants—namely, the Black Eagle stem which nevertheless seems to persecute him, turning up everywhere, with Expressionist-like results in the scene where the Judge finds himself right under the gigantic stone eagle which towers on the staircase of Dubrovsky's house, menacingly revealed by flashes of lightning during a storm.

On the other hand, Kirila the usurper is depicted as a rough-mannered country merchant whose greed results in distrust and disdain for everyone in his acquaintance, and who prefers the company of dogs to that of his men—a trait not unlike Freda himself. As portrayed by Gino Cervi, Kirila does not come off as an entirely unsympathetic character, as the actor's natural bonhomie comes through here and there, making his confrontation with Dubrovsky all the more interesting, and allowing for one of the film's best scenes: the intimate dialogue with Vladimir (posing as a French teacher) at night, with Kirila confessing his fears and solitude, and at one point even encouraging his adversary to shoot him, only for Dubrovsky to run away, torn between his hatred for the man and his love for the latter's daughter.

Freda's favorite of the trio, cinematically speaking, is clearly the despicable, leering Prince Sergei, the kind of venomous snake whose utter debauchery and duplicity enrages the audience. An early scene perfectly sums up the character, as Sergei indifferently burns the letter with which Dubrovsky justified his sudden leave and absence from the duel he was about to fight with him, and which Vladimir personally handed to the adversary, naively trusting in the prince's sense of honor. Sergei also provides the kind of sexual threat that could only be hinted at with cautious euphemisms in 1940s Italy: not only he is to marry the woman Dubrovsky loves, but before the wedding ceremony he sneaks into the bride's room with a bottle of champagne, claiming that "one has to try something before rejecting it," in a not-so-tacit attempt at prenuptial sex that borders on rape, and is interrupted at just the right moment by Vladimir's triumphant entrance in the room, announced by the hero's shadow stretching on the floor.

Dubrovsky is the epitome of Freda's heroes, "individualists who forge their destiny with their own hands and against all odds," in a blatant rejection of "Neorealism's unanimist grisaille, its more or less avowed resignation, as well as its prodigious attention to the present," to quote Jacques Lourcelles.[5] The role went to the 30-year-old Rossano Brazzi (1916–1994), soon to become one of the most popular Italian film stars abroad, thanks to his good looks and tumultuous love life—which resulted in his typecasting as a Latin lover in such films as *Three Coins in the Fountain* (1954, Jean Negulesco), *The Barefoot Contessa* (1954, Joseph Mankiewicz) and *Interlude* (1957, Douglas Sirk)—rather than to his acting chops. "He had done a couple of films with Goffredo Alessandrini during Fascism, *Addio Kira!* and *Noi vivi*…. After the war he had fallen into oblivion and played old types on stage. I offered him the role of the 'Black Eagle' on the good memories of Alessandrini's films. The movie made him popular again and Zanuck called him to Hollywood," Freda recalled.[6] The director had Brazzi made up to resemble the young Valentino, with striking results: still, the actor's handsomeness cannot overcome his wooden acting in the scenes where he poses as the effete French professor.

The rest of the cast was very strong, with Gino Cervi—now too old to play the lead in adventure films—making an impressive villain, the great Paolo Stoppa as yet another comic relief in the part of a bandit with a taste for good wine, and Pietro Sharoff, a renowned Russian stage actor and director who had moved to Italy and become an Italian citizen in the 1930s, as Vladimir's father. The despicable Sergei was played with gusto by Harry Feist, the hateful Nazi officer in Roberto Rossellini's *Roma città aperta* (a.k.a. *Rome Open City*, 1945)—further evidence of Freda's excellent eye for casting, and proof that even though he rejected Neorealism as a whole, he owed it at least a small part of the film's success.

For the role of Masha, the director cast the Brazilian-born Irasema Dilián (born Eva Irasema Warschalowska, 1924–1996), who had debuted in *Maddalena, zero in condotta* and had started a rather successful career in Italy, appearing in such important films as *Malombra* (1942, Mario Soldati). *Aquila nera* featured a number of gorgeous young ladies as extras, two of whom were headed to a bright future[7]: the 19-year-old Gina Lollobrigida (who made her screen debut as an odalisque, for a total of a four-day shooting, and was paid 1,000 *lire* per day) and the 20-year-old Yvonne Sanson as Kirila's mistress, who sits right by Gino Cervi in the banquet scene. When Freda cast her, he promised Sanson that even though she did not have a single line in the film, everyone would notice her. He was right. Within three years, Sanson would become one of Italy's most popular divas, especially after Raffaello Matarazzo's phenomenally successful melodrama *Catene*.

Compared to Brown's film, which focused on the love story between Vladimir and Masha (played by Vilma Bánky), Freda's version is decidedly more action-packed, comprising a number of show-stopping sequences. Unlike *Don Cesare di Bazan*, the director found it easier to put his ideas on screen with the help of d.o.p. Rodolfo Lombardi, who did not object to axis cuts, ellipses or bold tracking shots. Born in 1908, Lombardi was one of the pioneering cinematographers in Italian cinema since the 1930s, and worked with the major filmmakers of the period, such as Carlo Ludovico Bragaglia and Roberto Rossellini: it was Lombardi, and not the titular d.o.p. Ubaldo Arata, who shot *Roma città aperta*'s most famous sequence, the one where Anna Magnani runs after the truck on which her husband is being taken away by the Germans and is shot to death by the Nazis—an experience that would come handy in Freda's film.

One sequence in particular stands out as a testament to Lombardi's skills: the duel between Dubrovsky and Prince Sergei—which has been postponed since the film's beginning, when Vladimir had to run to his dying father's bedside. Freda here reprised the basic idea of a similar scene in *Don Cesare di Bazan*: as Vladimir and Sergei are crossing swords on an imposing staircase, their confrontation is duplicated by their own shadows projected on the wall, towering over their object of desire—Masha—who is watching the duelists. This way, we follow the action through the evocative game of lights and shadows as well as through the expressions of fear and anguish in the woman's eyes, while hardly seeing the two men. It is an exquisitely shot and lighted sequence that shows the director's commanding use of suspense and his flair for dramatic effects. Another showstopper is the wedding banquet scene, which Freda managed to shoot at the Quirinale palace in Rome, soon to become the residence of the President of the Republic, when on June 2, 1946, a popular referendum resulted in the abrogation of the monarchy. Here, the pairing of Freda's camerawork, extras' movements in the shot and tight editing (with an emphasis on the musicians' close ups as opposed to a long shot of the wide room which the camera explores on a crane) reaches its peak.

Aquila nera's filmic pièce de resistance is the rousing climax, with the Russian cavalry attacking Petrovic's castle. The extras were all Carabinieri, the national military police—the easiest and most effective way to portray convincingly an army of horsemen on the screen. The scene, likely inspired by the climax in John Ford's *Stagecoach*, was filmed with four cameras, one providing a lateral traveling shot from a jeep driving at full speed, quite a feat that Lombardi faced admirably. The result was breathtaking, and something unseen before in an Italian film, especially given the heavy, obsolete equipment Freda had to work with.

> We filmed with French cameras, the Debrie. They were heavy, but that was not the main issue. One could not see anything. There was no viewfinder, you could see what you had shot only when looking at the negative…. That sequence on horseback, we almost filmed it blindfold…. You needed a sixth sense to follow the placement of actors, set the frame composition and the lights…. As for film sensibility, we didn't even know what it was. It was necessary to employ a luminous intensity capable of illuminating Notre-Dame. At the time, lighting was a matter of hundreds of kilowatts. I've seen with my own eyes an actress' hair catch fire once….[8]

The scene's effectiveness was heightened by the fact that actress Rina Morelli, the servant who opens the castle's gate for the cavalry to enter, had trouble pulling the huge, heavy door, and succeeded in the nick of time: she can clearly be seen withdrawing at the very last second so as not to be run over by the galloping cavaliers. This, to Freda, was what realism was all about. Dubrovsky's pursuing of Kirila on horseback, which climaxes with the latter's carriage falling into a cliff right after Dubrovsky's spectacular rescue of Masha, was almost as effective, despite the scene's continuity flaws: at one point the characters seem to be converging from opposite directions.

Freda proudly claimed that "there is much more invention in my film than in the whole of Neorealism."[9] Still, *Aquila nera* did not age as well as its maker maintained. If on the one hand it shows Freda's virtues as a filmmaker, on the other hand it retains the director's weak spot, a tendency to rely on the sheer pleasure of narration while somehow undervaluing narrative logic and believability. For one thing, it is hard for a contemporary viewer to suspend disbelief in the scenes where Dubrovsky (wearing just a tiny black mask over his eyes) confronts Masha, and pretend that the girl does not recognize him as the French teacher she just spoke with several hours earlier.

Nevertheless, with its mere existence *Aquila nera* showed that there was room for another kind of filmmaking in post-war Italy, besides the grim Neorealism pursued by

Rossellini and the stale calligraphic formalism of the period films produced by Lux and Scalera Film. As a critic put it,

> Scalera's dusty touch, consisting of more concern toward the sets than to the script, survived almost undamaged the years of Salò and tried to resurface in the immediate post-war years, but was outclassed by the visual dynamism and the formal splendor concocted by Riccardo Freda, who ... relaunched adventure film by adopting, on the one hand, the Americans' mobility of shooting, while on the other hand retaining the taste for the plastic and figurative composition of the Italian pictorial tradition.[10]

In Italy—where commercial film production had just resumed, with 43 titles helmed in the year 1946—the film was a surprise hit, ending up second in the season's top box-office results after *Rigoletto* (1947, Carmine Gallone) and grossing about 200 million *lire*. As Freda proudly wrote,

> *Aquila nera* blasted off like a bomb to chase away the fetid miasms of Neorealism.... I remember the film's première at the Imperiale Theater, with Peppino Amato and Aldo Fabrizi roaring enthusiastically in celebration of my film, which they said ... had nothing to envy to the big budget overseas productions. I remember that a theater owner in Civitavecchia wrote us a letter, asking to alert him beforehand whenever another new film of that type came out, because the audience was so enthusiastic that they uprooted the theater's seats. Which certainly would not happen with *Umberto D.*[11]

The box-office success of *Aquila nera* paved the way for a number of literary adaptations with spectacular ambitions, such as Mario Camerini's *La figlia del capitano* (a.k.a. *The Captain's Daughter*, 1947), starring Dilián and Amedeo Nazzari, *Il corriere del re* (1947, Gennaro Righelli, based on Stendhal's *The Red and the Black*), which reunited Brazzi and his female co-star in Freda's film, and *Amanti senza amore* (a.k.a. *Prelude to Madness*, 1948, Gianni Franciolini), based on Leo Tolstoy's *The Kreutzer Sonata*. After her experience in Italy, Dilián (who was married to Italian scriptwriter Arduino Maiuri) moved to Spain and then to Mexico, where she starred in a number of important films, including Luis Buñuel's version of *Wuthering Heights*, *Abismos de pasión* (1954). Her last film role was in 1958.

The existing version of *Aquila nera* kept at Rome's CSC runs 111 minutes, three more than the one released theatrically in Italy, and conceals an unexpected Easter egg: a risqué scene of young girls bathing in the nude at Petrovic's house, shot for the foreign markets—not an uncommon occurrence, given the very strict censorship in the country—and featuring full frontal nudity on the part of several unnamed extras. Even though Freda claimed that he did not personally shoot it,[12] it stands out as the very first full nude scene in an Italian film.

Aquila nera was released in many European countries, including U.K. (in 1952, as *The Black Eagle*), whereas in the U.S. it became known as *Return of the Black Eagle*.

I miserabili

The phenomenal success of *Aquila nera* led Freda to adapt one of his favorite books, *Les Misérables*. First published in 1862, Victor Hugo's novel—a grandiose meditation on justice and redemption, human law and divine grace, with the turmoil of French post-revolutionary history from 1815 to 1832 serving as the background—had been adapted for the screen many times in the past since the early silent era, most notably in 1935 by Richard Boleslawski. The movie starred Fredric March as the ex-convict Jean Valjean, who turns his life around, builds a fortune and starts a new respectable life as a factory owner and town mayor, and Charles Laughton as the ruthless Inspector Javert, who pursues Valjean for decades as he does not believe in the latter's redemption.

The project came into shape thanks to the intervention of Riccardo Gualino, the head of Italy's most prestigious production company, Lux Film. A wealthy tycoon who had played a vital role in the development of Italian industries in the foreign markets, in such diverse fields as chemistry, naval engineering, banking and cars (he had been vice-president of FIAT in the early 1920s), Gualino (1879–1964) had undergone rough times during Fascism: he was openly adverse to the regime, and the excessive financial exposure he suffered during the great 1929 crisis resulted in the fall of his empire. He was sentenced to

French poster for *I miserabili* (1948).

internment in 1931 for fraudulent bankruptcy, and was interdicted from exerting administrative activity for ten years—an exemplary verdict which was meant to show the regime's iron fist against the non-aligned industrialists. Nevertheless, Gualino unofficially exerted control over his companies, and expanded his horizons. Already a theater enthusiast, to the point of having funded one of the most important playhouses in Turin, he started taking interest in the film business as well. First he contributed founding the French company Lux; then, under the regime's strict and suspicious surveillance, he constituted Compagnia Italiana Cinematografica Lux, in Turin. Always fascinated by art and modernity—he was a patron of arts and owned one of Italy's greatest art collections—Gualino saw the film industry as an ample opportunity: he was not just interested in producing, but in distributing pictures as well, so as to have a better grasp on the market.

In 1934, Lux started producing motion pictures and distributing foreign ones, favoring quality over quantity. The first five years were only mildly successful, though, and it was not until 1939, when Gualino relocated its offices in Rome, that the company experienced a decisive economic boost. In 1941, with the expiration of his ten-year interdiction, Gualino could officially take the seat as president of the firm, and until 1942 Lux was one of the main providers of entertainment during the difficult war days, producing twenty films in four years and distributing foreign pictures (from those countries that were not imposing an embargo, that is) in the theatrical circuit.

It is well known that Rossellini's *Roma città aperta* was filmed using leftovers of film stock, due to the dramatic lack of material immediately after the war. To make up for the shortage of silver, needed to produce film emulsion, Gualino deposited in the Bank of Italy the gold produced by one of his industries, Rumianca, and had it converted into silver and sent over to the Ferrania film factories. As a result, the Italian movie industry could breathe again, and new films could be produced so that the whole production and distribution chain would resume work. It was also because of gestures like these that in post-war Italy Gualino's Lux Film was seen as a beacon, a guiding light for all the people working in the movie business.

Similarly to what he had done in the other fields he had been involved in, Gualino gave the Italian film industry an international scope. In 1947 Lux Film was Italy's biggest and most ambitious production company, with a strongly focused policy that recalled those adopted by the Hollywood Majors. "It could rival with any American studio," as Freda pointed out, and rightly so. Lux did not produce its films directly: Gualino entrusted the greenlighted projects to a net of independent and capable executive producers, such as Carlo Ponti, Dino De Laurentiis and Luigi Rovere, who had a stable but not exclusive relationship with the company. These executive producers signed one-film deals, with a "fixed price" formula: they would guarantee a finished product to be delivered by a certain date and at a certain budget, which Lux would cover entirely. If the picture went over-budget, it was the executive producer who would put up the extra money, whereas if he managed to wrap it at a lower cost, he would keep the saved money for himself. Such a formula was obviously an invitation for executive producers to inflate the budgets and cut corners in order to get more money for themselves, but Gualino preferred to deal with secure costs.[13] On the other hand, Lux Films usually had much higher budgets at their disposal than the average productions, and its releases were characterized by elegant direction, accurately designed sets and a recurring number of first-rate actors who actually formed Italy's first attempt at a post-war star system.

Freda had first been approached by the then-current administrator of Lux, Guido Gatti, who asked him to become part of the production team, but—according to the director—his denunciation of the dishonesty within the company, and more precisely of the way the executive producers used to over-inflate the budgets, cost him the job. It was Gualino who, after *Aquila nera*'s commercial exploit, got in touch with Freda and asked him to direct a picture for his company.

Over the years, Freda spoke at length about Gualino, and always in enthusiastic terms. Their relationship went far beyond a mere commercial working deal: both men viewed cinema as something that could have a cultural and commercial potential as well. Even though he usually demanded that his executives take care of the directors' needs and demands, Gualino was unusually close to Freda, perhaps because of their mutual interests which went far beyond the moviemaking business. "We never talked about films, and discussed of art and literature instead. He was a very cultured person," Freda explained proudly. "With Gualino, I used to sign a deal in five minutes. That is to say, he simply asked me, 'Freda, what film do you want to make?' and that was that."[14]

The idea for *I miserabili* came to the director while on a taxi trip through Rome with Gatti and fellow directors Mario Soldati (*Malombra*) and Renato Castellani (*Un colpo di pistola*), with the four men frantically brainstorming to find stories worth adapting for the screen. When Freda came up with Hugo's novel, the other men looked at him in astonishment and mockery. "The book was very popular in Italy, but nobody thought it was possible to turn it into a film. My friends asked me if I planned to shoot on location in Paris, and I replied that Rome would suffice."[15]

Still, *Les Misérables* had been one of the most frequently adapted novels in those first fifty years of motion picture history, and the press responded ironically to the news of yet another film about Jean Valjean's vicissitudes. In an article in *Corriere d'informazione* that spitefully commented upon the lack of adventurousness on the part of filmmakers and producers, and mentioned a number of forthcoming titles based on oft-plundered books or plays—Alberto Lattuada's *Il delitto di Giovanni Episcopo*, Luchino Visconti's *Otello*, the latter never actually made—the illustrious Arturo Lanocita wrote: "The bottom has been reached with director Riccardo Freda, who, after thinking about it for a long time, decided to shoot the 39th version of *Les Misérables*, a novel which perhaps you've heard of."[16]

However, previous film adaptations of the book were not a deterrent to Freda, given his usual reliance on his cinephile memories as inspiration, and taste for a challenge and competition—not to mention his love for the source material. Years later, the director would speak at length about his admiration for the French novelist during a conversation with Bertrand Tavernier.

> I adore Victor Hugo. They said that his work has aged, but I think it has retained an amazing modernity. A character like Javert is of a burning actuality.... The theme of police inquisition, such as Hugo imagined it, has not aged at all—on the contrary.... As for the style, I would like the detractors to read again the description of Paris as written by Hugo. For me, these are the most beautiful pages of literature that I know of.[17]

For the second time in a row, Freda worked on the script with Vanzina and Monicelli, this time with the addition of another prestigious contributor: Vittorio Nino Novarese (1907–1983), a renowned art director who had started his career as a scriptwriter.[18] The adaptation retained many of the book's most famous moments—such as Valjean's attempted stealing of the candelabra at the bishop's house, or his escape in the sewers with the wounded Marius on his shoulders—but made several radical changes: Marius becomes the son of the Ministry of Police, and in the end Valjean does not commit suicide but is killed by the despicable Thenardier. Freda's concept of Valjean was pivotal in bringing to such changes, and once again reflected the director's idea of cinema as spectacle. As Jacques Lourcelles wrote, "Since the beginning of the film Jean Valjean is never seen, however little he may be, as guilty. He does not need any redemption, and his story is that of a free man even in his chains, who struggles to remain that way, within a violent society, hypocritical and full of prejudices."[19]

Freda confirmed such a vision:

> To me, Valjean had to be a hero, and not a character afflicted by his past. He does not ponder on metaphysical questions, he does not reflect upon the meaning of good and evil, he does what he wants.... Until the end of the story, my Valjean acts as he sees fit, he does not try to redeem himself.... Facing all of the human misery described by Hugo, I wanted a righter of wrongs, like the Black Eagle or later Casanova or Maciste.[20]

Even though the director did not elaborate on the subject, the same can be said about Javert, whose dogged perseverance turns into an out-and-out obsession—a trait that predates the director's much bleaker horror villains. Similarly to his counterpart, the restless inspector becomes a character devoid of any philosophical preoccupation until the very end; rather, Javert himself turns into a somehow metaphysical figure, an impassive, ubiquitous demon of human justice who materializes near Valjean when the latter least expects it.

Freda's reinterpretation of the source material is evident from the masterful opening ten minutes, which move at breakneck speed and are almost completely devoid of dialogue. The influence of silent cinema, from Chaplin to Murnau, can be seen in the introductory scene of Valjean stealing bread from a bakery, with the loaf finally ending up in a ditch where the starry sky is reflected—as poignant a reminder of man's misery on this Earth as anything the director ever filmed. On the other hand, the prison sequences draw from American cinema, from Mervyn LeRoy's *I Am a Fugitive from a Chain Gang* (1932) to John Ford's *The Prisoner of Shark Island* (1936). Moreover, Valjean's spectacular escape attempt is a disguised mini-Western of sorts, with all the genre's typical ingredients, such as the hero jumping on a horse's back and being chased by the guards at full speed; it also features the film's most amazing action bit, Valjean's escape on a mine carriage at breakneck speed down a hill. The technique on display is astonishing for a 1947 Italian film, as is Freda's use of the cinematic language: the passing of time in prison is conveyed through a tight series of cross-dissolves which illustrate Valjean's many unsuccessful escape attempts and the cruel punishments he undergoes as a result, alternated with the recurring sight of the inmates marching through a dark, Expressionist-like prison row. Another striking example of the use of lighting takes place later on, during Valjean's fight with Thernadier's goons, which happens in a darkened room during a storm.

"Adapting a novel I admired so much brought up insane problems, even more so because the film was made in Italy," the director commented, adding

> I think that it was in that adaptation of *Les Misérables* that I put the most of myself.... I had no foothold, as opposed to, let's say, *Il cavaliere misterioso*, which lied over a certain Italian tradition. There, everything was extraneous to me, and that was because of the condition of the shooting: the characters, the setting, the social background, everything had to be recreated.[21]

Still, faithful to his proposal, Freda shot the film entirely in Rome, reconstructing early 18th century-Paris in the studio, with the help of production designer Guido Fiorini. "I had never set foot in Paris, then we based our work on engravings, charts, old photos. I wanted the sets to be very precise and true to life. It was all built inside the studios at Rome's Centro Sperimentale," he pointed out: unlike other companies such as Scalera and Titanus, Lux did not own any film studio, but used to rent them so as to optimize costs—an exception to the rule at that time. Freda took advantage of the skills of Giovanni Piccolis, who recreated the views of old Paris through miniatures and *maquettes*. Born in 1892, Piccolis had been in the movie business since 1913, when he started working as a grip for Itala Films. Then he became head of crew workers at Fert, Pittaluga and Cines, and since the late 1930s he was the chief miniaturist at Cinecittà. Freda used to call him a genius.

Jacques Lourcelles labeled *I miserabili* as "only apparently expensive," adding that the relatively low budget "often stimulated the director's imagination but sometimes blocked it."[22] Indeed, now and then only Freda's visual flair distracts from the rather fake-looking sets. His choice to employ a filmic style that owed to the silent era (and to some of his favorite filmmakers, such as Murnau) resulted in sequences characterized by a careful attempt at stylization. That is the case with Fantine, Valjean's factory worker who is forced to become a prostitute to feed herself and her little daughter Cosette: Freda depicts her act of moral degradation in one extraordinary sequence, by showing the woman descending from her room into the street, the action underlined by a single long take, an elegant crane shot upwards to her room's window and then downwards to the street level again. According to Freda, Fantine's flash-backs were among the film's best moments, even though parts were cut during the editing phase. On the other hand, he judged the sequence of the 1832 barricades, with the cavalry attacking the revolutionaries in front of the Hotel de la Ville, as less personal.[23] However, the scene, shot in a single afternoon, allowed the director to satisfy once again his love for high-scale adventure and mass scenes, with remarkable results. As in *Aquila nera*, the extras on horseback were played by Carabinieri: despite Freda's recommendations that horses launch at full gallop only after his signal, as soon as the cavalry chief whistled on his horn the others lost control of their animals, resulting in a panic-ridden chaos, duly filmed by the five cameramen on the set.

According to film historian Tatti Sanguineti, the barricades sequence was one of the reasons—together with the choice of such an oft-filmed story—that determined Freda's fall from grace with the left-wing *intelligentsia*, since it dealt with a theme—the harsh clashes between the workers and the police forces—that ignited the early post–War years.

> In that seething 1948 in which Gualino explained to De Santis … that he better not shoot any scenes featuring soldiers … against the rice pickers [in *Riso amaro*, a.k.a. *Bitter Rice*], because the scene would not pass the board of censors…, Freda's fault was to show an army that charges, hits, shoots and massacres…. And to show it as a pure, compelling and colossal spectacle: on foot or on horseback … no police or army charge in Italian cinema is as beautiful as Freda's.[24]

Deprived of its ponderous philosophical digressions as well as of most of its historical background, in Freda's hands Hugo's novel became an out-and-out adventure story which nevertheless held a strong debt toward the so-called *feuilletons*, the 19th century serial novels published in installments as supplements to newspapers. In this sense, Valjean being shot at point blank by Thenardier is a great melodramatic twist conceived to make viewers scream in rage for such a blatant injustice—a poignant dramatic moment to top off three hours' worth of emotions and adventures, well-served by Alessandro Cicognini's music. Cicognini would work again with Freda on *Il cavaliere misterioso* before committing to the director's much hated Neorealism.

Over the years, Freda's take on the source material has gained him praise, especially on the part of the French, but it has also drawn its share of criticism. To literature scholar Carlo Testa, *I miserabili* is "a film of James Bond–like deeds and frenzied manhunts … an ancillary product whose basic paradox consists in the fact that the more it strives to compete with its original on an equal footing, the more it proves to be merely derivative from it."[25] Testa points to the fact that the film comes "in a form purged of all critical social content" whereas Hugo's novel clearly has a message to carry home, concluding that

> films like Freda's *I miserabili* are important documents that reveal, first and foremost, a deliberate will to blindness in the act of their production…. They are a historical continuation of the productions that in the first half-century after the invention of cinema in 1895 served as a substitute for literature for people who were barely, or not at all, able to read.

Testa even throws in the odd sarcastic remark, such as "one cannot help feeling skeptical about the director's praise of 'imagination' (and his attendant dismissal of the neorealist revolution) when one holds up to it such a long list of repetitive formula film"—an observation which makes the reader feel skeptical whether Testa had actually seen the works he is so scathingly dismissing, or he simply guessed their sticking to a formula by looking at their titles (which, by the way, are often misquoted).

Testa may have a point in underlining the film's obliviousness to any social message, but he himself is quite simply oblivious to Freda's thematic and stylistical approach, which goes far beyond a Fascist-minded over-simplification of the novel with no attempt at re-elaborating it. If Valjean's hunger and the revolutionaries' instances are merely instrumental to the plot, so is the key scene of the ex-convict's conversion to a honest life after the attempted stealing of the candelabra. The references to religion are distinctly devoid of pathos and look as if they were placed in the film merely to please the Catholic hierarchy, whereas the key scene of Valjean and Cosette taking refuge in a convent and being saved from arrest by the mother superior is played first and foremostly as a suspenseful moment, with the director underplaying the Christian symbology behind it.

Freda was never a believer, nor was he interested in affirming a superior entity to which conform one's moral. He believed in heroes, and in cinema as a way to celebrate them, and he pursued this aim with all his will: *I miserabili* is ample proof of that. Popular cinema may be a surrogate of literature for illiterate viewers, but its straightforward approach to narrative does not mean it carries a simple-minded approach to people, society and life. In this sense, the world of *I miserabili* according to Freda is strikingly pessimistic and downbeat, not unlike the fruits of Neorealism he dismissed so harshly. For one thing, the narrative is based on a continuous series of coincidences, of people repeatedly bumping into each other and even literally hanging around the same places—the same square with an octagonal fountain in the middle serves as the set for several scenes which are supposed to take place in different years and cities. Instead of diminishing the overall believability, the result recalls John Ford's use of Monument Valley in *The Searchers* (1956), with the characters passing over and over again beside the same stretches of landscape, in a sort of "eternal return" that perfectly suits the film's recurrent theme of a mechanistic universe where the main characters are continually doomed to meet again until they eventually fulfill their destiny. Even more than to his heroes, though, the director's sympathy goes to children: take the beautiful sequence where Valjean buys Cosette a doll before releasing her from the custody of the Thenardiers, which adopts the girl's point of view from under a table, or the way Freda focuses on the death of Gavroche, the little kid who takes part in the 1832 rebellion—an episode he might as well have cut from the whole picture, given its irrelevance to the plot, and which nonetheless makes for a poignant aside. In Freda's *oeuvre*, children are the innocent victims of the adult world, lost amid violence, scheming and calculations, exploited and victimized. And yet, their fragile innocence makes them ultimately the only thing worth living, and dying, for.

Working for the third time with Gino Cervi, Freda had to deal with his star's ego from the very first scene.

> He wore a bourgeois dress with golden buttons. I explained to him that he should look *miserable*, since he had to steal bread to feed his nephew. But he wouldn't understand. He only thought of the female audience: had he appeared in rags, his career would have ended.... So I had to film him in close-ups, framing only his hungry face and cursing his golden buttons.... He did not care about the story, the escape, the misery, only his public image mattered....[26]

A similar problem occurred while shooting the scenes of Valjean after his escape from Montreuil, with the actor still in his elegant mayor outfit. The director solved the problem by throwing talcum over Cervi's frock during takes so as to make it look old and ragged. Nevertheless, Cervi gives a commanding performance, perfectly conveying the character's physical strength and tenaciousness. As Javert, the German-born Hans Hinrich was a fine choice on Freda's part, as the actor's silent movie-like features perfectly suit the way his character is shaped. Due to his Jewish origins, Hinrich (1903–1970)—a stage actor and director in his home country, at Berlin's prestigious Deutsches Theater—had taken refuge in Italy in the late 1930s: after a number of films as a director he resumed his acting career, playing mostly villain roles. He became an Italian citizen in 1947, and adopted the name Giovanni. He returned in Germany in 1954, where he mostly worked on stage.

The 24-year-old Valentina Cortese played both Fantine and Cosette, with impressive results despite her tendency to overact: Freda's often underlooked ability at directing actors (his oft-claimed aversion to them notwithstanding) allowed him to use Cortese's somewhat stodgy theatricality (the tremors in her voice, the artificial whispers) as the "expression of the fragility of the humble."[27] Already a famous actress in her homeland, Cortese would experience a long and prestigious career and play in a number of foreign films, such as Jules Dassin's *Thieves' Highway* (1949) and Joseph Mankiewicz's *The Barefoot Contessa* (1954). Other prestigious titles in her filmography included Mario Bava's *La ragazza che sapeva troppo* (a.k.a. *The Girl Who Knew Too Much*, 1963), Federico Fellini's *Giulietta degli spiriti* (a.k.a. *Juliet of the Spirits*, 1965) and François Truffaut's *La Nuit américaine* (a.k.a. *Day for Night*, 1973), just to mention a few. In Freda's own recollections, she was as capricious as the star she would play in Truffaut's masterpiece. For her part, Cortese recalled the director's harsh methods: "Freda was a temperamental filmmaker: one day we were shooting a scene depicting the revolutionary uprisings, tomato sauce everywhere, shoots, extras running en masse, and Freda gave me a shove so as to push me into the frame under a restive horse. My God, what a scare!"[28]

As Cosette's love interest Marius, Aldo Nicodemi was yet another example of the director's absolute freedom of choice while working with Gualino. After Rossano Brazzi, his first choice for the role, demanded too high a salary from executive producer Carlo Ponti, Freda decided to settle with another actor. When Ponti asked him who he was going to hire, Freda simply replied that he would "pick up the first asshole that I'm going to meet on my way." And he did: he came across the wealthy and Adonis-like Nicodemi—not a professional actor at all—through a prostitute friend. Marius just had to look handsome, and Nicodemi obliged. After *I miserabili*, Nicodemi enjoyed a short-lived popularity, mainly thanks to his roles in Raffaello Matarazzo's melodramas. However, when he died at just 44 in a car accident, his film career had long since waned.

The rest of the cast featured a number of soon-to-be famous names, such as Gabriele Ferzetti (as Fantine's one-time lover, who seduces her, makes her pregnant and disappears) and a very young Marcello Mastroianni, in his film debut as one of Marius' revolutionist friends.[29] Cosette as a little girl was played by the daughter of Marquis Giraldi, Duccia, whom Freda discovered while strolling in via Veneto with his friend Matarazzo. For the scene in which Cosette starts crying after Valjean takes her doll away from her so as not to be discovered by Javert, Freda resorted to one of the oldest tricks in the book, by smearing his hands with onion juice and caressing the girl's cheek and hair. Little Duccia, who could not stand onions, started to cry like a river. She would never forget him, but the scene was a winner, and in just one take.

In one of his later interviews, the director told Giuseppe Tornatore an amusing anecdote which speaks volumes about his intolerance toward actors. When it came to shooting the scene in which Valjean and the little Cosette take refuge in a convent and Javert asks the mother superior if by chance the ex-convict is hiding in there, forcing the nun to lie, the woman playing the bit part of the nun who announces Javert's arrival could not speak a word. Freda got so pissed off that he threw the actress off the set.

> But then there was the problem about who'd take the part. So while I was looking around I saw the director's assistant who had a really angelic face. He was terrified because he saw I was staring at him and I said: "Him!" "What d'you mean him?" "He can be the nun. Don't piss me around!" And even though the poor sod wasn't too keen they got hold of him and dressed him as a nun.[30]

Unfortunately for Freda, actress Andreina Pagnani, who played the Mother Superior, had not been warned about the replacement. When Freda yelled "Action!" and she saw the young a.d. coming at her in nun robes, she had a hysterical laughing fit.

Freda's film surpassed the three-hour mark: not an excessive length if compared to the 359 minutes of the 1925 adaptation directed by Henri Fescourt, or the 281 minutes of Raymond Bernard's 1934 version. Still, *I miserabili* was submitted to the board of censors in December 1947 as two separate films which were released in Italy within the space of one week. The first part, *Caccia all'uomo* (Man Hunt), opened on January 21, 1948, while *Tempesta su Parigi* (Storm Over Paris) followed on January 28.[31] With box-office figures of 375 million *lire*, it was the top grossing Italian movie of 1948, making Freda the most successful filmmaker in Italian cinema with two smash hits in a row. However, this did not prevent critics and intellectuals to spit venom on him: the Neapolitan novelist, playwright and scriptwriter Giuseppe Marotta (1902–1963), the author of *L'oro di Napoli* and other popular works, used to direct mordant darts of irony against Freda in his newspaper column "Follie del cinema" in the *Corriere d'informazione*.

I miserabili was also distributed abroad, albeit in a form that did not reflect the author's vision. It would take four years before it was released in France, in a badly excised version (*L'évadé du bagne*) which ran only 110 minutes: Freda was not even consulted. Lux even released the film in the United States in March 1952, in a similarly truncated English-dubbed version, as *Les Miserables*, to tepid reviews. Joe Pihodna, of the *New York Herald Tribune*, passingly mentioned it running two hours, which suggests it likely being the same copy as the one released in France. While underlining Freda's "emphasis on movement rather than social significance," Pihodna called Gino Cervi's performance solid but uninspired, and objected to the excessive screen time given to the character of Thenardier. The reviewer blamed the awkward dubbing ("in attempting to use English words to fit the lip movements of Italian actors, the sound editors have come up with some pretty stilted lines.... The tendency to use formal phrases instead of the idiom, especially in dramatic action involving cops and criminals, is almost comical") and concluded: "The Italians have made a brave attempt to encompass the literary power of Hugo on the screen. They deserve a pat on the back for the try, but not much praise for the result."[32] The *New York Times*' reviewer was similarly unimpressed ("this, then, is somewhat less than a masterpiece, since Valjean and his implacable adversary, Inspector Javert, are, in the main, two-dimensional figures whose characters rarely, if ever, come to life") and named Luigi Pavese's Thenardier as the only fairly memorable supporting player, but praised Freda's work ("the director has managed to extract some of the excitement and movement inherent in the book"), pointing out that Valjean's attempted escape "makes for a momentary thrill," and similarly panned the jarring dubbing.[33] This last factor was commonly perceived as annoying and distracting, which gives an idea of the very few foreign dubbed European pictures that surfaced overseas during that period. The *Daily Boston Globe* was somewhat kinder, although calling the film overlong and slow, and blaming the poor editing for the character's lack of development,[34] while the *Los Angeles Times* called it "a fine version in many ways" despite being "too literally photographed."[35]

All reviewers, no exceptions, misspelled "Cortese" as "Cortesa."

Il cavaliere misterioso

For his next film project, Freda reunited with an acquaintance from the war days. He, Longanesi and Steno had met with Dino De Laurentiis in Torella dei Lombardi, near Avellino, in 1943, while hiding out from the Nazis in the chaotic days after the Armistice. When De Laurentiis approached Freda and asked him to make another picture for Lux, after viewing *I miserabili* in a small projection room at the company's headquarters, the director had no hesitation in proposing him a movie on Giacomo Casanova.

Violinist, professional gambler, alchemist, conspirator, swashbuckler, diplomat, stage impresario, poet ... and, most of all, an irresistible womanizer: had he not existed, Giacomo Casanova would have been an extraordinary literary creation. As it had happened with the director's previous projects, the Venetian adventurer had already been the subject of many films, including the Italian *L'avventura di Giacomo Casanova* (1937, Carlo Bassoli) and the French-made *Les Aventures de Casanova* (1947) by Jean Boyer.[36] Six years later, Steno himself would deliver a picture based on the adventures (and the loves) of the renowned 18th century Venetian adventurer: *Le avventure di Giacomo Casanova* (1954), starring Gabriele Ferzetti, ended up being one of Italy's most censored motion pictures

Italian 2-fogli manifesto for *Il cavaliere misterioso* (1948).

of the decade because of its alleged obscenity, and even had its visa revoked by the then-head of the head secretary of the Spectacle, future President of the Republic Oscar Luigi Scalfaro. When over twenty years later Federico Fellini brought Casanova to the screen, the times had changed: masterfully played by Donald Sutherland, Fellini's version of the character was a passionless, mechanical seducer, who goes through his love performances almost like an athlete of sex, without any emotion or pleasure, and eventually—in one of the most extraordinary scenes in Fellini's career—is seen dancing with his female double: an automaton. Other successful incarnations of Casanova were to be found in Luigi Comencini's delicious *Infanzia, vocazione e prime esperienze di Giacomo Casanova, veneziano* (a.k.a. *Giacomo Casanova: Childhood and Adolescence*, 1969), which dealt with Casanova's coming of age, whereas in Ettore Scola's *Il mondo nuovo* (a.k.a. *That Night in Varennes*, 1982), the Venetian seducer was played to perfection by Marcello Mastroianni (ironically, Fellini's icon on so many films) who portrayed a tired, elderly version of the character not dissimilar to the one seen in the last scenes of Fellini's masterpiece.

Freda's Casanova is none of the former. Even though he admitted that the character's sensual temper somehow reminded him of his own attitude, the director had no interest whatsoever in Casanova's badly-written memoir, nor in his love exploits: to him, Casanova was closer to the swashbuckling heroes of classical literature, from Balzac to Dumas—not to mention silver screen icons like Douglas Fairbanks, Errol Flynn or Ronald Colman. His Casanova is neither an intriguer nor a conspirator, but is moved by a frantical, reckless need for adventure, like a gambler who continually raises his stake: during his inexhaustible travels throughout Europe, rather than merely courting women—using his skills as a seducer to get what he wants, rather than out of sincere passion—it almost seems he is continually courting Death, which he calls "a rival against which it is impossible to fight." And still, his individualism is tampered down by the love for his brother: if there is one thing Freda's Casanova respects, it is family. In the end, though, just like in Fellini's film, he is condemned to loneliness: the unforgettable downbeat ending has the camera panning away from him as he leaves, silently walking across San Marco square after accomplishing his mission, but with his heart broken after the death of the only woman he ever loved. As Jacques Lourcelles wrote, Freda's vision of the 18th century allowed him to depict his vision of "a world of wickedness, calculation and cruelty, where sincerity is always losing, enlightened by an elegant crepuscular light."[37]

The narrative of *Il cavaliere misterioso* is structured like a mystery adventure, packed with incidents, twists, cliffhangers and a show-stopping chase scene in the snow. Freda throws in countless references to the literary loves of his youth, such as the stolen letter or the locker hidden in a clock, managing to keep them fresh and engrossing. The script follows scrupulously Hitchcock's golden rules of suspense: the compromising missive which Casanova pursues throughout Europe is nothing but a McGuffin that allows the director to play with his characters like a chess player does with his pawns. The result encompasses to perfection all the main elements of Freda's cinema: adventure, intrigue, romanticism, suspense and ribald humor—all blended together by Alessandro Cicognini's lively score.

Still, compared to the American adventure films the director was aiming at, his visual spirit is more on the Gothic side. In this respect, the opening scene is telling. Freda starts the film (as he will do with *Il conte Ugolino*) in a dungeon: there, a prisoner is being tortured by the Venetian inquisition. The shot opens on the close-up of a man spinning a huge wheel, while in the background we glimpse a semi-naked male figure tied to a St. Andrew's cross, his limbs being painfully stretched by the actions of two such wheels, operated in sync by a pair of executioners as the prisoner is being questioned by the inquisitor. It is a striking opening, and one which immediately puts Freda miles away from the kind of cinema his peers were making at that time. His sense of theatricality is enhanced in the following shots, where the executioner's shadow is projected over the wall behind the stolid inquisitor. This is not Neorealism—by a mile. Later on, a skull well in evidence over a table during a swashbuckling fight draws the viewer's attention, introducing an ominous note in an otherwise purely energetic scene: a reminder of Casanova's adversary, the one that will eventually have the upper hand, and which Neapolitans used to call *'a livella* (the level), because it makes all equal in their final hour; incidentally, a skull will play a similar role in the opening sequence of his 1963 Gothic horror film *Lo spettro*. The style is elegant throughout, and the images are often reminiscent of 18th century painters, such as Jean-Baptiste-Siméon Chardin (a master of still life, and an influence that would turn up again in Freda's work), and the Venetian Francesco Guardi, whose work the final shot strikingly resembles.

Filming for *Il cavaliere misterioso*—provisionally called *Le cento donne di Casanova* (Casanova's Hundred Women),[38] a title dropped possibly to avoid trouble with the censors—took place in summer 1948. Even more than in *Aquila nera* and *I miserabili*, Freda's exuberant visual style oozes from every shot, as he had the money and the technical resources to put to good use some of his views on filmmaking. And yet, during the shooting, the director had to deal with De Laurentiis' economizing habits:

> We had to shoot a minuet scene in Venice. Being a movie about Casanova, first we had to find very beautiful women, charming, attractive. And then instruct them, because the minuet has its own mandatory figures: the grace, the reverences ... every time I asked about it, De Laurentiis and his brother Luigi replied that they were rehearsing. Come the night when we had to shoot the minuet scene, in Mocenigo Palace, and they showed up with monsters—hideous, elderly, ugly women, chosen on purpose to make a grotesque scene. In five minutes' time, I had to come up with a totally new scene, cut out the minuet scene, have the cameramen's wives dress up as well as all the ladies on the set who gently obliged. The result was a scene undoubtedly wittier and more amiable than the minuet, which was a bit conventional: all the women asking Casanova questions, all the men in a corner. They [the De Laurentiis brothers] came up with such dirty tricks in order to cut costs.[39]

The scene Freda is referring to is indeed one of the best in the film, and displays the director's favorite habit of moving the camera from one character to another during a long take, here paired with an exquisite sense of humor. The shot opens on the orchestra violinist, and the camera withdraws graciously to the middle of the large hall, discovering the various men, standing without their dames, looking perplexed or annoyed; Casanova's adversary, the inquisitor played by Hans Hinrich, enters the frame, and refuses a glass of champagne offered by a valet; the camera then follows the valet's movement, turning leftward with a 120 degree movement and proceeding in the opposite direction, while a woman takes some pastries from the tray and turns back; meanwhile, the music is gradually overwhelmed by the sound of female voices and laughters; still moving forward, the camera shows that all the ladies in the room are standing in circle in a corner of a hall, an all-female audience surrounding Casanova, and delighted by his malicious jokes: "Are Parisian women so elegant?" "Well, I don't know.... I've seen so few of them with their clothes on!" It is a remarkable moment, not merely because of its elegance and wit, but also because with the use of camera movement, sound and characters' movements on the set, Freda conveys the essence of Casanova's character and myth, putting to best use his mastery of film language.

Eventually, Freda got so angry at De Laurentiis' money-saving tricks that he walked off the set after an argument with the executive producer. It took De Laurentiis' brother Luigi to make the director change his mind. "He brought along a blank sheet of paper signed by Dino De Laurentiis, and said: 'Listen Riccardo, you can write whatever you want on this piece of paper, that my brother is a son of a bitch, whatever you want, and he agrees, but he begs you to resume the shooting....'"[40]

Most outdoor scenes were shot in the region of Abruzzi, inside the National Park, which made for a convincing snowy Russia, and an ideal setting for the sequence of Casanova's troika being pursued by the Cossacks, which the director filmed in just two days. By shooting in exteriors, as he had done in *Aquila nera*, Freda was further detaching himself from the static, theatrical period films of the era, which emphasized dialogue over action, and were shot basically in studio, with minimal camera movements and blatant ellipses whenever a battle or another climactic event had to be shown. Primo Zeglio, the director of the 1947 version of *Genoveffa di Brabante* (which Freda would remake in 1964) once boasted about having shot a man falling from horseback without even having a horse at hand, but just through the use of camera movements and editing. In Freda's film, when a man falls from horseback, the scene features a real horse and the fall is done for real, often at a high risk. An example is the aforementioned climactic troika chase, which ends with the Cossacks spectacularly falling from a bridge: it was shot near Rome, on a bridge on the river Aniene, and Casanova's troika was trained by just two horses instead of three, since the viaduct was not large neither solid enough—still, no reviewer noticed that a horse was missing.[41] Such a reliance on spectacular stunts was something unseen and truly exciting in Italian cinema. Jacques Lourcelles, who considered *Il cavaliere misterioso* one of Freda's greatest efforts, included a long and detailed excerpt of the script in the special issue of the French magazine *Présence du cinéma* which in 1963 consecrated Freda as a top-notch auteur.

As Casanova, Freda cast the then-26-year-old Vittorio Gassman, a handsome stage actor who had debuted in the movies in 1945, but was still a little-known face. Once again it was a blessed choice, as Gassman provided Freda with the kind of energetic and athletic lead that he had been looking for in his earlier movies as well, plus the acting skills that *Aquila nera*'s Rossano Brazzi lacked.

> When I offered him the role of Casanova he accepted on the spot. We hadn't any problem during filming as he was an exceptional actor who could play everything. He was a sportsman and an acrobat—he had also been a basketball champion [the 6' 3" tall Gassman had played in Italy's professional basketball league and in the national University team]—and he had at the same time the sense of classical theater as well as of modern cinema. Exactly what I expected from him. His memory was exceptional and he never complained when I asked him to do another take. Each time it was better.... For a dueling scene, I put him opposite a real master of arms who had told me: "He can do whatever he wants and I'll just ward off the blows." Gassman threw himself in the duel like a tiger. And I saw the master of arms being pushed back by an actor who had never handled a sword before. After the take, he told me that Gassman was a dangerous madman![42]

On his part, this is what Gassman had to say about the director:

> I have always considered and keep considering him as a very anomalous case in Italian cinema. Surely a man of great intelligence, of amazing technical skills and with an exceptional knowledge of cinema, accompanied by an almost total cynicism. Nevertheless, as you know well, in France there are still cineclubs dedicated to him, and there are die-hard Freda fans.... And in fact the film was well-paced, it worked as a spectacle, as a narrative, emotionally.[43]

Following *Il cavaliere misterioso*, Gassman had the chance to play a totally opposite character, a charming yet wicked villain in Giuseppe De Santis' fascinating *film noir Riso amaro* (a.k.a. *Bitter Rice*, 1949), and over the following years he even acted in the United States in such films as Joseph H. Lewis' *Cry of the Hunted* (1953), Norman Foster's *Sombrero* (1953) and Robert Rossen's *Mambo* (1954). Yet it was Mario Monicelli's *I soliti ignoti* (a.k.a. *Big Deal on Madonna Street*, 1958) that showed Gassman's extraordinary qualities as a comedian, establishing him as one of Italy's leading thespians, as the stuttering dumb prizefighter who takes part in a heist that goes disastrously wrong. Interestingly, *I soliti ignoti* recycled almost verbatim a scene in *Il cavaliere misterioso* where Casanova instructs his servant to steal a lady's purse in order for the adventurer to catch the thief in the act and become acquainted with the woman—exactly the same trick used by Gassman's character and his accomplices in Monicelli's film to get in touch with a maid whom they plan to exploit for their ill-fated criminal plan, with more blatantly comic results. Eclectic and charismatic, Gassman was equally masterful at playing drama as well as comedy: some of his most memorable characters included the wily soldier in Monicelli's World War I epic *La grande guerra*, the small-time crook Bruno Cortona in Dino Risi's road comedy-drama *Il sorpasso* (a.k.a. *The Easy Life*, 1962) and the blind man who contemplates suicide in Risi's *Profumo di donna* (a.k.a. *Scent of a Woman*, 1974) for which he won a prize as Best Actor at the Cannes festival. He died in 2000.

The necessary comic relief is represented by Casanova's Neapolitan unpaid servant Gennaro, played by comedian Dante Maggio, a smart move that allows Freda to introduce a hint of down-to-earth cynicism into the story. But *Il cavaliere misterioso*'s most striking aspect, casting-wise, is the trio of glamorous ladies that play alongside Gassman. Freda worked again with Yvonne Sanson, now an established diva, who played the Tsarina Catherine, while the Spanish-born María Mercader (who in 1959 would marry Vittorio De Sica) was the love interest, Elisabetta.

For the minor but pivotal role of Countess Lehmann, the director cast the 21-year-old Gianna Maria Canale. Born in Reggio Calabria on September 12, 1927, from a family of Greek origins, Canale was just a company secretary when in 1947 she took part in the local Miss Calabria context and won: the next step was the national Miss Italy beauty context, where she ended up second, after Lucia Bosé; Gina Lollobrigida was third, thus confirming that 1947 was an exceptional year as far as female pulchritude was concerned.[44] Besides her passing resemblance to Ava Gardner, Canale's ravishing beauty and sultry looks were spellbinding. She was made for the silver screen, even though she never really enjoyed acting altogether. After all, however, she did not even really need to act—she just had to *be*.

Freda used to recall how he had met Canale by chance, coming across her as she came out of a glove shop in Rome. In the director's perhaps romanticized version, he followed her, found out where she lived, phoned her and asked her if she was interested in making movies. "She was rather rude. When I qualified myself, she just said: 'Oh, yes, *Aquila nera*, I liked it.'"[45] Having appeared on screen only once before, as an extra in Carmine Gallone's filmed opera *Rigoletto*, *Il cavaliere misterioso* was Canale's first major role. Freda memorably introduces her posing as a man, in male clothes, perhaps in a nod to Greta Garbo's appearance in *Queen Christina* (1933, Rouben Mamoulian): her subsequent scene at the inn with Casanova—preceded by an offbeat strip that provides the audience with the sight of the actress' hairy armpits—with the hero trying in every way he can to unravel her disguise, is priceless. It was during the shooting in Abruzzo that she and Freda, who was eighteen years older than her, became lovers. Ironically, a film about the seducer par excellence proved to be a love trap for his director. "To me, it was the great love. To her, I don't think so,"[46] Freda would bitterly comment about his relationship with the actress. For better or for worse, the love affair with Gianna Maria Canale marked deeply his life and career over the next decade.

5

Brazil ... and Back

Guarany

Il cavaliere misterioso did good business in Italy, with 180 million *lire*, even though Lux was perhaps expecting more after *I miserabili*. For his next movie, Freda went on to make one of the most unpredictable moves in his career. The opera film was a staple in Italian cinema of the period: audiences were eager for biopics of the country's most famous composers, which featured popular singers and were directed by such specialists as Mario Costa and Carmine Gallone. The lives of Verdi, Rossini and Bellini offered not only entertainment, but also a reminder of the country's past glory as a popular antidote to the misery and squalor unearthed by Neorealism. Freda, however, was saddled with a far less illustrious subject for his biopic. Antônio Carlos Gomes (1836–1896) was a Brazilian composer, author of many operettas, and not popular at all in Italy: his best-known work was the opera *Il Guarany*, based on a novel by José de Alencar, in turn inspired by an ancient Indian legend. Through the efforts of Giuseppe Verdi, Italy's greatest composer, Gomes managed to have his own opera staged at the Scala theater in Milan.

Freda had good reasons to accept the offer. One was that his old acquaintance Salvo D'Angelo (with whom he had worked on *Caravaggio, il pittore maledetto*, with the latter as set decorator) was now the head of Universalia, a Catholic-oriented production company founded in 1946 and financed by the Bank of Sicily and the Vatican. As Piero Regnoli, then the company's vice artistic manager, recalled: "The astonishing thing is that in 1946 Universalia had about one billion *lire* at disposal—cash. It was the biggest production company [in the country], and not only from a financial point of view, but because … it was the most sensational in appearance."[1] The artistic manager was Count Giuseppe Dalla Torre, the editor of the Vatican's official newspaper *L'Osservatore Romano*, and the Vatican had indeed a financial participation in the company—a fact that was evident from its very location. Universalia's headquarters were based at Castel Sant'Angelo, one of Rome's most famous monuments, and the owners used to give luxurious parties on the castle's terrace. According to Regnoli, D'Angelo managed to persuade Dalla Torre to play an active part in the company, whose statute was based on strict ethical principles, and was supposed to invest money in the production of films with a strong Catholic content. It was a project doomed to failure, though, mostly because of the company's lack of measure in administering its huge finances.

It is no wonder, then, that Freda claimed that for *Guarany* he was paid an unbelievably high sum, much more than he ever was in his career. The director confessed that he had asked a huge amount of money in the hope that D'Angelo would not accept and

Italian fotobusta for *Guarany* (filmed in 1948 but released in 1950).

he would not have to make a film he wasn't the least bit interested in: much to his surprise, the producer agreed to pay him that royalty sum. As a result, Freda could lead a luxurious life, becoming one of the wealthiest Italian directors of the period. He was not shy about his attachment to money: unlike some of his peers, he never denied that filmmaking was a job that he had chosen mostly for pecuniary reasons.

> Financial attractiveness has meant a lot in my decisions. I loved courting beautiful women and easy money. It is futile, but it is so. I loved this environment of millionaires, champagne and cruises in preparation. I'll be frank: if cinema hadn't provided me this superficial and luxurious life, I would have continued being a sculptor. Between sculpture and cinema, I would not hesitate for a second....[2]

Guarany was a drastic departure from the kind of cinema that Freda wanted to make. But then, in addition to the money he was being paid, the opportunity to fly to Brazil for a while with his beloved Gianna Maria was too much of a temptation. The prospect of a co-production with Brazil, albeit pioneering and poorly thought out as it might have been, represented a challenge for a director who loved adventure—of any kind. The cast, headed by the Portuguese António Vilar, featured Gianna Maria Canale as Jacqueline, contrasted to Mariella Lotti (real name Anna Maria Pianotti) as Lindita, whereas Dante Maggio played the comedy relief, a composer named Lauro Rossi who becomes Carlos' best friend.[3]

Filming started on June 11, 1948, in Rome, then Freda and the crew moved to shoot on location in Brazil. The result was, by all accounts, a mediocre film, which Freda claimed he never even watched. As customary, he managed to wrap up filming behind schedule, making the producers save money on the budget and earning a valuable bonus for himself (a reason that had a major part in his proverbial speed). One thing he recalled with satisfaction about the movie was filming the scene at the Emperor's palace at Titanus Studios in Rome. It was António Vilar's last day of shooting, and, as Freda explained, "there was no trace of the palace in the studio, except in the art director's drawings. And I had to shoot that scene the very next day. Well, I offered such a huge sum that all, I mean all the people at Titanus agreed to work for me on the movie. And in just one day and one night's work, they built a hall with huge columns, stuccos and so on—while all the other productions were halted, of course!"[4]

As of today, *Guarany* is unavailable in any form, not even at Rome's Cineteca Nazionale, but the voluminous, 303-page script kept at the CSC can at least give an idea of what the director had envisioned. Despite not being signed, it is very likely Freda's work, as suggested by the detailed division into numbered shots, with indications of camera movements and edit cuts. From the opening line ("This film tells the story of Carlo Gomez [sic], a great son of Brazil who with his worldwide acclaimed music gave glory to his homeland") *Guarany* wears its celebratory purpose on its sleeve. Freda tries in every way to convince us that Gomes—misspelled "Gomez" throughout—was a genius, saddling the viewer with his not-so-interesting life story and tribulations between Brazil, Portugal and Italy, but he is more successful when he opts for his favorite elements to enliven the standard biopic fare.

Only in parts does the story come alive, such as in the sequence where Gomes' mother is assassinated by the bandits before her son, which climaxes in a very quick tracking shot to an extreme close-up of the boy's eyes (a similar effect as the one employed in the climax of *Don Cesare di Bazan*), followed by a shot of the dead woman's hand falling over the bloody music sheet of Gomes' first composition, *Ave Maria*. The director stages one of his beloved feast scenes (here a dance in the village square), and concocts elaborate cuts and camera movements to enliven the proceedings, but cannot avoid slipping into cheap melodrama—as in Carlos' farewell to his father, the slapdash love triangle between Gomes, his longtime fiancée Lindita and the man-eater singer Jacqueline, and the climax where Lindita, dying of tuberculosis, witnesses Carlos' triumph during the first public performance of his opera, unbeknownst to her beloved. Freda was surely more at ease shooting the assault to a Guaraní tribe, which will inspire the titular opera: a scene worthy of a John Ford Western, complete with wild horses stampeding and the indios running away from the destruction of their village.

The part set in Milan benefitted from the odd historical detail of interest for music lovers, such as the portrayal of the opera world of the late 1800 and the references to such composers as Arrigo Boito, Amilcare Ponchielli and Giuseppe Verdi; a scene the director recalled with some satisfaction was the one where the desperate Gomes climbs atop the Cathedral of Milan after being told he cannot put his opera on stage. But it was too little to make this hagiographic mess come to life.

Guarany was submitted to the Italian board of censors in November 1949—almost a year after its making, and one month after the release of Freda's own *Il conte Ugolino*—and finally came out in theaters in January 1950. It was virtually ignored by the public and panned by the critics, who blamed its "unnerving slow pace," accused Vilar of "not having felt the role" and labeled Canale "a beautiful statue."[5] Nevertheless, the film was a huge hit in South America, which raised interest toward Universalia and gained the picture (and especially Gianna Maria Canale) dozens of magazine covers. However,

Universalia's days were numbered. Besides Freda's film and the incredibly expensive *Fabiola* (a.k.a. *Fabiola and the Fighting Gladiator*, 1949, Alessandro Blasetti), which cost 900 million *lire*, the equivalent of a Hollywood big budget picture, the company produced several more titles, including Visconti's *La terra trema* (1948), *Gli ultimi giorni di Pompei* (a.k.a. *The Last Days of Pompeii*, 1950, Marcel L'Herbier, Paolo Moffa) and René Clair's *La Beauté du diable* (a.k.a. *Beauty and the Devil*, 1950) before the senseless waste of money brought it to bankruptcy.

While shooting the indoor scenes for *Guarany* in Italy, Freda took advantage of the studio facilities and employed a number of young actors from the film (Rossella Falk, Paolo Panelli, Tino Buazzelli) in a couple of one-reel comedies he shot for his friend Attilio Riccio's company, Fortuna Film, *L'astuto barone (ovvero L'eredità contesa)* and *Tenori per forza*. The director signed them as Renato Dery and lent his voice as the narrator on *L'astuto barone*. "They are two one-reel shorts, made on a Sunday morning,"[6] he told Éric Poindron. Although allegedly shot in 1948, they were submitted to the board of censors a couple years later, respectively in October 1950 and September 1951, and were distributed by Documento Film.

Even though conceived as mere divertissements, the two short films showed an often overlooked side of Freda's character: his love for silent comedies. The format allowed him to pay homage to his beloved one-reelers, with a series of gags inspired by the silent era, similarly to what he would do in his 1955 comedy *Da qui all'eredità*. *L'astuto barone (ovvero L'eredità contesa)* (The Cunning Baron, or The Disputed Inheritance) is particularly interesting as it moves from a premise which underlines the director's flair for black humor, as the titular Baron Degubernatis invites his relatives at his villa to dispatch them and get hold of an inheritance. *Tenori per forza* (Tenors By Force) also revolves around a series of misunderstandings, and tells a story of two brothers who put themselves into trouble with some lowlifes, hide in a theater and are forced to pass themselves off as tenors, with the expected disastrous results.

Both *L'astuto barone* and *Tenori per forza* featured a number of young actors with a bright future ahead of them, such as the debuting Nino Manfredi and Rossella Falk: the latter, according to the director, "pushed comedy to the point of clownery."[7] Another soon-to-be famous face was that of Tino Buazzelli, who had showed up in a small role in *Il cavaliere misterioso*: a consistently popular character actor in his home country, Buazzelli would become a household name in the late 1960s after starring as Nero Wolfe in a hugely successful TV series based on Rex Stout's mystery novels. He died in 1980, when he was only 58 years old. Other soon-to-be-popular thesps turned up, such as Paolo Panelli, Bice Valori, and Luciano Salce, the latter an excellent filmmaker too. According to film historian Stefano Della Casa, *L'astuto barone* had a legal aftermath, as the real Baron De Gubernatis, offended by the homonymy with the film's character, sued the production.[8] *Tenori per forza* also featured a special participation on the part of António Vilar, who played Carlos Gomes in *Guarany*, and who had been persuaded by Freda that he was about to shoot a scene for that film: same set, same costumes, same technicians. Instead, he found himself right in the middle of a frantic cream pie war.

O caçula do barulho

After the end of World War II, Brazil was being seen by many as some sort of El Dorado: a new land full of untapped opportunities by immigrants and businessmen alike

Rare Brazilian press sheet for *O caçula do barulho* (1949, here spelled *O caçula do barulho*), featuring (left to right) Grande Otelo, Gianna Maria Canale, Oscarito and Anselmo Duarte. The text reads: "Gianna Maria Canale, the beautiful 'Miss Italia' is the star of this noteworthy dramatic comedy by Atlântida with Oscarito, Grande Otelo, Anselmo Duarte, Luis Tito, Sergio De Oliveira and others. The direction is by the famous Riccardo Freda, who made *Aquila nera*, *Don Cesare di Bazan* and *I miserabili*. Soon in the theaters of the Empresa Luiz Severiano Ribeiro."

from all over the planet. One of them was a Neapolitan by the name of Franco Zampari, an engineer and great fan of the theater who had settled in the country in 1922, to work for a steel factory owned by Brazilian millionaires of Italian extraction in São Paulo. Zampari quickly became known as a patron of the arts, and in 1948 he founded the Teatro Brasileiro de Comédia (TBC). The following year, Zampari invested money he had gotten from businessmen from all over the country and created Companhia Cinematográfica Vera Cruz. Located in São Bernando do Campo (a blue-collar city in the greater São Paulo area), on an area of approximately 300,000 square feet, it quickly became known as the "Brazilian Hollywood," topping in means and ambitions the existing companies such as Cinédia (funded in 1930 by Brazilian filmmakers) and Atlântida. Professionals from abroad were being hired to diversify the industry here. Austrians, Italians, Englishmen and Portuguese were brought to Brazil: one such was the Parisian-born Brazilian filmmaker Alberto Cavalcanti, the co-director of the classic horror anthology *Dead of Night* (1945), who was entrusted by Zampari as the head the company. Vera Cruz's first production also involved an Italian filmmaker: *Caiçará* (1950) was co-directed (together with Tom Payne and Cavalcanti) by Adolfo Celi, who was also TBC's first artistic director. Another Italian director who took his first steps in Brazil was Luciano Salce, who made a couple of movies back-to-back there, *Uma pulga na balança* (1953) and *Floradas na serra* (1954).

Freda and Canale arrived in Rio De Janeiro in September 1948, to shoot the exteriors for *Guarany*. What was supposed to be a short stay turned out to be a four-month-and-a-half period in Brazil, during which Freda was asked to direct three films by producer Luiz Severiano Ribeiro Jr., the owner of Atlântida Cinematográfica: he accepted on the spot due to the huge sum of money he was offered.

Founded in 1941 by Moacir Fenelon and José Carlos Burle, Atlântida Cinematográfica had been a pioneer in the development of the Brazilian film industry, and consolidated as the country's leading production company, with 12 films helmed between 1943 and 1947. Many starred a popular duo of comedians, the former circus clown Oscarito and the vaudeville artist Grande Otelo, who first acted together in 1944's *Tristezas Não Pagam Dívidas*, and became two of Atlântida's biggest stars. Otelo—who came from absolute poverty and a series of personal family tragedies having to do with his father's alcoholism—was a natural, with hardly any formal training; he was also a samba singer, lyricist and composer, and became a well-known face outside of his home country, doing bit parts in international features shot on Brazilian soil: Orson Welles' *It's All True* (1942–1993) the Claudia Cardinale vehicle *Una rosa per tutti* (1967, Franco Rossi), Werner Herzog's *Fitzcarraldo* (1982), and Julien Temple's *Running Out of Luck* (1987).

1947 marked a turning point in the history of Atlântida, with the advent of Luiz Severiano Ribeiro Jr.—already a leader in the distribution and exhibition market—as the main strongholder. With Ribeiro, the company consolidated its production of popular comedies and slapstick farces, the so-called *chanchadas* (as defined by Lisa Shaw: "a term coined in the 1930s by journalists and film critics to refer scathingly to the highly derivative, light musical comedies that were used to promote carnival music and were often modeled on Hollywood movies of the same era."[9]) Given the rapidly blooming motion picture industry, it is no wonder Ribeiro took the opportunity and secured the services of a respected foreign filmmaker (and an Italian rising diva). During that same period he also invested in other foreign technicians: he put under contract Edmond F. Bernoudy, Hitchcock's former assistant on *Rebecca* (1940) and *Foreign Correspondent* (1940), to direct *Terra Violenta* (1948), based on Jorge Amado's novel. Likewise, he embarked in co-productions, such as *Vendaval maravilhoso* (1949), a biography of the Brazilian poet Antônio de Castro Alves directed by the Portuguese-born José Leitão de Barros.

The first (and eventually only) film Freda directed for Atlântida was *Um caçula do barulho* (literally, A Troublemaker Kid[10]: Even though the title is usually listed as *O caçula do barulho*, the title on the only existing copy is *Um caçula do barulho*). It was shot in three weeks in Rio, in the fall of 1948, with an above-average budget. Freda worked with an entirely Brazilian crew and cast—save for Canale, who looks stunning but rather uncomfortable with the Portuguese-spoken dialogue, and director of photography Ugo Lombardi, who had moved to Brazil after the war. In addition to Oscarito and Grande Otelo (both top-billed although their roles are relatively minor, especially Otelo's), the cast featured Luiz Tito (as the main villain) and future film director Anselmo Duarte—winner of the Golden Palm in Cannes in 1962 with *O pagador de promessas*, released to some English-language markets as *The Given Word*—in his first starring role in an Atlântida pic.

Um caçula do barulho tells of the irresponsible Luis (Duarte), the youngest of seven brothers, who is overprotected by his mother, does not work and always puts himself into trouble, until his brothers come and save him. He falls for an Italian singer, Gianna (Canale), unaware that she is tied to a gangster who runs a white slavery ring. Freda came up with the story, which, according to the director, was based on a silent flick named *Ecco i nostri*, "an unassuming dramatic comedy ... which I had seen as a child during the silent era: I had fun turning out a Brazilian version of it."[11] However, no silent film with such Italian title seems to exist, so perhaps Freda's memory was failing him.

In an in-depth essay on the film published in the Brazilian magazine *Filmecultura*, film scholar João Carlos Rodrigues notes that "not everyone was happy with the story. Ugo Lombardi said that Freda 'ignored Brazilian reality,' Anselmo Duarte ... said that 'the script was written quickly, without too much care' ... Alinor Azevedo told Freda that the story was crap."[12] Azevedo was entrusted by Ribeiro to write the dialogue and add some comic interludes, mostly centered on Oscarito's character, which further underline the movie's hybrid quality: the dramatic subplot involving the white slave ring borders on *film noir*, and somehow clashes with the fatuous comedy bits.

Um caçula do barulho was one of the rare *chanchadas* of the period almost devoid of song numbers, save for the opening credit dance sequence (reprised later in the film), featuring a woman wearing a *baiana* costume (the *baiana* being the stylized female figure dressed in white, with head wrap and jewelry, typical of the Rio carnival and burlesque theater) made famous in Hollywood by Carmen Miranda, alongside a male dancer dressed as a toreador, and one scene where Canale sings a number on the stage of the Recreio theater in Rio. In the scenes set in the theater, the film has some things in common with Freda's early musical comedies *Non canto più* and *Tutta la città canta* for its depiction of the stage world.

From many records, Freda alienated many in the crew due to his incessant set tantrums and marital crisis with the lead actress.[13] He was obviously a gun-for-hire on a movie whose sociological implications he did not know or care about. Grande Otelo and Oscarito—one black, the other white—personified the so-called *zé-povinho*, the average Brazilian everyman, and were figures that the urban Brazilian audience could easily identify with, covering "a broad racial spectrum of the urban masses."[14] They would team up as a comedy duo until 1954. In the film, Otelo plays a pathetic figure: a meek and poorly-treated cleaner—the lowest rung of the social ladder, referred to as "*Maldito negro!*" (Damned negro!)—, who befriends Gianna and is eventually dispatched by the bad guys. The short and slender Oscarito is the main comic relief, and, as customary, embodies a cowardly, emasculated type: he is seen donning a fruit-laden head-dress, Carmen Miranda-style, while helping Gianna pack her bags, and in another scene he is asked to woo Gianna's maid in order to gain access to her home, but is horrified to discover that the maid is a matronly black woman, and later escapes her amorous advances by taking refuge atop a wardrobe. If the ethnic jokes play rather uncomfortable to today's audience, they were a routine element in *chanchadas*: as Rodrigues points out, the following year Azevedo wrote José Carlos Burle's *Também somos irmãos*, a sincere anti-racist pamphlet.[15]

However, not all the comedy veers on buffoonery: the film features some good dialogue scenes between Otelo and Luiz Tito, and the parts set in the family could have been better developed, had the brothers been played by real actors and not professional wrestlers. "All this, some 80 percent, can be credited to the Italian director. The rest, imposed by the producer, is pure *chanchada,*" Rodrigues sums up.[16] Understandably, Freda was likely indifferent toward the verbal jokes: he visibly put more effort in the slapstick comedy bits, which are blatantly inspired by American silent movies. The opening dance number segues into a bar brawl and a chaotic chase, filmed with a quick travelling shot following the action, which look like a modern-day version of the ones featured in some of the director's swashbucklers, as Duarte escapes a gang of pursuers by jumping over tables and atop a flight of stairs, accompanied by quick camera movements. In another remarkable action bit near the end of the movie, a backstage brawl spills over to the stage. These scenes marked a historical landmark in Brazilian cinema: for the first time, fights were shot using Italian film techniques, which influenced the inclusion of similar sequences in subsequent Brazilian *chanchadas*. Even though he could not count on experienced stuntmen as in his Italian works (the fistfights look a bit clumsy in places), the result displays the director's flair for these kind of set-pieces, with a remarkable use of depth-of-field, featuring bodies thrown at the camera and plenty of low-angle shots. Freda also included shots of car-filled avenues at night and speeding through road tunnels, giving a metropolitan image of the city not unlike in Hollywood *film noir* entries of the period.

Even more significant are the dramatic bits. Rodrigues praises the scenes involving the white slave subplot, and another typically Freda moment when Anselmo Duarte is imprisoned by the bandits:

> Gianna escapes and asks his brothers for help, but they refuse. She, then, always well-dressed, begs them, strong and semi-naked men, to save their younger brother. The shot of the beautiful woman among the males, a tremendous archetype, is an authorial trait which Freda will develop in the following years in his historical and mythological films.[17]

The movie opened in Brazil on January 1, 1949: despite less than favorable reviews,[18] it was a major success, becoming one of Atlântida's most popular *chanchadas* of the period, and was periodically re-released in theaters for over a decade. Given that *Terra violenta* and *Vendaval maravilhoso* were box-office flops instead, Ribeiro stayed within the commercially comfortable realm of *chanchadas*. Alinor Azevedo would recycle the same mixture of crime film and comedy the following year, in *Carnaval no Fogo* (1949, Watson Macedo)—another huge hit which would set the tone for the *chanchadas* made during the 1950s.

With his usual taste for exaggeration, Freda later claimed that he had to literally teach his colleagues the basics of postproduction, which seems a bit unlikely considering that Atlântida had been in business for several years and Ribeiro owned the country's most modern processing lab. The director also told Éric Poindron about his ill-fated attempt at establishing a Society of the Authors, similar to Italy's SIAE, which would take care of copyright matters—a project that ended quite abruptly.[19]

After *Um caçula do barulho* Freda was asked to replace Bermoudy when the American director was fired from *Terra Violenta*, but he refused, and the film was salvaged by editor Paulo Machado. The second picture Freda was supposed to deliver for the company was *Anita Garibaldi*: an ambitious project that likely suited the director much more, given Giuseppe Garibaldi's popularity in South America as well, since the Italian patriot spent twelve years in exile in the continent after being sentenced to death in Italy. The movie was possibly centered on the meeting between the hero and his future wife, the Brazilian Ana Ribeiro da Silva, commonly known as "Anita," and on Garibaldi's fight against the rebels in the Ragamuffin War and the Uruguayan Civil War, before his return to Italy and his role in the creation of the Kingdom of Italy in 1861 with the 1860 Mille expedition to Southern Italy—when he led a corps of volunteers, the so-called "*camicie rosse*" (Redshirts), which resulted in the conquest of the Kingdom of the Two Sicilies, ruled by the Bourbons.

Given such a challenging project, it seemed that Freda's Brazilian stay would last for a while. However, Gianna Maria Canale thought differently. "One morning she packed her suitcases and demanded to leave on the spot, or else she would kill herself...."[20] Thus, in February 1949 Freda and the actress returned to Italy.

As for Atlântida, it existed until 1962, when it produced its 66th and last film in its 21-year-course, *Os Apavorados* (1962, Ismael Porto), before embarking in several co-production deals with other national and international companies.

Um caçula do barulho never surfaced outside of Brazil. It was never released in Italy either.

Il conte Ugolino

Freda's first film after his short-lived Brazilian experience was another period work with literary ascendences, albeit peculiar ones. Count Ugolino della Gherardesca (1220–1289) was a historical figure whose tragic story had been brought to universal resonance by the poet Dante Alighieri in his allegorical poem *Divine Comedy*. Born in the Tuscan city of Pisa into a noble family of German origins, Ugolino took active part in the ongoing war between the Ghibellines, who sided with the Emperor, and the Guelphs, who sided with the Pope and sought to maintain the self-governing city-states. Appointed first *Podestà* and then *Capitano del popolo*,[21] Ugolino became the most influential man in Pisa.

Although he belonged to a Ghibelline family, and the party controlled the city of Pisa, Ugolino behaved in an ambiguous manner: a key historical episode that happened during the war with the rival city of Genoa was his withdrawing of his division during the naval Battle of Meloria, in August 1284. After the defeat, which cost Pisa losses and the capture of many Ghibellines, Ugolino had to deal with other rival cities such as Florence and Lucca, and repeatedly refused to negotiate peace with Genoa, as he feared that it would compromise his power. The decline of Ugolino's fortunes was partly caused by his feud with the local Archbishop Ruggieri degli Ubaldini, in 1288, while Pisa was undergoing a severe economic crisis, with food shortage and riots. After being attacked by a group of Ghibellines, Ugolino withdrew into the town hall, but eventually he had to surrender when the crowd, aroused by the Archbishop's accusation of treachery, set the building on fire. Ugolino, his two sons and two grandsons were detained in the Muda tower, and there left to starve by the new *Podestà*—the Archbishop himself.

Dante placed Ugolino in the lowest circle of the *Inferno*, reserved for betrayers of kin, country, guests and benefactors. The poet depicts him entrapped in ice up to his neck, together with Archbishop Ruggieri, and constantly gnawing at the latter's skull: "I saw two shades frozen in a single hole / packed so close, one head hooded the other one; / the way the starving devour their bread, the soul / above had clenched the other with his teeth / where the brain meets the nape." (Chant XXXII, lines 124–129). However, the most famous verses are those where Dante hints at Ugolino's starvation, with his dying sons begging him to eat their bodies: "'Father our pain,' they said, / 'Will lessen if you eat us you are the one / Who clothed us with this wretched flesh: we plead / For you to be the one who strips it away.'" (Chant XXXII, lines 56–59)—and Ugolino's ambiguous reaction: "And I, / Already going blind, groped over my brood / Calling to them, though I had watched them die, / For two long days. And then the hunger had more / Power than even sorrow over me." (Chant XXXII, lines 70–73).[22]

Dante's *Divine Comedy* had been used as a source of inspiration since the silent era of Italian cinema, and the story of Count Ugolino had already been adapted into film in 1909 by Giuseppe De Liguoro with *Il conte Ugolino*. Freda was not particularly enamored of Dante's work, which he claimed to have read as a child: he was more interested in the undergoing historical events that inspired the poet, such as the struggle for power between the cities and the cruelty that ensued, than in the symbolical meaning. Still, he was struck by the visionary quality of the poem. "Dante is imagination at its purest. The *Inferno* and the *Paradiso* don't have any equivalent or precedent. They are the most unsettling and fantasmagorical journeys that we have ever been allowed to make. To read Dante is to 'grasp' the Universe."[23]

Il conte Ugolino was definitely a lower-budgeted effort than Freda's previous efforts with Lux. It was produced by Forum Film, a small company that financed only a few pictures between 1949 and 1950, namely a few other dramas and three flicks starring Totò, such as *Totò le Moko* (1949) and *Totò cerca casa* (1950). The producer, Umberto Momi, would also finance a couple of the director's following films, *La vendetta di Aquila Nera* and *Vedi Napoli e poi muori*.

As with many Italian motion pictures of the period, including the second part of *I miserabili*, *Il conte Ugolino* opens with a book whose pages are being browsed, in an explicit reference to its literary source:

Italian 2-fogli manifesto for *Il conte Ugolino* (1949).

the emphasis on the illustrious background is further proof of the makers' will to detach from Neorealism. The opening titles are set over a series of etchings by Gustave Doré (1832–1883), who famously illustrated Dante's *Divine Comedy*, but overall the poem was merely a pretext to dwell into a historical melodrama, as it had been the case with the previous *Pia de' Tolomei* (1941, Esodo Pratelli) and would be with the contemporaneous *Paolo e Francesca* (1950, Raffaello Matarazzo). On *Il conte Ugolino*, Freda similarly focused on the historical scenario, with a period drama that in several ways predated his 1956 masterwork *Beatrice Cenci*. Nevertheless, the film actually takes many liberties with the historical facts, going so far as using the Battle of Meloria as the pivotal event that leads to the Count's imprisonment, whereas it actually took place five years earlier and was interpreted as treachery only starting with 16th century historians. Luigi Bonelli's story has the trappings of a turgid melodrama, but the script—by Steno (whose name is misspelled in the credits as Stefano *Vanzini*) and Monicelli, with the director's uncredited contribution—wisely bypasses such limitations.

The theme of power crosses the film like a tumultuous undercurrent. Freda's distrust of politics and organized religion can be glimpsed in the sympathy with which he depicts such an ambiguous, shady figure as Ugolino. Despite being a hothead and vindictive type, the libertine and voluptuary Count obviously has the director's admiration. He represents Freda's ideal of manhood—virile, patriarchal, independent, a man of action rather than words: "There are two kinds of appointment where a man of honor must go alone: those with love and those with death" he claims, echoing a famous line ("Well, there are some things a man just can't run away from") uttered by the Ringo Kid in *Stagecoach*—as opposed to the evil, effeminate Archbishop. Their confrontation becomes a struggle between the darkness of the Middle Ages and the Enlightenment: hypocrisy against sincerity, prejudice against reason, empty talk against action, the oppressive Church against an individual's free will.

Freda compared the Archbishop to *I miserabili*'s Javert, but the character seems actually closer to the French Ambassador in *Don Cesare di Bazan*, as he is not allowed Javert's last-minute redemption. It was a bold but not isolated move, for a filmmaker who would later depict religious characters in a shady manner, such as the Church seen as a crushing, cruel force in *Beatrice Cenci* and the greedy parish priest played by Umberto Raho in *Lo spettro*. Even though Freda used to minimize this aspect in later interviews, *Il conte Ugolino* stands out amidst the generally pious period films of the era, imbued with Catholicism and careful not to raise controversial matters that might result in a harsh judgment on the part of the Vatican in the reviews (or rather, "reports") by the powerful CCC—*Centro Cattolico Cinematografico* (Catholic Cinema Center).

Created in 1935, the CCC was an organism devoted to the review and classification of all motion pictures distributed in Italy. Its reviews, published in volumes named "*Segnalazioni cinematografiche*" (Film reports), were aimed at parish priests and managers of the parish theaters, and classified each film according to three basic categories, inspired by Catholic values: "Suitable," expressed with the abbreviation "T" as "*per tutti*" (for all audiences), "Tr" (less suitable for younger audiences), "A" (adults only) or "Am" (for adults with a "complete maturity of moral judgment"); "Suitable with Reservation," expressed with the abbreviation "Ar" and meaning films that, although not entirely negative, featured dangerous elements for adults as well and deserved "objective moral reservations"; and "Negative," that is "S," "*sconsigliato*" (not recommended, that is a film which "constitutes an objective danger for all categories of filmgoers") or "E," "*escluso*" (excluded, that is a "gravely immoral and harmful film for all audiences").

With its reports, CCC basically stated which films were to be considered moral or immoral, advisable or negligible, thus orientating the decisions of the parish theaters which formed an important economic resource for producers and distributors alike. Similarly, the Board of Censors rejected films that were considered offensive to Catholicism, such as Eisenstein's *Aleksandr Nevskij* (1938), because of the scene in which monks are seen blessing the Teutonic Knights before battle: first submitted to the board in 1946, Eisenstein's film was rejected twice (following the same fate as a number of Russian and Eastern European pictures) and finally granted a visa only in 1960. Apparently, *Il conte Ugolino*'s allegedly anti-religious quality did pass unnoticed in Italy, but not abroad: according to the director, Stalin's Russia acquired it for distribution based on this peculiarity.

In accordance to the story's gloominess, Freda adopted a style that was quite different from the airy, exuberant one of his previous adventure films: the lights are dim, the characters are invariably framed in lingering close-ups, the outdoor scenes are few and far between. "Each story has only one way to be told," he explained. "If I were to film *Aquila nera* the same way as *Il conte Ugolino*, I'd have to quit my job because I haven't understood anything about movies. To raise the drama and the plot, I had to observe my characters without ever leaving them."[24] The use of interior space and sets is often stunning, such as in the scene of the Pisa war council, or that of Ugolino leaving the lounge room of his castle after vainly awaiting the messenger, filmed with Freda's favorite sideways tracking shot across the hall.

To film the trial scene, having to deal with a lower budget than on his previous efforts with Lux, Freda recurred to a time-saving, innovative trick: instead of changing the camera's axis and filming shots and counter shots, the director simply had the background scenery behind the actors replaced, so as to keep the same lighting scheme. The trick (which soon was given the name "*flipperone*") would become one of his trademark speedy methods, and one often used in low-budget filmmaking to this day.

In spite of the story's overall claustrophobic quality, Freda managed to inject a few action bits in it, with top-notch results. Ugolino's confrontation with his enemies in a decaying hostel has the director employ his usual flair for low-angle shots and contrasted light-and-shadows games, and the scenes set in the forest have an ethereal, otherwordly quality, due to Sergio Pesce's impressive black-and-white cinematography, while Freda's love for classic adventure yarns results in one of the villains appearing as a mysterious black-masked rider.

Unlike in the director's other works of the period, evil wins in the end. Even the obligatory romantic subplot—Ugolino's daughter Emilia's love for the young Balduccio—turns out to be sour, as, unbeknownst to the woman, Balduccio is the Archbishop's accomplice in provoking Ugolino's ruin. The ending—like in so many Freda films—is perfectly circular: the story begins and ends in a dungeon, where Ugolino releases his friend Fortebraccio who had been condemned to starvation, and where he too will end up to face the same punishment. Here, *Il conte Ugolino* reprises to the letter the words of Dante's poem, which are recited off-screen as we witness the agony of Ugolino and his starving sons. Then, the epilogue: after obtaining grace on the part of the Pope, Emilia runs to the dungeon where her father has been buried alive. The guard knocks down the wall with a huge hammer and the woman advances inside the prison. There, a quick tracking shot onward—similar to the one employed in the climax of *Don Cesare di Bazan*—frames her in close-up, as Emilia's expression changes from anxiety to sheer horror. Her images freezes as Dante's famous verse appears: "Then, fasting got the mastery of grief." Even though he basically preserves the ambiguity of Dante's poetry through an ellipsis, by choosing not to reveal what Emilia sees, Freda clearly implies that an act of cannibalism has occurred, as Ugolino presumably devoured his own offspring. The director commented: "The main problem is to know whether Dante came up with this act of cannibalism or it actually had a historical basis.... Sure, in the film I remained in the vague.... According to several interpretations, Dante hints at cannibalism without ever stating it. On the contrary, I think Dante wrote it down clearly: 'Fasting got the mastery of grief,' hunger is stronger than love...."[25]

Not only the dark mood of *Il conte Ugolino* predates the director's grim horror stories of the following decades, but the film already contains in essence many elements of the Gothic horror thread which Freda himself will inaugurate with *I vampiri*. Not only does the story rely upon Gothic's typical imagery, but it moves toward a horrific *coup de théatre* which climaxes with the close-up of a woman exposed to the sight of a literally inconceivable horror. It is an emblematic image that will return over and over in Italian horror and *gialli*, starting with Freda's very own, from Duchess Du Grand (Gianna Maria Canale) screaming after she has reverted to her aged, horrible self in *I vampiri*, to Deborah (Silvia Dionisio) facing the final image of horror in *Murder Obsession*—not forgetting Anne's (Daria Nicolodi) desperate, endless scream in the final shot of *Tenebre* (a.k.a. *Tenebrae*, 1982), one of a number of references to Freda's work on the part of Dario Argento.

The casting of Gianna Maria Canale as Ugolino's firstborn Emilia was dictated by the filmmaker's affair with the actress; even though she had a minor role, Canale was given the film's very best moment, the extraordinary final close-up, one of the most memorable images in the history of Italian popular cinema. On the other hand, Carla Calò (herself the distributor's mistress) had a minor but interesting part as Ugolino's neglected and duplicitous mistress Haidée. Even though she redeems herself in the end by saving Emilia's life, her character somehow predates Freda's heroines of evil, most notably in the beautiful sequence where, as soon as her lover has departed, she lights a lantern and makes a signal to her other lover—Ugolino's sworn enemy Balduccio—from her balcony, a moment which brings to mind Barbara Steele's secret encounter with Peter Baldwin in *Lo spettro*.

As Ugolino, the stage actor Carlo Ninchi (the brother of Annibale, the star of Carmine Gallone's *Scipione l'africano*) gives a strong performance, but at times he is even topped by Peter Trent as the Archbishop. The British actor, born in 1917, started working in Italy right after World War II, as an extra, and was often cast as a villain: here he is constantly on the verge of camp, looking like a mixture between a silent movie vamp with a goatee and a sacred icon gone terribly wrong, either when he is casually caressing a kitten, lost in his thoughts (as Professor Bernard Hichcock will be seen doing in *L'orribile segreto del Dr. Hichcock*), or when he raises his eyes up to the sky, in a hypocritical, would-be pious posture that is subtly unsettling. The character's ambiguity has a sexual innuendo to it: when the Archbishop whispers that to him the dead Balduccio was "like a son ... more than a son..." one cannot help having bad thoughts. And, as Giulio Andreotti used to say, "'bad thoughts are a sin, but they get to the kernel." Freda would cast Trent again in *Il figlio di d'Artagnan* and *La vendetta di Aquila Nera*.

With box-office grossings of 87 million *lire*, *Il conte Ugolino* was a moderate success in Italy, and was allegedly distributed abroad as *The Iron Swordsman*. It paved the way for Raffaello Matarazzo's adaptation of another famous episode in Dante's *Inferno*, Chant

V's telling of the ill-fated love story between Paolo Malatesta and Francesca Da Rimini, *Paolo e Francesca*. Freda considered *Il conte Ugolino* one of his very best works.

Il figlio di d'Artagnan

After the gloomy *Il conte Ugolino*, the director returned to a more light-hearted kind of adventure story with *Il figlio di d'Artagnan*, a title which partially contradicted his later statement that he would never make a movie based on his favorite novel, Dumas' *The Three Musketeers*, since he so loved Fred Niblo's 1921 version starring Douglas Fairbanks, and especially George Sidney's 1948 adaptation starring Gene Kelly as d'Artagnan, "a magnificent film…. It was impossible to do better."[26] If Dumas' text was untouchable to him, at least Freda could evoke its mythical halo—and get ahead of Sidney's film, which came out in Italy in late 1950—by shaping the story around d'Artagnan's son Raoul, whom he imagines as a novice in a convent, who picks up the sword after his Prior has been murdered, and uncovers a conspiracy against the King. However, the project—financed by Freda's old acquaintance Raffaele Colamonici and produced by a small company named Augustus Film—was not destined to turn out as one of the director's most popular efforts. For one thing, the casting of the handsome but not much talented Piero Palermini (real name Giuseppe Palermini, 1925–1996) as Raoul, a move dictated possibly by the actor's passing resemblance to Gene Kelly, was an ill-fated choice, and one Freda would always regret.

The director's low opinion of actors is the stuff of legend: if Hitchcock referred to them as cattle, Freda was often more trenchant. For a filmmaker who thought of cinema essentially as a visual medium, and who tightly constructed his scripts with a precise numbering of shots and camera movements, he never wasted much time discussing the role or the approach to the character.

I never rehearse with actors," he stated.

> In essence, the actor must show up on the set already knowing his role. Yet, I regret to say, it is very rare that an actor has a clear idea of what he must do. He only sees the role through his own personality, which is usually very expansive. He exaggerates the effects and the importance of his part…. With bad actors, the best thing would be not to cast them, but whenever you have the misfortune of having them around, it's always difficult to get what you want.[27]

Freda had already cast Palermini on *Il conte Ugolino*, where he played Balduccio, and did not think very highly of him: he would have preferred the much more athletic and gifted Vittorio Gassman for the role. After *Riso amaro*, though, Gassman's salary had soared: the new-born star was too much of an investment for a modest B-picture, and most of the budget had been put in the climactic sequence at Castle Sant'Angelo. If Gassman had proven an instinctive, rousing swordfighter in *Il cavaliere misterioso*, poor Palermini was incapable of giving the action scenes the necessary intensity and verve. What is more, he constantly had to answer back to Freda's instructions—and, one suspects, the director's pungent remarks. Freda maintained that he was so dissatisfied with his leading man that, while filming the climactic battle on top of the tower, he even threatened to kill Palermini: "I grabbed him by the chest, leaned him over the void and said, 'One more word and I'm throwing you off!' And I would have done it! That's the only time when I really lost control."[28]

Palermini's subsequent career was spotty at best, consisting primarily of secondary

Set still from *Il figlio di d'Artagnan*: (left to right) Carlo Ninchi, Paolo Stoppa, and Gianna Maria Canale.

roles in 1950s adventure and historical flicks. From the mid–1960s onwards his appearances on the big screen became more sparse, with only a handful of titles between 1963 and 1985, when he turned up as the Fascist hierarch Farinacci in the TV miniseries *Mussolini and I*, starring Bob Hoskins as the Duce. Alongside him Freda cast Gianna Maria Canale as Linda, the love interest, and Franca Marzi, with whom he would work again on *La vendetta di Aquila Nera* and *Vedi Napoli e poi muori*. The buxom Marzi would often play the fatal woman in melodramas and comedies, often alongside Totò, but her most famous role is perhaps as Wanda, the prostitute who is Giulietta Masina's best friend in Fellini's *Le notti di Cabiria* (a.k.a. *The Nights of Cabiria*, 1957). The cast also featured several of the director's regular supporting actors, such as Paolo Stoppa, Peter Trent (again playing the villain) and Enzo Fiermonte. A curious presence was that of the three Meniconi brothers (Furio, Mario, Nello); the debuting Furio would become one of those familiar faces that showed up every so often in Italian genre films, sometimes concealed under such pseudonyms as "Men Fury."

So low was his own opinion of the film, that Freda even refused to discuss *Il figlio di d'Artagnan* in interviews, apparently out of superstition. In the end he curtly stated: "Jean-Louis Bory loved it very much, but I think it is unworthy of Dumas."[29] Ironically, the film was the inspiration for Freda's ultimate, and no less unlucky project, Bertrand Tavernier's *La fille de d'Artagnan*.

Even though the result was not up to *Il cavaliere misterioso*, nevertheless *Il figlio di d'Artagnan* has an excessively harsh reputation, possibly due to the fact that, as of today, it is almost invisible. The main problem lies in the script, penned by Freda himself under the alias "Dick Jordan." The absence of Steno and Monicelli is evident, as the story puts together a series of typical situations in the vein of the average swashbuckling adventure, without caring too much about characters or plot development. Nerio Bernardi's imposing monk is clearly modeled upon Friar Tuck in the Robin Hood stories and movies, the romantic subplot steals from *Cyrano de Bergerac*, a gloomy cell looks like something out of *The Count of Monte Cristo*, and so on. The director draws from classic literature to build an ideal universe, which looks like a boy's dreams come true, a hodgepodge of clichés comprised within the 90-minute space of a movie. Reviewers pointed out the film's derivative story: "Period adventure pics have considerable importance in a film industry, but must be treated with the necessary care to avoid far more conspicuous defects than the movies based on the events of contemporary life. Freda's effort is scripted awkwardly and there lie its major shortcomings. The key stages of the plot are carried out in a manner so incredible as to compromise whatever good might there be in the film."[30]

Similarly, *Il figlio di d'Artagnan* encompasses diverse cinephile suggestions. Sometimes Freda simply borrows from his own works: the introductory tavern scene in the village of Grecy looks almost identical to the opening of *Don Cesare di Bazan*, as does Raoul and Linda's marriage in prison; the moment where a man is tortured with a hot iron poker recalls the early scenes in the Venetian dungeon in *Il cavaliere misterioso*; the trial scene reprises the same situation as seen in *Il conte Ugolino*; and the rousing final attack to the fortress by an army of horsemen recreates to the letter the exciting climax of *Aquila nera*. But there are also nods to the work of Alfred Hitchcock, something rather surprising in a late 1940s period adventure Italian film. The sequence in which Raoul follows the conspirators to a windmill where he finds a tortured man, goes back to alert his father and returns to the place, only to find it populated with harmless peasants, is a typical Hitchcockian situation (shades of *Foreign Correspondent*, even though Freda had certainly in mind Dreyer's *Vampyr* for the depiction of the gigantic mill gears), which the director would reprise, in a different context (Pierre Lantin leading the police to the apartment where his fiancée has been kidnapped), in *I vampiri*; similarly, the detail of the missing finger that identifies the (not-so) surprise head of the conspirators is also typically Hitchcockian, and the scene where Freda's camera cranes down to a table where the traitors are sitting, to frame the mutilated hand in close-up, is reminiscent of a celebrated shot in *Young and Innocent* (1937).

Still, Freda makes up for the lack of originality with tight pacing and amiable humor, adopting a tongue-in-cheek approach that is always compelling, and often quite funny. In the beginning, after witnessing the murder of the Prior and swearing revenge, the inexperienced Raoul is about to leave the convent when he is abruptly stopped by an elderly friar (Nerio Bernardi), who picks up Raoul's sword and starts displaying unexpected fencing abilities, out of the blue. It turns out that all the other monks in the convent are former adventurers, and all of them are well-versed in fencing, fighting, gambling, and so on: what follows is a series of humorous vignettes depicting Raoul's speedy apprenticeship, in a similar way as in George Sidney's film. What is more, he gives ample screen time to the hero's sidekick, the Duke of Bligny (Paolo Stoppa), a comic relief very much in the same vein as the character played by Stoppa in *Don Cesare di Bazan*: when Raoul and Bligny sneak in the enemy fortress, they are forced by circumstances to act out as a couple of bungling doctors, summoned to cure the regent, with the expected comic results. Another endearing characterization is that of Richelieu, who turns up only at the end of the movie: far from the scheming Luciferian villain of Sidney's film, he is an amiable old rogue who plays with his kittens and decides Raoul's destiny by challenging one of the monks to a game of cards: he has three kings, but the other beats him by coming up with five (!) aces. "There are situations where kings have no value," Richelieu amiably comments, granting D'Artagnan's son the pardon.

The action sequences are almost all top-notch: Freda makes ample use of dolly and tracking shots, not only to explore the sets (as in the aforementioned tavern scene), but also to emphasize the scene's dramatic potential, as in a beautiful tracking shot onward near the beginning, where a man pursued by the conspirators emerges from the woods. He also takes an obvious delight in filming horsemen riding in the woods, and D'Artagnan's final assault on the fortress is the equivalent of the cavalry rides to the rescue in John Ford's cinema, with the camera mounted on a jeep riding at breakneck speed. The only slight drawback is a somewhat rough use of two cameras during a tavern brawl, to capture simultaneous details. On the other hand, the final battle in the Flemish fortress, shot on a large sound indoor set, is a triumph of vertical dollies and cranes, as the camera follows Raoul's feats against the enemies on the battlements; what is more, it also features impressive miniature work and a show-stopping climax, as Raoul blows up the fortress' dam, and the stream engulfs and wipes away the enemy soldiers, not dissimilarly to the "river of blood" at the climax of Antonio Margheriti's *I criminali della galassia* (a.k.a. *The Wild, Wild Planet*, 1965). Only the final part of the duel between Raoul and the evil Duke of Malvoisin was filmed on the ramparts of Castle Sant'Angelo—most likely thanks to Freda's acquaintances at Universalia Film after the making of *Guarany*.

In the opening credits, the names of Gianna Maria Canale and Franca Marzi are top-billed, although their roles are essentially vapid: Marzi's prominence was possibly due to her affair with the producer, whereas Canale's was the result of Freda attempting to push her to stardom. Whenever the camera frames her, Sergio Pesce's black-and-white cinematography—already prodigal with references to Flemish painters—pays full homage to her arresting beauty. Ultimately, *Il figlio di d'Artagnan* is a movie made by a man deeply in love, and the punchline sums up his thoughts, as Richelieu watches Linda and Raoul walk away in the sunset and comments, "Why talk of such a sad thing as war?"

When reviewing the picture, the president of the censorship commission Annibale Scicluna Sorge was unusually vocal about its formal qualities, stating: "It's a swashbuckling film, made with a large budget and technically very well-crafted. The final sequence (the explosion of the powderhouse and the subsequent collapse of a dam) stands out, as it is shot and edited with remarkable skill. The acting overall leaves a lot to be desired." In accordance with the dominant Catholic mentality, which resulted in all kinds of religious jokes and satire being excised from motion pictures, the board of censors demanded that a brief humorous scene be cut, in which a monk makes the sign of absolution and then pounces on his adversary. Curiously, the commissioners' nationalistic pride was untouched by the amusing moment in the climax where d'Artagnan shouts "*Vive la France!*"—no wonder *Il figlio di d'Artagnan* was released the next year in France by the Cocinor company. In Italy it did good business (201 million *lire*) but could not hold a candle to the year's top grossing films, such as *Gli ultimi giorni di Pompei* (841 million) and *Tormento* (726 million), respectively an Ancient Rome epic and a contemporary melodrama.

It was also picked up for distribution overseas: an article in the *Los Angeles Times* dated November 1950 mentioned that Sol Lesser's company Principal Pictures International was going to import the film (as *The Son of d'Artagnan*)[31]: however, the movie came out in the U.S. in late 1953, on the bottom end of double-bills,[32] with the singularly infelicitous title *The Gay Swordsman*, courtesy of Jules Weill.[33] Freda's name was changed to "Richard Freda" for the direction credit, whereas Gianna Maria Canale simply became "Maria Canale."

Magia a prezzi modici

In the early 1950s, Italian producers churned out a huge number of short films, to take advantage of the State financings introduced by the Andreotti law (#958, 29 December 1949), which redesigned the State's economic contributions to the motion picture industry. The law established the essential requirements for every short film in black-and-white, whose length was to be not less than 250 meters and not more than 2000 meters; whereas for those made in color the minimum length sufficient for the admission to the benefits of the law was 180 meters. The law granted, upon advice of a Technical Committee, an economic contribution on the part of the State equal to the three percent of the box-office gross introits of the screenings in which the short film was projected for a period of three years after the first public screening. It also granted, always upon advice of the Technical Committee, an additional contribution of a two percent of gross introits of said screenings, in cases of exceptional technical and artistic value. This way, besides strengthening the role of the Technical Committee, the Andreotti law favored color short films for mere economic reasons, compared to the use of black-and-white, by its nature more suited to filming documentaries. What is more, theater owners were obliged to screen Italian short films in each and every showing, paired with a feature-length movie, for at least half of the year, ditto for newsreels. Only a few, however, would benefit from the State's ample funds destined for short films, as not all of them obtained the so-called "*programmazione obbligatoria*" (mandatory programming), which indeed was denied to many of the best documentaries made by illustrious directors, affected and discriminated against for plainly political reasons. On top of that, the law caused the creation of a dangerous oligopoly that favored the big production companies and ended up suffocating the small and independent ones. Soon a cartel was formed by the most important producers (Edelweiss, Documento, Astra, Sedi, Gamma), which signed an agreement with distributors for the exclusive pairing of documentaries, promoted by the Technical Committee, to the most successful feature films. Small companies were then forced to sell their products to the cartel, which squeezed much higher profits out of them. Ultimately, short films and documentaries constituted one of the biggest speculations in Italian post-war film industry.

Financed by Freda's longtime friend Attilio Riccio, with whom the director would work again by the end of the decade and the early 1960s, shooting uncredited scenes for the latter's sword-and-sandal pictures, *Magia a prezzi modici* was a ten-minute short in which Freda dealt with one of his favorite themes—magic. In the ministerial papers, it is described as "a surprising reportage in the unexplored world of magicians and astrologists," but its approach is firmly tongue-in-cheek. As Freda recalled, "In Rome there was a fashion of satanism and the occult, and I wanted to report the phenomenon in mockery form."[34] Therefore, *Magia a prezzi modici* takes a decidedly ironic approach to the subject, through a first-person narrative which mixes little comic vignettes and historical digressions about superstitious beliefs.

The examples are often funny; some—like the fear of black cats or of the number thirteen—are well known, whereas others are more obscure and anthropologically interesting: for instance, crossing a fork and a knife on the table means that there will be obstacles on the way of some business, if your tablemate pours wine in your glass with his left hand, that means treason, and so on. The most interesting bit, however, is the scene where a man goes to a fortune teller to learn about his future: a tight montage follows, which plays humorously with horror movie clichés like pentacles, a "dead man's hand" and a skull, as well as a devilish-looking extra fixing the camera and menacing light-shadows inspired by Val Lewton-produced horror movies. "My film showed clairvoyants, a whole parapsychological fauna, absolutely not serious. But the audience believed them, and did not realize that it was an ironic film, about the kindred of Astarot, magicians and the devil."[35] To the director, it was a way to sneer at superstition as opposed to a true knowledge and study of the occult, a matter that always interested him.

The director spoke of *Magia a prezzi modici* with affection.

> The opening is amusing, there was a voice off saying, "I have a friend who really has no luck, when he comes across a black cat, his day is ruined...." The friend who has no luck, was me, I drove out of a superb villa on my Rolls. In the middle of the street there was a black cat. The car stopped abruptly, and I showed the action filmed backwards and speeded up. The car returned in the villa and the film started....[36]

Freda—driving the car only in the opening long shots—actually doubled for the real protagonist, played by Mario Siletti (1897–1977), a stage actor who was very active in the movies since the early 1930s and had worked with the director on *Aquila nera*. Freda would cast him again on *Teodora*.

Magia a prezzi modici was submitted to the board of censors on December 2, 1950, and obtained the visa on December 13. It was distributed in theaters in January 1951.

6

Under the Sign of Melodrama

Il tradimento (Passato che uccide)

Freda's return to the present times after a string of period films was mainly due to commercial shrewdness. A new popular trend was catching on, that of turgid, tear-jerking melodramas set in contemporary Italy, whose constant ingredients revolved around a Manichean view, with honest men wrongly accused of crimes they did not commit and despicable scoundrels, man-eating vamps and innocent girls whose good virtue was unjustly maligned. The plots offered somewhat unlikely twists and turns, which ultimately led to the triumph of family values as opposed to immorality, greed and falseness. The undisputed star was Amedeo Nazzari, one of the most popular Italian actors during the Fascist era, whose career had benefitted from a new start after the enormous box-office success of Raffaello Matarazzo's *Catene*, which he starred in alongside Yvonne Sanson and Aldo Nicodemi, two of Freda's discoveries. The critics disparaged such films, calling them "*Neorealismo d'appendice*" (Neorealism wannabe) for their tendency to water down Neorealism's characters into conventional, soap-opera narratives with little regard for the precepts of realism and barely sketched psychologies. Nevertheless, the audience loved them. On his part, Freda claimed that he and Monicelli almost forced Matarazzo to move to melodrama and write *Catene*: "We won his resistance, because he wouldn't even want to hear about it. So, Matarazzo got money and fame from films that made him almost throw up during the making, quite distant from his Croce-inspired spirit."[1] However, in spite of his alleged dislike toward the genre, Matarazzo's adherence to the stories he was telling in his melodramas (as *I figli di nessuno*, 1951, and *Torna!*, 1953, both starring Nazzari and Sanson) is evident and absolute, making them among the best efforts in his career.

The idea for Freda's first contemporary melodrama, *Il tradimento (Passato che uccide)* (Betrayal—The Past That Kills) came through Mario Monicelli, who read in a newspaper a curious true story that happened in 1922 and suggested to Freda that they make it into a film. The plot revolves around a wealthy engineer, Pietro Vanzelli, who is unjustly framed for murder by the malevolent Renato Salvi, who fakes his own death. Vanzelli is sentenced to fifteen years and his life is destroyed: his wife commits suicide and his daughter Luisa grows up away from him and in poverty. After being released, he accidentally comes across his estranged daughter, and then Salvi, who attempts to blackmail him: this time, Vanzelli kills Salvi for real, but he is acquitted and can finally reunite with his offspring.

The plot, which recalls in parts an earlier post-war melodrama, *Felicità perduta*

Italian fotobusta for *Il tradimento* (1951).

(1946, Filippo Walter Ratti), has its share of cheap twists and tearjerking situations—the most easily disposable being the subplot about Luisa's love story with a young nobleman named Stefano and his parents' disapproval of it. Monicelli's sharp eye for social criticism comes to the fore from time to time. A case in point are the scenes that depict Luisa being harassed by her greedy landlady, who explicitly pushes her to become a prostitute. A few years later, as a director, Monicelli would explore a similar topic in the excellent *Totò e Carolina* (1955): it met lots of trouble with the board of censors due to the plot centering on a poor country girl who resorts to prostitution after getting pregnant and is arrested by a good-hearted, if not too bright, cop (Totò) who will eventually take care of her. On *Il tradimento*, the script's anti-conformism goes as far as the strict censorship of the time would allow, in the thorny scene where the drunk Pietro finds himself in Luisa's room and, not yet knowing she is his daughter, makes a pass at her, believing she is a prostitute.

As film historian Emiliano Morreale observed, "the protagonist's comeback, after being in jail since 1935 to the present, makes him ideally a 'veteran' like many in Italian cinema of the period: his return is the nearest thing to Neorealism ever achieved by Freda, perhaps the most fiercely extraneous filmmaker to the Neorealist mood."[2] However, there are important differences from the typical melodramas of the period: as in the director's other foray in the genre, *Vedi Napoli e poi muori*, the story takes place in an upper-class setting (in Vanzelli's elegant house there is always room for a bottle of champagne), and the plot is not centered around "the dynamics of guilt and atonement that concern the female characters," as Morreale underlines, but on the male figures instead, especially that of the villain.

Even though he is basically detached from *mélo* as he was from Neorealism, Freda's handling of the melodramatic aspects is assured: that is the case with the vital plot element of the doll which Vanzelli gave Luisa as a child (shades of *I miserabili* here) and which he finds again, many years later, in the young woman's room, leading him to recognize her as his offspring. The trial scene—a situation where Freda would always give his best, from *Il conte Ugolino* to *Roger la Honte*—is also remarkable: the director's favorite sideways tracking shots are put to best use to show the onlookers' morbid curiosity as well as the judges' impassiveness, as opposed to Vanzelli's utter desperation.

Still, Freda was obviously more interested in the Hitchcockian situation of a man wrongly accused of murder, and in the paradoxical theme of the past returning in the form of the alleged victim reappearing and fate causing the protagonist to kill him again, this time for real. Thanks also to Enzo Serafin's accomplished black-and-white cinematography, the best scenes in *Il tradimento* have a distinct *film noir* feel to them: Salvi's despicable plan being hinted at little by little in the opening sequences, as he pretends to be drunk while scattering clues that will lead to the innocent Vanzelli's arrest; the two men driving at night in the outskirts of Rome and in the countryside; Vanzelli meeting Salvi again on a train years later, with the latter's face suddenly revealed by the light of a match; Luisa's nocturnal wanderings in the city before her casual meeting with the drunken stranger who turns out to be her father. Most impressive, though, is the two men's deadly fight in Vanzelli's apartment, which takes place in almost utter darkness and shows the director's skills and flair for strong dramatic images: the murder takes place off-screen and is suggested by Salvi's lifeless hand falling right onto the old newspaper which carried the news of Vanzelli's indictment—a moment which brings to mind the killing of Gomes' mother in *Guarany*. It is a shot that would have made Hitchcock proud. Ditto for the eerie scene in which Vanzelli retraces the same route as fifteen years earlier in order to get rid of Salvi's body, and comes across the son of the linesman he had met at a rail crossing: here, the concept of a cyclically returning destiny comes to the fore, a notion which Freda would later explore in his horror films and thrillers.

For *Il tradimento*, the director teamed up again with Amedeo Nazzari, whom he had met ten years earlier on the set of *Caravaggio, il pittore maledetto*. Even though Freda and Nazzari eventually became friends, and at one point even thought of setting up a production company together, their relationship did not start on the right foot. Nazzari had not changed since the days of his prima donna moods in *Caravaggio*, and claimed to have a word in directing, commenting on Freda's choice of camera set-ups and the like. Quite an ill-fated move, considering the latter's irascible temper.

> Nazzari thought that his celebrity status allowed him the right to direct the film or at least the director. At the end of the fourth day, when we were shooting near St. Peter's square, he started to make ironic comments on my work. I think I had had too much tea: the seamstress put cognac in the thermos, by order of Nazzari! I lost my patience, told him to go to hell and walked off the set. The next day, I explained my decision to the producers: either I'd continue the film without Nazzari, or I'd quit. But how to shoot the film without its leading man? It was sufficient to use a double, and by the end of the shoot another director would film Nazzari's close-ups. Once again, the producers thought I was crazy, but they accepted my decision. The next day I went back to work with Nazzari's double, a certain Di Carlo, who looked a lot like him and could imitate his attitudes. I shot very important sequences with Di Carlo.... In the evening, Di Carlo reported to Nazzari. And Nazzari, very upset, asked: "But you didn't pass near the camera, did you?" And Di Carlo: "Yes, I did, only three feet away

from the camera!" The second day, same report. The third day Nazzari came over to apologize and promised that he would never meddle again in my direction.³

Besides Nazzari's commanding performance, *Il tradimento* benefits enormously from Vittorio Gassman's turn as the villain. After *Riso amaro*, the Ligurian actor was being regularly cast as the bad guy, in roles that allowed him to give vent to his tendency to histrionics. Here, Gassman wisely avoids going over the top, and breathes life into a rather sketchy character, making the leery, abject Renato a study in duplicitousness, the kind of vile yet perversely fascinating opportunist that he will play to perfection in such films as *Il sorpasso*. As the actor recalled, "In Freda's *Il tradimento* I was a villain, and also [a] repugnant, filthy, coward, slapped by women as well as by Nazzari—I remember a scene on a train where he slaps me twice, and they were well-deserved slaps. I have few memories of it…. However, there are still fans of this film, who maintain it is an extraordinary movie, to be rediscovered. And perhaps they are right…."⁴

Of the three leads, Gianna Maria Canale comes off as the worst by far, as her beauty cannot hide her acting shortcomings in a role that does not suit her imposing beauty as it should have. For the brief part of Vanzelli's unfortunate wife Clara, Freda cast Caterina Boratto (1915–2010), one of the stars of Italian cinema in the late 1930s: *Il tradimento* was to be her last film in over a decade, and Boratto would return to the big screen in Federico Fellini's *8½* (1963). In her later career Boratto would appear in such works as Fellini's *Giulietta degli spiriti*, Mario Bava's *Diabolik* (a.k.a. *Danger: Diabolik*, 1968), Sydney Pollack's *Castle Keep* (1969) and Pier Paolo Pasolini's *Salò o le 120 giornate di Sodoma* (a.k.a. *Salò, or the 120 Days of Sodom*, 1975).

Il tradimento was one of the many melodramas that met the utter disapproval on the part of the Centro Cattolico Cinematografico, being classified *"escluso per tutti"* (excluded for all audiences). Nevertheless, it made good business in Italy with 311 million *lire*, even though not on a par with Matarazzo's *I figli di nessuno*, which grossed over 950 million at the box-office. It was distributed in the U.S. as *Double Cross*, in a dubbed, severely cut 77-minute version, directly on the television circuit.⁵

La vendetta di Aquila Nera

After a merely commercial project as *Il tradimento*, Freda pursued economic and creative independence by setting up a production company comprised of local distributors from various regions, including Carlo Caiano, the father of film director Mario Caiano. The result was A.P.I. Film, the acronym of Associati Produttori Indipendenti (Associated Independent Producers). During the first meeting, since the distributors failed to agree on a subject for their first production effort, Freda suggested a follow-up to one of his most successful films, *Aquila nera*. The proposal was met with enthusiasm by all involved, who asked the director for a treatment, that he promised to deliver the following day, *Seven Keys to Baldpate*-style. Armed with a typewriter and a secretary, he set out to the effort, not an uncommon task in the glorious days of Italian commercial cinema. "I slipped into *La vendetta di Aquila Nera* all of Pushkin's beautiful inventions that I couldn't fit into *Aquila nera*. We worked all night and the next day I delivered the story."⁶

With *Aquila nera*, Freda had paved the way for a series of films which were more and more loosely based on prestigious novels. The severing of ties with the literary sources

pushed these period yarns "toward out-and-out adventure, the depicting of great passions, violent conflicts, where the *raison d'Etat* is subjected to the individual's reasons," as noted by film historian Gian Piero Brunetta.[7] In more than a way, the ease with which scriptwriters and directors alike got rid of the awe toward the models was an anticipation of the habit of literally fabricating a prestigious literary descendance for their films during the Gothic horror heyday of the early 1960s. *La vendetta di Aquila Nera* goes even further, by piling up the heroics and the action with an abandon that harks back to the silent era, while at the same time reprising ideas from his own previous works: the scenes in the Siberian prison camp, reminiscent of *I miserabili*, and the hero's fake death drew back to *Don Cesare di Bazan*. Whereas its predecessor had at least the literary alibi of Pushkin's novel, here Freda pulled out all the stops to fabricate a cinematic spectacle that would rival his beloved childhood favorites.

La vendetta di Aquila Nera is the epitome of Freda's conception of popular cinema as a rollercoaster of emotions and events, populated with larger-than-life characters who perform superhuman feats, and hate and love like the gods on Olympus did, with an intensity unknown to most humans. That is, the total opposite of Neorealism. Dubrovsky is the embodiment of the director's favorite heroes: he fabricates his own destiny, for better or for worse, and when he chooses a path he goes all the way through. He is a *übermensch* in a Cossack bearskin hat, who believes in honor, family and passion, and who even enslaves the woman he'll eventually marry. "You don't kill men like Dubrovsky," the villain sums it up: "Death is a very small thing for them. They are not scared of it."

As the heroic protagonist, who utters such lines as "Justice won't be stopped by bad men's will," Freda once again cast Rossano Brazzi, who in the meantime had become one of Italy's most beloved film stars, while Gianna Maria Canale was the obligatory choice as the love interest, Tatiana. That year, Canale acted in a U.S. war film directed by Robert Pirosh, *Go for Broke!*, starring Van Johnson: an unsuccessful attempt at launching the ravishing actress in Hollywood, it was a box-office flop, and Canale, who had signed a contract with M.G.M., eventually stepped back from the deal. According to Freda, the studio did not understand Canale's charm ("It is absurd, they gave her the role of a peasant while she is a natural born princess!" he commented), whereas others claim it was because she couldn't stay away from Italy, an example being her sudden change of mood that forced Freda to leave Brazil.[8]

Always true to his sharp tongue, Freda later delighted in emphasizing not only Brazzi's shortcomings as an actor, but his lack of agility as well, which affected not only his horseback scenes but also the ones shot in the studio, on a rocking horse. But Brazzi's somewhat wooden performance is not the movie's sole flaw. The refined balance that made *Il cavaliere misterioso* stand out is lost in half-baked melodramatics and poor dialogue: the absence of Steno and Monicelli can be detected immediately, and despite resorting to the trick of splitting the villain into two, neither Cernicevsky (played by Peter Trent) nor Yuravleff (the renowned stage and voice actor Vittorio Sanipoli, playing one of Freda's scheming sexual predators) are particularly interesting figures, while Nerio Bernardi, as the Tsar, is a hollow caricature. Even more than in his previous adventure films, it is as if Freda overtly relied on the audience's hunger for adventure and emotion, treating the plot as a pretext for awesome showpieces and taking little care of his paper-thin characters. As usual, his heart was in the action scenes.

Opposite: **U.S. poster for** *La vendetta di Aquila Nera* **(1951).**

"There is an amusing story among stuntmen about *La vendetta di Aquila Nera*," Jacqueline Freda recalls:

> For the climax the stuntmen had to ride on horseback through a gorge and rocks were falling on them from the mountain. Of course the rocks were made of polystyrene. My father was not happy at all about the scene—he did seven, eight, ten takes, which for him were an enormity, but it just didn't work. So he got pissed off and started to yell: "You chickenshit! I want to see those horse galloping!" Eventually he said, "Ok, now the horses are tired, let's go home. We're shooting it again tomorrow." The stuntmen were all happy—you know, one day's worth of extra work, more money…. Next day they show up, all smiling and stuff, and while they are mounting the horses, just before calling "Action," my father adds: "Hey, guys, I forgot to tell you one thing: this time the rocks are *real* ones!" And just as they started galloping, they felt the earth tremble, and realized he wasn't poking fun at them. They rode through that gorge like daredevils! And in the end, my dad commented: "So, was it such a big deal?"[9]

Indeed, some sequences rank among the director's best, such as the climactic stunt, when Dubrovsky rides on horseback inside his enemy's palace, picks up Tatiana and launches his horse against a window to escape, a moment the director would remake in *Agi Murad—Il diavolo bianco*. The director's evocation of the silent movie tradition extends to the use of close-ups and reaction shots, and permeates entire sequences, such as those featuring Duccio Sissia as Dubrovsky's little son Andrei, who has become mute after witnessing his mother's murder (a moment patterned over an early scene in *Guarany*) on the part of the brigands, instructed by Dubrovsky's sworn enemy, Yuravleff. In the most memorable scene, borrowed from Pushkin, Yuravleff, who has kidnapped Andrei and is using him as bait to lure the Black Eagle into a trap, rolls an orange on the floor which the little child pursues down to a court where a ferocious bear stands up menacingly before him; his father rescues him at the eleventh hour. When Dubrovsky shoots the bear dead, off-camera crew had to pull ropes that had been tied to the animal so that it would fall on its back. The frightful encounter between the kid (who was not the least bit scared of the animal, so that Freda had to teach him to pretend) and the bear was shot with three cameras, with Freda acting also as cinematographer, a duty he performed throughout the whole movie.[10]

The most emblematic homage to the silent era comes when Dubrovsky makes his appearance in a room crowded with enemies, hinting that he is not alone: behind him, a pair of perfectly still shadows depict a couple of warriors with swords in their hands. Later, when Dubrovsky leaves the place, we find out what we had suspected in the first place: the two "warriors" are actually small paper cut silhouettes put before a candle. The scene is both fascinating, for its sincere evocation of magic lanterns and early cinema, and at the same time naïve: it was probably perceived as that even at the time of the film's release—to many viewers, Freda's conception of cinema was beginning to feel *passé*. Or rather, it was the context that worked against the film: even though it had proved successful in *Aquila nera*, the evocation of 18th century Russia was too far detached from moviegoers by then. The kind of popular adventure the director pursued would soon find a much more accommodating environment within another, much more commercially successful thread: the *peplum*.

Freda's eye for impressive set-pieces allowed him to recreate a fairytale-like Russia in Italian locations: the caves where the Cossacks hide are the Pastena caves, near Rome, while the Tsar's residence was recreated at the Royal Palace of Caserta, built for the Bourbon kings of Naples and often used as a film location, most recently for *Star Wars Episode*

I: The Phantom Menace (2001), *Mission: Impossible III* (2006) and *Angels & Demons* (2009). Despite the not-so-big budget, the director indulged in his favorite banquet scenes, filmed with his trademark tracking shots to guide the viewer through a crowded ambience. However, here and there the lack of money can be detected: a huge but fake-looking Orthodox church was decidedly less than convincing, whereas Freda himself recreated the interior—after the Rome authorities denied him the use of the church he had employed in *Aquila nera*—by adorning a huge empty wall with a painted Byzantine glass window depicting Christ's face and a couple hundred candles for the scene of Tatiana and Yuravleff's wedding, with impressive, atmospheric results.

The score was composed by Renzo Rossellini, Roberto's brother, in the first of three collaborations with the director. Even though Freda was satisfied with Rossellini's work for *Spartaco* and *Teodora*, he couldn't help noticing that "he always kept foisting off on me the same music," confirming the director's belief that "Italian musicians work with ready-made scores: one for the dramatic scenes, another for action scenes, another for kisses in close-up. They simply change a few notes and there you have a new score."[11]

La vendetta di Aquila Nera was moderately successful, both with the audience (grossing over 368 million *lire*) and the critics, who had words of praise for it, despite it being a unpretentious popular adventure flick. "Although it was made with a low budget, it is a picture that now and then hits the mark," one critic wrote, adding: "Overall, this violently-tinged melodrama is not lacking quite effective sequences, although it is long-winded and sometimes naive."[12] Other reviewers were less favorable: "Instead of entertaining, with its horseback rides, its duels and its acrobatics, the film eventually bores the audience: Let's hope that the public keeps being bored at every film of this type, forcing the producers and directors to make things seriously,"[13] wrote *L'Unità*. The movie was picked up for distribution in the States, in an English-dubbed version with the title *The Vengeance of the Black Eagle*.[14] Pushkin's story was used again in the late 1950s as the subject for William Dieterle's *Il vendicatore* (*Dubrowsky*, 1959), and in 1968 director Guido Malatesta helmed *Il figlio di Aquila Nera* (The Son of Black Eagle), starring Mimmo Palmara and a very young Edwige Fenech. Produced by Fortunato Misiano, it was an attempt to draw back to the atmosphere of old adventure flicks that came out too late for its own good: Italian cinema had drastically changed by then.

Vedi Napoli e poi muori

Following the commercial success of *La vendetta di Aquila Nera*, the second film Freda helmed through Momi and Caiano's production company A.P.I. marked a return to contemporary melodrama—a genre the director despised—merely for commercial reasons. The turgid, tearjerking *Vedi Napoli e poi muori*, written by the prolific Ennio De Concini and Alberto Vecchietti, crammed up all the usual ingredients for the recipe, all balanced to maximum effect: the typical characters (an unjustly maligned woman, a scheming ex-lover, an upright husband, a little child), the obligatory plot points (blackmail, sexual harassment, humiliation, prison), the inevitable final redemption and the triumph of truth for the much-awaited happy ending—after squeezing as many tears as possible out of the audience.

Unlike Freda's previous stab at melodrama, the above-average *Il tradimento*, the script features lazy characterization and stereotypes galore, not to mention a retrograde vision of marriage: "You talk to me about rights?! I don't know you, you are a stranger to me!" exclaims the embittered husband, who chases his wife from home and prevents her from seeing her sick child, in order to punish the woman for her alleged betrayal. Chilling but true, this was the way most Italian males reasoned back then, and bad acting on the part of Renato Baldini did not improve the scene. The most noteworthy thing about *Vedi Napoli e poi muori* is its unusual upper-class setting (at the beginning the protagonists are hosting an elegant party at their house, the kind that would normally be seen in American film), which evidently was more suited to the director than the habitual proletarian or petit bourgeois ones, and which further marked his detachment from the Neorealist poetics.

The result was primarily a showcase for Gianna Maria Canale, looking as ravishing as ever in a short, blonde-dyed hairdo as the unfortunate Marisa, despite her acting consisting mostly of crying in despair in almost all her scenes, and raising her eyebrows to underline whatever emotion she was supposed to feel. Canale's presence shadows her male partners, Renato Baldini, as her husband Giacomo, and Vittorio Sanipoli, as the villain, Roberto. However, like a number of melodramas made in those years, the film was also a vehicle for a musical celebrity: the then-25 year-old Claudio Villa, one of Italy's most popular singers, had a minor role in the film as Marisa's singing partner, who is hopelessly in love with her. Villa's songs feature prominently throughout the story.[15] Even though he looks uncomfortable and his voice is dubbed, Villa would stubbornly pursue an acting career. His first starring role was in *Serenata amara* (1952, Pino Mercanti), the first in a series of musical tearjerkers which blended the ingredients of the Matarazzo-style melodrama with a handful of popular numbers performed by the film's star.

Freda claimed he shot *Vedi Napoli e poi muori* in 15 days, three on location in Naples and the rest in Rome, at the CSC studios. Never one to waste time or stop against setbacks, when his female lead fell ill he simply

French poster for *Vedi Napoli e poi muori* (1952).

replaced her with a double and went on filming. The only thing the director boasted about the movie, which proved a good commercial success and earned him a fair amount of money as co-producer, was a song which he had written for it, both the words and the music. It would not be the last time Freda would try his hand at songwriting, although the result (and the film where the song was featured, *Estratto dagli archivi segreti della polizia di una capitale europea*) would certainly not be something to be proud of, at least for him.

Still, now and then the director's skills come to the fore. The opening camera-car that follows a pastry bellhop on his bike across the city of Naples is suitably impressive, and the scenes in the night club have a certain visual flair: Roberto's appearance in Marisa's dressing room, reflected in the multiple mirrors, has distinct shades of *The Lady from Shanghai* (1947) in it, and the climax set at a deserted amusement park at night exudes a convincing *film noir* mood. Freda even stages an impressive night scene in Marisa's bedroom, intermittently lighted by a huge neon sign just outside the window, in pure *film noir* fashion, which gives way to a series of tightly-edited flashbacks (all in cross-dissolves) about Marisa's happy marital life, under the notes of Claudio Villa singing the poignant 'A voce 'e mamma.

The film marked the first teaming of Freda and the man who would become his favorite director of photography, the Hungarian-Italian Gábor Pogány (1915–1999). Pogány had arrived in Italy in the late 1930s, as in that decade Italian producers were recruiting for technical competence in other countries. As many film historians have noted, this not only helped Italian cinema to quickly reach a top-notch technical level, but also gave room to the migration in the country of many Jewish professionals, who found in Rome a safe niche, since Luigi Freddi openly disapproved racial policy. Besides Pogány, who had started working with Amleto Palermi and Flavio Calzavara, and collaborated on *Un abito nero da sposa*, co-scripted by Freda, this exodus from the aryanised areas brought to Cinecittà such names as the Czech cinematographers Václav Vích and Jan Stallich, and the Hungarian scriptwriters Ákos Tolnay and László Vajda, among others. Technically, this led to a small revolution in Italian filmmaking, as Freda—who witnessed its advent first-hand—recalled. "It is quite astonishing, but it was the Hungarians and the Czechs who revolutionized cinematography in Italy. Stallich, Vích and Pogány. They reinvented the use of lighting on sets.... This trio remained famous in Italy under the name of 'Hungarian school.'"[16] Before the arrival of the Eastern European cinematographers, the set and actors were flooded in light. Everything had to be fully visible, clear, shining. With Stallich—the responsible for the extraordinary symbolical black-and-white of Máchatý's *Exstase* (1933)—and Vích, the Italians discovered the Expressionist use of light. In Italy, Stallich photographed among others *L'assedio dell'Alcazar* and the 1941 version of *Beatrice Cenci*, whereas Vích was responsible for Blasetti's *Ettore Fieramosca* and *Un'avventura di Salvator Rosa*.

An example of Pogány's will to experiment was the color sequence that he and Freda had devised when Marisa performs a song in a cabaret, to break the film's melodramatic atmosphere: a few months earlier, the melodrama *Luna Rossa* (1951) featured a similar sequence in color. Freda and the d.o.p. had decided to use incandescent light bulbs, so as to give the scene a dominant red color, something which was considered taboo at the time. Back then, color was still something of a novelty in Italian cinema: Ferrania Technologies had developed a color system which had supplanted Agfa's Ansco Color (used for one film in 1950, the religious-themed *Mater Dei*). By mixing incandescent bulbs with the then-common arc lights, Freda and his collaborators obtained surprising results with the Ferraniacolor film stock, paving the way for the advent of color film.

The episode is important as it shows Freda's tendency toward a dramatic use of color, something which would become evident in his later films and especially in his Gothic horror efforts, such as *L'orribile segreto del Dr. Hichcock*. He was possibly influenced by Rouben Mamoulian's approach to color filmmaking in such works as *Becky Sharp* (1935) and *Blood and Sand* (1940); sadly, the sequence is no longer to be found in the existing copies of *Vedi Napoli e poi muori*. A few months later, *Totò a colori* (1952) was the first widely distributed Italian film in color.[17]

Unfortunately, the director's experiments were lost on the critics, who generally panned the film, noting (and rightly so) that despite the title—a reference to a renowned Italian saying which implies Naples being the most enchanting place in the world[18]— "there is little or nothing of Naples in it, since the story could have been set in any other town."[19] This did not stop viewers from paying the ticket, and the film proved Freda's most successful melodrama, grossing over 381 million *lire*.

Vedi Napoli e poi muori was released theatrically in the U.S. in 1959 by Crown Pictures, in a subtitled version, under the literal title *See Naples and Die*. American critics were not kind, either. "Our heroine ... is probably one of the hardiest souls ever to tackle a sodden script," the *New York Times*' reviewer noted; "Gianna Maria Canale, as that pretty, luckless lady, is involved in nearly every cliché dear to the devotees of daytime detergent dramas on radio, but unsmilingly she comes through.... There are English titles but even without them it is fairly clear that sad is the word for the manufactured tragedies in *See Naples and Die*."[20]

La leggenda del Piave

After the two films produced by A.P.I., Freda embarked on yet another melodrama, this time set against the historical backdrop of World War I—a theme that spawned a small thread of films in the early 1950s, which had the aim of reviving the public's interest in the heroic gestures of the Italian army after the Neorealist wave: *Il caimano del Piave* (1950, Giorgio Bianchi), *Carica eroica* (1952, Francesco De Robertis), *Penne nere* (1952, Oreste Biancoli) and *I sette dell'Orsa Maggiore* (1953, Duilio Coletti), to name the most important. These pictures, with their openly nationalistic and militaristic undertones, were applauded by the government, and had the thinly veiled purpose of justifying the anti-communist block during the Cold War, rather than celebrating the virtues of the Italian army. They included openly anti–Communist allusions, and featured Socialist characters who abandoned their antimilitaristic stances in favor of a patriotic, interventionist view.

Freda's film, *La leggenda del Piave* (The Legend of the River Piave), was centered on the battle of Caporetto (October 24–November 12, 1917), which marked the biggest defeat in the history of the Italian army, so much so that the term "Caporetto" became synonymous with unmitigated disaster. After the crisis in Russia due to the Bolshevik revolution, the Austrian-Hungarian army transferred a consistent amount of troops from the Eastern front to the Western and Italian ones. Helped by the Germanic élite troops, the enemy broke through the lines and forced the Italian army to retreat behind the river Piave. General Cadorna, the main responsible for the defeat with his glaring tactical errors,

Italian fotobusta for *La leggenda del Piave* (1952).

resigned and was replaced by Armando Diaz. Later on, the Italian army managed to stop the Austrian-Hungarian troops in the so-called "first battle of the Piave," preventing them to invade Milan, and finally defeated the enemies at Vittorio Veneto. The obstinate, courageous resistance held by the army after Caporetto was the subject of a number of popular songs, and was still a much-felt subject matter after the disastrous Second World War, for Italians to rely on a heroic vision of the past before the Fascist era.

Freda came up with a story related to the battle events, inspired by the song *Il Piave mormorò*—at least according to the credits, even though there is actually very little in common between the song and the film. The plot revolves around Count Dolfin, who has enlisted the army to carry on a black market business, his estranged wife Giovanna and her little son, who have to endure the presence of the enemy troops in the castle after the Caporetto defeat. Eventually Dolfin redeems himself at the front, but he is gravely injured, and ends up an armless war hero. Since the producer Raffaele Colamonici had already financed a silent picture on a mutilated war veteran who was believed to be a coward, *La leggenda del Piave* was almost a remake. "My film is a historical melodrama. I make fiction and I exalt history,"[21] he claimed. Since the opening sequence set in the little child's bedroom, which depicts a carillon shaped as a windmill surrounded by other kid's toys, Freda enhanced the private, intimate dimension of the tale; what is more, in a homage to the rules of melodrama, singer Giorgio Consolini was cast in a brief role as a singing soldier.

La leggenda del Piave was made at a time where *Democrazia Cristiana* (Christian

Democracy) ruled the country, and a number of war films were made that depicted the bravery of Italian soldiers, with little or no attention to the bigger picture (i.e., the Fascist regime embarking on a war with the Nazis). In some ways, it was a response against the Neorealist dramas which portrayed the war years in a much bleaker way, an example being Carlo Lizzani's feature film debut *Achtung! Banditi!* (1951). Even though Freda was certainly not close to the ruling party, here he alludes to a political agenda that was very much felt at that time. During the banquet scene, the characters make a toast to "free Trento and Trieste." In 1952, Trieste was still partially a Yugoslavian territory, and would be reannexed to Italy only in 1954.

The film has its share of nods to Catholicism, in typical melodrama fashion. For instance, after losing sight of her son during a bombing, Giovanna makes a vow to the Virgin Mary in a ruined church to have him back. What is more, Renato Baldini plays a wise priest who tells a politician, "The difference between you and me is that your country is from the Alps to the sea, whereas mine is a little bit larger, and wars are not admitted in it…" and has an argument with a hypocritical, wealthy Socialist, who labels Proletarian revolution as "sacred" and proclaims that "violence is always on the side of warmonger Capitalism."

Still, despite the simple-minded plot and the overtly didactic dialogue, Freda managed to partially escape easy-minded Manichaeism when depicting the protagonist. Count Riccardo Dolfin is not the director's usual out-and-out hero; but on the contrary, he starts the film as a cowardly type who then manages to redeem himself at a high cost. The climax, which Freda rightly labeled as "diabolically melodramatic" and which in the director's words "made all Italy cry," has Dolfin meet his wife and son after the war. The Count, wearing a long cloak, refuses to hug the boy (Freda masterfully alternating high-angle and low-angle shots from their opposite points of view), and the Countess believes that such apparent coldness is caused by the man being ashamed of his own cowardice. But when the Count is about to leave, his little son embraces him and the cloak falls onto the floor, showing that the man has lost both his arms in battle. The Countess, and the audience as well, won't be able to hold back their tears…. In underlining the movie's fusion of melodrama, war yarn and historical fresco, Jacques Lourcelles analyzed Freda's attitude in depicting real-life accidents: "The film does not reject realism, but on the condition that it has an epic dimension and bypasses the anecdote and the simple truth of the moment. To Freda, it is about finding again, in the particular history of one place and one age, what it might have had in common, in the registry of the grandiose, the heroic and the passional, with other places and other ages."[22]

La leggenda del Piave was filmed in four weeks, mostly at the Titanus studios. Freda's direction is accurate and often elegant, such as in the long take that introduces the army banquet near the beginning, with a serpentine tracking shot backwards preceding two elderly female guests through various ambients, while the director's usually skillful use of extras' movement in the shot gives the viewer a vivid impression of the upper class' obliviousness toward the ongoing conflict, lost as they are in their own luxurious world. The battle sequences are uniformly impressive: for the spectacular Caporetto sequence, Freda had hundreds of extras at his disposal—provided by no less than the Mafia. Upon hearing that the director was going to put on screen one of the most shameful moments in Italian history, the Ministry of Defense denied him the availability of soldiers as extras as well as of arms and original costumes: "In France, they can make a film on Waterloo, in Italy we cannot make one on Caporetto," Freda later commented. Therefore, Colamonici—"a notorious Cammorist"[23] according to the director—suggested they employ Mafia men. "We slid two or three million *lire* inside two or three little suitcases and took the route to Calabria with a small crew. In Reggio Calabria we had our first contacts, secret rendez-vous worthy of *The Godfather*, and closed the deal. The cammorist took the order as if it was about leeks or potatoes.... A thousand extras, a hundred horsemen. Three hours later, in the main square, a real army was awaiting us!"[24] Whether fact, exaggeration or pure invention, Freda's tale is enlightening about the shady ways in which the Italian movie industry sometimes operated.

The crucial battle of the river Piave, accompanied by the aforementioned song, was filmed with several cameras, and featured a number of spectacular stunts of soldiers falling off their horses before the camera.

> I spoke to each cameraman to know if the falls had worked ... all of them were enthusiastic. One took care of the long shots, the other of the pannings on the horses, the other of the close-ups of the falls. Upon my return to Rome, when I watched the rushes, I didn't see anything.... I don't know whether it had been because of the fear, but none of my five cameramen had filmed anything. I had to redo all the stunts in Rome. I had a master shot, I had the gun shots, but no shots of falls.[25]

The result was yet another of the director's remarkable battle scenes, as dynamic and spectacular as anything he'd ever filmed: the sideways tracking shots accompanying the soldiers on the battle field are particularly impressive, and positively bring to mind Stanley Kubrick's *Paths of Glory* (1957). On the other hand, the archive World War I footage depicting the subsequent Italian victory over the Austrians that ends the film was added by the producer as a last-minute attempt at highlighting the heroic war context—a *captatio benevolentiae* if there was one.

On the other hand, the scenes where Giovanna is forced to stay in the family manor, occupied by the Austrian troops, deal with the director's bleakest side, and convey a suitably Gothic-like feel, accompanied by a few blackly humored lines of dialogue when portraying the devilish Austrians. "We destroyed the future of Italy, now let's abuse its past," a Teutonic officer says while his soldiers are sacking a castle. Freda's depiction of the enemy harks back to his taste for adventure stories where the adversaries have to be out-and-out cruel, vicious, menacing. Here, as played by character actor Edoardo Toniolo, the Austrian officer is a kind of distant cousin of Count Zaroff—a cultured man who delights in the pleasures of war as well as in those of the flesh. In a subtly Sadean scene, filled with sexual innuendo, he treats the Countess to a luxurious dinner (in her own house!) in an attempt to seduction which almost turn into a rape attempt as the woman proudly rejects his increasingly explicits passes, until he eventually blurts: "The Italians love only music, spaghetti and love—three useless things in war!"

For the third time in a row, Freda employed a young kid (Duccio Sissia, seen in *La vendetta di Aquila Nera* and *Vedi Napoli e poi muori*) as a crucial element in the plot and for maximum dramatic effect. Perhaps he was paying homage to Fritz Lang's *M* in one of the film's very best scenes, where the Countess' son is chasing a ball which bounces down the castle's stairs only to come across the menacing enemy.

Even though its box-office results were consistent, with over 361 million *lire*, *La leggenda del Piave* failed to gain much critical acclaim. Actually, a look at official papers shows how little the authorities themselves thought of it. Former Fascist exponent Annibale Scicluna Sorge (one of the many who recycled themselves in power positions after the war) commented that "the film is supposed to be a re-enactment of the tragic days of Caporetto and the subsequent victorious rescue, as the title itself suggests; in reality, however, it is a trivial family drama, artificially inserted into the frame of those events. Overall it is a very poor film … and especially unworthy of evoking, with its title, the 'Legend of the Piave.'"

The board of censors demanded a scene be cut, where a bare-chested officer is seen in an hotel room next to a scantily dressed prostitute, who wakes up from the bed and slowly starts dressing up. Their response to Freda's subsequent picture would be quite different.

7

Historia Magistra Vitae

Spartaco

The so-called *peplum* had been one of Italy's earliest and most popular genres since Enrico Guazzoni's epics (*Agrippina*, 1910; *Quo vadis?*, 1912; *Marcantonio e Cleopatra*, 1913; *Fabiola*, 1918; *Messalina*, 1922, to name a few) as well as Giovanni Pastrone's legendary *Cabiria*. After a brief resurgence during the Fascist regime with the notorious *Scipione l'africano*, which exalted the values and imagery of Ancient Imperial Rome as the ideal progenitor of Fascism, whose ambition was to revive the glory of its ancestors, the genre faded. It was the box-office success of Alessandro Blasetti's *Fabiola* (based on Nicholas Wiseman's novel and produced by Orbis-Universalia) that paved the way for a renaissance of the sword-and-sandal cycle in the 1950s.

If Blasetti's film had been the flicker of a flame, revived the following year by a new version of Bulwer-Lytton's novel *Sins of Pompeii* (*Gli ultimi giorni di Pompei*)—also produced by Orbis-Universalia so as to recover the costs of Blasetti's film—and then by Carmine Gallone's *Messalina* (a.k.a. *Messaline*, 1951), the fire had been properly lighted by the big-budget Hollywood epic *Quo Vadis?* (1951, Mervyn LeRoy), shot mostly in Rome and with an all-star cast led by Robert Taylor. Soon classical antiquity was "in" again, even though the serious works—such as Pietro Francisci's *La regina di Saba* (a.k.a. *The Queen of Sheba*, 1952) and *Frine, cortigiana d'Oriente* (1953)—rubbed shoulders with the parodies, namely *O.K. Nerone* (a.k.a. *O.K. Nero*, 1952, Mario Soldati), *Due notti con Cleopatra* (a.k.a. *Two Nights with Cleopatra*, 1953, Mario Mattoli) or *Mio figlio Nerone* (a.k.a. *Nero's Big Weekend*, 1956, Steno). Satire was the cheapest, easiest way to deal with the past in order to hint at the present, substituting spectacular values with laughter and the sight of gorgeous, skimpily-dressed women.

Like Gallone's *Messalina*, Freda's first *peplum* was an Italian-French co-production: the genre was popular in the transalpine market, due to its mild eroticism. The actresses' bodies were most liberally on display in the versions designed for the foreign distribution, an example being Mattoli's film, which starred a young Sophia Loren: the strict Italian censors closed one eye on this undercounter practice on the part of the producers. However, compared to his contemporaries, Freda's approximation to the genre was characterized by a more blatantly heroic, male-oriented angle, starting with the subject matter: the revolt of Spartacus the gladiator. Despite having been a voracious reader of the ancient Rome historians such as Titus Livius (whose magnum opus, the history of Rome *Ab urbe condita*, furnished him with the basic story) and Tacitus, Freda claimed that it had been *Cabiria* and Guazzoni's *Messalina* that had made him love Ancient Rome and the mythical

Gianna Maria Canale (left), Vittorio Sanipoli and Ludmilla Tchérina (right) in *Spartaco* (1953).

imagery associated with it. What is more, the Thracian hero had been the subject of a popular silent film, *Spartacus, il gladiatore della Tracia* (1913, Enrico Vidali), even though the director's most immediate inspiration was perhaps the publishing of Howard Fast's best-selling novel *Spartacus* (1951).

For the role of Spartacus, Freda cast Massimo Girotti, the handsome leading man in Blasetti's *La corona di ferro* and Visconti's *Ossessione*—that is, two opposite ways of conceiving moviemaking, the fantasy adventure and the dawn of Neorealism. Girotti's lack of enthusiasm for the project is not a secret: after abandoning cinema for a while, unsatisfied with the roles that he was offered, he focused on his stage career. But on his comeback to the silver screen he found out the situation was even worse. "When I came back to making movies, after a long tour, I did not have any offers, save for the usual ones, which I had always refused, for popular and more banal genre films. I resisted for a while, then, out of exhaustion and rage, accepted to do three of them in a row.... I didn't have the chance of making different choices, I was a bit forced to act that way."[1]

Predictably, Gianna Maria Canale played a seductress figure, Crasso's daughter Sabina (a character tailor-made for her by the director: Crasso had two sons, Marcus and Publius, but no daughters), whereas Monte Carlo dancer Ludmilla Tchérina (previously seen in Powell and Pressburger's *The Tales of Hoffmann*, 1951) came aboard mainly for co-production reasons as the slave Amitys, and was given a dance scene to show off her talents. Shooting lasted 40 days, from October to December 1952, since the higher production values and the complexity of the mass scenes forced the usually speedy director to spend some more time on several sequences. Nevertheless, the budget's shortcomings caused Freda to make do with *maquettes* where he could not afford to build the sets from scratch. Therefore, Rome was recreated on a modern Verona square, whereas the ship where Spartacus is enslaved was shown through a section plane which Freda could explore by way of a camera mounted atop a crane. The scene where the slaves attack the Roman camp was also shot in the studio, while the crowded Verona Arena was partially "reconstructed" via *maquettes* and puppets.

The director claimed to have had lots of trouble with the Italian censors. At that time, producers and filmmakers had to undergo a preemptive censorship: the scripts were examined before filming started and, if considered objectionable for a variety of reasons (moral, political, religious), the makers had to either change or abridge them as requested, or drop the project altogether. According to Freda, the shooting for *Spartaco* was interrupted on the third day and changes were requested on the part of the General Director of Cinematography, Nicola De Pirro, a former Fascist hierarch who, like so many of his peers, had survived the fall of the regime and recycled himself in a position of power. Ironically, De Pirro's office was in Palazzo Balestra, formerly the headquarters of Mussolini's Ministry of Popular Culture (Minculpop), as were those of his fellow officials, also former Fascist bureaucrats who sat in the ministerial seats thanks to Giulio Andreotti's governance: Andreotti was undersecretary in charge of entertainment from 1947 to 1953, and in such a position he *de facto* reigned over the Italian film industry, establishing import limits, screen quotas, and providing loans to Italian production firms, besides exerting a strict control over national productions.

De Pirro was one of Andreotti's key pawns: "a shy and honest man," in Andreotti's words, so much so that "he and another colleague had only one formal dress which they shared because they never wore it." Freda, who utterly despised De Pirro, loved to recall an episode which involved the renowned comedian Ettore Petrolini, who, upon meeting the bald General Director, started praising his looks: "How handsome thou are Nicola!" De Pirro blushed in pleasure, to which Petrolini added, "You look like the Roman forum," causing a puzzling look in his interlocutor, and ending with a venomous: "All in ruins underneath!" De Pirro's persona concentrated in himself the typical traits of the Fascist bureaucrat's way of thinking, and as such he was the perfect man to watch over the dangerous waters of post-war Italian cinema. His view on Freda's film was—and couldn't be otherwise—characterized by a heartful reverence toward the Ancient Rome values, exactly what Freda was aiming to criticize with *Spartaco*.

"You don't mess with Roman history. My film stayed at the periphery of the real history, the revolt of the slaves. You don't understand why they act out a rebellion.... You mustn't forget that Mussolini's political or artistic model was Ancient Rome. Impossible to criticize Nero, the founding fathers, the legionaries. De Pirro kept this rule in mind."[2] Freda's intention to show the cruelty of the Romans was therefore sabotaged, so much so that De Pirro imposed the adding of scenes that would portray their humanity toward the slaves. As Freda sarcastically commented, "I met the producers and told them, 'Everything that's in the film, you can find it in Titus Livius.' And they replied, 'Who is Titus Livius?'"[3]

Freda's claims were not exaggerated: some episodes in the film—such as the gladiators sieged on top of Mount Vesuvio, and using vine shoots to climb down the mountain on the opposite side of the Roman troops—are taken almost verbatim from ancient history books. Still, the director had to settle on making a less violent, more sentimental picture, giving more room to the love triangle between the gladiator, Amitys and Sabina. Traces of Freda's ironic approach can be detected in the character of Crassus, who is portrayed with subtly caricatural traits. Near the beginning, as he is about to condemn Spartacus to death, his daughter Sabina purportedly distracts him by telling him that a civil action against him, where he was defended by none other than Cicero, has ended "with justice triumphant." "Then I've lost the cause!?" he blurts. Then he remarks that "that little Cicero will be going places, I absolutely have to pay him!" Crassus is a Mussolini-type the way Leo Longanesi would have portrayed it, both pompous in his assertion of the moral strength of the Romans and yet attached to money, wealth and the pleasures of the flesh.

Nevertheless, Freda's explanations do not seem to take into account the fear on the part of De Pirro and the Christian Democracy party that the audiences might see the revolt of the slaves as a political metaphor of the rebellion of the proletarian masses against the capitalists, thus comparing them to the peasants and the factory workers, whose union claims often resulted in strikes that were violently repressed by the law enforcement. One of the main victims of Italian censorship during that period were, in fact, the documentaries financed by the Communist Party, and directed by such filmmakers as Carlo Lizzani, which portrayed the injust and harsh conditions of land workers, especially in Southern Italy, where landowners still forced them to inhuman labor. What is more, Spartacus himself, as the subject of a 1874 novel by Raffaello Giovagnoli, had been taken as an example of a national popular literature by none other than Vittorio Gramsci (1891-1937), the Communist thinker whose prison notebooks were published between 1948 and 1951. In 1952—presumably in the wake of the success of Howard Fast's novel—the newspaper *Vie Nuove*, ideologically close to the Communist Party, reissued Giovagnoli's novel with excerpts from Gramsci's letters from the prison. No wonder De Pirro was concerned about the subject matter.

By leaning on the obsolete view of Rome *caput mundi* as in the days of Fascism (which nevertheless still existed in the mind of many) and overlooking the more obvious ties to the contemporary post–War juxtaposition between the Christian Democrats and the Communist Party, Freda actually showed his detachment from the political reality of the period—or rather, from the ideals that were at the center of a heated debate. This somehow undermines the more openly ideological readings of the film, and on the other hand it underlines the director's fiercely individualistic position. It has been observed that while

> at first glance, the film seems to support Communist investment in the novel and its hero. Rome and the Romans are presented as Fascistic. The growing community of Spartacus' rebels, gathering in the countryside, clearly evoke the Italian resistance fighters who helped liberate Italy at the end of the Second World War.... However, unlike the partisan movement, Spartaco's rebellion ends not only in failure but devastation. Moreover, the film dramatically de-heroizes the protagonist.... In fact, Spartaco, having founded the revolutionary movement, ends up betraying it.[4]

Paradoxically, the additions made by Freda in order to comply to the requests on the part of De Pirro's—that is, the softening in the portrayal of Romans, or the inflation of the romantic subplot—become, in the critic's analysis, just as many clues of the author's disenchantment toward the revolution: the conclusion is that "the overwhelming sensation is of the annihilation of the rebel movement."[5] This may well be true, but in pointing out the analogies with both Soviet and Italian Communism, one ends up underestimating the director's cynical worldview. Freda graced his titular hero with a much more faceted psychology than the context would suggest, and unlike most of *peplum*'s future muscle-bound heroes, Spartacus is riddled with doubts and remorses.

As Derek Elley noted, "the film emerges more as a heightened tale of one man's heroism than one of epic implications"[6] like the Dalton Trumbo-scripted epic directed by Stanley Kubrick would be instead. If Spartacus is a hero, he is such exactly because he is doomed to failure, and he knows it. What is more, future revolts are destined to the very same ending. Even though Freda closes the film on an apparent hopeful note, with Spartacus handling Amitys his sword so that she will pass it on to their son, this does not mean that in the future the slaves will be free: Spartacus himself has previously confessed that "we are running like blind or mad toward destruction," adding that "we believe, by winning, that our freedom will be eternal. But who knows, who knows whether this is the right path. I feel that this freedom would slip between my hands like sand." More fittingly, then, the passing of the sword implies a concept of history as an eternal return where the next generations are doomed to repeat the same path of their predecessors and meet an identical fate. A circular vision that fits with the director's disenchanted worldview.

When *Spartaco* was submitted to the Board of Censors, in January 1953, the commissioners objected only to a few allegedly erotic bits, asking that a scene be cut in which Sabina appeared with "her breast almost exposed and a naked thigh, while she is lying on a couch, in her villa at Pompei," and that in the same sequence "be cut the scene in which Spartacus embraces Sabina." What is more, in the initial part of the banquet scene at Crassus' house, the brief shot of a couple embracing was eliminated. A sign that the movie was now harmless to them, just like any other *peplum*.

To Freda, the scenes featuring Sabina and Spartacus were the film's least successful part. And yet, they convey a vibrant eroticism, mainly thanks to Canale's sensual portrayal of Crassus' daughter—a man-eater who already has in her the seed of *I vampiri*'s Duchess Du Grand. A woman accustomed to having any man she desires, she immediately sets her eyes on Spartacus and treats him as a sexual object, and nevertheless the character rises from cliché status, as Sabina gradually shows an emotional density that cracks her arrogant surface. Her first encounter with the gladiator is memorably underlined by a pair of quick tracking shots onwards to each one's close-up: in a few years' time, a similar scene would be customarily solved via a much more economic zoom, even by Freda himself.

On the other hand, the hero losing his will before the woman's sensuality recalls a typical classical motif—Ulysses and Circe—and the inner struggle (itself doomed to failure) against her seductive power perfectly synthesizes the main conflict at the core of both the *peplum* genre to come and the Gothic—see, for one thing, Gorobec's confrontation with the spellbinding Asa in Bava's *La maschera del demonio* (a.k.a. *Black Sunday*, 1960). What is more, the casting of the handsome Girotti, who is often shown barechested, already predates *peplum*'s self complacency in the erotic depiction of barely dressed muscle types.[7]

The dualism between Sabina and Amitys also rises up a typical motif taken from melodrama (the virgin-type vs. the whore), which here is developed with impressive traits. Amitys' dance on a warship in the partially flooded arena pushes the concept along while showing Freda's flair for grandiose spectacles: the scene is staged like a ritual ballet, closer to *The Red Shoes* or *The Tales of Hoffmann* than to a Hollywood musical. As the choreography goes on, Sabina explains that it is based on the legend of a sacred virgin who falls in love with a sailor and is therefore condemned to death. When a listener objects that he never heard of such a legend, Sabina chillingly replies, "I made it up," thus hinting at her will to dispatch her rival.

Stylistically, *Spartaco* is one of Freda's most accomplished works. The ample use of crane shots gives the mass scenes a visual power which the director's previous films partially lacked, and fully conveys the sense of spectacle he was aiming at. Dozens of extras move against natural landscapes, with effects that are either exquisitely pictorial (such as in the scenes near the river, with mist coming out of the waters) or downright breathtaking. To Derek Elley, Freda's "potent use of tracking and crane shots ... is as emotive as anything by Delmer Daves and Anthony Mann."[8] The night sequences—all shot without ever resorting to day-for-night tricks—are also remarkable, especially the slaves' escape into the river, whereas for Sabina's visit to Spartacus in the gladiator dungeon Freda opted for a very impressive, Piranesi-style cutaway, with the camera vertically (and simbolically) accompanying the actress' descent through various levels. Much of the film's impressive atmosphere was the result of Gábor Pogány's masterful black-and-white lighting. The director noted: "Pogány was very cultured, curious and ready to try every kind of experiment. On *Spartaco*, he masterfully photographed the night scenes: the gladiators' escape, the attack at the Roman camp, at a time where we did not know about sensitive film stock. Pogány followed my slightest indications and proposed solutions or experiments."[9]

Even though he repeatedly dismissed *Spartaco* as badly flawed, Freda could not resist boasting about the gladiator fight shot at the Verona Arena, which in his words "even Kubrick would not have even dreamt of."[10] It was shot with Mario Bava as the director of photography, replacing Pogány for the occasion, thus marking the first official collaboration between Freda and the future director of *La maschera del demonio*. Still today, the result looks amazing, especially for the off-putting detail of the trireme on which Tchérina performs her dance routine, which is unlike anything seen in *peplum*. With the assistance of Darix Togni, a renowned circus man and lion tamer, Freda employed no less than twenty lions for the scene, and reinvented the typical gladiators-vs-wild beasts spectacle with utter disregard for historical truth, and a touch of utter sadism in the moment where a lion is seen devouring an unfortunate slave in close-up, an impressive shot accomplished through the use of a neat camera trick which paired an actor's face with a manikin's body, courtesy of Bava's magic.

Freda explained that the choice of partially filling the Verona Arena with water was mainly due to precautionary reasons. "Togni had told me that the lions were horrified by water, so I had the arena filled with it and placed the cameras on islets. But when the lions came out of the cages, they jumped into the water and naturally swam toward the cameras and the cameramen!" In order to film the wild beasts' entrance in the arena, Freda locked himself, Bava and the camera inside a cage. When the lions' cages were opened, the director and his d.o.p. found themselves surrounded by the felines. Freda yelled to the crew to raise the main iron gate that led to the arena. Nothing happened. It turned out that the rope that should have opened the gate had broken. Meanwhile, the lions were getting interested in those two humans inside the cage, and one big feline even mounted on top of it.

> Bava, who was filming, did not realize the drama because he had his face stuck to the camera under a black sheet ... when the cage started shaking dangerously he asked me what was going on. A lion stretched his paw between the bars and attempted to grab our faces. I simply answered to Mario: "No problem, there's just a lion above your head!" I wanted him to keep filming. And throughout the sequence, I kept yelling insults at the crew.... I struggled amid six cameras, twenty lions, in an arena which resembled Venice, filled with terrified extras and technicians. I had almost become Spartacus....[11]

The director's trademark tracking shots are restless and omnipresent, and truly function as an instrument to convey not only spectacle, but a worldview as well. Whether it be a long line of chained slaves or a Roman hall where an orgy is taking place, a gladiator game staged in the arena or a battlefield full of dead bodies, Freda's conception of cinema as marvel through discovery functions also as a way to make parallels between various states of the human conditions, and ultimately trace a neat line toward the ultimate stage: defeat, ruin, death—as masterfully conveyed by the final, protracted aerial crane shot that metamorphoses through a cross-dissolve into a panning over the aftermath of the slaves' defeat, while Amitys desperately searches for Spartacus' body on the battlefield. Despite the similarities with Kubrick's version of the story, it conveys a very different mood: the Christian symbology, with the image of the crucified gladiator and the newly born child, here is replaced by a vision of death and hopelessness. It is one of the very best moments in Freda's career, and one that any filmmaker would be proud of.

As usual, though, Italian critics were harsh: "There are no adequate words to say what this movie is. We were shocked of how cinema can descend so low," one particularly spiteful reviewer wrote: "There are occasionally some good shots of reconstructions, or rather of decors made at the Verona Arena. But all is lost in the abyss of nonsense that has its culmination in the dialogue…. It is one of Freda's worst."[12] Nevertheless *Spartaco* was a good box-office success in Italy, with about 450 million *lire*, and was distributed throughout Europe, including UK as *Spartacus the Gladiator*. The next year it was picked up for a U.S. theatrical release by RKO, in a severely truncated print, as *Sins of Rome*, a title which had nothing to do with the film's content and betrayed Freda's concept even further: "The audience anticipated a film portraying orgies, excesses and sexual violence, with which the American cinema usually associated the Roman world."[13]

Freda claimed that Kirk Douglas' company Bryna later bought all the negatives and the posters in order to prevent from eventual rereleases that could have damaged Stanley Kubrick's *Spartacus*, and all the copies were destroyed save for the French prints. However, since there is no official confirmation of such claim, this might be another of the director's exaggerations: the film had played on the bottom end of double bills, paired with such unlikely companions as Frank Tashlin's comedy *Susan Slept Here*,[14] John Farrow's Western *A Bullet Is Waiting*[15] and Allan Dwan's *Passion*,[16] and by 1960 it is unlikely that anyone was afraid of a little black-and-white European film which by then had likely disappeared into oblivion. However, in 1963 Universal did indeed demand that Sergio Corbucci's film *Il figlio di Spartacus* (a.k.a. *Son of Spartacus*, a.k.a. *The Slave*, 1963) be withdrawn from circulation in the States.

Nowadays *Spartaco* is widely available in the home video circuit in the U.S., in a variety of DVD releases.[17]

Teodora

For his second ancient period epic in a row, Freda resorted to another controversial historical figure: Theodora, the wife of Justinian I, Emperor of the Byzantine empire in the Sixth century A.C. A former courtesan, twenty years younger than him, Theodora was a "new woman" who rose from the lower classes to the throne, something impossible until Justinian's uncle, Emperor Justin I, passed a law allowing marriage between different social classes. The union was a scandal, but soon Theodora proved a savvy and influential figure, so much so that several historians considered her as empress regnant; the couple had no children and Theodora died at a young age, with her husband outliving her by

Gianna Maria Canale and Georges Marchal in *Teodora* (1954).

nearly twenty years. Later on, other emperors followed Justinian's example and married women who did not belong to the aristocracy.

Theodora's fascinating character had already inspired several silent films, *Teodora imperatrice di Bisanzio* (1909, Ernesto Maria Pasquali), *Teodora* (1914, Roberto Roberti—Sergio Leone's father) and *Teodora* (1921, Leopoldo Carlucci), plus the French *Théodora* (1912, Henri Pouctal). Similarly to what had happened with Spartacus, her popularity had been recently revived in France thanks to a historical novel written by the Romanian-French writer Marthe Bibesco, *Theodora, le cadeau de Dieu* (1953). To Freda, the love story between Theodora and Justinian was also a way to portray a troubled period in the history of the Roman empire, with the resurgence of class struggle between the people and the patricians. This time, though, since the setting was not Rome but Byzantium, he was confident that the censors would not meddle with the script.

At first the producers thought of adapting the empress' story as told by late antique historian Procopius or the stage play *Theodora* (1884) by the French playwright Victorien Sardou (written expressly for Sarah Bernhardt), later adapted into an opera by Xavier Leroux and used as a basis for Pouctal and Carlucci's films. Eventually the two sources were blended together: even though no less than four scriptwriters are credited, the main responsible was René Wheeler (1912–2000), a French screenwriter and a director on his own.[18]

The story displays the expected disregard to historical truth in favor of spectacular

U.S. poster for *Teodora* (1954).

values. Justinian married Theodora when he was not yet the Emperor; Theodora actually favored the Blue faction, and not the Green as in the film; Belisario (portrayed as an old man, with canute beard and hair) was actually 30 year old during the events depicted on screen; finance minister John the Cappadocian did conjure against Justinian, but under completely different circumstances as told in the movie. Needless to say, fabrication was the screenwriters' rule when it came to flesh out the story: Theodora's arrest and the chariot race leading to the marriage were invented, and so was the character of Theodora's lover, Arkal; as for the conspiracy against the Emperor, it was mostly invented, and retained only a few historical references, such as Theodora's line that "royal purple is the noblest shroud." Similarly, the opening and final scenes with Justinian in Ravenna's Basilica of San Vitale are dubious at least.

Teodora (also known as *Teodora, imperatrice di Bisanzio*) was the third and final collaboration between Freda and Riccardo Gualino's Lux Film. Legend has it that around the same time MGM was working on a similar project starring Ava Gardner as Theodora, and Gualino was understandably worried about that. Freda told the producer not to worry: as soon as the Hollywood executives would learn that *he* was making his own *Theodora*, they would drop the project, since Freda's film would be ready for release before they could even finish pre-production stage—and so it happened.[19]

The year 1954 was to mark the twentieth anniversary of Gualino's production company. Despite the celebrations that came with it, the year was also the beginning of the decadence for Lux. After Ponti and De Laurentiis had left the company to create their own independent Ponti/De Laurentiis venture, its fortunes had slowly started to decline. Perhaps as an attempt to reverse the trend, Gualino had agreed to launch into more expensive, spectacular productions, clearly influenced by the American pictures filmed at Cinecittà such as *Quo Vadis?* That year the studio released Visconti's challenging *Senso*, which failed to get a prize at the Venice festival, but relied more heavily than before on co-productions: Mario Camerini's *Ulisse* was the result of a deal with Ponti and De Laurentiis, while Pietro Francisci's *Attila* and *Teodora* were co-financed by the company's French counterpart, Lux France, which in the case of Freda's picture provided 30 per cent of the budget. As film historian Alberto Farassino wrote, "Lux still had prestige and financial resources, even though it resorted, now more regularly than before, to bank credit or to the group's capitals, but it had less and less an identity of its own."[20]

Newspapers saluted the filming of *Teodora* as "the biggest boat, together with *Quo Vadis?*, that cinema has launched in latest years," although the diffidence toward this type of big productions was patent in the way the film was described, as "a huge and hasty mishmash, in every way suited to the bombastic theme ... movie people don't care much about respecting history. What they are urged by is to create a 'show.'"[21] Having to deal with his most conspicuous budget to date—400 million *lire*—and with a filming schedule of three months, Freda could pay more attention to the set-pieces, costumes (Canale's alone cost over one million *lire*, he boasted) and the more spectacular sequences.

Filming took place mostly at the Safa Palatino Studios in Rome, but Freda managed to shoot the opening scene in Ravenna, a city marked by the Byzantine influence with its wonderful mosaics and churches, such as the Basilica of San Vitale. The director also took advantage of the EUR, the residential and business district in the South area of Rome that Mussolini had started building in 1938, in view of the World Fair that should have taken place in 1942 and would celebrate the twentieth anniversary of the Fascist regime, but was ultimately cancelled due to World War II: with its marble statues and palaces, and an architecture openly inspired by Ancient Rome, EUR was to portray the official image of Fascist Rome. It was a perfect setting for the outdoor scenes, including the celebrated chariot race, which—Freda claimed, and rightly so—was a patent influence on the one in William Wyler's *Ben-Hur* (1959). At first the producers had thought of using the Verona Arena as in *Spartaco*, but eventually settled for a huge site (about two acres wide) where a racetrack was built, about 500 feet long, and the leftovers from the construction sites—marble, travertine and porphyry—were used for the bleachers.

Despite the higher budget at disposal, as usual Freda's parsimoniousness prevailed. "I liquidated the extras in one day. They sent over 300 extras. In the morning I filmed them watching the chariot race, and in the afternoon I shot the people's revolt with the same extras: fires, battles, falls…. The extras were furious, because they thought they would work at least one week…!"[22] The race was shot in just four days, with three cameras. Freda took care of the main camera for the traveling shots—to such a passionate horse racing aficionado as him, it was nothing short of a delight—while another cameraman filmed the horses' paws galloping. Even though Gianna Maria Canale is patently (and understandably) replaced by a male stunt double in the long shots, the results are first-rate, and sport a remarkable dynamism in the choice and variety of shots. The scene was later recycled as stock footage in a number of titles, including *Maciste l'uomo più forte del mondo* (a.k.a. *Mole Men Against the Son of Hercules*, 1961), directed by Freda's assistant on *Teodora*, Michele Lupo. It also features glass matte shots that were the work of an uncredited Mario Bava.[23]

For the film, Freda collaborated again with Rodolfo Lombardi, whose brother Guglielmo was the credited first cameraman. The director claimed he took over the latter's duties: "In *Teodora* I was just first camera, it was still me, because I wanted to understand more directly, because … when you're fighting a battle or there's a rush of takes, how did it go, if you can't see it? So I had to be the cameraman. In *Teodora* I was the camera operator."[24] Being Freda's first color film after the brief experimental sequence in *Vedi Napoli e poi muori*, *Teodora* was one of the first Italian pictures shot with an Eastman Kodak film in Technicolor monopack (the so-called Pathecolor), that is only one negative, as opposed to the tripack procedure (three negatives, and three huge cameras) that was in use earlier. The negatives were to be developed and printed overseas, since no Italian lab was furnished with the necessary equipment. So, according to Freda, each evening the film reels had to be shipped to Rochester, New York, without even watching the rushes in color but only in a bad quality black-and-white, and within twenty days the lab would send back a telegram regarding the developing and color gradation.

> Which other producer but Gualino would have accepted…? To me, there was no problem at all. Because I knew beforehand the results of what I was filming, there were no surprises. I had simply accepted the responsability of making that film. But the money was Gualino's. He simply asked me, "Are you sure of what you are doing?" No other producer in the world would have accepted such a deal.[25]

Gualino's bet proved to be a winning one. *Teodora* is nothing short of outstanding, and paves the way for the visual symphony of *Beatrice Cenci*. Freda makes ample use of his trademark tracking shots, with impressive moments such as Justinian entering the tavern where he meets Theodora, the descent to prisons, and the obligatory palace feast scene. His penchant for framing results in several extraordinary moments, such as in the scene near the end, championed by Jacques Lourcelles, where Theodora is chased by the gigantic blind slave who has been ordered to kill her—a moment of mythical resonance, with the beauty menaced by the beast—and tries to break the lines of the guards preventing her from escaping. Another impressive sequence is the revolt, which confirms Freda's flair for mass scenes. The city is invaded by wild beasts, and the animals—panthers, lions, bears—wreak havoc: once again the scene was filmed with a good dose of recklessness, with six or seven extras running scared before a lion and the cameraman filming from inside a cage, and benefits from a tight, rousing editing.

On top of that, the use of color is stunning throughout, and results in neat pictorial images, such as a close-up of watermelons during the revolt, a still-life set against the action that is going on all around. Freda and Lombardi experimented with color, on several levels. Most notable is the contrast between light and shadows, accomplished by juxtaposing the bright outdoors (such as the chariot race) and the darkened indoor scenes, thus emphasizing the film's inner melodramatic values, but without the at times unbalanced excesses found in *Spartaco*. In addition to that, Freda and his d.o.p. used color to underline the different social environments, not only by having the main characters and extras wear red, green and blue robes, but coming up with strikingly different color schemes to portray the Emperor's court and the slums. The scenes set in Byzantium's subterraneans and prisons are characterized by the predominance of greens and reds, and some moments—such as the gypsy reading the ashes for Theodora's envious sister Saidia, and a slave being blinded with a hot iron—already hint at the pictorial richness of Mario Bava's adventure and Gothic films. On the other hand, the scenes at Justinian's palace are bathed in pale blue, with unreal, otherworldly effects, heightened by the use of studio sets, as in the scene of Theodora rejecting the Emperor's advances and suggesting that he marry her. The expert Lombardi, who in 1957 moved to the small screen, was later one of the pioneers in the development of color in Italian television.[26]

Even though the story is pretty standard, and the characters are very schematically sketched, *Teodora* nevertheless has a lightness of touch and a breezy rhythm that set it above most period films of the era. As Jacques Lourcelles noted, *Teodora*

> is one of Freda's few optimistic films. The union of sensuality and tenderness between Justinian and Theodora is mirrored, at a political level, in the happy marriage between aristocratic severity and popularly inspired liberalism. And so a continual correspondence (in Baudelaire's sense of the word) is established between the private life of the two characters and their public destiny. It gives a surprisingly positive hint about the political daydreaming of a director who is usually more cynical and bitter.[27]

Even though Freda sometimes referred to Theodora as "Spartacus' little sister," the empress and her relationship with her husband had more than a few traits in common with Gianna Maria Canale and her love affair with the director, resulting in a more personal and heartfelt work. Theodora is a strong female figure, proud and courageous to the point of challenging and defying her male opponents in the chariot race, but also wise and sagacious when it comes to ruling the empire—all this without ever sacrificing her sexuality, which oozes powerfully from her in each and every scene. Quite something, if compared to the typical figures of melodrama and adventure. *Teodora* is a love poem to Gianna Maria Canale, then at her popularity peak. "She immediately became a star," Freda recalled. "The people at Lux completely adhered to my casting demands, and whenever they asked me who I wanted to play the female lead I answered Gianna Maria Canale, and the matter was closed."[28] In *Teodora*, with the help of color, the director had his lead actress lighted like an American diva, and the results are astounding. Canale's first apparition on screen, when Justinian comes across her amid the Byzantium crowd after the woman's failed attempt at robbing him, has Freda linger on a close-up of the actress' impossibly beautiful features, her emerald eyes literally transfixing the camera. The effect is truly mesmerizing. Later on, when Theodora is imprisoned after being falsely accused of treason, a tracking shot to her face (predating the use of zooms in the following decade) achieves a poignant sentimental quality, and puts to best use one of the director's favorite stylistical features. Future film director Osvaldo Civirani, who was the still photographer on set, recalled in his memoir that "Canale was another of those actresses whom I would never get tired to photographing. She had perfect facial features and a pair of enchanting emerald pale blue eyes."[29]

Besides Canale, the cast featured Georges Marchal and Irene Papas. The French-born Marchal (1920–1997) was an athletic, handsome beau who had already starred in Gallone's *Messalina* and was very active in Italy during the 1950s and the 1960s, appearing in such adventure films as *Le vicomte de Bragelonne* (a.k.a. *Count of Bragelonne*, a.k.a. *The Last Musketeer*, 1954, Fernando Cerchio), *La rivolta dei gladiatori* (a.k.a. *The Warrior and the Slave Girl*, 1958, Vittorio Cottafavi) and Sergio Leone's *Il colosso di Rodi* (a.k.a. *The Colossus of Rhodes*, 1961). Marchal was also one of Buñuel's recurring actors, appearing in four films directed by the Spanish filmmaker: *Cela s'appelle l'aurore* (a.k.a. *That Is the Dawn*, 1956); *La Mort en ce jardin* (a.k.a. *Death in the Garden*, 1956); *Belle de Jour* (1967) and *La Voie lactée* (a.k.a. *The Milky Way*, 1969). The then-27-year-old Papas had been put under contract by Lux, a move which would have been unthinkable for the company just a few years earlier, as it was against Gualino's policy to sign exclusive deals with actors. Whereas Freda had good words about Marchal, he was slightly less complimentary about Papas, who seemingly refused to kiss her partners on scene.[30] The Greek actress is somehow sacrificed in the film as Theodora's sister Saidia, and her character really comes to the fore only near the end. Papas and Freda would work together again a dozen years later for *Roger La Honte*.

Even though it was passed with no cuts and rated "for all audiences," according to Freda *Teodora* was slightly trimmed by the producers before being submitted to the board of censors, in December 1953. It was an understandable move on the part of Lux, in one of the strictest periods for film censorship in the country: Canale's dance scene was rather daring for the time, and certainly would not meet the favor of the board, headed by Teodoro Bubbio. "They cut almost completely the dance scene in *Teodora*. It was the time when the moral judgment on the part of the Centro Cattolico Cinematografico counted a lot in terms of box-office grossings," Freda explained.

> Therefore, Lux wanted the film to be classified "for all audiences." So, before its release, they begged someone from the CCC to watch it in order to perform the cuts that they thought were necessary. So came this guy, whose name I don't recall, and we sat at the moviola. In the dance scene Gianna Maria Canale appeared with her belly uncovered, but she was wearing rather opaque see-through panties as well as a huge, thick bra. Well, there was nothing we could do. For the simple fact that she had her belly button exposed, the guy considered her terribly sinful. So I was forced to cut the scene where she was wearing that outfit.[31]

Freda stated that another sequence had to be redubbed because it was considered too virulent on a political plan: the long dialogue between the Emperor and the archbishop.[32] If this happened, it took place during the post-production stage, since there is no trace of complaints regarding the aforementioned scene in the official ministerial papers. Despite several sources claiming a running time of 124 minutes, the version submitted to the board was 2545 meters—approximately 92 minutes and 45 seconds. It took nine months before *Teodora* was finally released, in September 1954: meanwhile, the censorship situation had become even more strict with the appointment of the new Undersecretary to the Presidency of the council (and chief of the Board) Oscar Luigi Scalfaro, who would embark on several infamous crusades against vice and immorality in the movies.

Teodora was destined to be one of Freda's most popular films. Even the usually harsh Italian critics were slightly more generous, possibly because of the garish colors and indisputable spectacular values. "Compared to Freda's previous ... historical efforts, this film can be considered as a slight progress, and there is no doubt that the general public will be attracted by its lure,"[33] wrote film critic Umberto Tani. Although not properly a sword-and-sandal picture, since the action takes place several centuries later than *Spartaco* and other Ancient Rome pics, *Teodora* marked a vital step in the renewal of the genre—even though with the success of *Le fatiche di Ercole* (a.k.a. *Hercules*, 1958, Pietro Francisci) the *peplum* would soon take a turn toward the Fantastic which marked a radical dichotomy between the more historically-oriented works and the more fanciful, adventure-filled ones. Grossing over 590 million *lire*, it was a solid commercial success, although perhaps not the smashing hit the company had hoped for; *Ulisse*, on the other hand, grossed three times as much, with over 1,800 million *lire*, while *Attila* reached an estimated figure of 674 million *lire*.

The film was released theatrically overseas by I.F.E. as *Theodora, Slave Empress*. Compared to Freda's previous works, it benefitted from larger exposure and an impressive campaign. The U.S. poster, featuring prominently Canale (during a love scene with Marchal and running with a leash in hand, underlining the character's passionality and strength), promised "Passions ablaze! An empire aflame!" (hinting at the destruction of Rome as seen in *Quo Vadis?*), remarked the film's technical qualities ("Filmed on a scale beyond compare in Pathecolor") and mentioned "a cast of thousands." *Theodora* opened at NYC's Globe Theater on January 11, 1955,[34] announced by a pic in the *New York Times* of Canale leading the uprising during the film's climax, with the tag "Aroused Queen in Sixth Century Byzantium," and was granted an unusually in-depth and moderately praising review which started like this: "If there is some slight suspicion that Hollywood and/or Cecil B. DeMille have a corner on movie spectacle then such doubts should be dispelled by *Theodora, Slave Empress*, which crashed into the Globe yesterday." It was a remark that would make Freda proud for the rest of his days.

Predictably, the reviewer juxtaposed the film's lavishness with its alleged two-dimensional characters and stilted plot, but conceded that "the four scenarists, among whom is director Riccardo Freda, are not short-changing a viewer on eye appeal. For the vistas of Byzantium's teeming market places, palaces, hippodrome, caged and snarling lions, chariot races and hand-to-hand combats are likely to keep an observer on the alert." While panning the dubbing ("the stately phrases supposedly emerging from the principals' lips often have a dull, archaic ring"), the article had admired words for Gianna Maria Canale's screen presence ("What Signorina Canale lacks in histrionic ability is overshadowed by the physical requirements of the role") and concluded that "if the customers doze through these surface characterizations, it appears unlikely they will nod at the lush splendors of Byzantium. The talk may be dull but the action is lively."[35]

During the filming of *Teodora*, Freda made *I mosaici di Ravenna*, a color documentary short on the byzantine mosaics in Ravenna. The direction was credited to Giuseppe Fatigati, the production manager on the latter film. "While I was shooting in the S. Apollinare church in Ravenna, I asked Gualino: 'Why don't we take advantage of the fact that I am in Ravenna and I have all the lighting equipment, and shoot a documentary as well?' 'Sure, why not? How much would it cost?' I think it cost 6 million, a rather conspicuous sum. I shot a two-reels in a couple of Saturdays and Sundays...."[36]

As the director told Éric Poindron, "Aside from my personal interest, it was a complementary work, a way of understanding Byzantium. I have always loved frescoes, great paintings and mosaics.... I've said it time and again, a director is a slave to a film format and the lens; a painter, on the other hand, is free. Abel Gance tried to free himself from format, and I understand his endeavors. What I think would be ideal is to change format, focal length and screen according to the shot. A vertical screen, for example, for filming a tower, and a horizontal one for a banquet."[37]

Of course, besides the artistic motives, the main *raison d'être* for the documentary was the access to benefits as provided according to the Andreotti law.

Roland and the Finger of God

Teodora marked Freda's last collaboration with Lux Film. The director's subsequent project for Gualino's company was a prestigious literary adaptation which came close to materializing, but ultimately fell apart: a big-budget adventure film based on the 11th century epic poem *La Chanson de Roland*, set during the reign of Charlemagne, to be shot immediately after *Teodora*. Lux Film invested seven million *lire* for pre-production, sets and costumes. The script, provisionally titled *Orlando il paladino*, was penned by Freda and Vitaliano Brancati, and news of pre-production came out on the press in late 1954. Freda again asked the collaboration of Piccolis to build the main set pieces, and an ad was placed in newspapers, looking for a young male from 22 to 28 years old, with "the head of Apollo, the body of Hercules and the agility of the discobolus," to play Orlando, although the director later claimed that the production was in talks with Rock Hudson, while Gianna Maria Canale was to play Angélique.[38]

The movie was to be shot in Spain with the financial cooperation of Productora Toledo Films. However, when he travelled to Madrid, Freda found out that the Spanish censorship objected to the filming due to a historical motif: according to them, Charlemagne had not been defeated by the Moors, as the *Chanson* states, but by the Basques of Navarre. Therefore, Spain could not produce a motion picture about a Catholic King defeated by the Spanish. Freda claimed that he suggested shooting two versions, one with the Basques and the other with the Moors as the villains (ironically, the practice of double versions, one for the home market and one for the foreign ones, would be the norm in Spain in the following decades, so as to bypass the strict censorship on nudity), but to no avail. Whether this is fact or fabrication, one does not know: fact is, Lux could probably not afford such a big budget picture without a substantial co-production backup, and so the project was eventually shelved. Later on, Freda tried to resume it with producer Raffaele Colamonici, this time working on Ludovico Ariosto's 1516 romance epic poem *Orlando Furioso*, inspired by the same events as *La Chanson de Roland* but seen under a fantasy light. Cesare Zavattini collaborated to the script and master miniature maker Giovanni Piccolis was to devise the Hippogriff, a flying horse which is one of the many fantastic creatures Orlando meets in Ariosto's poem. Unfortunately, the project was too costly for Colamonici and was eventually abandoned. In 1956, though, Pietro Francisci directed *Orlando e i Paladini di Francia* (a.k.a. *Roland the Mighty*), starring Rik Battaglia and Rosanna Schiaffino and written by Ennio De Concini. Mario Bava was the director of photography.

The failure of an ambitious picture such as *La Chanson de Roland* caused Freda to move on to quicker, less challenging projects. He was called on to direct *Giove in doppiopetto* (1955), an adaptation of a successful stage musical by the acclaimed duo Garinei & Giovannini, Italy's first film in Cinemascope, after his use of color in *Vedi Napoli e poi muori* and *Teodora*. Even if it was not a project he cared about—especially since he could not stand the protagonist, comedian Carlo Dapporto—the money he was offered was enough to dissipate his reservations. However, he resisted behind the camera only one day.

> The set had been built in a pavillion of Turin's Exposition area, a hideous building near the river Po. I showed up, ready to shoot, but Dapporto started to have a tantrum: the set had to be changed, the costumes were so-so, maybe we could cast other comedians to strengthen the story.... I endured him for a few hours, then I explained to him that he was a nobody, and the film only served to exploit the success of the stage musical, what is more I liked to shoot fast and not waste any time. As soon as he began to answer back, I got up and left.[39]

Direction was taken over by Freda's assistant Daniele D'Anza, who later became a prominent TV director, with such popular works as the Gothic mini-series *Il segno del comando* (1971).

Another project possibly dating to the 1950s, which never reached production stage, was a script called *Il dito di Dio* (The Finger of God). It would have been an offbeat challenge for the director: an anthology movie in four episodes, all veering on black comedy and grotesque, a bit in the vein of that *commedia all'italiana* he definitely did not love, which nevertheless offered ample room for his biting sense of humor. The first episode was based on a story told to him by Enzo Fiermonte: a young kid who does not salute the passing Fascist troops is severely beaten by a Blackshirts hierarch and sent to hospital; years later the boy becomes a boxing champion, and one day he meets again the Fascist, who, not recognizing him, congratulates him for his exploits: for the prizefighter, it is time for vengeance. The second story was about a military shoemaker whose wife betrays him with an army officer: the man prepares a special pair of boots with dynamite concealed in the heels, so that when the officer stands to attention before his general and knocks his heels together, they will explode (a similar gag was later seen in Elio Petri's *La decima vittima*, 1965). For the third episode, Freda took inspiration from his stingy Roman antiquarian, called Veneziani: an antique dealer has a heart condition, undergoes many visits but cannot overcome his problem and eventually is visited by a world-renowned specialist who diagnoses him a small but harmless inconvenience; to pay for the expensive visit, the antiquarian offers the doctor to choose an item in his shop: the doctor agrees, but the object he picks up is such a priceless antique that the antiquarian has a heart attack. The fourth story was about the crown prince of Spain, who had not uttered a single word since his birth: the king entrusts a woman to assist and take care of the young man, and she dedicates her life to the prince's recovery, to the point of becoming his lover. Eventually she succeeds: but the prince's first words in front of her and his whole family are "I don't want to see this woman ever again."[40]

Da qui all'eredità

Freda's next movie after *Teodora* was another change of pace. *Da qui all'eredità* (From Here to the Heritage) was a low-budget black-and-white comedy shot in Naples whose title was a pun on Fred Zinneman's *From Here to Eternity* (1953, released in Italy in 1954 as *Da qui all'eternità*), one of the greatest box-office hits of the time. It was produced by the Naples-based Centauro Film, headed by Freda's friend Carlo Caiano, and featured the producer's son Mario—who later became a filmmaker on his own, with such titles as *Amanti d'oltretomba* (a.k.a. *Nightmare Castle*, 1965) and *L'occhio nel labirinto* (a.k.a. *The Eye in the Labyrinth*, 1972)—as assistant director.

The opening line states that "the film apparently takes place in Naples, but every reference to the city, its inhabitants, firms, people and things, is purely fanciful and casual." It was not merely a square-up of sorts to ingratiate the audience. Actually, even though he conceived the story as "an ode to Naples and the Neapolitans' way of life," Freda's take on the thread was quite different from the regional comedies that monopolized the screens, epitomized by the figure of the Neapolitan-born Totò.

Italian poster for *Da qui all'eredità* (1955).

Freda's consideration of Italy's greatest comic actor was opinionated to say the least, not unlike many others of his statements regarding Italian cinema. "He was a great comedian, sure, but a comedian Neapolitan-style.... Neapolitan pantomime is founded on the grimace, on wordplay, on the joke or the exaggerated gesture ... it was some kind of *commedia dell'arte*, frozen and devoid of gags."[41] By labeling Totò's comedy as purely verbal, Freda chose to omit the actor's extraordinary body language, such as his celebrated "string puppet" impersonation, seen for instance in *Totò a colori*. He even recalled having quit a film starring Totò around the same time as *Da qui all'eredità*. The movie, titled *Il coraggio* (1955), was eventually directed by Domenico Paolella and paired Totò with one of Freda's favorite thesps, Gino Cervi, and featured Gianna Maria Canale in a special participation; interestingly, it was one of Totò's films closer to Neorealist drama. Anyway, the director told Éric Poindron that he and Totò discussed the idea of making another movie together at one point, which Freda claimed he would shoot in two days—one of those challenges he fancied so much.[42]

Freda's dismissal of the typical wordplay-based Neapolitan comedy and his love for the early one-reels by Mack Sennett, Buster Keaton and Charlie Chaplin are on display in *Da qui all'eredità*: the director concocted an array of sight gags in the style of silent-era gagmen, and toned down the two leads' verbal jokes to focus on physical comedy. The opening sequence is a case in point: it focuses on a complex Rube Goldberg device of sorts concocted to wake up the two protagonists, Alberto and Beniamino. When their condo's porter pulls a rope, water is poured onto a system of gutters and ends up in a rivulet on Beniamino's face. The man wakes up and, without getting up from the bed, maneuvers a pair of rows which operate a mechanism that opens the windows and shakes Alberto's bed, so as to wake him up in turn. All this is rendered through Freda's customary sideways tracking shot (for the Rube Goldberg machine) and then through an imaginative tracking backwards from Beniamino's close-up to reveal the whole of the apartment, split into two levels like a dollhouse cutaway. The scene possibly pays homage to Buster Keaton and Eddie Cline's two-reel comedy *The Scarecrow* (1920) as well as to Keaton's masterpiece *The Navigator* (1924).

The director relied upon a couple of Neapolitan stage comedians, Beniamino Maggio and Alberto Sorrentino, whose mutual feeling allowed the many gags—each constructed like a small one-reel episode on its own—to hit the mark. Therefore we get to see the two wimps acting as plumbers, coachmen and electricians, with disastrous results. Their resort to petty theft and hoaxes (in true Neapolitan comedy tradition) is heightened by the emphasis on elaborate gags: in order to get the milk for their breakfast, Alberto and Beniamino steal a bottle from another hallway, but first make sure that nobody is in the proximity by way of a periscope. Another amusing bit has the two penniless protagonists arrange a dinner for their unaware guest by literally fishing out the various dishes (soup, wine, chicken, cheese...) from nearby apartments of the same condo. Once again, as in *Vedi Napoli e poi muori*, Freda opted to insert a brief color sequence in the climax, when Alberto and Beniamino wreak havoc in a nightclub where they have been recruited as electricians in order to fix the wiring. Their effort turns into a disastrous, amusing mess, complete with fireworks, explosions, sparks and assorted chaos, as the nightclub is literally destroyed by the two simpletons. Unfortunately the existing prints feature the scene in black-and-white.[43]

Da qui all'eredità is an amiable little comedy, where the director's visual gags spice up a bit the tiny, unpretentious story, centered on the inevitable romantic subplot about two lovers struggling to get married despite the girl's hyper-protective, tyrannical aunt: the latter was played by Tina Pica, a then-popular Neapolitan comedian whose limited, verbal kind of comedy (essentially a variation on the gruff, curmudgeon but golden-hearted type) was obviously quite distant from Freda's tastes. On the other hand, for the first time since their professional and personal encounter, the director did not cast his partner Gianna Maria Canale.

As customary with Italian genre films of the period, *Da qui all'eredità* featured a popular singer in an acting role. Domenico Modugno (1928–1994) was becoming a well-known name in Italy: since the beginning of his career he had divided himself between acting (he had debuted in 1949 in the Totò vehicle *I pompieri di Viggiù*) and singing, and in the mid-1950s he was having his first hits, such as *Lu pisce spada* and the beautiful *Vecchio frac*. He would become a star after his victory at the 1958 San Remo Festival with *Nel blu dipinto di blu*, one of Italy's most famous songs of the 20th century. For Freda's film, besides his acting turn, Modugno also wrote the score and sung *La donna riccia*.

His above-average acting chops would best be underlined by the likes of Pier Paolo Pasolini and Luigi Comencini, respectively in the extraordinary episode *Che cosa sono le nuvole?* (in *Capriccio all'italiana*, 1968) and in the grim black comedy *Lo scopone scientifico* (a.k.a. *The Scientific Cardplayer*, 1972), starring Alberto Sordi, Silvana Mangano, Bette Davis and Joseph Cotten.

Mario Caiano's recollections on Freda were not particularly kind. "Those who, like my father, used to deal with him in private life, swear that he could be a really sweet man; but I find it rather difficult to believe it," he wrote in his memoir, recalling Freda's attitude on set:

> Violent (to my knowledge only verbally), irascible, despotic and intolerant toward any opposition and conflict, he was one of those filmmakers to whom the fiction of cinema comes first and real life comes next. Therefore, if a comedian's wife has just passed away, that is not a good reason not to shoot a scene where he has to elicit laughs; if on the night in which five Roman soldiers must dive into the Aniene on horseback, dressed with only their armour, the temperature is only 26 degrees, that's an unimportant detail.[44]

During shooting, Caiano even performed before the camera as Alberto Sorrentino's double, for the scene in which Sorrentino, posing as a plumber, is working in a bathroom that is almost completely flooded by the water. Since it was early spring and the water was cold, Sorrentino panicked, prompting Caiano to dress in his plumber costume and do the take in his place—it was neither the first time nor the last that something like that happened in a Freda film. Despite the director's efforts, its strongly regional characters had that, even though it performed rather well in the South of Italy, *Da qui all'eredità* went almost unnoticed in the North. Box-office grossings amounted to roughly 142 million *lire*.

Beatrice Cenci

The sad and terrible story of Beatrice Cenci, the daughter of Count Francesco Cenci, made her one of Italy's most popular heroines, and the subject of countless works of art, including portraits and statues, over a dozen novels, tragedies and tales, plus a number of operas. The 22-year-old Beatrice was beheaded on September 11, 1599, after being convicted and submitted to torture for the crime of patricide. It is said that she plotted her father's murder as a revenge for the sexual abuse she was submitted to by the Count. The crime was the result of a teamwork, which included Beatrice's stepmother Lucrezia, her brothers Giacomo and Bernardo, the nobleman Olimpio Calvetti, and a blacksmith, Marzio da Fioran.

Francesco Cenci was a dissolute, violent man. He had put his daughter in a convent at the age of seven, and when she came back in the family at 15, he began to abuse her. Francesco, overwhelmed by debts and twice condemned to severe monetary penalty because of "heinous guilts" such as sodomy, kept Beatrice and Lucrezia segregated in his small castle in the Reign of Naples. Beatrice vainly tried to ask for help, with the sole result of being severely punished by her wicked father.

The murder of Francesco Cenci proved to be a hard effort. Despite suffering from mange and gout, he was a strong man. Two attempts at his life proved ill-fated: first Beatrice and her accomplices poisoned him, then set up an ambush with the aid of local bandits. The third attempt was finally successful: drugged with opium diluted in his wine,

French poster for *Beatrice Cenci* (1956).

Francesco Cenci was assaulted in his sleep. Marzio broke both his legs with a hammer, and Olimpio finished him off by hammering a nail through his cranium and throat. Then the conspirators attempted to conceal the murder by staging a fake fatal accident. However, soon the rumors about Cenci's demise started to spread, and the authorities exhumed the body. Eventually Beatrice and the other accomplices were arrested, and Olimpio confessed. He was later killed by one of the Cenci acquaintances, Monsignor Guerra, to avoid further revelations on his part. Marzio confessed too after being tortured, but when he was put face to face with Beatrice he retracted his accusations, and died shortly afterwards for the injuries. Giacomo and Bernardo confessed as well, as did Beatrice: the tortures she underwent eventually broke her down and she ended up admitting the crime.

The Cenci trial had a great resonance. During the debate, Beatrice's attorney publicly revealed that Francesco had repeatedly raped his daughter, but Beatrice denied it. Chronicles of the time state that the defense attorney could not even make his harangue, as he was admitted to court only after the sentence had been emitted. Despite the many requests for clemency, Pope Clemente VII refused it, so as to give an example to the people in the papal State. Beatrice and Lucrezia were sentenced to beheading by sword, a more merciful fate than Giacomo's, who was sentenced to quartering, while the younger brother Bernardo, who had not taken part in the murder, was condemned to a lifetime's rowing in the papal galleys. A large crowd attended the execution, and various riots and brawls took place, as the Pope's sentence was fiercely disapproved by the Roman people.

Such a tragic series of events was the ideal source material for many writers and artists. The story of the Cenci inspired among others a tragedy written by Percy Bysshe Shelley, a famous story by Stendhal included in his *Italian Chronicles*, a tale by the Italian Francesco Domenico Guerrazzi and, more recently, *Les Cenci*, a 1935 stage adaptation by Antonin Artaud, and a 1955 pièce by Alberto Moravia. The tale had been adapted for the screen several times as well since the silent era, in 1908 (*Béatrix Cenci*, by Albert Capellani), 1909 (*Beatrice Cenci*, by Mario Caserini), 1926 (*Beatrice Cenci*, by Baldassarre Negroni) and 1941 (Guido Brignone's *Beatrice Cenci*). Around the same time as Freda's film Vittorio Gassman was considering to make his directorial debut with his own version of the story, but eventually went on to make *Kean—Genio e sregolatezza* (1957, co-directed by Francesco Rosi); further versions would be helmed in 1969 by Lucio Fulci (*Beatrice Cenci*) and Bertrand Tavernier (*La passion Béatrice*, 1987).[45] Still, as Sandra A. Waters put it, "the 'real' events surrounding Beatrice Cenci have been clouded by romanticizations and exaggerations of the facts in drama, painting, film, literature, and opera," noting that writers, playwrights and filmmakers "have all depicted Beatrice through rose-tinted lenses, but the qualities that Guerrazzi assigns her in his novel would thrust her toward sainthood."[46]

Written in 1854, Guerrazzi's take on the story comes close to being a Gothic novel of sorts. The author hinted at the Fantastic genre with the depiction of the so-called "*notte delle fantasime*" (night of the spirits, in aulic Italian) concocted to punish Francesco Cenci of his sins, with the apparition of a cannibal ghost described as "pale, tall, horribly skinny, with lifeless eyes similar to a dead fish" who devours food, plates and table cloth, and repeatedly tells Cenci "I'm hungry!" It is followed by another vision of a naked dead girl, her face covered by the unkempt, bloody hair, with a knife's handle thrust in her chest and a rivulet of blood flowing from the open wound.

None of this, however, is to be found in Freda's version, originally to be titled *I maledetti*[47] (The Cursed). The script, written by Jacques Rémy and Filippo Sanjust under the director's constant supervision, takes many liberties with the story and characters (even introducing the fictitious Martina, played by Claudine Dupuis) and rejects almost entirely the Gothic implications of the tale, its closer influence being Stendhal's work—although it takes a different approach to the heroine compared to the French writer. Freda's words to Bertrand Tavernier are enlightening, not only regarding his vision of the Cenci tragedy, but also related to the kind of audience his film was aimed at:

> Eventually I decided to deliberately soften the story of that family. You see, I am a popular filmmaker, and I feel that I have responsibilities toward the many spectators who watch my movie and are not very cultured people. I have not the right to impose on them a story where there is no glimmer of hope. You could do that with a more aware audience. Unfortunately, they don't go and see my films.[48]

Although they sound patronizing, Freda's observations were true. The kind of motion pictures he made were aimed at lower-class audiences, the time's corresponding of the *pieds-noirs* he met as a kid in the Egyptian theaters. Their participation in the stories was unconditioned, their faith in the traditional narratives was absolute. Those were not the same people at whom Fellini, Antonioni and the like aimed their films—although they went to see those as well, mainly to spot a glimpse of a naked leg or a female décolleté, or driven by the scandals raised by newspapers, certainly not because of the issues addressed by the filmmakers. A revealing line in Risi's *Il sorpasso*, a few years later, has the exuberant Bruno Cortona (Vittorio Gassman) ask to his shy friend Roberto (Jean-Louis Trintignant): "Have you seen *L'eclisse*? ... it put me to sleep." Another telling moment, in Pietro Germi's *Divorzio all'italiana* (a.k.a. *Divorce Italian Style*, 1961) has a crowd gathering at a Sicilian cinema at a screening of *La dolce vita*, to savor the sight of blonde goddess Anita Ekberg taking a bath in the Trevi Fountain, in spite of the local parish priest's condemnation of such an immoral work. Whereas the cinema Freda pursued was a kind of popular moviemaking that the middle class snubbed, and which most critics hastily labeled with short, biased, unconcerned reviews—and, indeed, patronizing. The commercial exploit of popular film genres in the following decade would somehow even broaden such a distinction. Then came the ingredient that worked magic for the rich and the poor, the cultured and the illiterate alike: sex.

To Freda, then, Beatrice is innocent, and could not be otherwise, so that the viewers can better sympathize with her sad destiny, and the murderous events surrounding the Cenci family become the culmination of the ill-fated love story between Beatrice and Olimpio. In Freda's conception of cinema, heroines must be pure as lilies, even more so when they are doomed to a bad ending. "It's more interesting to film an innocent woman than a criminal," he stated, adding that "*Beatrice Cenci* is a modern *peplum*. Again a drama with no way out, like the Greek tragedies. We cannot fight destiny. And I filmed this diabolical fate in CinemaScope...."[49] Taking this concept to maximum effect, the director builds the final part of the film like a suspenseful race against time, as Olimpio collects the evidence to save Beatrice, but is killed before he can deliver it to the judge, who receives the letter that exculpates the young woman too late to save her. No matter that it liberally manipulates historical truth: it is filmmaking at its peak. As Freda knew too well, when fact becomes legend, film the legend.

Compared to the 1969 version directed by Lucio Fulci, Freda's adaptation also mitigated the most violent moments—understandably, given the different times in which the two movies were made. The over-the-top cruelty of Francesco Cenci's assassination had been vividly described by Stendhal: the victim had one nail driven into his eye and another in the throat, in front of Beatrice and her mother, who later extracted the nails and took the body to an abandoned part of the garden so as to stage a gruesome accident. Italian censors would have never passed such a scene, so Freda and his scriptwriters resorted to the Shakespearean romantic element of the balcony (see *Romeo and Juliet*), which here turns into a deadly trap. The torture scenes also rely on suggestion, and the director claimed that he gave up the idea of depicting the prison system of the period, where the poor were shut down in the subterraneans whereas the aristocrats were detained in sumptuous apartments where they could receive their friends and entertain guests. Historical films made in Italy, he inferred, must be harmless.

Nine years after *I miserabili*, Freda teamed up with Gino Cervi for the fourth time. The 55-year-old actor was cast against type, as the Luciferian Francesco Cenci. Beatrice was played by the 20-year-old Mireille Granelli, a semi-debuting actress who did not have much of a career, appearing alongside Eddie Constantine in *The Big Bluff* (1957) and then in minor roles in Italian productions, including a couple of sword-and-sandal films before virtually disappearing from the big screen since the mid–1960s. Freda cast her on the spot in Paris, despite Granelli not having any experience as an actress, and much to the producers' disbelief, because of her stunning beauty (put at risk by Granelli's addiction to *fettuccine* pasta, which made her gain weight during shooting[50]). The fact that, despite her debatable acting chops, she makes for a convincing and vibrant Beatrice, goes to Freda's merit. The cast also featured the French Micheline Presle (the star of Claude Autant-Lara's *Diable au corps*, 1947, and Fritz Lang's *American Guerrilla in Philippines*, 1950, among others), Fausto Tozzi and a young Antonio De Teffé, not yet known as Anthony Steffen.

The special effects were the uncredited work of Mario Bava, who embellished several locations and helped Freda stage Beatrice's final execution, by way of a *maquette* and mirrors, turning a small number of extras into a veritable crowd that watches the gruesome spectacle from atop the castle's battlements. Bava also created the *maquettes* of Castle Sant'Angelo, as well as the bridge crossed in the procession scene that leads Beatrice to the executioner: here, the melodramatic effect is heightened by the use of Tchaikovsky's Symphony No. 6 "Pathétique," and overall the scene somehow predates Freda's own *Maciste all'inferno*.

Beatrice Cenci is a luscious period melodrama, at a time when it was experiencing its decline in its contemporary form, before the industry would convert into genres: the *peplum*, the Gothic, the Western, the spy film, etcetera. According to film scholar Emiliano Morreale, the film can be seen as "an authentic compendium of the 1800s melodramatic tradition, an update of popular Romanticism based on music…. Here the taste for the opera film in color meets with an almost overwhelming horror style (the castle, the cobwebs, the darkened forest), and a morbid and exquisitely sadistic eroticism, with an original tension toward the fantastic and the visionary."[51]

Unlike, say, Fritz Lang, who notoriously detested it, Freda found himself immediately at ease with the panoramic CinemaScope format, which he was using for the first time. On top of that, even more than *Teodora*, *Beatrice Cenci* allowed the director to resort to a dramatic use of color, the missing element that would enable him to make films similar to pictorial compositions, along the lines of his favorite painters such as Caravaggio, Ruysdaël or Veronese. "To me, color cinema is magic," he would claim, adding that "When they say 'film in color' they think of 'colored film.' And they paint everything, from the chair to the bed sheet, from the ceiling to the floor. Whereas I think we have to smother it and create a certain general tone where we can bring out the color touches."[52]

Taking inspiration from the 16th century Venetian painter Vittore Carpaccio's huge canvas, minutely filled with assorted details (regarding architecture, costumes and everyday life) and featuring a variety of characters as if on an imaginary stage, the director worked on each and every visual element of the shot, from the lighting to the costumes, from the set-pieces to the *maquettes*, so as to give them a strong dramatic flair, like a painter does with color, perspective and composition. Freda's concept that his film be a "fresco, but a morbid one," were followed to the letter by the extraordinary work of his d.o.p. Gábor Pogány, as well as by production designer Arrigo Equini and costume designer Filippo Sanjust. This resulted in such exquisite moments as Beatrice and Olimpio's encounter on the bridge, which recreates the style and colors of Tintoretto, or the banquet scene, which openly refers to Leonardo da Vinci's *The Last Supper*; overall, the pictorial references are scattered throughout the picture—notice the exquisite table composition made of a mandolin and a crate of fruits that can be glimpsed in one room of the castle, a still life worthy of Caravaggio.

The most striking example of Freda's concept is the beautiful opening, a series of masterfully conceived long takes—completely devoid of dialogue and scored with Beethoven's 6th Symphony "Pastoral"—which stands out as one of the director's crowning achievements. The camera cranes down on Beatrice, running in the woods at night under the rain, pursued by the family servants on horseback. The girl—who has fled from home after learning that her father poisoned her brother—hides in a bush and then runs through the trees, under a pouring rain and intermittent lightning, accompanied by a sweeping tracking shot rightward. She eventually drops down senseless near a torrent where she is found by Olimpio, who takes her in his arms and back home. Bathed in deep blue, with Beatrice's white-and-yellow dress and porcelain-like skin standing out against the night backdrop, it is an unforgettable scene, which sets the tone for the whole film and at the same time displays the director's innate Gothic flair: several years later he would stage a very similar sequence featuring Barbara Steele in *L'orribile segreto del Dr. Hichcock*. However, here Freda does not aim at suspense or cheap scares, but creates a desperate romantic feel rendered with all the visual strength he could summon, and which masterfully blends with the music. As the director later remarked, "my favorite collaborators remained Beethoven and Tchaikovsky in *Beatrice Cenci*. They are the pillars of the film, and sometimes I have the impression that they wrote the music specifically for me...."[53]

The use of costumes as a visual counterpoint to the character's emotions is remarkable as well. Beatrice is provided with a mixture of pastel-colored robes, so as to signify the girl's inner purity, while during the trial she wears violently vivid dresses that underline her passion for Olimpio and her inner drama. On the other hand, Olimpio wears bright red jackets, making him look as if he was the only living person in the shot—he is Beatrice's only hope to get away from her nightmarish existence—as well as a reminder of the story's doomed ending. Similarly, the castle—a fully Gothic environment, with its huge, luxurious yet cold empty rooms and subterraneans adding to the characters' sense of loneliness and doom—somehow reflects Cenci's duplicitousness, whereas the still-lifes on display—dead rabbits, geese and pheasants—are a gloomy memento of the presence of death hovering over its inhabitants.

The results are as far from the contemporaneous lurid present-day *mélos* as they are close to the visual excellency of Visconti' *Senso*. Nevertheless, Freda's film fully belongs to the realm of popular cinema. It is not designed for the critics but for mass consumptions, and speaks to the cultured and the illiterate with the same strength. With all its symbolic power that literally imbues each and every frame, camera movement and set prop, *Beatrice Cenci* is Freda's final and most vibrant *j'accuse* against Neorealism, and the definitive manifesto of his conception of cinema. On the other hand, despite the director's will to create a popular entertainment, the film exudes a cruelty that borders on the monstrous, and reflects a view of the world that is relentlessly grim.

A debauched, perverted tyrant who kills his sons and rapes his own daughter, Francesco Cenci is a figure worthy of Cronos, the mythological Greek god who devoured his offspring, and is the most astounding embodiment of pure evil in a Freda film so far. At first, the director cleverly camouflages the man's inner monstrosity by showing him as a feasting, Epicurean nobleman, a lover of good food and wine who is equally voracious to all the pleasures of life. Just like Dr. Hichcock, though, the patriarch is devoured by a "horrible secret"—incest—that undermines his authority and the whole institution of family with it. In this sense, *Beatrice Cenci* is as powerful as Freda's later Gothic horror films in its depiction of mankind.

The Count's incestuous desire is never explicitly mentioned, though, but suggested as far as censorship would allow: "From now on you must obey me in everything," he says menacingly to Beatrice, who is lying on her bed after her failed attempt at escape, his hand almost casually uncovering her naked shoulder while grabbing her from behind—a gesture repeated several times during the film, which underlines Cenci's predatory, vampiric nature. In another scene, he asks Beatrice to wear a dress that belongs to her stepmother (who previously refused Francesco's sexual advances), in front of him, thus symbolically having her take the place of his wife. The rape is implied by an abrupt fade to black, while Francesco—carrying Beatrice on his knees, as if she was a little girl, and, again, caressing her naked shoulder—tells her that he is not an ogre after all, that she is the only person he cares about, and that he has at heart her happiness "more than anything else in the world." The fade-out, here, is not as much a self-censorship, as it is a horrified yield to the utter blackness of Cenci's world.

On the other hand, Beatrice is a fully-fledged Romantic heroine, who fights against her father's absolute power and is doomed to failure, as is her male savant. She is always the point to which all the light converges in the frame, underlining her purity, and is often seen in poses that recall classical paintings or statues. Through her, "Freda's anti-realist cinema avoids any trace of coldness, and on the contrary it shows traits of surprising proximity with the deep feeling of its own time."[54]

In retrospective, given the strict adherence of Italian censorship to the moral rules imposed by the Vatican, it is amazing that *Beatrice Cenci* was greenlighted. In a 1955 speech to the members of the Italian film industry, Pope Pio XII stated that the "ideal film" must "communicate to those who see and listen the sense of reality ... as seen through the eyes of those who know more ... so as to help and comfort them.... The ideal film has ... a high and positive mission ... at the service of man" in order to "maintain and implement the adfirmation of one's self in the sentiment of the right and good." Freda's film is quite the opposite. The idealistic image of the patriarchal family exhibited by Francesco Cenci during his initial meeting with Olimpio is just a make-believe, which hides an inner, unspeakable, grotesquely deformed double: the wife won't sleep with her husband, who in turn lusts over his teenage daughter, has killed his other son and will be killed by his closest relatives. It recalls a Greek tragedy indeed, but it denies the viewer the much-awaited catharsis. The innocent are condemned, the guilty are spared, human laws are unfair and justice acts by way of horrendous instruments—even more so if we think that it is inflicted by the Church.

The film's pièce de resistance is the climactic trial, with the tribunal trying to extort a confession to Cenci's young cadet son: by putting a harmless, naive boy against an overpowering authority, Freda once again juxtaposes childhood's innocence to adulthood's cruelty as he did in *La vendetta di Aquila Nera*—a theme he will return to again in *Agi Murad—Il diavolo bianco* and *Roger La Honte*. Human justice, as in *Il conte Ugolino* and *Il tradimento*, becomes a paradoxical role play, which obeys to rules that are openly revealed as inhuman, void and absurd. What is left is the mourning and the rage for beauty and love destroyed. It says much about the sensibility of a director who boasted about his own cynicism, and still in his most inspired films was able to dig to the core of the human condition.

Riccardo Freda considered *Beatrice Cenci* his best film. "It is more than a melodrama. It is a tragedy, it is a process that defies the genre. I put myself completely into it, for once I cared about an *auteur* direction, and the film seduces still today, when I watch it again I am shaken, haunted by a deep and unexplicable emotion...."[55] It was perhaps this picture that definitely made him an *auteur* into the eyes of the young French cinephiles, when it was released in France the next year as *Le château des amants maudits*.[56] As Bertrand Tavernier—who would helm a remake of sorts with his 1987 film *La passion Béatrice*, starring Julie Delpy—recalled,

> I will never forget the shock of watching *Beatrice Cenci* at a small cinema in Lyon behind the Brotteaux station, being struck by the close-ups, by the crane movement that focuses on a young girl running in a forest on a stormy night, this nocturnal chase scene, the sudden appearance of a knight who saves her at least for a little while, who gives her some rest. A masterly opening sequence in which Freda makes colors collide, the blues of night, of the water, the yellows of a dress or of a torch, in which he takes control of the space with the same dazzling force that propels his characters toward their own destiny.[57]

In his *Dictionnaire du cinéma*, Jacques Lourcelles celebrated the "marriage between melodrama and History. What History loses in truthfulness, melodrama regains in feverishness, lyricism, intensity, and in the depiction of a past relived in the present." He also pointed out the perfect balance between plasticity and dynamism, the accurate visual composition and the sudden accelerations in pacing, with "a lyrical and plastic juxtaposition of strong moments" that derives from opera, and noticed that "the dynamism and entertaining skill of Freda's *mise-en-scène* are such that the audience, near the end, starts dreaming that this story is invented, that it recreates itself progressively as he tells it, and that Beatrice, for who-knows-what miracle, can escape her fate in the end."[58] To Yves Boisset, "its splendor made one think of Visconti."[59]

Still, critical reception in Italy for *Beatrice Cenci* was almost nonexistent. "The only critic who wrote about it was a journalist in Turin, who claimed he had seen it on second-run,"[60] Freda bitterly recalled. However, after all the scrupulous prep work he had done and the care he had lavished on the film, *Beatrice Cenci*'s meager box-office results—a little over 220 million *lire*, it ended up at the 38th spot among Italian box office grossing of the year—were all the more disappointing. It was as if something had broken in the spiritual community between the director and his audience, that popular basin of low-cultured moviegoers whom he ideally made films for.

Beatrice Cenci was a landmark in Freda's career: the end of an age where the power of cinema could win over the senselessness of existence and the unbearable sight of mankind's misery, and perhaps also the end of a period in which, despite the critics' biased look at his work, he would be considered an A-list director due to his commercial success.

From then on, his works would become darker and darker, by choice and out of necessity, starting with his next one, Italy's first true horror film.

8

Diving into Genres

I vampiri

One of the most frequently recounted anecdotes regarding the birth of the Italian horror film is how Riccardo Freda came up with the idea for *I vampiri* during a conversation with producers Ermanno Donati and Luigi Carpentieri.

> I made a *fantastique* film as I had made adventure flicks. Fantastic cinema was a privilege of the Americans and the German Expressionists. And I wanted to prove that we could make fantastic films in Italy. I explained to Carpentieri that I could write a story in just one day and shoot the movie in two weeks. Carpentieri phoned Goffredo Lombardo, who was the biggest film producer, distributor and idiot in Italy. "Freda says he can make a horror movie in two weeks…" and Lombardo answered, "Well, it's not a big investment, we can give it a try." I dictated the scenario on the magnetophone, wrote the script with Piero Regnoli and we started shooting.[1]

I vampiri was a low-budget production: Donati and Carpentieri's Athena and Lombardo's Titanus invested 32 million *lire* each. The initial budget (97 million) increased to 142 million (including 20 million for post-production and release) after the switch to the panoramic format: it was the second time in a row Freda employed CinemaScope. To save on the budget, the director and crew utilized mostly existing sets: "There were the remains of a papier-maché castle abandoned in the heart of the studio. The sets were about to collapse at any moment…. The castle's garden was the garden at Titanus studio…. The only time we went outside was to shoot the scene were the body is found in the river. It's the Aniene, a tributary of the Tiber."[2]

True, *I vampiri* was born of a challenge. But why did this challenge occur in the first place? There is a blatant hiatus between the luscious, full-color atmospheric tragedy of *Beatrice Cenci* and the stark, if stylish, black-and-white of this modern-day story about girls being drained of their blood. One must consider, however, an interesting and usually overlooked moment in Freda's career, which allegedly took place in 1956, when he teamed up with the young mystery writer Sergio Donati to work on a script based on a James Hadley Chase novel, *You Find Him, I'll Fix Him*, published in the U.S. with the a.k.a. Raymond Marshall.[3] Between 1955 and 1956 Donati had written three interesting but not very successful novels published in the *Giallo Mondadori* series, *L'altra faccia della luna* (adapted in 1966 as *Tre notti violente*, by Nick Nostro), *Il sepolcro di carta*, which later became a film directed by Tinto Brass, *Col cuore in gola* (a.k.a. *Deadly Sweet*, 1967), starring Jean-Louis Trintignant and Ewa Aulin, and *Mr. Sharkey torna a casa*. Unfortunately the movie never got made due to lack of funds, but it helped Donati move his first steps in the movie business, and meet "a skinny, swindling assistant director with a big nose, named Sergio Leone...."[4] However, the choice of adapting the author of such hard-boiled stuff as *No Orchids for Miss Blandish*, *Eve* and *Safer Dead* signalled how Freda was definitely moving to darker territories.

"From a certain point on, I started making films I did not care much about. I made certain movies just to prove to myself that I could, in spite of a very limited shooting schedule and wretched means,"[5] the director would later confess. Whether this was the case with *I vampiri*, it is debatable. Some facts, then, are not: for one thing, Freda had a very precise vision of the horror genre, and yet the finished film is not what he had envisioned.

Once again, as with *Don Cesare di Bazan* and especially *Aquila nera*, Freda shaped a new genre out of nothing, like a sculptor turns inanimate, rough matter into a fully pro-

French pressbook for *I vampiri* (1957).

portioned figure. Even more than with those previous works, here he had basically to start from scratch, as he himself recalled. "In Italy there were just 'scary' movies which were very naïve, with a cheap supernatural angle, Carolina Invernizio-style," the director pointed out while explaining the innovative quality of his work. "Italian cinema never ventured into the realm of the supernatural, never tried to make something like Murnau's *Faust*, which I still recall vividly ... an extraordinary film. We couldn't even dream to have filmmakers of Murnau's strength."[6]

To Freda, horror had to be sought elsewhere, and his conception of classical Gothic monsters was strikingly bold. Proof of *I vampiri*'s innovative quality can be easily found by comparing it to the horror and science fiction films produced around the same time in the United States: the approximations to classic movie monsters—namely, *I Was a Teenage Werewolf* (1957, Gene Fowler, Jr.), *I Was a Teenage Frankenstein* (1957, Herbert L. Strock) and *Blood of Dracula* (1957, Herbert L. Strock)—uneasily tried to lure younger audiences by relying on characters of troubled teenagers and rebels without a cause. On the other hand, attempts at reviving the vampire figure within contemporary American settings were to be found in such low-budget fare as *The Return of Dracula* (1958, Paul Landres): there, the makers' reliance on traditional bloodsuckers, in juxtaposition with the ordinariness of middle America scenery, resulted in a shaky, intermittently interesting but ultimately awkward affair. Similarly, South-of-the-border productions such as Fernando Méndez's *El vampiro* (a.k.a. *The Vampire*, 1957) and *El ataúd del vampiro* (a.k.a. *The Vampire's Coffin*, 1958) drew back to the old Universal clichés, albeit with a refreshing Latin sensibility, to curious but somehow naïve results.

Freda, on the contrary, chose to overthrow the vampire film conventions altogether, both figuratively and substantially. His movie centered not on a single male figure, but on a fascinating woman who seemingly never ages, and surrounds herself with a court of servants who procure her the blood she needs to preserve her youth and beauty. Not coincidentally, the film's title is in the plural form. First of all, Freda's "vampires" don't wear tuxedo and cape, but white coats or black raincoats. They don't hypnotize their victims either, but narcotize them with chloroform, like ordinary gangsters. Most importantly, they don't have pointed fangs and don't bite the unfortunate girls' necks, but drain their blood in a lab, with cold medical efficiency. "Syringes are more shocking than either vampire's fangs or a bat. I transposed 'suction' with 'transfusion,'" Freda would comment. "This kind of vampirism is practiced every day in hospitals.... Therefore I gave my Fantastic film a medical nature. Abandoning the Anglo-Saxon imagery, I threw myself headlong into horror.... Horror and reality nowadays march side by side."[7]

With its utter rejection of the supernatural and its reliance on science, Freda's film was closer in spirit to the more experimental sci-fi works of the period, such as *The Man Who Turned to Stone* (1957, László Kardos), another example of an idiosyncratic re-reading of vampirism which features a similar trick as the one used by Mario Bava for the Duchess' sudden aging on camera, or Roger Corman's *The Wasp Woman* (1959). Yet the style was quite different. The U.S. productions looked cheap and unattractive, save for the occasional nod to Expressionism and *film noir*, whereas Freda's film exudes a luscious visual flair that often borders on Surrealism. The title itself is a nod to one of the director's beloved silent film serials, Feuillade's *Les Vampires* (1915), to which the story's structure and characters also pay reference repeatedly, starting with the choice of the reporter hero Pierre Lantin modeled upon Philipe Guérande in Feuillade's film.

The Parisian setting evoked by Mario Bava's *maquettes* incongruously reinvents some of the French city's best known monuments in a strikingly offbeat way: that is the case with the famous Saint-Jacques tower, which in the film becomes the tower of Castle Du Grand. Even though Freda's decision to set *I vampiri* in the present was mainly due to budget-saving reasons (a director like him, fascinated by period movies, wouldn't have lost the opportunity to play with an atmospheric horror story set in the past, had he had the means), the contrast between the 20th century Paris (or rather, its highly stylized makeshift) and the imposing interiors of Castle Du Grand is striking, and gives the picture its peculiar tone. Freda connects horror to popular chronicles, as a modern-day variant of the past's sensationalistic *feuilletons*, the popular novels that often revolved around horrific and mysterious events (such as *The Mysteries of Paris* by Eugène Sue) and suggests an ideal thread between the European tradition and the present day.

Then, more importantly, *I vampiri* does not focus on a millenarian being that feeds with blood in order to survive, but on an aging rich woman, Duchess Du Grand, who uses blood as means to retain her apparent beauty and youth, and turn into her alter ego, Giséle—therefore, not a predator but an exploiter. A parasite. "Vampires do exist and they stir close to us all the time, even though they can't be recognized by their incisors [*sic*], and even if a timely heart attack is enough to make them die," Freda commented, adding:

Being a vampire means to live near someone who is much younger than us and "suck," without him or her noticing, the best—intelligence, vital spirit, and especially freshness—of ideas, feelings, reactions. Woe be it to live with elderly people: they drag you to the abyss of their anxious waiting for death. Hence the modern idea of a vampire which must be objectified, in order to make audiences understand it, through an old woman craving for the blood of a young one.[8]

I vampiri's basic concept makes for a metaphorical reading, heightened by the film's setting and scenery. The story leans on the contrast between the sunny modern-day Paris, and the dusty aristocracy ("A bunch of dried-up mummies is what they are!" as Gisèle Du Grand admits) that celebrates—and unnaturally perpetuates—itself in the hall of the castle, which becomes the offshoot of a decaying noble class that is out of time (a notion also hinted by the relics of the past that adorn the Duchess' bedroom) yet still looks down on the world. The Duchess herself is a symbol and a keeper of such a hierarchical view: she invariably appears in a vantage position compared to her interlocutors, whether it be the castle's stairs (a striking moment which reinvents Dracula's first apparition in Tod Browning's film) or a throne-like armchair on which she sits while the men gather around her like her subjects. Her power is based on the ascendancy that she has because of her social and economic position, and she maneuvers her minions according to a strict hierarchical order.

The character of Duchess Du Grand is basically a re-reading of the historical Countess Erzsébet Báthory, who bathed in the blood of virgins to stay young, and Gisèle's sudden final transformation into her octagenarian self after suffering violent emotions, which make the precarious chemical balance created by Professor Du Grand's parascientific alchemies collapse, is a nod to the finale of Robert Louis Stevenson's *The Strange Case of Dr. Jekyll and Mr. Hyde* ("We wanted to create a double as terrifying as Mr. Hyde" Freda commented[9]): two sources that highlight the film's discourse. On the one hand, the image of an aristocrat who uses her power to exploit the lower classes; on the other, a psychophysical dissociation and a split of the social identity, stressed by the contrast between the social norms that the individual rationally forces himself to obey and the primary, irrational impulses that shake him (or, in case of Freda's film, her) from deep within. The director would explore the latter theme in his following Gothic works, with outstanding results.

Another major influence on *I vampiri* was Edgar Allan Poe's short story *The Fall of the House of Usher*, with the suggested parallel between the decaying, dissipated castle interiors (designed by the great art director Beni Montresor) and the "vampire" played by Gianna Maria Canale. The manor, "more disturbing and closer to us than Dracula's castle in Transylvania," as Freda commented, is no less than an architectural monster, conceived "like a putrefying organic structure, whose stones are corroded and almost falling apart, a metaphorical expansion of its inhabitant."[10] Ultimately, the duchess and her decaying lair—incongruously imprinted in the postcard-like Paris that surrounds it and therefore immediately hinting at the woman's abnormality, her being out of place in the present—are one and the same. "I really don't understand how she can live in a place like this," Pierre's friend says about Gisèle Du Grand; and the hero adds: "I don't know why, but I can't stand either her or this castle," unconsciously associating person and place as one entity.[11]

The director's refined cinephile culture brought him to draw from various sources throughout the film. The notion of a horror strictly related to technology recalls Fritz Lang's *Dr. Mabuse* films, and the scary Seignoret (the Swiss-born Paul Muller, one of the recurring faces in European horror films of the ensuing decades) is not simply a hybrid of Dracula's Renfield and the Frankenstein monster, as some critics have noted, but most of all a perverse contemporary variation on Cesare, the somnambulistic zombie of Robert Wiene's *Das Cabinet des Dr. Caligari* (1920), a testimony to Freda's love for German Expressionism.

> There was a trend in Germany that certainly influenced me more than any other: the vampire film series and Expressionism, *Nosferatu*, *Der Golem*, Dreyer's film [*Vampyr*], all the Fantastic motion pictures of that era. It's a common saying that movies leave a mark on children, but certainly they made a huge impression on me: I wasn't frightened, I liked them.[12]

There are also elements taken from U.S. horror and science fiction films of the 1930s and 1940s: the mystery subplot recalls *Mystery of the Wax Museum* (1933, Michael Curtiz), and the idea of a woman pursuing eternal youth draws from such classics as *She* (1935, Lansing G. Holden and Irving Pichel), although Freda was probably thinking of another famous movie history character, Queen Antinea in G. W. Pabst's *Die Herrin von Atlantis* (1932).

The most interesting choice on Freda's part, however, is the reference to Carl Theodor Dreyer's *Vampyr* (1932). The decrepit duchess Du Grand, who hides her octagenarian features behind a black veil, is modeled upon the disturbing old lady (Henriette Gerard) who is responsible for the vampirizations in Dreyer's masterpiece: a fact underlined by the name that the Duchess assumes in her juvenile incarnation after she has been injected with the rejuvenating serum—Gisèle, just like the young girl threatened by the old woman in *Vampyr*. Freda would use again the image of the veiled old lady in *L'orribile segreto del Dr. Hichcock*, where he also recreated one of *Vampyr*'s most celebrated shots, that of David Gray lying in his coffin, in the scene where Barbara Steele wakes up in a casket which has a small glass window at face level, just as in Dreyer's film.

All these influences notwithstanding, *I vampiri* is an astonishingly modern work for the time in which it was released. Besides all the aforementioned qualities, and in spite of the manipulation performed on its original plot, the film's sadistic core stands out, as an element that the director had already exploited in the past (*Beatrice Cenci* is a case in point) and would further develop in his following horror efforts.

That said, the film that came out in the theaters was quite different from Freda's original idea. Production started in November 1956, but for neither the first nor the last time in his career, the director had an argument with the producers—apparently because he couldn't keep up with such a tight schedule and asked in vain for an extension.[13] Freda walked off the set, and it was his director of photography Mario Bava who finished the film. As for the duration of the shooting, versions vary: Freda claimed he left on the twelfth day, other sources state he walked off on the tenth, whereas Bava reportedly said that he shot his part in two days.[14] Still, according to the papers kept at Rome's Archive of State, filming went on for a total of 20 days—that is, little less than three weeks.

Freda's abandon led to a substantial rewriting of the story—which likely explains the credit as co-scenarist and scriptwriter to the fictitious "Rijk Sijöstrom," as well as the many incongruencies that can be found in the version released in theaters. Originally, the director had envisioned the doctor and Julien Du Grand as *two* different characters: the former was a stereotypical mad doctor while Du Grand was a young man "guillotined for having killed and raped a little girl" (as written in the original synopsis kept at the Archive of State), brought back to life and re-assembled like a Frankenstein monster of sorts, to kidnap the young women that will serve for the doctor's rejuvenating practices. "My film started with the execution of a murderer played by Paul Muller," Freda explained. "He was guillotined at dawn by some men in black: the scene was quite shocking, and Bava's black-and-white cinematography underlined its horrific quality. You could see the head fall. After the execution, professor Du Grand ... purloined the body and the head. And after Frankenstein-like manipulations he gave new life to this dead body."[15]

The scene was cut, but a fragment survives in the trailer for the German release of the film, *Der Vampir von Notre Dame*: the camera cranes down from a high-angle long shot while Muller's character is taken to the guillotine, as an impassive crowd watches under their umbrellas—one figure elegantly posing as a silhouette in the foreground as the camera ends its descent. It is followed by an elliptical shot of the blade descending. It is a fascinating scene, which features several of Freda's trademark aesthetics, and recalls other similar moments in his career, such as Margaretha's funeral in *L'orribile segreto del Dr. Hichcock* and the "sack of Rome" in *Il magnifico avventuriero*.

Another scene which ended up quite different on film is the one in which Paul Muller's character is being questioned at the police station. In the theatrical version, the man suddenly falls unconscious to the floor, whereas originally his head would detach from the neck when the body hit the ground, as the reanimated manservant had run out of vital energy.[16] In fact, a close look at the scene reveals the Frankenstein-like sutures on Paul Muller's neck. Traces of the character of Julien Du Grand as imagined by Freda can also be found in the sequence where the duchess reaches the doctor's lab through the crypt: the close-up of the tomb has the inscription "Julien Du Grand, 1895–1957," implying that Du Grand was a man in his sixties, and was likely shot by Bava, whereas in the long shot the inscription "Julien Du Grand 1920–1956" can be glimpsed, hinting at a much younger Julien.[17] Another sequence that was either deleted or left unfilmed included the body of Ronald Fontaine (Angelo Galassi) being dissolved in a vat of acid, the same fate that the doctor's assistant had planned for Pierre's fiancée, Lorrette (Wandisa Guida). Such scenes display a reliance on blood and gore that was quite ahead of its time, and express a certain confidence in handling gruesome effects—a trait which would characterize most of Freda's subsequent horror and *gialli*, starting with *Caltiki il mostro immortale*. Definitely, in the director's original concept, horror would not "always occur offscreen."[18]

Bava's takeover pushed *I vampiri* toward a more conventional and tame crime territory compared to the grimmer, Grand-Guignol approach that Freda had envisaged—and which was a more likely reason for the director's disagreement with Donati and Carpentieri, who were considering as more commercially viable a product closer to the French *film noir*, with a hefty dose of mystery and detection. In fact, Italian critics labeled *I vampiri* as "a *noir* divertissement, Clouzot-style"[19] and a "crime film combined with terrifying macabre." This resulted in an emphasis on the young hero, Pierre Lantin, whereas the characters played by Paul Muller and Antoine Balpêtré became respectively the drug addict Joseph Seignoret (a character who is therefore understandably incongruent and rather unconvincing) and the new incarnation of Julien Du Grand. In the final dialogue between Lantin and the commissioner, the latter specifies that Seignoret was *believed* to be dead by the police, thus erasing any trace of Freda's original Frankenstein-like concept. In addition to that, Bava filmed new sequences according to the actors' availability on the set (one such was the first encounter between Pierre and Lorrette, in order to heighten the romantic subplot), shot additional close-ups that restored narrative coherence, and added the inserts of newspapers and rotary presses. He also filmed a totally new ending, which makes *I vampiri* end like a standard detective story, with the hero and the commissioner walking away from the Du Grand castle just like Humphrey Bogart and Claude Rains in *Casablanca* (1942, Michael Curtiz). Freda's original epilogue was far more dramatic: "[In the current version] They find the heroine locked inside a crypt, whereas I wanted her to be hanged. I did shoot that sequence. The young actress was suspended in the air and had to fall into some kind of abyss. She wasn't a real actress ... she was terrified at the idea of being suspended into the void ... and the poor thing screamed. I filmed her screaming. It was not the cry of an actress but a real scream of horror!"[20]

In spite of all this, *I vampiri* is a more personal work than it might seem at face value. It has been labeled as basically a *mélo* disguised as a horror story, and that is indeed true. The center of the film is Duchess Du Grand's obsession with youth and beauty, and with the son of the man whom she once had loved. Here, such typical Gothic motifs as the *doppelgänger* and the return of the past blend with Freda's own favorite themes. Fate causing humans to repeat their actions (and their mistakes as well), and cross each other's path again, for instance, was not only inherent in literary adaptations such as *I miserabili*, but would turn into one of Freda's leitmotifs in the horror genre, whether it be somebody's return to his own unspeakable obsessions (*L'orribile segreto del Dr. Hichcock*) or a man haunted by the memory of his late father and ultimately destined to become him in his mother's eyes (*Murder Obsession*).

Perhaps, what was not stressed enough is that the film's melodramatic texture goes beyond what is on the screen. Eight years after *Il cavaliere misterioso*, *I vampiri* marked the end of Freda's personal and working relationship with Gianna Maria Canale. At the time she starred in the movie, Canale was not even 30, yet the director had her play a character that recalls such mythical creatures as the silent film divas, and the embodiment of an idea of beauty that is about to fade. Duchess Du Grand is not unlike Gloria Swanson's in *Sunset Blvd.* (1950): a woman obsessed with aging, secluded from the outside world, in love with someone much younger than her, served and revered by a lover who is also her servant and succubus. All this conveys the sense of a fading idea of beauty that is about to be swept away by another female icon; no wonder Canale initially did not want to play the role, according to the director. If *Il cavaliere misterioso* had been Freda's first gift to Canale's beauty, and *Teodora* his shiniest tribute to the woman he loved, *I vampiri* was a bitter farewell letter.

The duchess' sudden aging on camera, extraordinarily achieved by means of colored make-up and filters, was Bava's idea ("Shooting in black-and-white, the makeup was invisible. But when Bava placed progressive filters before the camera, the wrinkles and the transformations on her face appeared ... she really looked as if she was visibly decomposing"[21]), possibly inspired by Fredric March's metamorphosis in Rouben Mamoulian's *Dr. Jekyll and Mr. Hyde* (1931)[22]; however, the concept was pure Freda. A memento that her beauty would not last forever, that she would ultimately become old and ugly and alone like her own octogenarian self in the film. Freda's prophecy became true: after her breakup with the director, Canale's star abruptly faded. According to some sources,[23] her early retirement from the scenes in 1964 came after a grim event that recalled the fate of Duchess Du Grand: a car accident left the actress temporarily disfigured by a facial paralysis. Such rumors are impossible to verify: however, in the mid–1960s Canale retired in the isle of Giannutri, and never appeared again in films or television, nor did she allow herself to be photographed. She died on February 13, 2009, at the age of 81, leaving the memory of a young, ageless beauty behind her.

Following the underwhelming performance of *Beatrice Cenci*, *I vampiri* was another disappointment at the box-office: grossing 126 million *lire*, it was a profitable but undistinguished result, and definitely not the success its makers hoped it to be. Another oft-quoted anecdote has the director explain why: "I remember I was at the film's opening in San Remo. Many people entered the theater lobby and stopped to look at the posters and read the names on them. When they saw mine, they exclaimed: 'My God, but this is an Italian movie!?' and left. Back then, people didn't think Italians were able to make horror films."[24] Freda would solve the matter on his next horror movie, by adopting an Anglo-Saxon pseudonym.

I vampiri had a more successful commercial life abroad, albeit at the cost of severe manipulations. It was released theatrically in France (as *Les Vampires*), Germany (as *Der Vampir von Notre Dame*) and the United States. The American version, distributed in 1960 by Jonathan Daniels and Victor Purcell's company RCIP (Releasing Corporation of Independent Producers) with the title *The Devil's Commandment*, and credited to "Richard Freda," played the bottom of double bills in very limited release.[25] It was reassembled by Ronald Honthauer (needless to say, without any assistance on the part of Freda: the "final revisions" are credited to J. V. Rhems), ran about 75 minutes and was heavily re-edited: about a third of the original footage was missing, replaced with haphazardly filmed inserts featuring scantily clad starlets. Another minor difference concerns Pierre's surname, which becomes La Salle in the U.S. dubbing.

More in detail, the American version starts with a completely new sequence, which would not have been out of place in some sexploitation roughie. Under a light lamp (which provides the background for the opening title) a man, seen from behind, is smoking a cigarette and watching a window in the upper floor of a building (very obviously an American one, given the presence of a fire escape). When a light is turned on, the man throws away his cigarette and disappears. Inside the apartment a record-player plays a stereotypical Parisian music, while an anonymous actress is sitting before a mirror in her bra and stockings. She slowly strips and steps into a bubble bath, offering a glimpse of her naked breasts. A black-gloved intruder comes in—a shot of his feet stepping by the woman's slippers is supposed to heighten the suspense—and abducts her, the sequence ending with a POV shot of the woman as the figure (whose eyes are seen in an extreme close-up) approaches her with prowling hands armed with a chloroform-imbibed handkerchief, filling the screen. Cut to: *two* silhouettes dropping the body off a bridge at night. Then we finally move to Freda's original opening near the Aniene River, Pierre's dialogue scene in the newspaper, and Paul Muller attacking the ballerina in the empty theater, which is therefore placed as the second "vampire abduction" in the new cut.

The second stalk-and-abduct insert comes after about 27 minutes, and precedes Lorrette's kidnapping. A woman is being tailed in the streets by a sinister figure: shot in broad daylight in some New York alley with a hand-held camera, the scene couldn't be more distant from Freda and Bava's style. The frightened lady enters a bistro and we are subjected to a would-be-funny humorous interlude, as she ignores the maître d's gastronomic recommendations ("I would suggest the *poulet-au-vin*—it is magnificent, made of the finest chicken. I've had it for supper myself...") and asks for a double scotch instead ("Scotch? We're famous in Paris for our food!" he protests), and to a so-so acrobatic dance number, courtesy of Ronny and Joy Holiday. The girl goes to a back room to make a phone call, and there she is attacked and strangled: the assailant then drains her blood via a syringe.

The third insert comes near the ending, when Lorrette is taken away in the crypt by Du Grand's assistant (played by Angelo Galassi), while the police is searching the castle. The U.S. version adds an insert featuring veteran character actor Al Lewis (better known for his role as "Grandpa" in the CBS series *The Munsters*), replacing Galassi and intent on ripping off the blouse of another anonymous lookalike standing in for Wandisa Guida. Besides its sleazy content, the scene looks absurdly out of place in its gratuitousness.

On top of that, RCIP added a number of brief shots that in the distributors' intentions were to heighten the film's shock value and adapt it to drive-in consumption: for instance, Lorrette's discovery of the skeletons in the secret passage is diluted with close-ups of a rat and a skull, whereas Canale's final transformation features a close-up of her claw-like hands, and ends on a close-up of the dead duchess' mummified, skeleton-like face. The latter, according to Tim Lucas, was possibly a remnant from the original footage, cut by Italian censors, but in fact *I vampiri* was given a V.M.16 rating without any cut, so it is likely that the trimming was performed by the producers (similarly to what happened with the prologue) before submitting the movie to the censors.[26]

On the other hand, no fewer than eight scenes were cut from the original edit. In detail: Inspector Chantal and Pierre visit Seignoret's apartment, where they find another tenant instead (it will later turn out that they entered the wrong building); Pierre checks with Lorrette's parents after his girlfriend has not shown up from school; the inspector is informed by one of Lorrette's schoolmates that she was asked to mail a letter from a blind man, interrogates him and finds out that the girl took the letter to an empty house; Pierre is reproached by his newspaper editor for his "silly vampire stories"; Pierre leaves Gisèle's party earlier, telling his friend Ronald that he can pursue her; the next morning, Gisèle asks Pierre to accompany her to an antique shop where she buys a painting: the dealer tells her that "To me, the Duchess and you, Mademoiselle, are the same person," thus providing yet another hint to the solution; Pierre interrogates the antique dealer; Pierre meets Inspector Chantal and persuades him to search Castle Du Grand.

A nudie version was rumored to have circulated, under the title *Lust of the Vampire*, but to this day it has not surfaced.[27]

Agguato a Tangeri

After *I vampiri*, Freda moved on to another story set in the present, this time an out-and-out crime film. Co-financed by Gino Cervi's son Antonio, *Agguato a Tangeri* was an unpretentious commercial Italian-Spanish co-production, characterized by an overtly moralistic view on drug addiction, no doubt because of the Catholic Opus Dei owning the Spanish production company that co-financed it.

Freda dismissed the movie as totally devoid of any interest, and complained at length about the troubled shooting, blaming the Italian producer for that. When he first arrived in Tangiers for location scouting with the production supervisor—and later a filmmaker on his own with such titles as *Vulcano figlio di Giove* (a.k.a. *Vulcan Son of Jupiter*, 1962)—Domenico "Emimmo" Salvi, later joined by his regular d.o.p. Gábor Pogány, the director found out that the agency that was supposed to pay for their accommodation did not even want to hear about the film. Freda and Salvi—who had checked in at one of the city's best hotels—were left clueless.

> At 5 p.m., every day, in the lobby, a little show took place which had the hotel's customers gathering around us. In the phone booth, which was located precisely in the hall, Salvi called the producer in Rome, and presented him "our" dramatic situation. But on the other end of the line, with an admirable poker face, the producer replied point by point to Salvi's grievances, with the most absurd reassurances, which would then prove groundless, while the latter's voice was reaching very high tones. The phone calls ended with Salvi, his face congested and furious for such an effrontery, yelling: "What the fuck are you saying … we don't even have a penny here!" to which the other replied with a chilling, "Don't worry … don't worry…."[28]

With no cash, cameras or film, Freda and his acolytes eventually left Tangiers for Madrid. Once in Spain things got even worse, and Salvi was forced to flee the hotel overnight, since he had no money left to pay the bill. After about a month stalling, the movie was seemingly about to be cancelled, as Edmund Purdom and Généviève Page were under contract for only forty-five days. The Spanish co-producer asked Freda if he could shoot the whole movie in less than eighteen days.

> They were certain of a negative answer. "Not even a single set has been built yet," they said, and I replied, "What's the use for a set?" … I started shooting in the empty studio, which I used as a set, without any decoration, for a scene that was supposed to take place at a dock's warehouse. The film was shot in fifteen days, much to Purdom's anger since he was expecting who-knows-how-many dollars as compensation, whereas on the sixteenth day the movie was wrapped.[29]

Given the circumstances under which *Agguato a Tangeri* was made, it comes as no surprise that Freda's direction is adequate but rather detached and cold, with lots of medium shots designed for the scope format and few close-ups. To the director's credit, the *film noir* mood is well-rendered, with striking night scenes—such as the opening bit, where a man is murdered in a lonely street by a trio of killers disguised as road workers—underlined by Pogány's elegant black-and-white and Lelio Luttazzi's jazzy score. But besides the visuals there is little to enliven the film. Despite the presence of four screenwriters (including Alessandro Continenza, with whom Freda collaborated on *La vendetta di Aquila Nera* and later on *L'iguana dalla lingua di fuoco*),[30] the script is badly concocted, with static expository scenes, an uninteresting mystery plot and slapdash action scenes, including a routine car chase.[31] What is more, the drug-related theme is simplistic and laughably handled. For instance, in the Italian version Purdom's character mentions that he pretended to be "intoxicated" instead of a "drug addict," an euphemism most likely designed not to displease the Italian censors, since drug use was one of the riskiest subjects at that time.

Freda and his co-scriptwriters were possibly taking inspiration from Orson Welles' *Mr. Arkadin* (1955) for the theme of a wealthy elderly man (the prosperous ichthyologist Henry Bovelasco, played by Gino Cervi) whose innocent daughter does not know about his shady past; on the other hand, the love-hate triangle between Bovelasco, his young adoptive daughter Mary (Page) and the undercover hero John Milwood (Purdom) draws also from Freda's own filmography—namely, *Aquila nera* as well as *Beatrice Cenci*. Like Francesco Cenci, Bovelasco seems morbidly jealous of Mary, his fatherly overprotectiveness hiding subtler and darker implications.

For the first time in his career, the director's indifference toward the protagonist is patent: even though he plays undercover in order to get close to his target like Casanova did in *Il cavaliere misterioso*, posing as a ruthless and despicable fortune-hunter in front of the woman he loves, and even employing a little bit of pre–James Bond gadgetry, Interpol agent John Milwood is a thoroughly bland, listlessly conceived hero—and Purdom's deadpan acting does not help. Page does not fare much better as the heroine: like her male partner, she is hardly committed to the role. Once again Gino Cervi delivers the most impressive performance of the lot as the affable and apparently harmless Bovelasco: white haired, visibly aged and overweight, the 56-year-old thesp looks like the distant shadow of the leading hero in *Don Cesare di Bazan* and *I miserabili*, but is still a superb actor. *Agguato a Tangeri* would be his fifth and final film with Freda, not counting the director's uncredited work on *Nel segno di Roma*, the following year. Since Bovelasco is an ichthyologist, Freda asked his art director to build a huge aquarium, nine feet tall, that would be put right in the middle of Bovelasco's lounge, giving the indoor scenes a much-needed visual flair. The aquarium broke down one hour before shooting started, with water flowing all over the set. Needless to say, it was not rebuilt.[32]

The picture marked the debut of Spanish film director Jorge Grau, whose recollections shed further light on the shooting, as well as on Freda's lack of commitment to the whole project, since at the time, having split with Gianna Maria Canale, he had a new mistress in Spain.

> I was hired as a second assistant director because I spoke fluent Italian, but really my job came down to chatting with the director. I knew almost nothing about cinema, and he was like a friend with whom we chatted about everyday topics. The shooting was short, just three weeks, and I remember that one day the crew had to split into two—half with destination Tangiers, led by the first assistant director, and the other half, including Freda and me, in Malaga. On the last day of shooting, Freda received a call from his lover in Madrid, who threatened to break their relationship if he did not join her at once in the capital. And so, he left me to take care of the shooting: luckily there were only several missing shots left to film: a car arriving at the port of Malaga, a foot pressing the accelerator....[33]

Grau's marginal contribution is certainly not enough to credit him as co-director as some sources (like the IMDb) do.

Grau recounted the circumstances that led to his directing debut, the short film *El don del mar* (The Gift of the Sea, 1957), which originally Freda was to co-direct. His words seem to confirm that, at the time of the making of *Agguato a Tangeri*, the director and Gianna Maria Canale had already parted ways.

> Suddenly a production assistant showed up looking for Freda, and took him to Barbate [a Spanish town on the Andalusian coast], since he had pledged to make a documentary on tuna fishing. In short, I had to go to Barbate as well to do his job and I had to write a short treatment to be submitted to the board of censors. When Freda came back, he did not even want to see my script, because he said that he did not need any to shoot that documentary. I got rather angry, and claimed my wages with the intention to leave, but the production assistant convinced me to agree to co-direct the documentary…. To make matters worse Freda brought with him his lover, who was just 24, whereas Freda was 50 [actually 48] and I was 25. So she and I got along quite well, which aroused Freda's jealousy: from that moment on he was a pain in the ass all the time, contradicting whenever I suggested something and playing tricks on me; for example, he left me in Córdoba without warning that he was leaving. Eventually the production assistant got tired and decided that I would conclude and sign the film.[34]

Agguato a Tangeri was given a distribution visa in Italy after a few cuts concerning the torture scene of the character played by Alfredo Molino Rojo, which were judged excessively gruesome and cruel: the victim is savagely beaten up and has his chest branded with a hot electric stove. It is an odd over-the-top moment for such a bland effort, which nevertheless predates the director's graphic approach to violence in his later work. The film was also distributed in the U.S. in 1960 by Twentieth Century–Fox, in a dubbed version titled *Trapped in Tangiers* and shortened to 77 minutes for double-feature consumption which was mercilessly panned by *Variety*: the reviewer commented that it would severely damage any double bill it was on, as "these spy-story cliches have, of course, been pursued many times in the past, but rarely with such lack of insight, grace and cinematic know-how."[35] A photonovel version was also published in the magazine *Super Star—Cineromanzo gigante* (#56, May 1959).

Agi Murad—Il diavolo bianco

It was a set of different passions that prompted Freda to return to his favorite genre, the adventure film. His love for Russian literature and the likes of Pushkin and Tolstoy; his childhood memories of the great Russian silent actor Ivan Mosjoukine, whom he had admired on the big screen as Michael Strogoff as well as in other adventure epics; and his predilection for full-fledged heroes, who were experiencing a new renaissance thanks to the *peplum* genre. It was because of the sword-and-sandal fever that the director could mount his project, starring the genre's hero par excellence, Steve Reeves.

After the success of his *Hercules* films, the bodybuilder-turned-actor was trying to re-establish his screen persona, and perhaps show that he was not only a musclebound body with a talking head attached to it. As Freda explained,

> Reeves, who did not decide anything but deferred all decisions to his agent (and future wife), had been persuaded that he had to move away from his Hercules character, given the risk of being forever trapped in the role. Which of course duly happened: if they took away from him the chance to show off his perfect body, he was interchangeable with many actors.[36]

However, the role of Hadji Murad looked like the perfect chance to avoid repetition while remaining in the realm of the adventure genre. "To ride on horseback in the steppes, to him it was almost a new career," the director observed.[37]

Leo Tolstoy had first heard of the legendary Hadji Murad while serving in the Caucasus. The great novelist was fascinated by the inner contradiction of a rebel who forges an alliance with the enemy to save his family, and the story he concocted featured several of his favorite themes, such as determinism (like in *War and Peace*) and the struggle between West and East. The result was a novelette somehow similar in tone to Pushkin's *The Captain's Daughter*—a fact that Freda was no doubt aware of, as Pushkin's novel was one of his favorites—and very well researched, since Tolstoy deliberately opted for a realist approach, based on actual events and characters. Written between 1896 and 1904, *Hadji Murad* was published posthumously in 1912.

The connection with Tolstoy's work was nominal, though: the script took the name Hadji Murad (Italianized in the title as "Agi Murad"), the historical rebellion of the Cossacks and little else from the Russian writer's work, while the rest was purely the fruit of the writers' imagination. In some ways *Agi Murad—Il diavolo bianco* predated an ongoing trend in Freda's work of the 1960s, the attempt to rely on previous models which had their roots in Italian cinema of the 1940s, just like in the previous decades he had done with silent movies, in a period where Italian genres were radically changing due to a number of key factors. For one thing, it was actually a remake of sorts, as a previous, loose version of Tolstoy's novelette (Nunzio Malasomma's *Il diavolo bianco*, starring Rossano Brazzi) dated from 1947.

On top of that, the director drew from his own adventure films of the past years, namely *Aquila nera* and its sequel *La vendetta di Aquila Nera*. Several scenes, such as Hadji Murad's assault to the stagecoach and his first encounter with princess Maria, are virtually identical to the 1946 film, whereas the subplot about the kidnapping of Hadji's little son, as well as the climactic sequence in which the hero escapes from jail, mounts a white horse, rides through a ballroom and out of the window (but not before gallantly handing a rose to Maria), are taken straight from the 1951 film. Similarly, Freda not only staged a typical love triangle, having Hadji Murad torn between the plebeian Sultanet and the aristocrat Maria—a blatantly old-fashioned element which nevertheless could be found in many *pepla*—but he also doubled the villains as in his previous adventure films, with a more blatant class gap: the noble prince Sergei on the one hand, and the despicable Cossack traitor Ahmed Khan on the other. It is as if, to quote Stefano Della Casa, "Freda, recalcitrant to the idea of pigeonholing himself inside a genre invented by others, answered to it by bundling materials," with the result being "a film built on contrasts, on the contamination of environments and situations."[38]

Another example of the director's attachment to an old-style conception of the adventure film can be seen in his reliance on extended banquet and dance scenes, the likes of which were becoming more and more erotic-tinted in the contemporaneous sword-and-sandal pictures. Freda, on the other hand, opted for the colorful, the pictorial, the choreographic, going as far as hiring the Yugoslavian National Theater for the dance numbers. Even though he relied on Mario Bava's beautiful color cinematography, the results are rather academic and inert, and probably looked dated to contemporary audiences as well. What Freda could provide, and did it, was his technical skill in the mass scenes, such as the Cossack's charge toward the fort amid the plan, filmed laterally with the camera placed on a car driving at full speed—yet another climax reminiscent of the cavalry rescue in John Ford's *Stagecoach*.

Times were changing, indeed, and the audiences started demanding more sex, something to which Freda would oblige in his later years. But in *Agi Murad—Il diavolo bianco* the concessions to eroticism are minimal: the director allows the viewers only the sight of Scilla Gabel in a semi-transparent gown—even less than he used to show in his 1950s sword-and-sandal films. Similarly, the attempts at Grand Guignol are softened by the use of ellipsis: a decapitation takes place while a horse conveniently steps in the shot in close-up, covering the sight of the unfortunate victim. Interestingly, according to Della Casa, the film's most violent scene—the opening assault to a Cossack village, in which a Russian soldier shoots a child in the back, harmless villagers are hanged, women are raped and the huts are set on fire—was actually shot by the second unit director Leopoldo Savona, to cut costs.

In one of the director's most exemplary bouts of cynicism, the opening massacre scene dissolves into an assembly of generals, shot from above, coldly discussing military operation over a map inside a luxurious room. "This would be our tactic," a General states. To them, it is implied, the previous bloodshed was simply regarded as yet another military operation. The still-unseen hero is immediately put against a coldly observed, inherently despised (notice the high angle long shot, which reduces the generals to insignificant figures) élite—a view in line with the director's disenchanted opinion on human history and organized politics. The Russians, however, have a caricatural side to them: the Tsar is seen awkwardly making a pass at the beautiful wife of one of his generals, whereas Prince Vorontzov—sketched like a Nazi officer in a war film, complete with monocle and military uniform—is introduced via a menacing low-angle shot as he is severely giving an order to someone, only for us to discover that (in one of the few bits lifted off the novel) such an order is aimed at the general's puppy dog. Too bad these touches are lost as the film goes along: Ahmed Khan is a much more stereotyped villain than Vorontzov.

The best thing about *Agi Murad—Il diavolo bianco* is Bava's cinematography. As Della Casa notes, it is a nocturnal film, whereas the *peplum* genre is basically sunny.[39] Bava lights the studio-shot night exteriors in an openly unrealistic way, giving them the same outlandish look—either blue-tinted for the hero's visit to Sultanet or with a green-red dominance in the Cossack camp scenes—as his subsequent color Gothic and *peplum* efforts. Similarly, the brief interlude between Hadji and his beloved Sultanet in the forest, with leaves falling all around them and blades of sunlight penetrating through the thick vegetation, has an almost magical fairytale-like feel: its abrupt interruption, as the hero is surrounded by the spears of armed soldiers, recreates a similar moment in *Teodora*. The indoor scenes—such as the Princess' visit to the wounded Hadji, tied to the bed, or Ahmed Khan's subsequent, and specular, visit to Sultanet—feature Bava's exquisite use of blue-filtered spots to simulate moonlight. Bava's skills as a director of photography are at their best in the brief, atmospheric scene in the prison, where the Russian prisoners are awaiting for their destiny, on the extreme right of the frame, lighted only by a tiny spot coming from the cell's door, and surrounded by utter darkness. It is a striking pictorial image, not unworthy of Goya, as well as an example of Freda's accomplished use of the scope format.

Shooting took place in Yugoslavia, in December 1958, with Tito's soldiers acting as extras and the renowned fencer Enzo Musumeci Greco—who had worked among others with Burt Lancaster on *The Crimson Pirate* (1952) and Errol Flynn on *Crossed Swords* (1954)—as master of arms. Among the local financers there was also a young Croatian who would become a renowned producer on his own: Branko Lustig.[40] The indoor scenes were then shot in Rome. Freda claimed to have wrapped up the picture in eighteen days,[41] and found Reeves to be one of the most disciplined troupers he ever worked with. "He was not an actor, that's for sure, but he was cooperative. I made him work a lot, and exhausted him: falls, horse rides, running, physical feats…. After filming, Reeves confided me that he had never worked so hard as in my film."[42]

Still, despite Reeves' imposing physical shape, he needed a stunt double (Sergio Ciani, later known as Alan Steel, who had already performed this role in *Ercole e la regina di Lidia*) for some of his action scenes, including Murad's final duel with Ahmed Khan. What is more, to please the distributor, who demanded that the actor's muscles be on display so as to sell the film to the *peplum* audience, Freda had to stage a gratuitous barechested fight scene between Hadji and a fellow cossack. Even though on one occasion he observed that the character of Hadji Murad should have been played by someone like Kirk Douglas, "an individual whose intelligence we feel exceeds his strength,"[43] he and his lead actor got along surprisingly well: "Freda was a very good director," Reeves observed. "He explained every scene perfectly, like he was a friend instead of a director."[44]

So high was his opinion of him, that several years later the American actor got in touch with Freda for a project that never saw the light.

> Steve Reeves had Western movie ideals: a farm, animals…. I think he lives like this nowadays…. A few years before Leone's film [*Per un pugno di dollari*] we concocted a Western centered on Steve. He

brought me a novel, the story of a veterinarian who did justice on his own, with his muscles only. It all came to nothing eventually. The Wild West was his origin and his aspiration. He was really like that."[45]

When Reeves managed to fulfill his dream, producing and starring in the Western *Vivo per la tua morte* (a.k.a. *A Long Ride from Hell*, 1968), he reportedly invited Freda to shoot it, but the director's asking price was too high: the movie was directed by Camillo Bazzoni, and marked the disastrous end of Reeves' career.

Alongside Reeves, and following one of the basic rules in the cinema, Freda cast a brunette (singer Georgia Moll,[46] with whom he worked again on 1961's *Caccia all'uomo*), and a blonde (Scilla Gabel) as the love interests. Born in 1938, Gabel had been Sophia Loren's double in Jean Negulesco's *Boy on a Dolphin* and Henry Hathaway's *Legend of the Lost* (both 1957), and became known to the general public after her groundbreaking role in *Capitan Fracassa* (1958). She went on to become a popular face in Italian cinema—starring in *Il mulino delle donne di pietra* (a.k.a. *Mill of the Stone Women*, 1960) and appearing in a number of sword-and-sandal films, including *Sodom and Gomorrah* (1962)—and television; she played Helen of Troy in *Odissea* (1968). On the other hand, the German-born Gérard Herter (1920–2007) was not a professional actor, but Freda's hallway neighbor: his innate aristocratic air impressed the director so much that he asked him to play a role in the movie. It was the beginning of a marginal film career: Herter played the despicable Austrian officer in *La grande guerra* and appeared in a number of genre films, including Freda's own *Caltiki*. His last role was in Luchino Visconti's *Ludwig* (1973).

Agi Murad—Il diavolo bianco was released in Italy by Galatea Films, the company that would produce Freda's next film, *Caltiki il mostro immortale*: Galatea had in fact granted 30 million lire as a guaranteed minimum for the foreign sales, which proved to be fruitful. The film came out to theaters in the United States in 1961, released by Warner Bros, as *The White Warrior* (and with the director credited as "Richard Freda"), in a 86-minute-long dubbed version[47] which softened the (already tame) violence: the opening village raid was trimmed, as were bits in the torture chamber and the decapitation of one of Hadji's men; in addition to that, a narrating voice was added, together with inserts of letters and maps. It played at the top of double bills, to satisfying commercial performance ($768,000 in domestic rentals) but unfavorable reviews. A predictably condescending critic dismissed it as "a bit on the silly side," ironically pointing out the "plenty of galloping up and down ... along with the customary amount of last-minute rescues, tortures and battles to the death," including "one of the most savage duels of the year," although praising Bava's "extravagantly-colored" cinematography. Also noteworthy was the patronizing take on Reeves' stardom in Italy:

> Not much of Tolstoy's novel can be recognized, perhaps, but there's much to see of Reeves who exhibits his rippling muscles whenever there is opportunity. Two lovely ladies, Georgia Moll and Scilla Gabel, go into near-swoons whenever he appears.... The dialogue had been dubbed somewhat ineptly but it isn't necessary to listen too much. The story is of less importance than is Reeves, who is said to be one of the heroes of the younger generation in Rome and other Italian cities, and whose physique is considered sufficiently magnificent to overwhelm mere plot.[48]

Another writer started his review by bluntly claiming that Tolstoy was turning over in his grave.[49]

Interestingly, *Agi Murad—Il diavolo bianco* was one of the works that marked Freda's critical rediscovery in Italy. In 1974, film historian Marco Giusti wrote an enthusiastic essay on it, which was published on the fanzine *Il falcone maltese* (The Maltese Falcon), the training camp for some of the most prestigious critics of the following decades such as Enrico Ghezzi and Teo Mora—the latter being another fervent admirer of Freda's work, which he praised in his pioneering *Storia del cinema dell'orrore*, a landmark work in Italian film criticism. After underlining the film's hodgepodge of almost incoherent narratives, Giusti remarked:

> What is left is the hallucinatory surprise of indoor scenes always shot at night and exteriors always shot at daytime, so that when Steve Reeves leaves the colonel's palace it is suddenly day, he arrives in his hometown for the duel (indoors) at night and Agmed Kan [*sic*] falls from the walls of this city under the light of day. All this is of little importance in the face of the beauty of the scenes, the pictorially rich reconstruction of the sets, the surprising narrative structure which amalgamates psychological dramatic situations (in the same style as *Lo spettro*), with adventurous or even comical ones.[50]

Caltiki il mostro immortale

For his second Fantastic-themed film, Freda hid for the first time under an English pseudonym which he would use again on several occasions: Robert Hampton (misspelled "Hamton" in the credits). It was an inevitable move on his part after the disappointing financial results of *I vampiri*, and the realization that Italian audiences were not yet used to the notion of horror movies being produced in their own country.

In the two years following *I vampiri*, though, many things had changed: the release of Terence Fisher's *Horror of Dracula* (1958) unleashed an appetite for the horror genre which was unthinkable just a few years earlier, resulting in the appearance of such paperback horror series as *KKK. I Classici dell'Orrore* (June 1959) and *I Racconti di Dracula* (December 1959), which in turn paved the way for the first bout of Italian vampire films released the following year—not forgetting Steno's amiable spoof *Tempi duri per i vampiri* (a.k.a. *Uncle Was a Vampire*), co-starring Christopher Lee, released in October 1959. Audiences were thirsty for stories about bloodsuckers and other assorted creatures. Still, for the umpteenth time in his career, Freda moved on to almost uncharted territory: science fiction.

1952 had marked the birth of the first Italian science fiction magazines such as *Scienza fantastica* and *Urania* (the latter still published to this day), and in 1957, with the launch of the "Sputnik 1" satellite, a second wave of mags (*Galassia, Cosmo, Galaxy*) turned up in newsstands: it was the beginning of the Italian Golden Age of science fiction. Young novelists and scriptwriters cut their teeth on sci-fi novels and short stories, published under Anglo-Saxon pseudonyms, and in 1959 the prestigious publishing house Einaudi released the short story anthology *Le meraviglie del possibile* (The Wonders of the Possible) edited by Carlo Fruttero and Franco Lucentini, which included works by H. G. Wells, A. E. Van Vogt, Ray Bradbury, Fredric Brown, Philip K. Dick, Robert Sheckley and others, including Fruttero himself, masquerading as Charles F. Obstbaum. *Le meraviglie del possibile* was a tremendous, unexpected success and paved the way for similar anthologies, such as the Gothic-related *Storie di fantasmi* (Ghost Stories), edited in 1960 by Fruttero and Lucentini, and featuring the original short story (*Dalle tre alle tre e mezzo*, signed "P. Kettridge"—actually Franco Lucentini) that inspired the episode *The Drop of Water* in Mario Bava's *I tre volti della paura* (a.k.a. *Black Sabbath*, a.k.a. *The Three Faces of Fear*, 1963).

Still, by the late 1950s, science fiction was kind of a novelty for Italian cinema. In the previous decades there had been a very small number of films only vaguely related to the topic, such as Sergio Corbucci's comedy *Baracca e burattini*, made in 1954. Then, in 1958, two films directly connected to the genre were released: Steno's *Totò nella luna* (Totò in the Moon), a parody starring Totò which paid homage to such works as *Invasion of the Body Snatchers* (1956, Don Siegel), and *La morte viene dallo spazio* (a.k.a. *The Day the Sky Exploded*, 1958, Paolo Heusch, co-produced by the then-declining Lux Film), Italy's first attempt at an out-and-out science fiction flick. The latter, however, consisted for a large part of newsreels and stock footage, actually assembled by the director of photography Mario Bava around a threadbare plot.

Compared to Heusch's film, *Caltiki* displayed a very different approach to the subject. For one thing, whereas *La morte viene dallo spazio* was influenced by early 1950s U.S. space operas, a much more specific model could be detected for Freda's work: Hammer Films' horror-tinged *The Quatermass Xperiment* (1955, Val Guest). For one thing, the character of Max (Gérard Herter, in his second Freda film), who is infected by a deadly blob, goes crazy and escapes from the hospital, is traced off the astronaut played by Richard Wordsworth in Val Guest's film, released in Italy to good success in June 1956 as *L'astronave atomica del Dr. Quatermass* (The Atomic Spaceship of Dr. Quatermass): interestingly, its sequel *Quatermass 2 / Enemy From Space* was distributed in June 1957, a couple of months after *I vampiri*, with the title *I vampiri dello spazio* (Space Vampires)—a sign that times were almost ready for a revival of the horror genre.

On the other hand, the concept of Caltiki as a shapeless, ever-growing unicellular creature was more akin to the titular organism of the U.S. science fiction film *The Blob* (1958, Irvin S. Yeaworth, Jr.); on top of that, whereas *La morte viene dallo spazio* was essentially a camera piece of sorts, not unlike those stagey period dramas made around the same time as *Don Cesare di Bazan*, Freda's film was all action from start to finish, with very little scientific mumbo-jumbo, and relied heavily on special effects—a field that was taking its first steps after the rise of the new wave of *peplum*, as expert sculptors, painters and technicians were developing their skills in a different trajectory. Given that, and the story's reliance on a suggestive, horrific mood, the director's scarce feeling for science fiction is evident.

Caltiki was produced by Nello Santi for Galatea Film: the company was willing to explore new paths after the success of *Le fatiche di Ercole*, and as such *Caltiki* was conceived for the foreign markets. Although it was neither mentioned in the credits nor in the ministerial papers, European sources list the participation of the French company Climax Film. It was an average budget picture, with no big stars: the lead, the Canadian-born John Merivale (seen in Roy Ward Baker's *A Night to Remember*, 1958, and later in John Huston's *The List of Adrian Messenger*, 1963, among others) was certainly not a box-office name, whereas the debuting Didi Perego would gain notoriety only the following year, after her role in Franco Rossi's *Morte di un amico* (1959, released several months after *Caltiki*) and Gillo Pontecorvo's *Kapò* (1960), which won her a Silver Ribbon Award. Similarly, Daniela Rocca—Santi's mistress at the time—was only starting her way to popularity, appearing in a series of *peplum* flicks and, most importantly, in Pietro Germi's *Divorzio all'italiana*.

When asked about *Caltiki*, Freda pointed out that he did not really consider the film to be his own, and not just because he did not care about science fiction. In a 1971 interview with Luigi Cozzi, the director claimed that he took on the project simply because he wanted to push Bava toward directing, as he was sick and tired of seeing his friend being continually exploited by other, untalented filmmakers, for whom the Sanremese director of photography did uncredited directing work.

> The movie was born out of sheer chance, just to help Bava: you see, during that period Mario was the director of photography in my films as well as in Pietro Francisci's. It had been him who led Francisci to success, because the latter used to show up on the set, sit down and fall asleep, while Bava set up the shots, created the special effects, directed the actors ... in short, it was he who actually made the film. And there was nothing wrong in that, but I came to know that, behind Bava's back, Francisci was saying horrible things about him, and humiliated him. So, as a friend, I forced Bava to part ways with Francisci: and he would do that, but he had to get by—his dog was sick, the taxes were impending, his wife was pregnant ... in short, he had to work for a living. So we met at his father's house and laid out a film: *Caltiki*. Then I proposed it to a producer who accepted it. I left it when there were just two days of shooting left. I did shoot it, yes, but it's Bava's type of film. I don't enclose it in my body of work. The only thing I remember with pleasure about it are the statues that decorated the sets: I sculpted them myself.[51]

On the other hand, in an Italian language book on Freda published in 2004, Cozzi returned to the matter, giving yet another perspective to it.

> Nowadays, sometimes I happen to read ... that Riccardo Freda is not the real director of *Caltiki il mostro immortale*, since that film would have been directed by Mario Bava. In fact, over thirty years ago it was I who first hinted at this story, and many have reprised my words, misinterpreting them. Whereas the truth is only one: the director of *Caltiki il mostro immortale* is Riccardo Freda, full stop. Mario Bava did take care of the cinematography, the special effects and directed the scenes with the miniatures (that is, mostly the tanks...), and in addition to that he filmed some shots of soldiers with flame throwers. That's all, and of course it cannot be enough to say that Bava directed that movie.[52]

Cozzi adds that, when speaking with Freda on other occasions, the director repeatedly stressed that he was not interested in the script, and shot the film as a mere working commitment, without really putting anything of his own into it—hence, the use of the pseudonym. What is more, Cozzi reports Bava's alleged words during a conversation they had about the film, around the same time:

> I did not direct *Caltiki*. The director of that movie is Freda. Only, at a certain point, after principal shooting ended, Freda started editing the picture and then he had a big argument with the producer, I think for a matter of money. Then Freda walked out, slamming the door, and did not take care of the movie any longer. At that point, since there were some things left to be filmed—some special effects, the scenes of the soldiers with the flame throwers for the ending, the miniatures of the house and the tanks ... well, I shot those myself, yes, on my own. But however, we already agreed with Freda that I would take care of that stuff myself, it was part of my job as cameraman as well as second unit director. But that does not mean I was the director of *Caltiki*: that is a Riccardo Freda film.[53]

If we take Cozzi's recollections for granted, trying to pick up similarities between *Caltiki* and Bava's work might be a fascinating but useless exercise. On other occasions, however, Freda himself offered sensibly different recollections. He told Éric Poindron: "After a week I told the whole world to go *ad patres* [i.e., to hell]. I collaborated on the scenario and the decorations, that's all,"[54] thus implying that Bava's involvement was much bigger. According to Bava's biographer Tim Lucas, after Freda's walk-off "there remained two or three weeks of filming devoted entirely to special effects, which in this case amounted to over 100 individual effects shots for the 76-minute production."[55]

This version is corroborated by scriptwriter Massimo De Rita, who at that time was working for Galatea as unit manager. De Rita, who spent quite some time on the film's set, claimed that at 90 percent Bava was also the director of *Caltiki*, Freda was away, he didn't know anything about what Bava was contriving. It was Bava who told the actors what to do, it was he who shot all the connecting shots with the monster; and since the movie *was* the monster, Bava shot over 50 percent of the scenes featuring actors; he shot all the death scenes: he knew how he would put together the special effects and the acting bits.[56]

In an interview with Italian film historian Simone Venturini, De Rita even speaks of *Caltiki* as Bava's

first film ... it was lots of fun, we kept shooting special effects for one month, with tripe, a disgusting thing, we had to replace it every six hours, every morning we had a supplier delivering fresh tripe, never in Rome has been consumed so much tripe ... and then the miniatures, the special effects. And so we convinced Santi to entrust him with more dignified films, such as *La maschera del demonio*.[57]

Bava's changed role during shooting is further proved by the ministerial papers: the final balance assigns a lesser sum to Freda than initially budgeted (5 million *lire* instead of 6) whereas Bava was ultimately paid circa 6.250 million *lire* instead of 3 million. Similarly, said papers make clear Bava's role in the conception of the story, as he is credited as co-scenarist while Freda appears as co-scriptwriter together with Filippo Sanjust, whose name is the only one that appears in the credits.

Undoubtedly, the scenes involving special effects bear Bava's mark all over the place. The impressive credit sequence features an ingenious mixture of glass mattes depicting a Mayan landscape, and a striking use of depth-of-field; moreover, the depiction of an erupting volcano, accomplished through a "water tank" effect, is much more spectacular and suggestive then the one seen in the final sequence of *Gli ultimi giorni di Pompei* (a.k.a. *The Last Days of Pompeii*, 1959, Mario Bonnard), to which Bava only marginally contributed. Then, the moment when the last survivor of the expedition, Nieto, appears behind a mound of rocks at the film's beginning is a striking anticipation of Javutich's resurrection in *La maschera del demonio* (interestingly, both roles are played by the same actor, Arturo Dominici), whereas the reliance on gruesome details predates both directors' future works, and displays their confidence in the use of gore. During the monster's first attack, for instance, an expedition member named Bob (Daniele Vargas) is turned into a skeleton, and soon after we are treated to the gruesome sight of Max's arm being reduced to little more than bare bones, with tendons exposed. As in *I vampiri*, the intention was clearly to come up with a much gorier product than the foreign competitors of the period.

Besides his duties as d.o.p., Bava also took care of the special effects: a now-legendary anecdote has that he fabricated the monster by using beef tripe bought from a nearby abattoir, which was maneuvered from beneath by a crew member. Even though there was more than just butcher's tripe used in the film,[58] it was one of the earliest example of homemade gore effects to be found in Italian horror cinema: in the following years, the resort to butcher shops would be a rather common occurrence for special effects technicians, from the pig's heart employed in Massimo Pupillo's *5 tombe per un medium* (a.k.a. *Terror-Creatures from the Grave*, 1965) to Aristide Massaccesi's liberal use of *pajata* (baby veal intestines, a staple of traditional Roman cuisine) in the deliriously over-the-top climax of *Antropophagus* (a.k.a. *The Grim Reaper*, 1980). In addition to that, Bava also had a field day with miniatures: he recreated a replica of the protagonist's home (by using a dollhouse!) for the scene where the now-gigantic Caltiki wreaks havoc inside it, and concocted the film's climax, which included toy tanks and the like.

Still, despite the director's scarce interest in the project, there are a number of elements in *Caltiki* that hint at Freda's sensibility and attitude at moviemaking. The opening scenes, featuring an eerie Mexico setting recreated in studio by way of *maquettes*, optical tricks and cardboard painted sets, display his taste for the exotic, highlighted in the extended tribal dance scene—choreographed by Paolo Gozlino[59]—which Daniele Vargas' character unwisely captures with his camera, causing the natives' wrath (like Oliver in *Murder Obsession*, they believe that pictures might steal one's soul) and possibly a curse that will bring to his death. Speaking of which, the mélange of sci-fi and supernatural in the script is as fascinating as it is refreshing, with its reliance on an ancient Mexican legend which allows the science fiction angle to be read in an offbeat way. Take, for instance, the references to the Mayan prophecies that predated, and foretold in cryptic oracle language, the same events which in the present day are the competence of scientists, like the passing of the comet that unleashes Caltiki's destructive power by raising the level of radioactivity on Earth. In some ways, the result exudes uncanny similarities to H.P. Lovecraft's Cthulhu cycle, as well as to the fascinating anthropological speculations of Nigel Kneale's TV serial *Quatermass and the Pit* (1958), even though Sanjust does not come close to the British writer's masterful treating of the subject, nor does he attain a feeling of universal terror. Freda's sensibilities toward the occult were more effectively triggered by such an ambiguity than by the mere, cold scientific background of the usual sci-fi scenario.

Freda and (or) Bava came up with a number of interesting visual tricks, sometimes employing a striking use of depth-of-field. When Nieto turns up in the expedition camp, we first see him as a tiny little silhouette in the distance, before he suddenly shows up right before the camera; his shadow projected over the painted landscape in the background underlines the set's fakeness with an almost surreal effect. The scenes inside the cave with the pond of water where Caltiki hides are truly remarkable, and the sequence in which Bob immerses himself in the pool and discovers human remains on its bottom can be considered an early influence on the celebrated pool scene in Dario Argento's *Inferno* (1980). Another striking moment, inspired by *The Quatermass Xperiment*'s silent filmed recording of the astronauts' unfortunate voyage, is the 8mm footage depicting Nieto and Ulmer's expedition found in Caltiki's cave, where the use of out-of-focus, handheld shots predates Ruggero Deodato's *Cannibal Holocaust* (1980) and the whole found-footage subgenre. As Tim Lucas underlines, "viewed in context of Bava's always impeccably stylized black-and-white photography, the sheer *artlessness* of this 8 mm fragment catapults the film into an alarming tense of heightened reality.... At the time, it was the closest thing to a snuff reel ever dared in a horror movie."[60]

The rest of the picture fares worse. Take, for instance, Max's mad run from the hospital, again patterned on Val Guest's film (at one point even seemingly contemplating an encounter between the fugitive and a little girl, which does not take place after all), which leads to him taking refuge in Fielding's country house, and results in a confrontation between Max, Ellen and Linda, where the latter surprisingly turns out to be the madman's accomplice of sorts. It is a moment whose melodramatic potential is not well-served by the script as it should—ditto for the less-than-convincing sight of the monster assaulting Bava's dollhouse reproduction of the villa. In addition to that, the main characters are hopelessly clichéd, and Merivale makes for a less than memorable hero.

Caltiki culminates in a rather awkward climax where even Bava's visual inventions cannot camouflage the shoestring budget: the blatant miniatures, when the Mexican army finally defeats the monstrous amoeba-like organism by way of tanks and flame-throwers, destroy whatever suspense the movie had attained. However, even more than the technical shortcomings, it is the very concept of the army at rescue that does not hold up: something too far from the Italian mentality (and its endemic distrust of the law enforcement and all things military) to become convincing on screen, even if in a foreign setting.

Caltiki marked the last time Freda and Bava collaborated officially on a film project, not out of personal animosity but because of the latter's directorial career, which started the following year with *La maschera del demonio*. Nevertheless, Bava would occasionally show up on the set and help his friend out on uncredited duties, such as during the shooting of *Le sette spade del vendicatore*. Freda's judgment of Bava as a filmmaker would always be praiseful: "He was a real artist in his experiments, even though his films are not always up to his talent. He loved cinematic adventure at a time where in Italy the directors of photography were content to apply the current dogmas."[61] Still, the two directors' approach at the Gothic genre would show their sensibly different ways to conceive the genre as well as the essence of the Fantastic itself.

Caltiki il mostro immortale was distributed in Italy in August 1959, by Lux Film, and performed rather poorly, grossing a little over 94 million *lire*. However, it found its way abroad: it was released theatrically in the U.S. in September 1960, by Allied Artists, as *Caltiki, the Immortal Monster* (the American prints bear the credit "A Samuel Schneider presentation," leading to some sources speculating it was an Italian/U.S. co-production), and in the United Kingdom in 1962. That same year it was also published in a photonovel version, in the quarterly magazine *I Vostri Film* (issue #13, July 1, 1962, 66 pages).

9

Exploring the Myth

I giganti della Tessaglia

Six years after *Teodora*, Freda's return to the *peplum* couldn't have been timelier. The genre had met a glorious, unexpected renaissance after the success of Pietro Francisci's *Le fatiche di Ercole*, and scriptwriters were rushing through their old school textbooks to put together stories based on the Ancient Greek and Roman myths. Freda and his collaborators Giuseppe Masini and Mario Rossetti (plus Ennio De Concini, involved in an uncredited participation as a mere supervisor[1]) opted for the tale of Jason and the Argonauts and the search for the Golden Fleece, which had already been used as one of the episodes in Francisci's film, and chose to stretch it at film's length. Unfortunately, the producers could not use the title *Gli Argonauti* (The Argonauts) which had already been legally deposited at the Ministry, and had to make do with the less inspiring *I giganti della Tessaglia*, perhaps in a nod to the Steve Reeves vehicle *La battaglia di Maratona* (a.k.a. *The Giant of Marathon*, 1959). A few years later, the most famous film adaptation of the myth came out: *Jason and the Argonauts* (1963), directed by Don Chaffey.[2]

The script was a hodgepodge of mythological references, liberally put together. Freda and his acolytes totally ignored Apollonius of Rhodes' poem *Argonautica*, the main source for the Argonauts' myth, and liberally piled invention upon invention. The story starts *in medias res*, with Jason already on the way to Colchis, thus ignoring the dynastic antefact and the journey's preparation: the hero is given a wife named Creusa and a little son, Iti, and the original usurper Pelia is replaced by the scheming Adrastus. What is more, although the sirens (the same as described in the *Odyssey*) appeared in the Golden Fleece myth as well, Freda borrowed several episodes from Homer, namely Circe—here replaced by Queen Gaia, yet another invention on the part of the scriptwriters—transforming the Argonauts into muttons and Jason's encounter with the Cyclops. On top of that, the characters often refer to other myths: Laerte speaks nostalgically of his little son Ulysses, whereas Orpheus bitterly evokes the memory of his long-lost wife Eurydice (whose death is actually posterior to the Argonauts myth!) The result is a curious anticipation of the self-reflexive tendency of post-modernist cinema, with mythologic references instead of cinephile ones. Freda even managed to squeeze in elements of Italian folklore: the opening sequence borrows from the "Festa dei Ceri" (Procession of candles) in Gubbio, a Catholic festivity where every year three gigantic wooden candles (weighing over 300 kilos each) are carried across the steep streets of the little Umbrian village.

Curiously, given the character's role in the genre's renewed commercial success, *I giganti della Tessaglia* does not include Hercules as part of the Argo crew. In Francisci's

Italian pressbook for *I giganti della Tessaglia* (1960).

film, also co-scripted by De Concini, which drew heavily from the Argonauts myth as told by Apollonius of Rhodes' as well as from other sources, the demi-God was depicted as the pre-eminent member of the Argonauts' crew, with Jason (played by Fabrizio Mioni) relegated to a supporting role. Other differences from the myth include the introduction of Euristeo (a character originally not among the Argonauts), who was a traitor in Francisci's film and here becomes a young hero who provides a romantic subplot,[3] whereas Heracles is nowhere to be found. An even more striking absence in the story is that of Medea. The king of Colchis' daughter—who marries Jason and gives him two children, whom she will slain out of vengeance against him, after Jason has left her to marry the king of Corinth's daughter, Creusa (sometimes referred to as Glauce)—was the center of Euripides' harrowing tragedy, and a character very much in league with Freda's own world (think of Anita Strindberg's role in *Murder Obsession*): her story was later told by Pier Paolo Pasolini in 1969's *Medea*, starring Maria Callas. In Freda's film, Medea appears only in one scene, only to be completely forgotten afterwards: according to the director, "mythology does not exist in the movies."[4]

Such a choice is revealing of the director's approach to the myth: by eliminating tragedy (or evoking it off-screen, as in Orpheus' recalling of his dead Eurydice), what is left is sheer adventure. *I giganti della Tessaglia* features a number of original touches that hint at Freda's interests: compared to Hercules, Jason is a more athletic character, less a muscleman than a sword-and-sandal tantamount of Dubrovsky or D'Artagnan, and the rousing climax is a typical swashbuckling situation transported into the *peplum* universe, with the hero interrupting the marriage between his beloved and the villain at the very last moment. Similarly, Adrastus is yet another rendition of Freda's favorite film villain, as duplicitous and backstabbing as he is lecherous, turning into a sexual menace for the hero's wife. The director relishes in characterizing him as vain (he contemplates his own image in the mirror) and with a body language that at times recalls Mussolini's theatrical gestures.

Speaking of classical movie references, the scene where the Thessalian people are massacred by Adrastus' men over a flight of steps looks like a homage to the famous "Odessa steps" sequence in Eisenstein's *Battleship Potemkin* (1925). On the other hand, the character of Queen Gaia is in the same league as the ravishing and deadly witches in Italian Gothic horror films of the period, with her seductive appearance concealing her horrible real features; her sudden aging directly draws back to *I vampiri*, even though the director did not recycle the same photographic trick from the earlier film but relied on a different one: by way of a game of lights, the beautiful woman reflected in a mirror is replaced by a an ugly hag.

Overall, though, the script is far too sketchy, crowded as it is with episodes which are only briefly mentioned and therefore have to occur off-screen and be evoked through clumsy expository dialogue which has the characters deliver lines in a stilted, contrived language that awkwardly apes classicality. One such example is the Argonauts' transformation into sheep: one moment we see Laerte courting one of Gaia's beautiful handmaidens, and in the next scene Licaone and Argo discover that the metamorphosis has taken place as they are being followed by a flock of sheep. We don't get to see them recovering human form either. Since similar ellipses take place elsewhere in the movie, one wonders whether Freda had to drastically cut on the script due to budget reasons—perhaps even tearing off pages at the eleventh hour as he would do with *L'orribile segreto del Dr. Hichcock*. What is left is not always first-hand: the subplot about Euristeo's love for Aglaia is half-baked and seems merely an excuse for the trial scene which gives Massimo Girotti's Orpheus his "big" moment in the picture. On the other hand, on-set stills show episodes that are not in the finished film (such as Jason about to hang one of his men, perhaps following a mutiny attempt): this does not necessarily mean that the final version suffered from drastic cuts, since the use of fabricated on-set images which had no correspondent in the movie was the norm.

Much of the running time functions as a preparation for several show-stopping scenes: the one which introduces the Argonauts, where Argo's ship is rocked in the middle of a violent storm; the encounter with the ferocious Cyclops; and Jason's climbing atop a huge statue and getting hold of the Golden Fleece. The storm sequence shows both the necessity to cut corners on the part of the director and his talent at achieving impressive results with minimal means. It alternates a miniature of the vessel, a long shot of the studio set with the Argonauts on the deck of the ship prop, and close-ups of the actors receiving huge splashes of water on the face—a far cry from Hollywood's expensive recreations, but it works. The director restlessly moves the camera alongside the ship and highlights the individuals' dramatic efforts (such as Jason grabbing a companion's arm in close-up and rescuing him from the ocean, another Argonaut desperately handing the helm), achieving a pictorial result that elicits comparison Theodore Géricault's painting *The Raft of the Medusa*. According to Michel Mardore, the scene allows the viewer

> to understand the cosmic, Claudel-like character of Freda's genius. A few scantily-dressed extras, a haphazardly-made ship, the ship's deck. Then, a greenish light and an adequate soundtrack underline the images, making them lyrical and otherwordly…. Freda did not demand anything but to shoot a

three or four-hour movie, full of fantastic sequences so as to amaze the audience—the typical audience of the 19th century, a time characterized by a materialist rationalism that vainly attempts to cancel a true interest for superstition and magic.[5]

Even though he was not very kind to the movie, writing that it marked a letdown compared to the director's previous works, and criticizing the photography and the lack of conviction in filming the "interminable deliberations of the Thessalian deputies," Bertrand Tavernier praised the storm sequence as well, calling it "one of the best maritime scenes seen at the movies."[6]

Unlike Don Chaffey in *Jason and the Argonauts*, Freda did not have Ray Harryhausen at hand. No stop-motion sequences, no walking skeletons here, just the good ol' Italian way at improvisation and resourcefulness: the special effects were courtesy of a young and still unripe Carlo Rambaldi. The confrontation between the cyclops and the Argonauts, for instance, alternates close-ups of the Rambaldi-designed monster with shots of a very tall man wearing a cyclops mask-and-suit and kids dressed as the Argonauts in the background, so as to stress the difference in height. The result is clumsy to say the least.

According to Tim Lucas,[7] Freda told him by phone that several scenes—the shots of a miniature of the Argos ship tossed about on a stormy sea; the long shots of the Colossus; the shot of the Argos sailing into a city's harbor—contained uncredited effects by Mario Bava, but Freda pointed out to Éric Poindron that the miniatures and *maquettes* were almost totally the work of Gianfranco Piccolis, whom he praised at length, calling him "unknown and brilliant," and stated that Bava only worked on the statue of the Colossus, atop of which Jason has to climb to get hold of the Fleece, which was sculpted by him and the director himself.[8] It is another excellent sequence, on a par with anything in *peplum*, and one that more than makes up for the wait[9]—even though once again the director sensibly detached from the myth, as Jason finds none of the impediments of the mythological tradition: in the poem, king Eete has the hero face a number of feats, such as fighting ferocious bulls, sowing a dragon's teeth and struggle against the giants that were born out of them, and eventually kill the dragon.

Despite the budget shortcomings, which resulted in some slapdash-looking sets, Freda made good use of the scope format, and also threw in one of his beloved feast scenes, the banquet at Adrasto's palace—an inclusion which this time, unlike *Agi Murad—Il diavolo bianco*, is more in tune with the *peplum*'s spirit, and is blessed by the presence of pictorial elements such as a vase of flowers in a corner of the frame in the foreground. Whenever possible, he employed long takes and indulged in his favorite lateral tracking shots, such in the scene right after the storm, as Jason and the shipwright Argo discuss the damages to the vessel, or during Jason's stay in Gaia's palace, with the camera revealing the environment in parallel with the characters' movements across the set, and in the aforementioned banquet sequence. The director also managed to use Rome's EUR in a similar way as he had done in *Teodora*: Jason and the Argonauts' meeting with Aglaia and her father, when they learn about the cyclops' menace, was shot at the Museo della Civiltà Romana (Museum of Roman Civilization), and once again the Fascist architecture does wonders in evoking a passable imitation of classicality.

What is more, the lighting gives many scenes an abstract quality, suitably heightened by Carlo Rustichelli's score, which pushes the picture closer to the Italian fantastic cinema of the period. Freda was quite pleased with Rustichelli: the two had collaborated on *La leggenda del Piave,* and to him the composer remained "the best [type of] musician because he understood cinema. I described the film to him and he invented the music without a pre-written score."[10] Several moments stand out in this respect: Jason's brief interlude with Gaia features a show-stopping bit where the two actors are crossing a pool of water atop a little vessel which apparently moves by itself, like a fairy carriage. Another eerie bit has the Argo ship advancing in the night mist, before the umpteenth curse against the Argonauts takes form: here, the way Freda bypasses the budgetary limits and puts to best use a virtually bare studio set predates Bava's brilliant reinvention of it in *Terrore nello spazio* (a.k.a. *Planet of the Vampires*, 1965). All in all, despite its flaws, *I giganti della Tessaglia* shares the same surreal quality as the best examples of the *peplum* genre and at times recalls either Bava's *Ercole al centro della terra* (a.k.a. *Hercules in the Haunted World*, 1961) and Freda's own *Maciste all'inferno*.

Keeping true to his reputation, Freda once again walked off the set, after a futile argument with producer Virginio De Blasi, who yelled at the tiny dog he had carried on set, sending the director into a rage. "Between the dog and him, I did not hesitate a second," Freda commented, and who would blame him? According to *Présence du Cinema*, "certain insert scenes were filmed by the assistants, at the producers' request, following Freda's departure." And yet, Freda himself stated that it was De Blasi who took over, but he was so hopeless a replacement that the director returned behind the camera after just two days, at De Blasi's mistress' insistence.[11] If we take Freda's words for granted, any involvement on the part of Mario Bava as uncredited director seems highly unlikely.[12]

The lack of budget also affected the casting. Still, despite considering it a minor effort ("I don't like *I giganti della Tessaglia* either. The story is idiotic and the actors are awful. I only like the storm sequence," he told Bertrand Tavernier[13]), Freda later had kind words about the lead, the Swiss/French stuntman Henri Louis Roland Carey (Burt Lancaster's double in *Trapeze*, 1956) whom he regarded as disciplined and courageous, and who did all his stunts himself; even though he has the *physique du rôle*, however, Carey partially lacks the charisma of other *peplum* stars. After a minor career in the genre, the actor later appeared in a few other forgettable productions such as the Gothic/*giallo* hybrid *La bambola di Satana* (1969, Ferruccio Casapinta) alongside Erna Schurer. After over a decade away from the big screen, during which he worked as voice actor at Fono Roma, Carey made a hardly spectacular but decidedly noteworthy comeback, enthusiastically taking part—despite being nearly 50 years old—in five hardcore porn films directed in 1981 '82 by Alexander Borsky, a.k.a. Aristide Massaccesi, namely *Labbra vogliose, Sesso acerbo, Le porno investigatrici, La voglia* and *Super Hard Love*. The jewel in the crown in his filmography, however, is probably his role as a drug dealer in Krzystof Kieslowski's austere *Trois Couleurs: Rouge* (a.k.a. *Red*, 1994).

The rest of the cast is varied but hardly memorable: *Spartaco*'s Massimo Girotti, who by then had suffered a drop in popularity, turns up in a sadly minor role as Orpheus; stunt ace Gil Delamare is one of the Argonauts; *Da qui all'eredità*'s Alberto Sorrentino is the comic relief Antineo; dancer Paolo Gozlino plays Laerte; Alberto Farnese (whom the director would cast again in *Caccia all'uomo*) is suitably unpleasant as Adrastus. The female cast does not shine either: the Israeli-born Ziva Rodann (seen in Samuel Fuller's *Forty Guns*, 1957, and John Sturges' *Last Train from Gun Hill*, 1959) fails to make much of an impression as Creusa. For the rest of her not-so irresistible career, she would be relegated to exotic roles (such as Nefertiti in a couple of episodes of the *Batman* TV series). Similarly, the French-born Nadine Duca (*née* Nadine Ducasse, later known as Nadia Sanders) would appear in another *peplum* flick, Luigi Capuano's *La vendetta di*

Ursus (a.k.a. *The Vengeance of Ursus*, 1961) and in a few Totò vehicles before briefly popping up in Fellini's *8½* and then disappearing into an oblivion of uncredited roles. Maria Teresa Vianello (whom the director would cast as Dr. Hichcock's wife Margaretha in *L'orribile segreto del Dr. Hichcock*) pops up in a brief role as Queen Gaia's sister Olivia—enough, however, to show that acting chops were not among her strong points.

With 408 million *lire*, *I giganti della Tessaglia* did OK at the Italian box-office, and was sold throughout Europe. As usual with sword-and-sandal flicks, it was picked up in the U.S., and released in 1963 as *The Giants of Thessaly* by Medallion Pictures. Although some sources indicate a theatrical release, the film seems to have gone direct to TV.[14]

Maciste alla corte del Gran Khan

The enormous success of *Hercules* had producers and scriptwriters squeezing their brains to offer the audiences other musclebound heroes who would perform their amazing deeds in a Roman-Greek. Some, like Samson, were taken from the Bible; others, like Ursus, were lifted off more recent literary works (namely Henryk Sienkiewicz's 1894 novel *Quo Vadis?*) Both, however, were reinvented as producers would see fit, deprived of their original qualities and turned into marketable substitutes for the Greek demi-god portrayed by Steve Reeves.

Unlike the aforementioned characters, however, Maciste was fully a creation of the 20th century, and Italian to the bone. Born out of the renowned poet Gabriele D'Annunzio's imagination, he first appeared in Giovanni Pastrone's majestic 1914 sword-and-sandal epic *Cabiria*, played by the ex-dock worker Bartolomeo Pagano: Maciste's memorable entry on screen has him wholly covered in coal, so that he looks like a black slave.

Maciste became one of the heroes par excellence of Italian silent cinema, and underwent a very peculiar screen trajectory: in fact, the character was taken from his original Ancient Roman setting to the present, in such epics as the war propaganda film *Maciste alpino* (1916) and *Maciste poliziotto* (1918). For a couple of years, in 1922 and 1923, Pagano played Maciste in a handful of German productions, before returning to Italy in 1924: some of Maciste's most famous silent films date from the Fascist era, such as *Maciste contro lo sceicco* (1926, Mario Camerini) and Guido Brignone's *Maciste all'inferno*, made that same year, which was one of Federico Fellini's favorite pics. As in the previous decade, the stories were set indifferently in the past as in the present.

It was Ermanno Donati's idea to exhume the old silent film hero in the reawakening of the *peplum* fever. "There had been Francisci's *Hercules* films, which did so well at the box-office that my brother told himself, 'Why don't we pull out Maciste too?'" as Donati's brother Piero, the production manager at Panda, explained. "In a sense, Maciste's films were in juxtaposition with Hercules, as they were even more vernacular. And so we moved to Egypt and then to Yugoslavia and shot *Maciste nella valle dei re*."[15]

Freda's first Maciste film was born, like many other Italian productions of the period, out of mere economic necessity: it was a typical case of a so-called "*film di recupero*" (recovery movie). Panda had invested lots of money in the expensive epic *Marco Polo—L'avventura di un italiano in Cina* (1962)—originally to be shot partly in Hong Kong—

Opposite: U.S. poster for *Maciste alla corte del Gran Khan* (1961). Maciste was renamed Samson for the American audience.

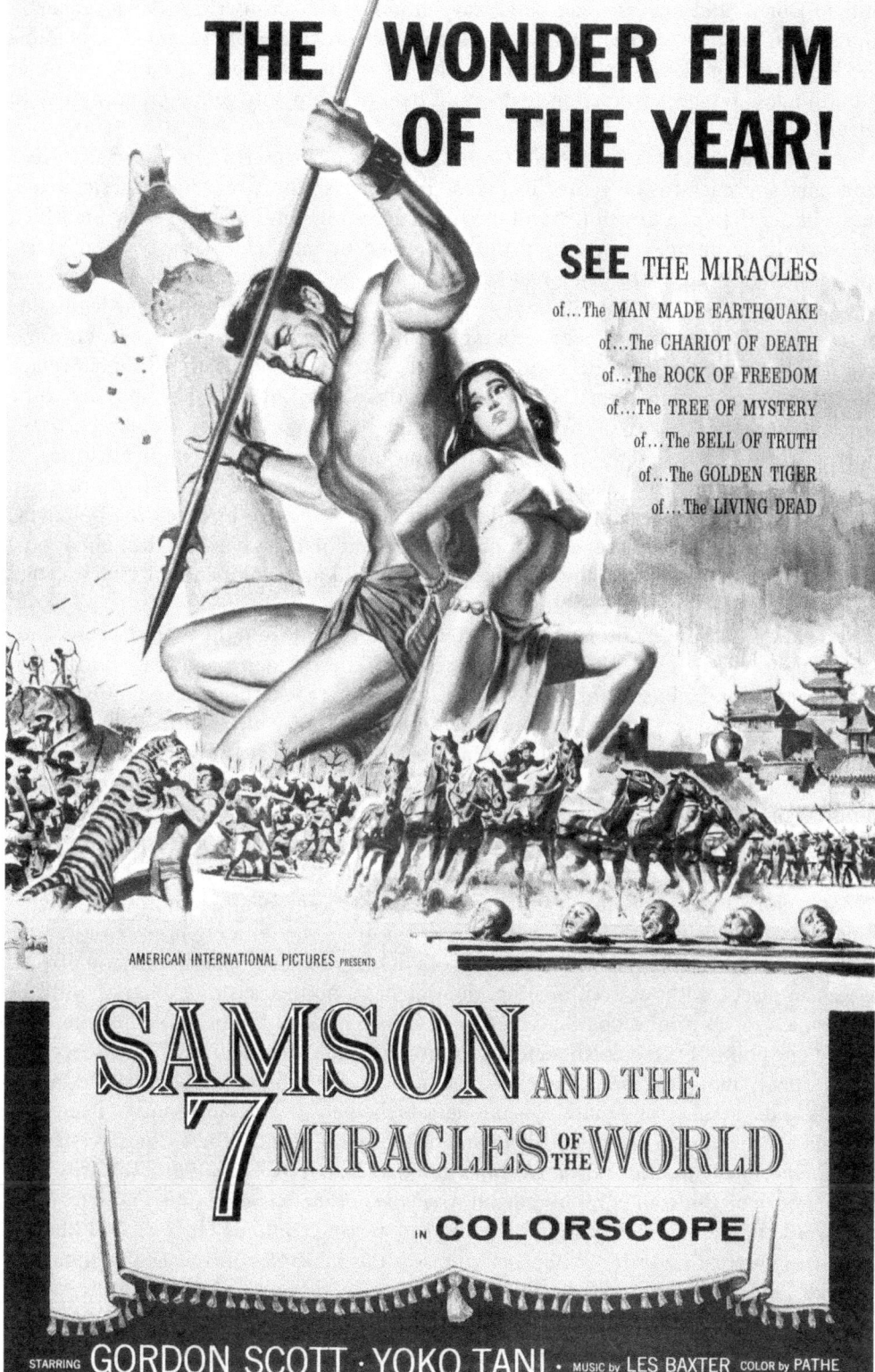

and so Donati and his associate Luigi Carpentieri urged scriptwriters Oreste Biancoli and Duccio Tessari to come up with a new scenario in order to exploit as much as possible the impressive outdoor sets, the interiors and the many extras employed for the other film, in a low-budget production that would help the company gain enough money to cover the costs.

The result, *Maciste alla corte del Gran Khan*, benefits from Duccio Tessari's far from routinary approach to the genre. To Freda, Tessari was "an extraordinary scriptwriter, much better than as a director,"[16] and the script accommodates unusual elements which are worth underlining. For one thing, the *peplum*'s recurring theme of the tyrant oppressing a population (here, the evil Great Khan Garak, who treacherously kills the Emperor of China and proclaims himself the regent, while attempting to get rid of the legitimate heirs, prince Tai Sung and princess Lei Ling) is enlivened with references to recent history: near the beginning, after a successful raid on the part of the rebels, the Mongols' retaliation is not long in coming. "For every Mongol soldier killed, 10 hostages are to be beheaded," a character says. The mind goes to the Nazi's reprisals over Italian partisans during World War II, and the infamous Ardeatine massacre in Rome, where 335 innocent citizens were summarily executed by the Germans on March 24, 1944, after a partisan attack resulted in 30 German soldiers dead. The Nazis retaliated by executing 10 Italians for each German killed. Other critics underlined the similarities between the fight opposing the Mongol oppressor to the Chinese people as told in the film and the civil war that led to the foundation of the Popular Republic of China in 1949.[17]

Tessari's take on the titular hero is also rather different from the typical sword-and-sandal figure. First of all, it is imbued with self-awareness. Maciste shows up for the first time from behind a bush—for an instant we are not sure whether it is a man or a tiger that is about to appear—like a star from behind the curtain onto the limelight. "*Io sono Maciste, sono nato dalla roccia*" (I am Maciste, I was born from a rock) is the first line he utters, a tongue-in-cheek nod to Gabriele D'Annunzio's fabricated mythology of the hero. In the film he is basically an outsider, as he will be in the director's next *peplum*. Bare-chested and wearing only a tiny red kilt, he looks otherwordly amidst the tiny Chinese extras, all dressed in green or gray—a presence from another time and dimension. What is more, Maciste is capable of irony and even sarcasm. A case in point is the hero's meeting with a patrol of Mongol soldiers, which gives way to a big brawl in a tavern. When the head patrol grabs his shoulder from behind, Maciste shakes the hand off as if it was an insect, without even turning, then he has a quite amusing exchange with the soldier, a not-too-bright looking type. "Hey, are you making fun of me?" the latter asks him at one point; "Even if I wanted to, I couldn't. You look too intelligent," Maciste replies in an openly mocking tone. The exchange goes on for a bit until eventually Maciste resorts to his main asset—muscles—and defeats the patrol. The same kind of irony surfaces in another Tessari-scripted *peplum* made that same year, Vittorio Cottafavi's *Ercole alla conquista di Atlantide* (a.k.a. *Hercules and the Captive Women*, 1961). Tessari would further develop this trait in his film debut *Arrivano i titani* (a.k.a. *My Son, the Hero*, 1962) and would follow a similar path in his Westerns starring Giuliano Gemma. But Maciste has other interesting traits. When he witnesses the rehearsal on the public square of Garak's Sadean execution device, the guillotine attached to a chariot, at first the hero is not interested in intervening: he shakes his head in disgust and is about to leave, when a woman's cry has him retrace his steps and decide to help the unfortunate prisoners—an interesting psychological notation for a usually monolithic character.

It is unlikely that Freda shared such a view, as he mostly focused on the idea of Maciste as a popular hero.

> Audiences loved a type of superhero such as Hercules and Maciste. Unconsciously they love it still nowadays because after all, whether it is strong, cocky or courageous, the audience identifies with him—every accountant dreams to pose as a superhero before his woman. The romantic subplot had a very minor importance, as these were romantic, barely sketched love stories. The sadistic part was non-existent. It was really all about adventure for adventure.[18]

As Della Casa notes, unlike in other films of the genre, here Maciste turns out to be asexual: even though for a brief moment Freda allows us to believe that a romantic attraction might blossom between the usurper's fascinating mistress Liu Tai and the hero during their night encounter in the palace, ultimately this doesn't happen, and the woman is mercilessly disposed of during the climax.

On the other hand, Garak is the typical Freda villain, all fake affability on the surface and Machiavellian plots behind the façade—plus the requested predatory sexual attitude. The way he gets rid of the Emperor by way of a hired assassin during a game of knife-throwing at court predates a plot element in the director's subsequent *Le sette spade del vendicatore*, where a political killing is supposed to take place during a stage play. Here, Tessari's script adds a further element of gleeful sadism, as Garak submits the killer to merciless tortures, since he knows the latter won't ever reveal the name of his mandator—he had the man's tongue cut off beforehand.

In spite of the low budget, the film looks gorgeous. Freda employs the scope format in a pictorial way, with the camera withdrawing to show the whole of a room filled with extras, such as during the Emperor's funeral, or in the dance bits, where the director's taste for picturesque choreography matches with the genre's required bouts of exoticism; whereas the scenes of Maciste sneaking at night into the deserted palace display his fascination for luxurious, awe-inspiring interiors: even the hero looks intimidated by such a display of wealth—courtesy of Cinecittà's expert set decorators. The torture scenes, on the other hand, have that same kind of Gothic feel as those of his 1940s and 1950s films, with elaborate machinery and executioners at work on infernal devices in damp, darkened crypts—courtesy of Riccardo Pallottini's accomplished lighting. The very talented Pallottini would go on to become Antonio Margheriti's regular d.o.p., starting with *Danza macabra* (a.k.a. *Castle of Blood*, 1964) and working with Margheriti on 18 films, before his untimely death in 1982.

Whenever possible, Freda resorted to his stylistic and visual leitmotifs. Lateral tracking shots are employed, such as in the hunting party scenes, with the camera slowly panning rightward as men come out of the woods and walk along an empty field, blowing horns; for the scenes set in the princess' hideout, on the other hand, the director reprises the same vertical movement as seen in the sequence set inside Spartacus' prison in his 1953 movie. The image of the slaves working in the quarry brings to mind *I miserabili*, whereas the rebel leader Cho leading the rebels' attack on horseback, preceded by the sight of the men on a hill's top in the distance, is typical Western material. At the end, Maciste proclaims that "destiny brought me here, now I must go wherever there's a fight between right and wrong" and leaves, while a monk closes the door behind him; willing or not on the part of the director, it is an almost literal nod to two of the finest moments in John Ford's filmography: Tom Joad's final monologue in *The Grapes of Wrath* (1940) and the celebrated ending in *The Searchers* (1956). It is a telling epigraph to Freda's conception of the mythological character, in a tale that can be read, even more than other examples of the genre, as a *roman de geste* which celebrates the individual hero and his strength, as the embodiment of the collective need for freedom and justice, in opposition to a modern world where the basic values seem to have been overwhelmed.

What makes the film memorable, is the way Freda approaches the story. By this time, he was rather disenchanted about the state of Italian popular cinema in general and of the *peplum* in particular. His view on the Maciste cycle of the late 1950s was sharp to say the least, and he looked at his own movie as a mere work-for-hire project. And yet, regardless of the plot's shortcomings, he tells the movie as if it were an epic adventure, trying to squeeze a sense of wonder and awe from every single shot, even though the not-so-luscious budget somehow spoils the hero's memorable early efforts—eradicating a tree over which several Mongols were hiding, and fighting a ferocious tiger with his bare hands. The scene where the rebels are buried in the ground, with only their heads protruding, and are about to be decapitated by a chariot, is another outstanding example of Freda's conception of cinema as spectacle: it predates a gruesome sequence in Tinto Brass' *Caligula* (1979) and allows Freda to stage a variation on the chariot race scene in *Teodora*, while paying the umpteenth homage to the Western with yet another reinvention of the celebrated Yakima Canutt stunt in *Stagecoach*, as Maciste jumps between the horses, slides underneath the chariot and reemerges on its back, before halting it by way of his extraordinary force.

The result, to quote the Spanish film critic Antonio José Navarro,

> by mixing instinct and experience, conviction and skill, puts into practice one of Walter Benjamin's most interesting reflections on the art of storytelling. As Benjamin said, more than half of it consists of keeping free from explanation the story that is being told. The marvelous, the extraordinary, is to be told with great accuracy, and a wide range of details, but without giving the viewer the psychological context of what happened. Thus, the audience will be completely free when it comes to arranging the things as they understand them, so that the story will reach an unexpected range of vibrations.[19]

In interviews as well as in his memoir, Freda boasted about the way he overcame the budgetary limits in the film's climax, which depicts the royal palace's spectacular destruction: "I managed to recreate the Beijing earthquake on a field in the suburbs of Rome. I had lots of fun shooting it and it was a great satisfaction to see the finished result, as it really seemed to be the real Beijing that was collapsing to the ground."[20] In addition to sculpting several props (such as an elephant statue which looks gigantic on screen), the director resorted to Mario Bava's help to accomplish a number of trick shots, such as the *maquette* of the palace, and the sight of hundreds of extras, skillfully multiplied on film by way of double exposure.[21] As usual, Freda ended up having an argument with Donati, who according to him was often trying to meddle with the direction.

After appearing in five feature films as Tarzan, Gordon Scott (born Gordon M. Werschkul, 1926–2007) headed to Italy in 1961, and appeared in many sword-and-sandal flicks, becoming one of the genre's most popular stars. *Maciste alla corte del Gran Khan* was the first of his solo starring performances in Italian *peplum*. Despite his shortcomings as an actor, Freda had unusually kind words for Scott: the actor was disciplined throughout, even in the most dire circumstances, such as in the sequence where he had to rescue the prince from a ferocious tiger's den, which formed the basis for one of *Divoratori di celluloide*'s most amusing anecdotes. The wild beast had been anesthetized so as to allow the filming, but the dose was not enough and the tiger had awakened. When he took the Korean actor who played the prince in his arms and got out of the tiger's ditch, Scott made a disgusted grimace, thus ruining the shot and making Freda angry at him. When he asked his lead why that face, the American actor replied that the prince had soiled his pants out of fear.[22] Scott's double in the action scenes, Pietro Torrisi, soon to be Mister Italy in 1963, would also enjoy a brief career in the sword-and-sandal genre, then became one of Italian cinema's most recognizable character actors: his muscular body granted him a renewed popularity as a leading man in the early 1980s, when a short-lived sword-and-sorcery cycle inspired by *Conan the Barbarian* (1982) blossomed.

Besides Scott, the cast was as diverse as could be expected in Italian productions of the period. As Garak, voice actor Leonardo Severini looks like he just stepped out of one of the director's earlier films, and relishes his role with gusto: the Khan was originally to be played by the Italian-American Dante DiPaolo, who refused to shave his beard and was then recast as Bayan, the head of the Khan's militia. DiPaolo told Tim Lucas that, "on the last day of filming, Freda demanded that he and a team of more experienced horsemen ride in their Mongolian makeup through a field rigged with explosives. DiPaolo was confused, as no such scene appeared in the script and later learned that it was an action scene Freda was directing for André De Toth's *I mongoli*."[23]

The female leads were Yōko Tani, the star of Nicholas Ray's *The Savage Innocents* (1960) who would also co-star in *Marco Polo*, and the alluring Hélène Chanel, who would turn up in Freda's next *peplum*. "When they offered me the part they told me 'Look, Riccardo Freda has chosen you because you remind him of Gianna Maria Canale, his favorite actress.' I felt like a makeshift, a poor man's Gianna Maria Canale" she recalled. Actually, it is likely that Chanel was cast to replace Chelo Alonso, who was initially slated to star in the film, according to a short untitled article in *Corriere d'informazione*, dated April 10–11, 1961.

Chanel was not particularly impressed with Freda's subsequent cult reputation, either. "Frankly I can't understand it; once I almost quarrelled with Francesco Laudadio, who directed me in a film starring Monica Bellucci [*La riffa*, 1991] in which I played a small role: he got really angry when I told him I had done Freda's Maciste films and also "much more serious stuff." Then I discovered he had studied *Maciste all'inferno* at Rome's CSC. I think Freda had a great technique, his brilliance showed during the shooting, but you can't really notice it in the finished film…. Freda's skills were evident in the stunts: he could make three extras look like an army, or turn a single calf into a stampeding herd of cattle. Considering the schedules and the budgets he had at disposal, he was great, but the result on screen is nothing special in my opinion … that's why I say his craftsmanship was purely technical."[24]

Maciste alla corte del Gran Khan was released in Italy in October 1961, and grossed over 468 million *lire*, quite an impressive result. American International Pictures imported it to the U.S. in December 1962 as *Samson and the 7 Miracles of the World*, advertising it with a bombastic poster that claimed: "SEE the Miracle of The Golden Tiger / The Tree of Mystery / The Chariot of Death / The Rock of Freedom / The Living Dead / The Bell of Truth / The Man-Made Earthquake," thus recapping the hero's main feats in the film. As it usually happened with the *pepla* featuring Maciste—a name which did not ring a bell to overseas audiences since it did not belong to classical mythology—Scott's character's name was changed to the more suitable Samson; similarly, *Maciste contro il vampiro* (1961, Giacomo Gentilomo and Sergio Corbucci) became *Goliath Against the Vampires* in the States. This led one reviewer to claim that the hero was "none other than the famous Biblical strongman transplanted to the Orient" while noting that "this Samson is beardless as a babe and seems to have learned about women."[25]

The American edit runs slightly less than 80 minutes and features a new music score by Les Baxter—a common occurrence with A.I.P. releases of foreign films—replacing Carlo Innocenzi's, as well as a number of differences compared to the Italian cut. The opening title sequence, with a long line of Chinese slaves at work along a mountain side, is slightly shortened and features a superimposed line: "China, the 13th century. Time of myth and mystery, conquest and courage." The whole opening part with Garak's murder of the Emperor and the torture scene is missing, and the U.S. version retains only a few shots of the Khan arriving in China before cutting to the images of the slaves working in the quarry, accompanied by an added-on voice-over which briefly exposes the Mongols' ruling over the country, plunging it "into the darkness of slavery and misery," before continuing:

> This is the story of the man who rose up against Garak and the Mongols, the young giant who was to strike terror into the hearts of the invaders. He assumed the name of Samson to match his size and feats of strength. His destiny was to perform the seven miracles, to ring the great bell of freedom which was China's ancient call to arms, to arouse the people from their apathy....

This was obviously done to anticipate Maciste/Samson's appearance, which in the original takes place about twenty minutes into the film. Several scenes—mostly dialogue ones—were either shortened or completely excerpted in order for the movie to accommodate double bills: Maciste carrying the fainted prince to the monastery, a monk delivering the fake news of the prince's death to Garak, Cho's encounter with the princess, Maciste's training of the rebels, his dialogue with Tao, a scene between Cho and the prince. Gone is also the amusing dialogue exchange between Maciste and the Mongol soldier: evidently Arkoff and Nicholson thought the hero's sense of humor would be an unnecessary distraction from the sight of his musclework—in some ways, they treated Maciste as yet another dumb big-bosomed blonde, all curves and no brain.

It was during the shooting of his first Maciste film, on a hot August day, that Freda received an unexpected visit on the set. "I was told that a French journalist wanted to speak with me. Had he been an Italian one, I wouldn't even have lost one minute of my time with him. Since he was a foreigner, I agreed to meet him. He was young, with mobile and smart Oriental-type black eyes. His name was Simon Mizrahi."[26] The young film critic would become one of the most important presences in the director's later career. He was not alone, though: the man who accompanied Mizrahi was Jacques Lourcelles. The two critics had run across most of Freda's filmography during a hectic week spent in the screening room at the Cineteca Nazionale, much to the staff's perplexity, and the result of their visit would be a special issue devoted to the Italian director by the magazine *Présence du cinéma* (#17, 1963), which included a long (and, as expected, frank and sharp) interview. It was not the only good news for the filmmaker: much to his delight, he learnt that the Cinémathèque Française in Paris was about to screen a retrospective of his works. At 52, Freda could proudly wear on his sleeve the title of *auteur*.

Caccia all'uomo

Shot in early spring 1961, before *Maciste alla corte del Gran Khan*, but released a couple of months later, *Caccia all'uomo* is definitely an oddity in Freda's *oeuvre*. Shot with the working title *Le avventure di Dox*, which then became *Dox, caccia all'uomo*, before sticking to the final version—curiously, the same title as the first part of *I miserabili*—

the film was inspired by true events and featured an unlikely hero: a police dog, a German shepherd named Dox. After winning the world championship of police dogs in 1953, Dox rose to the headlines due to its extraordinary feats: he took part in 171 police operations, contributed to the capture of over 500 wanted bandits, and had a vital role in locating and dismantling the Salvatore Giuliano gang in Sicily. Newspapers called him "the Italian Rin Tin Tin" and described at length Dox's amazing abilities: the dog could follow an odor trace across a traffic-ridden city; once he chased a thief for miles even after the criminal shot him and broke his paw; saved a girl's life by pushing her away from an oncoming car; found a missing skier on the mountains after a whole research party with police dogs had given up. Dox could even unload a gun without shooting it, and release a man tied to a chair, no matter how intricate

Italian 2-fogli manifesto for *Caccia all'uomo* (1961).

were the knots—a scene included in the script, incidentally. The idea for the film possibly came to Freda after the newsreel "Settimana Incom" dedicated a story to the dog's retirement from service in February 1960: Dox died in 1965, at the venerable age of 19.[27] What is more, at that time the Italian television was broadcasting a very popular series centered on a dog, *The Adventures of Rin Tin Tin*.

Freda's concept was quite daring on paper: "I wanted the dog to be the main character and the audience to follow its deeds through the animal's point of view, with subjective shots."[28] The concept of humanity and its misery as seen through the eyes of a dog was an interesting choice on the part of the director, which however told less about his love for simple-minded, engrossing adventure stories than of his disdain toward thesps—a chapter of his memoir is tellingly titled "Animals and Actors," and he would further develop the idea in his unfilmed project *Animal's Gang*. No wonder he claimed to love the film very much. However, the project eventually evolved into a half-baked police yarn that had little to do with the original idea. The result is not devoid of interest, and predates such later works as the German TV series *Kommissar Rex* (1994), also featuring a police dog. Still, it cannot be counted among the director's most successful works.

Caccia all'uomo consists basically of two episodes, introduced by a brief prologue in which Dox saves a woman who jumped from a bridge in front of Castle Sant'Angelo, and shakily tied together by the presence of Dox and its owner, vice-brigadeer Maimonti (played by Umberto Orsini), a character inspired by the real-life Giovanni Maimone, Dox's trainer. The narrative is somewhat rudimentary at times, on the level of a barely interesting crime story that never quite lights up. Mostly, that's because the two stories never really add up as a whole, making the film unbalanced and fragmentary. However, the juxtaposition was purportedly pursued by the director, as underlined by the stark difference between the sunny Sicilian settings in the first part and the shadowy Rome as depicted in the second.

Despite the impressive depiction of the Sicilian landscapes and ambients, however, the first half—tacked on to the pic at a later stage in order to reach a passable running time[29]—is a predictable variation on the usual stereotypes about the Mediterranean island: a libidinous Count, a sensual maid, a vindictive lover. It would take someone like Pietro Germi to reinvent those clichés in a satirical key, that very same year, in *Divorzio all'italiana*; here, the melodramatic love story between the bandit and his mistress appears clumsy and ineffective. On the other hand, the Rome-based segment, shot mostly at the EUR district, is rather different in tone and fares much better in comparison, with a sharper *film noir* look (heightened by Marcello Giombini's lively jazzy score) and several impressive light/shade sequences, such as the dog and two cops exploring an abandoned house, and a fistfight in a shady basement full of empty bottles. Still, it suffers from the somewhat naive depiction of the drug traffic ring (a flaw which already marred the mediocre *Agguato a Tangeri*) as well as from a forgettable romantic subplot featuring Georgia Moll.

Predictably, some of the most amiable sequences involve the German shepherd (played in the film by Dox's son), such as Maimonti and the dog's amusing arrival at the remote Sicilian village (with the Commissioner and his men openly disappointed that the only reinforcements sent from the Rome headquarters are a plainclothes cop and his dog) and the discovery of the kidnapped little girl. Sometimes Freda employs the dog's abilities for broad comedy, such as Dox jumping a ride onto a car and barking affirmatively to the driver's inquiry if he has to go to the police station ("Gee, this dog even understands dialect!"), and is immensely aided by Dox's acting, as the animal often steals the scene (presumably, much to the director's glee). Freda also concocted a very well-made action sequence, a car chase filmed in Rome's chaotic traffic at night (much to the disdain of the local newspapers: the days of the *poliziottesco* were yet to come), with police officer Armando Spatafora acting as a one-of-a-kind stunt driver. Himself a celebrity because of the acrobatic car chases he was involved in, Spatafora became the inspiration for Maurizio Merli's character in Stelvio Massi's entertaining crime flick *Poliziotto Sprint* (a.k.a. *Highway Racer*, 1977).

Caccia all'uomo's most impressive sequence, however, is the murder of the fashion model Clara Ducci. A somewhat jarring moment in a movie otherwise aimed at a younger audience, proving Freda's growing interest in a darker kind of films compared to his works of the 1940s and early 1950s, it definitely predates both his subsequent Gothics as well as the *giallo*'s typical stylistical traits, and deserves to be analyzed in detail. The woman is alone in her apartment when the lights go out during a thunderstorm. She lights a match and advances through the darkened place (Freda's camera accompanying her laterally, as customary, from one room to the next). She reacts in fear when a window suddenly opens due to the wind. Clara lights a candle and proceeds to another room, but the camera abandons her and zooms in on the door's handle, which is being opened, from the outside. Clara adjusts a necklace to which a key (a vital plot point) is attached and prepares to go out, when the phone rings. She has barely the time to answer: a black-gloved hand covers her mouth from behind. The killer repeatedly stabs her in the back. She falls on her back and is stabbed again in the belly, the camera zooming in on her face in close-up while the killer grabs the necklace and tears it off her neck. Besides the emphasis on atmosphere, the mise-en-scène of the act of killing (possibly influenced by Hitchcock's *Dial M for Murder*, 1954) is a stunning anticipation of what will be found in the forthcoming *gialli*, from Bava to Argento (see, for instance, Bianca Merusi's murder in *Il gatto a nove code/Cat O'Nine Tails*)—although little known because of the film's scarce circulation outside Italy. According to Freda,[30] originally the scene was even longer, with the victim being hit multiple times and painfully attempting to drag herself to the door, but it was judged too violent; since the censors did not intervene on the film, such cuts must have been the result of the producers' choice.

Stylistically, *Caccia all'uomo* is rather inconsistent. Freda's trademark tracking shots are well in evidence throughout—see, for instance, the scenes at the drug dealer's villa. Still, the difference from the director's work in the past decades is immediately evident by his embracing of the zoom lens as a time-saving trick and a stylistic resort (such as in Clara's murder scene), a trait which would become more and more prominent in the years to come. What is more, Freda was not happy with his d.o.p. Alessandro D'Eva, who had just risen to notoriety after his work on Franco Rossi's exotic drama *Odissea nuda* (1961), shot in Tahiti. "If you go to Polynesia and place the camera with only the aid of a small rulebook ... you will obviously have a wonderful photography. But it's not you who create the photography, it's nature that gives you the chance. Fellini took him as d.o.p. after watching the movie: he had him do some tests and fired him. It's a guy who's just not capable of placing lights."[31]

The human leads are the celebrated stage actor Umberto Orsini, here in one of his very first film roles, and the reliable Riccardo Garrone (1926–2016), the brother of film director Sergio, and one of Italian cinema's better known supporting actors, as the hard-boiled Commissioner who keeps rubbing his hands with a handkerchief as if to clean away all the violence and squalor he has to face daily. The cast features a number of well-known thesps in small roles: the great Andrea Checchi (seen the previous year in *La maschera del demonio*), the French-born Yvonne Furneaux, a young Philippe Leroy in one of his early film roles after Jacques Becker's masterpiece *Le Trou* (1960), and the beautiful Eleonora Rossi Drago, who—despite being top-billed—has a rather small but key role as the unfortunate Clara. Rossi Drago (born Palmira Omiccioli, 1925–2007) had been a very popular name in the 1950s, and the star of Michelangelo Antonioni's *Le amiche* (1955, co-starring Furneaux), Vittorio Gassman's *Kean* and Valerio Zurlini's *Estate violenta* (a.k.a. *Violent Summer*, 1959), which won her a Silver Ribbon award for best actress in her home country. By the 1960s, however, her career had started to go downhill: she would appear in decidedly more commercial flicks, such as the sword-and-sandal epic *David e Golia* (1960), the German *krimi* film *Der Teppich des Grauens* (a.k.a. *The Carpet of Horror*, 1962), Eugenio Martín's eerie mystery *Ipnosi* (a.k.a. *Hypnosis*, 1962), Radley Metzger's stylish *Camille 2000* (1969), Massimo Dallamano's *Il dio chiamato Dorian* (a.k.a. *Dorian Gray*, 1970) and Sergio Bergonzelli's trashy *giallo* oddity *Nelle pieghe della carne* (a.k.a. *In the Folds of the Flesh*, 1970) which turned out to be her last film role.

She married a wealthy Sicilian businessman and retired in Palermo. The controversial Giò Stajano—the nephew of a notorious Fascist hierarch and a well-known personality who in 1959 had published the autobiographical volume *Roma capovolta*, about his promiscuous sex life in Rome's high society—turns up briefly as Gabriellino, whose sexual inclination (at a time where homosexuality was still an unspeakable topic in Italian cinema) is suggested through him wearing an angora sweater—à la *Glen or Glenda*. In 1983 Stajano would undergo a sex reassignment surgery, becoming one of Italy's most famous transgenders.

Caccia all'uomo was released in late December 1961, to modest success: despite being distributed by Paramount Italia, it grossed only a disappointing 83 million *lire*. It came out in France the following year as *Chasse à la drogue*.

Maciste all'inferno

Freda's second Maciste film—shot in fall 1961 and released in Italy in April 1962—was yet another work for hire, which went on to become one of the director's weirdest efforts, although not one of his best. In his own words, Freda was called in at the very last minute, a mere two days before filming, by producer Ermanno Donati, to replace another unnamed director who was seemingly incapable of transposing the story's complex imagery onto the screen. He found himself dealing with a most peculiar script indeed.

Besides the concept of the titular hero descending into Hades, compared to Guido Brignone's 1926 film of the same name, the only thing that Oreste Biancoli and Piero Pierotti's screenplay for *Maciste all'inferno* had in common with the original was the title. Given that the *peplum* fever had viewers demanding more of the same, and the genre was eagerly embracing a number of fantasy elements, the scriptwriters inserted the muscular hero's journey into Hell within a narrative frame that was purely Gothic, in accordance to a thread that was gradually picking up steam after the international success of Mario Bava's *La maschera del demonio*, and which resulted in American companies picking up foreign horror flicks for U.S. distribution. Freda's film is not the only example of a peplum-cum-Gothic hybrid, though: Bava's *Ercole al centro della terra* also dealt with the hero descending into the netherworld, whereas *Maciste contro il vampiro* evoked the Gothic's monster par excellence, albeit in a rather offbeat fashion.

Overall, despite the more blatant differences, the Gothic and the *peplum* were like heterozygous twins, sharing the same directors, scriptwriters and crews, and dealing with a supernatural imagery that marked in both cases Italian cinema's most substantial approach to the Fantastic since its heyday. The *peplum* was commercially more relevant, at least in Italy, with a much larger number of titles and (at least apparently, given the use of color and recycled sets) bigger budgets, and a patent ease at depicting grotesque monsters: take, for instance, the flying zombies evoked by Lico (Christopher Lee) in *Ercole al centro della terra*, the faceless creatures at the orders of Kormak the vampire in *Maciste contro il vampiro*, the monsters designed by Carlo Rambaldi for *Perseo l'invincibile* (a.k.a. *Medusa Against the Son of Hercules*, 1963, Alberto De Martino) and the legions of the living dead in *Roma contro Roma* (a.k.a. *Rome Against Rome*, 1964, Giuseppe Vari). The same themes and characters would also turn up from time to time: Kormak's lab in *Maciste contro il vampiro*, complete with stills and petrified victims, recalls the one seen in Giorgio Ferroni's stylish Gothic *Il mulino delle donne di pietra*, and the hero faces his own evil double, predating a famous moment in Bava's *Operazione paura* (a.k.a. *Kill, Baby.... Kill!*, 1966). On top of that, both *Maciste contro il vampiro* and *Ercole al centro della terra* make ample use of colored filters that give the stories an eerie atmosphere, very similar in tone to the typical mood of the subsequent Italian Gothic horror films. Another key recurring feature of both threads was the dicothomy between the two female models—the wife and the lover—declined in a supernatural context.

Since Ennio De Concini, who provided the original idea, had also collaborated to *La maschera del demonio*, it is no surprise, then, that *Maciste all'inferno*'s opening recalls Bava's debut, centering as it does on a witch being burned at the stake and throwing a curse over a village and its inhabitants, that will hang over the place for centuries. Unlike Bava, though, Freda staged the scene in exteriors, near Manziana, a borough near the lake Bracciano, about one hour's distance from Rome,

U.S. poster for *Maciste all'inferno* (1962).

and filmed it at dawn under a copper-colored sky, with striking effects. As a result, the sequence is not so much a replica of Bava's celebrated prologue, but a mixture between Carl Theodor Dreyer's *La passion de Jeanne d'Arc* (a.k.a. *The Passion of Joan of Arc*, 1928) and *Vredens dag* (a.k.a. *Day of Wrath*, 1943), with an emphasis on low-angle close-ups of the witch and her nemesis, and the impressive scenographic presence of the withered tree—the work of art director Andrea Crisanti—that will have a fundamental part in the story. (Later on, though, the sequence where the innocent Martha Gunt is brought to the place of the execution in a caged carriage bears a stunning resemblance to the opening scene in the 1949 film version of the opera *Il Trovatore* directed by Carmine Gallone, a testament to Italian directors' re-reading of the Gothic imagery via the filter of melodrama.) It is not the only example of Freda spicing up the story and the visuals according to his sensibility: the scene of the collective madness that follows the witch's execution is introduced by an impressive high-angle, long panning shot leftwise from atop a hill, in one of the director's trademark stylistic figures.

The story proceeds in typical Gothic fashion, with some odd similarities with Roger Corman's *The Haunted Palace* (1963, based on H. P. Lovecraft's *The Case of Charles Dexter Ward*), as one hundred years later a young couple moves into a haunted manor (the Odescalchi castle in Bracciano) and experiences the effects of the curse. Here, Freda treats the supernatural with a matter-of-fact approach that recalls Méliès' cinema of illusions: the effects, such as a portmanteau inexplicably catching fire, take place directly on-camera. Unlike in other similarly-themed Gothic horror films of the period, the young and unfortunate Martha Gunt does not become an instrument of evil, nor is she a *doppelgänger* of the witch, save for bearing the same name: there is never any doubt about her innocence, not even when flames rise up from the Bible on which Martha swears her innocence during the trial. Rather than dwelling on ambiguity, Freda is more interested in portraying the drama of the innocent being thrown in prison, put to trial and condemned by an inflexible, obtuse court, thus reprising the theme of the individual alone against a judging, indifferent multitude: the affectionate viewer will recognize motifs from his earlier works, such as *Il conte Ugolino, Il tradimento (Passato che uccide)* and *Teodora*, and here the director perhaps drew inspiration also from Frank Lloyd's *Maid of Salem* (1937), where Claudette Colbert played a young woman accused of being a witch in 1692's Massachusetts. Similarly, in the earlier scene of the angry mob assaulting the castle (shades of *Frankenstein*) Freda added a touch of swashbuckling as Martha's husband (the hopelessly inept Angelo Zanolli) dispatches a couple of assailants on the stairs with his sword before being knocked out by the villagers.

The story takes a brisk turn with the introduction of the titular hero. Maciste's arrival in 17th century Scotland is as dumbfounding a moment as ever in Italian films of the period, even more than the infamous *peplum*-cum-Western hybrid *Sansone e il tesoro degli Incas* (a.k.a. *Hercules and the Treasure of the Incas*, 1964), again involving Piero Pierotti, this time also as director. Maciste shows up on horseback, wearing nothing but his red short skirt, without the villagers being particularly impressed by that unusual individual. Once and for all detached from its original Ancient Roman environment, after his appearance in Ancient Egypt (*Maciste nella valle dei re*) and middle age China (*Maciste alla corte del Gran Khan*) in Panda Cinematografica's previous outings, Maciste has become an out-and-out superhuman, timeless presence, a righter of wrongs who travels through time and space, a figure more akin to Lee Falk's *The Phantom* than to the original incarnation of the hero as seen in *Cabiria*.

This is actually underlined by the fact that Maciste does not utter a single word until over half an hour into the film. This was the result of one of Freda's curt choices on the set, due to practical reasons: the lead, 19-year-old Venetian ex-gondolier Adriano Bellini—whom Freda described as "weakling despite the appearances, cowardly and crybaby,"[32] because he was scared of performing such feats as opening a door engulfed in flames—had the physique but definitely not the acting skills. The director was so unsatisfied with Bellini's delivery that he simply dropped most of his dialogue. Other lines were suppressed in post-production: in the scene where Maciste opens the door to Hell, Bellini can be clearly seen uttering words that are replaced in the soundtrack by Carlo Franci's interesting, *musique concrète*-influenced score.

With Maciste's descent into Hell through a passage that opens under the roots of the withered tree near the site of Martha Gunt's execution, *Maciste all'inferno* becomes a multilayered riff on themes that belong to classical mythology as well as to its middle age reworking. Freda's Hell—actually the so-called "white cave" at the Caves of Castellana site, in the region of Puglia—is a mad mixture of Dante's *Inferno* as seen in Gustave Doré's engravings and Hieronymus Bosch's apocalyptic panels, with the damned being bitten and tortured by monstrous devil-like figures or standing up in their open graves, and peopled with such extraneous presences as Sisyphus (who is about to be crushed by the huge rock he is pushing up a hill), Prometheus (tied to a rock and condemned to have his liver eaten by an eagle), and a horde of raging bulls; on top of that, Maciste's mission in search of a woman is basically a rewriting of Orpheus' descent to Hades to find Eurydice.

The nonchalant mixture of Catholicism and Paganism reaches the odd surreal note, but the scenes in Hell are wildly uneven in quality. Some, like Maciste opening a gigantic flaming door, or a herd of bulls (actually cows in disguise[33]) falling off a precipice, are a spectacular reminder of Freda at his inventive best, whereas others—such as Maciste's fight with a puppet lion whose fur changes places from one shot to the next—are laughable and hint at the film's lower budget compared to Panda's previous Maciste entries. The hero's encounter with a ferocious giant is another awkward moment: as with the cyclops sequence in *I giganti della Tessaglia*, in order to portray the difference in height, Bellini is replaced by a kid in long shots, with unconvincing results, whereas in other shots the director makes a more apt use of depth-of-field and misleading perspectives. Overall, Freda's *Inferno* looks like a garish carnival funhouse, complete with eerie lights and assorted tricks and traps (such as the closing gates that trap Maciste and the descending spiked panel that threatens to kill him), whose papier-maché essence is exhibited more often than not—see the bouncing rocks that often fall down on the characters, and the stone which Maciste employs like an umbrella of sorts to protect himself from a rain of sparks. This impression is heightened by Freda following the hero in long takes while the special effects take place on camera, such as in the scene where Maciste walks amid a river of fire that rises under his feet.

Maciste's feats are observed at a distance by two figures, the old Martha Gunt and her former executioner, Judge Farris, who condemned her to the stake out of vengeance after the woman had rejected his advances in her youth. Therefore, the witch and the judge are both guilty, and both eventually reunited in the afterlife. Although barely sketched, the two characters' backstory is an interesting reminder of gender relationships as matters of power, a theme that Freda explored in the past in *Il conte Ugolino* (Ugolino's relationship with his mistress), *Spartaco* (Spartaco losing his will to fight in Sabina's arms), *Teodora* (where, again, power equals a different social class), and *I vampiri* (with the Duchess' ascendancy over Professor Du Grand). What is more, the Judge's righteousness is revealed to be only apparent, and in the end the statue that the villagers had raised to commemorate his memory falls to pieces, releasing them from the burden of a past which, unbeknownst to them, has proven deceitful. The same mistrust can be detected in the character of the burgomeister (played by John Karlsen), who is at the head of the court that judges Martha guilty, thus committing an even bigger injustice than his predecessor. Ultimately, Farris is more guilty than Martha, since he abused his own position within the community, whereas Martha's curse is a strange one indeed, resulting in the women turning crazy and thus rebelling against their submissive position in a male-dominated society. Even though the film plays the supernatural angle straight, the director seems more attracted to the various aspects of human wickedness: superstition, malevolence, abuse of power—not forgetting the dangerous obtuseness of the headless crowd, always ready to follow the leader without any objection and giving vent to the most hateful and vile instincts.

With the appearance of the ravishing Hélène Chanel as the witch's young incarnation Fania, who puts a love spell on the hero, *Maciste all'inferno* plays a riff on another typical Gothic leitmotif, the sorceress' seductive and perturbing power. As in *I vampiri* and *I giganti della Tessaglia*, evil hides its true ugly self behind an illusion of youth and beauty, and Fania's menace lies in her power to corrupt the hero's will. In another multiple reference to classical and Christian mythology (the lotus eaters in the *Odyssey*, the Judgment of Paris, Eve tempting Adam), Fania has Maciste bite an apple that makes him oblivious to his original mission.

For the scenes in which a kind deity helps the hero recover his memory by recalling his previous exploits, the film features some of the more spectacular footage from other Panda productions featuring Maciste: *Maciste nella valle dei re* (a.k.a. *Son of Samson*, 1960, Carlo Campogalliani, starring Mark Forest), *Maciste nella terra dei ciclopi* (a.k.a. *Atlas in the Land of the Cyclops*, 1961, Antonio Leonviola, with Gordon Mitchell as Maciste) as well as the chariot sequence of Freda's own *Maciste alla corte del Gran Khan*, featuring Gordon Scott. Despite the odd insert of Bellini's close-ups to tie it all together, in a number of shots it is pretty obvious that the Maciste in sight is not played by the same actor. Although basically a trick to cut costs and reach an acceptable running time, while at the same time keeping in with the audience's demands, this surreal expedient is quite significant indeed: according to Stefano Della Casa it shows "how an *auteur* discourse can manifest itself within the way of working of Italian cinema of the period."[34] What is more, it also underlines the utter interchangeability of *peplum*'s musclebound heroes, reducing their many different incarnations into one omnicomprehensive body.

The *peplum* tradition demands that the evil woman redeem herself in the end, and Favia willingly sacrifices her own life to save the hero. Like his Gothic counterparts, Maciste loses the object of his desire: in the moment his lips touch Fania's, the woman turns into a pile of ashes in his arms. It is a less gruesome but almost as equally powerful an image as Duchess Du Grand reverting to her old self in *I vampiri*, which hints again at mythology and has a romantic side to it: Orpheus lost Eurydice for good when he turned back to watch her, whereas here Maciste loses Fania in the moment he kisses her—a testament to the hero's destiny of celibacy. Like so many Western heroes the director loved so much (such as Shane in George Stevens' 1953 film of the same name), Maciste's fate is to disappear on horseback in the distance, alone, after fulfilling his mission.

Perhaps due to Freda's drastic countermeasures to his lead actor's lack of acting skills, Bellini fares rather well in the role, and definitely better than in some of his subsequent sword-and-sandal films. The quick decline of the *peplum* marked a brisque ending to Bellini's career: in the mid-to-late 1960s he appeared in such minor genre works as *2 + 5: Missione Hydra* (a.k.a. *Star Pilot*, 1966, Pietro Francisci) and *Sette baschi rossi* (a.k.a. *The Seven Red Berets*, 1969, Mario Siciliano). In the 1970s he devoted himself exclusively to photonovels, where acting was even less important than it had been during his sword-and-sandal days—and one did not even have to deliver lines.

Like the director's other films of the period, *Maciste all'inferno* was a rushed production. As Freda recalled, whenever shooting on a Panda production lasted over two weeks, problems rose with Donati, whose habit of putting his nose into the director's job had been the cause of many arguments with the irascible filmmaker over the years. Production manager Piero Donati had another explanation of Freda's notorious haste.

He could shoot a whole film in two weeks, because he already had it all in his head. But also because on the third week of shooting he was already tired, and was thinking about his dogs or horses. That was the case with *Maciste all'inferno*, which was done in a hurry and with a minimal budget, also because the distributors and theater owners were asking for it.[35]

The British journalist John Francis Lane, who gained a marginal popularity in the early 1960s after his acting turns in such films as *La dolce vita*, *Il sorpasso* and *8½*, had a brief role as Martha's servant. Lane was definitely not impressed by Freda's directing habits: "Actually, his merit was to shoot quickly…. I remember that he placed the camera in a certain position, and then, 'Now scene one, then number 50, then 122,' always in the same position, and he shot half an hour's worth of film in one morning!" a recollection which is pretty explicative of the director's time-saving working methods. Lane was also dismissive about Freda's personal attitude on the set. "He was a true tyrant! With his dog, with women, with his cohorts. A bit sadistic, too, with people as well as with the animals he employed in the film. Extras and crew members hated him, everybody knows that."[36]

Ermanno Donati's wife Vira Silenti, who played the young and unfortunate Martha Gunt, the witch's innocent namesake, had quite a different view on the director.

> I often saw Freda … outside the set as well, since he was a friend of my husband's, and I don't agree with those who say he had a bad temper. You had to know how to deal with him, that's all. To me, he was an unhappy man, perhaps because of his very intense but unfortunate sentimental life. Back then he was having a relationship with a French woman, I don't remember her name. He showed up on the set with his mastiff, she with her puppy. Anyway, he was a highly professional filmmaker.[37]

Crisanti also had quite a good relationship with the director, whom he recalled as "very nice, a cheerful man, who had had everything in life, and so he loved to have fun, eat, he loved women," and was very impressed by Freda's female companion: "Still today, I have this image of this very beautiful woman, with her leopard fur, and always accompanied by her very aggressive dog."[38]

On the set, Freda asked for Bava's uncredited assistance to supervise some special effects shots.[39] He also hired a young assistant named Marcello Avallone, who would later become a filmmaker. Avallone's father, a horse race lover just like Freda, asked the director to take his boy to the set and have him learn the job as a personal favor. Freda agreed, but in return he asked young Marcello, who was a good jockey, to ride his favorite horse every day for an hour.[40] "He was like a father to me," Avallone claimed, adding his own personal view on the director's legendary cynicism. "But perhaps you have to be like that not to become a victim. They [Freda, Risi, and Monicelli] kept the right distance. Freda, perhaps, was more cynical than others. He liked to draw attention to other things: gambling, horse races … he was a great *viveur*. Then, well, he wasted and gambled all he had."[41]

Maciste all'inferno did all right at the Italian box-office, with 277 million *lire*. Unlike *Maciste alla corte del Gran Khan* and so many other sword-and-sandal flicks, the U.S. version retained the hero's name as well, since the American distributor used the English language track recorded at the Fono Roma studios and directed by the American expatriate Mel Welles, who later helmed *La isla de la muerte* (a.k.a. *Island of the Doomed*, 1967) and *Lady Frankenstein* (1971). The film was released in the States in late 1963[42] by Medallion Pictures as *The Witch's Curse*, with an emphasis on the horror content—a sign that *peplum*'s fortunes were declining. It played at the bottom of double bills: one funny program had it paired with *Alone Against Rome*, one of several films to which Freda collaborated, albeit uncredited, during that period.[43]

10

Intermezzo— A Director for Hire

Freda's subsequent directing job after the ill-fated *Agguato a Tangeri* marked the first of several films, made between 1958 and 1963, on which he took care, at various levels, of the action and battle scenes, receiving marginal or no directing credit at all. All these assignments were acted out for mere economic reasons, perhaps suggesting that the split with Gianna Maria Canale had indeed had monetarian consequences. These productions were definitely bigger than the movies Freda directed after *Teodora*, with the partial exception of *Beatrice Cenci*, and allowed him to do what he did best: big, spectacular action sequences.

This was the case with the ambitious sword-and-sandal epic *Nel segno di Roma* (Under the Sign of Rome, 1959), whose director Guido Brignone—an elderly veteran of Italian cinema who started his career in 1916 and helmed among others the legendary *Maciste all'inferno*—fell ill during the shooting. To make up for the grave inconvenience and wrap up the filming on schedule, the producers hired two filmmakers that could not have been more distant from each other: Riccardo Freda and Michelangelo Antonioni.

Even though he was not yet an internationally established master of Italian cinema, Antonioni was undergoing a successful period: his latest work, *Il grido* (1957), starring Steve Cochran, had been critically acclaimed, even though it had caused controversy due to its bleak ending. To him, the job was mostly a way to help an elderly friend and mentor: every day he sat by Brignone's bedside, he reported in detail what he had filmed, and ask for instructions for the following day. On the other hand, Freda, no longer an A-director, was finding it more and more difficult to stay afloat in the increasingly turbulent waters of Italian popular cinema. Freda teamed up with Mario Bava (uncredited) as his director of photography, whereas Antonioni worked with the titular d.o.p. Luciano Trasatti, and each took care of different aspects of the film: Antonioni (whose contribution remained uncredited) directed the indoor scenes, whereas Freda (credited with the "battle scenes" shot at Cinecittà and mostly in Zagreb, Croatia) took care of the exteriors, the action sequences, the battles. Most amazingly, the two never met, not even once, during filming. "We were shooting in the same studio, had breakfast in the same cafeteria, hung around the same editing room and never met face for to face, not even for a coffee or by chance."[1] Freda never even met the leads, Georges Marchal and Anita Ekberg, who shot all their scenes with Antonioni. Another important name was involved in the making of the film, even though only at the scriptwriting stage: Sergio Leone, who would make his film debut under similar circumstances, having to replace Mario Bonnard on the set of *Gli ultimi giorni di Pompei*. As Stefano Della Casa quipped, "the new *peplum*, in conclusion, swept away the genre's helmers of the silent era."[2]

Freda's judgment on the film, and on his fellow director's work, was, as usual, mordant.

> Antonioni is probably ashamed of having fallen so low. Or perhaps he realized that he could not make that kind of cinema, being like a fish out of water. It's much more difficult to shoot a period film than a contemporary one. Just look at the sequences he directed, which couldn't make believable characters who dress or behave in a way that is necessarily completely different from ours. Evidently, it is much easier to lock a couple in crisis in a room and listen to their confessions for a hour and a half.[3]

Even though his direction is stylish, with ample use of tracking shots, Antonioni was reportedly listless on the set. Mimmo Palmara recalled: "He couldn't care less, didn't direct the actors. When I had a quarrel with Jacques Sernas on the set, he watched us without intervening."[4] Chelo Alonso, on her film debut, had an argument with Antonioni during a dance number which she felt the latter could not shoot properly.[5] On the other hand, Freda was reportedly as choleric as ever, and ended up having an argument with Palmara—and unsuccessfully courting Alonso.[6] The battle scenes—shot as customary with several cameras—are indeed impressive, even though some stunts were blatantly re-used several times in the editing room, with somewhat awkward results.

Filmed in 1958, *Nel segno di Roma* came out in Italy on March 5, 1959, one day before Brignone's death, to good box-office results. It was released theatrically in the United States in September of that year by American International Pictures, in a dubbed version,[7] as *Sign of the Gladiator*.[8] As Samuel Z. Arkoff recalled, "We also picked up a picture called *The Sign of Rome*, which had no gladiator, but in the dubbing we had the guy in it talk about the days when he was a gladiator, and we called the picture *Sign of the Gladiator* [laughs]!"[9] In the added opening narration we are in fact told that officers and generals of the Roman army were often recruited from the ranks of gladiators and that the foremost of the ex-gladiators was chosen to lead the army against Zenobia's hordes. Unlike with most foreign movies the company purchased for a U.S. release, AIP did not have Les Baxter re-score the film, and retained Angelo Lavagnino's music, except for the newly shot opening and closing credits. The main titles for the American version featured a scantily-clad girl dancing round a flaming altar, under Lavagnino's music cue taken from the scene where Marcus Valerius (Marchal) is tortured in the desert. The end titles featured a pop song, *Xenobia* (as Ekberg's character had been renamed), written by Dominic Frontiere with lyrics by Milton Raskin and sung by Bill Lee.[10]

In 1960, in the midst of a wave of Bible-inspired movies, Freda was planning to direct a big-budget Old Testament film. *L'arca di Noé (Il diluvio universale)* (Noah's Arc—The Flood) was to be a return to the limelight, a large scale epic to rival Hollywood products. According to the director, the project had first taken shape during his period at Lux: under Gualino's suggestion, Freda and Ermanno Gurgo Salice, Gualino's the latter's brother-in-law and the head of Lux France, had gone to New York to look for an American co-producer, but to no avail. The project eventually landed in the hands of Carlo Ponti, who financed it with his newborn company, Compagnia Cinematografica Champion: the budget was over 1,300 million *lire*, a remarkable sum for the time.

The script (penned by future film director Damiano Damiani, from a story by Freda) played very liberally with the Old Testament. It takes place in Sodom, ruled by the dissolute queen Machnet. Her daughter Elias has many lovers, including the warlord Bikra and the eunuch High Priest Rafa, who both aim at the throne; however, Elias falls in love with Noah's grandson Aron, who is building an ark on a mountain with his people in order to survive an impending flood. Seduced by Elias, Aron abandons Noah and moves to Sodom: there, a love triangle ensues, which leads to Aron killing Bikra and Rafa taking advantage of the murder to marry Elias. But God's wrath will be terrible: Sodom and all its sinners (including Elias and Aron) are destroyed by the flood, while Noah's ark sails, saving the pure of heart.

Freda's original story featured many familiar elements: Machnet "tries in vain to stem old age through inhuman blood sacrifices" like Duchess Du Grand; Elias hangs around taverns and alleys like Justinian in *Teodora*; there are plenty of spectacular sequences, including gladiator games in the arena and a fight between a man and a lion. Besides, Damiani's script described the sins of Sodom with a wild abandon that was quite unusual in Italian cinema of the period: Old men buy young girls at the slave market and enquire about their virginity; the queen indulges in sapphic pleasures; a ship full of semi-naked men assault a boat full of naked virgins; Elias performs a sexy dance covered only with pearls that eventually fall and leave her naked; the dialogue is full of allusive lines, including references to homosexuality and sodomy; lastly, in a scene two men are enticed by an underage prostitute "about ten years old."

Ponti provided Freda with an impressive cast: Gino Cervi (as Noah), Stephen Boyd (Aron), Joan Collins (Elias), Anthony Steel (Bikra), Massimo Girotti, Carlo Ninchi (Rafa), Claudio Gora, Giovanna Galletti (Machnet), Sylva Koscina and Gabriella Farinon; Gábor Pogány was the d.o.p., and Giovanni Fago was Freda's assistant. Shooting was supposed to start on August 15, 1960, and last for eight weeks. However, *L'arca di Noé (Il diluvio universale)* never took off. "Rarely, in a script, there happens to be such a large number of risqué scenes and details," wrote the board of censors that preventively examined it on that same month; the makers were quite aware of the risk, as proven by an opening note to the script which warned that "the most realistic scenes will be revised and filmed according to the more orthodox principles of the Italian and American censorship." The board concluded: "Therefore it is perhaps appropriate to wait for the result of such a work of self-revision before formulating a definitive judgment on the film." The response did not bode well, and convinced Ponti to shelve such a controversial and costly movie. The times were not ready for such a daring take on the Old Testament, and it would take a few years for preventive film censorship to disappear. The failure of his Biblical project led Freda to more work-for-hire directing jobs; he would draw again from the Scriptures for his 1970 film *Tamar Wife of Er*.

The presence of American filmmakers in Cinecittà had been a growing occurrence during the last decade. The less costly production values favored investments on the part of Hollywood-based production companies, which were able to shoot expensive-looking movies for much more sustainable budgets. Similarly, many actors who were finding it more and more difficult to get acting jobs in Hollywood were moving to Rome, where it was easier to get good roles and squeeze every drop of the respectability earned in their Hollywood years: young thesps had the chance to become stars, albeit less shiny ones, and has-beens were greeted by audiences who did not care if their fame had long since waned. On top of that, there was no lack of film crews either. Cinecittà had nurtured a veritable army of expert and skillful technicians, as well as painters, artists, set decorators, masters of arms, stuntmen, extras—hundreds of people who gravitated around costly productions as well as low-budget ones, which were often made with leftover sets and costumes.

A common occurrence had American directors being put under contract so as to sign a picture—thus giving it a respectability and, more important, a better marketability—while actually leaving most of the job to an Italian colleague, who would only receive a co-directing credit in the version for the home market. The reasons were basically financial ones: on the one hand, a "name" director would guarantee distribution abroad, whereas on the other hand the presence of an Italian filmmaker would satisfy the law requirements for the film to be labeled as Italian and benefit from economic facilities. That was the case with *I mongoli* (1961), officially André De Toth's second Italian effort after *Morgan il pirata* (a.k.a. *Morgan the Pirate*, 1960) starring Steve Reeves and co-directed by Primo Zeglio.

I mongoli was a big-budget Italian-French co-production starring Jack Palance and Anita Ekberg, and shot at the De Laurentiis studios in Rome and near Belgrad: De Toth acted as "supervising director," with Leopoldo Savona credited as second unit director. Yet Riccardo Freda was called in too, due to his skill at shooting action scenes: for the second time after *Nel segno di Roma*, he would do directing work on a picture signed by others—a much more remunerative job than his own pictures, and one which he could accomplish very quickly. As Ennio De Concini once recalled, by then Freda was selling his professional services by the scene[11]: a way to adapt himself to the new wave of big budget epics—the kind of films he always wanted to make—that, ironically, were credited to big name American directors whose skills were far less accomplished than his own. Freda's judgment on his colleague was as mordacious as ever.

> De Toth, like most American filmmakers in Italy, was lost. In Italy, the American director was a type entrusted with supervising and sticking on to a scenario which he hadn't written. He had a seat with his name on it, but his rights ended there. He would sign the script page by page, a commitment which prevented him from changing even a single comma. During filming, a script girl checked that the schedule was being followed to the letter.[12]

This is clearly an ungenerous judgment for a filmmaker who accomplished such extraordinary and creative works as *Pitfall* (1948), *Slattery's Hurricane* (1949) and *Day of the Outlaw* (1959), among others. Still, Freda's depiction of De Toth's attitude during his Italian stint is not an exaggeration, as it was common to other foreign moviemakers employed in Italian co-productions. Freda would discuss this at length, explaining how the U.S. directors he and Bava had worked with would show no interest in adding any creative input to the films, and just stuck to a workmanlike routine job. He recalled how Jacques Tourneur used to ask Bava for advice (to which he usually replied: "You are the director, not me...") on the set of *La battaglia di Maratona*, and how the cameramen were instructed to film master shots from every possible angle, just in case. Similarly, all the dialogue scenes were shot with close-ups of the actors which would be inserted in the sequence at will, according to the editor's choice. Freda also hated the practice of storyboarding, to which his foreign colleagues would stick to the letter, an occurrence he had witnessed during the filming of King Vidor's *War and Peace* (1956).

In the Italian prints of *I mongoli*, the opening credits are quite confusing. At first a card says "*Un film di André de Toth*" (A film by...), but then another one says "*Regia di Leopoldo Savona*" (Directed by...), followed by yet another which specifies, "*Regista delle scene di battaglia: Riccardo Freda*" (Director of the battle scenes: ...). Even though his contribution was seemingly confined to the battles, which were later re-used as stock shots on many low-budget productions, Freda claimed to have directed the majority of the film, which is quite plausible. The official co-director Leopoldo Savona (1913–2000) had been Giuseppe De Santis' assistant for many years, on some of the latter's best works—such as *Non c'è pace tra gli ulivi* (a.k.a. *Under the Olive Tree*, 1950) and *Uomini e lupi* (a.k.a. *Men and Wolves*, 1957). Savona also collaborated among others with Luigi Zampa, Camillo Mastrocinque, Alberto Lattuada and Freda himself (as second unit director on *Agi Murad—Il diavolo bianco*), and went on to work as technical advisor on Pier Paolo Pasolini's film debut *Accattone* (1961). His career as a director was spotty as best, though, with 18 titles between 1955's *Il principe dalla maschera rossa* (a modest adventure film which was released in France as *L'aigle rouge*, The Red Eagle) and 1977's *Le due orfanelle*, yet another rendition of Adolphe d'Ennery's tearjerking novel, which Freda himself had filmed in 1965. His *oeuvre* also comprises the weird Gothic horror *Byleth (Il demone dell'incesto)* (1972) and the obscure *giallo La morte scende leggera* (1972, released in 1974). All in all, Savona did not seem fit to handle a rather important production with a prestigious cast, whereas Freda had the experience and energy the other lacked.

Nevertheless, most of *I mongoli* is rather nondescript at best, and wavers between competently shot action scenes and turgid melodramatic interludes. As Genghis Khan's evil son Ogatai, Palance makes for a physically imposing if not wholly believable Mongol, although he is definitely better than John Wayne in the Duke's turn as Genghis Khan in the ill-fated *The Conqueror* (1956, Dick Powell)—here Genghis is played by the great Roldano Lupi, the grim-looking star of Ferdinando Maria Poggioli's extraordinary Gothic drama *Il cappello da prete* (1944), Pietro Germi's *Il testimone* (1945) and Alberto Lattuada's *Il delitto di Giovanni Episcopo*. Still, the film had its share of admirers: Jacques Lourcelles, in his pioneering essay "Un homme seul," praised the ending, with the barbarian hordes moving away into the sunset, as the best thing Freda had done in recent years, and so did Jean-Marie Sabatier in his book *Les classiques du cinéma fantastique*.

Working for hire was profitable but had its share of side effects—namely, having to swallow the employers' choices. Freda complained about the way De Toth and the producers had mercilessly cut a beautiful shot he had devised, as an introduction to the climactic battle between the Polish troops and the Mongols, thus breaking the scene's inner rhythm.

> Near the end of *I mongoli* there was a very long and very slow side traveling shot, about 50 metres long, when the Polish army, arrived before the Mongolian walls, stops since there are no external signs of activity. This shot was very important, because it balanced the whole sequence and served as a transition between the preparation of the battle and the battle itself.... There, the camera tracked slowly along the ranks of the Polish army, and progressively got closer to the soldiers' faces. One could see in their eyes the fear, the anguish, the astonishment and the anxiety that took hold of them in that moment. In fact, once they arrived under the city walls, nothing happened. There was utter silence, heavy and oppressive. And, all of a sudden, the doors opened down on the soldiers, with a terrifying rumble, which augmented the violence of surprise.[13]

Other cuts performed by the production (the film was passed uncut by Italian censors) involved Anita Ekberg's dance routine around the fire during a night scene, and the end of the sequence where Stephen of Crakow (Franco Silva) rescues Amina (Antonella Lualdi).

Working with Jack Palance—who in turn did not get along at all with Ekberg, despite the usual rumors of an on-set flirtation between the two—was nothing short of an ordeal. Freda called him "an extraordinary pain in the ass" and, once he got tired of his lead's constant bickering and interferences on the set (such as his habit of doing pushups just as Freda was about to call "Action!"), he resumed the trick he had played on Amedeo

Nazzari during the filming of *Il tradimento*: he found a German extra who looked very much like Palance and shot the whole final sequence of Ogatai's suicide atop his father's funeral pyre (to which the actor had objected, claiming it was not a honorable ending for his character) with the double, filmed in a long shot and mostly with his back to the camera.[14]

I mongoli surfaced in the States (as *The Mongols*) only in September 1966, a full five years after its making. It was distributed by Colorama Features.

According to Stefano Della Casa, Freda was initially supposed to shoot *Marco Polo— L'avventura di un italiano in Cina* after helming *Maciste alla corte del Gran Khan*. A big-budgeted epic starring Rory Calhoun in the role played by Gary Cooper in Archie Mayo's *The Adventures of Marco Polo* (1938), whose plot it closely resembled, the movie bore little adherence to the Venetian writer's *Il Milione* (a.k.a. *Book of the Marvels of the World*) and featured the expected nods to the current political situation.[15] *Marco Polo* was eventually directed by Piero Pierotti and Hugo Fregonese (although as usual the U.S. version is credited solely to Fregonese),[16] and was released in the States in a dubbed version by American International Pictures, with a new Les Baxter score replacing Angelo Francesco Lavagnino's. Since the sets and extras were the same as *Maciste alla corte del Gran Khan*, which he was shooting for producers Donati and Carpentieri, Freda allegedly filmed a number of battle scenes—twenty, according to Della Casa—which ended up in the film. It may well be that the argument with Donati on the set of the *Maciste* film resulted in the director walking away from the production of *Marco Polo*. However, Freda himself denied having taken part in the film when interviewed by Éric Poindron.[17]

A title which usually is not even listed in Freda's filmography, *Solo contro Roma* (1962) was a *peplum* vehicle for the ravishing Rossana Podestà, produced by her husband Marco Vicario and co-scripted by Vicario's brother Renato (under the a.k.a. Gastad Green, usually mistakenly referred to Ernesto Gastaldi[18]), the same team behind Antonio Margheriti's Gothic horror film *La vergine di Norimberga* (a.k.a. *The Virgin of Nuremberg*, 1963). *Solo contro Roma* was one of a handful of pictures credited to "Herbert Wise," a.k.a. Luciano Ricci, whose name was also associated with Warren Kiefer's *Il castello dei morti vivi* (a.k.a. *Castle of the Living Dead*, 1964) for tax reasons, even though Ricci did not even set foot on the set.[19] "You can imagine the disorder that reigned over Italian cinema and its co-productions," Freda commented. "It was my friend Attilio Riccio who often co produced those sword and sandal films. He had been protecting me at the Ministry during Fascism, and he had produced *Beatrice Cenci*. Whenever he was in trouble while shooting a *peplum*, he called me."[20]

Freda was hired to film a sequence set in the arena, where a wounded gladiator fights alone against a four-horse chariot, since, in his own words, the other director was "lost amid two thousand extras."[21] He did the job in just one day, using six cameras at once. The scene was shot in Pola, in the Yugoslavian territories of Istria. On the other hand, Freda did *not* direct the sequence of Lang Jeffries' whipping, which ended up in an amusing "100 best" list in a gay-themed book on the subject of male whipping on film.[22] In what was a customary practice during the age of *peplum*, the arena scene was later recycled in another Vicario production, Antonio Margheriti's *Il crollo di Roma* (a.k.a. *The Fall of Rome*, 1963), which consisted of stock footage for over a third of its running time.[23]

Solo contro Roma was released theatrically in the U.S. in December 1963 by Medallion Pictures (the Los Angeles opening took place on March 18, 1964) as *Alone Against Rome*, and gained tepid interest from the press. *The Boston Globe* wrote: "The drama, as one can readily see, is geared to an undemanding audience, but of even less distinction is the dialogue." However, the reviewer praised "the lovely Rossana Podesta [*sic*] ... a girl endowed bountifully by nature" and mentioned that "a great deal of the action takes place in a huge arena where big, brawny Jeffries Lang [*sic*] performs miracles of strength and agility...."[24]

Another film produced by Attilio Riccio which Freda is said to have taken part in was *Il dominatore dei sette mari (Sir Francis Drake)* (a.k.a. *Seven Seas to Calais*, 1962), a pirate movie signed by yet another odd American / Italian couple of filmmakers, Rudolph Maté and Primo Zeglio, and featuring a very young Mario Girotti, soon to be known as Terence Hill. According to Stefano Della Casa, Freda "took care of the editing of the naval battle scene," writing its *découpage*.[25] Still, the director vehemently denied his participation to the film, as he did with *Marco Polo*, when asked about it by Poindron: "It was again two Attilio Riccio productions, that's why everyone wants to put my name on these two films...."[26] However, if Freda's assertions seem true regarding *Il dominatore dei sette mari*, which was indeed produced by Riccio's company Adelphia, the producer surely did not have anything to do with *Marco Polo*, which was a Panda production. In the U.S. the film was credited solely to Rudolph Maté, in his final directing job.

Oro per i Cesari (1963), the last of Freda's largely uncredited works-for-hire, was an Italian-French *peplum* co-produced by Joseph Fryd, Freda's friend Attilio Riccio, and Bernard Borderie (the director of the *Angelique* series starring Michèle Mercier). The project, based on Florence A. Seward's historical novel of the same name, had been planned for filming by MGM as early as 1961, when Seward's book was first published, but was halted after the box-office failure of Nicholas Ray's *King of Kings* (1961): Fryd took over, and the original big budget production turned into a more economic one to be shot in Europe.[27] The story was also drastically altered from the novel, with emphasis on action over characterization.

Shot in the countryside near Terni in the summer of 1962,[28] with the breathtaking Marmore's Falls appearing in a number of scenes, *Oro per i Cesari* benefitted from the presence of Jeffrey Hunter, who co-starred in John Ford's *The Searchers* and *Sergeant Rutledge* (1960), and played Jesus Christ in *King of Kings*, as the protagonist, slave architect Lacer. For the second time after *I mongoli*, Freda (officially the second unit director) had to stand in for André De Toth, who was credited as director in the United States, whereas the Italian version listed Sabatino Ciuffini as director with De Toth credited as "supervising director" in accordance to co-production rules for the film to be listed as an Italian co-production and receive the subsequent law benefits. Given that Ciuffini was a screenwriter and this would be his only directorial credit, Freda's assertions shed a light on how things might have really gone on the set. "I claim the whole film as mine from start to finish. The producers put De Toth aside on the second day of shooting. André De Toth did not shoot *anything*."[29]

In his memoir *Fragments*, the Hungarian-American filmmaker never mentioned *Oro per i Cesari* (actually he gave scant mention to his film work overall), and in Anthony Slide's book *De Toth on De Toth* he dismissed his Italian experience as "a vacation, taking a breather between climbing new peaks. Unfortunately, I climbed the wrong one, and when I skied down one of the Swiss Alps, I broke my neck. And that wasn't on the schedule," he concluded, referring to an unfortunate accident that caused him a long hiatus from the set: he would return to directing only in 1968, with the excellent war movie

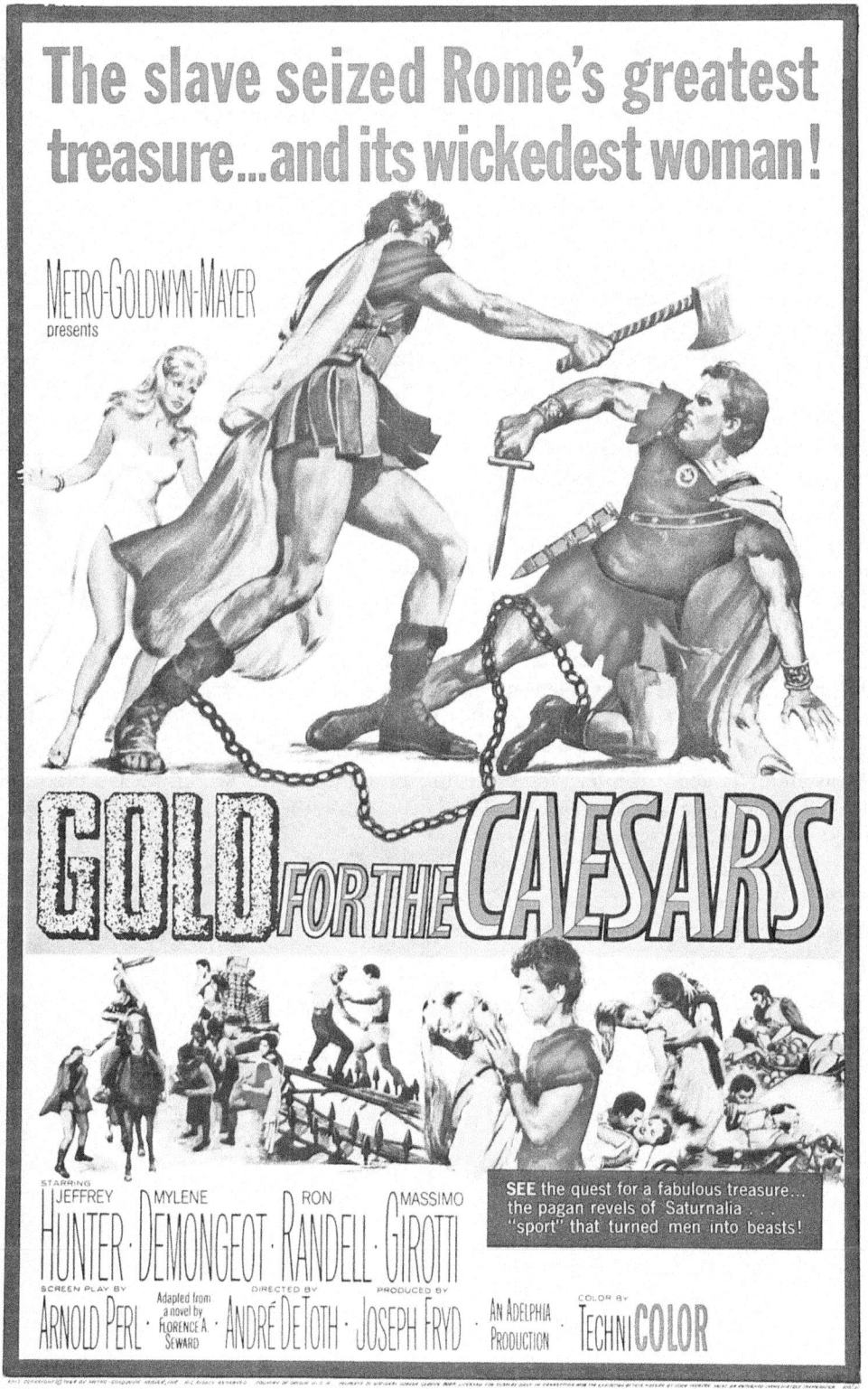

U.S. one-sheet poster for *Oro per i Cesari* (1963).

Play Dirty. Whether it be because of the producers' dissatisfaction, his own disinterest toward the material or the skiing accident, De Toth's involvement in his last Italian film seems almost non-existent. This is confirmed by *Oro per i Cesari*'s female lead, the French-born Mylène Demongeot, who in her autobiography *Tiroirs secrets* stressed the director's absence, thus reinforcing Freda's version. "De Toth seemed more interested in playing golf than in movies. He willingly left free ground to Riccardo Freda, who shot very spectacular scenes."[30]

Without venturing too far into stylistic analyses, given that Freda himself wasn't obviously that committed to the project and this was merely a work-for-hire job, one can sense the Italian director's touch in the film's most spectacular bits, such as the opening sequence depicting the building of a bridge, with the camera gradually exposing the environment via one of his customary tracking shots, or the climax featuring the final destruction of a dam. What is more, the gold fusion scene brings to mind the climax of Freda's own *Il magnifico avventuriero*, made the following year. On the other hand, the romantic subplot is indifferently handed, and despite Raffaele Masciocchi's atmospheric photography most studio scenes are uninteresting and feel outdated: the Saturnalia sequence ("See the pagan revels of Saturnalia" screamed a poster) depicts the kind of orgy one could find in the sword-and-sandal flicks made during the previous decade. The score retained some of Franco Mannino's cues from Freda's own *Le sette spade del vendicatore*.

Besides working for the third time with the ever-reliable Massimo Girotti, here in an unusual villain role, Freda had the chance to direct a Hollywood star, even if in a declining phase of his career. He went on at length praising Jeffrey Hunter as one of the most disciplined actors he worked with (discipline being apparently a thespian's best quality according to Freda). It was one of the rare occasions the director had kind words to say about an actor. Hunter reunited with Ron Randell, with whom he had played in *King of Kings*, while minor roles were played by Italian actors such as Ettore Manni, Furio Meniconi and Giulio Bosetti.

The film was distributed in the States by Metro-Goldwyn-Mayer in June 1964, as *Gold for the Caesars*, to little commercial and critical success, even though *Variety* called it "an acceptable piece of product that may satisfy the most undemanding filmgoers...."[31] It is currently available on DVD in the Warner Archives on-demand series.

11

The Gothic Years

L'orribile segreto del Dr. Hichcock

Readers who on July 13, 1962, purchased Milan's newspaper *Corriere d'informazione* could find on page 3 the umpteenth piece devoted to movie gossip. Among the expected news about Claudia Cardinale and Jane Mansfield, columnist Ugo Naldi briefly reported an amusing anecdote.

> The fashion has begun to pass off as foreign films that were produced and manufactured in Italy and interpreted by Italian actors. The trick is simple: you impose exotic names to the director and the actors and you're done. At least for the moviegoers, who think they are watching a foreign movie. Because the trick does not work the same way when it comes to submitting these pseudo-foreign films to the committee of experts for admission to the benefits of the law. There is a risk that experts deem these movies as foreign, excluding them from such benefits. This is what has happened to the film *L'orribile segreto del Dr. Hickock* [sic].... It was hard for the producers to prove that it was a very Italian film: they had to exhibit lots of papers and documents in order to prove the true identity of the director and actors. But the audience won't have access to such documents and will pay the ticket thinking they're about to watch an American movie, perhaps the latest exploit of the wizard of thrill. Because no one will even notice that, to avoid trouble, the producers used Hitchok's [sic] name in the title, but altered it into Hickock [sic].[1]

Even though the piece smells a lot like the brainchild of some cunning press office—it is really unbelievable that a film commission ever came close to being deceived by English pseudonyms, since producers were required to submit official papers with a complete list of the cast and crew (and their nationality) before the beginning of shooting, it is revealing of the way Freda's second Gothic horror picture was conceived and launched to an audience that, indeed, was still quite naive and inattentive when it came to decipher a motion picture's opening and closing credits.

L'orribile segreto del Dr. Hichcock blossomed in quite a different climate than *I vampiri*. Several years had passed since then, and in the meantime other directors had tried their hands at the genre. The first batch of Italian horror movies, although not particularly popular in their home country, had met a surprising success abroad, starting with *La maschera del demonio*, and favored the sudden reviviscence of a trend that seemed to have withered almost immediately (in 1961 only one horror film had been produced, Paolo Heusch's *Lycanthropus*, a.k.a. *Werewolf in a Girls' Dormitory*). Foreign sales rejuvenated Italian Gothic like blood transfusions did with Duchess Du Grand, and after the awkward early attempts, scriptwriters were learning to reshape their approach to the genre so as to give it a more defined identity.

When Ernesto Gastaldi received a phone call from Panda Cinematografica's Luigi

Carpentieri, asking him to write a horror script, he was some sort of a veteran in the genre, having helmed not only *Lycanthropus* but also Renato Polselli's *L'amante del vampiro* (a.k.a. *The Vampire and the Ballerina*, 1960) and *Il mostro dell'opera* (a.k.a. *The Vampire of the Opera*, released in 1964 but actually shot for the most part in 1961). A former CSC graduate, at just twenty-eight Gastaldi had been involved in the movie business for several years: after working as a ghost writer for Ugo Guerra, he had signed a number of scripts for such directors as Umberto Lenzi and Domenico Paolella, and published a number of crime and sci-fi novels, usually with the a.k.a. Julian Berry, a name borrowed from a friend of his, one Julian Birri. He was, one would say, a specialist.

"Carpentieri called and asked me to write an outline around a *giallo* story that he liked called *Spectral*. I wrote a treatment and called it *Raptus*," Gastaldi recalled.

> The story was different at first, because there wasn't any necrophilia in it. I don't remember now why I added this element later; perhaps one of the associates asked for something harder, more macabre. When you have to write many horror or thriller films, it's important to keep finding new topics. Necrophilia was just one of them. Here in Italy, no one was upset by this.[2]

There is the possibility that the suggestion came on the part of Freda, who on the other hand claimed, albeit unconvincingly, the paternity of the whole story ("It is entirely my idea. I nurtured it for a long time but it is Ernesto Gastaldi, a very good scenarist, who shaped it into form"[3]), although the scriptwriter's recollections seem to depict Freda as a mere executor.

> The producer summoned the director and gave him the script to read. The latter could say yes or no. He hardly ever met the writer. In fact on that occasion I met Freda by chance, and we chatted about football, politics and weather: not a word about the script he was about to be handed. When Donati, an imperious temper leaning on violence, slammed my script in his hands, saying: "Let's see if you have the balls to shoot this stuff, it's about corpses!" Riccardo did not even open the script or read the title; he put it under his arm and smiled seraphic: "As long as I get paid, I'm shooting even the phone book." And left without another word.[4]

The Italian locandina for *L'orribile segreto del Dr. Hichcock* (1962) hinted at the film's sexual theme.

Either way, the basic story—a widower, Dr. Hichcock, remarries and takes his second wife Cynthia to the family house, apparently still haunted by the presence of the first wife Margaretha, who eventually turns out to be alive and planning Cynthia's demise with her husband's help—was given a decisive extra kick by turning Hichcock into a man who is sexually attracted by the dead.

Consistently with his purpose of grounding horror within the individual's mind, in interviews of the period the director mentioned such influences as Richard von Krafft-Ebing's 1886 book *Psychopathia Sexualis*[5] and the historical episode of the killing of Marie-Thérèse Louise of Savoy-Carignan, princess of Lamballe, friend of Marie Antoinette, murdered by the *sans-culottes* in 1792 and turned into the object of necrophiliac practices by her executioners. More pointed references on Freda's part were Robert Louis Stevenson's *Strange Case of Dr. Jekyll and Mr. Hyde*, for the duality at the core of Dr. Hichcock's behavior, and Edgar Allan Poe. "I love the character and his decadence," as Freda explained, "I love his mélange of Fantastic and science. In Poe, the house becomes a character. He certainly influenced me in *L'orribile segreto del Dr. Hichcock*."[6]

Poe's work did surely drive Gastaldi's script, perhaps by way of the Roger Corman adaptations

Alternate Italian poster for *L'orribile segreto del Dr. Hichcock* (1962).

that were so popular at the time: the scriptwriter himself revealed that at the time of writing Mario Bava's *La frusta e il corpo* (a.k.a. *The Whip and the Body*, 1963) he was specifically commissioned something in the vein of AIP films.[7] *L'orribile segreto del Dr. Hichcock* features many elements in common with the works of the Baltimore-based writer: the widower who returns with his new wife to the family mansion, where the woman falls prey to rumors and mysterious presences, recalls *Ligeia*, whereas Margaretha's premature burial and Cynthia's attempted one are a nod to one of Poe's primary obsessions, and a common feature in contemporaneous Gothics. What is more, in a typical Poe-like process, the memory of Hichcock's first wife is associated with the presence of a black cat, Jezebel: on more than one occasion, the feline becomes Margaretha's emanation of sorts (even appearing by her side in the portraits scattered throughout the house), to the point of jumping over her coffin just after the funeral—a Poe moment if ever there was one.

Still, Gastaldi's main influence when writing the script was—as the title blatantly gives away, although with a minimal spelling trick so as to avoid legal trouble[8]—Alfred Hitchcock. The choice of making the character (named Stoltz in *Raptus*) a namesake of the British filmmaker drew on Hitch's enormous popularity in Italy: besides the steady box-office success of his movies, the TV series *Alfred Hitchcock Presents*, broadcast on Italian television since January 1959, made him a household name, and the British director's tongue-in-cheek appearances as himself in the episodes' introductions turned his face and silhouette into a synonym for the suspenseful and the macabre—even to people who had barely, if ever, seen any of his celluloid masterworks.

Overall, *L'orribile segreto del Dr. Hichcock* is a *pot-pourri* of homages to Hitch's *oeuvre*, starting with *Rebecca* (1940): Cynthia's bewilderment inside a huge and strange villa, her relationship with a hostile housekeeper clearly modeled on Mrs. Danvers, and the memory of Margaretha haunting the place are all elements borrowed from the 1940 film. But Freda and Gastaldi unearthed other Hitchcockian fetishes as well: the human skull found on the bed comes from *Under Capricorn* (1949); the poisoned glass of milk followed by the camera in close-up nods to *Suspicion* (1941); the complicity between Hichcock and Martha the housekeeper hints at the one between Claude Rains and his mother in *Notorious* (1946), and so do Cynthia's quest for the key to open the secret door and her being slowly poisoned by her husband; the sequence where Cynthia, wandering in the villa, discovers Martha intent on taking care of her insane "sister" (actually Margaretha), seen from behind on a chair, refers to *Psycho*. Last but not least, the funeral under the rain, with the parade of open umbrellas seen from an aerial shot, pays homage to a celebrated sequence in *Foreign Correspondent*.

However, the film includes just as many references to the Romantic tradition, namely to such works as *Jane Eyre* and *Wuthering Heights* and the so-called "female Gothic," which, according to Misha Kavka, "involves the haunting of a woman by another woman (usually a rival, a *Doppelgänger*, or a mother) and/or by her own projected sexual fears," and features a female protagonist "who is simultaneously a victim and an investigator of a haunting that is caused by anxieties about transgressive sexuality." Such a haunting may be real or simply paranoid, but as a consequence "the line between the supernatural and the psychological remains permeable, with the result that phantoms must equally be read as psychological manifestations, while paranoid fears always suggest the possibility of uncanny materialization."[9]

Gastaldi leans on typical fairytale-like elements, such as the forbidden door that the wife must not open, and plays as expected with all the requisite Gothic staples—thunderstorms, menacing noises and shadows, and so forth. Nevertheless, the result openly discards the supernatural so enthusiastically embraced by its peers. There is no room for monsters, save for a bizarre dream sequence, and the otherworldly angle is ultimately revealed as a red herring: the alleged ghastly presence that haunts the huge mansion where Cynthia and her husband have come to stay is a definitely human, tangible menace, not just the product of an obsession, and more than a true ghost—indeed a real, malevolent individual made of flesh and blood. This way, the film moves from the territory of *fantastique* and Gothic melodrama to mystery and out-and-out horror.[10] Whereas several plot synopses hint at Hichcock's plan to make Margaretha regain her beauty with Cynthia's blood, it is pretty obvious that said purpose is completely demented and has no factual basis: Hichcock is no mad scientist, nor does he have any secret lab where he performs experiments on rejuvenation. Margaretha's madness has infected and subjugated the other inhabitants, first Martha and then the doctor, who are now subdued to her: in a way, it is a similar situation to that of Duchess Du Grand—only, without any puerile rejuvenating serum. It is a mere delusional delirium, and it all takes place within the husband and wife's demented minds. Gastaldi maintains that the film's confused climax was the result of on-set alterations (debatably, since the synopsis for *Raptus* is identical to the finished film, save for the Swiss setting), and yet the story still stands up in its own weird way.

L'orribile segreto del Dr. Hichcock is characterized by a growing sense of bewilderment and misplacement that affects the viewer as well as Cynthia. Non-Euclidean geometries abound, surfaces have unexpected proportions and shapes, the interiors reflect the characters' inner selves and mirror their anxieties, fears and repressed feelings. For one thing, the planimetry of Hichcock's mansion is quite unclear and seems to change from scene to scene—a fact no doubt caused by the tight shooting schedule. And yet the effect of disorientation goes beyond a mere continuity error, as when in one scene we see Silvano Tranquilli's character emerging from a window that *should not be there*. It is as if the place has become a living organism, a labyrinth that attempts to engulf the characters within itself. Similarly, the underground tunnel that Cynthia walks through by candlelight becomes a boundless, endless path, just like in a nightmare. "I had fun in demolishing and rebuilding the house in order to better lose Barbara Steele and the viewer inside it,"[11] Freda would quip.

Even the passage of time in the movie is not quantifiable according to rational parameters. If this is to be expected in a purely supernatural work—as with the never-ending night in Margheriti's *Danza macabra*—such an occurrence is decidedly more unsettling when it takes place within a "rational" story. As in *Agi Murad—Il diavolo bianco*, the normal day/night sequence becomes blurred, and several environments are arbitrarily associated with a perennial low light or semi-darkness, as Hichcock's villa is, so that one is never sure which hour of the day it is. And, last but not least, the chronology of events becomes uncertain and deceitful. As film critic Glenn Erickson noted, when Hichcock and Cynthia first arrive at the doctor's mansion, Martha assures the latter that "tomorrow" she will be moving her crazy sister to a mental institute. The following evening, though, Martha claims to have sent her sister away "yesterday."[12] Such incongruences are the effect of hasty scriptwriting, disjointed editing, and a shooting schedule feverishly browsed in order to reach the expected number of setups per day. Nevertheless, the result has an undetermined quality that leads to a suggestive complexity which is proper to the realm of the *fantastique*.

The director was adamant about his attitude to the genre. In his memoir, he maintained that horror had

> nothing to do or deal with the objective depiction of some monster. That is an expedient which I consider of inferior quality, almost worthy of the Carnival of Viareggio [Italy's best known Carnival, taking place in the Tuscan town of Viareggio], with papier maché employed to scare the most

inexperienced viewers ... real horror is the one deep-rooted inside us since birth. It is an atavistic terror which likely dates back to the primordia of the cavemen, when the beings that still represented a transitional link between apes and the first humanoids burrowed in the deep of their caves, badly lit by the thin glare of a fire, while outside, in the immense darkness of those endless nights, apocalyptic violent storms rampaged ("the great flood") and frightening bellowings and roars of mastodontic animals echoed. And those poor, almost defenseless creatures crouched in fear, next to each other. The first terror is then the fear of the dark ... of blackness![13]

By focusing on a heroine persecuted by her own husband, Freda's film recalls such works as George Cukor's remake of *Gaslight* (1944: the 1940 version was not released theatrically in Italy), *Love from a Stranger* (1937, Rowland V. Lee, and its 1947 remake by Richard Whorf), Douglas Sirk's excellent *Sleep, My Love* (1948) and the more recent *Midnight Lace* (1960, David Miller), but with a peculiar emphasis on the bizarre, the unspeakable, the taboo. At the core, *L'orribile segreto del Dr. Hichcock* is the story of a bizarre sex triangle in which a man plots the murder of his second wife with the help of the first one—that is, the opposite of the stereotypical crime plot involving uxoricide. Quite a mordant idea in itself: a middle-aged man, who cannot have sex with his much younger and beautiful wife, teams up with his previous, older, partner—not only crazy after being buried alive, but ugly-looking as well after years of solitary confinement: yet another incarnation of the veiled old lady in *Vampyr*—with whom nevertheless he had found the perfect sexual communion.

Intricate and Machiavellian variations on the typical murderous love triangles were one of Gastaldi's favorite ploys, and he would recycle the husband-planning-to-turn-his-wife-crazy (or vice versa) plot in his own *giallo* scripts: take for instance his directorial debut *Libido* (1965) and *Le foto proibite di una signora per bene* (a.k.a. *The Forbidden Photos of a Lady Above Suspicion*, 1970, Luciano Ercoli), not to mention *Il tuo vizio è una stanza chiusa e solo io ne ho la chiave* (a.k.a. *Your Vice Is a Closed Room and Only I Have the Key*, 1972, Sergio Martino), also inspired by Poe. Still, the uneasiness that exudes from such a weird slice of marital life is very close to the core of Freda's cinema.

The theme of a mature man married to a much younger woman than him somehow reflects the director's bitterness toward his past relationship with Gianna Maria Canale (and will undergo an even more ruthless examination in the director's following Gothic horror film, *Lo spettro*), whereas his portrayal of family shows once again, like in *Beatrice Cenci*, an institution rotten to the core which relies on a façade of social conventions. Near the beginning, Hichcock returns home, craving sex, only to find out that his wife Margaretha has thrown a party, and is entertaining the guests with some piano playing. The professor instructs the maid to inform Margaretha about his desires, and the woman dutifully joins him in his secret alcove, where he has prepared a dose of the serum that will allow him to live out his necrophiliac fantasies. The refined wife, the impeccable lady of the house, becomes an obscene parody of the "sleeping beauty," a lifeless body that the prince charming fondles and kisses with obscene abandon.

Another striking moment, and one which perfectly encapsulates Freda's discourse, has the doctor and Cynthia sitting in the villa's lounge, in utter silence. Hichcock—fresh from having resumed his necrophiliac habits—is distractedly stroking his cat, aloof and almost annoyed by the presence of his spouse, lost as he is in his own erotic fantasies; on her part, Cynthia is resignedly playing the role of the good wife, drowning in boredom and vainly waiting for a sign of empathy, if not affection, on the part of her husband. Although they share the same room, they couldn't be further apart.

If *Beatrice Cenci* painted a horrifying picture of the patriarchal family, *L'orribile segreto del Dr. Hichcock* draws an upsetting slice of Victorian life: in a society based on the respect of strict moral codes, the doctor's "horrible secret" manifests itself as a violent, spiteful and irrational overturning of the bourgeois life's cornerstones. In this respect, Freda's mention of Stevenson's book acquires a more complex resonance: if on the surface the story is based on the theme of the female double, with the duality between Margaretha and her replacement Cynthia (heightened by such a typical Gothic element as Margaretha's portrait hanging on the lounge's wall), it is actually Hichcock who suffers from a split personality, like Henry Jekyll did. He is a respected member of the *haute bourgeoisie*, who in public is dedicated to saving lives, whereas in private he is driven by an irresistible impulse to consummate intercourse with the dead.

Hichcock's whole life system follows a series of rituals which perversely mirror each other and take on a radically different meaning according to the time, place and situation in which they are performed: his meticulous preparation of the syringe with the anesthetic at the hospital, before proceeding with surgery, is paired with the similar procedure that the doctor follows in his secret alcove, in preparation of the forthcoming sexual act. Ironically, then, Hichcock's self-imposed celibacy after Margaretha's apparent death, and his attempts at leading a normal sex life (which presumably leads to impotence and to a Platonic marital *ménage* with Cynthia) are mirrored with his professional failures: after giving up to his miraculous anesthetic, the doctor sees all his patients die on the operating table. There is a surrealistic element in the way the sets underline Hichcock's reversed world, in which death is associated with love and passion, whereas the living are seen and treated with coldness and detachment: the Professor's nuptial bed is a grotesque replica of a mortuary, and the preparation for the coitus has the timings and manners of a funeral wake; it is no coincidence, then, that Cynthia finds a skull on her nuptial bed, where she has never slept with her husband.

Despite Gastaldi playing it down in the aforementioned interview, necrophilia was a daring subject in Italian cinema of the time. It had been passingly evoked in other Gothic horror films such as *La maschera del demonio* and *Il mulino delle donne di pietra*, but releasing a movie that revolved around such a theme would be unthinkable just a few years earlier. Evidently times were rapidly changing, and censors were (most likely unwillingly) adapting to them. Still, the sequence in which Hichcock prepares the anesthetic and then, after a quick glance at his wife, decides to increase the dose to get even closer to the illusion of death, denotes a cinematic boldness on the part of the director that is quite far from the system of euphemisms and allusions that were typical of that era's horror films.

Hichcock's "horrible secret" is treated like an addiction—hence the emphasis on syringes, which will feature prominently in *Lo spettro* as well—and once again Freda depicts the main character as a vampiric figure, both metaphorically and literally. He preys on the dead, taking his pleasure from their bodies, and when he bends over the sedated Margaretha he looks like Count Orlok in Murnau's *Nosferatu*, his claw-like hands grabbing his wife's head and breast as he kisses her, in a further reference to the director's beloved Expressionism. What is more, Hichcock suffers from bouts of abstinence that distort his features, just like Duchess Du Grand bore on her face the marks of her sudden aging. Forbidden, irrepressible desire takes the form of a bright red light that fills the room and floods the doctor's face when he sneaks into the morgue of his London clinic and approaches the body of a dead young woman, covered with a sheet that belies her voluptuous forms. The abrupt fall of desire, as the doctor is disturbed by a noise that forces him to abandon his necrophiliac purposes, is represented by the red light's sudden disappearance.

Freda is not afraid to step into the grotesque in the attempt to scare the audience. Make-up artist Euclide Santoli recalled the nightmarish scene in which Hichcock's face swells and deforms right before the camera, assuming monstrous features. "I remember I did a double mask: the first was rather thick, and was identical to the actor's face. It had to be applied first, whereas the other was made of a very thin rubber skin and was stuck to the other all along the edges. Between them a sort of inner tube was formed, and there we blew air into it through a tube...."[14] The scene, the director later complained, was sabotaged by the producers:

> It was them, not the censors, that forced me to split the nightmare scene into several bits. In my version you could see Hichcock's face bloating and gradually transforming.... I was very disappointed when the producers forced me to edit a series of shots/countershots in what was originally conceived as a long take. They were afraid that the audience would not understand that it all took place within the woman's mind. They were also afraid that it would make people laugh, but I think that the original concept was much more startling.[15]

This time, Freda and his producers were determined not to repeat the mistake they had made on *I vampiri*. The director hid again under the same pseudonym he had used on *Caltiki*, the Brit-sounding Robert Hampton, and the whole crew adopted Anglo-Saxon pseudonyms as well, sometimes to amusing effects: for one thing, set designer Franco Fumagalli became "Frank Smokecocks," gleefully embracing the literal English translation of his surname.[16]

Freda was saddled with a tiny yet very strong cast, led by Barbara Steele: the actress, then at the apex of her fame, took a ten days' leave from the set of Fellini's *8½* to play what is perhaps her most conventional role in an Italian horror film, the designated victim, all wide-eyed stupor, faints and cries of terror. On the other hand, former stage actor Robert Flemyng (1912–1995) was mostly working on TV during that period, most notably in the TV series *Family Solicitor*. The British thesp recalled:

> My agent sent for me and asked me to meet with the producers. Carpentieri was in London and I met him, and he said that he spoke Italian, and very little English. He gave me the script. And I rather liked him. My agent said, "Would you like to do it?" and I said, "Well, I want to go to Rome, yes!" The script was in English, called *Raptus*, and it was hilariously funny. On the first page it said, "For some people, sex and death are indissoluble." I thought, "Oh, good gracious me!" By the time I got back to Brighton, I found the script was about necrophilia! I rang up my agent and I said, "Look, yes, I've got bills to pay, but I think this is a bit too much. I don't think I want to do this." He said, "It's too late, you've signed the contract." I particularly wanted to go to Rome, so I thought, "What the hell, no one will ever see it."[17]

Harriet White (1914–2005), had relocated in Italy since the end of World War II, when she flew from America to work on Rossellini's *Paisà* (1946). She married art director Gastone Medin and worked on a number of productions over the years, either as actress in bit parts (such as on *La dolce vita*) or as Gina Lollobrigida's dialogue coach (on *Beat the Devil*, 1953, and *Solomon and Sheba*, 1959). Her recollection of *L'orribile segreto del Dr. Hichcock* was less than glamorous:

> I don't know how they found me; there were no agents over there at that time. They might have found me through word-of-mouth. I suppose I got the role because I was an English-speaking actress.... I didn't know Robert Flemyng, but he called me up the night before filming began. He said,

"My dear, have you read the script?" I said, "Yes, isn't it terrible?" He said, "My God, we can't possibly do this; we'll be dead in the business." And I said, "Well, what can we do?" (Of course, I wasn't going to admit to him that I was willing to do *anything*!) And he said, "Well, we've signed our contracts, so I guess the only thing that's left to do is to play it so badly, that they'll never let it out of the vault!"[18]

They did not succeed, evidently, and whereas Flemyng's subsequent career in the U.K. included such titles as *The Deadly Affair* (1966, Sidney Lumet), *The Quiller Memorandum* (1966, Michael Anderson) and the cult horror oddity *The Blood Beast Terror* (1968, Vernon Sewell), White was called on to play the suspicious-looking housekeeper / neighbor in a number of Gothic and *gialli* flicks, namely Freda's own *Lo spettro*, Bava's *Sei donne per l'assassino* (a.k.a. *Blood and Black Lace*, 1964) and the Gastaldi-scripted *La lama nel corpo* (a.k.a. *The Murder Clinic*, 1966, Elio Scardamaglia, Lionello De Felice).[19]

Sporting Brit pseudonyms like the rest of the cast and crew, to hide their very Italianness, were the main supporting players, Montgomery Glenn, a.k.a. Silvano Tranquilli, and Teresa Fitzgerald, a.k.a. Maria Teresa Vianello. An experienced stage, TV and voice actor, Tranquilli (1925–1997) would become a recurrent face in Italy's 1960s and 1970s genre films, and turned up in another memorable Gothic, *Danza macabra*, as none other but Edgar Allan Poe. Vianello (b. 1936) enjoyed a brief film career in Italy (appearing in a bit role as a hostess in *La dolce vita*) and took part in the 1963 Miss Universe contest before moving to Mexico, where she married the film director José Bolaños, Marilyn Monroe's last lover. As customary, each cast member spoke his or her own language when filming.

Shooting took place in Villa Perucchetti in Via Pietro Paolo Rubens 21—a huge villa surrounded by a large green spot in the Parioli neighborhood of Rome, and the current home of the Bulgarian Embassy in Italy. It provided all the indoor sets for the film: the tiled kitchen was turned into Hichcock's lab and even provided the setting for the opening scene in the cemetery, with the addition of some earth, smoke and an apt camera angle. Steele recalled the feverish pace that characterized the filming:

> We worked 18 hours a day thanks to massive doses of Sambuca and coffee. If a dolly collapsed, Freda would just pull the camera on a carpet. Nothing would stop that man. He was obstinate, emotional, violent, animated by the energy of passion and, on top of that, he was an inveterate gambler.... The film seemed to deliberately take charge of its own voodoo magic as we proceeded at that wild rhythm.[20]

Despite the frantic working rhythms at which it was made, *L'orribile segreto del Dr. Hichcock* was not improvised on the spot. On the contrary, everything had been rigorously planned beforehand. As Santoli recalled, "these films were not made sloppily. They were simply made in ten days, like Bava's or Freda's, but there was a huge prep work before shooting. Then we rushed like crazy."[21] When Freda showed up on the set, the day's working schedule had been prepared so meticulously that he could film up to 50 or 60 camera setups. In previous films, when shooting in studio, he used to resort to one of his favorite tricks, by changing the scenery behind the actors while filming a dialogue scene, so that the director of photography would not have to change the lighting scheme. Shooting in a real villa did not allow for this, but there was another way to speed up the proceedings: employing three small crews at once. One of them was entrusted to the then 24-year-old Marcello Avallone, who had gained Freda's mentorship through their common love for horse racing.

As Avallone explained, "the first a.d. on that film was Giovanni Fago,[22] I think. We split into three units. One was mine: I shot several things, close-ups, pick-ups and cutaways, shit like that. All in three weeks."[23] Gastaldi, who paid a couple of visits to the set, recalled his marvel at Freda's time-saving methods: "The second time I went to the villa, I didn't speak to Freda, who was completely absorbed in his work. He was shooting with three cameras simultaneously—not shooting the same scenes from different angles, but shooting *different scenes!*"[24] According to Avallone, two versions of some sequences were shot: the Italian one, which was more suggestive and chaste, and another for the foreign markets, a bit more risqué: "Freda didn't shoot the more explicit scenes—I did, since he considered them to be just crap, pure butchery, blood and gore. He was always very strict about this kind of thing; he accepted this material into his film, but he refused to shoot it himself."[25] However, these spicier versions have not been unearthed so far.

Assistant cameraman Giuseppe Maccari, on the other hand, downplayed the effective role of such so-called second units: "We had two cameras. One was actually working. The other was used to prepare the shot, the following shot, the following scene. The villa had three stories plus a cellar, something like that. Freda would send one camera to the cellar with a little group of people—the assistant director and some stand-ins—to prepare the next shot, while he was with the actors, maybe on the roof, or the top floor, shooting a scene. When he finished that, he would rush down and make the next scene."[26] Maccari also maintained that multiple cameras were used only on some scenes, such as the climax with the fire in Hichcock's villa.

There are various versions as to *L'orribile segreto del Dr. Hichcock*'s actual shooting period. The movie was scheduled for filming from April 9 to May 5, 1962—with 21 effective shooting days, and a budget of 96 million *lire*. However, Freda always claimed that he wrapped up the film in two weeks, whereas film scholars Alan Upchurch and Tim Lucas wrote that the movie was filmed in 14 days.[27] On another occasion, Marcello Avallone recalled differently: "Think that it was all done in three weeks. Incredible, huh?"[28] Gastaldi, who showed up twice on the set, maintained the same figure and went on to explain how the sacrifice of his script's ending was a necessary move on the part of the director to keep up with his frantic schedule.

> That first day, Freda asked my permission to cut 10 pages from my script. They were important pages, important to an understanding of the plot. He told me that he had to finish shooting in a few days—the whole movie was filmed in only three weeks! He didn't have the time to film these pages, so I said, "Do whatever you want." So Freda cut the scenes in which my characters explained their motivations. The film became incomprehensible but people loved it!ced[29]

Such an approach, with Freda never doing more than three takes on a scene, obviously did not leave much time to focus on performances—not that he cared much about this aspect. To quote Marcello Avallone, "he just didn't give a shit about actors."[30] Avallone's claim is reinforced by an amusing anecdote which involved the young assistant director. Since Barbara Steele was often late on the set, one day Ermanno Donati had a heated argument with the actress, which ended with the producer slapping her in the face. Steele left the set in tears. Freda was not the least bit flustered, and for the umpteenth time he resorted to one of his specialties—that's when Avallone came handy. "He said: 'This next scene, we're shooting it without her!' 'What do you mean *without her*?' 'Yeah, you're playing her part!' You see, back then I was very thin, so they dressed me in Barbara Steele's clothes and I did a whole scene in a long shot, with a rather queer-like grace [laughs]. So, this is how much Riccardo cared about actors."[31]

Some cast members, such as Silvano Tranquilli and Harriet White, confirmed the director's autocratic attitude. According to Tranquilli, "he was easily irritated, and was explosive at the slightest provocation, and was a lot of trouble for the entire cast."[32] White went so far as describing him as "an ugly little man, always acting as though everybody was out to get him.... Bilious. He screamed at us ... perhaps more at me, because I wasn't very experienced in film technique and I kept doing things wrong. I don't remember any particular instances or stories, just that it was not particularly pleasant to go to work. I guess he was good; I guess he knew his job."[33] On the other hand, Flemyng got along very well with the director ("I liked him very much. He was very funny!") and pointed out how Freda agreed to his suggestions to make the dialogue more natural and colloquial.[34] Steele, who shot her scenes in eight days, painted quite a different picture than White, calling Freda "the only director out all of those Italian horror films I really felt a true connection with.... With Freda, I had an instinctive, emotional rapport. Freda is very seductive and intimate with his actors; he takes them aside, gives them little cookies and drinks, and tells them they're beautiful and wonderful. The roles I did with Freda were very emotional."[35]

The actors' professionalism (not to mention their safety) was put at stake when filming the climax: it was shot on the last day, with four cameras, and an in-depth recollection of it can be found in an excellent article on the making of the film, in *Video Watchdog* #49: according to Flemyng the whole place reeked of petrol, and Tranquilli would not play the scene as he considered it too dangerous. Flames had been prepared by the special effects technician with the use of a flammable liquid, but when shooting began, the director started screaming and cursing, yelling that the fire looked fake. Freda, whose early work as film doctor included the salvaging of *Fascino* by way of expanding and repeating the climactic fire in the movie, would not accept any compromise. The fire had to be *big*, and look real. The special effects man obliged. Soon the room, papered with wallpaper, was engulfed in flames, and the heat became unbearable, and as soon as the scene was over everyone was running for their life. A few crew members fainted, and Avallone maintains that some had to be hospitalized as they were poisoned by the smoke. Flemyng's vivid memories also share light on Freda's almost childish enthusiasm when filming adventurous scenes:

> Freda came and sat by me, and I said, "*Well!* What about *that!*" He said, "Oh, my dear, you are so nice, so calm, so English! These Italians are so hysterical." And I said, "Well, I'm not surprised, there are even people who were actually carried out with their hair taken off!" ... So, anyway, I asked him, "Did you get the shot?" And he looked at me, rather cunningly, and said, "*Bellissima!*"[36]

To Riccardo Freda, at that point in his career, horror was the realm where he could fully express his visionary imagination. It proved a challenge, as can be sensed by his declarations in an interview in the French magazine *Midi-Minuit Fantastique*:

> It's not that people really despise the genre. They say they do not consider all this as very serious. They consider the Fantastic as an easy genre, for imbeciles. It's a genre that I have practiced—I actually practiced all genres—and on the contrary I find it's the most delicate. It is so easy to slip into the ridiculous, and have a whole movie theater sneer. When one manages to achieve something that gives emotions, I mean strong emotions in a theater, it's a remarkable result.[37]

Horror also provided a type of material that demanded the same vigorous approach to storytelling as the adventure genre he liked so much, with suspenseful scenes instead of horseback rides and swashbuckling duels. Stylistically, this meant the use of color with a strong dramatic function, and a reliance on the zoom as means to achieve shock effects. For a filmmaker like Freda, the zoom lens was a mixed blessing. On one hand, it solved lots of technical problems, and made the director's job easier and faster, allowing him to totally bypass the dolly work which was previously necessary whenever one wanted to move from point A to point B within the same shot. It meant being able to cut corners and achieve a higher number of setups per day, speeding up the proceedings quite a lot. On the other hand, an aesthete like him understood quite well that such speed was reached at the expense of style. "The expressiveness of the zoom effect is certainly not higher than what could be achieved via a quick dolly onward," he wrote in his memoir. "In *Don Cesare di Bazan* there was a dolly shot onward made by shooting at 14 frames per second, which was quick, and which practically had the same effect as the zoom."[38]

Freda often criticized the abuse of zooms on the part of other filmmakers.

> There are directors who resort to the zoom even to show someone who's blowing his nose, convinced as they are that it conveys a particular effect, whereas the zoom must be used only for certain effects. Sure, if someone opens a door and finds himself in front of a terrifying scene, it is obvious that the result will be better if it is achieved with the camera reaching the eyes very quickly, because this gives the viewer some sort of a psychic shock. In horror movies the zoom is an almost indispensable tool, as it allows such an acceleration, which is useful to speed up the viewers' heartbeat.

Even a director he respected very much, Mario Bava, was not immune to Freda's criticism regarding his alleged abuse of the zoom. Freda pointed out *Lisa e il diavolo* (or rather, its bastardized version that came out in Italy as *La casa dell'esorcismo*) as an example: "The exorcist's house was portrayed in every shot with four or five zooms, and at that point the film lost its effectiveness because of the addiction to that effect."[39]

Still, Freda made a virtue of necessity. An example of his embracing the use of the zoom lens can be seen in the sequence where Cynthia discovers a human skull in her bed, screams in terror and faints. The scene consists of just two shots: a quick zoom-in on the macabre relic and a zoom-out from an extreme close-up of Cynthia's face to a full shot of the woman falling unconscious to the floor. In *I vampiri*, Freda had shot a similar scene (Wandisa Guida finding herself in a room populated with skeletons and rats) via a series of cuts between the terrified actress' close-ups and the human remains.

Music is also a vital part of the film's Gothic atmosphere. The opening credits, on a pitch-black background, are accompanied by Roman Vlad's remarkable main theme, which at a certain point abruptly halts. The ensuing silence is broken by a woman's scream. It is a very similar trick as the one in the opening credits of Argento's *Profondo rosso* (a.k.a. *Deep Red*, 1975): the irruption of an external element—represented in Argento's film by a child dirge and the brief Christmas scene that precedes a killing—acts as an anticipation of the horrors to come. Pity that such a moment was not featured in the heavily edited U.S. version, *The Horrible Dr. Hichcock*: besides displaying a will to experiment that will later take root, it further undermines how Argento's cinema was influenced by Freda's, perhaps in no less measure than by Bava's.

L'orribile segreto del Dr. Hichcock was submitted to the board of censors in June 1962, and was given a V.M.18 rating: it was the first time such a rating was employed for a horror movie after the entry into force of the new Italian law on censorship in April 1962, which abolished the earlier V.M.16 rating and introduced two new ones, V.M.14 (forbidden to audiences under 14 years-old) and V.M.18 (forbidden to minors). However, despite some sources—including the director himself—claiming otherwise, the board of censors did *not* demand that any cut be performed, although it pointed out that the film featured "many obsessive [sic] scenes in relation to the sensitivity of childhood."

The choice of using foreign pseudonyms ultimately worked. The movie did solid business in its home country, grossing 142 million *lire*, persuading Donati and Carpentieri to put together a sequel and leading Italian distributors to promote Ricardo Blasco's Spanish thriller *Autopsy of a Criminal* (a.k.a. *Autopsia de un criminal*, 1963) as a follow-up to Freda's film, *L'assassino del dott. Hitchkok* [sic]. Freda had fun recalling the alleged reactions on the part of the audience, claiming that "one part of the theater stated that the style was purely American, the others claimed on the contrary that it was an English film...."[40]

In France, where the director was by then an acknowledged *auteur*, critics had words of praise for the film, favorably comparing it to the milder British Gothic. As Gérard Legrand wrote in *Positif*,

> going beyond the threshold of parody as suggested by the title.... *L'orribile segreto del Dr. Hichcock* seems a hymn to necrophilia ... the storms, the excesses, the veneer of a modern chirurgical *décor* to cover a stylized *rococo* background, even the photography dominated by fascinating and artificial flashes of color ... everything warns us that the British "good taste" and the "scary" game of Terence Fisher's characters are irrelevant here.[41]

Donati and Carpentieri produced an English-language print (titled *Raptus: The Secret of Dr. Hichcock*) and offered it to AIP, confident that Barbara Steele's starring turn in it would be enough to sell it: however, Arkoff and Nicholson turned the movie down, as its content could not be possibly toned down and softened for general consumption.[42] It was released theatrically overseas in October 1964, in a dubbed version, by Sigma III Corp., as *The Horrible Dr. Hichcock*, playing on the top of double bills with Jesús Franco's *The Awful Dr. Orlof* (*Gritos en la noche*, 1961), to predictably harsh reviews.[43] British audiences would have the chance to watch the movie the following year, with the title *The Terror of Dr. Hichcock*.

The U.S. cut was severely trimmed: it ran only 76 minutes long, featured a somehow different edit (such as the opening graveyard sequence being turned into a pre-credit prologue), add many dissolves in place of direct cuts (such as the pairing of syringe preparations in the hospital and at home), and omitted some key scenes such as the domestic vision of Hichcock and Cynthia, thus spoiling Freda's pace and atmosphere. What is more, Sigma III added some unnecessary lines of dialogue (as when Hichcock decides to increase his wife's dosage of the serum, we hear Margaretha say "Darling, I've been waiting for you").[44] In addition to that, the English version was not on a par with the Italian one: the translation of Gastaldi's script was badly written, awkward and at times unfaithful; Flemyng so carelessly dubbed his own voice that it sounds like he was voiced by someone else, and the other dubbers were awful. Even though not on a par with the atrocious American butchering of *I vampiri*, it definitely did not do justice to the movie, and severely diminished its impact.

Strange but true, in 2015 a (very faithful) novelization was published in the U.S. by Raven Head Press, written by Florida-based writer Michael R. Hudson, who already transposed several Gastaldi scripts—including *My Name Is Nobody* and *The Case of the Bloody Iris*—into the novel format. It was a fitting closing of a circle for a film that always tried hard to pass off as an Anglo-Saxon one.

Le sette spade del vendicatore

The third Freda film released in the year 1962, *Le sette spade del vendicatore*, was a return to the past of some sorts for the director. When Robert De Nesle, who distributed *Maciste all'inferno* in France, proposed him to work together on a motion picture to be co-produced by his company C.F.F.P., Freda ended up remaking his first film, *Don Cesare*

U.K. poster for *Le sette spade del vendicatore* (1962). The film was paired with the Laurel & Hardy classic *The Flying Deuces* (1939).

di Bazan. He maintained that he loved the idea of shooting a new version of his debut with more apt technical means ("In 1942 technicians opposed so-called avant-garde ideas: complicated camera movements, elliptic cuts, subtle lighting"[45]) and turning out with a true-looking American-style swashbuckling epic. What is more, being a great fan of Dumas' work, perhaps the idea of returning to the same story twenty years later sounded also like a Gascon gesture to him, a way to show that at 53 he was as skilled and accomplished a director as ever, an indomitable musketeer despite the ever-changing moods of the Italian film industry.

However, the kind of cinema he thought of when working on *Don Cesare di Bazan* was now just a thing of the past: the dream of an Italian way to adventure films (and basically to popular genres) whose products would rival with Hollywood blockbusters had crushed against the reality of a movie industry which relied on a huge number of low-budget pictures, shot very quickly and without much expectations as far as box-office grossings went. These titles were aimed at the so-called "*mercato di profondità*" (in-depth market), the circuit of second and third-run theaters which stretched the movies' commercial life, but kept them away from the big numbers of the A-movie circuit. The exception to the rule would come within a couple of years, with Sergio Leone's Westerns, which in turn gave way to a flooding tidal wave of low-budget subproducts, one of them helmed by Freda himself.

The script for *Le sette spade del vendicatore* (originally titled *Sette spade per il re*, Seven Swords for the King) retained only a handful of elements from the original, such as the scene where the hero (here named Don Carlos) marries an unknown woman in prison. Together with scriptwriter Filippo Sanjust, Freda opted to revitalize the story while keeping in with the genre's classic ingredients, by piling on the action and suspense. Some scenes from the earlier version were rewritten so as to make them fit this new vision. For instance, Don Carlos' fake execution, which in the 1942 film relied on the character of the young boy whom the protagonist saved from punishment (absent in this version), here is made more suspenseful by a fortuitous accident: a member of the firing squad stumbles and drops his gun (which, unbeknownst to him, had been loaded with blanks) into a pool of mud, thus having to replace it with another, this time loaded with a real bullet, and putting the hero's life in danger. Carlos survives, even though he is badly wounded.

As a result, the story was imbued with a mélange of styles. *Le sette spade del vendicatore* offers an amazing blend of influences: horror, comedy, Western, Gothic. The opening scene sets the mood, and it is quite different from the one in Freda's debut. The tone is almost comical, as the king of Spain is busy having his court painters draw a portrait of a mysterious woman he met months earlier. Unsatisfied with the results, the sovereign puts together different parts from each portrait—the eyes, the mouth, the chin—in order to come up with a resembling identikit. Why is he looking for that woman? Like many other plot points, this is not revealed immediately so as to keep the viewer guessing, but we know that the unknown woman has a vital part in the story, and Freda enhances the concept by having his camera tracking onward to the portrait. It is the same camera movement as the one that will open his next horror film *Lo spettro*, but with quite a different meaning. It suggests viewers that they are in for a breezy, tongue-in-cheek, exciting ride—and for a filmmaker like Freda, what could be more exciting than asking the audience "*Cherchez la femme*"? This kind of approach—riddling the movie with mysteries and characters that are not immediately revealed as good or bad, thus keeping the storyline purposedly obscure in parts—gives *Le sette spade del vendicatore* a *feuilleton*-like feel, which makes for a breath of fresh air compared to the first version's straightforwardness.

Freda also spiced up the proceeding with elements that have a distinct Gothic flair: the mysterious prisoner in the castle whose screams Carlos hears overnight; the secret meeting in the dilapidated church, where Carlos infiltrates the conspirators; and, of course, the scenes in a dungeon—including the final duel, which takes place among braziers, ominously squeaking gigantic wheels and huge, menacing pendulum blades that openly pay reference to Edgar Allan Poe's *The Pit and the Pendulum*. "Once again, we looked for inspiration on Piranesi and his series of *Prisons* etchings. I asked my d.o.p. Raffaele Masciocchi for a blood red lighting, gloomy, with gigantic shadows so as to reenforce the darkness and mystery of the dungeon," the director explained.[46] Freda only complained about the piranha-ridden pool which, given the impossibility of using real piranhas, was filled with harmless goldfish, with unintentionally comic effects: the scene where an actor is locked in a cage and plunged into the pool, and then his fleshless skeleton emerges, was regrettably met with bouts of laughter on the part of the audience. Overall, the director was rather satisfied with the film's look. He told Bertrand Tavernier: "From a visual point of view, I obtained everything I wanted, especially concerning the lighting. Ordinarily, the directors of photography are paralyzed by certain rules and refuse natural light sources. They prefer a lifeless, flat photography, where objects and people are not reproduced truthfully."[47] This was not the case with Masciocchi, who had proven an excellent accomplice in his Gothic color films. The talented cinematographer unfortunately died at the untimely age of 44, in 1965.

The romantic subplot benefits from the more relaxed censorship, and is devoid of the old-fashioned romanticism of the earlier version, giving way to a more light-hearted, at times malicious approach. Namely, the sequence where Carlos meets his future wife Isabella, at an inn where their beds are separated by a curtain instead of a wall, is a nod to classic American comedy, such as Frank Capra's *It Happened One Night* (1934). Freda stages it as a theatrical farce, as first the man and then the girl notice how their bed is apparently creaking even when they are lying still: Carlos rips the curtain open with his knife ... and finds Isabella on the other side. What happens next is implied by the characters' reaction to the unexpected encounter: a malicious laughter, followed by the sight of the lovers in bed, lost in postcoital bliss—something unthinkable in an Italian film only a few years earlier, if one thinks about the censorial trouble of Steno's 1954 film on Casanova.

Le sette spade del vendicatore also benefits from a much-welcomed sense of humor. Like in the 1942 version, the Spanish court is depicted in a rather desecrating manner, and the young king is portrayed as an unrepentant womanizer. But this time the script adds a truly unforgettable character: the cardinal—a vain and self-important ecclesiastic who thinks of himself as a great playwright—played by the renowned stage actor Mario Scaccia, later seen among others in Francesco Barilli's *Il profumo della signora in nero* (a.k.a. *The Perfume of the Lady in Black*, 1974). The sequence of the staging of the cardinal's tragedy *The Temptations of the Christian Soul*—a pompous, boring, lousy stage play, during which the conspirators are planning to murder the king—is an amusing showpiece which shows Freda's oft-overlooked flair for comedy, and truly surpasses the 1942 film, where the *Don Juan* was hopelessly ravaged by Don Cesare and his men posing as actors. However, all the scenes involving the cardinal are missing from the French version, *Sept épées pour le roi*, thus making the film slightly incomprehensible at times. The director claimed that the cuts were made on the order of the French board of censors because of their "offensive" view of the Church, whereas according to film critic Jacques Lourcelles it was De Nesle himself who performed the cuts preventively, in accordance with the French Catholic Office—a practice which lasted up to the end of the 1960s.[48]

The film was shot mostly at Bracciano's Castle Odescalchi—seen in many pictures of the era, including Warren Kiefer's *Il castello dei morti vivi* and Freda's own *Maciste all'inferno*—over a six-week period; occasionally the director employed two cameras at once. The use of real-life ambients gives the story a much more compelling and authentic feel, and is a welcome change of pace from the phony-looking studio-shot interiors of Freda's earlier adventure films. The result is breezy and fast-paced: the action scenes— such as the beautifully shot duel in the mist-covered forest at dawn, or Carlos's escape at night from a trio of assassins through the town's roofs—also benefit from the realistic setting and ample use of exteriors. Freda even outdoes himself by staging a rousing assault to a convoy transporting gunpowder that is pure Western style, and literally blows away one of *Don Cesare di Bazan*'s best scenes.

The young and athletic Brett Halsey is much more convincing than the overweight Gino Cervi as the young hero. After many appearances in American B-pictures and TV movies of the 1950s, Halsey (b. 1933) rose to popularity by the end of the decade, after his roles in *The Revenge of the Fly* (1959) and *Return to Peyton Place* (1961, José Ferrer), in which he appeared with his then-wife Luciana Paluzzi, and won the 1961 Golden Globe Award for "New Star of the Year." He subsequently relocated to Italy for a decade. *Le sette spade del vendicatore* was his first Italian movie, which first of all meant lots of language issues on set. Halsey recalled:

> I didn't know any Italian then, and one of the first scenes I had, there were five actors in the scene, each one acting in his own language: five different languages. So you had to learn ... what you do is, when you learn your lines, you'd learn everyone else's lines as well. In the beginning, I would count: he talks, he talks, he talks, I talk, he talks, I talk, he talks, he talks, I talk.[49]

That's how the actor recalls his experience on *Le sette spade del vendicatore*:

> I had a very good and respectful relationship with Freda. He was always cheerful and friendly with me. I can remember him sometimes being tyrannical and maybe cruel with others on the set, but never with me. I liked and admired him. His direction was very simple. He let me know what he wanted and left it up to me to deliver the result. I do not remember any disagreement over my interpretation of his direction. I recall a particular incident that happened at my first lunch on location. Americans do not have the tradition of drinking wine with lunch, and on our first lunch together Freda very generously kept my wine glass quite full. After lunch I had a sword-fighting scene, and found myself neither as steady nor as self-assured as I wanted to be. Neither I nor my opponents were injured, but I hated the fact that I was not fully in charge of my faculties. It was a lesson that I never forgot, and never again drank wine with lunch before an action scene.[50]

Halsey embarked on a distinguished career in European genre cinema, most notably in spy films, swashbucklers and Westerns—including *Uccidete Johnny Ringo* (a.k.a. *Kill Johnny Ringo*, 1966, Gianfranco Baldanello), the Dario Argento-scripted *Oggi a me ... domani a te!* (a.k.a. *Today We Kill.... Tomorrow We Die!*, 1968, Tonino Cervi) and Mario Bava's *Roy Colt e Winchester Jack* (1970).[51] Actually, Halsey first met Bava on the set of *Le sette spade del vendicatore*, as Masciocchi fell ill and had to be replaced for a few days. "I remember how impressed I was over the fact that such a well-known director would come in and help Freda when his cameraman was indisposed," Halsey recalls, "But that was Bava!"[52] The actor also worked with Bava in the erotic comedy *Quante volte ... quella notte* (a.k.a. *Four Times That Night*, made in 1969 but released only in 1972), originally banned in Italy by the censor board, which at that time included Freda as well.

Alberto Sorrentino, in his third Freda picture, was cast as the comic relief, as Carlos' esquire Sancho, and Gabriele Tinti had a small but impressive role as one of the conspirators. Tinti (1932–1991) debuted in the early 1950s and worked with such directors as Alessandro Blasetti, Luigi Zampa and Camillo Mastrocinque. His career mostly took place within the realm of popular cinema (albeit with such striking exceptions as Florestano Vancini's extraordinary true crime story *La banda Casaroli*, 1962); by the mid–1970s, when he married Laura Gemser, he became a recurring presence in erotic films, including the *Black Emanuelle* cycle. *Le sette spade del vendicatore* was perhaps Béatrice Altariba's finest hour: the French-born actress, who had appeared in small roles in such films as the 1958 version of *Les Misérables* (as Cosette) and *Les yeux sans visage* (a.k.a. *Eyes Without a Face*, 1960, Georges Franju), would soon return to anonymity.

Freda also claimed to have had a part in the music score, signed by Franco Mannino, which was allegedly improvised like a jam session while screening a rough cut of the film. It was partially reused in *Oro per i Cesari*.

Le sette spade del vendicatore was released theatrically in the United States in 1963 by Medallion Pictures as *The Seventh Sword*. It rapidly surfaced on U.S. television as well.[53]

Lo spettro

"It is the story of a woman married to an old crippled man, a great surgeon (once again), who decides to kill her husband with the help of her lover. Until then, nothing out of the ordinary."[54] That is how, in an interview dated May 1963 in the French magazine *Midi-Minuit Fantastique*, Freda started to explain to Michel Caen and Jean-Claude Romer the basic plot of his last film, the still-unreleased in France *Lo spettro*—the "nothing out of the ordinary" being particularly enlightening, since we are talking betrayal and murder here. If, as he claimed to *Midi-Minuit Fantastique* (no doubt out of opportunity, being interviewed in a magazine devoted to that type of film), horror was "the genre that matches the most my character, and in any case it is the one that gives me the most pleasure,"[55] the idea of a claustrophobic picture about a deadly triangle was revealing of the director's by-now bleak world view. It was not a matter of personal unhappiness: his *oeuvre* had been discovered by the French critics and cinephiles, and the retrospective at the Paris Cinémathèque had been a sound revenge against the Italian movie industry. On top of that, by this time his personal life was undergoing a very happy streak after the encounter with a young woman, the 24-year-old Silvana Merli, born in Gallarate on August 8, 1939, who on December of that same year would give birth to his first daughter, Jacqueline.

It had been partly the disenchantment toward the film industry that led Freda to embrace a more economical form of moviemaking such as horror, since his latest works

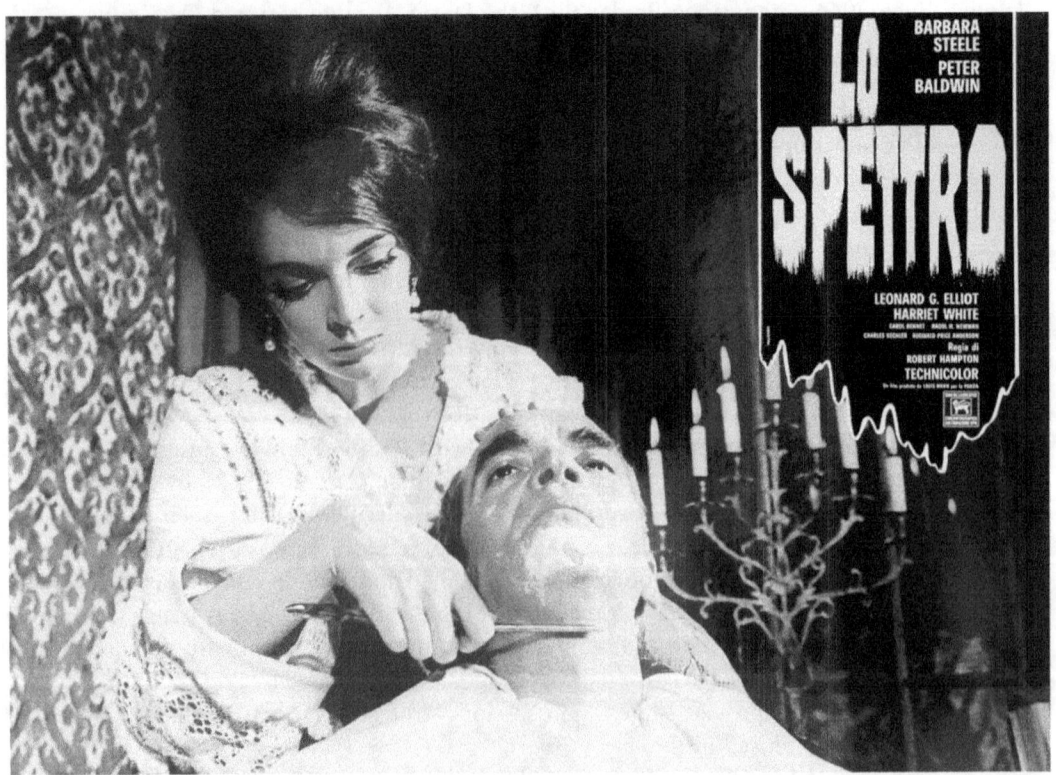

Barbara Steele and Elio Jotta in the Italian fotobusta for *Lo spettro* (1963).

in the adventure genre had mostly been work-for-hire jobs on films he would not even sign, credited to American directors that he felt were not even up to being his assistants. Switching from the territory of classic adventure to the darker realm of Gothic horror stories allowed Freda to let his darker side emerge: not only his admiration toward Poe and Stevenson, his interest for the occult, his love for Expressionism and his readings of Krafft-Ebing, but also his view on humanity. All this, while shaping a kind of cinema that would be up to his own vision of the medium: action, emotion, tension, velocity—minus the happy ending, that is.

Lo spettro is the exact opposite of the kind of films Freda loved as a child: almost a *kammerspiel* set entirely in a dark house, with a handful of characters coming in and out of doors and performing lengthy monologues. Still, it is one of his most personal works overall, starting from its genesis.

Dr. Hichcock (Elio Jotta) returns from the grave in this Italian fotobusta for *Lo spettro* (1963).

This time, unlike *L'orribile segreto del Dr. Hichcock*, Freda did not work on a preexisting script, but took active part in its writing. Despite his claims of being "entirely responsible for the screenplay,"[56] the story was credited to "Robert Davidson" (a.k.a. Oreste Biancoli) who penned the script with the director. A former journalist and playwright, Biancoli (1897–1971) had been a prolific scriptwriter since the early 1930s, and directed eight films of little interest between 1937 and 1943: after his final directorial effort, 1952's *Penne nere*, he had devoted himself entirely to scriptwriting, and his path had already crossed Freda's for the two *pepla* helmed by the director for Panda Cinematografica.[57]

Despite featuring a character whose surname is, again, Hichcock, *Lo spettro* is not a sequel to the 1962 film, to which it was tied merely by commercial necessity—to the point that the working title was *Lo spettro del Dr. Hichcock*. For one thing, the time and setting are different: whereas the first film was set in Victorian-age England, the second takes place in early 20th century Scotland. As played by Leonard G. Eliot, a.k.a. Elio

Jotta, Dr. John Hichcock has in common with his namesake the invention of a prodigious cure (this time for his paralysis, which consists in administering a small quantity of an otherwise lethal poison), a wife named Margaret and a sinister-looking housekeeper with the face of Harriet White. As Freda admitted, the story was basically a murderous triangle, with a fake supernatural element that came straight from H. G. Clouzot's *Les Diaboliques* (a.k.a. *Diabolique*, 1955), as the two lovers who got rid of the elderly husband are persecuted by the man's ghost, which manifests in traces of his presence, such as a wheelchair falling off the stairs (itself a nod to Henry Hathaway's *Kiss of Death*), or a carillon that only the murderers can hear (a wink at Poe's *The Tell-Tale Heart*).

What Freda added was the psychological exploration of the two lovers' relationship as it disintegrates: at first passionate and close, they become increasingly estranged and eventually turn one against the other, each of them suspecting the other of deceit. The supernatural menace which corrodes their union (a sexual attraction enforced by the mirage of the deceased husband's wealth that Margaret will inherit) basically demonstrates the transience of human feelings: love turns into hatred, trust evolves into suspicion, passion becomes homicidal frenzy. The self-destroying relationship between Margaret and Dr. Charles Livingstone is just a speeded up image of a marriage going to pieces, just like the one between Margaret and Hichcock did.

Like in Freda's previous Gothic horror film, the story focuses on an older man who cannot satisfy his young, desirable wife: in *L'orribile segreto del Dr. Hichcock* the main character's alleged impotency (or lack of sexual desire toward his second wife) was a consequence of his necrophilia, whereas in *Lo spettro* it is the dire consequence of age and physical decay. "I was a real man, then," Hichcock says while recalling his first meeting with Margaret, thirteen years earlier, in the extraordinary dialogue scene in which the woman is shaving him—an act that implicitly acquires a symbolical meaning of castration. "How happy we were then," he muses, recalling the days when she was "a beautiful, penniless young thing," while Margaret is tempted to cut him short—literally, by slashing his throat with the razor she is passing on his neck. "Pour me some gin," he asks her, "it brings back memories." ("You have some too," he tells Margaretha: drinking from the same glass is the closest intimate thing they can share now). Indeed, memories are all that is left, and those that are sweet for one party can be sour as poison to the other.

Freda depicts marriage as a role play, a pantomime of sorts in which both spouses play roles and wear masks that they cannot wait to get rid of. An exemplary moment in this respect is the one where Margaret holds up her elderly husband, escorts him to bed and undresses him like a nurse, immediately followed by Margaret's feverish, liberating race to the greenhouse, the meeting place where her lover awaits her—a scene which Freda depicts with a breathtaking tracking shot sideways, once again showing his mastery of film language. And yet, true love and passion are even more volatile. Immediately after the funeral, the couple's first night together (with both dressed in mourning, in yet another inversion of the bourgeois' mores as seen in *L'orribile segreto del Dr. Hichcock*) is spoiled by the first manifestations of Hichcock's "ghost," which makes Margaret so nervous she rejects Livingstone. So much for a honeymoon.

Margaret and Charles truly look like an early 20th century version of Lady Macbeth and her submissive male partner. And yet the disintegration of their bond, although carried on with open references to Shakespeare's tragedy (see the leitmotiv of bloodstains and a dialogue quoting the famous "What's done cannot be undone" line), moves on to a darkly ironically commentary on the dissipation of their mutual feelings, as the two partners reciprocally exchange accusations, blaming each other for the murder. Soon, very soon, they are just another unhappy couple. And when Margaret repeats that she loves him, Charles bitterly replies: "It's too late for loving feeling. You once loved your husband, didn't you?" The circle is over. Thus, even more than as a horror story, *The Ghost* is striking as an examination of marriage. Freda dismissed Bergman as "a very intelligent, maybe monstrously intelligent man, but one who does not make movies,"[58] and yet here he comes as close to make his own *Scenes from a Marriage*.

The film begins with the depiction of a séance, in which the psychic (Hichcock's housekeeper Kathryn) falls into a trance and starts speaking in tongues. Of all the other participants, only Hichcock seems to understand the meaning of her words. "That's Sanskrit," he announces, before translating what sounds like a sinister prophecy delivered by some soul from the afterlife. As the séance is over, Hichcock, his wife and Livingstone leave, while a couple of guests untie the still senseless Kathryn from the chair and take her away. Meanwhile, as the opening credits appear, the camera slowly tracks onwards to the table on which a human skull is placed, until the macabre object is in close-up. The main theme reaches its peak, the name "Robert Hampton" appears. Fade to black. It is one of the most powerful and stylish sequences Freda has ever filmed, and one that perfectly defines of Italian Gothic cinema: a "Triumph of Death" that harks back to the literary roots of the genre, referencing to the obsession with skulls and skeletons that pervaded Italian macabre poetry of the late 19th century. At the same time, it introduces a visual leitmotiv (the skull will appear over and over again during the film) and underlines Freda's vision—or rather, negation—of the afterlife. It is no use to look for the spirit, the director seems to imply: what is left are just bones.

Similarly, even more so than in the director's previous horror films, the supernatural element is evoked only to be eventually denied: the ending gives the right perspective to what has happened before, as in a 18th century anamorphosis. To Freda, horror is a Cartesian matter, a theorem to be proved by means of images: the thesis is the immanence of evil, while the supernatural is only a masquerade that allows us to bear our deepest, atavistic fears. "*True* horror is deep-rooted in each one of us from birth," he wrote in an oft-quoted passage of his memoir. A statement somehow confirmed by a line of dialogue in *L'orribile segreto del Dr. Hichcock* which sounded like a declaration of intents: "So much time has been wasted in the attempt to analyze the soul, while the material part of our being is still an unknown universe." Here, the none-too-intelligent priest played by Umberto Raho comments, "The Devil is more real a person than our modern world would have it."

The director claimed he tried to inject in his Gothic films Fritz Lang's conception of the Fantastic, which "exists because humans transgress good,"[59] and this is never more evident than in *Lo spettro*. "In Freda's film, fear is so everyday and tangible that it becomes flesh," as Italian film critic Carlo Bocci observed. "Not even once does *Lo spettro* slip into the *epouvante cocasse* of so many horror movies, neither can one be relieved with the apparition of the monster, as every single character in the film *is* a monster."[60] This might perhaps be an overstatement: the main characters are indeed monsters, whereas the secondary ones are merely caricatures, not unlike the Grand Duke of Florence's courtesans in *Il magnifico avventuriero*. Take Canon Owens, the priest: slightly effeminate, always sporting a rather obtuse smile, blissfully oblivious to his parishioners' real nature—as is the chief constable who loves playing chess with Hichcock—he looks like "the picture of health" and seems definitely more interested in the doctor's fortune than in the salvation of souls. Owens acts like a chorus of sorts, giving voice to the community's gossip and hypocritical morality, in turn criticizing the doctor's séances, Margaret not going to church, and Livingstone's presence in the widow's house. Yet another stab at organized religion, after the scheming Archbishop in *Il conte Ugolino* and the vain Cardinal in *Le sette spade del vendicatore*.

Even though he treats the supernatural with disdain in the film, Freda had more than a passing interest in the occult, and often claimed to have had first-hand experiences in the field: for example, he used to tell stories about his old princely apartment right by Rome's Spanish steps—the city's most prestigious spot—which was seemingly haunted by ghosts. Hence, it is no chance that the plot is filled with references to occultism. In a scene, while the objects around her seem to be possessed by an unknown invisible force, Margaret comes across an open book that discusses the astral body—a theme that will be featured prominently in the director's final film, *Murder Obsession*.

Ultimately, the critics who raised similarities between *Lo spettro* and Jean-Paul Sartre's stage play *Huis clos* were not astray. Like in Sartre's work, the characters are ultimately prisoners—of their state (Margaret's marriage and widowhood), of common morality (the impossibility for Margaret and Livingstone to live out their love), of their own feelings (greed, guilt, fear, hatred and remorse). And, ultimately, of the very house where the story takes place. In true Gothic fashion, the mansion itself becomes a character, with huge doors and high ceilings that seemingly squeeze and crush the inhabitants to their human misery. There are no more than a handful of outdoor shots in the whole film[61]: the outside world is seen through windows whose grids look rather like prison bars, or, worse still, it is evoked in passing through faded memories. At one point Margaret is looking out of the window one morning—one of the very few scenes set at daytime, in a movie dominated by darkness—at a beach which incongruously appears to be next to the house: it almost looks like a daydream, an image blossomed from the memory, as Margaret's face registers the woman's impossible desire to be free. As Lourcelles put it, "Satan affects the characters not only by stirring their usual vices (cupidity, jealousy, vengefulness, and so on) but also torturing them with the longing for a paradise and happiness lost."[62]

Lo spettro climaxes in one of Freda's circular endings, and truly one of the best: a grim family portrait where the roles are reversed. Margaret, poisoned and unable to move, is forced on the wheelchair where her husband once was, while Hichcock has regained all his self-assurance and virility as he delivers the monologue in which he explains his grand plan. But in a deliciously ironic twist, the gin that "brought back memories," and which he gleefully sips, turns out to be the poison that will lead him to his death.

Fittingly, whereas the opening scene is a reminder of Freda's vision, the final shot is a sinister punchline that culminates with the sight of a secret door behind which Dr. Hichcock is dying, unbeknownst to all, hidden like a rat. What will be left of him is not even worth seeing: he will disappear from view and from the world, doomed to become what the opening shot implied—no spirit, just bones. It is a chilling, nihilistic ending which rivals some of the director's most celebrated ones, like that of *Il conte Ugolino*. In *L'orribile segreto del Dr. Hichcock* the secret passage was a "forbidden door" which Cynthia should not trespass, as in the most classic fairytales; it was the key to move from one world to the other, from the reassuring order and luxury of the *haute bourgeoisie* to the hidden dimension of Hichcock's dark side, and the threshold between the two realities was a mirror. In *Lo spettro* Freda turns the essence of the secret passage upside down: no more a privileged instrument to reach inaccessible places and reveal secrets, but a blind alley, a street of no return where to end up and die like a wounded animal. "The Devil is a very real person," comments the priest upon leaving the room where a tragicomedy of horror has just been consumed. Curtains.

As with its predecessor, *Lo spettro* was shot in a very short time, possibly in late 1962.[63] Freda even boasted: "I wrote the script all at once, in one day. I shot it in twelve days, and yet I'm very satisfied with it."[64] This time Hichcock had the face of Italian stage actor Adelio "Elio" Jotta, while the unfortunate Dr. Livingstone was played by the American-born Peter Baldwin, who had relocated in Italy after an unmemorable Hollywood career, with bit parts in movies by Billy Wilder, Cecil B. DeMille and Jack Arnold. After starring in other interesting Italian films—such as *La donna del lago* (1965, Luigi Bazzoni and Franco Rossellini) and *Concerto per pistola solista* (a.k.a. *The Weekend Murders*, 1970, Michele Lupo)—he returned to the States and became a TV director; among his credits were such popular sitcoms as *The Brady Bunch* and the TV series *The Wonder Years*, which won him an Emmy award in 1988. Silvana Merli took part in the shooting as well, at least nominally, as assistant director, under the alias "Silvy Black," basing on the official papers kept at Rome's Archive of State.[65]

But the star, needless to say, was Barbara Steele. For his second collaboration with the British actress, Freda had words of admiration, calling her "extraordinary" and praising her "metaphysical eyes ... they are not real, it's not possible, they are De Chirico eyes...."[66] with reference to the "metaphysical art" of painter Giorgio De Chirico—and, to quote one of the artist's most famous painting, Barbara Steele was indeed the "Disquieting Muse" of Italian Horror. Freda also correctly pointed out how Steele's role was much more complex and interesting than the somewhat dull one she played in the previous film: the duplicitous Margaret lives a life of mystification, and is herself a prisoner of her character (the loving, considerate wife). Scene after scene, she goes from one extreme to the next: affectionate love and savage hatred, methodical scheming and irrational terror, utmost cruelty and willful self-destruction. Steele's final scene has Margaret—already paralyzed and unable to speak—communicating her feelings only with her now crazed eyes, a dramatic tour de force that fully demonstrates the actress' skills up to the very end, with Margaret madly laughing at fate's unfathomable ways.

Whereas Margaret is a complex, full-fledged character, a strong woman who dominates her male counterpart, her lover Dr. Livingstone (Freda ironically makes the poisoner a namesake of the famous missionary) is weak and spineless: like so many male figures of Italian Gothic, he is at the mercy of the weaker sex. Margaret maneuvers him like a puppet ("I thought you would do anything in the world for me," she complains at one point), and her every gesture toward him has both a sexual and a dominating innuendo, like the possessive way her rapacious hand closes over Livingstone's while the doctor is preparing the fatal dose of poison that will kill Hichcock (or so they think). Significantly, Freda shows Livingstone's death from the man's point of view: similarly to the famous shower murder scene in *Psycho*, the POV shot underlines the victim's helplessness.

As with *L'orribile segreto del Dr. Hichcock*, the director's use of the typical Gothic elements is assured and powerful: Hichcock's portrait looms over the scheming lovers, the crypt's niches (explored by a subjective shot) are decorated with skulls, a coffin is profaned to reveal a rotting corpse, a thunderstorm breaks out at night, the howling wind makes curtains and chandeliers alive.... The seemingly supernatural appearances are also remarkably conceived: an exquisite scene has the camera slowly tracking onwards to Margaret combing her hair before a mirror, to a close-up of the woman who suddenly turns back upon hearing a creaking noise in the room, only to see the specter emerging from behind a curtain.

Lighting and color have a distinct dramatic flair. Characters are usually lit from below, their bodies project towering, menacing shadows that look very much like the expression of their pitch black inner self, and their features are distorted, as in the apparitions of Hichcock's ghost, uneasily similar to the ghastly old lady in the final segment (*La goccia d'acqua*) of Bava's *I tre volti della paura* (a.k.a. *Black Sabbath / The Three Faces of Fear*, 1963). Also akin to Bava's film are the drops of blood falling from the ceiling on Margaret's bed, accompanied by expressionistic sounds in the score, which play a similar role as the drop of water in the aforementioned episode. As in *L'orribile segreto del Dr. Hichcock*, the color red is given a menacing, symbolic relevance: Hichcock's painting is bathed in crimson, as is Kathryn's face when the woman is seemingly in trance and speaking with Hichcock's voice.

Moreover, Freda enriches many scenes with pictorial elements, such as the presence of flowers compositions (as he did in *Beatrice Cenci* and *I giganti della Tessaglia*) often associated with Margaret, which take on a symbolic added value as well, again hinting at the character's still-life condition, and are juxtaposed with the bouquet of dead flowers that the ghost is seen carrying in his hands. Framing composition and camera movements are also imbued with a significance that goes beyond aesthetics; the camera eye becomes an instrument of moral judgment, as it approaches objects and moves away from them at the beginning and end of many sequences. Such movements express the fascination and repulsion toward evil and the physical tools with which it is perpetrated: a syringe, a razor, a vial of poison, a glass of gin. As Bocci noted,

> The real protagonists are the objects that we have seen before the horrible doctor's apparent death: the objects that become the tools of fear and death when the plot thickens. No one of the privileged objects as seen in the first part of the film escapes its fate of transfiguration. Freda's cold camera keeps framing them from low angles throughout the film, without a single impulse of sympathy for any of them: the director's cruelty toward his own creatures adds to the theatrical cruelty—we would be tempted to say, Elizabethan—of the *mise-en-scène*.[67]

Another noteworthy element is the presence of a *carillon* which has a diegetic function similar to the one in Sergio Leone's *Per qualche dollaro in più* (a.k.a. *For a Few Dollars More*, 1965) as well as the harmonica in *C'era una volta il West* (a.k.a. *Once Upon a Time in the West*, 1968) and Dario Argento's *Profondo rosso*. When we first get to listen to it, Hichcock recalls to have first heard that tune on the day he and Margaret met in Copenhagen; later on it becomes the sign of Hichcock's undead presence: again, the past memories come back to haunt the living, and poison their heart and mind.

The score is credited to "Franck Wallace," which—according to the list of aliases registered with the performing rights society SIAE as well as other sources such as the Italian magazine *Bianco e Nero* and the *Monthly Film Bulletin*—was the pseudonym of Franco Mannino. Other references suggest that "Franck Wallace" was actually a joint pseudonym for Mannino and Roman Vlad. However, when Beat Records released the film's soundtrack in 2008, it was discovered that the surviving tapes were attributed to Francesco De Masi, even though he is not credited on the picture. Filippo De Masi, the composer's son, is adamant that the whole score was written by his father, since Freda was unhappy with Mannino's score and replaced it at the eleventh hour, which explains the use of Mannino's pseudonym in the credits.[68] The musical accompaniment is one of the film's many highlights, and the striking, haunting title theme would turn up again and again in other Italian horror films of the period—such as Mino Guerrini's morbid *Il terzo occhio* (a.k.a. *The Third Eye*, 1966), starring Franco Nero—due to the typical recycling habits of Italian low-budget productions.

As he attempted to do in *I vampiri*, Freda pushed the pedal of the macabre and explicit violence. Even though it largely relies on suspense, *Lo spettro* features one of Italian Gothic's most utterly violent moments ever: the extraordinary scene where Margaret massacres her lover with a razor, shown through a tight editing of gory close-ups of the razor slashing the man's hands and climaxing in Livingstone's subjective shot while Barbara Steele savagely wields the weapon toward the camera—a scene later redone by Aristide Massaccesi in *La morte ha sorriso all'assassino* (a.k.a. *Death Smiles on a Murderer*, 1973)—and blood flows all over the lens. It is a chilling, savage moment that rivals the infamous opening of Bava's *La maschera del demonio* and predates a similar scene in Roman Polanski's *Repulsion* (1965), synthesizing Italian Horror's emphasis on gruesomeness. What is more, the film predates the *giallo* in the use of one of the latter genre's most fetishized weapons, especially in Argento's films. Overall *Lo spettro* showed Freda in top form, and is perhaps his best Gothic film: too bad it remained his last effort in the genre for years, despite the director claiming to *Midi-Minuit Fantastique* that he was working on another horror picture.[69]

Lo spettro received a predictable V.M.18 rating from the Italian board of censors, but no cuts were demanded. When interviewed by *Midi-Minuit Fantastique*, Freda claimed he was satisfied with the way the Ministerial commission had treated his film. "I didn't have any problems with the censors. Contrary to what one might expect, they proved to be intelligent."[70] With 175 million *lire*, it outgrossed *L'orribile segreto del Dr. Hichcock* at the Italian box-office. It came out in France in December 1964 (as *Le spectre du Dr. Hichcock*) and was given an early 1965 theatrical release in the States by Magna Pictures, as *The Ghost*.[71]

Il magnifico avventuriero

Freda's last effort for Panda Cinematografica was centered on a real-life character, the Florence-born Benvenuto Cellini (1500–1571): sculptor, goldsmith, draftsman, soldier and musician. A true Renaissance man, whose memoir—an incredibly adventurous, although fanciful and self-apologetic, reinvention of his own life—gained a huge popularity during the 19th century, even eclipsing Cellini's fame as an artist. The life and work of Cellini were a source of inspiration for other famous writers, such as Alexandre Dumas, *père* (whose 1843 novel *L'orfèvre du roi, ou Ascanio*, "The king's goldsmith, or Ascanio," about one of Cellini's apprentices, Freda tried to adapt for the screen in the early 1980s), Balzac (who mentioned Cellini in his 1831 novel *La peau du chagrin*), Melville, Hawthorne (*Rappaccini's Daughter* mentions a fictional work by Cellini) and Mark Twain; the latter often referred to Cellini's work and memoir in *The Adventures of Huckleberry Finn* (where Tom Sawyer cites the autobiography as inspiration while releasing Jim), *The Prince and the Pauper* and *A Connecticut Yankee in King Arthur's Court*.

Freda was fascinated by such a rogue, an artist who was also a bandit (or vice versa) and whose attitude informed his works and life in an inextricable blend. "I dreamt of being a pirate," he would confess to Éric Poindron, adding: "All brigands have my sympathy. Benvenuto Cellini has always been a model of independence for me. However, he was more of a great brigand than a great artist."[72] Himself an artist who had learned how to move in the shark-infested waters of Italian cinema, Freda knew that to survive in the movie business one had also to be some kind of a bandit, ready to do anything to bring his projects to life. Cellini embodied the kind of adventurer he loved, closer to the amoral Casanova (*Il cavaliere misterioso*) than to the virtuous Dubrovsky (*Aquila nera, La vendetta di Aquila Nera*) or Hadji Murad (*Agi Murad—Il diavolo bianco*) … in fact, whereas Robin Hood stole the rich to give the poor, Cellini steals gold and turns it into art, by molding it into exquisite pieces of jewelry.

What is more, the figure of Cellini offered the director the chance of going back to the kind of adventure biographies that were common in Italian cinema of the late '30s and early '40s, with such films as *Un'avventura di Salvator Rosa* and *Caravaggio, il pittore maledetto*, the latter supervised by Freda himself. Like in *Le sette spade del vendicatore*, he attempted to enliven the genre for the contemporary audience, with the complicity of the talented writer Filippo Sanjust, who later became one of the most prominent figures in the world of Opera, as producer and stage designer, until his premature death in 1992, at 67. The result was a work which was already out of its time—soon Leone's *Per un pugno di dollari* (a.k.a. *A Fistful of Dollars*, 1964) would wipe away the vapid adventure films of the period and impose a new type of cinematic hero—but nevertheless offered a vivid, engrossing spectacle.

Italian poster for *Il magnifico avventuriero* (1963).

The script (concocted with Freda's uncredited collaboration) does not follow even remotely Cellini's memoir, but takes the character and puts him into a totally invented scenario which, given the film's low budget, could not be a detailed rendition of Italy's Renaissance period as Freda dreamt. The sole reference to Cellini's own book were the infamous Sack of Rome, the invasion perpetrated in 1527 by Charles V's army of German mercenaries (the so-called lansquenets), and the remarkable ending in which the sculptor and his acolytes are feverishly working on his most famous work, the Perseus with the Head of Medusa.

Freda did not think highly of Cellini as an artist, and used to quote Michelangelo's dismissal of the Perseus ("The torso of a giant, the legs of a young girl, and the whole is none of these"); yet in the film he stages an odd encounter between the two artists at the court of the Grand Duke of Florence, as Michelangelo (played by Andrea Bosic) judges Cellini's work during an artistic competition held by the Grand Duke of Tuscany. "Benvenuto Cellini is a young dishonest man, while the other competitors are very honest ... but Benvenuto Cellini has more talent than all the others, combined."

Il magnifico avventuriero was shot (under the title *Le avventure di Benvenuto Cellini*) in March and April 1963 in Rome, at Castle Sant'Angelo, Castle d'Ostia, and at the De Paolis Studios. It benefitted from Julio Ortas and Raffaele Masciocchi's accomplished cinematography, which Freda personally supervised. As with *Lo spettro*, Silvana Merli—who was pregnant with their first daughter—was credited as assistant director. For the second time after *Le sette spade del vendicatore* Brett Halsey was cast as the lead, as he had the looks and the athletic skills to be a believable Cellini. Halsey recalled the howling of the director's mutts on the set, acting as a distracting factor ("These dogs would howl: '*Oooo-oooooh!*' Then, you'd complain about it, but those are *Freda's* dogs. No, you can't complain, it'd be like sending his *wife* away or something!"[73]), an element which the actor later used in his novel *The Magnificent Strangers*, set in 1960s Rome.

The film being a French co-production, a couple of renowned transalpine thesps were employed, namely the ravishing Françoise Fabian—as one of Cellini's love interests, the other being played by Adriano Celentano's soon-to-be wife Claudia Mori—and Bernard Blier, the latter playing Pope Clemente VII. Freda recalled that, due to his usual frantic working pace, all of Blier's scenes—scheduled for a week's worth of shooting—where done in just one day, with the seamstresses frantically changing the actor's costume after each take. Such an attitude was confirmed by Brett Halsey:

> Freda was interested in the mechanics of moviemaking. He liked, I think, setting up shots.... he didn't like shooting close-ups. So we'd get to the end of the picture and spend two days shooting close-ups: change costumes ... against the sky ... against the wall. He liked the big picture, the panorama. He'd shoot beautiful masters, but for the close-ups: "Aww, do it later."[74]

Freda had only words of praise for Filippo Sanjust, and rightly so. The scriptwriter's taste for sparkling dialogue and characterization is even sharper than in his previous collaboration with the director, and results in several amusing comedy bits. For one thing, the character of the pedantic Frangipani, who is writing a mammoth history of his own family, is basically a reinvention of the Cardinal in *Le sette spade del vendicatore*. However, the most memorable moment is perhaps when the Grand Duke of Florence, despite the strong contrary advice of his doctors ("It's sheer madness!") as well as of the bishop ("Where are we going to end, then? Will Florence become a circle of Pagans and non-believers?") finally makes up his mind and undergoes a perilous experiment: taking a bath (but with his trousers on). Visibly delighted by the new experience, he goes so far as claiming: "With social progress, I am certain that in the future people will take a bath even once a year!" To which the bishop comments, "Father, forgive them; for they know not what they do!" The scene—actually a humorous recreation of a somewhat similar moment in *Beatrice Cenci* where Francesco Cenci is taking a bath and receives gifts from his farmers and servants—once again shows Freda's often overlooked eye for comedy.

On the other hand, the director staged a number of vivid dramatic sequences. The Sack of Rome is synthesized in a beautiful crane shot on a square where the lansquenets wreak havoc, performing theft, rape and murder; several friars are tied around a huge barrel of wine, and the spilling liquid mixes with their blood in an uneasy sight. Cellini's night escape on the river Tiber is also remarkable, but perhaps the film's showpiece is the protagonist's duel with his enemy atop a speeding unguided coach, where once again the camera runs at full speed by the galloping horses and captures the drama and dynamism of the events. As a French critic put it, "Freda (and his cameraman) are able to recover the exact density of a fabric, a wood, a fitting, a handful of gold. The realism, the presence of detail manage to replace the overly expensive architectural compositions. One dreams of what Riccardo Freda might have made with *Cleopatra*'s millions."[75]

The final sequence—the making of the Perseus—is among the most intense in the director's career, and builds up to quite an unusual climax. Since the fire for the melting is too feeble, Cellini has his apprentices burn chairs, handrails, and whatever piece of wood they can find in order to melt the metal that has to be poured into the cast of the Perseus. Then, since the metal is not enough, they requisition whatever they can find— cups, jugs, tin plates. Freda's addition to the scene was having Cellini's girlfriend offer her earrings as well to help him. The artist throws one in the melting pot and puts the other at his fiancée's finger, as a wedding ring.

The scene—lifted from Dumas' *Ascanio*—works also a perfect metaphor of the filmmaker's creative fury at work: he molds the film from an array of diverse, rough elements, and works tirelessly, at an inhuman rhythm, so as to reach his goal—no matter what obstacles he has to deal with. What really matters is the final goal: in the end the Perseus emerges in all its exquisite, imposing beauty, out of a shapeless mold which is literally hammered away by its creators. Films—Freda's in particular—were something very much alike: works of artistry whose disguised, rough appearance made their beauty visible only to those who could see it. Among them, unfortunately, were not the critics—at least the Italian ones. But the director was content to have found attentive interlocutors among the French critics, as he confessed to Bertrand Tavernier: "You cannot imagine how I have been touched by the reception on the part of the French cinephiles. It comforts me to see that someone understands what I was trying to do, and I definitely needed that."[76]

With approximately 120 million *lire* grossed at the box office, *Il magnifico avventuriero* did nondescript business in Italy. It was released in France as *L'aventurier magnifique (L'Aigle de Florence)*, and was picked up for distribution in the States by AIP, for the television circuit, as *The Magnificent Adventurer*. It circulated also under the title *The Burning of Rome*. Several years later, in 1968, Alessandro Blasetti tried to put together another movie on Benvenuto Cellini, which was eventually dropped. As for Freda, he attempted to bring to the screen two more projects in the same vein, which unfortunately were destined to be shelved: *Casanova* (which the director claimed would be "totally different from *Il cavaliere misterioso*"[77]), and an adaptation of Michel Zévaco's cloak-and-dagger novel *Le pont des soupirs* (a.k.a. *The Bridge of Sighs*), which had already been brought to the screen several times, in 1921 (by Domenico Gaido), 1940 (Mario Bonnard's *Il ponte dei sospiri*) and, most notably, 1953, with Antonio Leonviola's remarkable *Sul ponte dei sospiri*, a failed attempt at a swashbuckling romance the way Freda himself would have done. *Il ponte dei sospiri* ended up being directed by Carlo Campogalliani, who fell ill during the shooting and was replaced by Piero Pierotti, and starring Brett Halsey and Gianna Maria Canale.

Around the same time, in the interview in *Midi-Minuit Fantastique*, the director claimed that he was developing a new horror movie, whereas that same year, speaking to Bertrand Tavernier,[78] he mentioned a script based on a famous novel with references to the "Affaire Audin," the disappearance of Maurice Audin, a French member of the Algerian Communist Party, who was arrested, tortured and presumably murdered by the French secret service during the Battle of Algiers in 1957. Sadly, no other information is known about these two elusive projects: however, it is unlikely that they reached an advanced stage. If anything, they proved how Freda was feeling more and more detached from his homeland.

12

In Exile

Romeo e Giulietta

The camera pans over a field surrounded by mountains, under a copper sky. Several men on horseback are destroying fences, pushing the enclosed cattle to escape. Then one announces: "The Montagues are coming!" A second group of men arrives, all brandishing swords. A violent battle ensues: the enemies come riding their horses at full gallop on a high plain. Two men are hiding atop a tree and aim their crossbows like Indians would do with bows and arrows. The others cross swords, exchange blows, jump off their horseback, in a fight to the death. A mortally wounded man, his face red with blood, drags himself on the ground in death spasms. Then, the title appears: *Romeo e Giulietta*. Wait—what is *this*? Is it supposed to be Shakespeare's play? No way, this is a *Western*. A cattle herd that looks like something out of *Red River* (1948, Howard Hawks), the theme of violence as means to take control of the herd, an ensuing battle that is, again, pure horse opera material—all this sums up, it must be added, to an idea of the Western that is still untouched by the germs of Sergio Leone's revolution.

Freda maintained that it was his idea to adapt Shakespeare's play. Having been an admirer of the Bard's work since adolescence, he chose to put one of his favorite tragedies on screen—in his own way. Shot in three weeks between Rome and Spain[1] (with the famous balcony scene filmed at the director's luxurious villa outside Rome), *Romeo e Giulietta* (1964) was one of Freda's own favorites among his works. For the occasion, he claimed that he even convinced Goffredo Lombardo, who had gone bankrupt after Robert Aldrich's costly Biblical epic *Sodom and Gomorrah* (1962), to create a new production company together, Imprecine, and set up a co-production deal with Spain for two films—the other being *Genoveffa di Brabante* (1964)—to cut costs. Other sources tell a different story: Freda was commissioned to shoot a Shakespeare adaptation by the Spanish company Hispamer Films, and accepted only because he saw the opportunity to make a period drama, in which he would inject ample elements of his favorite genre—the adventure film.[2]

Coming after George Cukor's 1936 adaptation and Renato Castellani's 1954 *Giulietta e Romeo*, Freda's film (which the titles state as a *"libera riduzione,"* a free rendering) is more akin to the director's sensibility than to the previous versions, even though it retains elements of both. Its retelling of Shakespeare, which would probably make the Bard's scholars turn green, is one of the first original examples of a bold literary adaptation: it is not as daring as *West Side Story* (1961), but it paves the way for the kind of treatment the Italian Western would often return to in the following years—think of Gianni Puccini's

The ball scene in *Romeo e Giulietta* (1964).

Dove si spara di più (a.k.a. *Fury of Johnny Kid*, 1967), which stages *Romeo and Juliet* in the Wild West, or Enzo G. Castellari's *Quella sporca storia nel West* (a.k.a. *Johnny Hamlet*, 1968), which does the same with *Hamlet*. The aforementioned pre-credit sequence reinvents the tone and the setting (a prairie instead of a Verona square), taking the viewer off-hand and hinting at what will come next.

However, despite the initial shock, Freda's film reveals itself as an essentially faithful adaptation of the tragedy, and retains many lines of the play almost verbatim, as the ensuing scene featuring the Prince's speech proves. Still, as noted by Shakespearian scholar Vincenza Minutella,

> an interesting addition emerges: the Prince's words "have thrice disturbed the quiet of our streets" become "hanno turbato tre volte la quiete delle nostre strade *e delle nostre champagne*" … (have

thrice disturbed the quiet of our streets *and our countryside*). In the following scene, another addition is made: Benvolio explains that the brawl was caused by "una razzia tentata dai Capuleti" (a raid attempted by the Capulets).[3]

Freda thus reinvents the Montague and Capulets as land and cattle owners, and imagines that their feud is caused by disputes over the land and pastures, just like in a typical Western scenario.

Another major addition on the director's part is the use of comic relief and typical adventure film elements in the key episode where Romeo comes to read the invitation to the Capulet's ball. Here, the illiterate servant Peter enters a tavern where Romeo, Benvolio and Mercutio are drinking and discussing women, and the scene soon evolves into something modeled upon the typical picaresque saloon brawl, with stuntmen disastrously falling off balconies and onto tables, breaking plates and chairs and generally wreaking havoc in the place. Eventually Romeo finds the invitation lists on the floor, under a table. In this sense, Freda is surprisingly akin to philosopher Benedetto Croce's reading of Shakespeare's drama as the "tragedy of a comedy."[4]

The director even managed to stage one of his trademark sequences. The masked ball at Capulet's house is unmistakably Freda, with the camera panning leftward through the huge hall from a group of musicians wearing weird tree masks, to show a quartet of dancing women who all have their hair made up with fruits and leaves to suggest the theme of Spring, and a table covered with plates of fruit and other foods, *à la Beatrice Cenci*. The scene allows him a take on the romantic theme of disguise after *Aquila nera* and *Il cavaliere misterioso*, as Romeo and his friends show up wearing masks in order not to be spotted by the Capulets. Romeo's courting of Juliet during the ball, as their faces come close and then retreat during the dance steps, is a beautiful moment that somehow reminds of Visconti.

Freda's depiction of the aftermath of Romeo and Juliet's night of passion is also remarkable: the camera explores the outside of Capulet's house, frames the balcony, then cuts inside the bedroom, panning across it while doing a 180-degree-turn, discovering clothes abandoned on a chair and finally advancing like an invisible presence to show the two lovers embraced on the bed and kissing, to the sound of Rachmaninoff's Piano Concerto. It is one of the director's best romantic scenes, and one of the film's most poignant moments, matched by the lovers' ensuing farewell, with the breeze slowly moving the windows' curtains that pose as a veil between the actors and the camera, before the latter almost imperceptibly advances to their faces.

The elements of the adventure film return in the next sequence—another addition from the play, naturally—in which Romeo escapes from the guards who caught him in Juliet's garden upon his leave from his beloved. After a chase on foot which has the young man perform acrobatic feats, Romeo jumps on a horse and gallops away in the countryside, pursued by the guards on horseback through the woods. He shakes them off by taking refuge inside a crevice in a rock, unseen to them. Devoid of dialogue and accompanied by Rachmaninoff's orchestral music, the sequence is the most blatant example of Freda's recourse to extraneous codes—taken from Westerns as well as from his own earlier adventure films—to flesh out Shakespeare's story and reshape it according to his own taste.

According to Minutella,

> The setting—woods, mountains and red rocks—reminds spectators of Spaghetti Westerns, which were shot in the same Spanish locations. The employment of quick camera movements, long silences, close-ups of Romeo and operatic music to underscore the character's mood and create suspense are

traits borrowed from Sergio Leone's films. On the other hand, the portrayal of Romeo as a handsome, positive hero seems more in keeping with the protagonists of traditional American Westerns than with Leone's anti-heroes.[5]

The analysis suffers from an incorrect historical perspective, though: Freda's film was made around the same time as *Per un pugno di dollari* (it came out in Italy several days earlier, on August 28, 1964, whereas Leone's film was released on September 12, 1964) and could not possibly be influenced by the latter's style. What is more, Freda usually dismissed Spaghetti Westerns as crap, and his only stab at the genre, *La morte non conta i dollari* (1967), presents quite peculiar traits when compared with Leone's work.

On the other hand, the climactic sequences share a distinct Gothic feel. As Juliet is about to drink the potion that will put her in a state of apparent death, Gábor Pogány's cinematography surrounds her with a growing dominance of the color red, not dissimilar to what happens in the scene of *L'orribile segreto del Dr. Hichcock* when the doctor is about to resume his necrophiliac habits. The sequence ends with a beautiful extreme close-up of Juliet's eyes, her face standing out, surrounded by a bright red, abstract background. Gothic staples return ominously in the brief scene at the apothecary's shop where Romeo purchases the poison: a skull is placed on a table near the alembics, *à la Lo spettro*, and a human skeleton can be spotted in the background.

Similarly, the climax in the darkened crypt, with Romeo committing suicide next to Juliet by drinking poison, and Juliet's awakening from the drug-induced sleep, pays reference to the Gothic genre. The girl, resting on a red cushion, slowly raises her head and looks around. The camera takes on her point of view, slowly panning around the crypt, revealing bones and skulls disposed in a weird cross-like decoration over a wall, a column's capital, a huge chandelier hanging from the ceiling, and ending over a somber-looking statue with a Modigliani-like neck (the work of Freda himself, perhaps?). Juliet gets up and starts walking around her catafalque with unsure steps. When she notices Romeo's body, Freda violently zooms in on her eyes, in a stylistic device that is fully part of the grammar of Italian Gothic horror films, and which the director himself had employed in *L'orribile segreto del Dr. Hichcock*, in the scene where Cynthia discovers the skull on her bed.

The movie ends with Friar Laurence descending into the crypt, his face eerily lit by a lantern, only to discover in horror the lifeless lovers; again the camera zooms in on his eyes, before symmetrically zooming in from Laurence's point of view on the dead bodies on the floor. The scene brings to mind the ending of *Il conte Ugolino*, by having a powerless individual witness a terrible tragedy. Only, this time Freda allows the viewer to see what the character is seeing, which is not horrific at all in itself but disquietingly peaceful: Romeo and Juliet look pacified in death, as if they finally found the happiness they vainly looked for in life.

The scene is also important because of the way it deals with the character of Friar Laurence, as Minutella points out.

> By making Friar Laurence arrive after Juliet's death, Freda relieves him from blame. This view of the Friar had previously emerged in the cuts and changes made by Freda to the character. Friar Laurence is subject to important alterations, which render him perhaps more earthly, less of a holy or philosophical man. His speech on Nature is shortened, many proverbs are omitted, while he is given lines which were not his in Shakespeare.

Ultimately, these modifications make the Friar "closer to Romeo and more practical"[6]— almost a revised, less cynical and more sympathetic version of Raho's character in *Lo spettro*.

It is moments like these which, by contrast, underline the awkwardness of the dialogue scenes, which stand uncomfortably by the accomplished atmospheric and action bits. This is partially due to the rather shakily assembled cast: Carlo D'Angelo (the Prince) was an experienced Shakespearian thesp, and dubbed Laurence Olivier's voice in his Shakespeare-based films, but most of the roles were played by undistinguished Italian and Spanish character actors—the best-known face possibly being that of Umberto Raho. As Juliet, the Anglo-Italian Rosemarie Dexter (1944–2010), in her second film role after Ugo Gregoretti's sci-fi political satire *Omicron* (1963), is a lively presence, but former teen idol Geronimo Meynier (b. 1941) does not seem to be up to the task as Romeo. This was his last film role. Originally, though, it was Brett Halsey who was to play the lead—a choice that would have undoubtedly made for a much more convincing and dynamic Romeo, and one that perfectly matched the director's vision of the play. As the actor explains,

> My only negative experience with Freda occurred when he asked me to play Romeo in his production of *Romeo and Juliet*. A principal feature of Shakespeare's plays is his dialogue. Freda told me he planned to shoot the film in the original English (Freda's English was "okay" but not great), in four weeks, with no rehearsal time. I think I am a pretty good actor, but with my limited training in classical theater, and without adequate rehearsal time, I feared I would not be up to the demands of the role. When I explained to Freda that these were my reasons for turning him down, he took my refusal as a personal affront and we didn't speak again until many years later.[7]

Freda never cared much about actors, but here it looks like his lack of attention (possibly due to the rushed shooting schedule) affected the result; each actor speaks in his or her language (judging from the labials, Dexter delivers her lines in English, Meynier and Raho speak Italian, whereas Toni Soler and Carlos Estrada stick to Spanish), and overall the Italian dubbing makes the dialogue sound stilted and redundant. Only occasionally does Freda overcome the issue, such as in Mercutio's death scene, after an impressive duel shot outdoors in a market square littered with extras (filmed in Ávila), where the director puts to best use his lateral dolly shots to follow the dueling adversaries. Ruggero Deodato, who was the assistant director on the film, recalled:

> Freda was a genius. I learned a lot from him. He was an intelligent person, cultured, and even a bit nasty on the set. He mistreated the crew, and to film a good chase on horseback, he did not hesitate to cripple the horses, even though he owned a stable ... he always came up with ideas which I hadn't thought of, both on set as in the editing room. I remember him at the moviola, amid a sea of film footage. "Pass on that segment, splice it with that other one...." Talking with him or Rossellini, it was almost the same thing.... When I met him, he had slightly declined to B pictures, and started being a producer, making two films at once, so as to earn money....[8]

Despite the director's claims that the film was bought for U.S. distribution and even screened at universities,[9] *Giulietta e Romeo* did disappointing business at the Italian box-office and remained virtually unknown abroad.[10] The French, however, seemed to like it, at least in the director's recollections of a Parisian audience enthusiastically welcoming the tavern fight scene, whereas "Marc Allégret looked aghast and in dismay."[11] Shakespeare's tragedy would be filmed again, within just a few years, by Franco Zeffirelli, who adapted for the big screen other Shakespeare works, including Freda's own favorite, *Hamlet* (1992). As usual, the director's view on his colleague's work was hardly diplomatic. "No one harmed Shakespeare more than Zeffirelli."[12]

Genoveffa di Brabante

The second co-production between Freda and Lombardo's company Imprecine and Madrid's Hispamer Film was *Genoveffa di Brabante*. Shot back-to-back with *Romeo e Giulietta* and featuring several cast members from the previous film, it was based on the character of Geneviève de Brabant, a legendary heroine made popular by *Golden Legend*, a 13th century collection of hagiographies (originally called *Legenda Sanctorum*, "Readings of the Saints") compiled by the monk Jacubus de Voragine, which in the Middle Age had been printed in more copies than the Bible.

Geneviève's tearjerking, educational story had also been the subject of a 17th century drama by P.C. Nivelle de la Chaussée, and had inspired a number of literary and musical works during Romanticism, including Friedrich Müller's tragedy *Golo und Genoveva*, Robert Schumann's opera *Genoveva* and Jacques Offenbach's *opera buffa*, *Geneviève de Brabant*. Cinema had taken inspiration from the character as well, and her story had already been filmed a number of times: in 1933 (*Genoveffa—Il figlio della foresta*, by Giulio Amauli), 1947 (*Genoveffa di Brabante*, by Primo Zeglio, starring none other than Harriet White) and 1952 (*La leggenda di Genoveffa*, by Arthur Maria Rabenalt, starring Rossano Brazzi as Siegfried). Marc Allégret's *I cavalieri dell'illusione* (1954) also featured Geneviève, played by Hedy Lamarr.

Freda wrote the screenplay himself. As the original title of the script kept at Rome's CSC—*Il cavaliere della spada nera* (The Rider with the Black Sword), 217 pages long and dated September 1, 1964—suggests, he once again attempted to blend the dramatic core into an adventurous narrative; as customary with the scripts the director penned, it is very detailed and filled with indications of camera movements and cuts. The script follows Geneviève's story rather closely: after her husband Siegfried has left for the crusades, she falls victim to her husband's counselor, Goto, who, having failed to seduce her, accuses her of adultery (whereas the woman is pregnant with Siegfried's child) and has her sentenced to death. Due to the executioner's mercy, Geneviève is abandoned in the forest, where she gives birth to a son, whom she raises in the wild. Upon his return, Siegfried punishes Goto and takes back Geneviève to his castle.

Compared to the previous versions, which were static, wooden melodramas, *Genoveffa di Brabante* adds quite a bit of action: for instance, in the 1952 movie the Crusades were left completely off-screen, and in the end Golo killed himself out of remorse, whereas here we are treated to extended battle scenes and a climactic swashbuckling duel. Perhaps the director was driven to the story because of its similarities with *Othello*, in the triangle of sorts between the jealous husband, the faithful and innocent wife and the scheming Golo. In Freda's films, the hero's best friend or right arm is also his worst enemy, or the maker of his ruin (see also *Spartaco*'s Ocnomas), but Golo easily tops all the previous incarnations of such a deceitful figure. The villainous administrator is the film's most compelling presence, much more so than the bland Siegfried or the unfortunate Geneviève. Like *Teodora*'s Arcas, *Agi Murad*'s Ahmed Khan and *I giganti della Tessaglia*'s Adrastus, Golo is the umpteenth villain in Freda's filmography whose desire for power must pass through the ritual profanation of his master's wife.

It is not simply the director sticking to a genre formula here, but the expression of a darker and more virulent view, which drastically detaches the story from its edifying original core. In this respect, the resort to graphic violence—resulting in a surprisingly gory scene in which Golo axes a servant to death, which comes off as yet another anticipation of Freda's descent into the splatter movie arena in the following decade—is not merely a nod to a fashionable thread, but the coherent result of a vision that is becoming more and more downbeat and nihilist, and therefore needs to be expressed in a grim, unpleasant way. Even though it is as crude as it gets, the sight of actor Franco Balducci's face covered in blood tops anything Freda had conceived in terms of violence in his Gothic diptych, and paves the way for a deliriously over-the-top Sadean scene in which Golo has Geneviève's maid tied to a St. Andrew's cross and mercilessly whipped by a bare-chested servant.

Genoveffa di Brabante works primarily as a lurid period melodrama in which the heroine is beaten, abused and humiliated with gleeful sadism. Thrown in a dark dungeon, robbed of her wedding ring, condemned to death, lost in the woods, Geneviève briefly becomes a Gothic heroine of sorts; then the film makes a sudden turn from which it never recovers, with Geneviève's miraculous encounter with a sheep which she milks to feed the baby: in addition to the heavy-handed religious symbology—possibly introduced to please the Spanish co-producer—the animal is obviously embalmed, causing the scene to slip into the involuntarily ridiculous. The scenes featuring Geneviève and her little son in the wild, including a fight with the wolf where the actress is visibly replaced by a double, don't fare better either.

Freda could film the early sequences, in which the wounded Siegfried is taken to the Duke of Brabant's castle, in and around an impressive-looking Spanish manor, with impressive results, whereas Siegfried's manor being the oft-seen Piccolomini Castle in Balsorano, Italy. Nevertheless, the lack of budget proved overwhelming for the three weeks' shoot in Spain,[13] and the director had to over-indulge in zooms. Sometimes, though, he used the zoom in an inventive way, just as Mario Bava did. An example is Geneviève's first appearance, conducted with a complex mixture of a backward tracking shot and a zooming in and out: the young woman is introduced through the sight of her shadow carrying a knife projected on the wall which the camera duly follows, before zooming in on the dagger and then back to reveal Geneviève's face, as she moves toward the room where the wounded Siegfried is resting. On the other hand, the remainder of the scene shows the lack of care with which the film was made. At the beginning, the Duke of Brabant and Siegfried are initially depicted as rivals, therefore the situation is supposed to be suspenseful (is Geneviève going to stab the man?), but the way we find out that she has actually come over to cure him is awkwardly rendered, with Geneviève standing motionless over Siegfried for what looks like an eternity, before she uses the knife to rip his shirt open and clean the wound.

The action is also subpar. The film opens rather abruptly with one of Freda's typical battle scenes. A knight on his horse is exchanging blows with a man standing before him. A panning shot to the right uncovers more dueling figures, yet the battle is rather poorly staged, with just a handful of extras crossing swords in a plain. A warrior appears in the distance, the horse rising on its back legs in an iconic image, then he gallops toward the other fighters, preceded by the camera at full speed, swirling his sword. A pair of crude, badly edited close-ups of enemies with their faces covered in blood paint ensue. Not only the scene is sabotaged by the sloppy editing—a knight's ruinous fall is recycled twice in a few minutes, although from different camera angles, and the close-ups of the wounded warriors don't match with the long shots as they wear different costumes and hoods—but it pales in comparison with what the director could achieve in his glorious past. Even worse is the climactic duel scene, where both actors are visibly replaced by doubles who don't even remotely look like them: Stephen Forsyth's is a very young Aldo Canti, later known to film fans as "Nick Jordan," who also plays the bit part of a soldier tortured by Golo. One wonders whether Freda still believed he could do anything with a double and the right camera angle or he simply did not care.

The director's overall attitude about the material is perhaps best exemplified by the way he keeps drawing back to his own work, as if on autopilot. A shot of the Duke of Brabant sitting at his table, on which a plate of multi-colored fruit stands out like a still life, is a nod to *Beatrice Cenci*, whereas Siegfried's imprisonment in enemy territory recalls *I miserabili*. The duel between Golo's henchmen in the forest near Geneviève's newborn baby—one about to kill the infant, the other attempting to save him—is another example of the director resorting to suspense by putting a harmless child in danger (see *La vendetta di Aquila Nera*), and in the same sequence he recycles the same trick as seen in the climax of *Aquila nera*: we hear a scream off-screen, and we don't know which of the two has died; then the bad guy returns, apparently the winner, only to drop down dead after a few steps. Sadly, this was old hat in 1964.

The cinematography (credited to Stelvio Massi and Julio Ortas) strives for the occasional colorful effect, but the outdoor scenes are often carelessly lit. Still, now and then the director comes up with the odd striking shot. After Geneviève has waved goodbye to Siegfried from the castle's bastions, she turns back in despair; the camera slightly moves leftward to show Golo. The two characters are standing on the opposite sides of the panoramic screen, divided by a huge battlement. A conflict is implied by their physical distance, and despite the man's reassuring words. Geneviève departs, leaving Golo at the center of the frame, alone—a grim omen of what will happen.

As for the leads, the Spanish María José Alfonso is a correct but unmemorable heroine, while Alberto Lupo (then very popular in Italy after his participations in many successful TV movies) is rather wooden as Siegfried. On the other hand, Stephen Forsyth makes an impressive turn as the wicked Golo. Although not a trained actor, Forsyth's cold stare, angular profile and controlled demeanor aptly suggest Golo's resentful feelings against his lord, and his latent wickedness is symbolically revealed by the Y-shaped scar that crosses his right cheek, almost a psychosomatic clue of his inner lust. The Canadian-born Forsyth would embark on a brief acting career between 1964 and 1970, with such films as Mino Loy's *Furia a Marrakech* (a.k.a. *Fury in Marrakech*, 1966), Freda's own *La morte non conta i dollari*, and Mario Bava's extraordinary Gothic thriller *Il rosso segno della follia* (a.k.a. *Hatchet for the Honeymoon*, 1970), before giving up acting and becoming a composer.

Forsyth described to this author how he became involved in the film business and his meeting with Freda:

> After studying in London at the London School of Economics I went to France and in Paris worked as a singer/songwriter. While on a short vacation to Rome I was approached by a photographer who asked to take my photograph for Gillette razors in Milan and this resulted an exclusive contract for me to do print and TV ads for Gillette in Europe. After acquiring an agent for acting, the first movie job I was sent out for was with director Riccardo Freda. Within minutes of meeting he offered me the lead in his upcoming movie *Genoveffa di Brabante*. He gave me the script to read and asked me to meet with him again and see if I was interested in doing the part. When I returned to see him I mentioned that I found the part of the antagonist more interesting than that of the protagonist that he had offered to me. He immediately said, "No problem, the antagonist part is yours and I'll let Alberto Lupo, the other lead, know the roles have been switched."[14]

Even though it was the very first movie in which he was cast, *Genoveffa di Brabante* was not technically Forsyth's debut.

> Shortly after signing the contract for the Freda film I was sent to meet director Gianni Puccini for a role in the movie *L'idea fissa*. I got the part which was for a one day shoot just prior to starting the Freda movie, so that was in fact my first time on a film set. *L'idea fissa* was very successful and as a result I was offered billing above the title in my next movie, *L'uomo di Toledo*.[15]

Working with Freda meant getting accustomed with his speedy working method and his use of multiple cameras, as Forsyth recalled.

> On my first day of shooting with Freda I didn't know what to expect, especially having had only one day of prior experience on a film set. I do remember there were multiple cameras, numerous marks for me to hit and dialogue that went on for pages and pages. It was all new to me so I dived in head first, did one take and that was it! Most of the scenes that followed were also multi-camera long takes.

Action scenes, such as horseback riding and swashbuckling duels, were rather more troublesome for the debuting actor, as proven by a humorous on-set anecdote.

> During out meeting, the only question Freda asked me regarding my past experience was, "Do you have experience with horseback riding?" Without having any real experience I answered I did, thinking I would have time before shooting to take some lessons. This would come back to haunt me! I did some preparation for the dueling scenes which went well but I never did get around to learning how to ride a horse. Before I knew it I was in Almería on a horse with an army of soldiers on horseback behind me about to charge a castle. I had a bit of trouble getting on the horse but figured I could fake my way through it. At "Action" I raised my sword and yelled to the army "Charge!" The only problem was I couldn't get my horse to move and the army behind me went charging by leaving me motionless in their dust. I knew I was in trouble and I could see Freda quickly advancing in a rage with his fist in the air and screaming "You said you could ride!" Taken aback by his rage I yelled back "There's something wrong with my horse!" Freda turned and yelled at the horse wranglers, "Get him another horse!" When the next horse arrived it was a black Arabian stallion, wild and agitated and the trainer said quietly, "Kick hard and don't pull the reins." I could barely mount the horse because it wouldn't stop moving. At this point I was thinking this is getting a bit scary as the horse was shaking and trembling underneath me. Next thing I knew there was another "Action" and before I could get my sword fully in the air the beast took off like there was no tomorrow. All I can remember was violently bouncing up and down hoping each time that I came down the horse would still be there. I realized later that if I had fallen off my horse with the army of horses charging behind me I could have been seriously trampled. It seemed that Freda was not too concerned about that. It was the last day of shooting and I didn't speak to Freda again. I found out later from one of the stuntmen that many of the most dangerous action scenes which included a principal actor were left to the last day of shooting in case there were any accidents. After this memorable incident I took the time to learn to ride well which would serve me well in other movies I made.[16]

Despite the director's irascible temper, Forsyth's relationship with him on set was quite smooth.

> I never witnessed Freda being a tyrant on the set and found him to be respectful and quietly in control. Freda was the first director to offer me a film role, and basically without knowing anything about me he trusted in my ability to do the job. His faith in me was empowering. Freda never questioned my ability to be able to meet the demands of the job. Most of the actors he used were very experienced and he expected a high level of professionalism from all involved. The atmosphere was always serious and business-like—no joking around. By the time I did my second film with him [*La morte non conta i dollari*] I had become quite a good horseman. Most often the principal actors were not allowed to ride when not shooting because of the possibility of an accident. Since I had free time between scenes, I wanted to go riding. I discussed this with Freda and he unexpectedly said it was okay for me to do this and then complimented me with a sly smile on my riding skills. I was quite

surprised and flattered to hear from somebody working on Bava's *Hatchet for the Honeymoon* that Freda had said I was one of the best actors he had worked with. It may have been on Freda's recommendation to Mario Bava that I was hired for *Hatchet for the Honeymoon*.[17]

For his part, Freda considered *Genoveffa di Brabante* a totally forgettable work, and later, in one of his bouts of self-deprecation, claimed he was satisfied only with María José Alfonso: "She was beautiful and mysterious as her character. She was a palm reader and a witch."[18] Possibly because of tax reasons, he did not even sign the film, which is credited to the Spanish José Luis Monter, who also acted as a front on Renato Polselli's trashy Western *Lo sceriffo che non spara* (a.k.a. *Sheriff Won't Shoot*, 1965).[19] *Genoveffa di Brabante* came out in Italy in late 1964, at a time when the Spaghetti Western fever had already started, and soon disappeared without a trace. It surfaced in the U.S. only in 2009 on DVD, in an English subtitled version titled *The Revenge of the Crusader*.

Les deux orphelines

After the failure of *Genoveffa di Brabante*, Freda finally had the chance to work on a French production. When producer Robert de Nesle invited him to direct a film version of *Les deux orphelines* for his company Comptoir Français du Film Production (C.F.F.P.), the director jumped at the opportunity: "If he'd asked me to film the restaurant's menu, I'd have accepted all the same," he later commented.[20]

First staged in 1874 as a five-act drama, the tearjerking story concocted by Adolphe d'Ennery and Eugène Cormon was then published as a novel in 1877, signed solely by D'Ennery. It focuses on two girls raised as sisters, Henriette and Louise, who are separated by events and undergo a series of sad experiences: Henriette is abducted by a libertine Marquis, and the blind Louise is exploited by a ruthless beggar, "Mother" Frochard. Eventually both girls will meet a happy ending, and Louise will recover her sight. *Les deux orphelines* met a long-lasting fortune in the movies, and was adapted for the screen numerous times since as early as 1907. The most popular version had been helmed in 1921 by D. W. Griffith, starring the Gish sisters, but there had also been two Italian versions, dated 1942 and 1954, directed respectively by Carmine Gallone and Giacomo Gentilomo—none of which Freda had ever seen, nor he had read the novel, for that matter. Nevertheless, the director revised the original script by Michel Wichard with the aim of adding more action and adventure to it, thus reshaping the original mélo into something closer to his vision of cinema.

Despite De Nesle's distrust that he could make the film in four weeks, Freda kept faithful to his promise to the producer. Shooting took place at a private property owned by one of the producer's acquaintances, a small village of sorts with streets and architecture, which recalled 18th century. The cast, comprised mostly of stage thesps (such as the great Jean Carmet) and led by Valeria Ciangottini (the innocent girl whose words Marcello Mastroianni cannot hear in the celebrated ending of *La dolce vita*) and Sophie Darès, served him well. As the male lead, Roger De Vaudray, Mike Marshall (Michèle Morgan's son) was merely adequate, though; Marshall's following film career was rather undistinguished, with mostly small roles (such as *Moonraker*) and the occasional lead. Fans of Euro cult may remember him as Greg in Jean Rollin's *La Morte vivante* (1982).[21]

Les deux orphelines marked a turn in Freda's life and career. In France the director found himself acclaimed as a master filmmaker, since his work had gained a consistent following in the country after the retrospective at the Cinémathèque Française, which according to the director had made Rossellini furious. He had moved to Paris in 1963, and during his Parisian stay he was interviewed by the prestigious *Midi-Minuit Fantastique* and met young film critics who admired his work, such as Bertrand Tavernier, who interviewed him for *Cinéma 63*. His first daughter Jacqueline was born there, on December 12, 1963, and Freda used to take his baby to the set and rock her pram during filming, in early 1965. A second daughter, Guislaine, would be born on July 10, 1965. It seemed that, in his adoptive country, the director had found happiness and peace. He would live in France for several years.

Compared to his previous couple of films shot in Spain, *Les deux orphelines* is much more accomplished stylistically, even though not quite "sumptuous" as Yves Boisset labeled it.[22] The camera moves restlessly in exquisite tracking shots that explore and reveal the sets in the director's characteristically elegant manner. An example is the opening arrival of the two orphan girls at the stagecoach station where destiny will divide them, during which Freda follows the trajectories of every single character (Henriette, Frochard, her sons…), thus metaphorically drawing the invisible lines that will tie them to one another and guide their actions.

Still, the film is even more revealing of the director's growing detachment from the paths of contemporary cinema. In Freda's universe time stopped in the 1940s, and the Nouvelle Vague never even existed in the first place. Hand-held camera was blasphemy, and self-reflexive complicity with the viewer was out of the question. The audience was taken for granted as a passive, inert flock which would respond to basic solicitations according to its primary instincts: sympathy for the heroes and hatred for the villains, awe or marvel at the costumes and portrayal of a past era, excitement at the swashbuckling duels, surprise at the plot twists. Unfortunately for the director, moviegoers had become a lot smarter than the masses he used to recall when he was a kid, and despite the young critics' praise—or possibly because of it—Freda's sticking to a stale idea of filmmaking was ultimately self-defeating. This is particularly evident given the literary source he tried his hands at. The pathetic story of the two orphan girls was definitely too old-fashioned for audiences, who would laugh at would-be-suspenseful scenes like the blind Louise clumsily walking dangerously near the edge of a 20-foot-high loft.

Had he had at hand a charismatic lead as Alain Delon instead of the bland Mike Marshall, perhaps Freda would have at least given its audience an excuse to sit through the predictable series of misadventures, dramas and agnitions. On the other hand, he stopped short from giving the material a thoroughly exploitative rereading, as, say, Roger Vadim would have done shamelessly. For all its requisite melodrama and action, *Les deux orphelines* is severely missing the titillation given by eroticism and violence. Even though the director claimed that "To me, the two orphan girls had to be very unfortunate, to the point that the viewer would be outraged…. I wanted to strengthen the sadistic and masochistic aspect of the story,"[23] the only mild attempt at giving the material a grim angle is when Frochard is pointing a knife at Henriette's throat, with the camera capturing a close-up of a thick line of blood coming out of the punctured skin—a moment, incidentally, which the Italian board of censors demanded be cut in order to give the film an "all audiences allowed" rating. Freda's intentions are best exemplified by the character of Mother Frochard, played with gusto by the Turkish-born Alice Sapritch, which the director wanted to be a bit like *The Mysteries of Paris*' Chouette, and who comes off as a female version of *Les Misérables*' Thenardier. Constantly over-the-top, and acting like a silent movie character, Sapritch steals every scene she is in, such as when she looks straight at the camera after hearing about Louise's blindness, jumping at the opportunity to employ the poor girl to raise money.

Unlike *Romeo e Giulietta*, where the paucity of means did not prevent him from boldly reinventing the story as a Western of sorts, in *Les deux orphelines* Freda seemed intimidated by the expectations that had been put on his shoulders. Here and there, though, the director's trademark cynicism pops up. There are some attempts at humor (such as when De Vaudray sees the portrait of his betrothed, a horrid-looking girl with a visible line of mustache) and ironic stabs at the clergy (an abbott who, instead of pushing a stagecoach through a countryside road, keeps reading his prayer book) and at the upper classes; the umpteenth banquet scene becomes the pretext to show the fatuous life of the élite, who indulge in the pleasures of gluttony and drink champagne that squirts out from a fountain maneuvered by a servant. However, this does not hint at a discourse on class struggle on the part of the director, as Freda is even more derisive when depicting the squalid ambience where the obnoxious Mother Frochard and her two sons live. As in *I vampiri*, here he seemed more interested in the theme of metaphoric vampirization, with elderly and disgusting people who are attracted by the pure, beautiful youth, and try to squeeze it from their victims by exploiting them in any way they can: in this sense, Marquis Presle and Mother Frochard are two sides of the same coin. One wonders what Freda might have done with De Sade's work.

Coplan FX 18 casse tout

The Eurospy fever provided Freda with the subject for his second film with C.F.F.P., on which he also took part as co-producer with the company Camera Films, together with the Milan-based Cinerad, owned by Luigi Radici. De Nesle's original idea was to adapt for the screen Gérard de Villiers' highly popular *S.A.S.* novels, but he could not get the rights, so Freda found himself saddled with the fourth installment in the *Coplan* series. The films featuring secret agent Francis Coplan were based on the novels by Paul Kenny (an alias for the Belgian writing duo Gaston Van den Panhuyse and Jean Libert), published since 1953. The series had started in 1957 with Maurice Labro's *Action immédiate* (a.k.a. *To Catch a Spy*), starring Henri Vidal. De Nesle revived Coplan with *Agent Secret FX 18* (a.k.a. *FX 18, Secret Agent*, 1964, Maurice Cloche), starring Ken Clark, and the same year a rival production company helmed *Coplan prend des risques* (a.k.a. *The Spy I Love*, 1964, Maurice Labro), featuring Dominique Paturel as Coplan.

For *Coplan FX 18 casse tout*, Freda was saddled with Richard Wyler, a British actor who had made his debut in George Sidney's *The Three Musketeers* and had become a minor star of Eurospy after his appearance in the U.K. television series *Man from Interpol*. *Coplan FX 18 casse tout* was Wyler's first European film; then he starred in Franco Prosperi's *Dick Smart 2007* (1967) and in a couple of Westerns—Eugenio Martín's *The Bounty Killer* (1967) alongside Tomas Milian, and León Klimovsky's *Un hombre vino a matar* (a.k.a. *Rattler Kid*, 1967)—before turning up in Jess Franco's stab at the Pop/spy universe *The Girl from Rio* (1969). Wyler would return to his birth name Richard Staples in the 1970s, appearing among others in Hitchcock's *Frenzy* (1972). The actor had very kind words toward Freda: "Oh, he was a wonderful man," he told film critic Robert Monell.

French poster for Freda's first Coplan film, *Coplan FX 18 casse tout* (1965).

A very good director whom everyone thought should be working on much better things than this low budget spy film.... he listened ... to the actors, the crew, anyone who had ideas on how to make the film better. Not all directors do that, you know.... Freda didn't talk very much. He wasn't very communicative. As I said, he was a very delightful man, very intelligent, he had a Doctorate in Art or something. He didn't speak much English. He would speak mainly in French.... He managed to communicate what he wanted, though, with a minimum of words.[24]

Beneath Wyler's impassible looks, Freda's Coplan is decidedly more violent and cynical than his contemporaries, though. As the actor explained, "I said to Freda that this kind of thing had been done so often that we might as well try to do something different with the character, give it a nihilistic feeling."[25] He goes through the usual routine of seducing and killing with the same coldness that he exhibits in the film's amusing opening sequence. In one of his trademark opening shots, Freda's camera reveals the setting (a nightclub where a band is playing a bawdy jazz tune while a *chanteuse* performs a risqué striptease) and introduces the hero, sitting at a table, who is handed a white rose by the stripper. In an amusing visual joke, the flower is revealed to be the vehicle of a secret message inscripted on its inner petal. Without anyone noticing, Coplan shoots an apparently harmless waiter who's about to open a champagne bottle at a nearby table, then pretends to be a doctor and diagnoses a heart attack: under the pretext of checking the man's identity card, he steals his wallet, which contains the key to decode a message. When the police arrives, the "doctor" has gone. His female accomplice joins him, right after Coplan has decoded the message. He hands her the agreed sum of money, but she replies: "I'm not here for that." After exchanging a lingering kiss, Coplain points at his watch, meaning there is no time. She takes the watch off his wrist and throws it on the floor, where it is joined by her hat, implying that for some things there is always time…

The rest of the film only sporadically lives up to its opening, and delivers a number of over-the-top violent bits, such as a dead body found inside a spike-ridden trunk, Virgin of Nüremberg style, a spy shot cold dead with a bullet to the head and another grabbed by the claws of a crane, a moment that somehow predates the opening scene of Tonino Valerii's excellent *giallo Mio caro assassino* (a.k.a. *My Dear Killer*, 1972). Women don't escape such violence either. When the body of a female Israeli agent (played by *Les deux orphelines*' Valeria Ciangottini) who has been tortured and murdered is found inside a coffin, Coplan's impassible face does not reflect the horrifying offscreen sight, but his visibly upset fellow agent's does.

Despite scriptwriter Claude-Marcel Richard's attempts at enlivening things up by way of codes, secret messages (the talking doll bit is amusing) and cool gadgetry such as a quick-draw sleeve gun that predates *Taxi Driver*, *Coplan FX 18 casse tout* relies on a bland intrigue like most other Eurospy films: Coplan uncovers a mad scientist's plan to destroy the Western and Eastern power blocks via a nuclear war, with the Chinese taking over the world as a result; the genre's umpteenth villain concocting world domination-cum-destruction is played by *Rififi*'s Robert Manuel. Two endings were filmed: one where Coplan ends up with a girl was discarded as the actress, a girlfriend of De Nesle, was so inept that the scene couldn't be used, as Wyler recalled.[26]

Most of the action is located in Turkey, and the opening credits, with a view of the Istanbul skyline at sunset from the Bosphorus channel, look like something out of a Jess Franco film. Besides Istanbul, Freda managed to shoot in the archaeological site in the Cappadocian district of Urgup, at the Göreme open air museum, with its ash and lava-formed soft rocks, and inside the church at Tokalı Kilise. The results are impressive and add a much-welcomed atmosphere to a standard plot, and somehow make up for the film's low budget, a testimony of Freda's professionalism and commitment even in the harshest conditions. As Wyler recalled, the director

> was busy concentrating on what he was doing, it was a very tightly budgeted and scheduled production. One day I saw him standing there looking very distracted and upset. I asked him what was wrong. Freda always seemed depressed about the way things were going. He had ambitions that went

way over the budgetary restrictions. He was having nightmares that he had to do this film, with all these special effects and stunts, without getting a chance to do second takes. We had very limited time on each location.... Later in the studio we shot some close-ups where he had the time to do multiple takes, but on the locations in France and Turkey virtually everything had to be done right the first time.[27]

Still, *Coplan FX 18 casse tout* is ridden with inventive sight gags and bravura shots, such as a sequence filmed through the point of view of a glass of Pernod, with the camera moving in sync with the glass, or the aftermath of a lovemaking scene as suggested through the characters' hands and featuring a nice James Bond joke. Freda even films a fistfight in a bathroom as one of his beloved silent movie gags, with people slipping on bars of soap and crashing through the walls. On top of that, he throws in an amusing nod to his previous work: when the villain recounts the horrors of Hiroshima, Coplan sharply replies: "Yet another version of *Les deux orphelines*...!" The use of zooms is also more laid-back than in the director's earlier Spanish co-productions, giving the film an internal rhythm that is right in tune with the genre.

In addition to Freda's energetic filmmaking style, ace stuntman Gil Delamare—with whom he had worked on *I giganti della Tessaglia*—came up with a number of show-stopping stunts that stand out among the usually slapdash action scenes of so many European James Bond rip-offs. Near the beginning, an amazing Hitchcockian sequence has a biplane attacking a truck on a lonely countryside road: after shooting one of the men dead, the pilot (Coplan) lands atop the truck, gets out and, while the plane falls off on the side of the road, catching fire, he sneaks into the cabin, kills the driver and stops the vehicle.

For a long chase with Coplan on a motorbike pursuing a sports car through canals, corn fields and countryside roads, Delamare asked the help of his friend, motocross champion Rémy Julienne. "I told him in advance that it was out of the question for me to do stunts, and I would only drive a motorbike," Julienne recalled. "But for him, I would do whatever I was able to.... We shot a lot of scenes and I suggested I jump over the sluice of Cepoy...."[28] The film's pièce de resistance features a car driving at full speed on Galata bridge and jumping from a dock onto a boat on the Bosphorus. The shot reportedly made the headlines in Turkish newspapers on the following day, and is a testament to the stuntman's exceptional skills. As Wyler recalled,

> he executed that stunt ... in one take! It just couldn't be done a second time. Freda and Gil were up the entire night before planning it out, that's all the time they had! There were 20 cameras set up all over the dock area so that it could be covered from all angles. This kind of stunt is done all the time today, but in those days it was a new thing and it was the first time anyone tried to do anything like it. Even the Bond films didn't go that far yet, and they had a much bigger budget. Gil had to have an air tank and a mask in the car in case he fell short of the ferry. He would have ended up in over 20 feet of cold water and could have easily died.... When the film opened in London, audiences were lined up around the block who had come just to see this scene, which everyone had heard about.[29]

Delamare, who also plays the Israeli spy Shaimoun in the film, would die the following year, at only 41, while performing a car stunt on the set of Christian-Jacque's *Le Saint prend l'affût* (a.k.a. *The Saint Lies in Wait*, 1966) where he worked as Jean Marais' double. *Coplan FX 18 casse tout* would be his last movie.

The film was moderately successful at the box-office but did not win the director any new admirers. Even the French critics were tepid: "Two or three gadgets and as many private jokes are not enough to save an insignificant mise-en-scène at the service of a stupid story,"³⁰ summed up *Image et son*'s reviewer. In Italy, under the title *Agente 777 missione Summergame*, it passed unnoticed among the flood of James Bond rip-offs of the period, Overseas, it did not have a theatrical release, but played on TV in Los Angeles only, in late 1968, as *FX 18 Superspy*.³¹

Roger La Honte

Published in 1886, *Roger-la-Honte* is one of the most popular *feuilletons* written by Jules Mary (1851–1922). Influenced by *Les Misérables* and by Naturalism in general, the story encompassed elements from the author's life, such as his service in the army during the Franco—Prussian war, and focused on one of Mary's favorite themes: mistrial. It was adapted for the screen several times over the years, starting with a 1914 short film. Other adaptation followed: after a 1924 picture directed by Jacques de Baroncelli and starring Gabriel Signoret, two more were produced in the sound era, respectively in 1933 by Gaston Roudés and in 1946 by André Cayatte, who helmed the diptych *Roger la Honte* and *La revanche de Roger la Honte*, with Lucien Coedel as Roger Laroque.

It is easy to see why Freda got involved in the film. Mary's novel had all the traits the director loved the most in a novel. It was the story of an innocent man who is humiliated, wrongly accused and imprisoned, and dedicates the rest of his life to proving his innocence—part *The Count of Monte Cristo*, half Eugène Sue, part Victor Hugo, as Freda synthesized it while commenting the film, one of his favorites. The script was written by his friend, the French writer Jean-Louis Bory (1919–1979), François Truffaut's replacement at the weekly magazine *Arts* since 1961 and later the literary and film critic for the prestigious *Nouvel Observateur*. The leftist Bory was not new to controversial positions: his rehabilitation of Louis-Ferdinand Céline (a surprising stand for a man near the Communist party) paired with his 1968 boycotting of the Cannes Festival that ended up with the competition being stopped. As for movies, unlike many of his peers Bory was resolutely against the so-called *films de boulevard* (such as those starring Louis de Funès, or made by such filmmakers as Henri Verneuil and Claude Lelouch), which he considered representative of the bourgeois art and values that he despised.

Bory was an admirer of Freda's work and met the director personally during the 1962 retrospective in Paris. Both men shared a passion for popular novels, which in Bory's case resulted in a number of influential essays on the topic, including *Eugène Sue, dandy et socialiste* (1962), a volume dedicated to the author of *The Mysteries of Paris*, as well as a number of TV adaptations of works by Sue, Balzac and Barbey d'Aurevilly. "I would like to retrieve the accordance that there existed in the 19th century between the general public and that type of popular literature ... and I am convinced that such an accordance can be reached through TV and cinema," the writer claimed. "Cinema represents what popular press had been in the last century, it is a tool technically equipped to keep this role. To fight against TV, anyway, it must move in two directions: cinema *d'essai* and spectacular cinema, cinema as a sanctuary and as a cathedral...."³²

According not only to Freda, but also to his friend Yves Boisset, who was assistant director on the film, *Roger la Honte* was a project the director truly cared about. "To me, it was a privilege to see Freda proud of what he was making," Boisset wrote.³³ The director had a good script to work with, decent production values and a formidable cast on top of that. Georges Géret, in a role that Freda had devised for Lino Ventura, gives a remark-

Irene Papas and Georges Géret in *Roger la Honte* (1966).

able performance as Roger Laroque, as does Jean-Pierre Marielle in his first dramatic role as Lucien, Roger's friend and lawyer who, after finding out his wife is Roger's lover, abandons the defense and later kills himself out of shame. After over a decade, the director worked again with Irene Papas, now an internationally popular name diva after her appearances in such productions as *The Guns of Navarone* (1961, J. Lee Thompson) and *Zorba the Greek* (1964, Michael Cacoyannis), who played Julia. Still, the director did not give up to his by now well-oiled timesaving methods. Shooting took place in four weeks, with Freda often using three cameras at once and employing a second unit (headed by Boisset) to speed up the proceedings. As the correspondents for the French mag *Cinéma 66* recounted after their visit on the set near the abbey of Châlis, for the last day of filming, on February 28, 1966, "one could witness an unusual sight: a squadron of Prussians in red and blue uniforms was charging on the park's lawns; and not far a theory of convicts jostled inside a prison van."[34]

For the opening, in which Roger crosses the battlefield littered with dead bodies to find his wounded comrade Lucien, carries the man on his back and leaves, Freda improvised the scene in the garden of the castle, much to the disbelief of his friend Bertrand Tavernier. "I had placed some fires here and there, some fake bodies of soldiers and horses, several overturned cannons. Very quickly, there was a real sense of carnage. It is an exercise I had already done in *Spartaco*. A very long side traveling shot on the bodies and the spears planted in vertical...."[35] Its making impressed the French journalists on the set, who described at length Freda's use of an extended traveling shot, about 50 meters long, to film the scene in just three takes while a second camera filmed the fire.

In a way, Freda was doing as a filmmaker what Jules Mary and the *feuilleton* novelists of the 19th century were doing as writers—working very quickly, since they were paid by the line. Still, this time his approach to the material was very self-conscious, and somehow along the same vein as Georges Franju's rereading of Feuillade's serials in *Judex* (1963): "We realized that it was necessary to cut out the frenzied side while maintaining a certain naivety. I wanted to give the film a resolutely modern form, even though in spite of that it remains a melodrama," Freda explained. Bory, on the other hand, employed his vast knowledge of the *feuilleton* to liberally squeeze from the novel (which he dismissed as of "a debatable literary quality") its main characters and feelings: love, hate, vengeance. In other words, taking a sub-par literary *Count of Monte Cristo* and turning it into an above-par cinematic one.

After the war prologue, which ends with Roger carrying his wounded friend on his shoulders, away from the battlefields, an abrupt cut brings us to a casino, on the close-up of a roulette's wheel spinning, for the enjoyment of an audience with their eyes fixed on the small white dancing sphere. The camera pans away with all the suaveness that we have come to expect from a Freda film, while the elegantly dressed players make their bets. The horrors of war have been forgotten, the upper classes are eager for pleasure. It is a hint at the film's main themes: fate, chance, and fortune. Roger's life will soon be like the ivory ball on the Roulette wheel, his future put at stake by forces he cannot even imagine.

With an almost imperceptible reversal of perspective, the same scene is then seen as reflected on a glass door, from which Julia enters the room. She heads toward a man with his back to her, that she has mistaken for Roger. The episode is subtly revealing: first, because it suggests an intimacy between the woman and the man she is looking for (we will soon learn she and Roger are lovers); and then because it also hints at the theme of the double, which clearly fascinated Freda and Bory. In the next scene, Julia reproaches Roger, telling him he is leading a double life, with his family and with her; later on, Roger finds that she as well has a double life: he knows Julia under a fake name, while she is actually his best friend's wife. Ironically, when Roger threatens to leave her, Bory has Julia burst out, "I bet my life upon you, on our love," thus subtly hinting to the opening images of the casino. Then there is the third man, Luversan, a.k.a. Mathias Hubert, the one Julia first mistakes for Roger. He appears in the first part of the film as a William Wilson of sorts, a distant and gleeful observer of Laroque's ruin. Later on in the film he is revealed to have a double identity as well: a former Prussian spy who has created a new identity for himself just like Roger will do after his escape from jail. The two men mirror one another, and even their identities blur: when Laroque's wife and little daughter glimpse Luversan murdering a man, they too believe it was Roger who did it.

By emphasizing the characters' duplicity, the Marxist Bory seems to reflect upon the hypocritical mores of the bourgeoisie—a condition Roger will eventually run away from by literally creating a new self. What is more, Bory gives the story a fresh quality by drawing liberally from other movies. Roger is framed for a murder committed by someone else and mistakenly identified as the culprit, like Henry Fonda was in Alfred Hitchcock's *The Wrong Man* (1956), and the scene where he is supposedly seen while committing the murder is a nod to *Rear Window* (1954). In this sense, *Roger la Honte* is a purely Hitchcockian melodrama, in the way it mercilessly piles up, one by one, the elements that will cause Roger's ruin, insisting less on the hero's moral drama than on the intricate plot that deprives him of his freedom, his honor, the love of his family and the respect of his best friend—all this, with a definite Sadean delight on the part of the makers in perfecting such an implacable narrative trap.

Bory claimed that he had written the adaptation and the dialogue exclusively in function of Freda's direction. "To me, the essential principle of a scriptwriter is to comply with the director's aesthetics, as he is and must remain the master, the author, until the end. Therefore, I choose the words in function of the images that I know by my knowledge of the filmmaker's other works."[36] And it is evident that he knew Freda's *oeuvre* very well indeed. Take, for instance, the trial scenes, which purposely recall those in *Il conte Ugolino* and *Il tradimento (Passato che uccide)*. In *Roger la Honte*, to portray the audience attending the trial, Freda employs the very same lateral panning shot he had used on *Il tradimento* when showing the jury. The director's tuning with the script is best shown by the extraordinary scene in which Roger's little daughter Suzanne is queried by the judge, with an insistence that soon borders on the sadistic, both for the poor girl and the audience. Far from being an impartial guardian of the law, the judge tries as best as he can to circumvent the little child, who has been instructed by her mother not to tell what she has seen (or rather, she *believes* she has seen—that is, her father committing a murder). Regardless of the little girl's desperate tears, he even threatens her by evoking a divine punishment, with the flames of hell awaiting perjurers, in order to make her talk. Here, the director's disdain of men's justice and organized religion is palpable.

With a sharp narrative cut, the film jumps from the moment where the jury retires to deliberate to a ballad singer who tells Roger's story, summarily drawn over a large canvas, to a small audience in a village: years have passed, one man's drama has become an exemplary tale to be passed from generation to generation. It is a remarkable narrative ellipsis, which proves Bory's skills as a scriptwriter, gives *Roger la Honte* an almost mythical quality, and at the same time underlines its essence as a popular story.

The second part of the film is patterned over *I miserabili*, as Roger returns under a new identity as Jean Valjean did, while commissioner Lacroix (Paul Muller) functions as a homologue to Javert; on top of that, Roger's confrontation with Julia, with the man wearing a pair of dark sunglasses to conceal his identity, brings to mind Rossano Brazzi's camouflage in *Aquila nera*. Bory's Marxist roots are also evident in his depicting of Roger's vengeance, which is economic as well: wealth becomes a tool for the stronger to crush and humiliate the weaker, and capitalism is a matter of the big fish eating the small one. In an exquisitely cruel scene, Roger has his own enemy, whom he just ruined economically, help him put on his coat like a butler would.

Compared to the first half, however, the story loses a bit of steam, despite some intense scenes, such as Roger's pursuing of Hubert on horseback, and Suzanne's confession to her father that she really believed she saw him murdering a man, filmed in a beautiful pictorial shot which encompasses Marie-France Boyer's close up and Georges Géret behind her, in an accomplished use of depth-of-field. Still, the director seems not as interested in the subplot concerning Suzanne's romance with Julia's son, played by Gabriele Tinti, which is rather inert and conventional. The overall impression is that the direction is quite rushed in places, as if Freda got tired of the material—or if, despite the larger means and better cast he was allowed on set, he was nevertheless accustomed to his speedy habits and would not consider a different, more careful approach. The scene of Suzanne's coach accident is an example of an awkward one-take job: as Marie-France Boyer's stunt double falls his dress rises, revealing a pair of decidedly masculine trousers, and the editor vainly tries to salvage the shot through an optical zoom that isolates the carriage and pushes the stuntman off-screen. Bertrand Tavernier, who was the press attaché on the film, recalled that Freda "filmed one of the essential scenes in one take, with three cameras, the equivalent of five or six pages of dialogue. Irene Papas was furious, and Georges Géret disappointed. And the scene looks botched."[37]

Roger La Honte picks up steam again near the end, with a climax that is purely Gothic in spirit, centered as it is on the cyclical return of the past which haunts and obsesses the characters: the final confrontation between Roger and Luversan takes place in the same room where the murder had occurred, and plays like a rerun of the earlier episode. Freda milks the scene for all it's worth, with such Expressionist effects such as Laroque's shadow towering over his adversary, and does not shy away in front of a classical melodramatic denouement. Once again he shows his basic respect for the tradition of the *feuilleton*, compared to the contemporaneous examples revisited with a pop and ironic sensibility such as the Fantômas cycle starring Jean Marais and Louis de Funès.

The film was enthusiastically received by the French critics. "We would like that all ... knew as much as Freda how to handle a camera (see the trial sequence) and its spectacular potential. That's what makes this cheap little film such a beautiful illusion and a definite pleasure…. Then? A must-see. This is cinema, indeed!"[38] enthused the reviewer on *Image and Son*. Future Cannes Film Festival president Gilles Jacob wrote: "It takes courage nowadays to face, were it through the mechanism of a double conspiracy, the sardonic sneers of enthusiasts made fussy by the subtle finesses of all the Audiards. Here, we do not despise the cries, nor the tears: vengeance dons a capital 'V,' love is draped in the magnification and effect, evil has an aura of inevitability."[39] However, as Boisset correctly pointed out, "melodrama was too devalued a genre to allow Freda to be truly acknowledged by the Parisian *intelligentsia*."[40] Or, as Jacob put it in his review, "let's face it, we would not go and see [the film], were it signed by Cayatte or Maurice Cloche."[41]

On the other hand, in Italy the movie was hardly noticed by the critics and the audience alike, also due to bad distribution. Even though some sources mention the English-language title *Trap for the Assassin* (the literal translation of the Italian one *Trappola per l'assassino*, which focused on the mystery aspect of the plot in the attempt to pass off as some kind of thriller[42]), it does not seem to have surfaced overseas. Freda and Bory then planned to adapt *The Mysteries of Paris*, but the project was shelved after the death of the producer.

Coplan ouvre le feu à Mexico

Freda's second Coplan film found the director coping again with an overly poor budget and assorted production issues. As with so many genre outings of the mid-to-late 1960s, *Coplan ouvre le feu à Mexico* was a co-production between France, Italy and Spain: besides Robert De Nesle's C.F.F.P., the other main backers were Edmondo Amati's Fida Cinematografica and Alfonso Balcázar's own company. The Spanish contribution was vital to the film, which was shot entirely in the suburbs of Barcelona and at the Balcázar studios with some recycled slapdash Western sets making for a poor man's impression of Mexico. Coplan was played by Lang Jeffries, who by then had specialized in spy flicks after the decline of *peplum*, while the rest of the cast comprised a number of genre character actors, such as the Italian Guido Lollobrigida and the Spanish José María Caffarel.

The script was co-written by Freda's colleague and friend Bertrand Tavernier. After directing a couple of nondescript episodes in a pair of omnibus comedies, Tavernier had reverted to journalism, and occasionally worked as press attaché, but Freda encouraged him to keep trying. Within a few years he would return behind the camera, with the extraordinary *L'horlogier de Saint-Paul* (a.k.a. *The Clockmaker*, 1973), and went on to become one of the top French film directors. Tavernier recalled the experience on working on *Coplan ouvre le feu à Mexico* this way: "He [Freda] was one of those who came over to my parents and convinced them to let me make movies. And it was he who asked me to work on that Paul Kenny novel that neither of us had read, because he believed it was useless."[43] Typically Freda.

Tavernier then came out with a delirious plot about a secret association of diehard Nazis planning to kidnap U.S. president Lyndon Johnson by way of a net of underground tunnels, replace him with a double and launch a missile attack against the major American cities. The script tried hard to keep in tune with the genre's pulp spirit, by coming up with all sorts of over-the-top inventions: the sequence in which Coplan and his aide jump off a biplane right into a car's backseat was probably concocted as some kind of a companion piece to *Coplan FX 18 casse tout*'s breathtaking plane-landing-over-a-truck scene, whereas a less spectacular but decidedly more bizarre bit has Coplan's contact agent (Guido Lollobrigida) meeting him on a rollercoaster to impart his secret information (with both actors appearing rather uncomfortable); after said contact is shot dead while diving off the Acapulco cliff, Coplan pursues the fleeing killers while parasailing. The list also includes: a funeral which evolves into a gunfight; a corpse found in an abattoir; the hero discovering his own coffin (a nod to *Thunderball*?) and then being trapped inside a room with a ceiling that closes on him mechanically, and so on. One of the best moments comes early on in the film and has Coplan show up at a female agent's flat which appears to be deserted. In the silent place, the sound of a drop of water coming from a faucet can be distinctly heard. Coplan turns the faucet off but the noise continues. The camera returns to the sink, showing that the noise is actually caused by drops of blood falling from above. Coplan goes upstairs and discover the dead girl's body. It is a very well conceived Hitchcockian scene, which also pays homage to the episode *La goccia d'acqua* in Bava's *I tre volti della paura*, possibly more on the part of Tavernier than Freda's.

Just like in the previous film, Coplan is as cynical a hero as any. He kills in cold blood, burns two men alive after lighting a cigarette, crushes a villain's head into a press, and at the end, when he is left alone, he plays a record of Chopin's "Funeral March" as a sarcastic requiem for his enemies. Still, by concocting a plot about the smuggling of invaluable paintings, which the Nazis use to finance their organization, Tavernier blatantly poked fun at the genre's uncultivated heroes, and inserted several amusing jokes about Coplan and his peers' utter ignorance. An example is the scene where a group of generals and heads of the secret service are watching a slide of a famous painting. "It looks like a Michelangelo," one observes. "Clearly Italian school," the other adds. The picture is then revealed to be a Rembrandt. Later on, during an auction, a character complains, "I like modern painting, when you don't understand a thing!" Coplan himself is bored to death by classical music and doesn't know the meaning of the word "pantheist."

The film is full of such in-jokes. In a scene, Coplan and Fondane (Frank Oliveras) contemplate a photo of the missing girl they are supposed to find, Francine (played by Silvia Solar); "She looks pretty," they agree: however, the photo is actually a set still from a scene that takes place later on in the film, when Francine is menaced in her apartment by a killer, and it depicts the woman in the act of screaming.

The tongue-in-cheek, spicy dialogue (credited to Christian Plume but written by Freda, at least according to Tavernier,[44] whereas the Spanish copies feature José Antonio de la Loma's name for co-production reasons) and plot twists partially make up for the chaotic storyline, and even Tavernier himself admitted that the result was far from brilliant. "I had concocted scenes susceptible to suit Freda's visual talent (such as the discovery of a dead body in an abattoir, for instance) but he shot them sloppily,"[45] he complained. Another soon-to-be prominent filmmaker, Yves Boisset, was part of the crew as Freda's assistant and second unit director, as in *Roger la Honte*: Boisset never hid his utter admiration for the Italian director, going so far as saying that "Freda, on the strict level of the *mise-en-scène*, the organization of images, is twice as strong as De Sica. Only, De Sica worked with a script that was a real script, and shot it with actors who were real actors."[46] This time, however, the director's lack of care was blatant. As Boisset recalled, the film was to be shot in Mexico, but Freda preferred Spain, claiming that "Barcelona was more authentic than Mexico." Which sounded like an unlikely excuse: the director—understandably, being the father of two little girls, the younger being less than two years old—simply did not feel like going to Mexico to make the movie. The French director added: "De Nesle was delighted, and it's this type of events, I think, that harmed Riccardo. He should have worked for more demanding producers. And so we shot in Spain, under unlikely conditions, a movie that I had prepared for another country."[47]

Following the tragic death of his favorite stuntman Gil Delamare, the director employed miniatures and *maquettes* for most of the stunts and explosion scenes, a choice which only heightened the film's sloppy feel, and perhaps Freda's disenchantment to the project, a much different approach to his previous Coplan film, where the need to adhere to the tight budget and schedule had stimulated his inventiveness. Here, the sight of a plane flying over a cardboard cut image of the Chichen Itza pyramid is just laughable—ditto for the Mexican "exteriors," made the same way. Even though Freda stages a dynamic fight scene featuring Oliveras that looks like it belongs to one of his early swashbucklers, and his use of long takes is notable here and there, zooms are often a quick replacement for tracking shots, and a number of sequences look rushed. The most blatant example of carelessness (not on the part of Freda, this time) is the moment where the story moves on to London, and the required establishing exterior shot is a very visible *still* of the Tower Bridge. Evidently, De Nesle could not even provide decent archive footage to his editor.

On top of that, Boisset claimed that Freda often stayed away from the set for several days, leaving his assistant director to shoot scenes he did not care about. "Contrary to the usual, it was not about filming chases, horserides or shoot-outs," Boisset explained.

> Freda loved filming the action scenes and therefore discharged on me the so-called 'psychological' ones. He much preferred the company of horses than of actors. Useless to add that such a distribution of competences perfectly suited me. Especially since, being credited with second unit and being the action scenes the best thing about the film, I acquired a bit abusively the reputation of having great skills in the direction of chases and other action scene.[48]

Reportedly, Freda let his assistant take care of the scenes featuring Sabine Sun, with whom he had worked on *Roger La Honte* and who had been once again imposed by De Nesle: "Monsieur Boisset, could you please direct this starlet?" he would say while leaving the set temporarily.[49]

Boisset's reports from the set only increased Tavernier's impression about Freda's lack of care on the project. As he recalled, "Boisset ... confirmed to me that Freda did not give a shit about it. I discovered scenes which were not in my script in the first place, and Riccardo, who had quarreled with the producer, didn't want to tell me what the characters were speaking. "You just have to sort it out yourself. The actors did, 'bla-bla-bla'.... We had to invent a dialogue based on the labials. Freda had made great films, but it also happened that he shamelessly rushed through."[50]

As readers will know by now, the quarrel Tavernier is referring to was one of Freda's recurring habits. During filming, he had an argument with De Nesle and left the set. *Coplan ouvre le feu à Mexico* was to be his last film with the French producer. That year, the director left France and returned to Italy. The film was finished by Yves Boisset, who—thanks to Freda's insistence toward De Nesle—would then direct the sixth and final installment in the series: *Coplan sauve sa peau* (a.k.a. *Coplan Saves His Sin*, 1968), starring Claudio Brook as Coplan and Klaus Kinski.[51]

Coplan ouvre le feu à Mexico was a financial flop in France, and did mediocre business abroad. In Italy, where it was announced as *Coplan contro i rapaci* (Coplan Against the Raptors), it was released in Summer 1967 with the unappetizing title *Moresque: obiettivo allucinante* (Moresque: Hallucinatory Target), to general indifference: reviewers did not even bother to mention Freda's name. In Spain, having made Silvia Solar (in a role initially destined for Mónica Randall) pass off as the film's protagonist in order to receive law benefits, Balcázar was fined for fraud by the Dirección General de Cinematografía (General Direction of Cinematography) and had to pay 10,000 pesetas.[52] A small mystery involves the presence of Italian actress Ida Galli (also known as Evelyn Stewart), who according to some sources worked on the film, although she is uncredited and cannot be spotted in the circulating copies. Galli herself stated: "I remember working with Freda, but this film I do not remember it at all...."[53]

It surfaced years later on tape in the U.S. in a severely truncated version, and with a lousy dubbing, as *Mexican Slayride*. About 30 minutes are missing from English language copies, mostly from the central part, including the scene in which Coplan is shut in the shrinking room and the killing of the Lady Lagrange (Sabine Sun) who, after securing Coplan's release from said room, is dispatched by way of her car's ignition gas in a locked garage from which she can't escape. On the other hand, the French official VHS release suffered from rough quality, with lots of missing frames and jumps. In Germany, Coplan was renamed "Frank Collins" and the film was retitled *Frank Collins 999—Mit Chloroform geht's besser* ("Frank Collins 999—With chloroform it gets even better"), with reference to the early scene where Coplan chloroforms Lady Lagrange, an affiliate of the Nazi organization, while they are in bed.

Freda's definition of *Coplan FX 18 casse tout* and *Coplan ouvre le feu à Mexico* pretty much summarizes his view on the spy genre, as well as his by then disillusioned vision of filmmaking:

> The Coplan films are like Maciste or modern *peplum* flicks. What matters is the action, and horses are replaced by cars. When I shot those movies, I did not expect to be listed in film dictionaries. It was very simple, we had to go to Turkey or Mexico, so as to make the result as exotic as possible, multiply the corpses and make the villain a real bastard. That was that.[54]

13

A Sort of Homecoming

La morte non conta i dollari

For his first film after his return to Italy, Freda had to cope with yet another trend that had caught on in the last few years: the so-called Spaghetti Western. The commercial exploit of *Per un pugno di dollari* had given way to a myriad of flicks in a similar vein—some good, some bad, some ugly. Freda did not love the genre—or rather, not the Italian approximations of it, which he dismissed as hardly distinguishable crap. Still, the once leading director who challenged the market by shooting ambitious adventure yarns such as *Aquila nera* and *Il cavaliere misterioso* was now forced to settle down with a low-budget subproduct whose main *raison d'être* was squeezing yet another few bucks from audiences that were seemingly never tired of more flicks in the vein of Sergio Leone's hits.

The story of *La morte non conta i dollari* revolves around two men, Lawrence White (who returns to his hometown of Owell Rock with his sister, to avenge his father's death at the hands of the gang led by Doc Lester, who rules over the town) and Harry Boyd, a gunslinger who is appointed as the sheriff of Owell Rock by Lester. Freda and his co-scriptwriter Giuseppe Masini blended together some typical Spaghetti Western motifs with more personal ideas. "For the script, I took inspiration from Mérimée's *Carmen*, it was the story of a vengeance," the director explained. Even though *Carmen* would provide the source for at least one other Italian Western, Luigi Bazzoni's *L'uomo, l'orgoglio, la vendetta* (a.k.a. *Pride and Vengeance*, 1967, starring Franco Nero and Klaus Kinski), the byzantine plot[1]—whose structure bore the inevitable nods to the theme of infiltrators with hidden agendas, which had been a staple of the Italian Western since *Per un pugno di dollari*[2]—takes a convoluted path which makes it look like a murder mystery of sorts, as the members of Lester's gang are being offed one by one by a mysterious killer. Then, a truly unexpected twist at about the hour's mark raises undetected similitudes with Freda's beloved *feuilletons*, with its reliance on secret (and switched) identities, which pairs with the classic theme of the sons avenging the father. All of this never really adds up; still it does not detract from the fun, and *La morte non conta i dollari* remains mildly enjoyable viewing, despite its many inconsistencies.[3] It climaxes in a rather complex, if haphazardly mounted sequence which—quite an oddity in the genre—has the hero take the villain to prison instead of shooting him dead in the customary duel.

Even though the material was second-hand at best, Freda's approach was closer in spirit to the Western directors he admired, starting with John Ford. A few minutes into the movie, Mark Damon appears from nowhere and hitches a ride on a stagecoach, just

Italian 2-fogli manifesto for Freda's only Western, *La morte non conta i dollari* (1967), signed as "George Lincoln."

like John Wayne did in *Stagecoach*. Dirty and sweaty, he accommodates between an impeccably dressed young man and an equally elegant city lady. More than a homage, it is almost a literal recreation of *Stagecoach*'s similar scene featuring Wayne, John Carradine and Louise Platt. The stagecoach is then attacked by the bandits, and after a rousing chase, which has the coachmen killed in the process, Damon (or rather, his stunt double) drops from the vehicle onto the horses's back, evoking Yakima Canutt's legendary stunt in Ford's masterpiece.

However, Freda's film is miles away from Ford's epics, as he himself admitted. "To make a Western, one needs the Grand Canyon, and all I had was the Italian countryside…." The exteriors were shot over the hills around Rome, and the definitely Italian landscape is a far cry from the Monument Valley. The main fault, once again, laid on the shoestring budget, which partially explains the overreliance on the zoom lens, even though the director managed to achieve a great sequence shot on a dolly in the scene anticipating the climax, as Lester's men take position in Owell Rock's main street and hide on the roofs to prepare their ambush.

The casting is flawed. Yves Boisset recalled that he had convinced Klaus Kinski (with whom he worked on *Coplan sauve sa peau*) to take the leading role, but the producer did not follow his advice.[4] Whereas Freda had to do with Mark Damon, the star of Roger Corman's *House of Usher* (1960) who had relocated in Rome and reinvented himself as one of the American stars of Italian cinema of the 1960s, and Spaghetti Western in particular, starring in *Johnny Oro* (1966, Sergio Corbucci) and *Johnny Yuma* (1966, Romolo Guerrieri) among others—which caused the film to be released in Denmark as a sequel to Guerrieri's Western, *Johnny Yuma vender tilbage* (Johnny Yuma Returns). As Boisset put it,

> when Mark Damon … arrived in Italy, he was barely an actor. Later he became a huge U.S. independent distributor, but never a great actor. He had the physique of a hairdresser's assistant. Freda liked Mark Damon very much because he agreed to work fast, but Damon didn't care about movies. What he wanted was to earn money to buy laundromats.[5]

Alongside Damon, Stephen Forsyth worked for the second time with Freda after *Genoveffa di Brabante*. He later observed about his role: "While watching the movie I was surprised at how good I was in my part but thought that if the roles had been switched like in *Genoveffa di Brabante* it would have been a more fun and interesting experience for me and perhaps would have resulted in a better movie."[6] Last but not least, the villains, headed by the unmistakable Nello Pazzafini, make for a rather uninteresting bunch.

Again, as in *Coplan ouvre le feu à Mexico*, Yves Boisset acted as second unit director. Still, this time Freda seemingly took care of the whole shooting, according to Forsyth: "I don't remember Boisset. I can't remember any scene that I did on a Freda movie that was done without Freda directing. In general it would be unusual for any scenes with dialogue and principal actors to be done without the director present and this would apply to any of the movies I worked on."[7]

Nevertheless, the French filmmaker confirmed the impression that *La morte non conta i dollari* was a rushed, indifferent job on Freda's part:

> Despite all the difficulties with the production and the actors, the Western was filmed in a sort of euphoria, but during the shooting everybody ceased to care. Freda was not the only one responsible for that; there was also the climate of vulgarity on the part of the producers, but he accommodated. I think Riccardo got engulfed in a ghetto by himself, working with third-rate producers and actors.[8]

Filming in a hurry meant, for instance, not having time to wait for a cloud to pass and allow d.o.p. Gábor Pogány to work out the correct lighting for a scene, even though it would be just a few minutes' waiting. Pogány dutifully obliged, but it was a humiliating experience for such an experienced, talented cinematographer.

In his memoir, Boisset went so far as stating that Freda was actually supposed to shoot two films back-to-back, with roughly the same cast. Through a substantial salary raise, he proposed to shoot them *at the same time*—same actors, same crew, same sets and costumes—in six weeks, instead of the scheduled four weeks per picture. The producer—according to Boisset, a butcher of the Roman suburbs who got bitten by the film bug—was so enthused with the proposal that he gave Freda a second-hand white Rolls Royce as extra payment for the job.

> In one of the two films, Mark Damon played the sympathetic hero, conveniently wearing white shirt, jacket and Stetson, and Stephen Forsyth—black shirt, jacket and Stetson—played the villain. In the other film, the roles and costume were the opposite. A spectacular saloon fistfight was the climax of each film. Surrounded by about twenty stuntmen who kept heartily beating each other up, Mark Damon and Stephen Forsyth faced each other during a fistfight in the grand tradition of John Ford. Freda had had the idea of having a big white line traced in the middle of the set. Whenever Mark and Stephen crossed that line, they stopped fighting, quickly exchanged jacket and Stetson and then immediately resumed their fistfight before the cameras of the other film, while all the stuntmen around them continued their big brawl. The scene was filmed in continuity by five cameras, three of which were mounted on a dolly. Thus Freda had at his disposal an exceptional richness and variety of shots. He had such a creative visual inventiveness that, even in the least successful films, there is always at least one magical scene.[9]

Anyway, since both Damon and Forsyth play the good guys and, even most importantly, there is no such climactic saloon brawl in the film, one wonders whether Boisset was simply making it up to pay homage to Freda's skillfulness—a suspicion that becomes fact once heard Forsyth's lapidary comment: "Two films being shot together is news to me and didn't happen."[10] The white-and-blue Rolls was a true detail, however, and the majestic vehicle was a familiar presence in Jacqueline Freda's early years. "You would buy my father with a fancy car, so it might as well have gone like that! It was *enormous*—I remember climbing on it on my tricycle and riding back and forth in the space before the back seats. And I used to hide in the hollow footrest compartment. There was so much room! And the smell of wood imbued with alcohol...."[11]

In his memoir, Boisset also recalled an anecdote about the shooting of one of *La morte non conta i dollari*'s key scenes, when the desperadoes are waiting for Lawrence White and his men to enter Owell Rock and kill them. One of the stunts, perched upon a stagecoach full of dynamite candles, had to head toward the bank and jump off the carriage just seconds before the inevitable explosion. On the first take, though, the stuntman panicked and jumped too early, so that the explosion came as a setback. The scene had to be shot again after rebuilding the set, a catastrophe for such a low-budget picture, and Freda—never one to hold back his tongue when it came to spit out sarcastic remarks—publicly humiliated the unfortunate stuntman. The next day the scene was ready to be filmed again, and the stuntman did his best. Only, this time he jumped too late and couldn't avoid being involved in the explosion, with fatal results. "Before his shattered body, Freda uttered this very lapidary eulogy: 'He wasn't a true professional.'" Yet, Boisset adds:

> This apparent cynicism on Freda's part concealed without a doubt a sincere emotion that his reservation and modesty prevented him to express. I am even more convinced of that since, some days later,

he had the heart to attend the stuntman's funeral. And, without anyone knowing, he sent money to the man's wife and children. That was Riccardo Freda. A sort of impassive commander whose philosophy could pass for arrogance, hiding immense qualities of heart.[12]

As significant and pointed as it may be, the anecdote is most likely yet another fabrication, or simply a variation of one of those urban legends that circulated on Italian sets about Freda's cynicism[13]: Forsyth is adamant in stating that there were no fatalities during the shooting of the movie, and no other source reported the episode.

La morte non conta i dollari came out in Italy almost unnoticed, grossing a little over 150 million *lire*, and the director had a good share of complaints about it. "They destroyed my edit," he stated. "I had little resources, and they cut the most violent scenes.... But I insist, I wrote the scenario, it was a cruel film."[14] The two scenes he was referring to are the one where a man has his tongue cut out and a violent whipping. However, Freda overstated the importance of said cuts on the film: the board of censors demanded only six seconds to be excerpted, and overall *La morte non conta i dollari* pales in comparison with other Italian westerns of the period as far as graphic violence is concerned. Anyway, the director was so dissatisfied with the result that he signed the film with the pseudonym George Lincoln, evoking not one but two presidents of the United States, so as to detach his name from it. Even the title—literally, "Death Does Not Count the Dollars"—he utterly disliked: "It doesn't mean anything, neither in French, nor in English, and not even in Italian!"[15]

Lucky ... or maybe not

If *La morte non conta i dollari* was the umpteenth work-for-hire, around the same time Freda was attempting to put together one of his most ambitious projects, a movie about Salvatore Lucania, better known as Lucky Luciano. The director claimed to have passingly met the Italian-American gangster at the racetracks, which both of them regularly attended, and a few years after Lucky's death he developed a film project called *L'imperatore di New York* (The Emperor of New York), involving his friend Bertrand Tavernier in the scriptwriting phase. A copy of the 216-page script is kept at Madrid's Filmoteca; it bears the line "A script by John Garnett from a treatment by Bernard [*sic*] Tavernier, translated from English by Riccardo Freda." It might well be that the elusive Garnett and Freda are the same person.

The script is accompanied by a letter, dated November 15, 1967, written on a headed paper by U.N.A.C. (Unione Nazionale Autori e Cinetecnici—National Union of the Authors and Cinema Technicians) and addressed to the Spanish producer Eduardo Manzanos Brochero, in the attempt at involving him in a co-production deal. The letter reads:

> Dear Edoardo [*sic*], with Riccardo Freda—a director whom you certainly know—we are preparing a big movie on Lucky Luciano. The script was completed tonight, and before discussing it with others I want you to read it and tell me if you are interested in making it with us in co-production. For the leading role, we are already in talks with Van Cliff [Lee Van Cleef], but we also considered Dirk Bogard [Dirk Bogarde], for whom Freda has gotten in touch with his American acquaintance. Italcid is interested in the distribution. We would like to shoot it in the month of March, 1968. Tomorrow morning I'll call you and you will tell me what to do. I must tell you that we are planning a big movie. Recommending you not to lose the script, I salute you affectionately.

As repeatedly stressed by the letter's author, *L'imperatore di New York* was meant to be a big budget picture, a return to the "A" category of the products Freda was making in the late 1940s and early 1950s, after over a decade in exile: the perfect movie to celebrate his return to his home country, after the nondescript *La morte non conta i dollari.*

The script for *L'imperatore di New York* opens with the harrowing images of the burning of the "SS Normandie" ocean liner in the New York harbor, in 1942. Allegedly, the fire was the result of a sabotage act organized by the U.S. Cosa Nostra boss Anthony Anastasio, who controlled the dockyards; it forced the authorities to ask for the Mob to provide intelligence and assistance. Part of the deal was commuting Luciano's pending sentence of 30 to 50 years in prison on condition that he not resist deportation to Italy. After the images of the Normandie fire, the script depicts a reunion at the Navy Intelligence headquarters and the subsequent visit of the authorities to the Clinton penitentiary. Lucky Luciano is introduced through his shadow on the cell's wall, as he is summoned to the warden's office, and the scene ends with a close-up of the book he is reading, the "Laws and Constitution of the United States of America."

After Lucky's confrontation with Lieutenant Deffenen, with the Mafioso asking for freedom in exchange for his service, a long flashback begins, which encompasses the Mafia boss' story since 1922 (due to a typo on the script it reads 1932), during the gang war between Jack Valenti (misspelled "Valente") and Joe Masseria. The young and ambitious Salvatore Lucania—then just a Mafia gunman—acts a decisive role as Valenti's killer and then works his way through the hierarchy of Cosa Nostra via treason and doublecross. Meanwhile, he runs a flourishing prostitution racket, circumventing unsuspecting young girls. The depiction of Lucky's poor-but-honest family, the Prohibition-era speakeasies and Mafia gun-machine shootouts in the early scenes look like something out of a 1930s Warner pic, although Lucky's ascent to power is shown with plenty of grisly details—such as an informer being tortured with a circular saw—as required by the audience's tastes in terms of graphic violence.

Freda follows Lucky Luciano's life story rather closely, although he throws in the expected embellishment: the infamous episode that had him kidnapped, beaten and disfigured, thrown into a river and left for dead (which, as Lucania seemingly confided in 1953, was organized by the police) is imagined to be the consequence of Salvatore's love for the fictitious Helene, the daughter of police Captain Petersen—which allows for a shaky, half-baked romantic subplot: in real life, Lucky was the lover of Broadway dancer Gay Orlova.

The episode, which leaves Lucania permanently scarred, also owns him the nickname "Lucky," and paves the way for his ascent as the chief Mafia boss in New York, after the murder of Masseria in a Coney Island restaurant, organized with the help, among others, of his lieutenant "Bugsy" Siegel (only a secondary character in the script, usually depicted filing his nails). After Helene is blown up in Luciano's car, he retaliates by annihilating rival boss Salvatore Maranzano and his gang. Maranzano's notorious murder also roughly follows the chronicle of the period, with Luciano's men penetrating his headquarters dressed as cops. The sequence, and the ensuing massacre of Maranzano's henchmen, is perhaps the script's most impressive action bit, and leads to Luciano earning the title of Godfather or "*Capo di tutti i capi*," the "boss of all bosses," and his confrontation with District Attorney Thomas E. Dewey, who will eventually try and convict him for compulsory prostitution.

The final scenes of *L'imperatore di New York* depict Luciano's release (with the allusion that he helped the Allies' invasion of Sicily, by providing the U.S. army with Mafia contacts in the isle) and his return to Italy in 1946, the final image—in one of Freda's customary circular endings—being of Luciano throwing the "Laws and Constitution of the United States of America" tome into the ocean.

Despite being undeniably compelling, the script for *L'imperatore di New York* seems to lack the necessary weight for Freda's ambitions. It reads like a solid genre film, with a good dose of clichés and violence, but does not offer any real insight on the main character, whose ambitions (leave poverty behind, become rich and powerful) are illustrated in by-the-numbers, predictable monologues and didactic bits of dialogue. The script is more felicitous in capturing the ruthlessness within the Mafia, and sporadically it gives a convincing view of Cosa Nostra's inner struggle for power, depicting Luciano as the symbol of the new generations of Mob men (smarter, well-dressed, able to deal with America's system and laws) compared to the older generation of Italian mobsters, still somehow tied to their homeland, nostalgically eating spaghetti and listening to Neapolitan songs. In a sense, the director seems somehow fascinated by Luciano's cynical attitude and ability to turn events and manipulate people in his favor. The odd visual detail (such as a bouquet of roses withering near a woman whose face has been disfigured with vitriol) hints at Freda's aesthetic mastery, and further evidence at the director being the responsible for the script might be a sequence set at the Saratoga racetrack. Unlike other Freda-penned scripts, however, the indications of camera movements are sparse, except for the depiction of several sequences, such as Luciano's introduction in jail.

It was the right time for a period gangster film, after the release in Summer 1967 of Roger Corman's *The St. Valentine's Day Massacre* (1967) and Arthur Penn's *Bonnie and Clyde* (1967), which led to a small trend of Italian/Spanish films set in the 1920s—including a couple co-produced by Brochero's Copercines, *Tempo di Charleston / Tiempos de Chicago* (a.k.a. *They Paid with Bullets: Chicago 1929*, 1969, Julio Diamante) and *La vera storia di Frank Mannata / ¡Viva América!* (a.k.a. *Cry Chicago*, 1969, Javier Setó), the latter being Jeffrey Hunter's final film appearance. Nevertheless, the Spanish producer did not feel like investing a huge sum in the movie, or perhaps the Italian distributor did not offer a substantial amount of money: in retrospect, Italcid (a minor company specializing in releasing cheap genre stuff such as the comic book-like adventure flick *Devilman Story* or the Western *Sangue chiama sangue*) was the weak link in the deal.

L'imperatore di New York was doomed to be another of the director's unmade projects. Salvatore Lucania's story was later made into a film in 1973 by Francesco Rosi, with *Lucky Luciano*, starring Gian Maria Volonté. It was quite a different approach to Freda's, more documentary-like and with attention to Luciano's life in Italy after 1946.[16]

After the failure of *L'imperatore di New York*, Freda's name was attached to an unlikely Italian/Spanish co-production, a war movie called *Morte in Indonesia* (Death in Indonesia), to be co-produced (on a 70/30-percent deal) by a small company by the name of Garigliano Films (active primarily as a distributor)[17] and by Jaime Jesús Balcázar's production company, the Barcelona-based Producciones Cinematográficas Balcázar. It was a low-budget affair, with an estimated cost of 162 million *lire* (to be provided with the participation of the personnel involved: director, actors, technicians...) and a cast of little-known names led by the elusive John Kilwood (real name Giancarlo Da Roma) as the film's hero, Balis, and the exotic beauty Seyna Seyn (*Kiss the Girls and Make Them Die*, *The Drums of Tabu*). Other cast members listed were Frank Oliveras (Gutar), Alfredo Varelli (Vintra), Carlo Hintermann (Sergeant), Félix Dafauce (Governor), Mario Donatone

(Tinkar), Gérard Tichy (Dutch Sergeant).[18] Freda's partner Silvana Merli is listed as script girl in the papers deposited at the Ministry (unearthed by Italian film researchers Alessio Di Rocco and Stefano Raffaele). The same papers credit the story to Balcázar and the screenplay to the Spanish producer and Freda. However, although it is not signed, the film's script kept at Rome's CSC is written in a very precise style (with a detailed shot-for-shot division and many technical indications of camera movements), the same as most other Freda-penned scripts such as *Guarany* and *Genoveffa di Brabante.*

Morte in Indonesia is basically an old-style war movie whose main claim at originality lies in the subject: the story of Indonesia's fight against the Dutch colonial government, which led to the country's independence in December 1949, as seen through the eyes of a partisan named Balis, who in the impressive opening scene is shown as the sole survivor of a violent attack carried on by the Dutch army. Having returned to his village, and after witnessing the violence and destruction committed by the enemies on his people, he leaves on a mission with a small group of partisans; their objective is to take over the Dutch House of Resident (the Resident being the colonial administrator), the symbol of the colonial power, and give a decisive turn to the Indonesian fight for independence. The group is parachuted into the jungle and the film follows their difficult march, with all the typical genre trappings, including the encounter with a young woman who is actually a spy of the enemy, and whom Balis has to kill in cold blood. *Morte in Indonesia* climaxes in the assault to the Dutch headquarters, resulting in a massacre in which Balis is killed as well, before the final triumph of the Indonesian partisans.

The script has a number of traits that are typically Freda, such as the figure of the Dutch Resident, an aristocratic, coldly ruthless figure who in the end is seen dying while grabbing the crown of his country's coat-in-arms—the memory of Dubrovsky's family stem towering over the President of Court before his demise in *Aquila nera* comes to mind. Moreover, Balis is reserved a melodramatic heroic ending: "He remains still for a moment, as if crucified, then collapses to the ground, while in the sky, like wonderful flowers, the partisans paratroopers descend toward the finally liberated ground." On the other hand, there are a number of idyllic, lyrical moments that feel forced or didactic, due to cringe-inducing dialogue and a rather banal use of symbols, like a flashback of a boy flying a kite which gets stuck in a plane wreck—a moment that nevertheless predates one of the central images in Freda's unmade script *Francesco Baracca.* Sometimes, however, the descriptions become almost literary in the choice of words and images: this is especially true for an intense sequence in which the partisans travel through the forest that is described as "an immense, monstrous cathedral whose gigantic arcs have trapped those tiny human beings who dared violate its secrecy and silence."

The concessions to the public's tastes in terms of eroticism on screen are reduced to a brief love interlude between Balis and his wife and to a rather violent torture scene where an Indonesian girl undergoes a rape attempt, kills her torturer and is eventually gunned down by another Dutch soldier. The ending is distinctly downbeat: after the paratroopers' triumphal landing, the final scenes show a funeral procession of coffins, while a crying woman wonders at what price her country has gained freedom, and "a chorus, grave and slow in its dramatic incisiveness, underlines the march of the ceremony. The tragic image of the woman's crying face returns in extreme close-up." The End.

According to the notification of start of production, dated September 9, shooting was scheduled to begin on September 28, 1968, for a total of 60 days, in Spain, Italy (at the Tirrenia Studios) and Indonesia. Possibly the makers thought that the ongoing Vietnam war would make the story more palatable for the audience, but one wonders what market such a film would have had, at least in Italy, since it was rather distant from the trends en vogue at that time (albeit a small run of World War II films were being produced in the country in that period, in the wake of U.S. big-budget efforts). What is more, the cast of unknowns added no commercial value to the project, even more considering that—according to the papers—the makers were planning to use Caucasian actors in Oriental make-up, as in Hollywood's glory days. However, there seemed also to be bureaucratic and economic issues: by contemplating an economic participation on the part of the personnel, the makers were expecting to have access to the benefits of law,[19] but the papers submitted were judged as vague and incomplete by the Ministry, whose request to Garigliano Film for further details about the co-production deal apparently had no answer whatsoever. No wonder it all eventually fell apart.

A doppia faccia

The somewhat disordinate last phase of Freda's career brought him to try his hand at yet another commercially viable subgenre, the German *krimis* inspired by the works of Edgar Wallace. The director was summoned by the Italian producer Oreste Coltellacci, who had set up a deal with the German-based company Rialto, the main helmer of the Wallace series. The thread, which had been in vogue since Harald Reinl's *Der Frosch mit der Maske* (a.k.a. *Face of the Frog*, 1959) was undergoing a transformation of sorts: after 1968, the company's head Horst Wendlandt and his partner Preben Philipsen wanted to head on to a new direction with their *krimis* and allow more room for eroticism, given the rising presence of sex and nudity in films. Freda obliged, and *A doppia faccia* featured ample female nudity—not a novelty for the director, if one considers the nude bathing scene included in the foreign version of his 1946 film *Aquila nera*, still an important step for a notoriously conservative filmmaker. Even more than before, Freda had to bow down to what the market demanded.

The co-production nature of the project resulted in different commercial approaches. The film was released in Germany as *Das Gesicht im Dunkeln* (The Face in the Dark) and advertised as being based on Edgar Wallace's 1924 novel *The Face in the Night*: the pre-credit sequence ended with the customary sound of gunshots, followed by blood-red bullet holes appearing on the screen, from which the letters Edgar Wallace emerged, accompanied by a metallic off-screen voice (courtesy of film director Alfred Vohrer) announcing "*Hallo, hier spricht Edgar Wallace*" (Hello, Edgar Wallace speaking), after which the credits began to roll. However, the connection was merely a commercial trick, as the script had nothing to do with the book whatsoever: Wallace's novel, centered on the stealing of a diamond chain that belongs to the Queen of Finland, had been adapted for the screen in 1960 with *The Malpas Mystery*, directed by Sidney Hayers as part of the British TV series *The Edgar Wallace Mystery Theatre*.

The wholly original story was concocted by Lucio Fulci, Romano Migliorini and Giambattista Mussetto, whereas Freda took care of the screenplay with the assistance of the Austrian-born Paul Hengge—although it is likely that Hengge was credited only for co-production reasons (or simply worked on the script as translator) and that the script was solely the work of the director. In a 1994 interview Fulci claimed that he "wrote" the film for Freda, but whether his contribution extended beyond the story and treatment phase is uncertain. His touch can perhaps also be glimpsed in the sequence where Inspector Gordon (Luciano Spadoni) discusses with Alexander the latter's hobby of repairing clocks, and in the idea of linking the main clue to the solution with a defective chronograph, time being one of Fulci's primary obsession—think of *Sette note in nero* (a.k.a. *The Psychic*, 1977) and *La casa nel tempo* (a.k.a. *House of Clocks*, 1990), for instance. When asked if he was happy about the way his story had been filmed, Fulci admitted he didn't like it, claiming that Freda "had completely crushed it down to a pulp; at that time, he just didn't care anymore." However, he spent words of sincere esteem for the director, in his own way:

> In today's contemporary cinema, they are all so incredibly sad.... Whereas Bava was fun, malicious. Another one who had fun was Freda: think of *L'orribile segreto del Dr. Hichcock*, a very entertaining movie ... he is a very cultured, witty man, of a unique wickedness—perhaps the most wicked person I have met in my long life, together with Mario Monicelli. They are so wicked, they will never die.[20]

In Italy the movie was titled *A doppia faccia* (Double Face) and the Wallace reference was nowhere to be found, and understandably so: besides their somewhat old-fashioned appeal, *krimis* were not as commercially profitable as the new wave of erotic thrillers such as Romolo Guerrieri's *Il dolce corpo di Deborah* (a.k.a. *The Sweet Body of Deborah*, 1968), released in March 1968. The same would happen with other Italian-German co-productions such as *Cosa avete fatto a Solange?* (a.k.a. *What Have You Done To Solange?*, 1972, Massimo Dallamano), *Sette orchidee macchiate di rosso* (a.k.a. *Seven Bloodstained Orchids*, 1972,

Italian locandina for *A doppia faccia* (1969).

Umberto Lenzi) and even Dario Argento's *L'uccello dalle piume di cristallo* (a.k.a. *The Bird with the Crystal Plumage*, 1970)—all of them marketed as Wallace-based thrillers in Germany. Nevertheless, continuity with the Wallace series was guaranteed by the casting of Klaus Kinski in the lead alongside Günther Stoll, in one of his customary commissioner roles, and Christiane Krüger. On the other hand, the gorgeous Margaret Lee, Kinski's frequent partner on the set, played an extended cameo as Helen, while the ravishing Annabella Incontrera—a recurrent presence in *gialli*—and Barbara Nelli were given other important roles, with the latter performing an erotic scene with Kinski. An interesting presence was that of Charlie Chaplin's son Sydney, whose erratic film career had eventually brought him in the welcoming arms of Euro genre cinema.

Freda met the notoriously mercurial Kinski at the latter's villa in Rome. At first, the actor flatly refused, sick and tired at the thought of playing yet another psycho, but Freda claimed that he changed his mind after learning that for once he would play a victim instead. Shooting with Kinski—whom the director called "the crown Prince of assholes"[21]—proved to be an ordeal, and the two men almost came to blows on set. Freda claimed that he resorted to one of his usual tricks and proceeded shooting with Kinski's double.

> I found the double on a set at Cinecittà. He was an actor who worked with Fellini. I went to see Federico and told him: "That one, I'll borrow him, he'll be perfect as the lead." Fellini was very amused. When Kinski knew about it, he proposed to make peace. It was an armed peace but we finished the film. Kinski was a lousy person but a dazzling actor, on the set and in life. He could play anything, he was one of the actors that impressed me the most.[22]

When interviewed in Dominik Graf and Johannes Sievert's documentary about German B-movies *Verfluchte Liebe deutscher Film* (2016), Christiane Krüger confirmed Kinski's idiosyncratic attitude on the set, as the actor utterly refused to learn his dialogue and started reciting numbers instead: not an uncommon practice back then, since everything was dubbed afterwards.

Filming took place from January 20 to March 15, 1969, with an estimated budget of around 1,300,000 German marks, with 30 percent provided by Rialto and 70 percent by Coltellacci's company. After the shabby-looking Italian exteriors of *La morte non conta i dollari*, which made a poor substitute for American landscapes, this time Freda got the chance to film on location in London, capturing footage at Piccadilly Circus and a suitably evocative Wallace-like atmosphere. Additional shooting took place in Liverpool and Rome. However, during the filming Wendlandt became increasingly dissatisfied with the results, and believed that the director and the Italian co-producers did not have the situation under control. Wendlandt seemed to distance himself from the project by refusing to have his name in the credits for the first time since 1961.[23] As a consequence, Rialto did not follow their initial intentions of entrusting Freda with the direction of their next Wallace-based film *Der Engel des Schreckens* (The Angel of Terror).[24]

Following the story of a man, industrialist John Alexander (Kinski), haunted by the possibility that his dead wife (purportedly killed in a suspicious car accident which he is suspected to have caused in order to gain the inheritance) might be alive, although badly disfigured, *A doppia faccia* seems like it was born out of the same mold as Fulci's own *Una sull'altra* (a.k.a. *Perversion Story*, 1969), released in Italy only one month after Freda's film. Still, *Una sull'altra* thoroughly embraced the new wave of thriller, whereas *A doppia faccia* does not, and its stylistic unevenness puts it aside from contemporaneous Italian thrillers. Both films draw from very visible models, namely Henri-Georges

Clouzot's *Les Diaboliques* and generally the works of Pierre Boileau and Thomas Narcejac, which inspired Clouzot's film as well as Hitchcock's *Vertigo* (1958), whereas any influence on the part of Umberto Lenzi's *Orgasmo* (a.k.a. *Paranoia*, 1969) must be ruled out, at least in the case of *A doppia faccia*, since Lenzi's film was released in Italy in February 1969, when Freda was already shooting his own movie.

Like in *Les Diaboliques*, the idea that someone who should be dead might actually be alive is expressed by way of physical objects that belonged to that person: an elaborately designed ring, a pearl necklace, furs, a puppy dog, a lighter. The Boileau-Narcejac reference can also be seen in the element of the song (*A doppia faccia*) which obsessively remarks Helen's supposed presence, even though Freda had employed a musical motive in a similar way in *Lo spettro*, where the sound of the carillon persecuted Barbara Steele's character. Evocatively sung by Nora Orlandi (here hiding under the a.k.a. Silvie St. Laurent), it functions as a sound leitmotif that recalls their novel *A Coeur perdu* and Etienne Périer's film adaptation of it, *Meurtre en 45 tours* (a.k.a. *Murder at 45 R.P.M.*, 1960). The score–which some sources credit mistakenly to Carlo Rustichelli—was actually written by Orlandi herself with arrangements by Robby Poitevin, and is one of the film's assets: the singer-cum-composer hid under the a.k.a. Joan Cristian, a the pseudonym chosen after the name of her two kids, Gianfranco and Cristina, and described her experience with Freda on *A doppia faccia* as "unforgettable and very instructive."[25] Incidentally, the following year Orlandi would come up with a very similar tune to *A doppia faccia*'s titular song: *Dies Irae*, included in Sergio Martino's *Lo strano vizio della signora Wardh* (a.k.a. *The Strange Vice of Mrs. Wardh*, 1970).

On the other hand, the theme of the undead woman returning from the grave nods to Edgar Allan Poe, which allows the director to linger on the Gothic suggestions in the film's best sequence: Alexander returns home, only to find it is apparently inhabited by the ghost of his dead wife, announced by the sound of the song she used to play. Here the director is immensely aided by Gábor Pogány's symphony of lightning bolts and candlelights that accompany John to his discovery of an unannounced but definitely pleasant female guest. Spanish film critic Antonio José Navarro underlined the Gothic quality of the relationship between Alexander and his wife, "a sinister fatal woman, Keats' *belle dame sans merci*, who openly flirts with her female lover before her husband's bewilderment." John's obsession with his dead wife at times mirrors that of Dr. Bernard Hichcock: still, as Navarro pointed out, "there is nothing in this profane mixture of Ligeia and Berenice that lends itself to necrophile fetishism. Not by chance, the sensual body that appears in the shower ... belongs to a young hippie woman."[26]

A doppia faccia contains other elements akin to the director's *oeuvre*. The idea of a persecution led by someone close to the protagonist is also typically Freda, and so is the thin line between beauty and horror, desire and repulsion: the alleged Helen, after surviving a car accident that horribly disfigured her, has turned into a monstrous, sexually predatory creature, like *L'orribile segreto del Dr. Hichcock*'s Margaretha, and hides her horribly scarred face under a veil like *I vampiri*'s Duchess Du Grand. The element of vampirism is also briefly hinted at, with an overtly erotic significance, as the hippie girl, Christine, recalls that the Countess bit her in the neck during a particularly sultry sapphic embrace. Last but not least, even though the character is only superficially sketched, Sydney Chaplin's Mr. Brown is another in the long line of debauched, monstrous father figures in Freda's work. On the other hand, some moments seem to hint at the director's more personal ghosts: John and Helen are a detached couple that is quickly falling apart (she has a lesbian affair with a woman named Liz), and their early scene at the horse races, although perfunctorily shot, portrays their distance with surgical precision.

The theme of voyeurism is prominent throughout, and hints at the makers' attempt to give their audiences a little spicier recipe than usual. In an early sequence John comes home, finds Liz and Helen in an intimate moment and keeps spying them from behind a door, unable to react, as if transfixed by the sight; later on in the film, he similarly discovers an uninvited female guest taking a shower in his bathroom; consequently, he is led to watch the porn film which features—or so he is led to believe—his own, supposedly dead wife as one of the performers. Preceded—in a humorous joke on Freda's part—by a zany silent one-reel, it is much more stylishly shot than the stag films which were to be found in Soho in the period, and has a Radley Metzger–like quality in the emphasis on fetish objects (a knife employed to cut a necklace, a large scar on the woman's neck *à la Crash*) and sex rituals.

Later on, in a variation of the typical no-one-believes-me scene that has the other characters question the hero's mental stability, John screens the porn for another audience but finds it devoid of the details, which had convinced him in the first place that the faceless woman making it with another girl on screen was actually Helen. In a way, it is a metaphor of the double versions that were all too common back then: the same movie, two different edits—and that was the case with *A doppia faccia* too. The scene functions also as an unintentional parody of what went on when a movie was submitted to the board of censors: the film commissions—and Freda knew it all too well—were often presented with much tamer copies than the ones screened in theaters.

However, unlike the director's previous Gothic efforts, the style is not always up to Freda's standards. The pre-credit sequence, featuring a white Rolls Royce (the director's own?) chased by the police, ends with the car being crushed by a speeding train at a rail crossing and turning into a metal wreck engulfed in flames—the crash rendered through blatant miniatures. The other car, carrying John Alexander and another character (whom we will later find out is the police inspector, played by production designer Luciano Spadoni in one of his rare acting stints) stops nearby. Kinski's impenetrable face, lit by the fire's glare, does not betray any emotion, while a voice-over comments: "It was all over, tragically over … and still, the plan had been studied in the slightest details." The sequence is baffling as it tries hard to be thrilling: the Gothic-tinged piano-driven score and the cinematography are impressive, and yet the laughable special effects and poor voice-over ruin the overall result. The shots of Kinski and the commissioner are missing from the German version, which keeps the suspense on the identity of the man in the car. A wise choice, but one that makes the prologue rather shaky, as with the absence of the voice-over it lacks any relation with the rest of the movie. Similarly, the opening flashback, as John recalls the blossoming of his love story with Helen during a holiday in the Alps, is marred by a slapdash use of back-projection when Kinski and Margaret Lee are supposedly descending a slope on a sleigh, and falling off it in a very visible studio set. Like in his second Coplan film, Freda's use of miniatures for the car stunts is as distracting as it is annoying, not only giving away the low budget but harming the viewer's involvement in the story.

When shooting in real interiors, the director made use of hand-held camera shots, which somehow detract from his usual stylishness. Still, Pogány's cinematography is often the backbone that keeps the film afloat, and it prevents John's descent into a Swingin' London-ish wild party in a warehouse (filled with psychedelic lights, bikers and a girl dancing with only her boots and panties on) from slipping into the ridiculous. There, Freda comes up with one of his best stylistic choices in the film, by following Kinski's passage through a dancing and inebriated crowd via one of his trademark lateral panning shots, which acquires an almost hallucinatory quality due to Pogány's bravura lighting. The scene in the deserted photo lab, with rooms lit in bright red, yellow and green, also brings back fond memories—namely, the use of color in the Dr. Hichcock films—in a half-heartedly shot movie.

The Italian soundtrack adds unnecessary off-screen jokes in the porn reel scene (a man is heard saying: "They are *sadochist* [*sic*!] too!"), perhaps reflecting the embarrassment of the Italian ordinary viewer before a real porn flick. It is perhaps the more blatant sign of the makers' discomfort with their time: as it happened in the Gothic horror films of the 1960s, a lesbian relationship is presented as unnatural and menacing, despite John's awkward attempts at coping with Helen's liaison with Liz, and the view of youth culture is distrustful to say the least. Girls are portrayed as "easy," and drug use is suggested to be at the order of the day. On the other hand, the scene where John attempts to seduce the uninhibited Christine in order to obtain precious information from her is an overturning of the typical female-to-male seduction, and perhaps an attempt at re-establishing the hero's virility, severely undermined by his wife's betrayal with another woman.

Freda claimed he was interested in playing with the hero's ambiguity, but *A doppia faccia* hardly keeps with the director's intentions. If the viewer is unsure whether Alexander is innocent or guilty, that is simply because of the casting of Klaus Kinski, who manages to convey doubt and uneasiness in the viewer with his mere presence. His nonchalant demeanor and opaque stare—he was one of the rare actors who could turn his disinterest toward a film into an asset—make his every little gesture ominous and menacing, such as when he squeezes a red rose in his hand and casually drops the petals. Whenever he is not on screen, the story slides disastrously: the scenes with Günther Stoll and Luciano Spadoni are conventional in the worst sense of the term, and a further confirmation of Freda's utter disinterest in police procedural films. On top of that, the scriptwriters could not come up with a satisfying denouement, and the dialogue exchange between the culprit and the policemen, who discovered the criminal plan by tapping his phone, borders on the ridiculous: "But this is illegal!" the murderer protests. "Illegal, but handy!" is the reply. But then, twist endings were never the strong point of the Edgar Wallace series.

Like many other Freda films, *A doppia faccia* ends circularly. Not only does the villain find a fatal retribution by perishing in a car accident as horrible as the one in which Helen lost her life, but Freda reprises the opening chase and closes the story with the same image as the title sequence, a car wreck burning in the night. Even though there is a happy ending of sorts (John is acquitted from suspicion, avoids death and becomes the sole heir of the Brown empire), it is colored with a bitter undertaste, as the hero realizes that the "second chance" he had been apparently given by destiny was only delusional. The woman he loved has gone for good, and he is and will forever be alone.

Released in early July 1969, a month later than expected due to the prolonged post-production, the film did not do good business as expected in Germany, possibly because of the "18" rating it was given by the board of censors. With figures of about 600,000 viewers, it was the least successful Wallace film so far, causing Wendlandt to halt the production of two further titles; *Der Engel des Schreckens* eventually came out in 1971 as *Die Tote aus der Themse*, and was directed by Harald Philipp, whereas *Das Geheimnis der grünen Stecknadel* was made in 1972 as *Cosa avete fatto a Solange?* For his part, the director insisted that once again the producers ruined his work.

The German version of the film runs ten minutes shorter than the Italian one. Most of the cuts result in severely shortened transitional scenes (Liz and Helen preparing to leave, Alexander returning to his office and exchanging a few lines with his secretary, John waking up after his beating in the photo lab, etcetera). The hippie party scene is drastically shortened, and gone is also the amusing bit of the comic one-reel that precedes the screening of the stag film. What is more, two scenes turn up in different spots in the two versions: in the Italian cut the POV shot of Alexander heading to the phone and the ensuing phone call comes right after the inspector's visit, whereas in the German version it introduces the climax, as Alexander is summoned at the cathedral by the alleged Helen. Similarly, the sequence where Alexander gets drunk in a Soho bar is placed right before Alexander's return home and his meeting with Christine in the German version, whereas in the Italian one is right before the climax at the cathedral.

For the domestic release, Freda resorted to his habitual pseudonym Robert Hampton, whereas in the German prints he was credited as "Richard Freda." Still, even though he later claimed that the producers had shot additional sex scenes behind his back, partially destroying the story's ambiguity, in a 1970 interview (conducted by a young Luigi Cozzi) the director admitted to have shot double versions of several scenes. "In *A doppia faccia* the pubic hair, so to speak, can be seen only in the foreign version. In the Italian one the girl keeps her panties on, and only her breasts are exposed: pretty normal, huh?"[27] The nudity was removed altogether for the U.S. television screenings.

The French version, *Liz et Helen*, is in fact slightly more risqué than the Italian one, with several additional nude shots in the two sequences featuring a stag film, and in the aforementioned scene between Kinski and Nelli. Adding insult to injury, several years later Freda's former acolyte Robert de Nesle acquired the film for distribution and added hardcore inserts to it for a 1976 re-release in France in the X circuit under the title *Chaleur et jouissance* (Heat and pleasure). The explicit sex scenes were directed by Claude Sendron (the Count in Jesús Franco's *Exorcismes*, a.k.a. *Demoniac*, 1974) and featured Alice Arno. "Tavernier told me that it is amusing, in quotation marks, because it's not amusing at all for me," Freda commented. "There's a guy who opens a door and comes across some awful pornographic stuff, and one wonders why, what it represents! But what can you do then?"[28]

Interestingly, at the time he made *A doppia faccia* Freda was a member (*not* the head as incorrectly stated by some writers) of one of the censor boards that were to rate the pictures submitted to the Ministry and give (or deny) them the visa and therefore the permission of public screening: after having to deal with censorship as a filmmaker, now he was on the other side of the fence. This, according to Yves Boisset, heightened his isolation within the movie industry: "Freda's passage to the board of censors is the key of the fierce hatred, even the contempt in which many filmmakers held him—not to say the whole of Italian cinema. Freda was never tender, and even took advantage of it to settle certain private matters, understandably."[29]

"How do you reconcile your activity as a filmmaker with that of a censor?" Cozzi asked him. "Quite well," Freda answered. "One thing is to be a filmmaker and the other is viewing and judging films." The director went on at length explaining why he and his fellow members banned Richard Marquand's *Candy* (1968), which later came out in Italy in a heavily censored and abridged version, and even Bava's *Quante volte ... quella notte*:

"A horrible film," Freda commented when interviewed by Cozzi, "so bad that Mario doesn't even claim it as his own, but he did direct it. By preventing it from being distributed in Italy, I think I have done him a real favor as a friend."[30] However, one must not think of Freda as a narrow-minded moralist: once again, his main concern was aesthetic. Hence, he fought hard (but in vain) to defend Visconti's *La caduta degli dei* (a.k.a. *The Damned*, 1969), which depicted incest, against the cuts demanded by the majority of the members of the board of censors: "When the son goes to bed with his mother, the Italians were outraged; on the contrary I thought it was the work of an immense artist. It is as stupid as putting panties over Michelangelo's frescoes."[31] Perhaps the memory of Visconti's film came to the director's mind years later, when shooting *Murder Obsession*, a movie revolving around the theme of incest.

Incidentally, *A doppia faccia* was passed in Italy with a V.M.18 rating, after the producers agreed to cut the scene where Kinski gropes Nelli's naked breast in bed. It did modest business, with something in excess of 175 million *lire*: *Una sull'altra* grossed over 867 million, almost five times as much. Freda's film surfaced to home video in the U.S. in a badly panned-and-scanned, incomplete version (on the Unicorn Video label) which did not do justice either to its direction nor to Pogány's top notch cinematography.

Tamar Wife of Er

A bizarre occurrence in Freda's later filmography, *Tamar Wife of Er* is notable mainly for being one of the few Italian movies filmed in Israel in that period, like the bizarre Western *Black Jack* (1968, Gianfranco Baldanello) starring Robert Woods. The project was financed by Giuseppe "Peppino" Maggi's Filmar, together with the Spanish company Hispamer and Erwin C. Dietrich's Urania Filmproduktion, and was initially supposed to be filmed in Italy (at Tirrenia Studios) and Spain (Almería), with a budget of 320 million *lire* and for a total of 39 days, starting in January 1970. Things evolved in a different way when Maggi devised a way to involve an Israeli-based subsidiary, Filmar Studios of Israel (among the producers was Alexander Hacohen, later the president of Cannon Film). According to actor Michael Maien, who had a role in the movie, "interiors should at first be shot in Rome. A small studio in Tel Aviv offered us to film there, which was also cheaper."[32] The whole crew moved to Israel, to film in Jerusalem, the Dead Sea and Negev, for a total of six weeks, and the movie was eventually submitted to the Italian board of censors as an Israeli co-production.

The director's view on the project was trenchant to say the least. "The Italian producer, Maggi, who specialized in worthless crap, swore that the Israelis were attempting to develop the movie industry in their country and create studios as important as Cinecittà in Rome. That's why I accepted."[33] Freda's scarce appreciation of Maggi's work as a producer was not unmotivated: Filmar was specialized indeed in producing (and distributing) low-budget genre films with very little value. Bruno Mattei, one of Filmar's administrators and the editor on many of their films (often reshaping cheap foreign dreck for the Italian market), stated that "When I saw the Neptune brand [Filmar's trademark logo] I did not go in the theater."[34] It was exactly the same kind of third-rate producers' ghetto Yves Boisset had been referring to when talking about *La morte non conta i dollari*—only worse.

However, things get a little confused when one compares the official data with Freda's declarations and the papers deposited at the Ministry of Spectacle in Rome. According to most sources (such as a 1972 review in *The Jerusalem Post*), as unlikely as it might sound, the script was reportedly the work of Israeli novelist Yigal Mossinson, taken from his own novel of the same name, published in 1947, whereas the Italian papers credit Freda as the author of the story and screenplay, the latter together with María del Carmen Martínez Román, most likely for co-production reasons. On the other hand, the director was adamant in denying any involvement: "I did not take part in the scripting. I arrived in Israel several days before filming."[35] Unfortunately the script kept at Rome's CSC is not signed.

Tamar Wife of Er takes inspiration from the story of Tamar and her brother-in-law Onan, as told in the Book of Genesis, Chapter 38. After Onan's brother Er was slain by God, his father Judah told him to fulfill his duty as a brother-in-law by having intercourse with the woman (the so-called levirate marriage) and giving her offspring. The episode is perhaps more known because of Onan's withdrawing before the climax, spilling his semen on the ground, since according to the rules of the tribe any newborn child would not legally be considered his heir, but Er's. Disregarding the principle of a levirate union caused the wrath of God, who slew Onan. The passage of the "wasted seed" has been often misinterpreted as referring to masturbation (hence the term "onanism") instead of coitus interruptus. However, the script makes many changes to the original story, adding a fair share of eroticism, with the development of the love story between Tamar and her father-in-law, and combined the tale with the story of Dina, Jacob's daughter.

The project seemed to fit Freda's sensibility and taste. It was set in the remote past, allowing the director to explore a fascinating era—Old Testament's Palestine, the same setting he had attempted to bring to screen with his aborted 1960 film *L'arca di Noé (Il diluvio universale)*—which would allow him to immerse himself once again in the kind of cinema he loved, far and away from realism and everyday mediocrity. What is more, the story focused on the obscure, illicit and forbidden passions that nurture within the family, with the unconfessed attraction between a woman who has been purchased as a wife and her husband's father: a theme that now and then had surfaced in the director's past works, from *Beatrice Cenci* onwards. Unfortunately, the results were a bitter disappointment.

Shooting took place near the Jordan border, in a zone presided over by the army, and to Freda the experience turned out a paid vacation in an exotic country. "He came back totally fascinated by Israel. Never mentioned the movie, all the time he talked about how the Israeli people had managed to turn the country into a garden in the desert," Jacqueline Freda recalled.[36] According to Michael Maien, traces of the nearby conflict were all around: soldiers (both male and female) marched past the set, and work had often to be interrupted, with the blasts of bombs being heard from afar.

Filming was plagued with problems. Maien recalls that

> the circumstances were not the most favorable, as it was very hot during the day, and quite cold at night. Bedouins observed our work suspiciously, and the extras consisted of lay people from the area. There is a scene where Onan sets some place on fire, and the pyrotechnician used too much of the wrong material. The village set went up in flames, and eight valuable Arab stallions were burned. Gruesome. Ettore Manni and I were slightly injured because we were overrun by the horses in panic. Thereafter, the owner, a Bedouin, came and took us up in hostage to pay him a larger sum of money. The crew was in dread.[37]

What is more, despite Maggi's reassurances the director found out that the production resources were laughable, if not worse. "I filmed with one camera because the second didn't work. I couldn't watch the rushes because the film was developed in the States. And when I saw the footage, it was about thirty-per-cent of what I filmed, so I got disinterested in the editing."[38]

Tamar Wife of Er is a very slapdash, sometimes ugly-looking film, with little or nothing of Freda's usual stylistic flair. The lack of any dolly caused the director to avoid tracking shots and overdo on the zoom; moreover, many shots are even out-of-focus and the photography (by Peter Baumgartner, a frequent presence in Erwin Dietrich productions and the d.o.p. in a number of mid–1970s Jess Franco films) is poor, with dramatic lighting changes between one shot and the next. Not that the script was very good in the first place, anyway. It is likely that its basic idea was to investigate on the barbaric tribal laws in view of the contemporaneous process of female liberation, focusing on the female role in a retrograde male-oriented society and presenting a woman who is treated as an object and eventually chooses independence, solitude and freedom—not forgetting to affirm Israeli people's rights on the land they had settled in after World War II, with the final Biblical quotation of the words of the Almighty, "I will make of thee a multitude of people; and will give this land to thy seed after thee for an everlasting possession." The results are nevertheless poor, wavering between half-baked melodrama and low-brow exploitation. It would have been hard for any filmmaker to instill a spark of life in such a stodgy mess.

The opening scene, in which Judas and his acolytes kill a man whom they found raping Dina, gives away Freda's routine approach to the material. It plays like an up-to-date version of the razor attack in *Lo spettro*, with a subjective shot of the victim; the murderer, shot from a low angle, swirls his sword to the camera and buckets of blood splash in the air onto the lens, intercut with close-ups of Dina screaming in anguish. Here the director is playing safe by resorting to his own cinematic past; however, the result is both gratuitously over-the-top and badly executed in technical terms, with an off-screen crew member all too obviously throwing blood paint in the air the way one would expect from a Herschell Gordon Lewis flick.

For much of the running time, Freda seems content to direct on autopilot. He films his characters wandering or riding on horseback in the arid Israeli landscape, as if it was some sort of Middle Orient version of the Monument Valley, and stages the requisite feast and dance scenes (such as the exhausting sequence of the banquet after Tamar's marriage with Er, with a stretch of hora-dancing that seems to go on forever) as he used to do a couple of decades earlier, regardless that times have changed. On the other hand, he provides the expected quantity of eroticism. What is more, in what was by now a customary habit, he had Baumgartner shoot some scenes. Whether this was just cynicism, carelessness or incapability on his part to adapt to the current threads of filmmaking, it is of little importance. The Freda who shot *Tamar Wife of Er* was a distant relative to the masterful filmmaker who had helmed *Il cavaliere misterioso*, *Teodora* and *Beatrice Cenci*.

Even the actors look bored. Ettore Manni, as Judas, had been one of Italy's beaus in the 1950s, when he worked with Lattuada (*La lupa*, a.k.a. *The Devil Is a Woman*, 1953), Matarazzo (*La nave delle donne maledette*, a.k.a. *The Ship of Condemned Women*, 1953), Antonioni (*Le amiche*, 1955), among others. Over the years he put on weight and settled on secondary roles in genre films, with several exceptions, the most remarkable being Tony Richardson's extraordinary *Mademoiselle* (1966) where he played alongside Jeanne Moreau. His last film role was in Fellini's *La città delle donne* (a.k.a. *City of Women*, 1980). A notorious womanizer (Maien recalls that he liked flirting with the women on set) and an avid gun collector, Manni died in 1979 after shooting himself in the groin: there are still doubts whether his death was the result of a tragic accident or suicide.

Another familiar face for genre fans was that of the imposing American actor Paul Lawrence Smith (1936–2012), who at the time was living in Israel, where he had returned (after visiting the country in 1960 on occasion of his first film role, in Otto Preminger's *Exodus*) as a Mahal volunteer in the Six-Day War. Smith stayed in Israel until 1973 before moving to Italy, where he would reach some popularity as a Bud Spencer lookalike, starring alongside Michael Coby (born Antonio Cantafora) in a series of films that exploited the comedy/adventure formula made popular by Bud Spencer and Terence Hill. He then appeared in minor roles, usually as a villain, in such popular pictures as *Midnight Express* (1978, Alan Parker), *Popeye* (1980, Robert Altman, playing Bluto) and *Dune* (1984, David Lynch). According to Michael Maien, Smith was also executive producer. Maien, possibly chosen for the role of Er after Dietrich showed Freda excerpts from *Mark of the Devil* (1970, Michael Armstrong), where he played alongside Udo Kier, has positive memories of the director. "He was an elderly man, and behaved calmly and rationally with the actors. The most important thing for him was the camera set-up, and that everything worked on set."[39]

Due to the erotic scenes, *Tamar Wife of Er* was given a V.M.18 rating by the Italian board of censors after cuts were performed for about one minute and 20 seconds.[40] It came out in Italy in May 1971, several months after its German release in September 1970, as *La salamandra del deserto* (The Salamander of the Desert), a title concocted to make it pass off as an erotic flick along the lines of Alberto Cavallone's *Le salamandre* (1969), which had been a surprise minor hit. It was not enough to save the movie from a well-deserved oblivion. Dietrich did not like the finished movie very much, so he decided to give it only a very limited cinema release in West Germany, as *In der Glut des Mittags*. it was one of his very few flops.

The Israeli press was not kind either: "To say of this film that it is a sub-standard B picture is to be kind," wrote the film critic who panned the movie in *The Jerusalem Post*.

> Biblical stories rarely fare well on the screen but this is one of the poorest I have seen. The script halts (there is a lot of padding), the direction is uninspired, the acting is downright bad ... and the colour photography ... is muzzy. Much of the time the screen is so dark that one cannot see what is happening, the consolation being the knowledge that one is not missing anything worth while."[41]

Amen.

L'iguana dalla lingua di fuoco

Once upon a time in Italy, a young film critic by the name of Dario Argento ... thus begins one of the favorite tales for Italian cinema lovers. The phenomenal success of Argento's feature film debut, *L'uccello dalle piume di cristallo*, gave way to a new season of thrillers, with directors, scriptwriters and producers cramming their films with black-gloved killers, gory murders, stylish and/or bizarre camera movements, and an animal's name in the title. Having been by now recognized as one of the founding fathers of the Italian horror film together with Mario Bava, to Freda the most obvious thing to do was to try his hand at the modern-day descendance of the genre, the *giallo*. If *A doppia faccia* tried to cash in on the waning *krimis*, *L'iguana dalla lingua di fuoco* (a.k.a. *The Iguana with the Tongue of Fire*) saw the director embrace the Argento-style thriller, with the story of a tough commissioner investigating on a mysterious killer, somehow connected to the personnel of the French embassy in Dublin, who slashes women's throats and disfigures the victims with acid.

Unlike most *gialli* of the period, the film boasted its descendance from a literary source—the novel *A Room Without Door* by the elusive Richard Mann—which was most likely an invention on the part of the makers: the script is the work of screenwriter Sandro Continenza (the co-scriptwriters Gunther Ebert and André Tranché were credited solely for co-production purposes) with the director's pseudonymous contribution. With over 150 films to his credit, Continenza (1920–1996) was one of Italian cinema's most prolific screenwriters, having moved to comedy (he penned his first scripts in the 1940s for Totò) to Western, from spy flicks to *gialli* and horror: among the scripts he knocked out in the 1970s were *Sette scialli di seta gialla* (a.k.a. *The Crimes of the Black Cat*, 1972, Sergio Pastore) and Jorge Grau's zombie cult film, *Non si deve profanare il sonno dei morti*, a.k.a. *Let Sleeping Corpses Lie*, 1974).

Italian locandina for *L'iguana dalla lingua di fuoco* (1970).

L'iguana dalla lingua di fuoco duly obliges to the Argento-inspired trend of titles featuring animals, whose explanation is improbably evoked in some stilted dialogue; here, the chief of police observes that the murderer, like an iguana, "is very skilled at camouflaging," but whereas said reptile is ugly but harmless, the criminal has "a tongue of fire" represented by the vitriol employed to disfigure the victims (a method which, an uncomforting line of dialogue states, is "typical of women and negroes") and the razor that slashes their throats. Like a number of early 1970s *gialli*, though, the plot does away without such elements as the missing detail, the imperfect eyewitness, the big twist in the end. Even though it does feature the customarily black-gloved killer, the whodunit angle is risible: despite a character evoking the ghost of Agatha Christie's Miss Marple, there are no clues at all to discover the murderer. Freda seems content to zoom in on every character who at some point is wearing shades, in a crude attempt at enlivening the mystery, accompanied by an underlining screech in Stelvio Cipriani's score; on top of that, a chauffeur (Renato Romano) is even seen wearing shades at night as well—because of conjunctivitis, it turns out. If their attempts at building a satisfactory enigma were lazy at best, Continenza and Freda did not stint on the gore: within minutes, a woman's face is disfigured with acid and her throat is cut in extreme close-up, with bright red blood copiously flowing from the open wound, whereas the equally unpleasant climax features an old lady being bashed on the head and a semi-naked teenage girl having acid thrown in her face as well.

If Dario Argento's cinema has been undoubtedly influenced by Freda's work, the director of *I vampiri* spoke words of admiration toward his younger colleague, at least regarding Argento's early career: "He was one of my favorite filmmakers until *Profondo rosso*," he claimed, deploring Argento's later descent in the blood and gore arena. Nevertheless, the murder sequences, starting with the opening one, are singularly flat and by-the-numbers, which is kind of surprising since Freda had explored the aesthetics of fear in his earlier Gothics and even in the flawed crime film *Caccia all'uomo*, in the remarkable sequence of Eleonora Rossi Drago's murder. In *L'iguana dalla lingua di fuoco*, he completely bypasses Argento's customary stylishness while emphasizing the inner ugliness of violence, devoid of any redeeming formal quality. To quote Spanish film critic Antonio José Navarro, the sequence where the maniac attacks the protagonist's mother and daughter "shakes the viewer not for the details of planning and *mise-en-scène* ... but because of the dry exhibition of cruelty that goes far beyond the realistic limits of thriller."[42] In addition to the savage throat-cuttings or face-disfigurings, that is also the case with the recurring flashback in which protagonist John Norton (Luigi Pistilli) recalls how a young man he was interrogating (with decidedly objectionable methods, one shall add) grabbed Norton's pistol and shot himself in the mouth to escape more violence and torture on the part of the policeman. Freda's camera zooming in on the man's brains splashing over a white wall marks quite the opposite in comparison with Argento's visual symphonies of death. Overall, Freda's film is one of the period's very first Italian attempts at gore, such as Bava's *Reazione a catena* (a.k.a. *Bay of Blood*, 1971), Fernando di Leo's *La bestia uccide a sangue freddo* (a.k.a. *Slaughter Hotel*, 1971) and Giorgio Ferroni's *La notte dei diavoli* (a.k.a. *Night of the Devils*, 1972).

The idiosyncratic manner in which Freda copes with the required blood and gore quota shows a director who was no longer comfortable with contemporary filmmaking. "I did not believe in cinema anymore, movies were just a good excuse for travelling.... My concerns were far from cinema. I used to walk, admire the fauna, drink whisky, forget about movies," he recalled when discussing his later work.[43] Still, one of the most puzzling thing in Freda's later *oeuvre*—from, say, the Grand-Guignol bits in *Lo spettro* and *Genoveffa di Brabante* to the over-the-top gory excesses of *L'iguana dalla lingua di fuoco*, *Estratto dagli archivi segreti della polizia di una capitale europea* and *Murder Obsession*—is the blatant contradiction between the director's oft-proclaimed distaste for graphic violence on screen and his over-reliance on it. As Freda explained,

> Horror, to me, is suggestion, not exhibition ... on one hand, there are the puddles of blood and the fangs of Grand-Guignol, on the other hand the fear of suggestion ... the less I show and the more the viewer is involved in the horror, becomes the screenwriter and gets scared by himself. I pull the rug from under the audience's feet and leave them to their own imagination.[44]

Basically, it was simply a matter of "give the people what they want," as cynical as that, as exemplified by the recycling in the climax of the razor-through-the-palm effect employed in *Lo spettro* as yet another trick to make the audience squirm. In another gratuitous scene, Norton is medicated by a doctor (one of the film's pointless red herrings, incidentally, that turn up in the most diverse moments and places with a blatantly suspicious look) who sews a wound in the back of his head, and we are treated to a bogus-looking close up of a needle suturing the cut.

Nevertheless, it seems as if Freda's sadistic vein was given free rein. By piling up the shock effects, in "a sort of bloody bulimia which spasmodically invokes the presence of a supernatural terror that never manifests,"[45] he employed gore in the same way as he faced the action scenes in his earlier films, going for an over-the-top presentation that led (at least in the maker's intentions) to maximum effect. The viewers that screamed or turned their eyes away at the sight of gallons of blood and exposed viscera were experiencing that same raw feeling of identification with the movie as the *pieds noirs* in the Egyptian theaters in Freda's early recollections. What mattered, in the end, was having his audience under control, by any means necessary.

Another curious thing about *L'iguana dalla lingua di fuoco* are the characterizations. Norton—who in a passing and unexpected in-joke, at one point passes himself off as a "horse trainer"—is quite a different type compared with Freda's earlier heroes, and his portrayal as a violent cop who has pushed a suspect to shoot himself seems to pay reference both to hard-boiled fiction and to the contemporaneous Italian reality, with shades of Giuseppe Pinelli's "suicide" while being questioned by Commissioner Luigi Calabresi after being arrested for the Piazza Fontana bombing that took place in Milan in December 1969. Calabresi was a controversial public figure, whose popularity in the media was balanced by the hatred toward him on the part of the left-wing press, an attitude which grew even stronger after Pinelli's death—incidentally, the man did not have anything to do with the bombing, which was the work of extreme right-wing agents and part of the so-called "Strategy of Tension"—and culminated in Calabresi's murder in May 1972.[46] Calabresi's figure leaned like a shadow over the crime films made in Italy in the early 1970s, and inspired a number of its protagonists: in Freda's film, John Norton's casual turtleneck-sweater-cum-jacket look seems an explicit nod to Calabresi's typical dress code.

Freda and Continenza's choice to pattern a *gialli* hero on a tough cop rather than mold it on Argento's "imperfect eyewitnesses" speaks volumes, even more so if we consider how the murderer is characterized. Whereas *gialli* often lean on sexually ambiguous maniacs, here the killer is explicitly labeled as "abnormal" (i.e., homosexual, even if the word is never uttered), and portrayed as a debauched hippie who hangs around in saunas and revels in all-male parties, but even more off-putting is that the reference to the murderer's ability to camouflage must actually be read as the viewers' inability to identify him. In fact, the director plays with the audience by making the character's identity confused in the first place, rather than diverting suspicion from him.[47]

Freda's film has a couple of very dark stings in the tail for the viewer. The first is a visual gag—perhaps supposed to explain at least in part the killer's motives—as the murderer is revealed to have an ugly (and fake-looking) bald spot on the head, which looks like a venomous sneer directed to the so-called "longhairs." The second is the revelation of another culprit in the film's coda, which makes for the depiction of yet another dysfunctional family in Freda's filmography: not only is Ambassador Sobiesky (Anton Diffring) the umpteenth variation of the icy cold, stiff upper-lip villain the director loved to hate since his early works, but—the film implies—his debauchery has infiltrated and corrupted his whole parenthood. On the other hand, Norton's likeable, seemingly idyllic family is doomed to a paroxistically cruel retaliation, as if the murderer was punishing them for their moral integrity.

Stylistically, *L'iguana dalla lingua di fuoco* has little of Freda's earlier work. It is mostly efficient but also quite impersonal, a fact underlined by the opening scene, a listless montage of the various characters' vehicles driving through the Dublin streets: despite the notable use of dolly shots, it is a far cry from the director's usually remarkable openings. At times, as in *Tamar Wife of Er*, the mise-en-scène is surprisingly slapdash: a case in point is the bogus slow-motion of Norton desperately running to stop his prisoner from blowing his brains out, which brings to mind the infamous flashback in Jess Franco's *Frauengefängnis* (a.k.a. *Barbed Wire Dolls*, 1975). Besides the crudeness of the murder scenes, marred by the over-reliance on sub-par gore effects, Freda employs hand-held camera in the indoor shots (mostly real ambience, with no visible studio sets around) for practical reasons, as in *A doppia faccia*; to his credit, he makes a decent use of the Irish locations, with an impressive helicopter shot that leads to the discovery of a dead body near a cliff, and a few colorful bits, such as when, during an outdoor telephoto shot near the Dublin shore, the camera zooms in on a group of people in the distance, walking in the low tide. On the other hand, the scenes in St. Moritz—where Norton shows up in a failed attempt at questioning Sobiesky's son—seem just a diversion to pad out the running time, with the inclusion of some stock bobsled footage.

A couple of suspenseful scenes are decently concocted, though, such as Dagmar Lassander's character being chased through the foggy streets of Dublin to a drawbridge; and the climax, as unpleasant as it is, is undeniably effective, since the director makes the viewer identify with Norton' elderly short-sighted and deaf mother, menaced by the killer—a welcome change of pace from the typical young-woman-in-peril cliché. Interestingly, through the old woman's blurry eyes, the murderer—glimpsed as an out-of-focus figure wearing shades, wig and women's clothes—looks a lot like the razor-wielding transvestite maniac in Brian De Palma's *Dressed To Kill* (1980).

The director was not particularly fond of the film, let alone the cast. "I should have had Roger Moore in the lead, but at the last minute I got Luigi Pistilli,"[48] he remarked. But it is debatable that Moore would have done better than the Italian actor, with whom Freda worked again the following year on his next film. The female lead, Dagmar Lassander, was at the height of her fame in Italy, after Piero Schivazappa's *Femina Ridens* (a.k.a. *The Frightened Woman*, 1969), Mario Bava's *Il rosso segno della follia*, and Luciano Ercoli's *Le foto proibite di una signora per bene*. The Czech actress had pleasant memories of the set and the director as well: "Riccardo was a tough one ... he was a real eccentric character: he showed up on the set on his white Rolls Royce. A truly sophisticated man."[49]

One of the few things Freda was happy about *L'iguana dalla lingua di fuoco* was working again with Valentina Cortese, almost a quarter of century after *I miserabili*. Saddled with the thankless role of the Ambassador's vapid wife, who conceals her past as an *entraineuse* behind would-be elegant mannerisms and the constant use of French terms,

Cortese displays her usual wall-to-wall overacting. The actress shot all her scenes in 24 hours, flying to Ireland and back during a break in the filming of Franco Zeffirelli's *Fratello sole, sorella luna* (a.k.a. *Brother Sun, Sister Moon*, 1972). Lassander's recollections of Cortese's method on set bring back fond memories of the latter's role in *La nuit américaine*.

> I remember when Valentina arrived in Ireland where we where shooting the film and Pistilli told me, "Now you'll see how Cortese works ... she does not recite the dialogue, she counts." And in fact it was just like that. "One, two, three, four..." up to eighty. It was incredible! I asked myself how she managed to get to the right line with the numbers. She kept the rhythm of the dialogue with numbers....[50]

However, judging from the actress' labials in many shots, most of the times Cortese is actually delivering her lines in English.

Freda—who made a rare cameo appearance, sporting his inseparable coppola hat, as the doctor who cures Lassander's characters after she's jumped from a bridge to escape the murderer—adopted an idiosyncratic one-of-a-kind pseudonym to sign the film. Instead of resorting to the usual "Robert Hampton" or the "George Lincoln" he employed on *La morte non conta i dollari*, he came up with the rather incongruous-sounding Willy Pareto. It may well be that the alias was a reference to Vilfredo Pareto (1848–1923), an Italian sociologist, economist and philosopher, who made important contributions in the study of income distribution and individuals' choices, and popularized the use of the term "élite" in social analysis. Given that *L'iguana dalla lingua di fuoco* deals with members of the economic élite, who consider themselves above the law, the choice was undoubtedly fitting, and perhaps an evidence of the director's sarcastic attitude to such a project.

The emphasis on violence and sex (including a hot lovemaking scene between Pistilli and Lassander and the uneasy sight of Norton's teenage daughter in the nude during the murderer's final attack) caused the movie some trouble with the Italian board of censors. It was given a V.M.18 rating "due to the continuing and persistent gruesome scenes, relating to homicides, suicides and ruthless violence and some erotic scenes," but only after Freda and the producer agreed to perform a number of cuts (two lovemaking sequences between Norton and Helen Sobiesky and the one where Markos' friend picks up the phone in bed, next to a nude woman), whereas one member of the commission insisted it be banned since, even after the cuts, it was offensive to the common morality.[51]

Released in late August 1971, *L'iguana dalla lingua di fuoco* did rather poor business in Italy, with a total of 169 million *lire* grossed at the box-office, at a time when Argento's *Il gatto a nove code* made almost 2,400 million and a pretentiousless release such as *La notte che Evelyn uscì dalla tomba* (a.k.a. *The Night Evelyn Came Out of the Grave*, 1971, Emilio P. Miraglia) collected 450 million. A photonovel version of the film was later published in the adults-only mag *Cinesex* (issue #53, January 1972), featuring a more risqué version of Pistilli and Lassander's sex scene. The movie had a marginal theatrical distribution abroad (Turkey and Spain) and was later rediscovered by *gialli* fans thanks to home video: in the glory days of video cassettes, the English language Greek release (on the PVP label), albeit fullscreen, was the only way to savor an uncut version.

Estratto dagli archivi segreti della polizia di una capitale europea

"I forgot the time where I could see on the screen a movie resembling my work," a disheartened Freda confessed to Éric Poindron.[52] This was most likely the case as well with a film that he did not even mention once neither in interviews nor in his memoir, vehemently denying he ever had anything to do with: *Estratto dagli archivi segreti della polizia di una capitale europea*, a co-production financed by the Spanish producer José Gutiérrez Maesso. "Robert Hampton"'s last credit appearance has long been a mysterious object. The absurd Italian title (literally: Excerpt from the secret archives of the police of a European capital), which seems to belong to some politically committed crime film *à la* Damiano Damiani, is like a smoke halo that conceals the picture's true nature, that of a gory supernatural horror story (whereas the definition "a *giallo* on black magic" which appeared in press advertising of the period seems far-fetched). The original title was likely *Quella maledetta sera* ("That Doomed Evening"), whereas the Spanish one was the more apt *Trágica ceremonia en villa Alexander* ("Tragic Ceremony at Villa Alexander").[53]

Italian 2-fogli manifesto for the little-seen horror movie *Estratto dagli archivi segreti della polizia di una capitale europea* (1972).

After the disastrous Israelian experience with *Tamar Wife of Er*, Freda had been trying to put in motion a project he was much more interested in than his recent ventures into the *krimi* and *giallo* territory: *Francesco Baracca*, a biopic of a famous Italian aviator who died in World War I. Instead, he settled with another low-budget flick: a supernatural horror movie about a bunch of hippies—including the rich and introverted Bill and the beautiful and mysterious Jane—who end up at a villa whose owners, Lord and Lady Alexander, celebrate satanic rites. Shooting took place mostly in Spain, and began in June 1972.

Freda was not involved in the script, written by Mario Bianchi. "In addition to writing the story and screenplay, I should have done it [as assistant director], but I didn't," Bianchi recalled, "because since the assistant director starts collaborating with the director well before the shooting, I realized that he was a person with an almost inhuman nastiness inside him, and therefore I renounced just because I did not want to have anything to do with him."[54] Still, Freda co-authored the title song, written by Stelvio Cipriani, and sung by Ernesto Brancucci, *La vita*, a macabre little number whose lyrics sound like a modern take on a famous poem by Iginio Ugo Tarchetti, *Memento*, unfortunately devoid of any irony: "*Questa è la vita / Un uomo ride felice / La bocca già piena di terra / Danza una donna / Brulicante di vermi*" (This is life / A man laughs happily / His mouth already filled with soil / A woman dances / Teeming with worms). Some sources claim that the director left the set after a few days, and was replaced by Filippo Walter Ratti,[55] a veteran director who had jumped the sex-horror bandwagon with the weird Gothic horror flick *La notte dei dannati* (1971) and then helmed the equally bizarre erotic *giallo I vizi morbosi di una governante* (a.k.a. *Crazy Desires of a Murderer*, shot in 1973 but released in 1977). However, judging from first-hand testimonies, Freda's participation in the filming seems to have been much more substantial.

Carlo Rambaldi, who took care of the crude gory effects, recalled: "I did a film in Spain with him. Very likeable. A master at bypassing obstacles."[56] Which at least confirms Freda's presence on the set, and the fact that there *were* obstacles during filming. The director and Rambaldi would become good friends. On top of that, Freda's eldest daughter Jacqueline, who accompanied him in Spain with her mother and her younger sister and served on the set as a factotum—or, in her own words, as "assistant slave"—even though she was only 8 years-old, has a vivid recollection of the experience:

> Despite being a skinny little girl I woke up early in the morning with dad, and he made me do any kind of job on the set, in the most disparate ways. And when I didn't know what to do, he would say, "Go help the electricians mount the dolly!" The things I remember the most about the film are Rambaldi, the stuntmen, and my decision to become a stuntwoman myself. When I saw the action scenes I went to my father and said, "Dad, when I grow up I want to do this!" And he: "Sure, sure, why not... " Perhaps he thought it was like that other time when I told him I wanted to be a CIA agent![57]

Jacqueline is adamant in stating that Freda stayed for the whole shooting, and shot most of the film.

> My father directed all the action scenes. But, you know, on practically every film he left after finishing the action scenes, because to him the movie was over. He shot all the scenes in the villa, the action scenes, all of Rambaldi's splatter stuff, the black mass ... but also the boring stuff, such as the girl in the bathtub.... He never talked about the movie? Of course—he thought it was crap![58]

Producer Alfredo Leone, who at that time was working with Mario Bava in Spain, was introduced to Freda by his production manager Enzo Boetani; he paid visit on the set, and recalled Freda's attitude with actors.

> He was a tyrant on the set! Very strange man. Very intelligent, cultured, physically and mentally strong—and he had no respect for the actors. None! He'd set up the shot, and he had his 8-year-old daughter direct them! He would walk off the set. And they used to get furious! That was his character![59]

By comparing the original screenplay with the finished film, Ratti's contribution can perhaps be circumscribed to a couple of scenes that are not in the script: namely, the flashback in which Bill (Tony Isbert) gives his mother (Irina Demick) the pearl necklace and tells her the legend that accompanies it, and the epilogue in the asylum, where a doctor (played by Paul Muller) recapitulates the story and offers the viewer a (rather indigestible) explanation for the baffling supernatural events that have been going on, disserting about astral bodies with a raving, demented look. This addition might have been either the result of the need on the part of the producer to come up with enough footage for a feature length, since the rest barely reaches the 70-minute mark, or a consequence of the film's awkwardness. On the other hand, Bianchi's script encloses the story within one long flashback, after an opening set in the asylum where Jane is being questioned by a police inspector and a (female) doctor, a scene that in the movie takes place near the end; what is more, there are some differences here and there,[60] and a few bits were cut or possibly never shot, such as a scene in which Lord Alexander screens a 16mm film shot in India, where he first met Lady Alexander, thus hinting at the woman's supernatural nature.

It is no surprise that the producers attempted to give some sort of sense to such a wildly incoherent plot: at times the movie bears to mind the delirious circular pattern of Bava's *Lisa e il diavolo* (a.k.a. *Lisa and the Devil*, 1973), with which it shares the element of the travelers seeking shelter at a villa whose inhabitants are in league with evil forces, and the enigmatic figure of a Devil with a playful, catty attitude that acts as a factotum-servant—here a gas station attendant played by the Spanish character actor José "Pepe" Calvo. The way the latter mocks the young hippies and refuses to help them, coming up with every sort of excuse not to fill their car's tank, brings to mind the spiteful attitude of the butler played by Telly Savalas in Bava's film, and Calvo adds some nice touches, such as his character sniffing at the traveler's checks book handed to him by the wealthy Bill, in a fun variation of the Latin saying *pecunia non olet*.

However, whereas Bava's film opts for a surrealist, poetic approach to its tale of cyclical reincarnation, Freda's is all over the place, uncomfortably wavering between pale reminiscences of 1960s Italian Gothic, frantic splatter scenes and ill-fated nods to the present. A theme that harks back to the past decade is the pairing of beauty and horror, one of Italian Gothic horror's staples since *I vampiri* and *La maschera del demonio*: the diaphanous Jane (Camille Keaton), the object of desire of Bill and his young hippie friends, becomes a ghastly presence and the instrument of a vengeful force that seduces her unfortunate lovers, and at one point she displays a fleshless, putrescent face which is the equivalent of Barbara Steele's rotting torso in Bava's debut. The same idea would be developed in a much more convincing way the following year in Aristide Massaccesi's *La morte ha sorriso all'assassino*, which also included a grim razor-slashing subjective shot, patently influenced by a similar scene in *Lo spettro*. The biased view of the hippie phenomenon is typical of many films of the era: one particularly grating moment is the hilarious TV newscast which shows the killing's aftermath at Villa Alexander, and includes a totally gratuitous reference to the Bel Air massacre and Sharon Tate's murder, something not uncommon in the period: see also Steno's *giallo* parody *Il terrore con gli occhi storti*, made the same year.

Overall, the mixture of metempsychosis and black magic is fairly pointless, and the additional scenes only make matters worse. From Bill's monologue about the doomed necklace, at first we are supposed to think that evil is unleashed by said object (a returning fetish from *A doppia faccia*, incidentally) which Jane seemingly cannot take off her neck, and which is paired with a bracelet worn by Lady Alexander, that might function as a link between the two women; all this is more clearly outlined in the script, though. In the end, however, the diabolical presence is revealed to be Lady Alexander, with the help of her devilish factotum-driver (Calvo again), whereas Paul Muller's incoherent babbling fails to make much sense.

For his part, Freda did little to improve upon such a mess. One can only guess that he was uncomfortable with such a down-at-heel potboiler, given his overt interest in the occult. Stylistically, there are some moments of undeniable suggestion: the two scenes set at the gas station—which, when the hippies come back after the massacre, appears abandoned and in decay, providing one of the film's most impressive moments—filmed with the director's trademark panning shots, are suitably atmospheric, thanks also to Francisco Fraile's accomplished cinematography. Furthermore, at times the director resorted to his own cinematic past: the sight of Jane descending the villa's stairs, holding a candlestick, while the night breeze eerily raises the windows' curtains by her side, brings to mind both the President of the Court's wandering through Dubrovsky's house in *Aquila nera* and the Du Grand castle scenes in *I vampiri*; besides, the moment where the pearls slip out of her necklace and bounce down the steps echoes not only Bava's *5 bambole per la luna d'agosto* but its earlier antecedent, the scene of the little child's ball bouncing down the stairs in Freda's own *La leggenda del Piave*. Some themes are closer to the director's sensibility, though. Bill's morbid, vaguely incestuous attraction toward his fascinating and promiscuous mother predates *Murder Obsession*, and the story's original circular narrative is in tune with his vision of a deterministic universe where events are doomed to repeat over and over.

Freda's use of hand-held camera and wide-angle shots shows that he had put to good use the lesson of contemporaneous *gialli*, much more so than in *L'iguana dalla lingua di fuoco*, but the climactic "tragic ceremony" is rendered with an overreliance on weird angles and wild-eyed extras that recall Sergio Martino's *Tutti i colori del buio* (a.k.a. *All the Colors of the Dark*, 1972), released early that year, and soon become tiresome. At one point an on-set light and a cameraman can clearly be seen popping up the frame during a low-angle shot, underlining both the director's habit of using two or three cameras to film a scene and the sloppiness with which the film was made. Still, it is one of the most bizarre and over-the-top gore scenes ever seen in an Italian 1970s film, and one of the very first, in a year when Rambaldi also concocted the equally crude, but more coherent massacre at the climax of *La notte dei diavoli*: gunshots to the belly give way to abundant blood spilling, a man has his face bisected via a sword, Pistilli's character receives a bullet to the head which results in a geyser-like stream of blood from his forehead, a woman's head is chopped off, another one catches fire. For all its crudeness, it is a triumph of Grand-Guignol which tries hard to top *Reazione a catena*'s creative murders in just a handful of seconds. The black mass' splattery climax is repeated several times throughout the picture in order to maximize its gory quota, with the result of drastically cutting down its impact. The movie also features a couple of horrific scenes not included in the script: Bill ends up dead and blue-faced inside a wardrobe (Tony Isbert's make-up recalls the otherworldly presences seen in yet another awkward Italian/Spanish Gothic, Mario Siciliano's *Malocchio*, a.k.a. *Evil Eye*, 1975), whereas another bizarre gory scene plays like a variation of the throat slashings seen in *L'iguana dalla lingua di fuoco*, paired with a bizarre (and likely coincidental) nod to Scorsese's short film *The Big Shave* (1968).

As for the cast, Luigi Pistilli (whose first apparition, as a silhouette in close-up, is a striking moment) and Luciana Paluzzi, although top-billed, actually have minimal roles. The main spot goes to the 25-year-old Camille Keaton, who, after her debut in Massimo Dallamano's *Che cosa avete fatto a Solange?*, enjoyed a brief popularity as a horror starlet. She was the centerfold of the November 1972 issue of the Italian *Playmen*, and went on to make a handful of mostly bad movies such as the sex/Gothic horror *Il sesso della strega*

(1973, Elo Pannacciò) and the psychological drama *Madeleine, anatomia di un incubo* (1974, Roberto Mauri), before returning to the U.S. and starring in the controversial *I Spit on Your Grave*, a.k.a. *Day of the Woman* (1978), directed by her then-husband Meir Zarchi. Despite her unripe acting, the pale, fragile-looking Keaton makes for an unsettling presence, partly because of the visible scars on her face, the result of a car accident in her youth. She makes an uneasy pair with a very young, creepy-looking Tony Isbert.

Estratto dagli archivi segreti della polizia di una capitale europea was submitted to the Italian board of censors in December 1972, and was given a V.M. 18 rating "in relation to the theme of the film, the seriously gruesome scenes of violence (such as the rite that ends up in a massacre), linked to drug use, as well as the foul language used in several sequences." Curiously, the ministry papers state that the commission "auditioned the director, who claimed he would accept the prohibition to minors since he could not adhere to demands of cuts, not being authorized to." One wonders who the "director" was (Freda, whose name was clearly included in the ministerial papers, or maybe Ratti?) and why he was not authorized to allow cuts.

The movie performed very poorly in Italy, and was released in Spain only in September 1974, as *Trágica ceremonia en villa Alexander*. For years only the Spanish copy circulated among collectors, until *Estratto dagli archivi segreti della polizia di una capitale europea* was "rediscovered" at the 2004 Venice Film Festival as part of the retrospective "Italian Kings of the Bs"—a screening which ended with audience booing, and definitely not an apt choice to celebrate a master filmmaker (and not a "King of the B," whatever this means) such as Freda. A U.S. DVD titled *Tragic Ceremony* was released in 2008, marking the film's final rise from oblivion.

14

The Twilight Years

Silvana

After eight years away from the set,¹ Freda had the chance to make his directorial comeback in 1980. Eight years is an eternity for a filmmaker, especially one who used to knock out a movie in a few weeks. Why such a long stretch? "Maybe because of the rampant pornography, which broke the last levees against stupidity, allowing anyone to deal with the world's easiest job, that of film director, or maybe because the current mindset considers good only those filmmakers who have the luck of making movies with good actors and aimed at safe commercial success," Freda wrote, adding: "And maybe also because of my extremely difficult temper which only Riccardo Gualino could stand.... In Italy there are no producers, and mostly there lacks a distribution net, which has always been the connective tissue of this lucky film industry of ours."²

In spite of the growing critical reappraisal of his work in his home country, which culminated in a retrospective at the 1981 Mystfest (the International Festival of Crime and Mystery in Cattolica), in the mid-to-late 1970s the director went through a hard patch. A number of his projects failed to materialize, due to the disinterest of film producers and television, and to the ongoing crisis of the Italian film industry; moreover, the director's personal life was undergoing troubled times as well.³ Soon after the shooting of *Estratto dagli archivi segreti della polizia di una capitale europea*, he and Silvana Merli (who were not married) split up. Then Freda sold his princely villa in Vermicino, near Frascati, and moved back to Rome. He and Silvana lived in two different residences, in the northern part of the city, only a few minutes' away from each other.

"Selling the house at Vermicino was a huge pain for us, and for him as well. He said it cost too much money, but the real reason was another, which I found out only later," Jacqueline Freda explains. "He felt that there was something wrong with my mother, and realized he could not leave us alone with Mom without any control. So, the only solution was to sell the villa—too distant from the school I went to—and move back to Rome. That's why they lived separately but actually very close to each other, only a couple of minutes' walk. So he could watch over us."⁴

Silvana Merli's illness had been looming over the family for years. In 1968, the three-year-old Guislaine had been sent to a private college to keep her away from her mother, who, possibly suffering from postpartum depression, had become very aggressive toward her; Guislaine stayed with her sister and father (but never with her mother) about one month a year, during summer vacations.⁵ Then, after the separation, Silvana Merli was diagnosed with schizophrenia: the woman's illness forced Freda to radically revise his priorities. At almost 70, the director had to reinvent himself as a father and a mother substitute for his older daughter, take back home Silvana and become her male nurse. "That is a part of Riccardo Freda's private life that no one knows," Jacqueline comments.

> From being a Don Juan who cared only about luxury cars, horses and women, he became a full-time father and mother substitute, [raising] two teenage girls, ironing the white shirts of our school uniforms, preparing breakfast and dinner, picking me up from school and taking me to horse training school ... and in the few spare moments, if there were any, write a new movie ... and in my opinion he kept on dedicating himself to new projects mainly to escape from a life he would never want and he was trapped in, even though in his heart he knew he would probably never direct again. He was stoic. And he was a wonderful father to us, but that went to the expense of his career. You cannot be a director, scriptwriter, producer *and* a full-time father as well. Not to mention being the male nurse of a schizophrenic woman.[6]

Francesco Baracca

To a film historian, Freda's long absence from the sets after *Estratto dagli archivi segreti della polizia di una capitale europea* looks like a deep, elusive, insidious swamp, where the most unlikely projects rub shoulders with one another, in what patently look like frustrated attempts to keep up with the flow, no matter whether it be jumping on the post–*Exorcist* bandwagon or hoping to benefit from the scandalous aura of Tinto Brass' long-awaited *Caligula*—with the exception of one, his dream project, and the summation of all the things he loved most, in movies and in life: *Francesco Baracca*, a biopic on the World War I Italian flying ace which the director tried to bring to the screen for the best part of two decades.

Freda began working on the movie in the early 1970s, envisioning Fabio Testi in the lead (a perfect casting choice, because of the physical resemblance as well as Testi's charismatic screen persona), and struggled for years to make it, working on the script and perfecting it with dedication. Jacqueline Freda recalls the hours she spent writing and rewriting scenes at the typewriter, with her father dictating, and states that the screenplay was written by Freda in collaboration with Alessandro Continenza: "Being a General of Aviation, Continenza had the possibility to have access to air facilities and so on. He would have the Carabinieri squadron 'Pastrengo,' the trainees of the Military Riding School at Montelibretti for the scenes of the horse show...."[7] However, a detailed, 271-page long script, kept at Rome's CSC and dated October 4, 1973, is signed by Giuseppe Masini, a former aviation general who had been Freda's collaborator on *I giganti della Tessaglia* and *La morte non conta i dollari*, and the director of four films between 1952 and 1961. The opening line gives away the celebrating intent of the movie, on which Freda likely counted in order to gather financings: "On the 50th anniversary of the establishment of the Italian Air Force [March 28, 1923], with the evocation of Francesco Baracca's story, we also intend to remember all our aviators who fell in the line of duty, from the beginnings to the present."

Unfortunately Freda's dream would never materialize: first it was rejected "by that debts factory, pouring useless Hungarian film, that was Italnoleggio."[8] So, he was forced to turn to television, "that vile microbe," only to have a TV executive tell him: "Your project cannot be taken into account. It is not rich enough in spectacular elements."[9] Neither RaiUno nor RaiDue accepted to finance it, despite French television's willingness to coproduce it. In August 1984 the project was finally approved by RaiTre and seemed on the verge of finally surfacing from the limbo as a TV miniseries under the tentative title *L'uomo dei 45 colpi*, as reported by a newspaper article dated April 1986, which mentioned also Steno and Enzo De Caro as co-scriptwriters with Freda and Masini. The director claimed he wanted Christopher Reeve to play Baracca.[10] Jacqueline Freda adds bitterly, "it seemed *Francesco Baracca* was about to take off, but never did. Since my father truly cared about it, he never accepted any compromise. Either he would make the film his own way, or he wouldn't make it at all. And in the end there was not enough money to make it as he wanted to."[11]

In 1991, the French mag *L'avant scène cinéma* dedicated its special 400th issue to excerpts from unreleased screenplays by Michel Audiard, Jean Gruault, Jacques Tati, Pierre Véry and Riccardo Freda. Thus *Francesco Baracca* finally saw the light, albeit on paper, in the form of a 14-page scenario which follows the 1973 script very closely[12] but is divided into six parts, perhaps for TV consumption in the form of a mini-series. A passing read immediately gives an idea of the epic scope of Freda's most heartfelt project, and the way the director managed to blend his favorite themes into it.

The first part, *A Horse*, establishes the basis of Baracca's character and develops his heroic traits. It depicts the encounter and friendship between the young Francesco and the Neapolitan lieutenant Lampugnani, nicknamed "*Ingerenza*" (Interference) because of his nosy behavior. The opening scene sets the tone for the film, as the two men meet for the first time at a horse training camp (in Tor di Quinto, near Rome), where the unknown young officer impresses Lampugnani with his impeccable skills, gracefully descending on horseback along a steep slide to a pond, a feat that none other rider had managed to achieve. Lampugnani asks the young man his name. The answer is "Baracca…. Francesco Baracca."

The tale of the friendship between the two men is squeezed into a few spirited lines, with Lampugnani described as a character from a Pushkin novel, who juggles love affairs, gambling debts, card games and duels, and culminates with Francesco's encounter with a timid shop assistant, Nellina, who is quite different from the high society dames he regularly dates. The scene, beautifully conceived, takes place at sunset, after Baracca's triumph at the Piazza di Siena horse show in Rome, and has an Ophüls-like delicacy, as Francesco and the girl return on carriage across the streets of Rome while a mutual feeling blossoms. Theirs will be an unfulfilled love, which Baracca—despite being a great heartthrob—chooses not to consummate, so as not to soil Nellina's purity.

The grandson of a cavalry officer, and a horse lover since childhood, Freda had always loved filming horses more than actors, and on *Francesco Baracca* he allowed himself ample opportunity to stage as many scenes as possible featuring his favorite animals, such as Francesco's triumph at the 1910 horse show. After that, the first part depicts the origin of Baracca's symbol, the black prancing horse, which would later become the Ferrari logo, and does so with epic tones. After the umpteenth duel, Lampugnani is punished and sent to a remote barrack in Maremma, Tuscany, and Baracca pays him a visit. Ingerenza is frantically practicing billiards, in anticipation of a challenge with a wealthy landowner, a renowned billiard champion: the prize will be a wonderful black stallion, owned by the latter. Lampugnani wins, but his opponent refuses to give him the horse: when Francesco and his friend show up, they have to face the landowner's servants on horseback, armed with lashes. A duel ensues, in which the two army officers have the advantage on their adversaries. Their return at the barrack with the horse, whose magnificence and beauty will cause Lampugnani to be forgiven by his commander, ends the first part.

The second part, *The Kite*, shows the fulfillment of Baracca's destiny through an event that will mark his existence, juxtaposed with the blossoming of a second romantic subplot: at a high society party, Francesco meets the beautiful Countess Hamilton, a *belle dame sans merci* nicknamed "*Tigre reale*" (Royal Tiger, a reference to Giovanni Verga's novel), a true maneater that attracts Baracca irresistibly. Freda once dictated a tongue-in-cheek epigraph for his own obituary: "He loved women and horses too much,"[13] and here he imagined the courting, which ends with the woman ultimately rejecting Francesco, as the unsuccessful attempt to train a rebel thoroughbred. After that, the decisive event in Baracca's life is portrayed by the director in a magnificently evocative scene: during a horse training maneuver with his men, Francesco sees an airplane falling and crashing to the ground. "Suddenly, piercing the clouds, some kind of a huge, crackling kite appears," the script reads; the plane loses altitude, leaving a trail of smoke, and crashes into a hill. Baracca runs to the site of the explosion, and assists the dying pilot. The episode makes him decide to leave the cavalry and enroll in aviation. It is possible that Freda envisioned the scene as an omen of sorts, given Baracca's tragic fate: as a famous line in one of his favorite films recites, "there are things no man can escape," and it is fitting that a vision of beauty and death (a plane falling to the ground like a broken kite, its fragile grace suddenly reduced to a powerless fight against the law of gravity) drives him to follow the same route as his nameless predecessor. The scene evokes images from the Greek mythology (Icarus' fall from the sky after his wax wings have been melted by the sun) and hints at the theme of man trying to win the elements and eventually being defeated—a trait of classical heroes, and Baracca was one.

The Kite ends with a double farewell: to the Countess, who confesses to Francesco that she has given up romantic dreams for richness and comfort by marrying a much older man, with poor health and enormous wealth; and to Nelly, who runs in tears after learning of Baracca's decision while he disappears in the opposite direction. The juxtaposition between Francesco's platonic love for Nellina and his attraction toward the Countess reprises melodrama's typical dichotomy, with the protagonist divided between two women who are poles apart, as in *Agi Murad—Il diavolo bianco*; first and foremost, though, Baracca is a man alone, whose inner torments find relief in the thrill of his almost Promethean challenge to the skies.

The third part, *Friends and ... Enemies*, is about Baracca's training in Reims, where he becomes friends with the French aviator Roland Garros and meets his nemesis, Baron Von Kleist. Whereas the former is a real historical character, the latter is a pure invention, modeled on the typical villain figure that Freda loved to have us hate (think of Sergei Ivanovic as played by Harry Feist in *Aquila nera*): Von Kleist hates Italians and is jealous of Baracca's exploits, both as a pilot and with French women. The training ends with the final exam in the skies over Reims, with a spectacular simulated aircraft duel that ends with Francesco as the winner, much to Von Kleist's shame and Roland's joy.

Back in Rome, Baracca finds neither Nelly nor the Countess, but soon terrible news upsets a great ball of the Roman upper class in which he is taking part: the outbreak of World War I, after the assassination of the Archduke Franz Ferdinand of Austria. The scene recalls the opening of *La leggenda del Piave*, as the news "strikes like an axe on the partygoers. It is the end of an era ... of the *belle époque*, for sure.... The officers receive the order to return immediately to the barracks ... then they run downstairs ... running, the long cloaks fluttering on their shoulders, they resemble dismal bats."

The fourth segment, *War*, depicts the difficulties of the aircraft war: the Italian army, stationed in Udine, is armed with a few tatty and outdated airplanes ("When the pilot lands, he can only raise his eyes to the sky as a thankful gesture"), and the local population is diffident, considering the aviators shirkers compared with the soldiers fighting in trenches. The hostility increases after the Austrians' first air raid: led by Von Kleist, the enemy causes many casualties among the civilians, while Baracca and the other pilots are vainly waiting for the arrival of the new Fokker biplanes, that would allow them to face the Austrians successfully. At the Udine headquarters, where he has gone to protest, Francesco meets his old friend Ingerenza, who is outraged as well because of those planes, "unworthy cuckoos made of canvas and wood, assembled with wire, which cannot be even remotely compared to the powerful assembly of muscles and generous blood that constitutes the essence of a horse"—a line that sums up Freda's love for the noble animal.

Finally the Fokker planes arrive, led by Baracca's friend Roland Garros. Freda imagines their arrival as a pure exhibition of grace and power, similar to those displayed by Francesco's beloved horses: the description of the perfect landing, made possible by the planes' maneuverability, shows what was the film's spectacular core to the director's eyes. Not by chance, in the next sequence, Ingerenza has a black prancing horse painted on the fuselage of Baracca's plane. Perhaps, in a sense, this ideal of beauty that suffuses the film makes Freda's Francesco Baracca close to the dreamer engineer Jiro Horikoshi in Hayao Miyazaki's *Kaze tachinu* (a.k.a. *The Wind Rises*, 2013).

The war sequences are dense with action and events, even just passingly mentioned, and fully display the scope and production effort that *Francesco Baracca* would have demanded. In addition to the period recreation, the story also depicts challenging aerial combat sequences, in which the pilot's chivalrous attitude would shine: Baracca spared the opponents who were injured or had run out of bullets, saluting them militarily, and even assisted those that he had brought down ("It's the aircraft I aim at, not the man," he was quoted to have said). Freda also sketches other real-life Italian aviators, such as Natale Palli, who, after finishing the ammunition, shot down an enemy balloon by crossing it with his own airplane. The director also contemplated a few sequences set in the trenches, with Baracca carrying hot coffee and food to his men shivering in the cold of the harsh winter on the Alps.

Melodrama surfaces again with Francesco's unexpected meeting with Nelly, on a foggy night in Udine, which seems to foreshadow the long-awaited romantic rendezvous. But Baracca, upon following the young woman, finds out that Nelly is on the front to assist her seriously wounded fiancé at the military hospital: their love meeting will never take place. Freda underlines his hero's ultimate solitude, juxtaposing this encounter with another that takes place in the trenches, where Francesco meets a former servant of his family, Giovanni, who held the drone during his amorous raids: the flashback depicting Baracca's escapades, halfway between a Lubitsch-style pochade and an old Hollywood swashbuckler (with Francesco fleeing in haste from his latest conquest's window just before the husband's arrival, and the expected display of acrobatics) is perhaps a superfluous interlude, but it underlines the director's love for certain priceless characters embodied by Douglas Fairbanks and Errol Flynn—a hint that this time he wanted to have it his own way. What is more, said flashback is a much-welcomed moment of levity before the fifth part, *The Duel*, that finally sees the confrontation between Baracca, commanding a vastly outnumbered squadron, and the Austrians led by his arch-enemy Von Kleist.

The description of the duel as featured in the subject published by *L'avant scène cinéma* is long (one full page out of 14) and thrilling, described with the dramatic tones that show how Freda pursued an idea of classic adventure cinema: first the treacherous and cowardly Von Kleist mercilessly strikes the aircraft of a young and inexperienced pilot; then, forced to fight against Baracca, he simulates a failure in order to exploit his adversary's chivalry, deceive him and shoot at him treacherously: but with an extraordinary aerial maneuver, the Italian flying ace has the better of Von Kleist, bringing his plane down. At the military hospital, where he is visiting the young pilot shot down by the enemy, Baracca meets the "Royal Tiger," who, in the throes of an existential crisis after her husband's death, has become a nurse. This is the prelude to a brief love idyll in the Venice canals, during a short leave. Once again, the director slows down the pacing and chooses an interlude as a necessary step before the impending tragedy.

The final part, *The Apocalypse*, opens with the reconstruction of the defeat of Caporetto, already evoked in *La leggenda del Piave* and here seen from the Austrians' point of view, after the enemy, guided by the young captain Erwin Rommel, the future Desert Fox, break into the enemy lines. During the retreat, Baracca runs across Ingerenza, in command of a squad of lancers on horseback, heading to the front, and vainly attempts to join them. The lancers' suicide attack against the enemy lines in Razzuolo is edited in alternation with the preparations and take-off of Baracca's air squadron, in a desperate and vain attempt to bring his friend help, in the director's umpteenth reference to Eisenstein; Freda also explicitly refers to the "600 of Balaclava," and the scene first and foremost pays homage to the celebrated ending of Michael Curtiz's *The Charge of the Light Brigade* (1936), starring Errol Flynn.

After the Battle of the Piave the situation is reversed, and the Italian army regains its positions. Francesco is called to give a hand in a battle of infantry on the Montello hill. As Baracca's plane is passing along the side of the hill, returning to base, an Austrian sniper fires one single shot from a trench, without conviction, "to that kind of bird of ill omen." Only one shot, but fatal. Baracca, hit in the forehead, crashes with his plane on the mountainside. When the news reaches the enemy headquarters, the Austrian aviators leave the room without a word, take off and throw wreaths on the aircraft wreck. The final shot has the camera move forward to the wreck, until the prancing horse on the fuselage is framed in close-up. Jacqueline Freda recalls a slightly different ending: "You did not see the plane crashing. There was a fade-in on the black prancing horse on the fuselage, and a fade-out on a red Ferrari on a racetrack."[14]

Freda wanted *Francesco Baracca* to be the story of the last heroes in a century that engulfed the most precious values, such as friendship, courage, loyalty. A summation of the director's view of life and cinema, which was destined for a similar fate as its hero. As he himself put it, commenting the ending, "in that case it was television who put a bullet in Baracca's forehead, and in mine as well."[15]

Forgotten ... Almost

If *Francesco Baracca* was the film Freda wanted to make, sadly the same cannot be said about the other unfilmed pictures he was attached to for the remaining part of the decade. Luigi Cozzi's recollections about a couple of Freda's aborted projects in the 1970s suggest how the director was basically treading water. "Once he asked me to write a thriller with him, but I had too many other commitments, and could not accept such a truly interesting offer. On another occasion I met him at a production company's office … and he was developing a project of a rather sexy flick about the Ancient Romans (it was the time of *Caligula*…)."[16] Cozzi explained to this author:

> The first episode dated back soon after we met for the first time, around 1970, more or less after I started writing for Antonio Margheriti, who wanted to launch new Italian thriller directors with his production company. But soon after I met Argento and, having immediately understood that Dario was definitely another category, I gave up the experiences with Freda and Nini [Margheriti]. My other meeting with Freda happened several years later, I don't remember exactly when but roughly between late 1978 and 1980. On that occasion Freda made me a bit sad, seeing such a talent (I have always admired him very much as a director) wasted on projects which you could tell he did not care about in the least bit; he dedicated to them only not to be left out of the Roman film industry.[17]

If Freda despised *Estratto dagli archivi segreti della polizia di una capitale europea* to the point of removing it from his own filmography, one can only guess what he thought of *Gli esorcisti* (The Exorcists), a script he developed from a story by Mario Righi, who was to finance it with his company Alexander Cinematografica Internazionale. An attempt at cashing in on the success of Friedkin's film (which was actually released in Italy in October 1974), like other similar titles such as *L'ossessa* (a.k.a. *The Eerie Midnight Horror Show*, 1974, Mario Gariazzo) and *Un urlo dalle tenebre* (a.k.a. *Cries and Shadows*, a.k.a. *Naked Exorcism*, 1975, Franco Lo Cascio and Elo Pannacciò), *Gli esorcisti* was certainly not destined to stand out in the group, at least judging from Righi's terribly written, ungrammatical three-page scenario (provided courtesy of Alessio Di Rocco and Stefano Raffaele), which goes on at length describing the horrible transformation caused by diabolic possession: the protagonist, "a beautiful young successful actress about 22–25 years old" by the name of Patrizia, becomes "a beastly creature" whose beauty

> completely disappears, leaving room to a frightening being, with the eyes almost completely coming out of the orbits, the tongue coming out for four inches from the mouth, the hair turning fraught and stingy like bushes, the skin becoming old and wrinkled in a scary manner, inhuman and beastly yells coming out of her mouth, her body floundering in an epilectic way as threads of drool come out of her mouth, mixed with vomit.

Classy stuff.

To label Righi's story as "threadbare" would be an understatement: it is basically the tale of a series of exorcism attempts undergone by Patrizia, as her uncle desperately attempts to cure her, entrusting her to the cure of two "witch doctors." As expected, there is ample room for sex: the second witch doctor takes advantage of the situation to rape the girl, only to witness her metamorphosis in the midst of sexual intercourse, and be attacked in what the scenario laconically describes as "a scary scene." Eventually Patrizia is exorcised by a friar summoned by her fiancé Roberto: "The scene becomes more and more chilling; eventually Patrizia vomits the Devil in the form of toads, vipers and rats, then falls unconscious and healed." The light of God washes the room. The End. The cast list in the papers deposited at the Ministry featured Antonia Santilli—seen in Di Leo's *Il boss* (a.k.a. *The Boss*, 1973)—as Patrizia, Adolfo Lastretti, and Claudio Cassinelli as Roberto.[18] Scheduled to be filmed starting on March 11, 1974, *Gli esorcisti* stopped dead at pre-production stage, and it was definitely better this way for all those involved.

After his meeting with Alfredo Leone on the set of *Estratto dagli archivi segreti della polizia di una capitale europea*, Freda and the Italian-American producer worked on some projects to be shot in Spain in the mid–1970s. As Leone recalls,

We became very very close. We used to have dinner together, and I took him to Turkey, in Istanbul, they wanted me to open a studio and I was going to have Freda run the studio for me. As much as I did with him, it was more a friendship. He came to my office, almost every day. On occasion he'd bring his daughter. We talked about doing three big pictures in Spain, but ultimately he never did a movie for me. These three movies I was going to do in Spain with Bava, but he decided to do *Cani arrabbiati*. I was very upset, and that's where Freda came into the picture. I was going to do the movies with Freda in Spain, but then I decided not to do them. My production manager, Joe De Blasio, wasn't very dependable, and I had a falling out with the Spanish producer. So Boetani stepped in.[19]

Eventually, however, these project came to nothing.

Leone also recalled an evening out at a Roman restaurant with Freda, Jacqueline (whom he called Rusty after the character in the *Adventures of Rin Tin Tin* TV series) and Gianna Maria Canale, still ravishing in her mid-forties: evidently the past rust had been settled.[20] Freda's affectionate and yet amusing relationship with his elder daughter deeply touched the producer: "She was an equestrienne, I remember: she was a beautiful girl, but Freda raised her as a boy, dressed her like a boy, and made her work hard on the set too! So I asked him, 'Riccardo, why do you treat this little girl like a boy?' He turned to her and said, 'Tell him, Rusty: Are you a boy or a girl?' And she would answer, 'I'm a *boy*!'"[21]

In the late 1970s Freda stayed for some time at Piero Regnoli's guest house. A longtime friend of Freda's, with whom he had written *I vampiri*, Regnoli was one of the most extravagant figures in Italian cinema. Formerly the film critic for the Vatican's newspaper *L'Osservatore Romano*, his career in the movies was not something his ex-employers would have been proud of: besides the 11 directorial credits to his name (or his a.k.a. Dean Craig), which included the Gothic horror *L'ultima preda del vampiro* (a.k.a. *The Playgirls and the Vampire*, 1960) and the sexy fairytale spoof *La principessa sul pisello* (shot in 1973, but released in 1976), Regnoli was an incredibly prolific screenwriter, with over 110 scripts, most of which were heavily tinged with eroticism and perversions galore. As Jacqueline Freda recalls, "they wrote a lot of stuff together, one page after another, because Regnoli was a war machine! They worked with Bacharach's music as a background, my father dictating and Regnoli tapping on the typewriter. Then they stopped and discussed the next scene, and again on to the next, and the next, and the next…."[22]

Regnoli and Freda had much in common, including their passion for ancient Egypt, esoterism and séances: it is not surprising, then, that at a certain point the director was attached to a couple of movies written by his friend. The first, *Thanat 82*, is perhaps the most elusive in Freda's career, as we know nothing about the story, except for the title. However, the rest of the information we have can at least give us a clue of what the film was about. According to the papers kept at Rome's SIAE (provided courtesy of Alessio Di Rocco and Stefano Raffaele) and dated May 2, 1978, *Thanat 82* was to be produced by Cooperativa Cinematografica Internazionale, a cooperative presided by Freda himself and based at Regnoli's own house in via Casperia, in Rome. The script was written by Regnoli and the director, and the crew would include Gábor Pogány (with his son Cristiano acting as cameraman), editor Carlo Reali, assistant director Luigi Ferrara and art director Arrigo Equini, while Stelvio Cipriani would compose the score. The notification of start of production also listed a tentative cast list and a budget of slightly over a billion *lire*: 200 million would come from the guaranteed minimum provided by the Italian distributor, whereas 500 million would be the result of foreign pre-sales, and 150 would be guaranteed by an Indian participation. The film would star Ursula Andress—by then a recurrent presence in Italian cinema: Sergio Martino's *La montagna del dio cannibale*, a.k.a. *Slave of the Cannibal God* would come out later that year—as Thanat, and the tentative cast included many well-known names: Ettore Manni (as the President of the United States), Hardy Krüger (Cooper), Agostina Belli (or Carole André) as Helene, Renzo Palmer, Salvo Randone, Raoul Grassilli and Giampiero Albertini.

Filming was scheduled to start in September 1978: the shooting schedule plan consisted of nine weeks (two of them on location in India), plus four more weeks of post-production at Cinecittà for special effects—which, together with the indication of the various filming locations (a grotto, a submarine cave) and some characters' names, leads to speculations on the story's content. There is little doubt that *Thanat 82* was an esoteric story, centered on Indian mysticism and on the mysterious titular woman—possibly a deity incarnated? Certainly it was a theme that fascinated both Freda and Regnoli. The director had only marginally touched upon it in *Estratto dagli archivi segreti della polizia di una capitale europea* (where a scene depicting Lord Alexander's journey to India had been deleted from Mario Bianchi's script), and he would return on the theme of reincarnation in the unfilmed script for *La Dernière Momie d'Egypte*. The climax, to be set at the Pentagon, possibly hints at some apocalyptic finale, but we don't know for sure.

What is certain is that *Thanat 82* was quickly shelved, most likely because of the impossibility of gathering the esteemed budget, and Freda fell back on a decidedly less expensive project, a horror movie again written by Regnoli, together with Jaime Comas Gil and Roberto Montero (who was originally to direct it), from a story by Franco La Marca: *Satan's Night*. The project, originally entitled *Sensory*, had been announced in the Italian trade press as early as 1978; when Freda came aboard, and the notification of start of production was deposited by Cooperativa Cinematografica Internazionale, it had been blessed with a blatantly lurid title, *Qualcosa penetra in noi (Le notti di Satana)* (Something Penetrates Us—Satan's Nights).

Shooting was scheduled to start on February 12, 1979, but the movie never materialized. Judging from the screenplay kept at Rome's CSC (titled *Satan's Night*, dated March 1978 and running 215 pages), the story was a rather drab mixture of horror and eroticism, with an emphasis on the latter. In a typical *The Old Dark House*–style opening, a group of people meet during a thunderstorm at a villa in the woods, owned by the rich Diana Cronkite and her brother Paul: psychiatrist Bill Howard, his assistant Carla, journalist Lynne Sanders, ex-gynecologist Norman Schneider, black mannequin Cleo Kaufman and black magic scholar Vladimir Slokov. The villa is littered with "abstract-symbolic paintings" portraying the devil, and soon—but not before a couple of gratuitous nude scenes—the conversation switches to the occult: the inevitable séance follows, even though this time the guest must stay each in a different room of the house and await for the ancient demon Tolka ("the monster of the abysses of conscience") to materialize at Slokov's summoning.

The one interesting idea in Regnoli's script is, to quote Slokov's monologue, that "the devil is a puerile exemplification of what is commonly considered evil, but objectively it does not exist," since "man has called "angels" his positive energies and "demons" the negative ones." Hence, Satan "exists only within the individual, and never independently. That's why fear is nothing but the moment in which we learn as if through a mirror about the horror that is inside us." Too bad the demonstration for the theorem leans on the most hackneyed genre clichés and serves mostly as a pretext for erotic scenes. Predictably, Slokov dies during the séance, and soon the other guests—unable to leave the house for unexplicable reasons, *à la El ángel exterminador* (a.k.a. *The Exterminating Angel*, 1962, Luis Buñuel)—are offed by a malevolent presence that seems to feed on their most obscure secrets, which inevitably relate to sexuality (Diana's lesbianism and her incestuous past relationship with her brother, Lynne's masturbatory and voyeuristic tendencies, plus an over-the-top flashback with Schneider sodomizing a teen patient to death in his ambulatory). Nudity abounds, whereas gore is kept to a minimum: one of the few horrific descriptions in the script mentions Diana's fingers running over "a shaggy, hairy mass, pitch black and so slimy it looks wet" and the sight of a monstrous figure, a facsimile of what in the Ancient Testament is referred to as "The Beast."

Eventually, Bill discovers an old book on demonology which gives out the solution: Tolka "is born and grows in the subconscious and assumes the shape that the sense of guilt of every single individual tends to give to it. Tonka, in short, is the other side of the coin, the one which we desperately try to hide even to ourselves…." At dawn, Bill and Carla are about to leave, but the girl falls prey to yet another manifestation of the demon: however, the script calls for a hasty happy ending which sounds very much like old-school horror fare, in contrast with the liberal amount of sexuality on display throughout. All in all, there wouldn't probably be much that Freda could do to salvage such a mess: among other things, Regnoli would recycle the bit where a man is slayed by a couple of ferocious dogs in his script for *Patrick vive ancora* (a.k.a. *Patrick Still Lives*, 1980) by Mario Landi, who might as well have been a more suited director for this type of film.

According to the notification of start of production (from Alessio Di Rocco and Stefano Raffaele's personal archives), shooting was scheduled to start on February 12, 1979, for five weeks, at the De Paolis studios. The cast list included Gabriele Tinti (Bill), Silvia Dionisio (Carla), Olga Karlatos (Diana), Ettore Manni (Schneider), Laura Gemser (Cleo), and the Swiss François Simon (the film's most interesting casting choice) as Slokov. The crew list included Sandro Mancori d.o.p.), Otello Colangeli (editor), Stelvio Cipriani (music).[23] Interestingly, the papers deposited at SIAE make no mention of Montero and Comas Gil's names, which were instead included in the CSC script. Eventually the movie was cancelled, and probably it was a blessing for Freda: however, Gemser and Dionisio would turn up in the director's next film.

Murder Obsession

The opportunity to return to filmmaking finally came in the form of a low budget horror movie. Its genesis is as surprising as it is emblematic of the subterranean threads that ran across Italian cinema of the period, connecting and tangling up people, ideas and stories like in a spider's web.

A former assistant director to Lucio Fulci, Edoardo Mulargia and Giuliano Carnimeo, in the early 1970s Fabio Piccioni had penned a short story called *Il grido del Capricorno*, which he adapted into an adult comic book in the *Oltretomba* series (*Oltretomba Gigante* #9, February 1974, with drawings by José María Bellalta). Set in 1894, *Il grido del capricorno* was the story of a young musician, Ludwig von Mayer, who lives in the shadow of his late father, a composer and orchestra conductor, and is oppressed by a domineering mother who wants him to follow in his father's footsteps and become as famous as him. Meanwhile, a black-gloved killer starts dispatching the young man's lovers and friends in gruesome ways (and with ample display of nudity and sadism). The police and a criminologist start suspecting Ludwig, who is revealed to have killed his own father as a child, but bears no memory of the event. Then, after Ludwig's wife-to-be Helga is horribly murdered too, a shocking truth is revealed.

Being in severe shortage of cash, Piccioni approached Salvatore Argento, with whom he was in good terms and whose office was just in front of his house in Rome, and sold him *Il grido del capricorno* for 500,000 *lire*. The deal had an ironic side which perhaps came unnoticed to both parts, given that a couple of scenes in the comic were blatantly stolen from *L'uccello dalle piume di cristallo*, namely the killer terrorizing a woman in bed and ripping off her panties, and the maniac attempting to penetrate Helga's house, by jimmying the door with a knife, as the woman watches in terror.

Very little of *Il grido del capricorno* ultimately migrated in the basic core that became *Profondo rosso*, but it was vital to the film's plot: the relationship between (Gabriele Lavia) and his oppressive mother (Clara Calamai) comes from it, as does the brief opening flashback in which a child is seen picking up the knife that just killed his father, an image taken

Italian locandina for *Murder Obsession* (1981).

almost verbatim from Piccioni's story (and the *Oltretomba* comic). The rest, of course, was all Dario Argento's invention. Still, it is no surprise that Argento chose not to follow the outrageous final twist, where the murderer is not only revealed to be Ludwig's mother, but the elderly woman turns out to be a man in disguise, his father's

Riccardo Freda on the set of *Murder Obsession*.

longtime lover—shades of Gunnar Hellström's bizarre thriller *The Name of the Game Is Kill!* (1968).

Piccioni then recycled several elements from *Il grido del Capricorno* once more, a few years later, in a contemporary setting: again there were a young man obsessed by the memory of his late father, an orchestra director; a domineering, overly possessive mother; and a flashback that reveals the child's apparent role in his father's murder, which ends with the boy holding a bloody knife in his hand, as if hypnotized by the red liquid on the blade. The resulting script—concocted with the participation of Antonio Cesare Corti and Freda—was *Murder Obsession*.[24] It is the story of a young disturbed actor, Michael, who—after almost murdering an actress during the filming of a scene in a horror movie—returns to his secluded mother's house for a brief vacation, together with the film's director, the latter's a.d., the aforementioned actress, and his fiancée. Unsettling, horrific events ensue at the sinister house: Michael's girlfriend experiences an eerie nightmare, supernatural forces seem to materialize, and most characters meet gruesome deaths. Eventually the horrible truth behind Michael's shady past is revealed, as is the (not-so-surprise) murderer.

According to Jacqueline Freda, her father's aim when taking on the project was merely "to resurface on the market in order to find room (and money) to finance his project on Francesco Baracca, which indeed obsessed him. It was an embarrassing situation, he was annoyed, did not want to make it … well, he was always annoyed when making a movie—anyway, there was no concentration on his part."[25] Some sources list the script's original title as *L'ossessione che uccide*, whereas the script included in the

Simon Mizrahi fund at the BiFi (Bibliothèque du film) in Paris is titled *Deliria*, signed by Corti (as "Tony Blond") and Piccioni, and dated 1976. The 4-page synopsis retained at Rome's CSC is already titled *Murder Obsession*. Marked January 18, 1980, it dates the project slightly after *Qualcosa penetra in noi (Le notti di Satana)*; it is basically identical to the finished film, save for the characters' different names: Michael's fiancée is named Francis, the director's name becomes Ken and Michael's deceased father was a Wilhelm von Holbach.

Murder Obsession was a majoritarian Italian/French co-production. The Italian producer was Enzo Boetani, with his company Dionysio Cinematografica. Freda had become acquainted with Boetani since the days of the *peplum* fever, when the latter collaborated as executive producer with Carlo Ludovico Bragaglia, but the two had never had the chance to work together, although they had tried to mount other projects, but to no avail. One such was a horror movie to be co-produced with a French company, whose title Boetani does not recall (perhaps *Thanat 82*?), whereas another was *Superhuman*, announced in the January 1979 issue of the *Foreign Sales Italian Movie Trade* magazine. According to the producer, it was in the vein of the superhero-cum-wrestler films that were all the rage in South America, and was aimed specifically at that market, with Freda attached to direct it, but it all came to nothing because of problems with the South American buyer.[26]

"It was Riccardo who came to me with the script for *Murder Obsession*, and suggested an Italian/French co-production," Boetani recalls. The French producer would be his the director's friend Simon Mizrahi.

> The relationship between me and Freda was of mutual esteem, and honestly I must say I agreed to make the film for Riccardo—to make him and the crew work, since it was a difficult period for many of us—rather than because of the script's inner qualities. It was a low-budget movie, I think around 120 or 130 million *lire*, and we had to follow a tight shooting schedule. However, with Simon the situation was not so idyllic in the end, as there were problems with the French financers.[27]

Filming went on for three weeks, in April 1980, mostly in palace Borghese in Artena—one of the staple locations of Italian Gothic since Renato Polselli's *L'amante del vampiro*—and at Parco della Mola, in Oriolo Romano, where Laura Gemser's murder was filmed. Boetani cast three actors who had just finished working in a film he produced, *Prima della lunga notte (L'ebreo fascista)* (1980, Franco Molè, based on a book by Luigi Preti): Ray Lovelock, Silvia Dionisio and Martine Brochard. Dionisio was cast as the fiancée, now called Deborah, a part originally to be played by Janet Agren, whereas Lovelock (who even recalls having been prepared for the role and having made a screen-test) was replaced at the last minute by Stefano Patrizi for the role of Michael.

Born in Milan in 1950, the blond and handsome Patrizi had arrived in Rome in 1971, and took his first steps in the movie business thanks to his fiancée Barbara Mastroianni (Marcello's daughter), first as assistant editor (for Ruggero Mastroianni, on Visconti's *Ludwig* and Francesco Rosi's *Lucky Luciano*), and then, thanks also to his looks, as an actor, on Visconti's *Gruppo di famiglia in un interno* (a.k.a. *Conversation Piece*, 1974), followed by a number of often prestigious titles, including George Pan Cosmatos' *Cassandra Crossing* (1976), the grim crime film *Liberi, armati, pericolosi* (a.k.a. *Young, Violent, Dangerous*, 1976, directed by Romolo Guerrieri and written by Fernando di Leo) and the controversial *Lion of the Desert* (1980, Moustapha Akkad), starring Anthony Quinn and Oliver Reed.

Michael's mother, Glenda, was played by Anita Strindberg, a oft-seen presence in

1970s *gialli*, such as *Una lucertola con la pelle di donna* (a.k.a. *A Lizard in a Woman's Skin*, 1971, Lucio Fulci) and *La coda dello scorpione* (a.k.a. *The Case of the Scorpion's Tail*, 1971, Sergio Martino); John Richardson (*La maschera del demonio*) was cast as the enigmatic butler, Oliver. The bare-bones cast also featured Laura Gemser (the star of the *Black Emanuelle* series) as Beryl, the actress, and a couple of French thespians, Martine Brochard—seen among others in Umberto Lenzi's *Gatti rossi in un labirinto di vetro* (a.k.a. *Eyeball*, 1975), also starring Richardson—and Henri Garcin.

Filming was not a pleasant experience for most of the people involved. "*Mamma mia* what a nightmare!" Laura Gemser recalled.

> I remember that I had to shoot a scene with Anita Strindberg who had to grab a real knife and pretend to stab me. I shouted at Freda: "You're crazy? What if she really hits me?!" He said: "What are ya gonna do?" They would have done anything to save money on these sets. On top of that, I was naked, just for a change, and I was lying on the bank of a lake and it was freezing![28]

Martine Brochard's recollections were not happy either: "I remember I did not have much fun doing it, especially a scene where there was a glass which had been cut expressly so that I could put my head over it, and the camera was over a chainsaw that came closer and closer, and there I must confess I was really scared."[29] Brochard was not kind about Freda too:

> He was a very tough type, of a wickedness I did not expect and which upset me, so much so that on the very first day I answered him back, but then I took him aside, talked to him and he softened a bit. There were two French actors in the film and he treated them so badly that there was this actor, who worked on stage and was an important name in France [Henri Garcin], who was desperate, and I used to translate him everything because on that set nobody translated anything.[30]

As for Silvia Dionisio, who had recently separated from her husband Ruggero Deodato, according to Brochard she just looked forward to finishing the movie; it was her last film role, followed in 1982 by Daniele D'Anza's TV mini-series *La sconosciuta*, before her early retirement.

Similarly, Stefano Patrizi was on the verge of retirement as well: Freda's film was his last movie, and then he moved to Milan to work in an advertising agency:

> I did not like being an actor, and was bored to death by such a job: the endless waits and the estrangement from the working reality on set were undermining. I had decided to quit that job, and sincerely I really did not consider myself apt to it ... after six months in Africa shooting *Lion of the Desert* I was spent, and had decided to move away from Rome, with the aim of settling in Milan and starting over with something that would give me a more solid future and a full involvement....

Patrizi candidly admitted to this writer that he has no recollection whatsoever of *Murder Obsession*: "I vaguely recall Freda as a harsh man, of a few words and not very affable."[31]

Boetani—who maintains that Freda always behaved deliciously with him, and even introduced the producer to his future wife, script girl Maria Luce Faccenna, the daughter of producer Angelo Faccenna—adds that "Once I came on the set, and watch him direct a scene. He set up the camera, yelled 'Action' ... and turned his back on the actors! (laughs) 'But Riccardo, why are you doing that?' 'Well, you know, I can't make them act to save their life! Even if I don't watch them, that's the same—if it's good for the camera, then it's good for me too!' (laughs) You know, he was joking, but I think he really meant that...."[32] Overall, the feeling between the director and the cast was mutual: "He hated them," Jacqueline maintains. "He thought they were just terrible."[33]

Murder Obsession was submitted to the censors board on October 15, 1980, and given a visa on October 31; yet it took some months before it came out to theaters. Released in Italy in February 1981, it did mediocre business: Boetani blames the distributor, who also failed to pay back the expected sum, and adds that the production lost over 50 percent of the production costs on it. Nevertheless, the film was met with enthusiasm by a small group of fierce supporters, including the eminent film critic and historian Goffredo Fofi (who helped Freda put together his memoir, *Divoratori di celluloide*, released in 1981 as well, and mostly derived from the interviews the director had given in the previous decades in France) and critic/scriptwriter Patrizia Pistagnesi. Over the years, Freda's final film underwent a peculiar fate: on the one hand it was harshly dismissed by its author—who went so far as labeling it "shit."[34]—, and on the other it was overrated and championed by some as the director's testament and a culmination of his whole body of work, with a blind eye to its many flaws, both in style and substance, starting with the blatant budgetary limits and the compromises on the part of Freda in order to adapt to a market that demanded conspicuous bouts of nudity and violence. Most reviewers would rather focus on the overall mood which conveyed the feeling of the end of an era—the same that exudes from the pages of Freda's own autobiography.

The film opens with a self-explanatory line, allegedly an excerpt taken from the work of a 17th century philosopher named Hieronimus A. Steinback: "For centuries, theologians, philosophers, and poets have delved into the universe in search of proof of the existence of the devil. It would have sufficed to look into the depths of their own souls." In the glorious tradition of Italian Gothic, the line is totally made up, and the name "Hieronimus A. Steinback" is a fabrication on the part of the scriptwriters. Still, besides functioning as a commentary to what we will witness in the following 97 minutes, it is in tune with Freda's vision and ideally reconnects to Umberto Raho's line about the proximity of the devil in *Lo spettro*.

It is just appropriate that *Murder Obsession* begins as it does, with a little bit of self-referential, film-within-a-film oddity. A beautiful girl returns to her flat, engulfed in darkness. She goes at the window to open it, and, revealed by a sudden lighting in a quasi-Expressionist shot, a male silhouette appears behind the curtain. The man grabs the girl by the neck, rips off her clothes and starts choking her. His face is splashed with a bright, unexplained red light, almost like in a Bava film—or rather, in Freda's earlier Gothics, such as *L'orribile segreto del Dr. Hichcock* or *Lo spettro*. It all turns out to be part of a low-budget horror movie, the kind John Travolta's character works on in De Palma's *Blow Out* (1981). As the camera recoils with an exquisitely fluid movement, revealing the tiny set on which the film is being made—as well as the very dolly it is mounted upon—we can glimpse an elderly man on the right corner, leaning on an armchair and wearing a plaid cap. It is Riccardo Freda. As the scene continues, his unmistakable voice is heard in the background, commenting: "It was not quite a brilliant idea…" One wonders whether this bit reflected the director's own reservations about the uneasy pairing of stylish *mise-en-scène* and cheap material, old-style lighting and sound effects and gratuitous nudity.

Freda did not have a very good opinion of the script, and it is obvious in the way he deals with the ultra gory scenes—an axe to the head and a decapitation via chainsaw, courtesy of Angelo Mattei's workshop, with a very young and still inexperienced Sergio Stivaletti in his debut[35]—which are as crude and unpleasant as those in *L'iguana dalla lingua di fuoco* and *Estratto dagli archivi segreti della polizia di una capitale europea*. According to Boetani, Martine Brochard's decapitation scene was concocted by the director himself: "He shot it right in my office," the producer recalls. "He employed a trick with mirrors. It was amazing, one of the brilliant things I saw him do. He was a genius in this respect! And he shot it all with just a cameraman, the actress, and three mirrors...."[36]

Even though *Murder Obsession* falls in the realm of the splatter film, Freda despised such practices, and such scenes further remark his distance. And yet, *Murder Obsession* contains at least one remarkable moment in this respect, when Michael wakes up next to the naked Beryl, and slowly starts caressing her leg, contemplating her nudity—as the audience does—until the camera pans on the woman's torso, revealing the gruesome gash on it. Only then he realizes (as we do) that she is dead. Desire becomes disgust, the perspective is reversed. Despite a somewhat imperfect framing that gives away the macabre twist a bit too early, it is a remarkable reflection over the forms of horror and desire in cinema, and one that exudes an almost pornographic visual power.

Murder Obsession is usually labeled as a *giallo*. Still, despite the presence of a black-gloved killer who employs such gruesome tools as an axe and a chainsaw, and a negative film capturing the murderer's identity *à la Blow-up* (1966), the whodunit elements—Beryl's attempted drowning in the bathtub *à la Sei donne per l'assassino*, the close-ups of the murderer's gloved hands, Schwartz and Shirley's killings—feel tacked on to a Gothic-oriented storyline, and not the other way round. Take the central role played by the mansion where the characters move, eat, sleep, make love, dream and die: with its tight stairs, eerie basements and old-style half-lighted rooms, it acts as a character of its own, and seems to control the protagonists' feelings and actions (take the intermittent lights that go out every now and then, forcing them in the dark), A haunted house which feeds on old memories and secrets, and does not let anyone come out alive: when the massacre is seemingly over, the doors close by itself, arbitrarily shutting the survivors inside. Such a *huis clos* seems to belong to an indefinite era, and the odd contemporary details—such as Oliver's blue jeans and tennis shoes—are as disruptive as the sudden bursts of gore, adding to the film's overall sense of unease. The theme of the double, a Gothic staple, here becomes a further instrument to disrupt the difference between past and present, which, as in Bava's *Lisa e il diavolo*, ultimately get confused and indistinguishable: not only does Michael look exactly like his father (Freda did not even try and have Stefano Patrizi made up in a different way, but simply relied on different clothes for the flashbacks depicting the man's death), but in the end he becomes one and the same with him in the eyes of his crazed mother.

The distance from the *giallo* can also be detected in the pacing and plot construction. It takes almost an hour before the first killing occurs (and offscreen, too: we get to see only the aftermath of Beryl's demise), and the following murder sequences are carried out in a rather idiosyncratic way, with the director avoiding the use of POV shots of the killer—*giallo*'s trademark—and relying on abrupt bursts of violence. The resolution is also as tortuous as the path in the woods across which Michael lead his friends in a scene; what is more, rather than a typical whodunit twist, the final revelation of the murderer's identity and its motives comes off as rather disregarding of the surprise in itself, and unrolls as one of those digressions that were typical of the director's beloved popular novels: Oliver's taped confession which Michael listens to is a case in point.

Instead of going for a tight pacing, Freda lingers on the interiors of palace Borghese and sets up slow and elegant camera movements, leaving aside the direction of his clueless cast. He also avoids *gialli*'s visual frenzy, and often comes up with stylized frame compositions that even recall the silent era, as in Michael's flashback of his father's alleged death. Despite not being satisfied with the actors, the director went along very well with the young d.o.p. Cristiano Pogany, the son of the great Gábor[37]: "He adored him," Jacqueline Freda recalls. "He was one of the few people my father really cared about and treated well on the set—and believe me, on the set my father was a wild beast! In his private life he was extremely good-natured, but when it came to his job he was frightful—with me as well! Whereas with Cristiano, he was incredibly sweet...."[38]

Indeed, the cinematography is quite good in spite of the painful budgetary shortcomings. Freda claimed that he thought of Bava while making the film,[39] and some photography tricks (such as the jellies in the "astral body" scene) recall the work of the Sanremese director. The use of miniatures and *maquettes*, on the other hand, is typical of both filmmakers, but several moments hark back unmistakably to Freda's past, for better or worse. The crude night views of Michael's house—incidentally, the same camera angle as that of Hichcock's mansion in *L'orribile segreto del Dr. Hichcock*—were obtained via a photo of the palace before the camera, and recall *I vampiri* and *Caltiki*, but also the awkward "exterior" shots in *Coplan ouvre le feu à Mexico*. What is more, the nightmarish bit when Silvia Dionisio's character is running across a wood of malevolent branches brings to mind Barbara Steele's mad run in the villa's garden in *L'orribile segreto del Dr. Hichcock*; later on, in the scene of Deborah fleeing from the haunted house at night during a thunderstorm, the obvious blueprint is *Beatrice Cenci*'s extraordinary opening sequence. Freda was likely drawing from his cinematic memory and career in order to reshape a half-baked project into something as close as he could to his own vision, and come out unscathed as far as possible.

Still, *Murder Obsession* shows an in-depth involvement with the supernatural and the occult which was always part of Freda's character. Rather surprisingly for such a disenchanted and rationalistic figure, the director repeatedly professed his interest for superstitious beliefs and magical practices. "I have always been fascinated with esoterical and magic problems, and instead of *Little Red Riding Hood* I used to read Eliphas Lévi's manuals. My adolescence was dotted with Seals of Solomon and elderberry twigs plucked in nights with no moon."[40] Magic had been a recurring presence throughout his career, too. In 1946, when Freda could not find anyone interested in financing his next film, his elderly maid performed a ritual to chase away the "evil eye" from him: that very day he got in touch with Nino Angioletti, who would produce *Aquila Nera*; in 1948 he and Gianna Maria Canale witnessed a macumba ritual in Brazil which resulted in the actress falling ill; in 1950 he directed the self-explanatory short *Magia a prezzi modici*.

Murder Obsession's story and dialogue are literally packed with esoteric references, and each character seems to have a connection with magical practices, which manifests itself through a physical object (often a jewel) they have on them. Beryl mentions the voodoo rites she witnessed and took part in, in her home country of Martinique; Shirley owns a bracelet depicting an *ouroboros*, the serpent eating its own tail (in the dialogue, though, it is referred to as a "winged serpent"), a symbol of eternal return and an alchemical sigil; Glenda is revealed to wear a necklace with occult symbols, including a vampire bat, whereas Deborah is spared because she is wearing the Seal of Solomon. But there is more: "The camera is my third eye," Hans Schwartz quips, and later on Oliver covers his face so as not to be photographed by him (displaying the same annoyance as the natives in *Caltiki* when their dance ritual was disturbed by the explorers). Beryl hypothesizes that this is because he is scared that the camera might capture his soul.

As in Paul Muller's final monologue in *Estratto dagli archivi segreti della polizia di una capitale europea*, there is much talk of an "astral body," and we find out that Oliver can actually detach himself from his physical body and wander through the house at night, in a scene rendered in a rather crude yet endearing manner through subjective shots distorted by a jelly and the stop-motion appearance of muddy footprints on the staircase, in a perhaps fortuitous homage to Bava's *La frusta e il corpo*. Of all the characters summoned at Michael's house, Hans Schwartz—not just a film director but one resembling Freda: notice the glasses and cap he wears and the cigar he smokes—seems to be the more aware of the role of magic in the universe. "It's the only way to solve the mystery of life … magic," he observes, and when we see him leafing through an occult book in plain sight in the lounge, it is clear that he is not simply trying to waste time during an insomniac bout.

Hans Schwartz's monologue on the astral body and on the necessity to analyze the moment when the soul separates from the body ("But to do this, we must be capable of killing with our own hands so that no breath of life escapes us") strangely predates the theme of *Martyrs* (2008, Pascal Laugier) and its obsession with the afterlife. Schwartz also points out that he believes in reincarnation as "the only way to explain the moral and material unhappiness of mankind because of its bestial, degrading past life"—a line that is 100 percent Freda. His dialogue with Glenda, carried out like a subterranean seduction scene, is a fascinating and often overlooked moment that provides *Murder Obsession* its core. It is also one of several scenes absent in the version originally released to home video in the States, *The Wailing*, which also attempted to make the film pass off as a standard *giallo* by way of adding a trivial synth score to flesh out (and replace in parts) Franco Mannino's haunting piano rendering of classical music by Bach and Liszt, itself another element that remarked Freda's distance from the contemporary ways of horror cinema.[41]

Another interesting example of the film's emphasis on the occult is Deborah's nightmare—one of *Murder Obsession*'s most derided sequences, and understandably so, given the ridiculous appearance of patently fake bats flapping about on wires and a giant rubber spider which the girl runs across at one point. Deborah is chased in the mansion's crypt by a pair of hooded, monstrous-looking figures, finds a way out in the garden, experiences horrid visions (such as skulls hanging from a tree like ripe fruits and dripping blood from their empty eye sockets), is tied to a St. Andrew's cross and subjected to an incomprehensible ritual. At first glance, the scene seems pointless, a shock segment whose only function is to provide cheap thrills to an undemanding audience. And yet, despite its sloppy effects work, which elicits comparison with a similarly awkward moment in Luigi Batzella's awful *Nuda per Satana* (a.k.a. *Nude for Satan*, 1974)—or, again, an adults-only comic book like Ediperiodici's *Lucifera*, which in one issue featured a panel depicting a woman being raped by a giant spider—, the sequence is not devoid of interest. On the technical side, it is characterized by the use of fluid long takes, whereas thematically it carries out several of the plot's key themes and further underlines the director's fascination for the subject matter.

Scattered with magic symbols, Deborah's dream becomes the key to penetrate into the true nature of the mystery. Note, for instance, the presence of the spider. In *Estratto dagli archivi segreti della polizia di una capitale europea*, a stone spider figure could be glimpsed on the fireplace during the occult ceremony at the Alexander mansion, and since Freda sometimes took care of sculpting props for his films, that could have been the case as well (after all, he even bothered writing the words for the bad song heard throughout the movie). Here the arachnid figure returns, with an overly symbolic significance. First Deborah runs into its web; then, during the rite, the spider reappears and takes a semi-human form, its paws eerily turning into furry, vaguely human hands which lusciously caress the girl's legs. The spider is an ancient symbol of mystery, power and growth: in India it is associated with the term "Maya," meaning the illusory nature of appearances, whereas in Egypt it is paired with the process of creation and recreation, and other civilizations saw it as a spinner of fate. Christian cultures have linked it with duplicitous meanings, but mostly as an evil force that sucks blood. As we will find out in the end, Michael himself has been trapped into a web of deception, and his own mother is revealed to be the spider-like spinner of the events that—in typical Freda fashion—lead to a circular ending, an eternal return that mirrors the ineluctability of fate.

On *Murder Obsession* the director returned to the primordial core of his conception of Gothic: a family melodrama, excessive and morbid, soaked with psychoanalytic undertones, in which the horror blossoms and feeds on the dynamics of parental relationships. As portrayed by the ravishing 43-year-old Anita Strindberg, Glenda is Freda's last and perhaps ultimate monster, the true point of no return after the incestuous father of *Beatrice Cenci*, the beauty-obsessed nubile old lady of *I vampiri*, the necrophile husband of *L'orribile segreto del Dr. Hichcock* and the scheming wife of *Lo spettro*. She is a young-looking, sexy, desirable mother, who meets her son in bed while dressed in a transparent nightgown, and whose feelings for her offspring leave no room for doubt. She is also a vampire of sorts, feeding off other men's lusts for her, and using them like puppets.

"The story nevertheless interested me. What can happen in our tragic childhood? What are the consequences when guilt and murder mingle?"[42] the director observed, while offering a psychoanalytic reading to his film. The weight of the past is connected to a horrific primary scene that is repeated twice—half-*Rashomon*, half-*Marnie*—to bring to the surface the torments of the unconscious which previously took the shape of grotesque nightmarish creatures. Freda's ultimate mockery is to load his unhappy Oedipus with a burden of guilt that is not his own; here the sins of the mother are literally passed on to the son, who has to cope for the better part of his existence with the fabricated notion of having murdered his father. The process of discovering the truth—that is, his own innocence—leads him to ruin all the same. To Freda, as it has ever been, evil is a vital part of human nature, and as such it will always win.

The director's reversal of the ancient Greek myth is sneering: not only it is Jocasta who lusts after her son, but she ends up killing the object of her desire in order to forever keep him with her. Freda ends the film with a final and blasphemous act of annihilation, with one of the most powerful—perhaps at least in part because unexpected—endings in his *oeuvre*, one that openly recalls those of *Il conte Ugolino* and *Lo spettro* and which truly lives up to Jacques Lourcelles' definition of the director as "one of the great aesthetes in cinema history."[43] The scene recreates one of the most awe-inspiring icons of classical art, Michelangelo's Pity, in a way that is as elegant as it is cruelly mocking. The image of the Virgin Mary cuddling Jesus on her womb after crucifixion becomes the sight of a murderous mother who cries over the dying son whom she has just killed; a "hellish composition" in which "through the harmony of Renaissance art, dear as always to Freda as a painter and sculptor, and within the most reassuring image, the mother with her son … earthly monstrosities thrive."[44] As Jacqueline Freda recalls, "we spent one day on that scene. It was the only one in the movie which took a whole day to shoot—and one day, to my father, was like a whole week on a normal set! But he really cared about it. I think it was probably the only thing he really cared about in the movie...."[45]

Once again, as in *Lo spettro*, the camera's eye takes on a moral function. Nevertheless, the film's memorable final image can be read in many ways. Perhaps, to Freda, it was also an ideal way to connect to his own past, to his early days as a sculptor in Adolfo Wildt shop, where he tried his hand at reproducing the *Pietà*; in a way, it was yet another circular ending, like the ones he loved most. What is more, it even works as a biting metaphor on the state of the Italian film industry, murdered by the maternal hands of the State by way of absurd and useless laws, its remains exposed for us to mourn. Therefore, the door that closes by itself, peremptorily, subtracting the mother, the son and the heroine to the world and to our view, and delivering them to oblivion, acquires a further, powerful symbolic meaning. It is Freda's hand that closes that door, sealing—with this premature yet late burial—his own film career, and a whole season of Italian cinema.

Epilogue

"We lived through a wonderful time and never even realized it!"[1]

Far from being a summation of his own work, Murder Obsession was supposed to be a shortcut for Freda to return to the limelight, and have the chance to develop more ambitious projects. One such was an adaptation of Alexandre Dumas' *Ascanio*, on which Freda worked in late 1980, immediately after filming Murder Obsession, whereas the other, co-written with the French critic Jacques Lourcelles, was *La Dernière Momie d'Egypte* (The Last Mummy of Egypt), a story of love and reincarnation that should have been produced by Tarak Ben Ammar. Excerpts from both are included in Stefano Della Casa's 1993 book *Riccardo Freda. Un homme seul*.

Freda had been dreaming of making a film of Dumas' novel for a long time. When interviewed by Bertrand Tavernier in 1963, he claimed: "for nothing in the world I would 'make Neorealism' or 'Antonioni-like' stuff. I am horrified by those. No, if I had the chance there are certain stories I'd like to make: I think of several extraordinary novels by Dumas, such as *Ascanio*. But will I therefore propose that to producers? By Dumas, they only know *The Three Musketeers* or *The Count of Monte Cristo*. They only vaguely heard of that and they know it makes money. But the rest, nothing."[2]

The director penned a ten-page synopsis for *Ascanio*, in which he reprised the character of Benvenuto Cellini, the protagonist of *Il magnifico avventuriero*, here accompanied by his young apprentice Ascanio. After taking refuge in France, at the court of King Francis I, the sculptor and his pupil face a series of adventures that revolve around the scheming Madame d'Étampes, who is infatuated with Ascanio and attempts to destroy his love for the young Colombe. Divided into five parts and accompanied by a brief set of notes, dated December 1980, the synopsis' tone and style show a tangible enthusiasm; whereas Murder Obsession had been just a passing commitment, *Ascanio* was much closer to the director's heart. The story is packed full with all the adventure novel staples that the director loved: intrigue and twists, romanticism and thrill, mystery and picaresque humor, courageous and clever heroes and despicable villains. Freda even managed to restage the ending of *Il magnifico avventuriero* (which in turn he had lifted off Dumas' novel in the first place) for the scene where Cellini burns all the furniture of his room in order to make a gigantic statue of Jupiter for the king of France, and since the gold is not enough he merges the tableware.

In the notes accompanying the synopsis, the director went on at length explaining how he wanted to reach a compromise between two different approaches to the story: a romantic one, closer to Dumas' version, and a modern one. Therefore, his intention was to tone down the characters' more naive traits ("they are all too good, sentimental and naive like Ascanio ... too villainous, like Madame d'Étampes or Colombe's father, or too "generous" like Cellini"),[3] and portray them in a way that would fit contemporary tastes. Given the novel's plentiful intrigue, it was useless to invent new plot twists, he added: it would be sufficient to drop the outdated ones. Another option was to either develop the story into a five or six-hour TV series or a two-hour movie. In either case, though, Freda had quite clear what kind of mood he would go for: "The film, in my view, will have to keep essentially a romantic and decorative atmosphere. The splendor of the scenery and costumes, the vivacity of a photography rich in 16th century light and shade effects, so as to leave little breaks in a story dense with twists, will have to serve as a juxtaposition to those characters as seen with a more actual look." For instance, Freda underlined that "his" Cellini had to be very different from Dumas' selfless character, and closer to his own *Il magnifico avventuriero*. He also planned to add "a brief erotic-sexual parenthesis" when Ascanio finds shelter in the home of a beautiful courtesan, and to characterize Colombe's love for the young man with a more concrete sexual element. Basically, it was the same approach as in the director's 1960s adventure films: remaining faithful to his favorite themes, while adapting himself to the times. Such good intentions, however, were to remain on paper: *Ascanio* was destined to become yet another unfulfilled dream.

Penned in 1981–1982, *La Dernière Momie d'Egypte* was no less ambitious, and even more daring in tone and scope, blending costume melodrama, mystery, *amour fou* and a bit of horror. The film would start in ancient Egypt, under the reign of Amenhotep III: the pharaoh's wife, Nepherta, in love with a soldier named Thaiber, kills herself with her lover, in the belief that they will reincarnate and be together in the next life. The woman is given a majestic funeral, while the soldier's body is thrown in a hole in the desert. The two lovers reincarnate in the 20th century, looking for each other, between New York and modern Egypt. Nepherta is a rich woman, Joan Adamson, who has financed an expedition conducted by the archaeologist Ashley, to locate the princess' mummy; she believes to recognize Thaiber in a Greenwich village drug addict, John Simpson, who was the model for a statue of Thaiber that Joan keeps in the garden. When Joan realizes she has been cheated by Ashley, who wanted to exploit her money, she murders him and Simpson. Having failed to reunite with her beloved, the woman blames the god Ra, whose wrath puts an end to the reincarnation cycle. All the mummies in the world turn into dust. The film ends in the future, "when the humans have gotten rid of gods and of the fear of gods," as the director put it: in the last scene, an old man and a child walk in the desert to the ruins of the temple of Ra. The child asks the grandfather what is a god, and the answer is: "Something that existed once, long time ago. When men still ignored courage, the courage of simply being men...."

As with *Ascanio*, it all came to nothing, as did other less adventurous attempts. Boetani and Freda traveled to New York, several months after the making of *Murder Obsession*, to discuss the possibility of other low-budget horror movies with American producers. Freda was trying to cash in on his by-now established fame as the father of the Italian horror film, but the timing and circumstances proved unfavorable. "Since Riccardo was not in good economic conditions in that period, I agreed to go with him and help him find a deal," the producer recalls. "We went and stayed there for a couple of weeks, but without really coming up to anything concrete, because we realized that those potential financers were not so brilliant and, so to speak, reliable."[4]

In the 1980s and 1990s, Freda's work met a renewed interest on the part of critics, film festivals and young cinephiles: to quote Stefano Della Casa, "to organize an homage was a necessary step, a revendication of cinephile militancy."[5] This resulted in a renewed visibility for the septuagenarian director. He was the special guest at the Lux Film retrospective during the 1984 Locarno Film Festival; three years later he was a member of the Jury at Salsomaggiore; and in 1989 he attended a retrospective of his films in Bologna. The next year it was Turin's Sport Film Festival that paid homage to him, while in 1991 he had the chance to talk about his early involvement in the *telefoni bianchi* comedies at the Pesaro Festival, and enjoyed yet another retrospective of his work in Locarno, followed in 1993 by another one in Bergamo—both accompanied by monographic volumes. His status of "master of horror" was also celebrated in a three-part TV program called *Il cinema della paura*, directed by his former assistant Marcello Avallone (who underwent a brief moment of popularity after directing the horror film *Spettri*, 1987) and Patrizia Pistagnesi, and broadcast in November 1986 on RaiTre. The elderly director appeared in the first installment: sitting on an armchair by a fireplace, in a studio set made to look like a castle hall, complete with thunder and lighting, he played with gusto the part of the world-weary lord of the castle, explaining for the umpteenth time his conception of fear and of the horror film in general with his usual eloquence and property of language.

Despite his age, Freda was as sharp and intellectually brilliant as ever, but the many sincere homages only served to underline his belonging to a past age that would never come back. By 1990, Italian cinema was a sleeping corpse, like one of Dr. Hichcock's favorite diversions, and there was no way it could be reanimated. Too much sedative—this time, lethal for good. The economic hemorrhage that had led to the closing of so many theater houses (later recycled as banks or shopping malls) was only one factor. There was also the invasion of television, which had caused cinema to lose its centrality. And then there was politics, which had destroyed any chance of the decaying tissue to recover. Who would allow Freda to shoot a film in two weeks, if there was no distribution circuit to grant a release? And who would even think of financing a movie like, say, *L'orribile segreto del Dr. Hichcock*, after the Mammì law in 1991 had practically submitted the film production to the supremacy of television? Freda had often criticized Neorealism, but the landscape that was before him in his eighties was much more chilling: a never ending parade of harmless, cookie-cut comedies designed for TV consumption. The other genres were reduced to a few names (such as Dario Argento) who were finding it harder and harder to keep the commercial relevance they had enjoyed in the previous decades. It was bitterly apt, then, that the man who had witnessed the birth of Cinecittà was now sitting by the river's edge, watching Italian cinema die, little by little.

When evoking those times of grandeur and creativity, Riccardo Freda sounded like a survivor from a distant past, an old sage who still breathed cinema and could well give a lesson to any of those semi-improvised young filmmakers born with a silver spoon in their mouth, who kept churning out undistinguished dreck, and blissfully fulfilled his prophecy about the world's easiest job being at the mercy of a bubbling idiocracy. And yet, there was no room for him behind the camera—not even in the safe waters of the small screen. In an article that appeared in the Winter 1987 issue of the magazine *Shock Xpress*, writer Ed Senior recalled that when Bruce Beresford was making *King David* (1985), shot for the most part in the Italian regions of Abruzzo-Molise, Basilicata and Sardinia, Freda was called in to direct exterior action sequences, but when he arrived, he "was treated dismissively by his Australian colleague, who told the press that this Italian was of no use to the production, as his experience was not suitable."[6]

Freda had been toying with the idea of remaking *Beatrice Cenci*, and asked Bertrand Tavernier's wife Colo O'Hagan to work on a scenario, but could not manage to find a producer.[7] Tavernier became interested in the project, which would became *La passion Béatrice*, with the story transposed from Renaissance Italy to 14th century France, during the Hundred Years War. Out of respect, the French filmmaker invited Freda on the set as technical advisor, and dedicated the film to him. The Italian director's contribution, as he admitted, was minimal, though: "I took care of the horses a bit and gave him some suggestions, which he did not need. He had entrusted me with a second camera, which was a plaything rather than a true necessity. But I shot very few things. I suggested him to film a *maquette* ceiling in order to squeeze the characters a bit, but his art directors opposed it."[8] In the late 1980s, during a Parisian stay, Freda even showed up in one of his rare acting roles in the only film directed by stage director Pierre Pradinas, the intimate drama *Un tour de manège* (1989), starring Juliette Binoche and François Cluzet and featuring a young Denis Lavant; aptly, he played a movie director named Riccardo.

The only other trace of Freda's presence during the decade is *Stille di sangue e lacrime di rospo* (1987), a shot-on-video directorial essay made by the alumni of the Promovies film school in Padua, one of the very first film schools that were born and developed in the country outside Rome's CSC, where Freda taught a course in 1987–88. Promovies founder Gianni Vitale, who invited the director over to Padua, recalled: "It was quite a bold move for the period, to have someone like Freda teaching a film course. Back then, he was not considered an *auteur* but a B-movie director—actually, not even someone like Mario Monicelli, or Ettore Scola, was considered as such. There was a very closed-mindedness on the part of the academic teachers, and consequently by the local authorities."[9]

Filmmaker Pietro Reggiani, who attended Freda's lessons, recalls:

> I remember him as an affable person, who always showed up with his wife but was very happy to interact, with extreme grace and finesse, with a group of girls who proposed themselves as preferred interlocutors. He told us many anecdotes, which I believe were all in his memoir, which had been published in those years, such as the one about the lions in the Arena of Verona, flooded to shoot a scene for *Spartaco*.... He often told about his skills as a director, as when he managed to shoot a film in two weeks, or when he salvaged a movie where the only good scene was a fire, which he repeated throughout the entire film. He said he would like to shoot a movie in Padua, the bloody and adventurous story of Ezzelino da Romano.[10] He said that with a few tricks we could easily recreate the medieval town—I have to say that the subject was far away from what we would like to do, so that, delay after delay, he finished the course without having decided what essay we'd make. But some enterprising students decided to make a two-hour documentary about him, *Stille di sangue e lacrime di rospo*.[11]

The movie includes excerpts of interviews with Freda, who plays the director everyone loves to hate with amiable coherence (with such sharp-tongued, provocative statements as "If in Papuasia there was a film industry, it would be better than ours..."), as well as footage from his movies interspersed with excerpts from pictures by other filmmakers who shared a very similar vision and spirit, and sometimes seem to have been directly inspired by him. Whether Steven Spielberg had actually seen or not *I miserabili* is debatable; still, by juxtaposing Jean Valjean's escape on a mine carriage from Freda's film and the celebrated rollercoaster sequence in *Indiana Jones and the Temple of Doom* (1984), one cannot help thinking that, despite the almost 40-year hiatus, both filmmakers had the same aim: cinema as fable, entertainment, wonder, escape from everyday reality.

Stille di sangue e lacrime di rospo was shown at the 1988 Venice Film Festival, in a collateral section, to good critical praise; however, because of technical problems (a somewhat low audio recording) as well as for the use of music whose rights had not been paid, it did not circulate outside the festival circuit.

In 1990, the news came that Freda was being evicted from his house in Rome.[12] Again, France seemed to be a refuge—or rather, a mirage. He took Silvana with him, and had her hospitalized in a clinic where she was submitted to experimental cures with lithium, from which she drew some benefit. Moreover, in France, the director could nurture the dream of returning behind the camera. His daughters had grown, and moved on with their lives: there was no need for him to be a father anymore. And he was surrounded and supported by admirers, who kept remarking their love for his work whenever possible: in June 1988 he had even received the prestigious Medal of Commander of Arts and Letters at the Cinémathèque Française. To the Italian press, this seemed incomprehensible, especially given the sharp judgments that Freda kept distributing about Neorealism and the sacred cows of Italian cinema.

Still, his economic conditions were problematic: during the 1993 Bergamo retrospective, a petition was launched in order to admit the 84-year-old director to the benefits from the "Bacchelli law," which granted a pension to illustrious personalities from the cultural and artistic world in dire straits. The first signer of the petition was Bertrand Tavernier.[13]

Out of friendship and respect, the French filmmaker tried again to bring the octagenarian colleague behind the camera during the early 1990s. In July 1991, Freda announced to newspapers that he was going to make his comeback with "a Disney-like movie": a French/Italian co-production aimed at kids with a financial participation on the part of the European Economic Community, with the French filmmaker acting as guarantor, titled *Animal's Gang*. "A magical and popular adventure, full of fights and twists, with plenty of action and lots of humor, according to those that have always been the characteristics of my films," he enthused.[14]

The main concept drew on his 1961 movie *Caccia all'uomo*, about the adventures of a police dog who at one point releases a kidnapped little girl, and pushed further the comedy and fantasy element. An early draft of the script (which seems to be identical to the movie Freda wanted to make), kept at Rome's CSC and titled…. *E se gli animali parlassero…?* (…What If Animals Could Talk…?), is dated October 30, 1984, proving that the director had had the project on the shelf for years.[15] His daughter Jacqueline helped out as usual: he dictated, she typed.

The subtitle, "a modern fairytale by Riccardo Freda," sets the tone for the whole film, which opens on a dark stormy night, with the kidnapping of Count Lugnano's younger sons, Alessandro and Claudia, by a gang of masked bandits. The kidnappers demand a 5 billion *lire* ransom, and the vice-chief of police Rinaldi and his bumbling, obtuse men suspect the Count's introverted elder son Roberto (a biker whose only concern seem to be the animals in his stables—actually a sort of zoo, with not just horses but also lions, a panther, a falcon, a boa, dobermanns, a chimp…) and the two grooms, a couple of Brit sisters by the names of Mary and Joan. The animals, led by a mynah bird, gather together in the stable and discuss the situation: it turns out that they communicate through speech and that they are even smarter than humans. The animals conceive an elaborate plan to locate and release the kids.

The story moves on predictably, with Bob and the two girls carrying out a mysterious plan to put together the ransom money (which has the police assume they are actually the kidnappers), and a wild motorbike chase in the country. Eventually Bob and the animals team up to defeat the bad guys—who, in a rather annoying aside, are revealed to be Sardinians, like the most infamous kidnappers operating in Italy in the 1970s—with the extra help of a Collie shepherd dog, a flock of sheep, and a skunk, whose stinking exhalations act as a diversion before the big climax. The director described the animals' attack to the kidnappers' shack, as "*The Alamo*, with the animals on one side and the bandits on the other."[16] Here, however, Freda was probably drawing from his earlier films, such as *Spartaco* and *Teodora*, as the script imagines the lion and the panther assaulting and immobilizing (with no bloodshed this time) the villains.

Overall, the script for *Animal's Gang* reads like Freda's attempt to turn into reality one of his favorite axioms—he'd rather direct animals than actors; what is more, the characters of the two dynamic British girls are likely patterned on his own daughters Jacqueline and Guislaine. Still, the result is pretty dire. The would-be funny dialogue exchanges between the animals border on the embarrassing: a falcon speaks in a foul language worthy of a seasoned longshoreman, the chimp refers to evolutionism ("If we hadn't existed, there would be no men"), whereas the mynah bird quotes von Clausewitz ("Surprise guarantees success"), name-drops the famous Italian circus celebrity Moira Orfei and even references the infamous pseudo-Masonic lodge, "Loggia P2." All this sounds unfunny on paper, and despite Freda's technical ability one wonders how the director would have managed to make the movie work with such a lazy script. Chris Noonan's *Babe* (1995) showed that a motion picture about talking animals could be an extraordinary effort, but even with all of Freda's good will, *Animal's Gang* looked at best like a tired, outdated rehash of some modest Disney movie from the 1960s.

The director resumed *Animal's Gang* from the shelf after his meeting with a young filmmaker, Roberto Torelli, who got in touch with him to have advice on the film he was trying to put together, and which featured many action scenes. Freda persuaded Torelli to abandon his project and help him on his directorial comeback instead. Like the French critics who had met Freda two decades earlier, Torelli was struck by the elderly director's personality, so much so that he dutifully agreed to become his esquire in yet another assault to the windmills.[17] Freda suggested involving Bertrand Tavernier in the project, as a producer; Ettore Scola joined them too.[18] The script[19] was granted financing on the part of the EEC, and the makers attempted to have access to a grant by Italy's Istituto LUCE, but to no avail.

Tavernier was also involved in Freda's next project. It was another of the Italian director's longtime admirers, Pierre Rissient, then working as artistic consultant with the Paris-based production company Ciby 2000, who got a project off the ground which Freda had conceived with his biographer and friend Éric Poindron, *La Fille de d'Artagnan*—the result of his longtime dissatisfaction with *Il figlio di d'Artagnan*. The story was basically a remake of the 1950 film: this time, though, d'Artagnan's young son, Raoul, turned into a beautiful young girl, Eloise. It was itself a Dumas-like effort, a *Twenty Years After* with the octagenarian filmmaker as a modern-day d'Artagnan who resumes his cape and sword and launches himself at full gallop against the enemy—that is, nearly everyone else in the movie business. And wins. This is probably how Riccardo Freda saw it.

The project seemed to be born under a good star: Ciby 2000 greenlighted the project, with the participation of Little Bear and Tavernier once again serving as patron, and a first-rate cast led by Sophie Marceau as Eloise, and with the special participation of Philippe Noiret as d'Artagnan. The scriptwriting credits feature a long list of names: Freda and Poindron are credited with the idea, while the scenario is by Michel Léviant, who took care also of the screenplay adaptation together with Tavernier and Jean Cosmos, while the dialogue is credited to Léviant and Cosmos.

Unfortunately, *La Fille de d'Artagnan* (1994) was doomed to be Freda's ultimate and most bitter failure. Newspapers of the time reported that he had been replaced at the eleventh hour by Tavernier himself. The French filmmaker told the press:

> The idea of replacing my friend Riccardo Freda was not mine, but came from our common producer, Fred Bourboulon. Concerned about the rising costs of the project, about the director's advanced age (would an 84-year-old manage to shoot a movie this rich with action and hold off all those actors?) and worried by the lackluster feeling between the gruff Italian filmmaker and the young heroine (the project was born around Sophie Marceau: without her, no film), a week after shooting started, the producer decided to replace the director.[20]

Freda's lack of diplomacy with actors was notorious, and he and Marceau did not get along at all from the very beginning. The rehearsals were marked by a heated argument between them, after which the director refused to make peace with the actress, despite the intervention of Tavernier and his son Nils. Freda proposed to leave the set whenever Marceau was to be part of a scene, a solution Bourboulon promptly discarded, and a compromise was eventually reached: Tavernier would join Freda as co-director, in order to prevent Marceau from leaving the picture.[21] But when the crew moved to Portugal to start filming, the situation got quickly worse, leading to Freda walking off the set. Stefano Della Casa maintains that Freda left after only one day, after a violent argument with the actress.[22] Jacqueline Freda is even more tranchent: "He couldn't stand Sophie Marceau, not even for one day. So he told her to fuck off and left. And that was that. And of course it damaged his friendship with Tavernier...."[23]

However, it was not simply the result of a personal clash between the filmmaker and the movie's star, but also a matter of budget: Freda's intention to shoot fast ("I'll make the film in four weeks ... cinema is action, emotion, tension, speed...") and without live sound clashed against the economic demands of contemporary filmmaking. As Philippe Noiret later told the press,

> Freda wanted to shoot it quickly, leaving a lot of freedom to the actors, and Sophie Marceau got worried that she wouldn't be helped enough. So she demanded that Tavernier assist Freda. Then, when we arrived in Portugal for the shooting and Bertrand saw the locations chosen by Riccardo, he got worried too. So he decided to take hold of the situation, and Riccardo, understandably, got angry and left the set. It was a painful but necessary choice. I too, after meeting him, got convinced that Riccardo couldn't physically endure such a challenging film, shot in midwinter and with so many action scenes.[24]

Practically ostracized on the set after his clash with Marceau, and in the absence of Tavernier, who had gone scouting for missing locations with the rest of the crew, Freda did what his pride, honor and temper demanded him to do. He flew back to Rome. There, he received a telegram from Tavernier, who vainly tried to have him back on the set to co-direct at least the big battle on the galleon. "Riccardo, come back, we adore you." He didn't. As a result, a film about a daughter who reunites with her father, produced by a virtual son in order to celebrate his spiritual father, ended with the latter abandoning (and being abandoned by) the former. What was meant as an act of love and friendship turned sour for everyone involved. Freda was more than embittered—he was outraged.

He felt betrayed, backstabbed by the friend who was supposed to put him back in the saddle. "It was the most obscene thing that ever happened in my life. I would perhaps have expected something like that to happen in Italy, but from a Frenchman?!"[25] Perhaps, what he didn't want to admit was that what had stabbed him in the back was cinema itself, now a very different creature from the one he had learned to know and master since his early years in Egypt. And that creature did not need someone like Riccardo Freda anymore.

Upon returning to Rome, Silvana's condition got worse. And worse. More hospitalizations followed. "My mother's illness drained him in his last years. Guislaine and I were grown-ups, had our own lives, could not give him a hand. He had to do all by himself," Jacqueline commented.[26] Nevertheless, Freda kept dreaming about making movies, even though he seemed mostly interested in the challenge itself and not in the film—as a way to feel alive and kicking again, in short. During an interview with Luigi Cozzi at the latter's "Profondo Rosso" shop in Rome, he claimed:

> Thanks to video technique, today I feel ready to shoot a whole movie in one day. Yeah, write it down: I am convinced I could easily shoot a *giallo* or a crime film in one day, today, using videocameras. And who knows, sooner or later I might really make it. We could shoot it right here, all in this shop and in its fabulous basement: then, the next morning, we could screen it right here, to friends and fans ... what do you say?[27]

If cinema was now only a matter of dreams, his daughter Jacqueline was Riccardo's pride: first, fulfilling the dream she had followed since working on the set of *Estratto dagli archivi segreti della polizia di una capitale europea*, she had become a stuntwoman: "I was so mad about stunts that I took my father at the movies to watch *Hooper*, starring Burt Reynolds as 'the greatest stuntman alive'—eight days in a row! Eventually he gave up: 'Do what the fuck you want about your life but I'm not gonna watch this movie ever again!'"[28] Then, sharing the family's love for horses, she had become Italy's greatest jockey. Freda was overwhelmed with joy, as Luigi Cozzi recalls:

> I was a friend of the critic Vittorio Giacci, then the head of Cinecittà and Istituto Luce, who often organized dinners and invited top executives, politicians, directors, actresses, etc. For a period Freda showed up at these dinners, because Giacci and Cinecittà had organized a retrospective of his works at Locarno, which had been a huge success. Freda was so proud of his daughter, who won a lot of horse races, that he practically forced us all to watch them on TV, on the Teleippica channel![29]

In recalling the director's liveliness, Jacqueline Freda maintains:

> My father's modernity was astounding. I mean, for a man born in 1909, having to raise two adolescent daughters would seem a desperate challenge. And yet the way he taught us about life could be compared to that of a much younger parent. Our relationship was based on mutual trust, and we used to tell him about everything. I remember one morning, I was 19, and the night earlier I had smoked my first joint. It had been a rather weird and unpleasant experience, and I just couldn't wait to have breakfast with dad and tell him everything about the experience, because I felt guilty. So, we're having breakfast, and I go, "You know, Dad, yesterday I smoked weed," and he, "Oh really? And what did it feel like?" He was very calm and understanding, he did not reproach me at all but just advised me not to go too far. We were talking about it as if we were a couple of friends sitting at the table, regardless of the fact that there were three generations between me and my dad. And that was that.[30]

In his late years, Freda was paid homage by young colleagues—a sign of the steady reappreciation of his work on the part of the new generations. In June 1996 Giuseppe Tornatore, whose *Nuovo Cinema Paradiso* (a.k.a. *Cinema Paradiso*, 1988) had won the Academy Award for Best Foreign Film in 1989, met Freda for an informal interview: the conversation was published in 2007 by the Taormina Festival in a bilingual version, Italian and English, as *Il quarto moschettiere / The Fourth Musketeer*,[31] and formed the basis for the Tornatore-directed episode of the series *Ritratti d'autore*, dedicated to prestigious Italian directors, which aired in November 1996.

In 1998 Rome's CSC entrusted Mimmo Calopresti (the director of the intense drama *La seconda volta*, 1995) to make a documentary on the 89-year-old Freda. The 45 minute long *Un uomo solo* (A Man Alone), displays a moving empathy for a director apparently so distant from Calopresti's approach to filmmaking: the result is "almost a sentimental education of the new Italian cinema toward a director so far in age and tastes."[32] Filmed by Calopresti during a pilgrimage to several significant sites in his career and life (Rome's Centro Sperimentale, the now-dilapidated studio backlot where he shot a memorable scene of *I miserabili*, the terrace at Trinità dei Monti near the house where he once had lived), Freda looks indeed a man alone; yet, when Stefano Della Casa asks him about his past, the elderly director displays the usual nonchalant frankness, and wipes away any attempt on Calopresti's part to present him in a melancholic, pitiful way, thanks to his customary dose of cynicism. But he cannot help injecting such a disenchanted look on a long-gone era with a lively sense of humor: when asked why he had chosen to shoot the opening sequence of *Beatrice Cenci* with a long take, he replies "Maybe I was drunk that day."

A portrait of Riccardo Freda taken in 1998 by André Bakker, during the Rotterdam International Film Festival.

It was an apt epilogue, one last reverent bow to the retired musketeer.

Even in his late days, Freda had not lost his sharp tongue and will to provoke the listener, such as when he told Giuseppe Tornatore, the author of the outstanding Camorra drama *Il camorrista* (a.k.a. *The Professor*, 1986) that after all the Cammorists were better than most people he had known. And there was some kind of *cupio dissolvi* in the mordant way he recalled his past glory, even if that meant telling for the umpteenth time the same anecdote on the birth of *I vampiri*. When it's all over, and all you have are memories, better be the good ones that lead to your grave. As he himself put it, "I can't have any regrets, because I've had everything that a man could possibly desire from the movie business: money, wealth, beautiful women, an easy life, cars, the most beautiful cars in the world."[33]

Riccardo Freda died on December 20, 1999. Like with Bava and Fulci's before him, his death coincided with (and was partially obscured by) the passing of a renowned film director, Robert Bresson, deceased on December 18. Up to a few months prior to his death, he had been lucid and active as ever. Then, as Jacqueline put it, "he just did not make it anymore. All of a sudden, he surrendered. He had a physical and mental collapse, and in the blink of an eye it was over. I think those last years had been too much for him."[34] Silvana Merli—whom he had married in 1996, as a way to at least guarantee her the legal benefits of marriage—followed him three months later, on February 27, 2000. That same year, Jacqueline ended her career as jockey and returned to Cinecittà, where she has established herself as a top-notch stuntwoman and horse master. "I think it was the need to return to an environment where my name was his name again. In the racetrack, Freda was me; here in Cinecittà, Freda was my father. And I felt the need to keep that name, and its memory, alive."[35]

I have never visited Riccardo Freda's tomb, but I like to fancy that there is an epitaph engraved on it. A cinephile quote which he might have surely appreciated.

"I am big, it's the pictures that got small!"

Filmography

This filmography has 3 sections: Collaborations 289; As Director 302; Films on Freda 328. The films in each section are listed chronologically, based on release dates. If a movie was given a visa in December 1938 and was released theatrically in January 1939, it is dated 1939. Italian visa numbers are given for a few foreign productions to provide both the Italian release dates and those for other countries. Running times are based on the effective length in meters of the copies submitted to the Italian board of censors.

Abbreviations

The following abbreviations are used in the credits list for each entry:

Crew: AC: Assistant camera; ACO: Costume assistant; AD: Assistant director; AE: Assistant editor; AMU: Assistant makeup; APD: Production design assistant; ArtD: Art director; B: Boom man; C: Camera; ChEl: Chief electrician; CHOR: Choreographer; CO: Costumes; CON: Continuity; D: directed by; DialD: Dialogue coach / Dialogue director; DOP: Director of photography; DubD: Dubbing director; E: Editor; El: Electrician; G: Grip; GA: Gaffer; Hair: Hairdresser; KG: Key grip; LT: lighting technician; M: Music; MA: Master of arms; Mix: Sound mixer; MU: Makeup; OE: Optical effects; PD: Production designer; PrM: Property manager; S: Story; 2ndAD: 2nd Assistant director; SC: Screenplay; SD: Set decoration; SE: Special effects; SO: Sound; SOE: Special sound effects; SP: Still photographer; SS: Script supervisor / Script girl; W: Wardrobe.

Production: ADM: Administrator; AP: Associate producer; EP: Executive producer; GM: General manager; PA: Production assistant; PM: Production manager; PROD: Produced by; PS: Production supervisor; PSe: Production secretary; PseA: Production secretary assistant; UM: Unit manager; UMA: assistant unit manager.

Collaborations

Lasciate ogni speranza

Italy 1937, b&w, 84 minutes

D: Gennaro Righelli. S: based on the play *L'agonia di Schizzo* by Athos Setti. SC: Riccardo Freda, Camillo Mariani dell'Anguillara [and Edoardo Antonelli, uncredited]. DOP: Carlo Montuori. M: Cesare A. Bixio.

Cast: Antonio Gandusio (Pasquale Grifone), María Denis (Gina Grifone), Rosina Anselmi (Filomena Grifone), Giorgio De Rege (Giovanni), Guido De Rege (Arturo), Elli Parvo (Gemma), Maria Dominiani (Assunta), Mario Siletti (Jack Hilton), Angelo Bizzari, Mario Colli, Rocco D'Assunta, Walter Grant, Edwige Masing, Giulio Mostocotto, Luigi Pellegrini, Edoardo Toniolo.

PROD: Juventus Film (Rome). Visa n. 29792 (9/22/1937, m. 2324). Release date: October 1937. Distribution: Juventus Film.

Pasquale Grifone, a modest theatrical agent, wins a huge sum by playing at the lottery a series of numbers he 'saw' in a dream. However, the winning has a downside: the dream predicted the exact moment—in days, hours and minutes—of Pasquale's death. Was it a premonition after all? Even though they have become rich, Pasquale, his wife Filomena and his daughter Gina await in despair the alleged moment of the man's demise...

L'allegro cantante

Italy 1938, b&w, 78 minutes

D: Gennaro Righelli. S: Edoardo Anton [Edoardo Antonelli], Riccardo Freda, Camillo Mariani Dell'Anguillara. SC: Edoardo Anton, Riccardo Freda, Camillo Mariani Dell'Anguillara, Gennaro Righelli. DOP: Carlo Montuori. M: Cesare A. Bixio, Armando Fragna, Pasquale Frustaci. E: Gennaro Righelli, Filippo Walter Ratti. PD: Alfredo Montuori, Giorgio Pinzauti. AD: Filippo Walter Ratti.

Cast: Giovanni Manurita (The tenor), Germana Paolieri (The tenor's girlfriend), Vandina Guglielmi (The little girl), Giorgio De Rege, Guido De Rege, Giovanni Barrella, Rubi D'Alma, Nicola Maldacea, Olivia Fried, Maria Dominiani, Cesare Zoppetti, Guglielmo Sinaz, Gino Viotti, Walter Grant, Maria Polese, Ornella Da Vasto, Alessandro Antonelli, Guelfo Chiarini. Tina Lenzi, Lia Rosa, Franca Barale, Olinto Cristina.

PROD: Juventus Film (Rome). PM: Raffaele Colamonici. Visa n. 30004 (1/25/1938, m. 2160). Release date: February 1938. Distribution: Juventus Film.

Following the terms of a will, which appoints them as the heirs of a prominent heritage on the condition that they locate the father of a little girl, two bumbling brothers—assisted by a friend and the latter's girlfriend—carry out their investigation in the upper-class world. After many adventures they discover that their friend (who is also a talented tenor) is the little girl's father. However, when it comes to cash in on the inheritance, the brothers find out that it has gone up in smoke following a collapse of the stock market. Meanwhile the tenor has become famous, and has embarked on a brilliant career. He and his girlfriend get married and raise the girl.

Fuochi d'artificio

Italy 1938, b&w, 76 minutes

D: Gennaro Righelli. S: based on the play by Luigi Chiarelli. SC: Riccardo Freda, Gennaro Righelli, Luigi Chiarelli. DOP: Domenico Scala [and Carlo Montuori, uncredited]. M: Cesare A. Bixio, Franco Casavola. E: Fernando Tropea. PD: Alfredo Montori. ArtD: Camillo Del Signore. MU: Arcangelo Aversa. AD: Filippo Walter Ratti. SO: Ovidio Del Grande. SS: Gennaro Balistrieri.

Cast: Amedeo Nazzari (Gerardo di Jersay), Gery Land [Linda Pini] (Daisy D'Elsing), Vanna Vanni (Elena D'Argirò), Giuseppe Porelli (Scaramanzia), Luigi Carini (Prince Tommaso D'Angiò), Romolo Costa (Rodolfo Meseri), Talia Volpiana [Neda Naldi] (Diana), Carlo Bressan (Giorgio), Corrado De Cenzo (Duke Ottimo D'Alfa), Anna Valpreda (Gisella); *uncredited*: Renato Chiantoni, Alba Ferrarotti, Carmine Garibaldi, Jucci Kellerman, Pino Locchi, Giorgio Malvezzi, Renato Navarrini, Gennaro Sabatano, Aura Sortis, Germana Vivian.

PROD: Juventus Film (Rome). PM: Raffaele Colamonici. PSe: Gennaro Masullo. Visa n. 30375 (10/25/1938, m. 2098). Release date: December 1938. Distribution: Juventus Film.

A young man, Gerardo, returns from America even more penniless than when he left. At the hotel where he is staying, though, his old friends are convinced that he is very wealthy. The word spreads and Gerardo's secretary attempts a bold shot at the stock exchange, in order to save him from humiliation. The coup succeeds: Gerardo becomes truly rich and marries the girl he loves.

La voce senza volto

Italy 1939, b&w, 69 minutes

D: Gennaro Righelli. S: Corrado D'Errico. SC: Corrado D'Errico, Aldo De Benedetti, Riccardo Freda, Ivo Perilli. DOP: Domenico Scala. M: Cesare A. Bixio. E: Gisa Radicchi Levi. PD: Alfredo Montori. MU: Arcangelo Aversa. AD: Filippo Walter Ratti. SO: Ovidio Del Grande.

Cast: Giovanni Manurita (Gino Malversi), Laura Nucci (Doris), Vanna Vanni (Mirella Bonardi), Elsa De Giorgi (Actress), Carlo Romano (Maurizio Sala, the tenor), Romolo Costa (Riva, the film director), Claudio Ermelli (Tabarrini), Adele Garavaglia (Gino's mother), Anita Farra (Hostel Owner), Corrado De Cenzo (Producer), Nietta Zocchi (The Actress' Maid), Lidia Bartolini, Gianni Cavalieri (Man with the Pen), Vasco Creti (Doctor), Ilia Duchini, Aldo Fiorelli (Moviola Technician), Ernesto Gentili, Giorgio Malvezzi (Kramer), Antonietta Marchi, Angelo Montagna (Assistant Director), Peppino Nicolosi (Rossi), Pietro Nofri, Jone Romano (Maria), Domenico Serra (Assistant Director), Anna Valpreda (Actress).

PROD: Juventus Film (Rome). PM: Raffaele Colamonici. Visa n. 30451 (12/16/1938, m. 1906). Release date: 1/5/1939. Distribution: Juventus Film.

Gino, a shipyard worker whose voice is similar

to that of a famous tenor, is hired by a Cinecittà production company to dub the singer on a movie after the latter has lost his voice. Gino realizes too late that he has been deceived, because the terms of the contract commit him to absolute secrecy. However, he eventually achieves the fame he deserves after challenging the singer whose voice he has dubbed to a singing duel, and finds true love in the person of the producer's secretary, Doris.

Piccoli naufraghi

Italy 1939, b&w, 83 minutes

D: Flavio Calzavara. S: Giuseppe Zucca. SC: Leo Bomba, Flavio Calzavara, Riccardo Freda. DOP: Arturo Gallea, Aldo Tonti. M: Renzo Rossellini, conducted by Ugo Giacomozzi. E: Ferdinando Maria Poggioli. AD: Riccardo Freda. PD: Italo Cremona. SO: Mario Amari. SD: Savino Fino. SS: Gino Betrone, Maria Cecchi.

Cast: Romolo Aglietti (Donghi), Mario Angelini (Grandi), Mario Artese (Colella), Guglielmo Brunetti (Bruno), Remo Castagnoli (Ferrini), Nello De Rossi (Silvestri), Luigi Lucifora (Perché), Leo Melchiorri (Esposito), Roberto Pironti (De Renzis), Gerolamo Prestigiacomo (Minutillo), Pietro Signoretti (Rossi), Rolando Vona (Pisani), Ali Ibrahim Sidali (Simba), Giovanni Grasso (The Commander), Riccardo Santelmi [Riccardo Freda] (Professor Giannini), Felice Minotti (The Petty Officer), Carlo Duse (Chief Smuggler), Mario Terchietti (Godfather), Galaor [Alfredo Boccolini] (Tattooed Man), Salvatore Cuffaro (Loony), Pietro Baldi (Cabin Boy), Giuseppe Angelini, Roberto Angelini, Renzo Brunetti, Franco Caruso, Elio Dalilla, Enrico Effernelli, Felice Minotti, Alfredo Petroni, Alvaro Zerboni.

PROD: Eugenio Fontana for Mediterranea Film (Rome). PS: Piero Cocco. Filmed at Pisorno Studios (Tirrenia). Visa n. 30478 (1/4/1939, m. 2282). Release date: 1/30/1939. Distribution: Mediterranea Film.

Also known as: *Piccoli avventurieri* (U.S.A.), *Pequeños naufragos* (Spain).

Note: Freda's pseudonym is actually spelled as "Riccardo Santelini" in the Spanish language credits of the copy kept at the Cineteca Nazionale.

Following their school teacher, twelve boys embark clandestinely on the merchant ship Perseo, en route to Oceania, where the father of one of them has emigrated. However, the boys are soon discovered and the Perseo deviates toward Suez to land them. Unfortunately, a thick fog causes a collision at sea which results in a shipwreck. By means of a lifeboat, the boys reach a remote island where they settle as best they can. One day a sailing ship lands on the isle: the captain and crew are shady types, and turn out to be arms dealers. The boys cleverly manage to get hold of the ship, after a fierce fight with the crew, and return to Italy aboard it.

Il cavaliere di San Marco

Italy 1939, b&w, 76 minutes

D: Gennaro Righelli. S: Alessandro De Stefani. Adaptation: Luigi Chiarelli, Gennaro Righelli. SC: Alessandro De Stefani, Gherardo Gherardi, Edoardo Anton, Renato Castellani, Riccardo Freda. DOP: Domenico Scala. M: Cesare A. Bixio, Franco Casavola. E: Vincenzo Zampi. PD: Alfredo Montori. CO: Gino Sensani. MU: Arcangelo Aversa. SO: Ovidio Del Grande.

Cast: Mario Ferrari (Daniele Orsenigo), Dria Paola (Stefania), Laura Nucci (Teresa), Romolo Costa (Tito Orsenigo), Sandro Ruffini (Orsenigo's father), Renato Cialente (Commissioner Von Krauss), Vanna Vanni (Bianca), Augusto Di Giovanni (Bauer), Michele Malaspina (Andrea), Ruggero Capodaglio, Pina DE Angelis, Corrado De Cenzo, Anita Farra, Giovanni Ferrari, Pietro Nofri, Massimo Pianforini, Ivano Viganò, Loretta Vicni, Liliana Zanardi.

PROD: Renato Cogliati Dezza for Juventus Film (Rome). PM: Raffaele Colamonici. Visa n. 30552 (3/14/1939, m. 2112). Release date: 4/10/1939. Distribution: Juventus Film.

Also known as: *The Knight of San Marco* (English title—World-wide)

Early 19th century. During the Italian unification period, the young Venetian patriot Daniele Orsenigo is heading to Parma with an important document for his fellow revolutionaries. At an inn he meets a young woman whom he falls for. Overnight the paper is stolen from him and is found the next morning on the person of Daniele's brother, who is sentenced to life imprisonment. Daniele goes in search of the mysterious woman and, after various vicissitudes, he finally discovers that she is the wife of the new governor of Venice. She tries to protect him, but to no avail. Chased by the police, Orsenigo returns home just in time to catch his father's last breath. The dying man tells Daniele that he was the Knight of St. Mark, the mysterious head of the revolutionary patriots, and leaves his son the legacy of his name and mission.

Fascino

Italy 1940, b&w, 81 minutes
D: Giacinto Solito. S: Sebastiano A. Luciani, Henry Clark. SC: Sebastiano A. Luciani, Camillo Mariani Dell'Aguillara, Henry Clark. DOP: Piero Pupilli. M: Franco Casavola. E: Giuseppe Fatigati [and Riccardo Freda, uncredited]. PD, SD: Salvo D'Angelo. CO: Luciano Forzano Roncato. AD: Mario Monicelli.
Cast: Iva Pacetti (Ada, the singer), Silvana Jachino (Liliana), Cesare Bettarini (Paolo), Bella Starace Sainati (The Aunt), Guglielmo Sinaz (The Impresario), Liliana Aloy, Guglielmo Barnabò, Vasco Creti, Lilli Dusi (Liliana as a child), Anita Farra, Camilla Lo Faso, Elodia Maresca, Carlo Mariotti, Giacomo Moschini, Mario Pucci, Mario Siletti, Elio Steiner.
PROD: Virginio Albarello for Viralba Film (Rome). Visa n. 30756 (10/25/1939, m. 2234). PM: Giacinto Solito. Release date: March 1940 Distribution: Tirrenia Film.

Ada, a famous soprano singer, is not willing to star in Bellini's "Norma," since ten years earlier, during a recital of the opera in which she starred, a sudden fire broke out on stage. In the ensuing panic, Ada's little sister Liliana was overrun by the crowd and the shock left her mute. Liliana, who has become a renowned dancer, rejects a pianist, Paolo, who is in love with her but does not know about her trauma. After he learns the truth, Paolo asks Liliana to marry him. Liliana accidentally joins Ada on stage during a performance of "Norma." She undergoes a nervous breakdown, but recovers her voice. She and Paolo get married.

Il barone di Corbò

Italy 1940, b&w, 76 minutes
D: Gennaro Righelli. S: based on the play by Luigi Antonelli. SC: Luigi Antonelli, Riccardo Freda, Gennaro Righelli. DOP: Domenico Scala. M: Ezio Carabella. E: Vincenzo Zampi. PD: Alfredo Montori. AD: Filippo Walter Ratti. SO: Ovidio Del Grande.
Cast: Enrico Glori (The Baron of Corbò), Laura Nucci (Gabriella), Armando Migliari (Teodorico Belmonte), Vanna Vanni (Lulù), Dina Perbellini (Didone, Teodorico's wife), Corrado De Cenzo (Giacomo), Wandina Guglielmi (Doretta), Diana Torrieri (Lulù's mother), Giovanni Ferrari (Madman), M. Dotri (Madman), Renato Chiantoni, Augusto Di Giovanni, Lina Tartara Minora.
PROD: Renato Cogliati Dezza for Juventus Film (Rome). PM: Raffaele Colamonici. Visa n. 30696 (7/31/1939, m. 2092). Release date: May 1940. Distribution: Juventus Film.

Several deranged patients escape from a mental hospital, and the news spreads panic among the inhabitants of the nearby villa Belmonte. The landlord, Teodorico, who was about to leave for a secret meeting with his mistress Gabriella, is embarassed when she shows up at the villa, accompanied by a young man, the alleged Baron of Corbò. To avoid his jealous wife's suspicions, Teodorico introduces the two guests as newlyweds. During the night, the Baron's strange behavior convinces the others that he is one of the escaped lunatics. The butler, Giacomo, is sent to the asylum to ask for aid, but the escapees show up at the villa, passing themselves off as male nurses and doctors. The situation is about to escalate tragically when the real nurses show up to restore order. The baron of Corbò asks to marry Teodorico's daughter.

In campagna è caduta una stella

Italy 1939, b&w, 85 minutes
D: Eduardo De Filippo. Collaborator to direction: Riccardo Freda. S: based on the play *A Coperchia è caduta una stella* by Peppino De Filippo. SC: Eduardo De Filippo, Riccardo Freda. DOP: Mario Albertelli. M: Luigi Avitabile; songs: Cesare A. Bixio. E: Guido Ricci. PD: Giovanni Brancaccio. SO: Raoul Magni.
Cast: Rosina Lawrence (Margaret), Eduardo De Filippo (Pasquale Montuori), Peppino De Filippo (Luigino Montuori), Oretta Fiume (Rosina), Dolores Palumbo (Clotilde), Gorella Gori (Teodorico's wife), Elena Altieri (Margaret's sister-in-law), Adele Mosso (Aunt Rita), Gina Amendola (Montuori's Housekeeper), Armando Migliari (Teodorico), Guido Notari (Margaret's father-in-law), Edoardo Toniolo (Margaret's fiancé), Emilio Petacci (Clotilde's father), Carlo Marazzini, Ruggero Capodaglio (Brigadier), Antonio Gradoli (Margaret's brother), Giuseppe De Martino; *uncredited*: Celio Bucchi.
PROD: Peppino De Filippo for Defilm (Rome). PM: Oscar Gaeta. Filmed at Pisorno

Studios (Tirrenia). Visa n. 30763 (11/7/1939, m. 2352). Release date: 11/11/1939. Distribution: Tirrenia.

Also known as: *In the Country Fell a Star* (U.S.A.)

A young American woman, Margaret, shows up in a small village: she has come to Italy to marry a penniless nobleman she has seen only in a photo. Upon learning that the man is not as good-looking as he appears in the picture, the girl flees by car and takes refuge in a country house owned by two brothers, Pasquale and Luigino. Her presence puts the whole village in turmoil and excites the brothers' mutual jealousy. Luigino, who is engaged with Rosina, even tries to withdraw from the marriage. In the end, Margaret's parents locate her and take her back home. The two brothers reconcile and return to their quiet existence.

La granduchessa si diverte

Italy 1940, b&w, 85 minutes

D: Giacomo Gentilomo. S: loosely based on the play *La corona di strass* by Ugo Falena. SC: Riccardo Freda, Giacomo Gentilomo, Mino Caudana [and Aldo De Benedetti and Mario Monicelli, uncredited.] DOP: Mario Albertelli, Giuseppe La Torre. M: Salvatore Allegra. E: Renzo Lucidi. AD: Mario Monicelli. SD: Savino Fino. CO: Gino Sensani. SO: Mario Faraoni.

Cast: Paola Barbara (Marinella the Grand-Duchess / Fanny the dancer), Carlo Campanini (Police Prefect), Giacomo Moschini (Prime Minister), Otello Toso (Maurizio), Sergio Tofano (Prince), Rosetta Tofano (Zelmaide), Giulio Alfieri, Ernesto Almirante, Oreste Bilancia, Romolo Costa, Vasco Creti, Rudi Dal Pra, Jone Frigerio, Tullio Galvani, Ethel Maggi, Nino Marchetti, Erzia Mariani, Evelina Paoli, Emilio Petacci, Checco Rissone.

Produced by Mario Borghi for Industria Cinematografica Italiana (Rome). PM: Carlo Benetti. Visa n. 31029 (6/28/1940, m. 2338). Release date: 7/20/1940. Distribution: Tirrenia Film.

Also known as: *La Gran Duquesa se divierte* (Spain).

In the capital of a small European state, Fanny, a dancer who performs with a ballet company, turns out to be a dead ringer for the reigning Grand Duchess, Marinella. The prefect of police and some ministers expel the dangerous impersonator; but, on a whim of the sovereign who wanted to meet her lookalike, it is the Grand Duchess who ends up being expelled while Fanny takes her place. After the exchange, many misunderstandings ensue: the false Grand Duchess must get engaged to a prince's cousin, while the false dancer receives a marriage proposal from her boyfriend. Eventually the two women resume each other's place and it all ends in the best way ... at least for Fanny.

Cento lettere d'amore

Italy 1940, b&w, 68 minutes

D: Max Neufeld. S and SC: Alberto Consiglio, Mino Caudana, Alessandro De Stefani, Riccardo Freda. DOP: Giuseppe La Torre. M: Enzo Masetti, Eldo Di Lazzaro. E: Renzo Lucidi. PD: Luigi Ricci. ArtD: Gino Brosio. AD: Raffaele Delago. SO: Italo Rivosecchi.

Cast: Armando Falconi (The Financer), Vivi Gioi (The Secretary's Wife), Giuseppe Porelli (The Secretary), Alfredo Martinelli (The Baronet), Lilian Hermann, Enzo Biliotti, Maria Jacobini, Gemma D'Alba, Vasco Creti, Luigi Erminio D'Olivo, Alfredo Petroni, Alba Wiegele [Marina Doge], Ori Monteverdi, Bianca Camarda, Lydia Johnson, Loretta Vinci, Giacomo Almirante, Eugenio Duse, Bebi Nucci.

Produced by Mario Borghi for Industria Cinematografica Italiana (Rome). PM: Fabio Franchini. Visa n. 31067 (9/8/1940, m. 1873). Release date: 9/8/1940. Distribution: Tirrenia Film.

By sheer chance, one hundred compromising letters sent by a married woman to her lover are found by her husband's secretary. When the latter's wife reads the letters in turn, she believes that her husband is cheating on her. From here on a series of misunderstandings and embarrassing events ensue...

Notte di fortuna

Italy 1941, b&w, 86 minutes

D: Raffaello Matarazzo [and Ugo Lombardi, uncredited]. S: Raffaello Matarazzo. SC: Raffaello Matarazzo, Riccardo Freda, Camillo Mariani Dell'Aguilara. DOP: Ugo Lombardi [and Václav Vích, uncredited]. M: Dan Caslar. E: Angelo Comitti. PD: Piero Rosi.

Cast: Peppino De Filippo (Biagio Natalini), Leda Gloria (The Principal's Sister), Vera Bergman (The Mysterious Girl), Olinto Cristina, Gorella Gori, Nino Marchetti, Guido Notari, Fausto Guerzoni, Giulio Alfieri, Iginia

Armilli, Gino Baghetti, Luigi Barbieri, Ciro Berardi, Michele Malaspina, Nicola Maldacea, Lina Tartara Minora, Silva Nova, Giovanni Petti [Giovanni Petrucci], Cesare Pianigiani, Domenico Serra, Edda Soligo, Olga von Kollar.

Produced by Atesia Film (Rome). PM: Icilio Sterbini. Visa n. 31234 (1/31/1941, m. 2350). Release date: 2/2/1941. Distribution: Atesia Film.

Biagio, a pharmacist's clerk in a small village, is invited to the town of San Remo by an eccentric millionaire. Attracted by the hope of winning a fortune, he leaves his job and moves to the Riviera; there, at the local casino, Biagio actually wins a huge sum. However, to meet the demands of a woman he met there, he keeps gambling and eventually loses all the money. Back to his hometown, Biagio is triumphantly welcomed by the villagers, who have learned of his extraordinary winning from the newspapers. The woman he met in San Remo shows up too, with a valuable pearl necklace that he had bought for her during his lucky streak. The necklace will allow them to marry and settle down.

Caravaggio, il pittore maledetto

Italy 1941, b&w, 108 minutes

D: Goffredo Alessandrini. S: Bruno Valeri, Vittorio Verga. SC: Bruno Valeri, Ákos Tolnay, Riccardo Freda, Gherardo Gherardi, Goffredo Alessandrini. DOP: Aldo Tonti [and Jan Stallich, uncredited]. M: Riccardo Zandonai, conducted by Ugo Giacomozzi. E: Giancarlo Cappelli. PD, SD: Salvo D'Angelo. CO: Veniero Colasanti. AD: Umberto Scarpelli. SO: Franco Croci. MA: Enzo Musumeci Greco. Technical advisor: Gustavo Brigante Colonna. Collaboration to the making: Riccardo Freda.

Cast: Amedeo Nazzari (Michelangelo Merisi, the Caravaggio), Clara Calamai (Madonna Giaconella), Lamberto Picasso (Knight d'Arpino), Nino Crisman (Alef of Wignacourt), Lauro Gazzolo (Uncle Nello), Beatrice Mancini (Lena), Olinto Cristina (Cardinal Dal Monte), Felice Romano, Pina Gallini, Achille Majeroni (Cardinal Borghese), Luigi Garrone, Maria Dominiani (Alessandra), Renato Malavasi (Mauro), Alessandra Adari, Giulio Alfieri, Oscar Andriani, Angelo Bassanelli, Luciana Campion, Franco Castellani, Liana Del Balzo, Anna Maria Falchi, Jolanda Fantini, Arnaldo Firpo, Salvatore Furnari (Dwarf), Tullio Galvani, Olga Vittoria Gentili, Walter Grant, Mario Lodolini, Carlo Mariotti, Mario Mazza, Piero Pastore, Amina Pirani Maggi, Mario Revera, Tino Scotti, Vinicio Sofia, Umberto Spadaro.

Produced by Francesco Curato for Elica Film (Rome). Visa n. 31229 (1/31/1941, m. 2981). PM: Aldo Salerno. PS: S. Farina, E. Ruffo. PSe: Emilio Gerosa. PA: Adolfo Lengyel. Filmed at SAFA Studios (Rome). Release date: 2/6/1941. Distribution: Minerva.

The painter Michelangelo Merisi da Caravaggio arrives in Rome, uncertain of his own art but restless in life. In a short time he is reduced to poverty and is forced to become the assistant of a mediocre but famous painter, D'Arpino. Tired of painting still lifes, and helped by the poet Marino, Caravaggio manages to obtain an important painting job by himself. However, his unbridled nature and tormented love life lead him to fight in a duel with a Roman gentleman, that Caravaggio kills. The painter flees to Malta where, after ten years of exemplary life, he joins the order of the Knights of St. John in Malta. The nostalgia for Italy leads Caravaggio to attempt to return illegally to his home country, but he is located by the police. Despite having been granted a safe conduct, the painter dies in the swamp where he is hiding from the soldiers.

L'avventuriera del piano di sopra

Italy 1941, b&w, 81 minutes

D: Raffaello Matarazzo. S: Raffaello Matarazzo. SC: Raffaello Matarazzo, Riccardo Freda, Edoardo Anton. DOP: Tino Santoni. M: Giuseppe Anepeta. E: Riccardo Freda. PD: Veniero Colasanti. SO: Franco Croci.

Cast: Vittorio De Sica (Fabrizio Marchini), Giuditta Rissone (Clara Marchini), Clara Calamai (Biancamaria Rossi), Camillo Pilotto (Rossi), Carlo Campanini (Arturo), Dina Romano (Matilde the maid), Jucci Kellerman (Nella the maid), Olga Vittoria Gentili (Biancamaria's mother), Ernesto Almirante (Cesare, Biancamaria's father), Gisella Gasperini (Lucrezia the maid), Cesare Fantoni (Florist).

Produced by Francesco Curato and Giorgio Genesi for Elica Film, Artisti Associati S.A. Produzione Filmi (Rome). PM: Celestino Cairella. UPM: M. Damiani. Filmed at SAFA studios (Rome). Visa n. 31420 (10/23/1941, m. 2244). Release date: 10/21/1941. Distribution: Artisti Associati.

Also known as: *La aventurera del piso de arriba* (Spain).

Note: Although credited as scriptwriter, Freda denied having taken part in the script. Like with other movies made during wartime, the film was given the official visa a few days *after* the release. The same happened with Freda's *Don Cesare di Bazan* and *Aquila nera*.

A young lawyer, Fabrizio, is married to the very jealous Clara. One night, while Clara is away, the upstairs neighbor, Biancamaria, takes refuge in Fabrizio's apartment, hiding from her possessive husband. Fabrizio gallantly offers her to sleep in his bed, and after a vain attempt at seduction he falls asleep on a sofa. When he awakens, Bianca Maria is gone and, much to his surprise, he finds out that Clara's valuable necklace has disappeared. Mistakenly believing that Biancamaria is a thief, Fabrizio sets out to the rescue, to regain possession of the necklace and give the woman a lesson. After a series of comic events the misunderstanding is finally clarified and the two couples reconcile.

L'abito nero da sposa

Italy 1945, b&w, 96 minutes
D: Luigi Zampa. S: based on the play *The Cardinal* by Louis N. Parker. SC: Mario Pannunzio, Ennio Flaiano, Riccardo Freda, Gherardo Gherardi, Luigi Zampa [and Leo Longanesi, uncredited.]. DOP: Gábor Pogány, Aldo Tonti. M: Carlo Piero Giorgi. E: Maria Rosada. PD: Fulvio Jacchia. CO: Bianca Emanuele Baciochi. MU: Roberto Pasetti. AD: Aldo Quinti. SO: Enrico Palmieri. C: A. Postoini.

Cast: Fosco Giachetti (Cardinal Giovanni de' Medici), Jacqueline Laurent (Berta Chigi), Enzo Fiermonte (Giuliano de' Medici), Aldo Silvani (Bartolomeo Chigi), Carlo Tamberlani (Andrea Strozzi), Domenico Viglione Borghese (Governor Baglioni), Manoel Roero (Raffaello), Fausto Guerzoni (Beppe), Evelina Paoli (Madonna de' Medici), Peppino Spadaro (Luigi), Renato Chiantoni (Bernardino), Emilio Petacci (Merchant), Franco Pesce (Party Guest), Giuliana Pitti (Berta's friend), Elena Sangro (Celestina), Bruno Smith (Strozzi's comrade in arms), Armando Furlai (Witness for the prosecution), Luisa Alliani (Onoria), Walter Grant, Alessandra Adari.

Produced by Vittorio Vassarotti for Vi-Va Film (Rome). PM: Folco Laudati. PS: Ernesto Gentili. PSe: A. Cappelli. Visa n. 47 (5/17/1945, m. 2645). Release date: 5/17/1945. Distribution: Produttori Associati.

Also known as: *La Confession tragique* (France), *El cardenal* (Spain).

Florence, 16th century. The mercenary soldier Andrea Strozzi is refused the hand of Berta because her father, the wealthy banker Chigi, has already promised her to Giuliano de' Medici. Andrea kills the banker, and Giuliano is wrongly accused of the crime. He is arrested and locked up in jail, awaiting trial. Andrea, feeling safe, confesses the crime to Cardinal Giovanni de' Medici, Giuliano's brother, who is bound by the secrecy of confession. But on the day of the execution the cardinal pretends to have gone crazy, and thus he manages to make Andrea confess his crime next to some hidden witnesses. The truth is revealed and the real culprit is arrested.

07 ... tassì

Italy 1945, b&w, 89 minutes
D: Alberto D'Aversa [and Marcello Pagliero, Riccardo Freda]. S: Marcello Pagliero. SC: Leo Bomba, Alberto D'Aversa, Marcello Pagliero. DOP: Emanuel Filiberto Lomiry. M: Tarcisio Fusco. E: Riccardo Freda. PD: Nino Maccarones. AD: Isa Bartalini.

Cast: Vera Carmi (The Actress), Tito Gobbi (Taxi Driver), Rosetta D'Este (His Daughter), Carlo Campanini (Driver), Franco Scandurra (Driver), Luigi Almirante, Osvaldo Genazzani, Lily Granado, Germana Paolieri, Nico Pepe, Corrado Racca, Bella Starace Sainati, Fausto Tommei.

Produced by Artisti Associati, Quartafilm, Società Italiana Produttori Cinematografici (SIPAC) (Rome). PM: Max Calandri, Dino Sant'Ambrogio. PSe: Rosario Restivo. Visa n. 7 (11/16/1944, m. 2463). Release date: 12/25/1945. Distribution: Artisti Associati.

Note: The film was started by Pagliero. Frieda briefly took over the direction, but the film was eventually finished by D'Aversa.

A taxi driver, a widower with a daughter, invites to his home a penniless girl who tried unsuccessfully to become a stage actress. The two become romantically involved and decide to marry, but a series of misunderstandings result in the girl leaving the taxi driver and returning—this time successfully—to acting. Several months later the two meet again and, having cleared up all misunderstandings, fulfill their love dream.

Giove in doppiopetto

Italy 1955, color, 102 minutes.

D: Daniele D'Anza. S: based on Pietro Garinei and Sandro Giovannini's musical stage play; DOP: Enzo Serafin; M: Gorni Kramer; E: Eraldo Da Roma. PD: Luigi Scaccianoce. CO: Giulio Coltellacci. AD: Ernesto Guida. SO: Alberto Bartolomei. C: Sandro Serafin, Aldo Scavarda. AE: Marisa Mengoli, Pina Soletti.

Cast: Carlo Dapporto (Jupiter), Delia Scala (Juno), Lucy d'Albert, Gino Ravazzini, Franca Gandolfi, Gianni Agus, Annabella Cerliani, Lilo Weibel, Françoise Rambert, Rina Mascetti, Lile Larson, Renato Tovaglieri, Silvio Crescenzi, Domenico Crescentini.

Produced by Film Costellazione Produzione. Visa n. 18742 (3/28/1955, m. 2780, V.M.16). PM: Gino Rossi. Release date: 4/9/1955. Distribution: Cei-Incom.

Note: Freda was originally to direct the film: he claimed he walked off the set on the first day of shooting.

The goddess Juno plays a trick on her unfaithful husband Jupiter. The God has landed on Earth to look for easy female prey, and his wife follows him: Jupiter starts courting a beautiful girl, unaware that she is actually Juno in disguise...

Nel segno di Roma

Italy / France / West Germany/Yugoslavia 1959, color, 98 minutes

D: Guido Brignone [and Michelangelo Antonioni, uncredited]. S and SC: Francesco Thellung, Francesco De Feo, Sergio Leone, Giuseppe Mangione, Guido Brignone. DOP: Luciano Trasatti [and Mario Bava, uncredited] (Eastmancolor, Dyaliscope). M: Angelo Francesco Lavagnino, conducted by the author (Ed. Nord-Sud). E: Nino Baragli. ArtD: Ottavio Scotti. SD: Ugo Pericoli. CO: Vittorio Nino Novarese. MU: Giuliano Laurenti. Hair: Ada Palombi. AD: Michele Lupo [and Sergio Leone, uncredited]. 2nd unit director—Battle scenes: Riccardo Freda. DO: Adriano Taloni, Mario Amari. SE: Joseph Nathanson. C: Franco Villa. W: Enzo Bulgarelli. SS: Gigliola Rosmino. CHOR: Claude Marchant. SP: Vaselli.

Cast: Anita Ekberg (Zenobia), Georges Marchal (Marcus Valerius), Folco Lulli (Semantius), Jacques Sernas (Julianus), Lorella De Luca (Bathsheba), Alberto Farnese (Marcello), Mimmo Palmara (Lator), Alfredo Varelli (Vithos), Sergio Sauro (Flavio), Remo De Angelis, Paul Muller (Slave master), Chelo Alonso (Erica), Gino Cervi (Aurelianus).

PROD: Enzo Merolle for Giomer Film, Lux Film (Rome), Société Cinématographique Lyre (Paris), Tele Film GmbH (Munich), Dubrava Film (Zagreb), Filmiski Studio (Sarajevo). PM: Rino Merolle. PS: Sergio Merolle, Fernando Cinquini. PA: Sante Chimirri, Tonino Garzarelli. Filmed in Yugoslavia and at Incir-De Paolis Studios (Rome). Visa n. 28773 (3/5/1959, m. 2700). Release date: 3/5/1959. Distribution: Glomer Film (Italy), AIP (U.S.A.)

Also known as: *Sign of the Gladiator*; *Sheba and the Gladiator* (U.S.A.), *La regina del deserto* (Italy: reissue title), *Sous le signe de Rome* (France), *Bajo el signo de Roma* (Spain), *Im Zeichen Roms* (West Germany; Austria), *Zenóbia e o Gladiator* (Portugal), *O Escudo Romano* (Brazil), *La carga de los gladiatores* (Mexico), *Róma csillaga* (Hungary), *Pod znakiem Rzymu* (Poland).

Queen Zenobia of Palmyra defeats the Roman troops led by the consul Marcus Valerius, who is captured, forced into slavery and tortured. However, he escapes and presents himself before the Queen, offering her his services, so as to convince her to annex her kingdom to Rome. Valerius' plan is about to succeed, but he falls for Zenobia, and is torn between love and his loyalty to Rome. What is more, general Marcello orders a sudden attack on Palmyra. Zenobia is defeated and conducted to Rome as a slave. Marcus Valerius, who has saved the queen's life from a coup led by her treacherous minister Semantius, has her released and keeps her in his house as a concubine, while an African successor chosen by Rome is preparing to assume the domain of Palmyra...

I mongoli

Italy / France 1961, color, 115 minutes

D: André De Toth, Leopoldo Savona; battle scenes: Riccardo Freda. S and SC: Ugo Guerra, Luciano Martino, Ottavio Alessi, Alessandro Ferraù [and Ernesto Gastaldi, uncredited]. DOP: Aldo Giordani; 2nd unit DOP: Renato Del Frate. M: Mario Nascimbene, directed by Franco Ferrara. E: Otello Colangeli. PD: Angelo Zambon, Aleksandar Milovic. ArtD: Ottavio Scotti, Milan Todorovic. SD: Arrigo Breschi. CO: Enzo Bulgarelli. AD: Alberto Cardone. C: Giovanni Bergamini, Sergio Bergamini. Stunts: Milan Mitic. SP: Guglielmo Coluzzi, Aldo Galfano. CHOR: Dino Solari.

Cast: Jack Palance (Ogatai), Anita Ekberg (Hulina), Antonella Lualdi (Amina), Franco Silva (Stephen of Crakow), Gianni Garko [Gianni Garkovich] (Henri de Valois), Roldano Lupi (Genghis Khan), Gabriella Pallotta (Lutezia), Gabriele Antonini (Temugin), Pierre Cressoy (Igor), Mario Colli (Boris), Lawrence Montaigne (Prince Stefan's ally), George Wang (Subodai), Andrej Gardenin, Vittorio Sanipoli; *uncredited:* Janine Hendy (Harem dancer).

PROD: Guido Giambartolomei for Royal Film (Rome), France Cinéma Productions (Paris). PM: Carlo Bessi. Visa n. 35404 (8/22/1961, m. 3157). Release date: 8/31/1961. Distribution: Cineriz.

Also known as: *The Mongols* (U.S.A.), *Les mongols* (France), *Los mongoles* (Spain), *Raubzüge der Mongolen*; *Brut des Bösen*; *Schreckensreiter der Mongolenwölfe* (West Germany), *Die Mongolen* (Austria), *O maior império do mundo* (Portugal), *Bogotai—O Bárbaro Mongol*; *Os Mongoís* (Brazil), *Mongolit* (Finland), *A mongolok* (Hungary), *Môko no arashi* (Japan), *De Mongolen* (Netherlands), *Mongolowie* (Poland), *Mongolernas sista strid* (Sweden).

While the army of the Mongols led by Genghis Khan threatens to invade Europe, a Diet is urgently summoned in Warsaw. The participants establish to acknowledge the invaders the possession of the lands that have already been conquered, provided that they won't advance further. The task of dealing with the enemy is entrusted to Prince Stephen of Crakow. Ogotai, Genghis Khan's son, who commands the Mongols in his father's absence, rejects any peace proposal; what is more, his counselor, the beautiful and ruthless Hulina, attempts to kill Stephen. Having survived the attack, the Prince goes in search of Genghis Khan's camp. Wounded and hungry, Stephen wanders amidst the Mongolian territories until he is admitted in the presence of the emperor. Genghis Khan is willing to negotiate peace but Ogotai, determined to conquer the whole of Europe, kills him. War ensues, and Stephen has no choice but to draw the Mongols into a trap...

Marco Polo—L'avventura di un italiano in Cina

Italy / France 1962, color, 103 minutes
D: Piero Pierotti, Hugo Fregonese. S: Piero Pierotti, Oreste Biancoli. SC: Duccio Tessari, Piero Pierotti, Antoinette Pellevant, Oreste Biancoli [and Ennio De Concini, uncredited]. DOP: Riccardo Pallottini. M: Angelo Francesco Lavagnino [U.S. version: Les Baxter]. E: Ornella Micheli. PD: Zoran Zorcic. ArtD: Aurelio Crugnola, Franco Fumagalli, Miodrag Miric, Jovan Radic. CO: Mario Giorsi. MU: Euclide Santoli. Hair: Lina Geleng. AD: Michelangelo Panaro. ASD: Aldo Fumagalli. ACO: Silvano Giusti. CHOR: Franca Bartolomei.

Cast: Rory Calhoun (Marco Polo), Yōko Tani (Princess Amuray), Camillo Pilotto (Great Khan), Pierre Cressoy (Cuday), Michel Chow (Ciu-Lin), Thien-Huong (Tai-Au), Franco Ammirata, Tonino Cianci, Paola Falchi, Angelo Galassi, Anna Maestri, Spartaco Nale, Ching Jen Pai, Roberto Paoletti, Ada Passeri, Bianca Pividori, Franco Ressel, Poing Ping Sam, Giacomo Tchang (Old Chinese man), Janine Tramony, Robert Hundar [Claudio Undari] (Mongka).

Produced by Ermanno Donati and Luigi Carpentieri for Panda Cinematografica (Rome), Trans Film Orsa (Paris). PM: Gianni Minervini, Lucio Orlandini. PS: Livio Maffei. Visa n. 36921 (3/10/1962, m. 2841). Release date: 6/21/1962. Distribution: Unidis.

Also known as: *Marco Polo* (U.S.A.)

Note: Freda's name is nowhere to be found in the credits. According to some sources he filmed several battle scenes, but he denied his involvement in the film.

Marco Polo leaves Venice on the day of his marriage and heads East. Once in Mongolia, he becomes acquainted with a local guide and gets past the Great Wall of China. One night Marco saves the Great Khan's daughter, Amuray, whose caravan has been assaulted by the rebels. He meets the rebel chief, Cuday, the Khan's nephew, and learns that he is revolting against the cruel Prime Minister Mongka. Marco arrives in Beijing, where he is arrested during a protest in the main square. Released from prison and received at court, Marco recognizes Amuray as the Khan's daughter and falls for her. Mongka has the Khan imprisoned and leads Marco into a trap, but the hero escapes death and joins the rebels. Together they attack Beijing and release the Great Khan and the princess: Mongka perishes during the assault. Once peace has been re-established, Marco leaves toward the South.

Solo contro Roma

Italy 1962, color, 94 minutes
D: Herbert Wise [Luciano Ricci]. S and SC: Ennio Mancini, Gianni Astolfi, Gastad Green [Renato Vicario]. DOP: Silvano Ippoliti. M: Armando Trovajoli. E: Roberto Cinquini. PD: Piero Poletto. CO: Paolo Caracò. 2nd unit director: Riccardo Freda. 2nd unit DOP: Riccardo Pallottini, Raffaele Masciocchi. C: Michele Cristiani, Franco Di Giacomo, Antonio Schiavo Lena. AC: Franco Frazzi, Osvaldo Massimi, Giovanni Ciarlo. AD: Stefano Delic. SS: Paola Salvadori. 2ndAD: Natalino Vicario. MU: Vittorio Biseo. AMU: Cesare Biseo. Hair: Anna Cristofani, Maria Arié. W: Vera Ceffarelli, Flora Baldassarre, Agnese Tonnini. SO: Roy Mangano. SE: Vitantonio Ricci. MA: Goffredo Unger.

Cast: Rossana Podestà (Fabiola), Lang Jeffries (Brenno), Philippe Leroy (Silla), Gabriele Tinti (Goruk), Luciana Angiolillo (Saron's servant), Renato Terra (Gladiator Trainer), Frederico Hunger [Goffredo Unger], Angelo Bastianoni, Rinaldo Zamperla (Light Blond Prisoner), Djordje Nenadovic (Centurio Caius), Giancarlo Bastianoni (Darker Blond Prisoner), Alfredo Danesi, Franco Nonibasti, Janez Albreht.

PROD: Marco Vicario for Atlantica Cinematografica Produzione Films (Rome). PS: Antonio Palumbo.

Visa n. 38250 (9/5/1962, m. 2593). Release date: 9/6/1962. Distribution: Atlantica Cinematografica (Italy), Medallion Pictures (U.S.A.)

Also known as: *Alone Against Rome* (U.S.A.), *Vengeance of the Gladiator* (U.K.), *Seul contre Rome* (France), *Einer gegen Rom / Kampf der Gladiatoren* (West Germany), *Solo contra Roma* (Mexico), *O Império de Roma* (Portugal), *Rooman valtakunnan orjat* (Finland), *Upornik* (Slovenia).

Note: in the Italian prints, Freda is credited as follows: "The Arena sequences were directed by Riccardo Freda."

After conquering the city of Alesia, the Roman consul Lucius Suetonius leaves the tribune Silla to rule it. Soon Silla disobeys Suetonius' orders and harasses the population, seriously undermining the peace treaty sealed with the tribal leaders. The son of the head of the city, Gor, his daughter Fabiola and her fiancé Brenno are arrested, and Brenno is made to fight in the arena as a gladiator. One day he kills a centurion and is sentenced to death. Meanwhile, unable to bear the arrogance of the tribune any longer, the citizens of Alesia start a revolt. Brenno, Gor and their friends escape from prison and join the rebels. Brenno is wounded and is captured by Silla, while Gor reaches Suetonius' camp and informs him about the situation in Alesia. The consul returns to Alesia and allows Brenno to fight against Silla, who succumbs. Peace is restored in the region.

Il dominatore dei sette mari
(Sir Francis Drake)

Italy 1962, color, 103 minutes
D: Primo Zeglio [U.S. version: Rudolph Maté]. SC: Filippo Sanjust. DOP: Giulio Gianini. M: Franco Mannino. E: Franco Fraticelli. ArtD: Nicola Cantatore. CO: Filippo Sanjust. MU: Maurizio Giustini. SO: Primiano Muratori. SE: Eros Bacciucchi, SS: Anna Gruber.

Cast: Rod Taylor (Sir Francis Drake), Keith Michell (Malcolm Marsh), Edy Vessel [Edoarda Vesselovsky] (Arabella Ducleau), Mario Girotti (Babington), Basil Dignam (Sir Francis Walsingham), Anhtony Dawson (Lord Burleigh), Gianni Cajafa (Tom Moon), Irene Worth (Queen Elizabeth I), Arturo Dominici (Don Bernardino De Mendoza), Marco Guglielmi (Fletcher), Esmeralda Ruspoli (Mary of Scotland), Rossella D'Aquino (Potato), Umberto Raho (King Philip), Aldo Bufi Landi (Vigeois); *uncredited*: Giuseppe Abbrescia (Chester), Luciana Gilli (Indian wife), Massimo Righi (Lord of the Royal Court), Anna Santarsiero (Indian wife), Gianni Solaro (Admiral Medina Sedonia), Jacopo Tecchi (Garcia), Bruno Ukmar (Emmanuel), Franco Ukmar (Francisco), Adriano Vitale (Recalde).

Produced by Attilio Riccio for Adelphia Compagnia Cinematografica (Rome). Visa n. 37674 (6/20/1962, m. 2837). Release date: 6/20/1962. Distribution: MGM (U.S.A.)

Also known as: *Seven Seas to Calais* (U.S.A.), *Le corsaire de la reine* (France), *Pirat der sieben Meere* (West Germany), *Schrecken der Meere* (Austria), *El pirata de su majestad* (Mexico; Venezuela), *O Corsário da Rainha* (Portugal), *O Pirata Real* (Brazil), *Pirat på de syv have* (Denmark), *Kuninkaallinen merirosvo* (Finland).

Note: Freda's name is nowhere to be found in the credits. According to some sources he took care of the editing of the naval battle scene, but he denied his involvement in the film.

After a series of daring exploits against the Spaniards, the pirate Francis Drake and his men return to England, where the followers of Mary, Queen of Scots, who was imprisoned by Elizabeth, are attempting to release the former and kill the Queen of England. Drake manages to foil the plot. The conspirators and Mary of Scotland will be beheaded. One of Drake's men, who is in love with a young woman who had been implicated in the plot without her knowledge, marries the girl thanks to the Queen's intervention. Then the pirate leaves with his men to new adventures...

Oro per i Cesari

Italy / France 1963, color, 100 minutes
D: André De Toth. [Italian version: and Sabatino Ciuffini]. 2nd unit director: Riccardo Freda. S: based on the novel *Gold for the Caesars* by Florence A. Seward. SC: Arnold Perl [and Sabatino Ciuffini, Millard Lampell, uncredited]. DOP: Raffaele Masciocchi (Technicolor). M: Franco Mannino, conducted by the author. E: Franco Fraticelli. ArtD: Ottavio Scotti. SD: Arrigo Breschi. CO: Mario Giorsi. MU: Maurizio Giustini. H: Giancarlo Marin. AD: Jerzy Macc. SO: Giovanni Rossi. SE: Eros Bacciucchi. C: Antonio Schiavo Lena. AC: Remo Grisanti. SP: Angelo Pennoni. SS: Anna Gruber. MA: Bruno Ukmar.

Cast: Jeffrey Hunter (Lacer), Mylène Demongeot (Penelope), Ron Randell (Centurion Rufus), Massimo Girotti (Pro-consul Caius Cornelius Maximus), Giulio Bosetti (Scipio), Ettore Manni (Luna the Celt), Georges Lycan (Malendi the Celt), Furio Meniconi (Dax the Gaul); *uncredited*: Omero Capanna, Laura Nucci, Jacques Stany.

Produced by Joseph Fryd, Attilio Riccio and Bernard Borderie for Adelphia Compagnia Cinematografica (Rome), Compagnie Industrielle et Commerciale Cinématographique (Paris), Films Borderie (Paris). PM: Luciano Cattania. APM: Paolo Gargano. Visa n. 39565 (2/19/1963, m. 2756). Release date: 3/9/1963 (Italy), 6/1964 (U.S.A.). Distribution: MGM (U.S.A.)

Also known as: *Gold for the Caesars* (U.S.A.), *L'or des Césars / De l'or pour César* (France), *Das Gold der Cäsaren* (West Germany), *Oro para el césar* (Spain; Mexico), *Escravos do Império* (Portugal), *Ouro para os Imperadores* (Brazil), *Veristä kultaa* (Finland).

Note: Freda claimed he shot the whole film.

Spain, end of first century A.D.*; Penelope, the lover of Maximus, Rome's proconsul of Spain, falls for Lacer, a slave who is an expert manufacturer and geologist. Emperor Domitian, afraid of his proconsul's popularity in Spain, entrusts him with a difficult mission in the territory of the Celts: to find and exploit the gold mines of the Sil, so as to replenish the coffers of the Empire. Maximus, who plans to use the knowledge of Lacer in his search for the gold, hopes to conquer the throne with the wealth thus obtained and at the same time dispatch the slave, who has become his rival in love. Once inside the Celts' territory, the Roman expedition suffers many losses. The final fight between Maximus and Lacer, driven by opposing interests, ends with Maximus' death. Lacer defeats the Celtic army by destroying the dam he himself had built, and starts a free life with Penelope in Gaul.*

La passion Béatrice

France/Italy 1987, color, 134 minutes
D: Bertrand Tavernier. SC: Colo Tavernier O'Hagan. DOP: Bruno de Keyzer. M: Ron Carter. E: Armand Psenny. PD: Guy-Claude François. CO: Jacqueline Moreau. MU: Paul Le Marinel. AMU: Annick Legout. SO: Michel Desrois. B: Jean-Michel Chauvet. Mix: Michel Barlier, Gérard Lamps. Foley artists: Alain Lèvy, Jérôme Lévy. AC: Laurent Fletout. G: Jean-Yves Freess. SP: Georges Pierre.

Cast: Bernard-Pierre Donnadieu (François de Cortemart), Julie Delpy (Béatrice de Cortemart), Nils Tavernier (Arnaud de Cortemart), Monique Chaumette (François' mother), Robert Dhéry (Raoul), Michèle Gleizer (Hélène), Maxime Leroux (Richard), Jean-Claude Adelin (Bertrand Lemartin), Jean-Louis Grinfeld (Maître Blanche), Claude Duneton (Curate), Isabelle Nanty (Nurse), Jean-Luc Rivals (Jehan), Roselyne Vuillaume (Marie), Maïté Maillé (Swarthy), Albane Guilhe (Recluse), Marie Privat (Marguerite), Sébastien Konieczny (François as a child), Vincent Saint-Ouen (Little François' father), Tina Sportolaro (Little François' mother), François Hadji-Lazaro (Priest at war), Érick Bernard (Lover), Nicole Siffre (Pauline), Myriam Thomas (Mariette), Christophe Rea (Jacques), David Ordonez (Thomas), Jacques Raynaud (Joseph), Pétrus Léo Crombe (Gildas), Béatrice Abatut (Blandine), Jean-Claude de Brou (Flayer), Stéphane

Bédrossian (Flayer), Christophe Poiron (Flayer), Yves Frexinos (Flayer), Raymond Pazzaglia (Flayer), Marie Cosnay (Nicolette), Sylvie Beyssen (Prostitute), Anne Bolon (Prostitute), Frédérique Figuero (Prostitute), Agnès Hick (Prostitute).

Produced by Adolphe Viezzi for AMLF, Cléa Productions, Les Films de la Tour, Little Bear, TF1 Films Production, CNC (Paris), Scena Film (Rome). Visa n. 83662 (6/1/1988, m. 3700, V.M.18). Release date: 11/11/1987 (France), 13/4/1988 (U.S.A.), 6/9/1988 (Italy). Distribution: Medusa (Italy).

Also known as: *Quarto comandamento* (Italy), *Beatrice*; *The Passion of Beatrice* (U.S.A.), *La pasión de Beatriz* (Spain; Argentina), *Die Passion der Beatrice* (Germany), *Intohimojen kekiaika* (Finland), *Béatrice passiója* (Hungary).

Note: The film is dedicated "to my friend Riccardo Freda."

14th century France. The devout Béatrice is impatient to see her father François de Cortemart return from English captivity after the Hundred Years' War. However, upon his return Cortemart—who killed his mother's lover as a child and has grown up hating women—submits Béatrice to abuse and humiliation which eventually leads to incest...

Un tour de manège

France 1989, color, 80 minutes

D: Pierre Pradinas. S and SC: Alain Gautre, Pierre Pradinas, Simon Pradinas. DOP: Jean-Pierre Sauvaire. M: Albert Marcoeur. E: Chantal Delattre. PD: Michel Vandestien. CO: Valérie Pozzo di Borgo. AD: Gabriel Julien-Laferrière, Gábor Rassov. PM: Thierry Rouxel. SO: William Flageollet, Antoine Ouvrier. SP: Marion Stalens.

Cast: Juliette Binoche (Elsa), François Cluzet (Al), Thierry Gimenez (Duc), Daniel Jégou (Sylvain), Jean-Chrétien Sibertin-Blanc (Olivier Rateau), Denis Lavant (Berville), Thierry Fortineau (Jo), Albert Prévost (Montaigne), Brigitte Catillon (Karine), Michel Aumont (Bank manager), Riccardo Freda (Riccardo, the film director), Jean-Claude Lecas (Benoît), Claire Pascal (Ju), Soizic Arsal (Jeanne), Michel Francini (Emilio Giliotti), François Monnié, Anne Lévy, Alain Aithnard, Simon Pradinas, Gábor Rassov, Henri Behar, Pierre Large; *uncredited*: Eric Prat, Marion Stalens.

PROD: Jean Achache, Robert Guédiguian, Albert Prévost for MP Productions, AB Films, Gaumont, Orly Films, Au Progrès du singe, Chapeau Rouge Films, Les Productions du 3ème Etage (Paris). EP: Albert Prévost, Frédéric Bourboulon, Michel Propper. Location manager: Gilles Sacuto. Filmed in Paris. Visa n. 66410. Release date: 3/29/1989. Distribution: Gaumont.

Also known as: *Roundabout* (U.K.), *Rotonda* (Spain).

Al and Elsa have been a couple for some time, but Al is dependent on the woman for his every emotional need, and has a drinking and gambling problem. After a period of separation Elsa show up again, and when Al is cast in a movie role, the couple move to a better apartment and rekindle their romance, but their old issues return...

La fille de d'Artagnan

France 1994, color, 125 minutes

D: Bertrand Tavernier. S: Michel Léviant, from an idea by Riccardo Freda and Éric Poindron. SC: Michel Léviant, Bertrand Tavernier, Jean Cosmos. Dial: Michel Léviant, Jean Cosmos. DOP: Patrick Blossier. M: Philippe Sarde. E: Ariane Boeglin. PD: Geoffroy Larcher. SD: Frédéric Duru, Marie-Laure Valla. CO: Jacqueline Moreau. MU: Eric Pierre. AMU: Magali Ceyrat, Sano De Perpessac, Caroline Philipponnat, Muriel Truque. Hair: Beya Gasmi, Fernando Mendes. AD: Jean-Marc Tostivint, João Pedro Ruivo. 2ndAD: Michel Ganz, Tiffany Tavernier, Alexis Quentin. C: Benoît Chamaillard, Nathalie Durand. AC: Amílcar Carrajola. 2ndAC: Jean-Pierre Méchin, Tony Costa, Jérôme Alméras, Miguel Sales Lopes. Steadicam operator: Pierre Morel, Patrick de Ranter, Marc Koninckx. KG: Yves Van der Smissen. G: Nils Moreau, Miguel Efe, Carlos Silva, Thierry Van Laere. ChEl: Rafael de Sousa, Rachid Madaoui. El: Philippe Pantanella, Mouloud Kakrout, Benoit Kemercier, Helder Loureiro, Mário Soares. Generator operator: Bernard Caroff, Domingos Batista. SP: Etienne George. ACO: Agnès Evein, Anne-Marie Drean, Rosário Moreira, Catarina Santos. W: Bruce Lignerat. AE: Benoît Alric, Louise Genis, Lisa Pfeiffer. Color timer: Bruno Patin. Head painter: Marie José Arnautin. Props: Franck Hugot, Fernando Assunção, Jacques Pélissier, Christophe Serraz. AsstArtD: Denis Renault, João Torres. 2ndAsstArtD: Thierry

Chavenon, Bruno Madesclaire. SD: Denis Mercier. Construction coordinators: Luc Compère, Pierre Cotte, José Matos, Jean-Claude Tenes. Carpenter: Manuel Swieton. Upholstery: Hervé Poeydemenge. SO: Michel Desrois. B: Jean-Michel Chauvet. SOE: Minh-Tam Nguyen, Eric Tisserand. Mix: Gérard Lamps. Foley artist: Jean-Pierre Lelong, Mario Melchiorri. Foley mixer: Jacque Thomas-Gérard. SE: Louis Gleize, Rui Alves. Visual effects: Thomas Duval, Antoine Simkinge, Rip Hampton O'Neil. Armorer: Raoul Billerey, Lionel Vitrant. MA: Claude Carliez, Michel Carliez. Horse master: Mario Luraschi. Press attaché: Dominique Segall. SS: Zoe Zurstrassen. Stunt coordinator: Claude Carliez. Stunts: Jean-Louis Airola, Michel Anderson, Guylaine Arnoult, Joëlle Baland, Alain Barbier, Jean Blats, Michel Bouis, Jean-Claude Braquet, Daniel Breton, Alain Brochery, William Cagnard, Rémi Canaple, Michel Carliez, Gilles Conseil, Jean-François Demange, Albert Goldberg, Pascal Guégan, Philippe Guégan, Pascal Lopez, Patrick Médioni, Philippe Neunreuther, André Obadia, Leslie Rain, Pierre Rousselle, Bernard Sachsé, Patrick Steltzer, Frédéric Vallet.

Cast: Sophie Marceau (Eloise), Philippe Noiret (D'Artagnan), Claude Rich (Duke of Crassac), Sami Frey (Aramis), Jean-Luc Bideau (Athos), Raoul Billerey (Porthos), Charlotte Kady (Eglantine de Rochefort), Nils Tavernier (Quentin la Misère), Luigi Proietti (Mazarin), Jean-Paul Roussillon (Planchet), Pascale Roberts (Mother Superior), Emmanuelle Bataille (Sister Félicité), Christine Pignet (Sister Céline), Fabienne Chaudat (Sister Frédegonde), Josselin Siassia (Slave), Jean-Claude Calon (Slave Trader), Stéphane Legros (Louis XIV), Maria Pitarresi (Olympe), Jean Martinez (Duke of Longueville), Patrick Rocca (Bargas), Michel Alexandre (The Hallebardier), Fanny Aubert (Sister Huguette), Grégoire Barachin (Fencing Pupil #1), Jean-Pierre Bouchard (Conspirator), Daniel Breton (Recruiting Sergeant), Canto e Castro (Singing Monk), Carlos César (Innkeeper), Vanina Delannoy (Courtesan #1), Raymond Faucher (Painter), Filipe Ferrer (Conti), Guilherme Filipe (Duke of Condé), Philippe Flotot (Spanish Ambassador), Adrien Frank (Young Brother), Jean-Claude Frissung (Doctor), Yves Gabrielli (Man of the Right), Michel Ganz (Peasant), Albert Goldberg (Associate), José Gomes (Duke of Beaufort), Laure Guillaume (Courtesan #2), Françoise Johannel (Harpist), João Lagarto (Jules), Philippe Lazoore (First Maître), Jean-Pierre Lebrun (Footman), Emmanuel Legrand (Postmaster), François Levantal (Courtier), Mario Luraschi (Henchman), André Mala (Duke of Conflans), Jean-Sebastien Pinel (Fencing Pupil #2), Carole Pommes (Sister Germaine), Rémy Riflade (Police Officer), François Sinapi (Riccardo), Severine Truquet (Servant), Sylvie Van Den Elsen (Anne d'Autriche), Lionel Vitrant (Dying Man), Vincent Dumestre (Musician #1), Eric Martinez (Musician #2), François Nicolet (Musician #3).

Produced by Véronique Bourboulon for CiBy 2000, Little Bear, TF1 Films Production, in association with Canal +, Sofica BNP Images (Paris). EP: Frédéric Bourboulon, António da Cunha Telles. UM: Emmanuel Legrand, Rui Louro, Pascal Ralite. UMA: Grégoire Barschin, José Borges, Sylvain Bouladoux, Benoit Charrie, Eric Gueret, Francisco Santos, Nathalie Grouard. Production coordinator: Martine Vergnes. Location manager: Patrick Lambert, Bertrand Vuarnesson. PA: Florence Dard. PSe: Clara Santos. Adm: Françoise Gavalda, Ágnes La Pont. AsstAdm: Nicole Tiramani.

Visa n. 90721 (2/29/1996, m. 3450). Release dates: 8/24/1994 (France), 4/2/1996 (Italy). Distribution: Bac Films (France), Cecchi Gori (Italy).

Also known as: *Revenge of the Musketeers* (U.S.A.), *Eloise, la figlia di d'Artagnan* (Italy), *La hija de D'Artagnan* (Spain), *D'Artagnans Tochter* (Germany), *A Filha de D'Artagnan* (Portugal), *D'Artagnan ja tytär*; *D'Artagnanin tytär* (Finland), *D'Artagnan lánya* (Hungary), *Córka d'Artagnan* (Poland), *D'Artagnans dotter*; *Musketörernas hämnd* (Sweden), *D'Artagnan'in kizi* (Turkey).

Note: Riccardo Freda was originally set to direct the film, but he was sacked right after the beginning of shooting. Bertrand Tavernier took over the direction.

France, 1654. Eloise, the daughter of d'Artagnan the musketeer, lives in a cloister. When the convent she calls home falls victim to villainy, Eloise uncovers a murderous conspiracy to overthrow the king of France. The young woman takes up her father's adventurous ambitions, and calls upon her ageing parent and his retired brothers-in-arms to reunite in the name of justice...

As Director

Don Cesare di Bazan

Italy 1942, b&w, 77 minutes
D: Riccardo Freda. S: from the play *Don César de Bazan* by Adolphe d'Ennery and Philippe Dumanoir. SC: Sergio Amidei, Vitaliano Brancati, Riccardo Freda, Cesare Zavattini [and Giacomo Debenedetti, uncredited]. DOP: Mario Craveri. M: Franco D'Achiardi (Ed. S.A.F.E.M.). E: Rolando Benedetti. PD: Gastone Medin. AD: Fede Arnaud. SD: Guglielmo Borzone. CO: Gino Sensani, Maria De Matteis. SO: Tommaso Barberini. AC: Ubaldo Marelli, Amleto Dessie.

Cast: Gino Cervi (Don Cesare di Bazan), Anneliese Uhlig (Renéè Duras), Enrico Glori (Viscount of Beaumont), Paolo Stoppa (Sancho), Enzo Biliotti (King Philip IV). Giovanni Grasso (Don José of Nogueira), Sandrino Moreno (The kid), Carlo Duse ("The Crow," the Viscount's messenger).

PROD: Riccardo Freda for Elica-Artisti Associati (Rome). PM: Piero Cocco. PS: Paolo Frascà. Filmed at Pisornio Studios (Tirrenia). Visa n. 31761 (10/7/1942, m. 2118). Release date: 10/4/1942. Distribution: Artisti Associati. Domestic gross: n.a.

Also known as: *La lama del giustiziere* (Italy; alternate title), *Don César de Bazan* (France), *D. César de Bazan* (Portugal).

Note: as with other movie made during wartime, the official visa dates a few days after the release date.

Spain, 1650. At a tavern in Barcelona, the courageous Don Cesare, Count of Bazan, glimpses a beautiful, mysterious lady. The woman is Renéè Duras, a French spy who is part of a conspiracy against King Philip IV, concocted by the French Ambassador, the Viscount of Beaumont. The Ambassador is secretly supporting the Catalan separatists, and has arranged for a load of gunpowder to be delivered to the rebels. When Don Cesare and his valet Sancho casually discover the cargo, concealed inside barrels of champagne, the Count alerts the Prime Minister Don José, unaware that the latter is also part of the conspiracy. To get rid of Don Cesare, Don José and Beaumont have the hot-tempered nobleman duped into a duel (which a court edict has deemed illegal) and arrested. In prison, the Ambassador persuades Don Cesare to marry an unknown woman—actually Renéè—and in turn he will save his life: however, this is part of a plan to eliminate the Count, have Renéè gain the title of Countess of Bazan and invite the King over to the castle of Avila, where the sovereign will be murdered. Don Cesare is brought before the firing squad, but a boy saves his life by charging the guns with blanks. While everyone believes him to be dead, Don Cesare destroys the gunpowder, dispatches Don José and sneaks into the castle, posing as a member of a performing company. Eventually he uncovers the plot and faces the Ambassador for one last swordfight atop the castle battlements...

Non canto più

Italy 1945, b&w, 79 minutes
D: Riccardo Freda. S and SC: Vittorio Metz, Steno [Stefano Vanzina], Riccardo Freda. DOP: Alfonso Frenguelli. M: Nuccio Fiorda. E: Rolando Benedetti. PD, SD: E. Verdozzi, A. Tagliolini. AD: Franco Fanfani.

Cast: Enzo Fiermonte (Giulio Revi, the tenor), Vera Bergman (Lisa Baratti), Paola Borboni (Greta Arden), Lamberto Picasso (Inspector Carter), Olinto Cristina (Carlo Baratti, Lisa's father), Giuseppe Porelli (Adolfo), Arturo Bragaglia (The Commissioner), Agnese Dubbini (The Cook), Virgilio Riento (Roberto).

PROD: Vittorio Vassarotti for Vi-Va Film (Rome). PM: Ernesto Gentili. Filmed at Titanus Studios (Rome). Visa n. 30 (3/22/1945, m. 2191). Release date: 9/30/1945. Distribution: Variety Film. Domestic gross: n.a.

Note: Filmed in 1943.

Mexico. Ruthless theatrical agent Greta Arden simulates the theft of a precious necklace for a publicity stunt, in order to launch the career of the talented young singer Giulio Revi: he will be blamed for the theft so as to mount a sensationalist press campaign, only to be exonerated during the trial. Giulio refuses to take part in the hoax, but Greta goes on with it regardless; what is more, she provides Giulio's unmistakable singing voice as the main clue for the police. As the manhunt progresses, Giulio—who has become a hobo and is unaware of what is going on—meets Lisa Baratti, the young daughter of a wealthy cattle farmer, and falls in love with her. As the wedding approaches, Lisa attempts to have Giulio perform at an audition, but her intervention only results in the young man being arrested, as his voice is recognized as that of the alleged thief. Once in prison, Giulio is acquitted by Greta, who also plans to announce her engagement with him, but it turns out that the necklace has been stolen for real. The culprit is Greta's jealous secretary, Adolfo, but despite the latter's attempt to frame him, Giulio proves his innocence and obtains a role in an opera. Now, he and Lisa can get married.

Tutta la città canta, a.k.a. 6 × 8 / 48 (*Tutta la città canta*)

Italy 1945, b&w, 86 minutes

D: Riccardo Freda. S and SC: Riccardo Freda, Marcello Marchesi, Vittorio Metz, Steno [Stefano Vanzina] [and Federico Fellini—SC: uncredited]. DOP: Tony Frenguelli (Ferrania Pancro C6). M: Gorni Kramer, Giovanni D'Anzi, Gino Filippini, Oscar De Mejo (songs: "Altalena d'amore," "Tutta la città canta" and "6 × 6" by Kramer/Marchesi). E: Riccardo Freda. AD, CO: Angela Freda.

Cast: Nino Taranto (Orazio Babila), Vivi Gioi (Pepita), Natalino Otto (Natalino), Kramer [Gorni Kramer] (Accordionist), I 3 Bonos [Gianni Bonos, Luigi Bonos, Vittorio Bonos] (Themselves), Nanda Primavera (First aunt), Guido Riccioli (General Inspector Gingirelli), Franca Casalboni (Lucia), Angelo Calabrese [Carmelo D'Angeli] (School Principal), Lello Nati (Cousin Cocco), Maria Pia Arcangeli (Second aunt), Umberto Silvestri (Butler), Piero Carnabuci (Theater owner), Edoardo Toniolo (Hotel valet), Alfredo Tupini, Erminio Nazzaro; *uncredited*: Giuseppe Addobbati (Hotel receptionist).

PROD: Appia Cinematografica, ICI—Industrie Cinematografiche Italiane, Littoria Film, SAFIR—Società Anonima Film Italiani Roma (Rome). GM: Mario Tugnoli. PM: Bruno Bolognesi. Filmed at Pisorno Studios (Tirrenia). Visa n. 61 (7/18/1945, m. 2380). Release date: 8/15/1945. Distribution: Effebi. Domestic gross: n.a.

Harassed by his two stingy aunts and engaged to the school headmaster's ugly daughter Lucia, whom he truly dislikes, the timid school teacher Orazio Babila receives a telegram which informs him that he has inherited a goldmine from a deceased uncle. The "goldmine," unbeknownst to him, is actually a stage company— "The Gold Mine Company"—on the verge of financial breakdown. When Orazio checks in at the city's most expensive hotel, the company's soubrette Pepita believes he is a millionaire. In order to prevent Orazio from rejecting the heritage, she flirts with him, while her colleagues concoct a plan to sell out their next show so as not to disappoint Orazio. Meanwhile, Babila's aunts—who have already started buying expensive cars and art objects and have moved in a luxurious palace—are planning to keep the inheritance for themselves, in cahoots with the greedy headmaster. Eventually Orazio finds out the truth and returns home; he confesses to his aunts and surrenders to the impending wedding with Lucia. Pepita and her acolytes set up a plan to save him: on the day the Ministry inspector visits the school, the Gold Mine Company wreaks havoc in the place, ruining the headmaster's reputation. Eventually, Orazio joins the company and he and Pepita get married.

Aquila nera

Italy 1946, b&w, 108 minutes

D: Riccardo Freda. S: Riccardo Freda, based on the novel *Dubrovsky* by Alexander Pushkin. SC: Riccardo Freda, Mario Monicelli, Steno [Stefano Vanzina], Braccio Agnoletti. DOP: Rodolfo Lombardi. M: Franco Casavola (Ed. Marletta). E: Otello Colangeli. SO: Raffaele Del Monte. AD: Giorgio Lastricati. MU: Alberto De Rossi. ArtD: Arrigo Equini. CO: Vasco Gori.

Cast: Rossano Brazzi (Vladimir Dubrovsky), Gino Cervi (Kirila Petrovic), Irasema Dilián (Masha Petrovic), Rina Morelli (Irina), Harry Feist (Sergei Ivanovic), Paolo Stoppa (Erkar, a bandit), Inga Gort (Maria), Pietro [Petr] Sharoff (Count Andrea Dubrovsky), Luigi Pavese (Kolia, the Servant), Angelo Calabrese (President of the Court), Angelo Bassanelli, Dante Carapelli, Pietro Ciriaci, Magda Forlenza, Armando Franco, Luigi A. Garrone, Loris Gizzi, Carlo Monteaux, Piero Pastore, Cesare Polacco (Spizhin), Silvio Rizzi, Felice Romano, Yvonne Sanson (Girl at the banquet), Ugo Sasso, Mario Siletti; *uncredited*: Gina Lollobrigida (Circassian slave).

PROD: Nino Angioletti for Cinematografica Distributori Indipendenti (Rome). PM: Romolo Laurenti, Franco Palaggi, Felice Romano. Filmed at the Centro Sperimentale Studios (Rome). Visa n. 1260 (9/26/1946, m. 2986). Release date: 9/21/1946. Distribution: Cinematografica Distributori Indipendenti (CDI) (Italy), Lux Film Distributing Corporation (U.S.A.). Domestic gross: 195,000,000 *lire*.

Also known as: *Return of the Black Eagle* (U.S.A.), *The Black Eagle* (U.K.), *L'aigle noir* (France, Belgium), *Schwarzer Adler* (West Germany, Austria), *Águila negra* (Spain, Argentina), *De zwarte arend* (Belgium—Flemish), *Águia negra* (Portugal, Brazil), *O aetos tis steppas / O mavros aetos* (Greece), *Czarny orzel* (Poland), *Svarta örnen* (Sweden), *Kara kartal* (Turkey).

Russia, early 19th century. Vladimir Dubrovsky, a young officer of the Imperial guard, learns from a faithful servant that the merchant Kirila Petrovic has confiscated all his family properties. Vladimir—who was about to fight prince Sergei Ivanovic in a duel the next morning—leaves the regiment in a hurry, and Ivanovic makes him pass as a traitor and a coward. After his old father dies in his arms, Vladimir swears vengeance and becomes an outlaw, under the name "Black Eagle." His first victim is the corrupt judge who helped Kirila get hold of Dubrovsky's land. Soon his exploits make the "Black Eagle" a notorious name among the Russian people. During an assault on a stagecoach, Vladimir meets Kirila's young daughter, Masha, and falls in love with her. In order to be received at Petrovic's mansion and court Masha, Vladimir passes off as a French professor. Having failed to murder Kirila, Vladimir's true identity is discovered when Ivanovic—who has been entrusted with the task of capturing the "Black Eagle"—shows up at Kirila's place. Despite Ivanovic and Petrovic's efforts, Dubrovsky manages to escape. Kirila gives Masha in marriage to Ivanovic, and when Vladimir learns about the wedding he returns to the castle to save her. He kills Ivanovic in a duel and, just as he is about to be overwhelmed by Kirila's men, his faithful Cossacks storm the castle. Kirila escapes with Masha in a carriage but Dubrovsky pursues him and saves the girl, while her father falls to his death in a precipice. His name now cleansed, Vladimir is re-admitted in the army and marries his beloved Masha.

I miserabili

Italy 1948, b&w, 189 minutes

D: Riccardo Freda. S: based on the novel by Victor Hugo. SC: Riccardo Freda, Mario Monicelli, [Vittorio] Nino Novarese, Stefano Vanzina. DOP: Rodolfo Lombardi (Ferrania Pancro C6). M: Alessandro Cicognini, conducted by Fernando Previtali. E: Otello Colangeli. C: Memmo [Guglielmo] Lombardi, Ugo Lombardi, Giorgio Orsini, Nando Ferrazza. AD: Giorgio Lastricati, Valentino Trevisanato. PD: Guido Del Re. CO: Dario Cecchi. MU: Alberto De Rossi. APD: Ivo Battelli. ACO: Maria Baroni. SE: Giovanni Piccolis.

Cast: Gino Cervi (Jean Valjean), Valentina Cortese (Fantine / Cosette as an adult), Giovanni [Hans] Hinrich (Javert), Aldo Nicodemi (Marius), Luigi Pavese (Thenardier), Jone Romano (Mrs. Thenardier), Joop van Hulzen (Baron Gillenormand), Delia Orman, Gino Cavalieri (Police archivist), Massimo Pianforini, Duccia Giraldi (Cosette as a child), Alba Setaccioli, Andreina Pagnani (Sister Simplicia), Ugo Sasso (Enjoiras), Luigi A. Garrone, Nino Marchetti, Dino Baronetto, Franco Balducci, Marcello Mastroianni (Revolutionist), Giuseppe Pierozzi; uncredited: Rinaldo Smordoni (Gavroche), Cesarina Rossi, Gabriele Ferzetti (Tholomyes).

PROD: Carlo Ponti for Lux Film. PM: Clemente Fracassi. PS: Bruno Todini. Filmed at CSC (Rome). Visa n. 3462 (12/15/1947, m. 2536), 3461 (12/27/1947, m. 2669). Release date: 1/21/1948, 1/28/1948. Distribution: Lux Film (Italy), Lux Film Distributing Corporation (U.S.A.). Domestic gross: 375,000,000 lire.

Also known as: *Les Miserables* (U.S.A.), *L'évadé du bagne* (France), *Die Elenden* (Germany), *Kurjat* (Finland), *Os Miserávles* (Portugal), *Samhällets olycksbarn* (Sweden).

Note: The film was released in Italy in two parts: *Caccia all'uomo* and *Tempesta su Parigi*. The second part received visa n. 3461, whereas the first had no. 3462. Nino Novarese is credited as scriptwriter only in the second part. Overseas it came out in a shortened version that blended the two parts together.

"*Caccia all'uomo*." Paris, 1781. A poor young man, Jean Valjean, is sentenced to five years in prison for stealing a loaf of bread. His repeated attempts at escape cost him a 18-year conviction, and undying hatred on the part of the ferocious policeman Javert. Upon his release, Valjean is embittered and penniless, but he starts out a new honest life thanks to the generosity of an elderly bishop. Under the identity of Monsieur Madeleine, he becomes the mayor and a respected industrialist of the city of Montreuil. But fate is against him: Javert arrives in Montreuil where he has been appointed as Inspector. Valjean helps out a poor woman, Fantine, a single parent who has been discharged from his factory and forced to become a prostitute, but Javert recognizes him. Valjean escapes arrest, and while on the lam he meets Fantine's little daughter, Cosette: Valjean takes the child with him to protect her from the abusive innkeeper Thenardier, but is accused of abduction, and once again he has Javert on his heels. Valjean and Cosette take refuge in a convent. "Tempesta su Parigi." Paris, 1832. A young revolutionary, Marius, hides at the house where the elderly Valjean (who rebuilt his fortune under a new identity) lives with Cosette, whom he raised as his daughter, and falls in love with her. Marius' landowner is Thenardier, who recognizes Valjean and vainly tries to blackmail him. Marius' father, the Minister of Police, tries to protect his son with Javert's help. When Valjean realizes that Cosette loves Marius, he joins the revolutionaries on the barricades and saves the young man's life from the execution squad. Javert arrests him, but ultimately he is won over by the realization of Valjean's honesty: overwhelmed by guilt, he commits suicide. Cosette and Marius are about to marry, but once again the evil Thenardier obstructs their happiness: Valjean faces him and provokes his death, but is himself mortally wounded.

Il cavaliere misterioso

Italy 1948, b&w, 92 minutes

D: Riccardo Freda. S and SC: Riccardo Freda, Mario Monicelli and Stefano Vanzina. DOP: Rodolfo Lombardi. M: Alessandro Cicognini, conducted by Ugo Giacomozzi. E: Otello Colangeli. PD: Piero Filippone. ArtD, CO: Vittorio Nino Novarese. AD: Valentino Trevisanato. C: Guglielmo Lombardi. MU: Otello Fava.

Cast: Vittorio Gassman (Giacomo Casanova), María Mercader (Elisabetta), Yvonne Sanson (Empress Catherine II of Russia), Gianna Maria Canale (Countess Lehmann), Alessandra Mamis (Countess Ipatief), Giovanni [Hans] Hinrich (The Great Inquisitor), Dante Maggio (Gennaro, Casanova's servant), Guido Notari (Count Ipatieff), Vittorio Duse, Elli Parvo (The Doge's wife), Antonio Centa (Antonio, Casanova's brother), Tino Buazzelli (Josef), Aldo Nicodemi (Count Orloff), Renato Valente (Count Polsky).

PROD: Dino De Laurentiis for Lux Film (Rome). PM: Dino De Laurentiis. PS: Fernando Pisani. PSe: Renato de Pasqualis. Filmed at Parco Nazionale d'Abruzzi and at Cinecittà Studios (Rome). Visa n. 4670 (10/14/1948, m. 2550). Release date: 11/1/1948. Distribution: Lux Film (Italy), Lux Compagnie Cinématographique de France (France). Domestic gross: 180,000,000 lire.

Also known as: *The Mysterious Rider* (U.S.A.), *Le chevalier mystérieux* (France), *Der geheimnisvolle Chevalier* (West Germany), *El caballero misterioso* (Spain), *O cavaleiro misterioso* (Brazil), *Aventura na Rússia* (Portugal), *De geheimzinnige ridder* (Belgium—Flemish title), *Kazanovas* (Greece).

Secret agents hired by Catherine of Russia steal a compromising letter from the Doge of Venice's wife. The document has a special importance for the Empress, as Catherine intends to annex some Venetian territories to her empire, while the Doge opposes it. With the letter in her hands, she will be able to break the Doge's resistance. The Doge's Secretary, Giacomo Casanova's brother, is wrongly accused of the theft and sentenced to death. Casanova is in exile, and a price has been put on his head in Venice. Despite this, he secretly returns to his hometown and is able to meet his brother: he obtains valuable information from him, and starts to investigate on his own. In Vienna, Casanova meets a young maid, Elisabetta, with whom he falls in love, and gets in touch with the conspirators. He escapes an ambush with the help of Countess Ipatieff, the wife of the head conspirator, and finds out that the carrier of the letter is a woman, Countess Lehmann, whom he follows to Russia. There, Casanova saves the Empress' life during a bear hunt and eventually manages to get hold of the letter in the nick of time, at Catherine's palace. In order to escape, he seduces Countess Lehmann, and then flees on a sledge with Elisabetta. They escape from the Cossacks, but the wounded Elisabetta dies in Casanova's arms. The adventurer accomplishes his mission and then leaves Venice alone, accompanied by the memory of his beloved.

O caçula do barulho

Brazil 1949, b&w, 87 minutes

D: Riccardo Freda. S and SC: Riccardo Freda. Dial: Alinor Azevedo. DOP: George Dusek, Ugo Lombardi. E: Carla Civelli, Serafim Moura, Nélson Chult [Schultz]. ArtD: Murillo Lopes. MU: Paulo Carias. AD: Hélio Tálamo. C: Amleto Daissé. SO: Sylvio Rabello, Aloysio Vianna. Songs: Alberto Ribeiro.

Cast: Oscarito [Oscar Lorenzo Jacinto de la

Imaculada Concepción Teresa Diaz] (Luis' sidekick), Grande Otelo [Sebastião Bernardes de Souza Prata] (The Cleaner), Gianna Maria Canale (Gianna), Anselmo Duarte (Luis Oliveira), Luiz Tito (Boss), Belmira de Almeida (Luis's mother), Sérgio de Oliveira (Luis' father), Lídia Vani, Antonio Sá Barbosa, Zulmira Miranda, Francisco Martorelli, Sebastiana Feliciana, Waldir Madeiros, Reginaldo Racy, Maia, Moraes, Nena Napoli, Grijó Sobrinho, Beyla Genauer, Walkiria Rosas, Aurora Labela, Pérola Negra.

PROD: L. Bruni for Atlântida Cinematográfica (Sao Paulo). AP: J. Parente Sobrinho. Release date: 1/1/1949. Distribution: UCB (Brazil). Domestic gross: n.a.

Note: Negatives and prints in 16 and 35 mm of the film are kept at the Fundação Cinemateca Brasileira in São Paulo. Even though sources list the title as *O caçula do barulho*, the only existing print (very worn-out and running 76 minutes and 35 seconds) is titled *Um caçula do barulho*. Maia and Moraes are two wrestlers of the "Escola dos Professores." A "special thanks" credit is dedicated to Walter Pinto. The credits are taken from said print.

Rio de Janeiro. Luis, the youngest of seven brothers, is a handsome slacker who always manages to get himself into trouble, usually with his cowardly friend. Each time it is up to his brothers to get him out of danger. Trouble comes again when Luis falls in love with an Italian singer, Gianna: he and Eliseo discover that she is tied to a seedy stage impresario who heads a white slave ring. Luis is captured by the gangsters, but Gianna warns the other brothers just in time...

Il conte Ugolino

Italy 1949, b&w, 88 minutes

D: Riccardo Freda. S: Luigi Bonelli. SC: Stefano Vanzina and Mario Monicelli [and Riccardo Freda, uncredited]. DOP: Sergio Pesce. M: Alessandro Cicognini (Ed. Bixio-S.A.M.). E: Roberto Cinquini. ArtD: Alberto Boccianti. AD: Valentino Trevisanato.

Cast: Carlo Ninchi (Count Ugolino Della Gherardesca), Gianna Maria Canale (Emilia), Peter Trent (Ruggieri), Piero Palermini (Balduccio Ubaldini), Carla Calò (Haidée), Luigi Pavese (Sismondi), Ugo Sasso (Fortebraccio), Ciro Bernardi (Lanfranchi), Armando Guarneri (Gualandi).

PROD: Forum Film (Rome). GM: Raffaele Colamonici. AP: Umberto Momi. Filmed at S.A.F.A. Studios (Rome). Visa n. 6619 (10/28/1949, m. 2437). Release date: 11/1/1949. Distribution: Forum Film. Domestic gross: 87,000,000 lire.

Also known as: *The Iron Swordsman* (U.S.A.)

Pisa, 1284. Count Ugolino della Gherardesca is the most powerful and wealthy man in the Republic of Pisa, but he has many enemies. Archbishop Ruggieri, who holds the Council of the Republic and is apparently a friend of Ugolino's, is actually a devious and cunning man who takes advantage of the situation. He submits a treacherous plan to the Count, suggesting to him attracting the fleet of the rival Republic of Genoa into a trap, and destroy it. Ugolino submits the plan to the Council and retires in his castle, waiting for the Council's message that entrusts him with the command of the Pisan fleet. But the Archbishop destroys the message and sends the Count a fake one, which orders him not to move. Therefore, the Genoese fleet advances undisturbed and the Pisan one is destroyed. Accused of treason, the Count cannot defend himself effectively, because the Archbishop denies the existence of the fake message that he has destroyed after retrieving it from Ugolino. The Count is condemned to die of starvation and is buried alive in a dungeon along with his children. Following the intervention of Ugolino's daughter Emilia, the Pope has the Archbishop arrested, but it is too late...

Guarany

Italy 1950, b&w, 87 minutes

D: Riccardo Freda. S: Riccardo Freda. SC: Riccardo Freda, Goffredo D'Andrea. DOP: Rodolfo Lombardi, Ugo Lombardi. M: Antônio Carlos Gomes, arranged by Vincenzo Tommasini, conducted by Fernando Previtali. E: Riccardo Freda. PD: Ettore Laccetti, Sergio Baldacchini. AD: Renato D'Andrea, Manoel Poeta. C: Guglielmo Lombardi. CO: Maria De Matteis. SO: Armando Parmegiani.

Cast: António Vilar (Antônio Carlos Gomes), Gianna Maria Canale (Jacqueline), Mariella Lotti (Lindita), Luigi Pavese (Carlos' father), Anita Vargas (Carlos' mother), Dante Maggio (Rossi), Andrea Forte (Carlos as a child), Guglielmo Barnabò, Tino Buazzelli, Pina Pallanti, Vittorio Duse, Pietro [Petr] Sharoff, Nino Marchetti, Tina Lattanzi, Fulvia Mammi, Rossella Falk, Paolo Panelli, Carlo Jachino, Mary Genni, Maria Da Glória, Mario Volpicelli, Elio Pandolfi.

PROD: Salvo D'Angelo for Universalia Film (Rome). GM: Goffredo D'Andrea. PM: Renato Silvestri. PS: Anna Davini, Gioacchino Colizzi. Pse: Claudio Forges Davanzati. Visa n. 6733 (11/16/1949, m. 2398). Filmed at Universalia Film Studios (Rome) and on location in Brazil. Release date: 1/3/1950. Distribution: Universalia Film. Domestic gross: 8,750,000 lire.

Also known as: *O Guarani* (Brazil).

Note: Filmed in 1948. A Brazilian pressbook lists the following as scriptwriters: Freda, Esodo Pratelli, Cesare Zavattini, Steno and Mario Monicelli.

Antônio Carlos Gomes, the son of a musician, lives in a remote village in Brazil. As a boy, he shows an inclination to music, but his passion is obstructed by his father, whereas Carlos' understanding mother dies when he is just a boy. Once an adult, Carlos abandons the village and his fiancée Lindita. In Rio de Janeiro he casually comes in contact with the Emperor Pedro II, who grants him a scholarship to study music composition. Carlos travels to Europe, and once in Lisbon he falls for a singer, Jacqueline, who accompanies him to Italy; for her Gomes composes very successful operettas. However, Carlos is not satisfied with his work, and Lindita urges him to write more serious music. He composes the opera "Il Guarany," but many obstacles, and Jacqueline's hostility, prevent it from being staged. Unbeknownst to Gomes, Lindita manages to give the music sheet to the great composer Giuseppe Verdi, who makes it possible for the opera to be staged at the Scala theater in Milan. The audience welcomes "Il Guarany" enthusiastically: having learned about Lindita's role in the triumph, Gomes returns to her.

Il figlio di d'Artagnan

Italy 1950, b&w, 86 minutes
D: Riccardo Freda. S and SC: Dick Jordan [Riccardo Freda]. DOP: Sergio Pesce. M: Carlo Jachino. E: Renato Cinquini. PD, SD: Alberto Boccianti. CO: Maria De Matteis. AD: Valentino Trevisanato. SO: Umberto Picistrelli.

Cast: Gianna Maria Canale (Linda), Franca Marzi [Francesca Marsi] (The Countess), Piero Palermini (Raoul d'Artagnan), Carlo Ninchi (Marshal D'Artagnan), Paolo Stoppa (Duke of Bligny), Peter Trent (Duke of Malvoisin), Nerio Bernardi (Friar), Enzo Fiermonte (Viscount of Langlass); *uncredited*: Ugo Sasso, Furio Meniconi, Mario Meniconi, Nello Meniconi, Miranda Campa.

PROD: Raffaele Colamonici and Umberto Montesi for Augustus Film. Visa n. 7416 (3/4/1950, m. 2788). Release date: 3/8/1950. Distribution: Augustus Film (Italy), Cocinor (France). Domestic gross: 201,000,000 *lire*.

Also known as: *The Gay Swordsman* (U.S.A.), *Le fils de d'Artagnan* (France; Belgium), *El hijo de d'Artagnan* (Spain), *Mönch und Musketier* (West Germany), *D'Artagnans søn* (Denmark), *Zoon van D'Artagnan* (Netherlands; Belgium—Flemish title), *O filho de d'Artagnan* (Portugal; Brazil).

Note: official ministry papers list a running time of approximately 102 minutes (2788 m.), but this is highly unlikely, and perhaps the result of a typo. The copy available at the Spanish filmoteca runs 86 minutes and shows no signs of cuts whatsoever.

Raoul d'Artagnan, the son of Marshal d'Artagnan, has entered a convent as a novice. When a mysterious knight kills the Prior, who was opposing the arrest of a courier sent over by Richelieu, Raoul starts investigating on his own. First, though, he is trained by the other friars in the art of fencing, horse riding, shooting, playing cards.... Dressed as a knight, Raoul goes to Grecy where his father has his headquarters. There he meets the Duke of Bligny and Linda, a beautiful pastry girl, whom he falls for. Raoul aims to track down and punish the mysterious knight, but the latter unsuccessfully attempts to have him killed. Then he frames Raoul, who is accused of having stolen a war plan to attack a Flemish fortress that bars the way to the troops. Raoul is sentenced to death for treason, but he escapes execution by volunteering to blow up the enemy fortress. Once inside with Bligny, Raoul discovers that the mysterious knight is the Duke of Malvoisin, his father's military advisor, who is double-crossing the French. The dangerous mission is carried out successfully: the French troops burst into the citadel and Raoul kills the traitor in a duel.

Magia a prezzi modici

Italy 1950, b&w, 10 minutes
D: Riccardo Freda. DOP: Enzo Serafin.
Cast: Mario Siletti.
PROD: Attilio Riccio for Opus Film. Visa n. 9092 (12/13/1950, m. 270). Release date: 1/11/1951. Distribution: Astra.

A superstitious man sees a black cat crossing the road in front of his car and panics: he drives the car back in the garage and goes out on foot. He then makes several examples of events and gestures which can be interpreted in a superstitious way. A brief digression follows, on superstition through the ages as well as on historical characters who believed in magic, from Socrates to Galileo, ending with Adolf Hitler. The story then cuts back to the present, as the protagonist goes to an astrologer to understand what fate awaits his unborn nephew, but to no avail. Worried about his future, the protagonist then meets another fortune teller who tells him he has a long way in front of him—a prophecy which turns out to be correct, as the man has to walk his way home throughout the city.

L'astuto barone
(ovvero L'eredità contesa)

Italy 1950, b&w, 10 minutes
D: Renato Dery [Riccardo Freda]. S: Renato Dery. SC: Riccardo Freda, Paolo Panelli, Tino Buazzelli. DOP: Rodolfo Lombardi. M: Franco Mannino. E: Otello Colangeli.
Cast: Paolo Panelli, Tino Buazzelli, Nino Manfredi, Rossella Falk, Bice Valori, Luciano Salce, Orazio Costa, Riccardo Freda (narrator).
PROD: Attilio Riccio for Fortuna Film. Visa n. 8744 (10/13/1950, m. 300). Distribution: Documento Film.
Note: Filmed in 1948.
After learning that his nephews, whom he always kept at distance, have received a huge inheritance, Baron Degubernatis invites them to his villa, with the intent of dispatching them and getting hold of the inheritance, but things don't go as planned...

Il tradimento (Passato che uccide)

Italy 1951, b&w, 94 minutes
D: Riccardo Freda. S: Mario Monicelli. SC: Mario Monicelli, Ennio De Concini, Riccardo Freda. DOP: Enzo Serafin (Ferrania Pancro C7). M: Carlo Innocenzi, conducted by Ezio Carabella; singer: Rino Salviati. E: Otello Colangeli. C: Aldo Scavarda. PD: Sergio Baldacchini. SD: Francesco Contardi. MU: Angelo Malantrucco. AD: Valentino Trevisanato. SO: Karl Schwartz. CO: Casa Montorsi.
Cast: Amedeo Nazzari (Pietro Vanzelli), Gianna Maria Canale (Luisa), Vittorio Gassman (Renato Salvi), Caterina Boratto (Clara Vanzelli), Armando Francioli (Stefano Soldani), Arnoldo Foà (Luigi, the Attorney), Camillo Pilotto (Soldani), Rita Livesi, Anita Durante, Oscar Andriani, Nerio Bernardi (Judge), Ciro Berardi, Attilio Dottesio (Dr. Bianchini).
PROD: S.A.F.A. Palatino (Rome). PM: Luigi Nannerini. PS: Valentino Pavoni. Filmed at S.A.F.A. Studios (Rome). Visa n. 9670 (4/6/1951, m. 2590). Release date: 4/11/1951. Distribution: Variety. Domestic gross: 311,000,000 lire.
Also known as: *Double Cross* (U.S.A.), *Trahison* (France; Belgium), *Traição/ Traição: Passado que mata* (Portugal; Brazil), *Dipli tragodia* (Greece).
1935. The malevolent Renato Salvi courts a married woman, Clara, the wife of his friend, engineer Pietro Vanzelli. After she refuses his advances, Salvi organizes a diabolical plan to get rid of her husband. Apparently drunk, he shows up at Vanzelli's place and asks the engineer to give him a lift home. Overnight Salvi disappears: the morning after his wallet is fished out of the river Tiber. Salvi actually faked his own death, by throwing a body with his clothes and documents into the river: wrongly accused of murder, Vanzelli is tried and sentenced to fifteen years in prison. Once released, he learns that his wife has died. His daughter Luisa, who was staying with a noble family in Livorno, has been fired because of her love affair with the nobleman's son; she has returned to Rome and is unemployed. One night Luisa gives assistance to a drunkard, whom she brings to her room. The man is Vanzelli, who eventually recognizes his daughter. The meeting is providential for both: Vanzelli rebuilds his position, Luisa returns to her beloved and marries him. But Salvi reappears and attempts to blackmail Vanzelli: a fight ensues, and Vanzelli kills Salvi in self-defence. Brought again to trial for the murder of the same man, this time Vanzelli is acquitted.

Tenori per forza

Italy 1951, b&w, 10 minutes
D: Renato Dery [Riccardo Freda]. S and SC: Renato Dery. DOP: Rodolfo Lombardi. M: Franco Mannino. E: Otello Colangeli.
Cast: Paolo Panelli, Tino Buazzelli, Nino Manfredi, Rossella Falk, Bice Valori, Luciano Salce, Orazio Costa, António Vilar, Riccardo Freda.
PROD: Attilio Riccio for Fortuna Film. Visa

n. 10577 (9/29/1951, m. 270). Distribution: Documento Film.

Note: Filmed in 1948.

Two young brothers learn that they have inherited a huge sum. To celebrate, they go to a tavern attended by lowlifes and bandits. The brothers are mistaken for cops and invited to a dice game which they end up winning. However, the bandits realize the misunderstanding and chase them to a theater, where the brothers are mistaken for tenors and forced to go on stage...

La vendetta di Aquila Nera

Italy 1951, b&w, 106 minutes

D: Riccardo Freda. S and SC: Riccardo Freda, Ennio De Concini, Sandro Continenza. DOP: Tony Frenguelli (Ferrania Pancro C7). M: Renzo Rossellini (Ed. Radio Record Ricordi). E: Otello Colangeli. PD: Piero Filippone. AD: Antonio Greco, Valentino Trevisanato. C: Enrico Betti Berutto. SO: Raffaele Del Monte, Giovanni Nesci. SS: N. Dorgo. MU: Manrico Spagnoli. SD: Egidio Campori; CO: Werther.

Cast: Rossano Brazzi (Vladimir Dubrovsky), Gianna Maria Canale (Tatiana), Vittorio Sanipoli (Boris Yuravleff), Peter Trent (Igor Cernicevsky), Attilio Dottesio (Boris' Guard Officer), Nerio Bernardi (Tsar Paul III), Fausto Guerzoni (Shepherd Witness), Ileana Semova (Maruska), Dante Carapelli (Selim), Giovanni Del Panta (Ivan), Franco Jamonte (Ilya), Arnaldo Mochetti (Innkeeper), Guido Moroni Celsi (Sermentoff, Prison Doctor), Raffaele Tana, Ughetto [Ugo Bertucci] (Kurin), Guido [Duccio] Sissia (Andrei Dubrovsky), Franca Marzi (Katia).

PROD: Umberto Momi and Carlo Caiano for A.P.I. Film—Associati Produttori Indipendenti. GM: Carlo Caiano. PM: Domenico Bologna. PS: Luigi Fanano. PSe: Luciano Momi. Filmed at S.A.F.A. Studios (Rome). Visa n. 10768 (10/25/1951, m. 2920). Release date: 10/25/1951. Distribution: A.P.I. (U.S.A.: J.H. Hoffberg). Domestic gross: 368,150,000 lire.

Also known as: *The Vengeance of the Black Eagle* (U.S.A.), *Revenge of the Black Eagle* (U.K.), *La Vengeance de l'aigle Noir* (France), *Die Rache des schwarzen Adlers* (West Germany; Austria), *La venganza de Águila Negra* (Spain), *A vingança do Águia Negra* (Portugal), *A vingança do Água Negra* (Brazil), *Den sorte ørn* (Denmark), *Svarta örnens hämnd* (Sweden), *Mustan Kotkan kosto* (Finland).

Note: Freda claimed that he acted as cameraman throughout the whole film.

Russia, 1782. During the Crimean war between Russia and Turkey, Vladimir Dubrovsky, a.k.a. Black Eagle, now commanding a regiment of Cossacks, discovers that Captain Cernicevsky is in cahoots with the Turks and has him arrested. Governor Yuravleff, Dubrovsky's sworn enemy, releases Cernicevsky and persuades the Tsar to proceed against the Black Eagle instead. While Dubrovsky is at war, the governor and his goons penetrate his castle, kill his wife and servants, and kidnap Vladimir's little son, Andrei. Dubrovsky swears revenge and, in order to force Cernicevsky to confront him, kidnaps the latter's sister Tatiana; but Cernicevsky has already been murdered on the orders of Yuravleff. Dubrovsky snatches a mute child from the hands of an innkeeper and gives him to Tatiana, whom he releases; only later on he finds out that the little boy is his own son, whom he hadn't seen since birth. Using the child as bait, Yuravleff has Dubrovsky captured and sends him over to Siberia, but the Black Eagle escapes after pretending to be dead. He kidnaps Tatiana—who has agreed to marry Yuravleff to save Vladimir's life—and is about to kill her; but Andrei, who has suddenly regained the power of speech, prevents him. Pursued by Yuravleff and his goons, Dubrovsky kills them all. He will marry Tatiana, whom he has fallen for.

Vedi Napoli e poi muori

Italy 1952, b&w and color, 87 minutes

D: Riccardo Freda. S and SC: Ennio De Concini, Alberto Vecchietti. DOP: Gábor Pogány (Ferrania Pancro C7; Ferraniacolor). M: Carlo Innocenzi (Ed. Radio Record Ricordi). E: Otello Colangeli. ArtD: Piero Filippone. C: Mario Capriotti. SO: Pietro Seriffo, Raffaele Del Monte. SS: Mario Tota. Artistic assistant: Luciano Momi. AD: Lodovico Borgo. SD: Enzo Costantini. AE: Fernanda Materni. MU: Angelo Malantrucco. H: Fulvia Dulac.

Cast: Gianna Maria Canale (Marisa Marini), Renato Baldini (Giacomo Marini), Vittorio Sanipoli (Roberto Sanesi), Carletto Sposito (Alfredo Bruca), Duccio [Duccio Sissia] (Giorgio, Marisa's son), Cicola Custureri (Valeria), Franca Marzi (Wanda, Sanesi's lover), Claudio Villa (Claudio).

PROD: Umberto Momi and Carlo Caiano for A.P.I. Film—Associati Produttori Indipendenti (Rome). GM: Carlo Caiano. PM:

Domenico Bologna. PS: Marcello Simoni. PSe: Gino Fanano. Filmed at the Teatri del Centro Sperimentale di Cinematografia (Rome) and on location in Naples. Visa n. 11506 (2/29/1952, m. 2405). Release date: 2/29/1952. Distribution: A.P.I. Domestic gross: 381,384,000 lire.

Also known as: *Perfido ricatto* (Italy), *See Naples and Die* (U.S.A.), *Le passé d'une mère*; *Chantage* (France), *Ver Nápoles ... e Depois Morrer* (Brazil).

Note: The songs *Ho pianto per te*, *A voce 'e mamma*, *Vedi Napoli e poi muori*, *Mattinata d'oro*, *Marechiaro* and *Malafemmina* are sung by Claudio Villa.

Before meeting her husband, bank official Giacomo Marini, the ex-singer Marisa was the fiancée of Roberto Sanesi, a shady crook who has just been released after seven years in jail. Sanesi, who has kept Marisa's love letters, intends to use them to blackmail Marini. Marisa, believing her husband is away, accepts to meet Roberto; however, Giacomo has been warned by Sanesi's jealous lover, Wanda, and becomes convinced that his wife is cheating on him. Shortly afterwards, the police arrest Sanesi, who is accused of drug trafficking, as well as Marisa, whom they believe is his accomplice. Marini does not listen to his wife's explanations and repudiates her. Driven away from home, Marisa is forced to resume her singing career in night clubs. Several years later, Sanesi comes out of prison and goes in search of the woman, with the intention of blackmailing Sanesi again. He kidnaps Marisa's little kid, who lives with his father, and demands a huge ransom. Marisa unexpectedly shows up at the meeting place and kills Sanesi in self-defense, even though she is badly wounded herself. The woman proves her innocence during the trial and finally reconciles with Giacomo.

La leggenda del Piave

Italy 1952, b&w, 77 minutes

D: Riccardo Freda. S: based on the song *Il Piave mormorò* by E.A. Mario [Ermete Giovanni Gaeta]. SC: Giuseppe Mangione, Riccardo Freda. DOP: Sergio Pesce (Ferrania Pancro C7). M: Carlo Rustichelli, conducted by Ugo Giacomozzi (Ed. Casa Editrice Nazionale). E: Mario Serandrei. C: Elio Polacchi. AD: Foen, Sante Chimirri. ArtD: Alfredo Montori. SD: Camillo Del Signore. SS: N. Costa. MU: Guglielmo Bonotti.

Cast: Gianna Maria Canale (Countess Giovanna Dolfin), Carlo Giustini (Count Riccardo Dolfin), Enrico Viarisio (Corporal Mainardi), Elena Cotta-Ramusino (Gabriella), Luigi De Filippo (Giorgio, a soldier), Edoardo Toniolo (Austrian officer), Giovanni Vari, Marcello Pedrini, Renato Baldini (Don Carlo, the chaplain), Giorgio Consolini (Singing soldier), Duccio Sissia (Mario, the countess' son).

PROD: CO.TU. (Produzione Film Colamonici Tupini) (Rome). PM: Manlio Maria Morelli. PS: A. Fanano, A. Fabrizi. Filmed at Titanus Studios (Rome). Visa n. 13047 (10/30/1952, m. 2135). Release date: 10/29/1952. Distribution: Regional. Domestic gross: 361,000,000 lire.

October 1917. During World War I, Count Riccardo Dolfin returns from the front to his castle in Veneto where his young wife, Giovanna, lives with their little son Mario. The Countess is a fervent patriot, whereas her husband had enlisted in the army only to carry on a shady black market business behind the lines. When she goes to Verona to visit her sick son, Giovanna discovers Riccardo's double life and decides to leave him. Meanwhile, the enemy has forced the defensive lines in Caporetto, resulting in a terrible defeat for the Italian army; despite the advice of friends, the Countess returns with her son to her castle over the Piave. All the territory is under control of the Austrian army, and the enemy settles in the manor: an Austrian officer attempts to rape Giovanna, but the Countess is saved by the intervention of a servant, who is then executed. The misfortunes of war have deeply shaken the soul of Count Riccardo; he demands to be sent to the front, where he fights heroically and is seriously injured. After the war, the couple meet again to agree on the terms of the separation, but they reconcile when Giovanna learns of her husband's bravery.

Spartaco, a.k.a. Spartaco— Il gladiatore della Tracia

Italy/France 1953, b&w, 105 minutes

D: Riccardo Freda. S: Maria Bory. SC: Jean Ferrey, Maria Bory, Gino Visentini. DOP: Gábor Pogány [and Mario Bava, uncredited]. M: Renzo Rossellini, conducted by the author. E: Mario Serandrei. ArtD: Franco Lolli. C: Guglielmo Garroni. CO: Dina Di Bari.

Cast: Massimo Girotti (Spartacus), Ludmilla Tchérina (Amitys), Yves Vincent (Ocnomas, Spartacus' lieutenant), Gianna Maria

Canale (Sabina Crassus), Carlo Ninchi (Marcus Licinius Crassus), Vittorio Sanipoli (Marcus Virilius Rufus), Carlo Giustini (Artorige), Umberto Silvestri (Lentulus), Teresa Franchini (Spartacus' mother); *uncredited*: Renato Baldini (Gladiator), Nerio Bernardi, Cesare Bettarini, Darix Togni (Gladiator).

PROD: Carlo Caiano for A.P.I. Film (Rome), Consorzio Spartacus Film (Rome), Es Establissments Sinag (Paris), Rialto Film (Paris). GM: Carlo Caiano. PM: Roberto Fabbri, L. Goulian. Visa n. 13564 (1/28/1953, m. 2900). Release date: 1/28/1953. Distribution: A.P.I. (Italy). Domestic gross: 450,000,000 *lire*.

Also known as: *Sins of Rome* (U.S.A.), *Spartacus the Gladiator* (U.K.), *Spartacus* (France), *Spartacus, der Rebell von Rom* (West Germany; Austria), *Spartaco* (Spain), *Spartacus de bevrijder der slaven* (Netherlands), *Spartaco, o Gladiador de Trácia* (Portugal), *Spartacus* (Finland), *Roma Kanlar Içinde* (Turkey).

Rome, 74 B.C. Spartacus, a Roman soldier of Thracian origins, is enslaved by Crassus after coming to the defense of the beautiful slave Amitys. Enlisted in Lentulus' gladiators, he tries repeatedly to escape. When the gladiators, shaken by his clarion call, begin a revolt, Spartacus becomes their leader and leaves Rome with them. Wounded by Rufus' soldiers during a patrol, he takes refuge with Crassus' young daughter Sabina, who is in love with him. After recovering, Spartacus returns to his men, and leads his army in a victorious assault on Rufus' fortified camp. The unexpected defeat throws the senate in a panic: Crassus summons Spartacus, who manages to obtain the promise of freedom for himself and his followers. Meanwhile, though, the rebels, troubled by their leader's absence, decide to carry on a frontal attack on the Roman troops. Spartacus joins them and falls in battle, which turns into a carnage for the slaves.

Teodora, a.k.a. *Teodora, imperatrice di Bisanzio*

Italy/France, color, 92 minutes
D: Riccardo Freda. S: André-Paul Antoine, Riccardo Freda. SC: René Wheeler, Claude Accursi, Ranieri Cochetti, Riccardo Freda. DOP: Rodolfo Lombardi (Pathecolor). M: Renzo Rossellini, conducted by Franco Ferrara. E: Mario Serandrei. C: Guglielmo Lombardi, Mario Alberti, Giorgio Attili. PD: Antonio Valente, Filiberto Sbardella. CO: Veniero Colasanti. SD: Flora Capponi. SO: Aldo Calpini, Giovanni Nesci. AD: Giuseppe Divita, Ranieri Cochetti. 2ndAD: Mario Mambretti, Roland Stragliati. MU: Giuseppe Annunziata, Giuseppe Peruzzi. H: Renata Longari, Lina Cassini. SS: Agostino Zanelli. SP: Osvaldo Civirani.

Cast: Georges Marchal (Justinian), Gianna Maria Canale (Theodora), Renato Baldini (Arkal), Irene Papas (Saidia), Carletto Sposíto (Scarpios), Nerio Bernardi (Belisario), Olga Solbelli (Egina), Alessandro Fersen (Metropolita), Loris Gizzi (Smirnos), Umberto Silvestri (Blind Athlete), Mario Siletti (Magistrate), Oscar Andriani (Scarpios' Advocate), Giovanni Fagioli (Clerk of Court), Henri Guisol (John the Cappadocian), Roger Pigaut (Andres); *uncredited*: Armando Annuale (Sandals' Vendor), Fortunato Arena (Guard), Pietro Capanna, Gualtiero De Angelis (Andres, Head of the Imperial Guards), Libero Intorre, Giorgio Murri, Michele Riccardini.

PROD: Lux Film (Rome), Lux Compagnie Cinématographique de France (Paris). GM: Riccardo Freda. PS: Angelo Fanano. PSe: Franco Adrono. Shot at S.A.F.A. Studios (Rome). Visa n. 15641 (12/14/1953, m. 2545). Release date: 09/29/1954. Distribution: Lux Film (Italy), Lux Compagnie Cinématographique de France (France), I.F.E. Releasing Corporation (U.S.A.). Domestic gross: 592,000,000 *lire*.

Also known as: *Theodora, Slave Empress* (U.S.A.), *Théodora, impératrice de Byzance* (France; Belgium), *Theodora-Kaiserin von Byzanz* (West Germany; Austria), *Theodora, keizerin van Byzantium* (Belgium—Flemish title), *Teodora, Imperatriz de Bizâncio* (Portugal; Brazil), *Teodora* (Denmark), *Teodora—en gatflickas karriär* (Sweden), *Teodora—orjakeisarinna* (Finland), *Teodora, cesarzowa bizantyjska* (Poland).

547 A.D. Emperor Justinian I consecrates the basilica of San Vitale, in Ravenna, and recalls how he met his wife, years earlier.... While wandering incognito in a poor neighborhood of Byzantium, Justinian meets a dancer, Theodora, who earns her living with petty thefts, and robs him of a valuable medallion. Torn between desire and guilt, Justinian has her condemned to a severe penance, but Theodora escapes. A chariot race has been ordained, pitting the rich against the poor, and the winning charioteer will be proclaimed king for a day: seeking revenge, Theodora takes the place of her lover Arkal and wins the race, beating Justinian. Eventually the two fall in love and get married. Once on the throne, Theodora displays extraordinary political qualities, and uses her power to improve upon the conditions of the population. But she makes herself an enemy: Justinian's greedy minister, John the Cappadocian, who is secretly conspiring against the emperor. John and Andres, the head of Justinian's guards, send Theodora's former lover Arkal to kill her, but Theodora makes him change his mind and leads the people of Byzantium against the traitors. However, the Cappadocian persuades his mistress Saidia, Theodora's envious sister, to tell Justinian that Theodora is plotting against him. The emperor learns the truth just in time to save Theodora from death.

I mosaici di Ravenna

Italy 1954, color, 10 minutes

D: Giuseppe Fatigati [actually Riccardo Freda]. DOP: Rodolfo Lombardi. M: Renzo Rossellini. E: Riccardo Freda. Commentary: Paola Ojetti.

PROD: Lux Film. GM: Riccardo Freda. Visa n. 17939 (12/16/1954, m. 258). Distribution: Lux Film.

A documentary short film about the early Christian mosaics in the churches of Ravenna.

Da qui all'eredità

Italy 1955, b&w and color, 86 minutes.

D: Riccardo Freda. S: Carlo Veo, Carlo Moscovini. SC: Riccardo Freda, Carlo Moscovini, Carlo Veo. DOP: Mario Albertelli. M: Domenico Modugno (Ed. Bixio-S.A.M.), conducted by Ranieri Romagnoli. E: Otello Colangeli. AD: Mario Caiano. PD: Arrigo Equini. C: Silvano Ippoliti. MU: Giorgio Garbini. SO: Amelio Verona.

Cast: Beniamino Maggio (Beniamino), Alberto Sorrentino (Alberto), Tina Pica (Aunt Tina), Domenico Modugno (Mimmo), Pina Bottin (Marisa), Nerio Bernardi (Commissioner), Luigi De Filippo (Mr. Tortelli), Carlo Delle Piane (Waiter), Loris Gizzi (Pipitone), Ughetto [Ughetto Bertucci] (Don Alonso), Ciccio Barbi (Male nurse), Lia Cancellieri (Ivana), Pietro Carloni, Pasquale De Filippo, Rosanna Fabrizi, Adriana Facchetti, Mariangela Giordano, Enzo Maggio, Gina Mascetti, Nino Milano, Piero Pastore, Enzo Petito (Movie Theater Owner), Pina Mascetti.

PROD: Carlo Caiano for Centauro Film (Naples). GM: Carlo Caiano, Riccardo Freda. PM: Mario Damiani. PS: Renato De Pasqualis. PSe: Bruno Fenocchi, Michele Lupo. AsstPSe: Mario Basile. Filmed at Istituto Nazionale Luce Studios (Rome) and on location in Naples. Visa n. 19562 (8/13/1955, m. 2485). Release date: 8/14/1955. Distribution: Centauro Film (Regional). Domestic gross: 142,000,000 lire.

Naples. Alberto and Beniamino share an apartment without water, electricity, gas and basic necessities. They spend their time concocting extravagant hoaxes and trying to remedy their disastrous consequences. Their aunt Tina, a rough-mannered and resolute elderly woman, threatens to disinherit them if they keep behaving in such a silly and inconvenient way. Aunt Tina would want their pretty little cousin, Marisa, to marry the son of lawyer Tortelli, but the girl is in love with another man, a singer named Mimmo. One night, Tina, Alberto, Beniamino and Marisa show up at the nightclub where Mimmo is performing. With Alberto and Beniamino's unwilling help, Tina unmasks Tortelli's falsehood and pitfalls. Eventually, the elderly lady decides to take Alberto and Beniamino home with her, so as to prevent them from taking any other disastrous initiative, and Marisa will marry Mimmo, who has won the grumpy aunt's heart.

Beatrice Cenci

Italy/France 1956, color, 98 minutes

D: Riccardo Freda. S: Riccardo Freda and Attilio Riccio. SC: Jacques Rémy, Filippo Sanjust. DOP: Gábor Pogány (Eastmancolor, CinemaScope). M: Franco Mannino. E: Riccardo Freda, Giuliana Taucer. PD: Arrigo Equini. AD: Piero Mussetta. 2ndAD: Mario Raffi. C: Mario Capriotti. SD: Maurizio Serra. CO: Filippo Samjust. SO: Ennio Sensi. SP: Angelo Pennoni. SE: Mario Bava.

Cast: Mireille Granelli (Beatrice Cenci), Micheline Presle (Lucrezia Cenci), Gino Cervi (Francesco Cenci), Fausto Tozzi (Olimpio Calvetti), Frank Villard (Judge Ranieri), Claudine Dupuis (Martina), Antonio De Teffé (Giacomo Cenci), Emilio Petacci (Marzio Catalano), Guido Barbarisi, Vittorio Vaser, Isabella Raffi, Carlo Mazzoni.

PROD: Electra Compagnia Cinematografica (Rome), Cinecittà (Rome), Franco London Films (Paris). PM: Luigi Sanjust. PS:

Tommaso Sagone. PSe: Claudio Agostinelli, Andrea Fantacci. Visa n. 22028 (6/25/1956, m. 2694). Release date: 9/6/1956. Distribution: Cei-Incom. Domestic gross: 223,400,000 lire.

Also known as: *Le château des amants maudits* (France), *Ein zarter Hals für den Henker* (West Germany)

1598, Papal State. Count Francesco Cenci is hated and feared because of his cruelty, which he also displays toward his own family: word of mouth has it that he poisoned his son Cristoforo. Francesco's wrath comes to a head when he learns that his daughter Beatrice—to whom he is morbidly attached—is in love with Olimpio Calvetti, his castle's steward. Cenci's son Giacomo is having an affair with his stepmother Lucrezia; after Francesco's unsuccessful attempt to have him killed, Giacomo and the woman plan to suppress him in turn. However, Lucrezia does not have the courage to poison her husband. Giacomo flees, but before leaving he saws the planks that support the balcony of his father's room. Meanwhile Olimpio, who dared to stand up to his master, is chased from the castle and threatened with death if he returns. When Olimpio shows up again to meet Beatrice, Francesco is about to shoot him, but falls from the balcony and dies. Lucrezia, Giacomo and Beatrice are about to leave the castle and move to Rome, when the judge Marcantonio Ranieri shows up to investigate. In Rome, Beatrice meets Olimpio again, and suspects that he is responsible for the death of her father. Olimpio manages to convince the girl of his innocence, but when Ranieri accuses Giacomo of patricide, Lucrezia defends him by blaming Olimpio, who is in turn defended by Beatrice. The two women are arrested, tortured and put on trial: Lucrezia resists out of love for Giacomo, whereas Beatrice confesses to the murder and is condemned to death. Olimpio collects evidence to save her, but is shot to death before he can deliver it to the judge. Beatrice is decapitated.

I vampiri

Italy 1957, b&w, 80 minutes

D: Riccardo Freda [and Mario Bava, uncredited]. S: Piero Regnoli. SC: Piero Regnoli, Riccardo Freda. DOP: Mario Bava (CinemaScope). M: Roman Vlad, conducted by the author (Ed. Titanus); E: Roberto Cinquini; PD, CO: Beni Montresor; ACO: Adriana Berselli; AD: Piero Regnoli; MU: Franco Freda; Hair: Ada Palombi; SO: Mario Messina; SE: Mario Bava (uncredited); C: Corrado Bartoloni.

Cast: Gianna Maria Canale (Gisèle Du Grand / Marguerite Du Grand), Carlo D'Angelo (Inspector Chantal), Dario Michaelis (Pierre Lantin), Wandisa Guida (Lorrette Robert), Angelo Galassi (Ronald Fontaine), Renato Tontini (Rinaldo), Charles Fawcett (Lonette's father), Gisella Mancinotti (Schoolgirl), Miranda Campa (Lorrette's Mother), Antoine Balpêtré (Julien Du Grand), Paul Muller (Joseph Seignoret); uncredited: Riccardo Freda (Autopsy doctor), Piero Regnoli (Mr. Bourgeois). *The Devil's Commandment*—extra cast: Barbara London, Al Lewis, Bert Goldstein, Larry Boston, Barbara Wohl, Ronny and Joy Holiday.

PROD: Ermanno Donati and Luigi Carpentieri for Athena Cinematografica (Rome), Titanus (Rome). PM: Piero Donati; PA: Claudio Agostinelli. Filmed at Titanus—Appia Studios (Rome). Visa n. 23894 (4/3/1957, m. 2220; V.M.16). Release date: 4/5/1957. Distribution: Titanus (Italy); Les Films Marbeuf (France), RCIP (U.S.A.). Domestic gross: 125,300,000 lire.

Also known as: *The Devil's Commandment* (U.S.A.-re-edited 1960 version), *Les Vampires* (France), *Der Vampir von Notre Dame* (Germany), *Los vampiros* (Spain), *El vampiro* (Argentina), *Os Vampiros* (Brazil).

Paris, the present day. The city is plagued by mysterious killings which the newspapers claim to be the work of "vampires," since the victims—all women in their twenties—have been completely drained of their blood. Journalist Pierre Lantin investigates, but his involvement in the case becomes much more personal when his fiancée Lorrette is kidnapped. The executor of the crimes, a man named Seignoret, is arrested: before mysteriously dying, he reveals that the culprit is Professor Du Grand, a renowned physician who lives in a gloomy castle owned by his cousin, the elderly Duchess Marguerite Du Grand. Marguerite's niece, the ravishing Gisèle, is hopelessly in love with Lantin, just like Marguerite had loved his father before him, but Pierre is strangely repulsed by Gisèle. Eventually it turns out that Marguerite and Gisèle are one and the same, and that the old woman is rejuvenated with the blood of the young victims by Professor Du Grand, who faked his own death in order to escape the police and continues his experiments in the castle's underground lab.

However, the effects of Du Grand's serum are only temporary, and Gisèle ages to her true self before Pierre and the police. Lorrette, who was being held prisoner in the castle, is released just in time.

Agguato a Tangeri

Italy / Spain 1957, b&w, 94 minutes

D: Riccardo Freda. S and SC: Alessandro Continenza, Vittoriano Petrilli, Paolo Spinola, Riccardo Freda. DOP: Gábor Pogány [Spanish version: Francisco Sempere] (Supercinescope). M: Lelio Luttazzi, conducted by the author. E: Nino Baragli, Margarita de Ochoa. PD, SD: José Alqueró, Gil Parrondo. AD Paolo Spinola, Juan Serra. MU: José Luis Ruiz. 2ndAD: Federico Vaquero [and Jorge Grau, uncredited]. PDA: Luis Paton. C: Miguel Agufo. AC: Alvaro Lanzoni. AE: Alicia Santacana.

Cast: Edmund Purdom (John Milwood), Géneviève Page (Mary Bovelasco), Gino Cervi (Prof. Bovelasco), José Guardiola (González's henchman), Félix Dafauce (Inspector Mathias), Antonio Molino Rojo (Pérez), Mario Moreno (Chief of Police), Amparo Rivelles (Lola), Luis Peña (González), Enrique Pelayo, Alfonso Rojas, Juan Olaguivel, Félix Bafara.

PROD: Antonio Cervi for Antonio Cervi Produzioni Cinematografica (Rome), Producciónes Ariel (Madrid), Rodas P.C. (Madrid). PS: Emimmo Salvi. UM: Rafael Carrillo. PSe: Rafael Carrillo, Rafael Crespo. Visa n. 25397 (10/23/1957, m. 2593). Release date: 11/8/1957. Distribution: Euro International Film (Italy), Twentieth Century-Fox (U.S.A.). Domestic gross: 168,500,000 lire.

Also known as: *Trapped in Tangiers* (U.S.A.), *Un hombre en la red* (Spain), *Guet-apens à Tanger* (France), *Brennpunkt Tanger* (West Germany), *Kovaa peliä Tangerissa* (Finland), *Tânger* (Portugal), *Cilada Sangrenta* (Brazil). Filmed in Madrid (Spain).

Note: The song *The Last Phone Call* (Edward Brody) is sung by Gin Maureen.

Tangiers. John Milwood, an American allegedly expelled from the United States, is courting Mary, the adopted daughter of the wealthy ichthyologist Henry Bovelasco. The latter does not look kindly upon the young man, whom he believes to be a fortune hunter: when he realizes it, John leaves Mary, who has fallen for him. Milwood spends his evenings at the Sheherazade nightclub, owned by a certain González, a drug dealer, and asks him to become part of his organization. González entrusts John to get rid of the body of a federal agent, who was posing as a barman at the Sheherazade, and collected evidence of the clubowner's shady deeds. But John is actually an undercover Interpol agent, on a mission to crack the drug ring that is operating in Tangiers. He evades a trap set up by a corrupt police official, and is believed dead by everyone except Mary, to whom he reveals his secret. Eventually John manages to vanquish the gang of traffickers, whose leader is Bovelasco, formerly a Chicago gangster by the name Nick Dobelli.

Agi Murad—Il diavolo bianco

Italy / Yugoslavia 1959, color, 95 minutes

D: Riccardo Freda. S: based on Leo Tolstoy's novelette *Hadhi Murad*. SC: Gino De Santis, Ákos Tolnay [and Riccardo Freda, uncredited]. 2ndUD: Leopoldo Savona. DOP: Mario Bava (Eastmancolor, Dyaliscope). 2nd unit DOP: Frano Vodopivec. M: Roberto Nicolosi, conducted by Pierluigi Urbini. E: Riccardo Freda. CO: Filippo Sanjust. PD: Kosta Krivokapic. ArtD: Alessandar Milovic. SD: Andrea Fantacci. AD: Odoardo Fiory, Milo Djukanovic. C: Ubaldo Terzano, Sekula Banovic, Kreso Grcevic. SO: Ovidio Del Grande. MU: Antonio Marini, Mirko Mackic. H: Anna Cristofani. MA: Enzo Musumeci Greco. AsstArtD: Kaja Zilko. CHOR: Branko Markovic.

Cast: Steve Reeves (Hadji Murad), Georgia Moll [Giorgia Molinella] (Sultanet), Renato Baldini (Ahmed Khan), Scilla Gabel [Gianranca Gabellini] (Princess Maria Vorontsova), Gérard Herter (Prince Sergei Vorontzov), Milivoje Zivanovic (Tsar Nicholas I), Nikola Popovic (King Shamil), Jovan Gec (Aslan Bey), Nicola Stefanini (Gonzalo), Milivoje Popovic-Mavid (Doctor Eldar), Marija Tocinoski, Pasquale Basile, Goffredo Ungaro [Unger]; *uncredited*: Dragomir Felba, Antun Nalis (Melders, Murad's Lieutenant), Massimo Righi (Tsar Orderly).

PROD: Mario Zama for Majestic Films (Rome), Lovcen Film (Belgrad). PM: Tommaso Sagone, Milan Zmukic. PS: Ermete Paolucci, Dusan Perkocic, Branko Lustig. Filmed in Yugoslavia. Visa n. 29387 (6/4/1959, m. 2615). Release date: 6/21/1959. Distribution: Lux Film (Italy), Warner Bros. (U.S.A.) Domestic gross: 483,160,000 lire.

Also known as: *The White Warrior* (U.S.A.),

Beli djavo / *Bijeli djavo* (Yugoslavia), *La charge des Cosaques* (France), *El diablo bianco* (Spain; Mexico), *Hadschi Murad—Unter der Knute des Zaren* (West Germany), *O diabo dranco* (Portugal; Brazil), *Bialy diabel* (Poland).

Note: Leopoldo Savona is credited in Italian prints as "collaborator to the direction."

Russia, 1850. Hadji Murad, the so-called "white devil," is a rebel who fights with his army of Cossacks, together with other tribes under the command of elderly king Shamil, for the independence of his people against Tsar Nicholas I, who has occupied the region. Tired of the ongoing, costly war, the Tsar entrusts Princess Maria Vorontsova, the wife of his main general, Prince Sergei Vorontzov, to bring over to her husband the authorization to start peace negotiations with the enemy. Meanwhile, Hadji Murad meets the other tribe chiefs, and his plan to lead an attack against a strategic Russian fort is disputed by fellow tribe chief Ahmed Khan. The assault on the fort is victorious, but Ahmed Khan—who lusts after Murad's bride-to-be Sultanet—spreads discord between Shamil and the hero, causing the latter to leave the tribes' council. Hadji ritually abducts Sultanet for the wedding, but is captured by the Russians, who have been alerted by Ahmed Khan. The badly wounded Hadji is held prisoner by Vorontzov, who has him tortured in order for Murad to sign a treaty, but the hero finds an unexpected ally in Maria, who is in love with him. Meanwhile Ahmed Khan takes Hadji's little son hostage. Hadji escapes and takes his revenge upon the traitor.

Caltiki il mostro immortale

Italy / France 1959, b&w, 76 minutes

D: Robert Hamton [Riccardo Freda] [and Mario Bava, uncredited]. SC: Philip Just [Filippo Sanjust] [and Riccardo Freda, uncredited]. DOP: Mario Bava. M: Roberto Nicolosi (Ed. Nord-Sud). E: Mario Serandrei. SE: Mario Bava. AD: Edoardo Fiory. Scientific Consultant: Elle Bi.

Cast: John Merivale (Dr. John Fielding), Didi Sullivan [Didi Perego] (Ellen), Gerard Haerter [Gérard Herter] (Max Gunther), G. R. [Giacomo Rossi] Stuart (Rodriguez), Victor André [Vittorio André] (Prof. Rodriguez), Daniela Rocca (Linda), Daniel [Daniele] Vargas (Bob), Arthur Dominick [Arturo Dominici] (Nieto), Black Bernard [Nerio Bernardi] (Police Commissioner), Rex Wood, Gay Pearl (Dancer).

PROD: Nello Santi for Galatea Film (Rome), Climax Pictures (Paris). EP: Bruno Vailati. Visa n. 29967 (8/4/1959, m. 2103, V.M.16). Release date: 8/8/1959. Distribution: Lux Film (Italy), Allied Artists (U.S.A.). Domestic gross: 94,150,000 *lire*.

Also known as: *Caltiki, the Immortal Monster* (U.S.A.), *Caltiki, le monstre immortel* (France), *Caltiki, Rätsel des Grauens* (West Germany), *Le monstre immortel* (Belgium).

Note: Freda is credited as "Robert Hamton" [sic]. English-language prints of the film feature more English pseudonyms: Mario Bava is credited respectively as "John Foam" (as d.o.p.) and "Marie Foam (for the special effects). Roberto Nicolosi is credited as "Robert Nicholas." Lee Kressel was the dubbing director.

Biologist John Fielding, his wife Ellen and their assistant Max Gunther are travelling through the Mexican jungle, looking for traces of the ancient Mayan civilization. Suddenly a member of the expedition disappears and another goes mad. John and Max investigate so as to discover the causes of these mysterious events: in a cave, near a pond of water, they discover the statue of Caltiki, the goddess of death. A monstrous creature emerges from the pond and severely wounds Max. In Mexico City, a fragment of the monster's flesh is detached from Gunther's arm: it is discovered to be a giant primordial unicellular creature, which grew thanks to radioactivity. John brings the sample home to study it; during his absence, the passage of a radioactive comet awakens the inert mass, which begins to grow again and multiply. Meanwhile, the crazed Max escapes from the hospital and sneaks into Fielding's house, where he threatens to abduct Ellen, and murders his own lover Linda: eventually, he is killed by the now gigantic monster, which destroys the house. Upon his return, John turns to the military command for help: a task force armed with flamethrowers and tanks attacks the monster and destroys it.

I giganti della Tessaglia
(Gli Argonauti)

Italy / France 1960, color, 87 minutes

D: Riccardo Freda. SC: Giuseppe Masini, Mario Rossetti, Riccardo Freda [and Ennio De Concini, uncredited]. DOP: Václav Vích, Raffaele Masciocchi (Eastmancolor, Totalscope). M: Carlo Rustichelli, conducted by Franco

Ferrara. E: Otello Colangeli. ArtD: Franco Lolli. CO: Mario Giorsi. ACO: Tony Randaccio. AD: Odoardo Fiory. C: Carmelo Petralia, Antonio Schiavo Lena. AC: Enrico Cortese. SE: Carlo Rambaldi. MU: Giuseppe Peruzzi. H: Anna Graziosi. SD: Antonio Visone. SP: Alfio Quattrini. SO: Renato Cadueri, Luigi Puri. SS: Vittoria Vigorelli.

Cast: Roland Carey (Jason), Ziva Rodann (Creusa), Alberto Farnese (Adrastus), Massimo Girotti (Orpheus), Nadine Duca [Nadine Ducasse] (Queen Gaia), Luciano Marin (Euristeo), Cathia Caro (Aglaia), Alfredo Varelli (Argo), Gil Delamare (Alceo), Maria Teresa Vianello (Olivia), Nando Tamberlani (Aglaia's father), Alberto Sorrentino (Licaone), Massimo Pianforini (Argo's father), Paolo Gozlino (Laerte), Raf Baldassarre (Antinoo), Nando Angelini, Taki Karas, Franco Gentili, Jacques Stany (Jason's companion), Gualberto Titta, Alfredo Zammi, Salvatore Furnari, Pietro Tordi, Raimondo Magni, Giovanni Sabbatini, Tino Vetrani, Pietro Capanna, Alice Clements (Dancer).

PROD: Virgilio De Blasi for Alexandra Produzioni Cinematografiche (Rome), Lyres Societé Cinématographique (Paris). EP: Virgilio De Blasi. PS: Enrico Bologna. PSe: Giuliano Sambati. Filmed at Cinecittà Istituto Luce Studios (Rome). Visa n. 33588 (12/6/1960, m. 2399). Release date: 12/6/1960. Distribution: Filmar (Italy), Medallion Pictures (U.S.A). Domestic gross: 408,000,000 *lire*.

Also known as: *The Giants of Thessaly* (U.S.A.), *Le géant de Thessalie* (France; Belgium—French title), *Das Schwert des roten Giganten* (West Germany), *Los gigantes de la Tessaglia* (Spain), *De reus van Thessalie* (Belgium—Flemish title), *Os gigantes de Tessália* (Portugal), *Los gigantes de Tesalia* (Mexico), *Os Argonautas* (Brazil).

1250 B.C. Jason, king of Thessaly, has left toward Colchis with a crew of trusted men, the Argonauts, in search of the Golden Fleece that was stolen from his land, in an attempt to save his people from Zeus' wrath. Meanwhile, his cousin Adrastus—whom the king had entrusted to rule over Thessaly during his absence—aims to seize the throne and craves for Jason's wife, Creusa. After facing a furious storm and an attempt at mutiny on the part of several men, Jason and his crew reach an island inhabited only by women. There, Jason is cordially met by the beautiful Queen Gaia, but he discovers that she is actually an ugly witch who has put a malevolent spell on his men, turning them into sheep. The Argonauts resume their journey and face more perils: on another island, they save the inhabitants from a ferocious Cyclops that demanded human sacrifices. One of Jason's men, Euristeo, falls in love with the young Aglaia and brings her onto the ship, unbeknownst to the others. After Aglaia is discovered and survives a rape attempt on the part of another Argonaut, Euristeo is put on trial, but Orpheus intercedes for him. Meanwhile, Adrastus—who has proclaimed himself king—tries to win over Creusa's resistance by threatening to kill her son Iti if she doesn't marry him. Eventually the Argo ship reaches Colchis. Jason climbs atop a huge statue where the Golden Fleece is placed and takes it away. Hurrying on the way home, he is informed by Euristeo of Adrastus' evil plans: back in Thessaly, he confronts the usurper just in time to save Creusa and his people.

Maciste alla corte del Gran Khan

Italy / France 1961, color, 94 minutes

D: Riccardo Freda. S: Oreste Biancoli. SC: Oreste Biancoli, Duccio Tessari. DOP: Riccardo Pallottini (Technicolor, Supercinescope). M: Carlo Innocenzi, conducted by Carlo Savina (Ed. Cinque Continenti) [U.S. version: Les Baxter]. E: Ornella Micheli. AD: Giuliano Betti. C: Stelvio Massi. AC: Giulio Spadini. SO: Mario Del Pozzo, Raffaele Del Monte. MU: Piero Mecacci. ArtD: Piero Filippone. SD: Athos Zanelli, Ennio Michettoni. CO: Massimo Bolongaro. CHOR: Wilbert Bradley. Chinese consultant: Tseng Yu.

Cast: Gordon Scott (Maciste; U.S. version: Samson), Yōko Tani (Princess Lei Ling), Hélène Chanel (Liu Tai), Dante Di Paolo (Bayan), Gabriele Antonini (Cho), Leonardo Severini (Garak, the Great Khan), Valéry Inkijinoff (Taoist high priest), Franco Ressel (Captain of the Khan's guards), Chu Lai Chit, Sergio Ukmar, Antonio Cianci, Giacomo Tchang (Old priest), Luong Ham-Chau, Tonino Chou, Ely Yeh.

PROD: Ermanno Donati and Luigi Carpentieri for Panda Cinematografica (Rome), Gallus Film (Paris). PM: Mario Damiani, Livio Maffei. Filmed at Incir-De Paolis Studios (Rome). Distribution: Jolly Film (Rome). Visa n. 35995 (10/25/1961, m. 2603). Release date: 10/31/1961. Distribution: Unidis (Italy), AIP (U.S.A.). Domestic gross: 468,200,000 *lire*.

Home video: Bayview Entertainment/Widowmaker (DVD, U.S.A.—as *Samson and the 7 Miracles*), Impulso (DVD, Spain)

Also known as: *Samson and the 7 Miracles of the World* (U.S.A.), *Le géant à la cour de Kublai Khan* / *Kublai Khan et le géant de Mongolie* (France), *En la corte del gran Khan* (Spain), *Maciste at the Court of the Great Khan* (U.K.), *Maciste in der Gewalt des Tyrannen* / *Die wilden Horden des Dschingis Khan* / *Maciste—Der Felsgeborene* (West Germany), *Maciste à la cour du Gran Khan* / *Goliath and the Golden City* (Belgium), *Den grusomme Khan* (Denmark), *Maciste ja Idän prinsessa* (Finland), *Sanson y los Siete Milagros* (Mexico).

China, 13th century. To halt the Tartars, who are threatening to invade the country, the Emperor of China asks Garak, the Great Khan of the Mongols, for help. However, Garak treacherously kills the Emperor and proclaims himself the regent of the Celestial Empire until the two legitimate heirs, Prince Tai Sung and Princess Lei Ling, reach adulthood. Ten years later, China is still under the Khan's tyranny, and its inhabitants are treated like slaves. The Khan is plotting to kill Tai Sung during a hunting party so as to keep the power for himself, but Maciste shows up and saves the Prince. The hero takes Tai Sung to a monastery in the mountains and meets the rebel leader, Cho, who is setting up a revolt against the usurper. Garak captures Lei Ling, and plans to marry her to become the legitimate sovereign, thus causing the jealousy of his lover Liu Tai. Alerted about the imminent wedding, Maciste arrives in Beijing, where he releases Lei Ling with Liu Tai's unexpected aid. Garak finds out about it and tortures Liu Tai. The Mongols attack the rebels' hideout: most of them escape with Maciste's help, but Tai Sung is killed in the process, and the princess spontaneously returns to Beijing to marry Garak. According to an old oracle the revolt will begin only after a gigantic bell tolls: Maciste succeeds in the feat, and the rebellion ensues. However, Maciste is captured and falls, apparently dead: he is subsequently buried in the depths of the Emperor's palace, while the rebels are about to be executed. The hero miraculously revives and comes out of his grave, provoking a terrible earthquake during which the Khan is finally killed. Princess Li Ling Chu marries Cho, and Maciste leaves toward new adventures.

Caccia all'uomo

Italy 1961, b&w, 101 minutes

D: Riccardo Freda. S and SC: Marcello Coscia, Dino De Palma. DOP: Sandro D'Eva (Kodak). M: Marcello Giombini, conducted by the author (Ed. Sinphony). E: Otello Colangeli. AD: Franco Loquenzi, Valentino Trevisanato. C: Giovanni Scarpellini. MU: Marcello Ceccarelli. SOE: Aurelio Pennacchia. ArtD: Piero Filippone. SD: Arrigo Breschi.

Cast: Eleonora Rossi Drago (Clara Ducci), Yvonne Furneaux (Maria Pardino), Umberto Orsini (Giovanni Maimonti), Riccardo Garrone (Commissioner Nardelli), Andrea Checchi (Inzirillo), Alberto Farnese (Paolo), Philippe Leroy (Mazzarò), Georgia Moll [Giorgia Molinella] (Anna), Aldo Bufi Landi (Baron Raimondo Platania), Luigi Visconti (Marshall), Vincenzo Musolino (Salvatore Pardino), Peter Dane (Schultz), Nando Angelini (Bandit), Mario Laurentino (Vice commissioner), Giò Stajano (Gabriellino), Franco Ressel (Headwaiter).

PROD: Mario Cecchi Gori for FairFilm (Rome). PM: Pio Angeletti. PS: Umberto Santoni. PSe: Franco Recine, Adriano De Micheli. Filmed at Incir-De Paolis Studios (Rome) and on location in Rome and Sicily. Visa n. 36089 (11/24/1961, m. 2787). Release date: 12/23/1961. Distribution: Paramount. Domestic gross: 83,000,000 lire.

Also known as: *Chasse à la drogue* (France), *Agent 0-1-7 auf heißer Spur* (West Germany).

Sicily. Commissioner Nardelli conducts the investigations against the bandit Mazzarò, who has murdered a notary and kidnapped a little girl, the niece of Baron Platania. The key to the case is a young woman, Maria Pardino, who is Platania's mistress and also the bandit's lover. The arrival of a police dog, Dox, trained by the young vice-brigadier Maimonti, lends a twist to the investigation, despite Nardelli's initial perplexities. Dox locates the bandit's hideout, releases the kidnapped girl and captures Mazzarò, after Maria has plunged into a ravine. Dox and Maimonti, both injured during the raid, are decorated with a medal and transferred to Rome: here, Maimonti flirts with a young girl and takes part in another difficult police investigation into the murder of an American, John Cooper. The inquiry leads Nardelli and his vice Inzirillo to uncover a drug trafficking ring that smuggles heroin hidden in lipstick tubes. *After one of the couriers, a model named Clara, is murdered, it is up to the dog to capture the head of the ring, the wealthy Schultz, and earn a second medal.*

Maciste all'inferno

Italy 1962, color, 91 minutes

D: Riccardo Freda. S: Eddy H. Given [Ennio De Concini]. SC: Oreste Biancoli, Piero Pierotti. DOP: Riccardo Pallottini (Technicolor, Cinemascope). M: Carlo Franci, conducted by the author (Ed. Nazionalmusic). E: Ornello Micheli. PD, CO: Luciano Spadoni. ArtD: Andrea Crisanti. AD: Giorgio Gentili. SS: Paola Salvadori. MA: Remo De Angelis. C: Alvaro Lanzoni, Maurizio Scanzani. AC: Luigi Conversi, Guido Cosulich De Pecine. SO: Fernando Pescetelli. MU: Giuliano Laurenti. H: Elda Magnanti. ACO: Marina Grugnola. SE: Serse Urbisaglia [and Mario Bava, uncredited]. SP: Angelo Pennoni.

Cast: Kirk Morris [Adriano Bellini] (Maciste), Hélène Chanel (The Witch / Fania), Vira Silenti (Martha Gunt), Angelo Zanolli (Charley Law), Andrea Bosic [Ignacio Božič] (Judge Edgard Parris), Donatella Mauro (Doris), Gina Mascetti (Innkeeper), Antonella Della Porta (Doris), John Karlsen (Burgomeister), Antonio Ciani (Villager), Puccio [Pietro] Ceccarelli (Giant), Remo De Angelis (Prometheus), Evar Maran [Evaristo Maran] (Villager), Charles Fawcett (Doctor), John Francis Lane (Matha's servant).

PROD: Luigi Carpentieri and Ermanno Donati for Panda Cinematografica (Rome). PM: Lucio Bompani. GM: Piero Donati. PS: Livio Maffei. PSe: Carlo Zanotti. Filmed at Grotte di Castellana (Bari), Manziana and the Odescalchi Castle (Bracciano). Visa n. 37190 (4/3/1962, m. 2502). Release date: 4/11/1962. Distribution: Regional (Italy), Medallion Pictures (U.S.A.). Domestic gross: 277,000,000 lire.

Also known as: *The Witch's Curse* (U.S.A.), *Maciste en enfer* (France), *Maciste, der Rächer der Verdammten* (West Germany), *Maciste en el infierno* (Spain), *Maciste no Inferno* (Brazil).

1522, Loch Lake, Scotland. Judge Parris condemns the witch Martha Gunt, whom he had loved in his youth, to burn at the stake. While engulfed in flames, Martha curses the judge and the whole village. One hundred years later, a girl who bears the same name as the witch arrives in Loch Lake with her husband Charley on their honeymoon. The village has been plagued by episodes of madness among the local women, and the villagers, who think Martha Gunt is a reincarnation of the witch, storm the castle where she is residing. Martha is dragged before the judges and condemned to the stake. Maciste shows up and descends into hell to fight the malevolent curse that haunts the village. There he has to face many perils, such as a ferocious lion and a door engulfed in flames, and is badly injured. He is cured by a young and beautiful woman, Fania, who turns out to be the witch in disguise. Fania has Maciste lose his memory, making him oblivious of his mission. Eventually, though, the witch, who has fallen in love with the hero, sacrifices herself to save him, and Maciste accomplishes his task, saving Martha Gunt just as she and Charley are about to be executed.

L'orribile segreto del Dr. Hichcock

Italy 1962, color, 88 minutes

D: Robert Hampton [Riccardo Freda]. S and SC: Julyan Perry [Ernesto Gastaldi]. DOP: Donald Green [Raffaele Masciocchi] (Kodak Eastmancolor). M: Roman Vlad. E: Donna Christie [Ornella Micheli]. ArtD: Joseph Goodman [Aurelio Crugnola]. SD: Frank Smokecocks [Franco Fumagalli]. CO: Inoa Starly [Itala Scandariato]. AD: John M. Farquhar [Giovanni Fago] [and Marcello Avallone, uncredited]. C: Anthony Taylor [Antonio Schiavo Lena]. AC: Giuseppe Maccari (uncredited). SO: Jackson McGregor [Renato Cadueri]. MU: Bud Steiner [Euclide Santoli]. H: Annette Winter [Anna Fabrizi]. SP: Angelo Pennoni (uncredited).

Cast: Barbara Steele (Cynthia Hichcock), Robert Flemyng (Prof. Bernard Hichcock), Montgomery Glenn [Silvano Tranquilli] (Dr. Kurt Lowe), Teresa Fitzgerald [Maria Teresa Vianello] (Margaretha), Harriet White [Harriet White Medin] (Martha, the housekeeper), Al Christianson [Aldo Cristiani] (Hichcock's assistant), Evar Simpsom [Evaristo Signorini] (Inspector Scott), Nat Harley [Giovanni Querel] (Gravedigger), Spencer Williams [Lamberto Antinori] (Franz, male nurse).

PROD: Louis Mann [Ermanno Donati and Luigi Carpentieri] for Panda Cinematografica (Rome). PM: Lou D. Kelly [Piero Donati]. PS: Charles Law [Livio Maffeo]. Filmed at Villa Centurini (Rome). Visa n. 37710 (6/26/1962, m. 2422, V.M.18). Release date: 6/30/1962.

Distribution: Warner Bros. (Italy), Sigma III Corp. (U.S.A.). Domestic gross: 142,000,000 lire.

Also known as: *The Horrible Dr. Hichcock*; *Raptus—The Secret of Dr. Hichcock*, *The Horrible Secret of Dr. Hichcock*, *The Terrible Secret of Dr. Hichcock* (USA), *The Terror of Dr. Hichcock* (UK), *L'effroyable secret du Dr. Hichcock* (France), *El horrible secreto del Doctor Hitchcock* (Spain) *El terrible secreto del Dr. Hichcock* (Mexico), *Raptus—O Diabólico Dr. Hichcock / O Demônio e o Dr. Hichcock* (Brazil).

Note: In Gastaldi's original story *Raptus*, the main character is named Bernard Stoltz.

England, 1885. The renowned Professor Bernard Hichcock has perfected an anesthetic which allows him to perform surgery even to patients in desperate conditions. Hichcock, who is actually a necrophile, also uses his invention to "put to sleep" his willing wife Margaretha and have sex with her, while pretending that she is dead. After Margaretha dies from a fatal dose of the anesthetic, Hichcock leaves England, only to return twelve years later with his second wife, Cynthia. The young woman is welcomed coldly by Martha, the housekeeper, and a series of weird events convince her that Margaretha has returned as a ghost. On the other hand, Hichcock can no longer control his necrophiliac impulses: he discovers that Margaretha is still alive, although insane, and hiding in the house. The doctor conjures up a deadly plan to restore his first wife's beauty at the expense of Cynthia's life...

Le sette spade del vendicatore

Italy / France 1962, color, 101 minutes

D: Riccardo Freda. S and SC: Filippo Sanjust [and Riccardo Freda, uncredited]. DOP: Raffaele Masciocchi (Technicolor). M: Franco Mannino. E: Franco Fraticelli. PD: Antonio Martini. AD: Marcello Avallone. SO: Leopoldo Rosi. C: Antonio Schiavo Lena. AC: Giorgio Pasquali, Remo Grisanti. MU: Maurizio Giustini, Massimo Giustini. H: Giancarlo Marin. SP: Angelo Pennoni. MA: Bruno Ukmar. SE: Eros Bacciucchi.

Cast: Brett Halsey (Don Carlos de Bazan), Béatrice Altariba (Isabella), Giulio Bosetti (Duke of Saavedra), Gabriele Antonini (King Philip II), Mario Scaccia (The Cardinal), Gabriele Tinti (Manolo), Jacopo Tecchio (Intendant), Alberto Sorrentino (Sancho), Anita Todesco (Catherine); *uncredited*: John Karlsen (Actor).

PROD: Cino Del Duca and Robert De Nesle for Adelphia Compagnia Cinematografica (Rome), Francisco Film (Paris). PM: Luciano Cattania. PS: Gino Peccerini. PSe: Giuseppe Rispoli, Salvatore Chetri. Visa n. 38671 (10/13/1962, m. 2795). Release date: 10/30/1962. Distribution: Cino Del Duca (Italy), Medallion Pictures (U.S.A.). Domestic gross: 140,000,000 lire.

Also known as: *The Seventh Sword* (U.S.A.), *Seven Swords for the King* (U.S.A.), *Sept épées pour le roi* (France), *Die sieben Schwerter der Rache* (West Germany), *Las siete espadas del vengador* (Mexico), *Musta naamio* (Finland).

Spain, early 17th century. Upon returning to his castle after the war, Carlos, the young Earl of Bazan, learns that his father has been murdered by bandits. The castle and the lands are now the property of his cousin, the Duke of Saavedra. That night Carlos survives a murder attempt: after leaving the castle he saves the beautiful Isabella from the bandits, and has a one-night affair with her. Later on, though, when he comes across Isabella again, she pretends not to know him. After enduring another ambush, Carlos stumbles upon a plot against King Philip II. He tries to alert the Prime Minister, but when the latter is killed, Carlos is framed for the murder and sentenced to death; to save himself, on the advice of his cousin, the Earl marries an unknown woman. What he does not know, though, is that the Duke of Saavedra is the head of the conspiracy: he wants to dispatch Carlos so as to inherit his wealth and carry out his plans. Carlos's unknown bride is Isabella, who has a key role in the conspiracy: she will invite the King to Bazan's castle where a deadly ambush has been set up for him. Carlos miraculously escapes death at the very last moment with the help of a handful of generous bandits who are loyal to the king. He is taken prisoner again by the duke, but Isabella saves the sovereign from certain death. Carlos takes the king's defense, and in the final duel he kills Saavedra. Carlos and Isabella live up to their marriage commitment.

Lo spettro

Italy 1963, color, 100 minutes

D: Robert Hampton [Riccardo Freda]. S: Robert Davidson [Oreste Biancoli]. SC: Robert Davidson, Robert Hampton [Riccardo Freda]. DOP: Donald Green [Raffaele Masciocchi] (Technicolor). M: Franck Wallace

[Francesco De Masi]. E: Donna Christie [Ornella Micheli]. PD: Sammy Fields [Mario Chiari]. CO: Mary McCarthy [Marilù Carteny]. AD: Silvy Black [Silvana Merli]. C: Anthony Taylor [Antonio Schiavo Lena]. AC: Piero Servo. SO: Christopher Curtis. MU: Max Justins [Massimo Giustini]. Hair: Charles Seaman [Giancarlo Marin].

Cast: Barbara Steele (Margaret Hichcock), Peter Baldwin (Dr. Charles Livingstone), Leonard G. Elliot [Elio Jotta] (Dr. John Hichcock), Harriet White [Harriet White Medin] (Kathryn Wood, The Housekeeper), Reginald Price Anderson (Albert Fisher), Raoul H. Newman [Umberto Raho] (Canon Owens, The Priest), Charles [Carlo] Kechler (Chief of Police), Carol Bennett (Woman).

PROD: Louis Mann [Ermanno Donati, Luigi Carpentieri] for Panda Cinematografica (Rome). PM: Lou D. Kelly [Lucio Bompani.] PA: Rommy Deutch [Romolo Germano], Lucky Reed. Visa n. 39641 (2/28/1963, m. 2790, V.M.18). Release date: 3/30/1963. Distribution: De Laurentiis (Italy), Magna Pictures (U.S.A.). Domestic gross: 175,000,000 *lire*.

Also known as: *The Ghost* (U.S.A.), *Le spectre du Dr. Hichcock* (France), *Frygtens time* (Denmark), *Hayalet* (Turkey).

Scotland, 1910. Bound to a wheelchair because of a grave disease, the elderly Dr. John Hichcock is a regretful old man. His obsession with the afterlife has Hichcock conduct séances in his mansion in order to get in touch with the spirits of the dead through his housekeeper, Kathryn, who is a medium. He is lovingly assisted by his much younger wife, Margaret, and by Dr. Charles Livingstone, who administers Hichcock small doses of poison as an experimental treatment to cure his condition. However, Margaret and Livingstone are actually lovers, and have concocted a plan to murder Hichcock by poisoning him, so as to inherit his wealth. They apparently succeed, but are forced to stay in the house, as the key to her husband's safe has mysteriously disappeared. It turns out to have been buried with the doctor: Margaret and Charles retrieve it but find out that the safe is empty. Soon Margaret is haunted by what appears to be her husband's ghost, and she begins to suspect that Livingstone has kept the jewels for himself. Hichcock's spectre, speaking through Kathryn, reveals to Margaret that the jewels are hidden in a box underneath the doctor's coffin. But the box is empty too. When Margaret confronts Livingstone, who has decided to leave her out of guilt, she finds out that he is taking the jewels with him: despite the man protesting his innocence, she savagely kills him with a razor. Only then she discovers that Hichcock faked his own death and orchestrated all the events, in order to perform a cruel revenge on her and her lover. Intoxicated by the same deadly poison she had used on her husband, Margaret is forced to attend to Hichcock's triumphant revelation. After dispatching the faithful Kathryn, who had been his accomplice all along, Hichcock plans to disappear with his wealth and lay the blame on his wife. But fate has a cruel joke awaiting him as well…

Il magnifico avventuriero

Italy / France / Spain 1963, color, 92 minutes

D: Riccardo Freda. S: Filippo Sanjust [and Riccardo Freda, uncredited]. SC: Filippo Sanjust (French adaptation: Antoinette Pellevant). DOP: Julio Ortas, Raffaele Masciocchi. M: Francesco De Masi (Ed. Nazionalmusic). E: Ornella Micheli. C: Antonio Schiavo Lena, Claudio Ragona. AD: Silvana Merli, Michel Autin. MA: Goffredo Unger. MU: Maurizio Giustini. H: Adalgisa Favella. CO: Marisa Crimi. ACO: Luciana Fortini. PDA: Franco Fumagalli. SO: Pietro Ortolani. SD: Aurelio Crugnola, Gianni Gianese (sculptures). SE: Eros Bacciucchi.

Cast: Brett Halsey (Benvenuto Cellini), Claudia Mori (Piera), Françoise Fabian (Lucrezia), Giampiero Littera (Francesco), Félix Dafauce (Frangipani), José Nieto (Constable of Bourbon), Jacinto San Emeterio (Francisco I), Rossella Como (Angela), Bernard Blier (Pope Clemente VII), Andrea Bosic [Ignacio Božič] (Michelangelo), Umberto D'Orsi (Grand Duke of Tuscany), Dany París (Francisco's wife), Elio Pandolfi (actor), Diego Michelotti (Charles V), Carla Calò (Angela's aunt), Bruno Scipioni (Guard), Sandro Dori (Angela's uncle).

PROD: Luigi Carpentieri and Ermanno Donati for Panda Cinematografica (Rome), Les Films du Centaure (Paris), Hispamer Films (Madrid). PM: Lucio Bompani. PS: Alfredo Melidoni. Filmed at Incir-De Paolis Studios (Rome). Visa n. 40754 (7/9/1963, m. 2537). Release date: 8/3/1963. Distribution: Regional. Domestic gross: 121,000,000 *lire*.

Also known as: *The Magnificent Adventurer*;

The Burning of Rome (U.S.A.), *L'aventurier magnifique (L'Aigle de Florence)* (France), *El magnífico aventurero / Las aventuras de Benvenuto Cellini* (Spain), *Mit Faust und Degen* (West Germany), *O Magnífico Aventureiro* (Brazil).

Benvenuto Cellini knows no bounds when it comes to creating a work of art or winning the heart of a woman. He steals from other goldsmiths the gold he needs to create a sculpture for a competition held by the Grand Duke of Florence, and then is forced to flee from the city. Attracted by the beautiful Countess Frangipani, Cellini joins a mission decreed by the King of France to the papal court; there he wins the favor of Pope Clement VII, who appoints him head of the Mint. However, to conquer Lucrezia's heart, Cellini breaks the law again, by fabricating counterfeit currency. Locked in the prisons of Castle Sant'Angelo, he is released by the Pope himself, who entrusts him with the command of Rome's troops against the army of Charles V. The mercenary militia conquers the city and commits every sort of injustice, in the so-called "Sack of Rome." Clemente VII takes refuge in Castle Sant'Angelo and orders Cellini to bring a message of peace to Charles V. The mission is completed and Rome is safe. Clemente VII allows Cellini to return to Florence.

Romeo e Giulietta

Italy / Spain 1964, color, 96 minutes

D: Riccardo Freda. S: loosely based on William Shakespeare's play. SC: Riccardo Freda. DOP: Gábor Pogány (Eastmancolor, Cromoscope). M: Bruno Nicolai. E: Anna Amedei. AD: Ruggero Deodato. AC: Mario Capriotti, Miguel Vaquero. ArtD: Teddy Villalba, Piero Filippone. CO: Rosalba Menichelli. MA: José Luís Chinchilla. MU: Adolfo Ponte. H: Elda Magnanti. SO: Giovanni Rossi.

Cast: Geronimo Meynier (Romeo), Rosemarie Dexter (Juliet), Carlos Estrada (Mercutio), Andrea Bosic [Ignacio Božič] (Capulet), Toni Soler (Nurse), Umberto Raho (Friar Laurence), Antonella Della Porta (Lady Capulet), José Marco (Paris), Elsa Vazzoler (Lady Montague), Franco Balducci (Benvolio), German Grech (Tybalt), Mario De Simone (Peter, the servant), Antonio Gradoli (Father Montague), Bruno Scipioni (Balthasar), Carlo D'Angelo (Prince of Verona).

PROD: Imprecine (Rome), Hispamer Film (Madrid). GM: Lucio Bompani. PM: Angel Rosson. PS: Romolo Germano. PSe: Roberto Natrici. Filmed in Spain and at Titanus Studios (Rome). Visa n. 43276 (6/26/1964, m. 2640). Release date: 8/28/1964. Distribution: Titanus. Domestic gross: 50,000,000 lire.

Also known as: *Romeo and Juliet* (U.S.A.), *Giulietta e Romeo* (Italy—Alternate title), *Los amantes de Verona* (Spain), *Roméo et Juliette* (France), *Liebe in Verona* (West Germany), *Julieta y Romeo* (Venezuela.)

Verona. The powerful Montague and Capulet families are divided by a long-running feud. Romeo Montague and his friends Mercutio and Benvolio show up uninvited at a ball held at the Capulets' house. There, Romeo meets Juliet and the two fall in love. A bloody brawl, during which Juliet's cousin Tybalt kills Mercutio and is in turn killed by Romeo, forces the latter into exile. While Romeo is away from Verona, Messer Capulet decides to give Juliet in marriage to Count Paris. To evade her father's will, on the eve of the wedding the girl swallows a sleeping pill, given to her by Friar Laurence, which puts her in a state of apparent death. Romeo, who does not know about this, kills himself in desperation. When she awakens, Juliet finds his lifeless body next to her, and commits suicide with Romeo's dagger.

Genoveffa di Brabante, a.k.a. La lancia della vendetta

Italy/Spain 1964, color, 89 minutes

D: José Luis Monter [actually Riccardo Freda, uncredited]. S: Riccardo Freda, based on the *Legenda aurea* by Jacobus de Voragine. SC: Riccardo Freda. DOP: Stelvio Massi, Julio Ortas (Eastmancolor, Tecnostampa). M: Carlo Rustichelli, conducted by Pierluigi Urbini (Ed. C.A.M.). E: Anna Amedei [Spanish version: Antonio Jimeno]. PD, CO: Carlo Leva. AD: Lamberto Benvenuti. C: Claudio Ragona. AC: Roberto Forges Davanzati. SO: Guido Mardone. MU: Libero Politi. H: Nicla Palombi.

Cast: Alberto Lupo (Count Siegfried of Treviri), María José Alfonso (Geneviève de Brabant), Stephen Forsyth (Golo), Andrea Bosic [Ignacio Božič] (The Count of Brabant), Antonella Della Porta (Geneviève's mother), Franco Balducci (Rambaldo), Rosita Yartza (Reibert's wife), Beni Deus (Reibert), Ángela Rhu (Berta), Bruno Scipioni, Loris Loddi; *uncredited*: Aldo Canti (Tortured soldier).

PROD: Imprecine (Rome), Hispamer Film (Madrid). GM: Lucio Bompani. PS: Rolando

Pieri. Visa n. 44364 (12/18/1964, m. 2461). Release date: 12/24/1964. Distribution: Regional. Domestic gross: 84,000,000 *lire*.

Also known as: *The Revenge of the Crusader* (U.S.A.—Home video), *Genoveva de Brabante* (Spain, Mexico), *A bosszú lándzsája* (Hungary), *La lancia della vendetta* (Greece—Home video)

Count Siegfried, seriously injured by a group of bandits, is brought to the castle of the Duke of Brabant, where he is cured with loving care by Geneviève, the Count's daughter. The two are married, and when Siegfried leaves for the Crusades, he entrusts his wife—not knowing she is pregnant—to the care of Golo, his administrator. However, Golo takes advantage of Siegfried's absence to undermine Geneviève, who strongly rejects his proposals and unleashes the man's wicked and vengeful nature. He has her accused of adultery and thrown into prison, where she gives birth to a son. Geneviève is sentenced to death, but one of the executioners spares Geneviève's life out of pity. She takes refuge in the forest and raises her son in the wild. Siegfried, who had been imprisoned by the Muslims, escapes and returns to the castle, oblivious to what happened. There, he discovers the truth; he punishes Golo, goes in search of his bride and son and comes back home with them.

Les deux orphelines

France / Italy 1965, color, 97 minutes

D: Riccardo Freda. S: based on the novel *Les deux orphelines* by Adolphe d'Ennery. SC: Michel Wichard, Riccardo Freda. DOP: Jean Tournier (Eastmancolor). M: René Sylviano. E: Jean-Marie Gimel, Patrick Clément-Bayard. PD: Jacques Mawart. MA: Claude Carliez, Antoine Baud. AD: Philippe Lefébvre. SS: Lily Hargous. SO: Gérard Brisseau. MU: Janine Jarreau. H: Huguette Lalaurette. CO: Sylvie Poulet. 2ndUC: Paul Souvestre.

Cast: Mike Marshall (Roger de Vaudray), Valeria Ciangottini (Louise), Sophie Darès (Henriette Gérard), Simone Valère (Countess of Linières), Jean Desailly (Count of Linières), Jacques Castelot (Marquis of Presle), Michel Barbey (Jacques Frochard), Denis Manuel (Pierre Frochard), André Falcon (Dr. Hébert), Jean Carmet (Picard), Alice Sapritch ("Mother" Frochard), Marie-France Mignal (Marianne), Roger Fradet (LaFleur), Bernard La Jarrige (Rumagnac), Virginie Rodin, Orlando [Roland] Catalano (Marest), Patrick Balkany, Lucia Amram (Florette), France Delahalle (Sister Angela), Max Vialle (Herald), Gabrielle Doulcet (Marion), Jean-Pierre Laverne (Gentleman next to Presle), François Brincourt, André Tomasi (M. Martin), Corinne Claire, Virginie Solenn, Christine Aurel (Françoise Morand), Dominique Delpierre (Girl in prison), Christian Brocard (Donuts Seller); *uncredited*: André Cagnard, Georges Guéret (False lumberjack), Rico López, Colette Mareuil, Gilbert Servien (Abbot), Eric Vasberg.

PROD: Robert de Nesle for Comptoir Français du Film Production (Paris), Roal Films (Paris), Cine Italia Film (Rome). PM: Jean Maumy. GM: Raymond Dupont. UPM: Louis Seuret. Filmed in Chaussy, Val-d'Oise (France). Visa n. 30212 (France, 5/20/1965, m. 2714), 46185 (Italy, 11/16/1965, m. 2677). Release dates: 5/24/1965 (France). Distribution: CFF (France), Regional (Italy). Domestic gross (Italy): n.a.

Also known as: *Le due orfanelle* (Italy), *The Two Orphans* (U.S.A.), *Las dos huérfanas de París* (Spain).

Henriette and Louise, two girls raised as sisters, come to Paris where Henriette hopes to cure Louise from blindness. However, Henriette is abducted by the Marquis of Presle, who has fallen in love with her, and Louise falls into the hands of a cruel hag, "Mother" Frochard, who forces her to become a beggar. Roger de Vaudray, the fiery nephew of the severe Chief of police, opposes Henriette's abduction and saves her. He and Henriette fall in love, but the Chief of police has both of them arrested. Henriette and Roger manage to escape and begin searching for Louise, whom they eventually locate, and rescue from the clutches of Mother Clochard and her sons. Roger's aunt recognizes Louise as the daughter she abandoned many years earlier on the steps of a church, and has her undergo eye surgery. Louise recovers her sight, and Henriette and Roger are married.

Coplan FX 18 casse tout

France / Italy 1965, color, 96 minutes (Italian version: 83 minutes)

D: Riccardo Freda. S: based on the novel *Stoppez Coplan* by Paul Kenny. SC: Claude-Marcel Richard. DOP: Henri Persin. M: Michel Magne. E: Renée Lichtig. SE: Gil Delamare. PD: Jacques Mawart. SO: Michel Fioni.

Cast: Richard Wyler [Richard Staples] (Coplan), Robert Manuel (Hartung), Jany Clair (Héléna Jordan), Valeria Ciangottini (Gelda), Maria-Rosa Rodriguez (Sheila), Gil Delamare (Shaimoun), Jacques Dacqmine (The "Old Man"), Robert Favart, Christian Kerville (Argaz), Bernard La Jarrige (Bruno Schwartz), Guy Marly (Said); *uncredited*: Fernand Bercher, Jackie Blanchot (Henchman), André Cagnard (John), Yvan Chiffre (Henchman), Jean-Pierre Janic (Henchman), Ham-Chau Luong (Chinese engineer), Tony Moreno, Tony Sandro.

PROD: Robert de Nesle for Comptoir Français du Film Production (Paris), Camera Films (Paris), Cinerad—Cinematografica Radici (Rome). PM: Jean Maumy. Filmed on location in Korem, Turkey, and Paris. Visa n. 30585 (France, 10/5/1965, m. 2639), 46646 (Italy, 3/15/1966, m. 2298). Release dates: 10/11/1965 (France), 3/26/1966 (Italy). Distribution: C.F.F.P. (France), Fida Cinematografica (Italy). Domestic gross (Italy): n.a..

Also known as: *Agente 777 missione Summergame* (Italy), *FX 18 Superspy*, a.k.a. *The Exterminators* (U.S.A.), *Objetivo: matar* (Spain), *Agent Secret FX-18 casse tout* / *Geheimagent FX 18 in de bres* (Belgium) *Geheimauftrag CIA—Istanbul 777* / *Phantom FX 18* (West Germany), *Clave FX18—Contraespionaje* (Mexico), *Rött betyder fara* (Sweden), *Agent Coplan FX 18 slår til* (Denmark), *Agentti FX-18 Istanbulissa* (Finland), *Coplan FX-18 Strike Again* (Hong Kong).

Entrusted with the task of shedding light on the kidnapping of a nuclear scientist, Coplan finds the man's dead body inside a trunk. Together with an Israeli agent, Shaimoun, he follows a message concealed in a talking doll which leads the two men to Istanbul. There, they meet a bizarre archaeologist, Hartung, who is actually planning to launch an atomic missile, perfected by the murdered scientist, against New York. In Hartung's plans, the destruction of the U.S. city will lead to a nuclear war between the Eastern and Western power blocks, which will end with the Chinese ruling the world. Coplan and Shaimoun locate Hartung's secret base in Cappadocia: the Israeli agent is killed, whereas Coplan is taken prisoner. However, the intervention of the Turkish police saves the day and, after a spectacular chase, Coplan secures Hartung to justice.

Roger la Honte

France / Italy 1966, color, 105 minutes

D: Riccardo Freda. S: based on the novel *Roger-la-Honte* by Jules Mary. SC: Jean-Louis Bory. DOP: Jean Tournier (Eastmancolor, Franscope). M: Antoine Duhamel, Georges et Jean-Luc (Ed. Eco-Music). E: Michèle Boehm [and Riccardo Freda, uncredited.] PD: Jacques Mawart. AD: Yves Boisset. C: Robert Florent, Daniel Vogel. CO: Christiane Courcelles. SO: René Longuet. AE: Catherine Moulin. SS: Lily Hargous. W: Georgette Fillion. MU: Gisèle Jacquin. Hair: Simone Knapp-Dugue.

Cast: Georges Géret (Roger Laroque / William Farnell), Irene Papas (Julia de Norville), Jean-Pierre Marielle (Lucien De Norville), Jean Topart (Luversan / Mathias Hubert), Sabine Sun'O [Sabine Sun] (Victoire), Gabriele Tinti (Raymond de Norville), Germaine Delbat (Mother Brun, Laroque's maid), Paul Sorèze, Guy Saint-Jean (Jean), Roger Fradet (Farney's Servant), Guy Marly (Usher), Claude Bahier (Noirville's collaborator), Fernand Bercher, Dominique Zardi (Convict), Henri Attal (Convict), Pierre Duncan (Luversan's Servant), Clément Harari (Larouette), Sabine Haudepin (Suzanne Laroque as a child), Joëlle LaTour (Luversan's girlfriend), Paul Muller (Commissioner Lacroix), William Sabatier (Advocate General), Marcel Cuvelier (Coroner), Jean Michaud (President of the Court), Jean Carmet (Tristot), Jacques Monod (President of the Assizes), Anne Vernon (Henriette Laroque), Marie-France Boyer (Suzanne Laroque); *uncredited*: Jean Danet (Judge), Arlette Gilbert (Housemaid), Henri Guégan (Convict), Bernard La Jarrige (Bernadit), Roland Malet (Valet at club), Pierre Vaudier (Priest), Lionel Vitrant (Convict).

PROD: Robert de Nesle and Alvaro Mancori for Comptoir Français du Film Production (Paris), Mancori (Rome). PM: Jean Maumy. UM: Raymond Dupont. Location manager: Pierre Lefait. Visa n. 31502 (France, 5/10/1966, m. 2895), 47731 (Italy, 9/22/1966, m. 2880). Release dates: 5/17/1966 (France), 10/21/1966 (Italy). Distribution: Regional (Italy). Domestic gross (Italy). N.a..

Also known as: *Trappola per l'assassino* (Italy), *Trap for the Assassin* (U.S.A.)

France, 1871. During the Franco-Prussian war, Roger Laroque saves the life of a fellow soldier, Lucien de Norville. Fourteen years later

Roger has become the owner of an industry inherited by his father-in-law, which stands on the brink of bankruptcy. Married and with a daughter, he also has a lover, Julia. Roger meets again Lucien, who has become a lawyer, and—much to his chagrin—finds out he is Julia's husband. Roger decides to leave the woman, who in turn threatens to ruin him. The sudden recovery of a huge sum allows Roger to remedy his ruinous economical situation. Meanwhile, though, his main creditor is killed, and all the evidence points at him. Roger is arrested and defended in court by Lucien, but he is unable to reveal that the money has been given to him by Julia. An anonymous letters reveals the truth to Lucien, who resigns. Roger is sentenced to life imprisonment. However, he manages to escape. Fifteen years later, posing as a wealthy American, he returns to exact revenge. His daughter Suzanne falls for Raymond, De Norville's son—Laroque's old friend committed suicide—but rejects his marriage proposal because she believes her father is guilty. Roger sets out to find the real culprit, Luversan, who is actually Mathias Jubert, a former comrade who swore to take revenge upon him for having been unmasked by Laroque as a traitor during the course of the war. Luversan blackmailed Julia and framed Roger for murder. Suddenly revealing his true identity to Jubert, Roger lays a trap for him so that he can finally prove his own innocence.

Coplan ouvre le feu à Mexico

France / Italy / Spain 1967, color, 97 minutes (Italian version: 96 minutes)

D: Riccardo Freda. S: based on the novel *Coplan fait peau neuve* by Paul Kenny. SC: Bertrand Tavernier. Dial: Christian Plume, Bertrand Tavernier. DOP: Paul Soulignac, Juan Gelpí (Technicolor, Techniscope). M: Jacques Lacome. E: Claude Gros, Vincenzo Tomassi, Teresa Alcocer. PD: Jacques Mawart, Juan Alberto Soler. CO: Marina Rodríguez. 2UD: Yves Boisset. AD: Juan Gabriel Tharrats. C: Ricardo Gonzales [French version: Gérard Brisseau]. AC: Antonio Peneiro [Piñero]. MU: Umberto De Martino. SO: Guy Rophé. SOM: L. and M. Kikoïne. Press attaché: Pierre Rissient, Bertrand Tavernier.

Cast: Lang Jeffries (Coplan), Sabine Sun (Countess Lagrange), José María Caffarel (Langis), Robert Party (Chief of the Secret Service), Frank Oliveras (Fondane), Lee Burton [Guido Lollobrigida] (Arturo Montes), Osvaldo Genazzani (Police Commissioner), Guy Marly (Dr. Krauz), Luciana Gilli (Maya), Silvia Solar (Francine Lamotte); *uncredited*: Francisco Cebrián, Antonio Orengo (Don Felipe), María Dolores Rubio, Tomás Torres (Lieutenant Hernandez; French version: Fregonese).

PROD: Robert de Nesle, Edmondo Amati, Alfonso Balcázar for Comptoir Français du Film Production (Paris), Fida Cinematografica (Rome), Producciones Cinematográficas Balcázar (Barcelona). PM: Jean Maumy, Maurizio Amati [Spanish version: Valentín Sallent]. PSe: Fernande Meunier. Visa n. 32006 (France, 2/10/1967, m. 2681), 49418 (Italy, 6/27/1967, m. 2650). Release dates: 2/15/1967 (France), 7/29/1967 (Italy), 11/8/1967 (Spain). Distribution: C.F.F.P. (France), Fida (Italy). Domestic gross (Italy): n.a.

Also known as: *Moresque: obiettivo allucinante* (Italy), *Mexican Slayride* (U.S.A.), *Entre las redes* (Spain), *Frank Collins 999—Mit Chloroform geht's besser / Todesspur* (West Germany), *0777 Ataca no México* (Brazil), *Tulit usta Meksikossa* (Finland).

After the discovery of a microfilm containing information on the smuggling of priceless paintings stolen in France by the Nazis during the war, Coplan becomes acquainted with the charming Countess Lagrange, who turns out to be part of a mysterious organization. Coplan follows her to Mexico, where he poses as a geologist. He escapes several attempts on his life and investigates on the mysterious murder of a geologist, and the disappearance of the victim's fiancée, Francine. After the death of his sidekick Fondane, Coplan ends up at the Moresque, the residence of the wealthy, elderly Don Felipe. There, he finds out that an organization of diehard Nazis have designed a diabolical plan to annihilate the United States. Financing themselves with the sales of the paintings, they have built a net of underground tunnels, one of which leads to the residence of President Johnson: Don Felipe and his men are planning to kidnap the president, replace him with a double and launch a missile attack against U.S. cities. Coplan escapes death and vanquishes the conspirators.

La morte non conta i dollari

Italy 1967, color, 92 minutes

D: George Lincoln [Riccardo Freda]. S: Giuseppe Masini, George Lincoln. DOP:

Gábor Pogány (Tecnostampa, Cromoscope). M: Nora Orlandi, Robby Poitevin, conducted by Robby Poitevin (Ed. R.C.A.). E: Anna Amedei. ArtD: Piero Filippone. SD: Carlo Gervasi. CO: Rosalba Menichelli. AD: Yves Boisset. Stunts: Giancarlo Bastianoni. SS: Bruna Malaguti. C: Idelmo Simonelli, Vittorio Bernini. SO: Aldo De Martini. MU: Angelo Roncaioli. AC: Sabino Tonti, Mario Lommi. SE: Erasmo Bacciucchi.

Cast: Mark Damon (Lawrence White), Stephen Forsyth (Harry Boyd), Luciana Gilli (Jane), Pamela Tudor (Lisbeth), Alan Collins [Luciano Pigozzi] (Judge Warren), Pedro Sanchez [Ignazio Spalla] (Pedro Rodriguez), Giovanni [Nello] Pazzafini (Doc Lester), Hardy Reichelt (Sheriff), Lidia Biondi (Mrs. Gilbert), Aldo Cecconi (Nolan), Mariella Palmich (Helen Warren), Spartaco Conversi (Bud Lester), Alessandro Gottlieb (Doctor), Francesco Tensi, Dino Strano (Mike Lester), Maurizio Tocchi (Lester Brother); *uncredited*: Renato Chiantoni, Bruno Arié (Helen's Guest), Renzo Pevarello (Lester Henchman).

PROD: Enrico Cogliati Dezza for Cinecidi (Rome). PM: Mario Perelli. PS: Valentino Trevisanato. PSe: Romano Di Casimiro. Filmed at Cinecittà (Rome). Visa n. 49416 (6/27/1967, m. 2545). Release date: 7/21/1967. Distribution: Warner Bros. (Italy). Domestic gross: 151,000,000 lire.

Also known as: *Death at Owell Rock*; *No Killing Without Dollars*; *Death Does Not Count the Dollars* (U.S.A.), *Der Tod zählt keine Dollar* (Germany), *Quand l'heure de la vengeance sonnera / Quand la vengeance sonnera* (France), *La muerte no cuente los dólares* (Spain), *Johnny Yuma vender tilbage* (Denmark), *De dood betaalt in dollars* (Netherlands).

Lawrence White returns to Owell Rock many years after the death of his father, killed by Doc Lester. In town Lawrence meets his sister Jane, who urges him to avenge their father, but Lawrence is hesitant and his attitude reassures Doc Lester. Meanwhile, another man has arrived in Owell Rock: a gunslinger named Harry Boyd. Some mysterious events begin to occur and one at a time the people who were involved in White's murder—including a doctor and the local sheriff—are killed by an unknown hand. Suspicion falls on Lawrence, and Lester appoints Boyd as sheriff. However, it turns out that the two young men are actually in cahoots, and have swapped each other's identities. In fact, Boyd is actually the real Lawrence White, while the alleged Lawrence is in fact Jane's boyfriend, Harry Boyd. After collecting all the evidence against Lester, Lawrence convinces Judge Warren, whose drinking habit has turned him into a puppet in the hands of the Lester family, to re-open the case. Lester's men set up an ambush, but Lawrence, Harry and their acolytes get the better of them. In the end only Doc survives, and Lawrence delivers him to Warren so that justice is served.

A doppia faccia

Italy / West Germany 1969, color, 90 minutes (German version: 80 minutes)

D: Robert Hampton [Riccardo Freda] [*German version*: Richard Freda.] S: [Italian version only] Lucio Fulci, Romano Migliorini, Gianbattista Mussetto. SC: Robert Hampton [Riccardo Freda], Paul Hengge [*German version*: Paul Hengge, Richard Freda]. DOP: Gábor Pogány (Eastmancolor, Tecnostampa). M: Joan Cristian [Nora Orlandi], conducted by Robby Poitevin (Ed. Generalmusic). E: Anna Amedei, Jutta Hering. PD, CO: Luciano Spadoni. AD: Ignazio Dolci [Dolce], Eva Hebner. AE: Rossana Coppola. SS: Maria Pia Rocco, Vivalda Vigorelli. C: Idelmo Simonelli. AC: Mario Lommi, Cristiano Pogany, Sabino Tonti. SO: Carlo Diotallevi [*German version*: Hubertus Schmandke]. SP: Angelo Pennoni. MU: Vittorio Biseo. H: Emilia Foschini. PDA: Umberto Turco. ACO: Francesca Romana Panicali. W: Vera Ceffarelli. SE: Eros Bacciucchi.

Cast: Klaus Kinski (John Alexander), Christiane Krüger (Christine), Günther Stoll (Inspector Stevens), Annabella Incontrera (Liz), Sydney Chaplin (Mr. Brown), Barbara Nelli (Alice), Margaret Lee (Helen Alexander, *née* Brown), Gastone Pescucci (Peter), Claudio Trionfi, Luciano Spadoni (Inspector Gordon), Carlo Marcolini (Butler), Ignazio Dolci [Dolce]; *uncredited*: Bedy Moratti, Fulvio Pellegrino (Policeman), Domenico Ravenna (Man at horse race).

PROD: Oreste Coltellacci and Horst Wendlandt for Colt Produzioni Cinematografiche (Rome), Mega Film (Rome), Rialto Film—Preben Philipsen Gmbh (Munich). PM: Antonio Girasante. PS: Kilian Rebentrost, Albino Morandini. PSe: Cicala Innocente, Giuliano Principato. Filmed in London, Liverpool and at Cinecittà Studios (Rome). Visa n. 53823

(6/14/1969, m. 2489, V.M.18). Release dates: 7/4/1969 (West Germany), 7/26/1969 (Italy). Distribution: Panta. Domestic gross: 175,626,000 lire.

Also known as: *Das Gesicht im Dunkeln* (West Germany; July 4, 1969), *Double Face*; *Puzzle of Horrors* (U.S.A.), *Liz et Helen* (France), *Chaleur et jouissance* (France: X-rated version), *Mit doppeltem Gesicht* (Switzerland), *A Dupla Face no Escuro* (Brazil).

Note: The songs are sung by Nora Orlandi, under the a.k.a. Silvie St. Laurent.

The sole shareholder of a large industry, Helen Brown—whose marriage to John Alexander is in crisis because of the woman's lesbian relationship with a stage actress, Liz—is killed in a car accident caused by a bomb planted in her vehicle by an unknown hand. Her death is officially dismissed as accidental, but the police opens an investigation: meanwhile John, who has returned home after a period of absence, is haunted by the memory of his late wife. One night he finds a young girl, Christine, in his house. She leads him to a party where a lesbian porn loop is screened. John recognizes Helen as the mysterious woman (whose face is never shown) performing with Christine. He purchases the film and learns from Christine that the elusive veiled woman, nicknamed the Countess, asked to be called Helen. John shows Helen's father the film, which turns out to be different from the one he saw: the veiled woman is not the same. John pays a visit to Liz, who confesses that Helen is still alive but badly scarred after the accident, and he even glimpses the veiled Helen leaving in a car. Eventually, though, John finds out that his wife really died in the car accident, and that he has been the victim of a diabolical plan...

Tamar Wife of Er, a.k.a. Tamar Eshet Er

Italy / West Germany / Spain / Israel 1970, color, 86 minutes

D: Riccardo Freda. SC: Yigal Mossinson, based on his book. DOP: Peter Baumgartner (Cinescope, Technicolor). M: Walter Baumgartner, Gianfranco Plenizio, conducted by the author (Ed. C.A.M.). E: Jordan B. Mattews [Bruno Mattei]. AD: Michael Thomas [Erwin C. Dietrich]. PD: Eduardo Torre De La Fuente. C: Modesto Rizzolo. AC: Eitan Zur. SO: Giovanni Laureano. CO: Vanni Castellani. ACO: Dafne Ciarrocchi. MU: Gianfranco Mecacci.

Cast: Claudia Wiedekind (Tamar), Ettore Manni (Judas), Yosef Shiloah [Joseph Shiloach] (Shimon), Léa Nanni (Dina), Michael Maien (Er), Angel Martín (Onan), Yelena Samarina (Bat Shua), José Jaspe (Hira), Sabi Dorr, Aryeh Itzaik [Itzhak], Gideon Eden, Paul Smith (Blacksmith), Nisim Aharon, Vala Yannun, Manuel Benito, Attilio Dottesio (Blacksmith), Maria Teresa Zago (Tamar's Mother); *uncredited*: Peter Baumgartner.

PROD: Erwin C. Dietrich, Alexander Ha-Cohen, Margot Klausner, Giuseppe Maggi for Filmar Compagnia Cinematografica (Rome), Filmar Studios of Israel (Tel Aviv), Hispamer (Madrid), Urania Filmproduktion (Berlin). PM: Mario Damiani. GM: Sergio Newman. EP: Amatsia Hiuni. PS: Moshe Afriat, Alfonso Cucci. Filmed on location in Israel. Visa n. 58177 (5/27/1971, m. 2360, V.M.18). Release dates: 9/25/1970 (West Germany), 8/5/1971 (Italy). Distribution: Seven Stars Cinematografica (Italy). Domestic gross: n.a.

Also known as: *La salamandra del deserto* (Italy), *In der Glut des Mittags* (West Germany)

Judas, the head of a Jewish community of shepherds, buys the beautiful Tamar as a wife for the eldest of his three sons, Er. However, the girl falls in love with the father and rejects the young husband, driving Er to commit suicide. According to the law of the community, Judas' second son Onan acquires the right to marry Tamar. Since the woman does not want him either, Onan weaves an illicit affair with his father's sister, which ends tragically. After Onan's death, Tamar escapes, torn by remorse. Judas, who loves her too, reaches her. Tamar becomes pregnant and is subjected to the judgment of the elderly. She is acquitted, thanks to her lover's defense, and decides to leave into the wilderness.

L'iguana dalla lingua di fuoco

Italy / France / West Germany 1971, color, 94 minutes

D: Willy Pareto [Riccardo Freda]. S and SC: Sandro Continenza, Riccardo Freda. DOP: Silvano Ippoliti (Eastmancolor). M: Stelvio Cipriani. E: Willy Pareto. PD, ArtD: Giuseppe Chevalier. CO: Nadia Vitali. MU: Lamberto Marini. AD: Leo Jahn. C: Enrico Sasso. AC: Renato Doria, Ennio Marzocchini. SO: Aldo De Martino. SP: Leo Massa, Mario Mazzoni. AE: Bruno Micheli, Gertrud Petermann. DubD: Nick Alexander. SS: Vivalda Vigorelli.

Cast: Luigi Pistilli (Detective John Norton), Dagmar Lassander (Helen Sobiesky), Anton Diffring (Ambassador Sobiesky), Arthur O'Sullivan (Inspector Lawrence), Werner Pochath (Marc Sobiesky), Dominique Boschero (The Ambassador's mistress), Renato Romano (Mandel), Sergio Doria (Walter), Valentina Cortese (Mrs. Sobiesky), Ruth Durley; *uncredited*: Niall Toibin (Doctor), Riccardo Freda (Doctor).

PROD: Oceania Produzioni Internazionali Cinematografica (Rome), Les Films Corona (Nanterre), Terra Filmkunst (Berlin). PM: Alfonso Donati. PS: Franco Fumagalli, Fritz Hammel. PSe: Giuseppe Bruno Bossio. Filmed on location in Dublin. Visa n. 58746 (8/11/1971, m. 2595, V.M.18). Release date: 8/24/1971. Distribution: Euro International Film. Domestic gross: 169,405,000 *lire*.

Also known as: *The Iguana with the Tongue of Fire* (English title—World-wide), *L'iguane à la langue de feu* (France), *Die Bestie mit dem feurigen Atem* (Germany), *La lengua de fuego de la iguana / La iguana de la lengua de fuego* (Spain)

Note: according to the opening credits, the story is based on the novel "A Room Without Door" by Richard Mann.

Dublin. The police are on alert for a string of mysterious and ferocious killings. Inspector Lawrence, unable to follow a trail that leads to the local French embassy—protected as such by diplomatic immunity—decides to call upon the services of John Norton, a former police inspector expelled from the ranks due to a violent incident against a criminal. Norton is able to establish a relationship with Helen, the stepdaughter of Ambassador Sobiesky, which allows him to investigate closely into the life of the diplomat, his family and the people surrounding them. The chain of murders continues, and various people related in some ways to Sobiesky—including his mistress and his driver—are horribly killed off, whereas Helen barely escapes an attempt on her life. On top of that, Norton' inquiry puts his own family in danger, as the killer retorts upon the cop's elderly mother and teenage daughter...

Estratto dagli archivi segreti della polizia di una capitale europea
Italy / Spain 1972, color, 85 minutes

D: Robert Hampton [Riccardo Freda]. S and SC: Mario Bianchi. DOP: Francisco Fraile (Eastmancolor, Telecolor). M: Stelvio Cipriani (Ed. C.A.M.). E: Iolanda Benvenuti. PD: Amedeo Mellone. AD: Rachel Griffiths. C: Giorgio Di Battista. AC: Enzo Tosi. AE: Alba di Salvo. PDA: Renato Pandolfi. SO: Eugenio Rondani. MU: Renzo Francioni. SE: Carlo Rambaldi.

Cast: Camille Keaton (Jane), Luciana Paluzzi (Lady Alexander), Luigi Pistilli (Lord Alexander), Giovanni Petrucci (Fred), Tony Isbert [Antonio Spitzer Ysbert] (Bill), Máximo Valverde (Joe), Pepe [José] Calvo (Sam David), Irina Demick (Bill's mother), Paul Muller (Doctor), Beni Deus (Ferguson), Milo Quesada (Cop), Alejandro de Enciso, Elsa Zabala (Devil worshipper), Ambra Mascarello, Adriana Facchetti (Woman in Alexander's house), Fulvio Mingozzi (Police Inspector), Carla Mancini.

PROD: Produzioni Internazionali Associate (Rome), Tecisa (Madrid). PM: Sergio Merolle. PS: Marco Claudio Merolle. PSe: Felice Rufini. Filmed in Spain and at Safa Palatino Studios (Rome). Visa n. 61507 (12/9/1972, m. 2334, V.M.18). Release date: 12/20/1972. Distribution: P.I.A. Domestic gross: 7,680,000 *lire*.

Also known as: *Tragic Ceremony* (U.S.A.—Home video), *Trágica ceremonia en villa Alexander* (Spain).

Note: According to some sources Filippo Walter Ratti took over the direction. José Gutiérrez Maesso and Leonardo Martín are credited as scriptwriters on the Spanish version, solely for co-production purposes. Carla Mancini's name features among the cast list but she does not actually appear in the film. The opening credits song *La vita* (Freda-Cipriani) is sung by Ernesto Brancucci.

Bill, an introverted rich young man, invites three acquaintances on his boat, including the laconic Jane, to whom he is attracted. Bill gives her a necklace that he has stolen from his mother, and which is said to have once belonged to a woman possessed by the Devil. On the way home, the group's dune buggy runs out of gas: after an encounter with a weird gas station owner, the four hippies end up at a villa whose owners, Lord and Lady Alexander, turn out to be members of a satanic cult. Jane falls into their hands and is about to be sacrificed during a black mass, but the ceremony climaxes in a massacre: Bill accidentally kills Lady Alexander, and all the devil worshippers are driven to kill each other by a mysterious force. Bill and friends flee the villa and take refuge first at Bill's place and then, after having been chased away by his mother, at his father's country house. There, even stranger things happen, and one by one they are dispatched by Jane, who has herself been possessed by a mysterious force. In the end we find Jane in a state of shock, at a mental institution: there, she is murdered by a supernatural presence ... that is revealed to be Lady Alexander.

Murder Obsession (Follia omicida)

Italy/France 1981, color, 97 minutes

D: Riccardo Freda. S: Antonio Cesare Corti, Fabio Piccioni. SC: Antonio Cesare Corti, Fabio Piccioni, Riccardo Freda. Dialogue adaptation: Simon Mizrahi. DOP: Cristiano Pogany (Telecolor). M: Franco Mannino. E: Riccardo Freda [uncredited]. PD, CO: Giorgio Desideri. AD: Antonio Cesare Corti, Bernard Cohn [and Jacqueline Freda, uncredited]. C: Roberto Lombardi Dallamano, Guglielmo Vincioni. AC: Stefano Guidi. ACO: Alberto Tosto. AE: Anne Barrault. MU: Lamberto Marini, Sergio Angeloni. Hair: Agnese Panarotto. SO: Davide Magara. SE: Angelo Mattei, Sergio Stivaletti. SP: Debora Beer. KG: Gianni Savini. ChEl: Alberico Novelli. SS: Maria Luce Faccenna.

Cast: Stefano Patrizi (Michael Stanford), Martine Brochard (Shirley Dawson), Henri Garcin (Hans Schwartz), Laura Gemser (Betty; English language: Beryl Fisher), John Richardson (Oliver), Anita Strindberg (Glenda Stanford), Silvia Dionisio (Deborah Jordan); *uncredited*: Fabrizio Moroni (Michael as a child), Riccardo Freda (Elderly man on the set).

Produced by Enzo Boetani, Giuseppe Collura, Simon Mizrahi for Dionysio Cinematografica (Rome), Societé Nouvelle Cinévog (Paris). PS: Antonio Boetani. PSe: Salvatore Carrara. Filmed at Palazzo Borghese, Artena (Rome) and at Incir-De Paolis Studios (Rome). Visa n. 75784 (10/31/1980, m. 2660, V.M.18). Release date: 2/24/1981. Distribution: Regional. Domestic gross: n.a.

Also known as: *Murder Obsession*; *Fear*; *The Wailing*; *Unconscious*; *Murder Syndrome* (U.S.A.—home video), *Angoisse* (France), *Obsessão Assassina* (Portugal), *Satan's Altar* (Greece), *Himomurhaaja* (Finland).

Note: On the poster for the foreign English language release titled *Unconscious*, Freda is credited as "Robert Hampton."

Following a violent raptus on the set that almost led him to strangle his co-star Beryl, actor Michael Stanford returns to the family home in Surrey after a fifteen-year absence, for a period of rest. He explains to his girlfriend Deborah, who accompanies him, that as a child he murdered his own father to protect his mother, and the event left him traumatized. His still younglooking mother, Glenda, instantly takes a dislike to Deborah, whom Michael has introduced as his secretary. A few days later a director friend, Hans Schwartz, shows up with his assistant Shirley and Beryl. The three seem to be poorly tolerated by Oliver, the enigmatic butler. Meanwhile, strange events occur: someone tries to drown Beryl in the bathtub, while Deborah experiences an upsetting nightmare in which she is subjected to a horrendous black magic ritual. The next day, during a walk in the woods, Michael and Beryl find an isolated spot and have sex: when Michael wakes up he finds Beryl's dead body next to him. Schwartz, who has witnessed and photographed the murder, is brutally dispatched with an axe, and soon it is Shirley's turn to be slaughtered by way of a chainsaw. All evidence points at Michael, to whom Glenda confesses that she was Oliver's lover: when Michael's father discovered them in the act of having sex, he killed the man and blamed the child for it. However, Michael finds out that Oliver has committed suicide, leaving a taped confession where he reveals that it had actually been Glenda who murdered her husband, and she is also the responsible for the gruesome killings. The woman, a practitioner of black magic, is morbidly jealous of her own son whom she believes is her husband reincarnated, and won't stop at anything to keep him with her...

Films and Documentaries on Riccardo Freda; Video Interviews; Appearances as Himself

Riccardo Freda by Barbara Steele

France 1968, color, short film

D: Jacques Baratier, Philippe Laïk, Jean-Daniel Simon.

Il cinema della paura

Italy 1986, color, 3 parts, 49 minutes each

D: Marcello Avallone, Patrizia Pistagnesi.
Note: Freda appears in the first installment, alongside with Dario Argento, Pino Donaggio and others.

Stille di sangue e lacrime di rospo
Italy 1987, color, 120 minutes.
D: Gianni Vitale.
Produced by Promovies.
Note: Directorial essay made by the alumni of the Promovies film school in Padua. Freda appears as himself.

Les Mystères du Premier-Film
France 1995, color, 52 minutes
D: Jean-Pierre Améris. M: Pierre Adenot.
Note: Based on an idea of Bertrand Tavernier. It is a sort of "making of" of the first film in cinema history shot by Louis Lumière, filmed on a site which still contains a few remaining vestiges of the former Lumière factories. Freda appears alongside Youssef Chahine, Stanley Donen, André De Toth, Stephen Frears, Karel Reisz, Alain Resnais, Claude Sautet, Jerry Schatzberg, Robert Parrish, Bertrand Tavernier, Paul Vecchiali, among others.

La regola del gioco (Cinema italiano in genere)
Italy 1995, color, 5 parts, 49 minutes each.
D: Sergio Grmek Germani.
Note: includes an interview with Freda, on top of the Spanish steps near the Trinità dei Monti church in Rome, next to the house where the director lived for two decades.

Ritratti d'autore. Quattro chiacchiere con Riccardo Freda
Italy 1996, color, 18 minutes
D: Giuseppe Tornatore. DOP: Marcello Montarsi. E: Massimo Quaglia. SO: Marco Fiumara.
Produced by Cristiano Bortone for O.R.I.S.A. Films, Tele +.
Note: Filmed as part of the TV documentary series "Ritratti d'autore," cured by Valentina Pascarelli. In 2007 a longer version (40') was shown, entitled *Ero il regista più pagato d'italia. Conversazione tra Riccardo Freda e Giuseppe Tornatore.*

Il mondo di Dario Argento 3: Il museo degli orrori di Dario Argento
Italy 1997, color, 90 minutes
D: Luigi Cozzi. SC: Luigi Cozzi. E: Gianmaria Scibilia.
Note: Documentary on Dario Argento, which focuses mostly on special effects. It features interviews with Argento's peers and associates as well as various film clips. Mostly shot inside the "Profondo Rosso" shop in Rome. Freda is one of the interviewees, alongside Daria Nicolodi, Tom Savini, Claudio Simonetti, Antonella Vitale, and Argento. It was included as an extra of the Japanese laserdisc of Argento's *Phenomena*.

Un uomo solo— Incontro con Riccardo Freda
Italy 1998, color, 44 minutes
D: Mimmo Calopresti. Supervisor: Stefano Della Casa. DOP: Paolo Ferrari. E: Massimo Fiocchi. AD: Manuela De Marchi. SO: Gianluca Costamagna. AC: Franco Robust. AE: Mario Di Chiara. SP: Paolo Pisanelli. Music excerpts courtesy of Stefano Bigazzi and Franco Piersanti.
Produced by Centro Sperimentale di Cinematografia—Scuola Nazionale di Cinema (Rome). EP: Minnie Ferrara. GM: Giovanni Saulini. PA: Luca De Risi, Francesco Colletta.
Note: Filmed in Rome and Bracciano in April 1998. Issue #2 of the anthology series "Archivio della memoria. Ritratti Italiani" produced by Rome's CSC and directed by Lino Miccichè. Included as an extra on the French DVD of *Don Cesare di Bazan*.

Kino kolossal— Herkules, Maciste & Co.
Germany 2000, color, 58 minutes
D: Hans-Jürgen Panitz, Inga Seyric. SC: Hans-Jürgen Panitz.
Note: Made-for-TV documentary on the *peplum* genre, with interviews to filmmakers, actors and other protagonists of that era.

Érase una vez en Europa
Spain 2001, color, TV series, 13 episode, 30 minutes each
D: Manel Prayol, Carles Prats. SC: Joan Ferrer, Carlos Aguilar. DOP: Pere Ballesteros, Angel Puig. M: Salvador Rey. E: Lolo Muñoz. ArtD: Frank Plant.
PROD: Sara Gibbings.
Also known as: *Once Upon a Time in Europe*.
Note: Made-for-TV documentary series on

European genre cinema between 1955 and 1975, presented by Christopher Lee. Freda is one of the interviewees, alongside Ennio Morricone, Martine Beswick, Jose Giovanni, Wolfgang Preiss, Giuliano Gemma, Antonio Margheriti, Jacques Deray, Dario Argento, Ingrid Pitt, Caroline Munro, Sergio Sollima, Franco Nero, Jack Taylor, Alessandro Alessandroni, Tonino Valerii, Bud Spencer, Marianne Koch, Jesús Franco, Paul Naschy, Amando de Ossorio, Aldo Sambrell, Jorge Grau, Joaquin Romero Marchent, Antonio Isasi and Eugenio Martin.

Chapter Notes

Introduction

1. Riccardo Freda, *Divoratori di celluloide* (Milan: Edizioni del Mystfest, Il Formichiere, 1981), 81.
2. Bertrand Tavernier, "Riccardo Freda," *Cinéma 63* #81, December 1963, 74.
3. Jacques Lourcelles and Simon Mizrahi, "Entretien avec Riccardo Freda," in *Présence du cinéma* #17, Spring 1963, 20.
4. Éric Poindron, *Riccardo Freda. Un pirate à la camera* (Lyon-Arles: Institute Lumière/Actes Sud, 1994), 293.
5. *Cinématographe* #13, 1975.
6. Poindron, *Riccardo Freda*, 363.
7. Franca Faldini, and Goffredo Fofi, eds. *L'avventurosa storia del cinema italiano raccontata dai suoi protagonisti 1960–1969* (Milan: Feltrinelli, 1981), 210.
8. Jacques Lourcelles, *Dictionnaire du cinéma. Les films* (Paris: Robert Laffont, 1992), 1440.
9. Freda, *Divoratori di celluloide*, 6.
10. Poindron, *Riccardo Freda*, 316.
11. Jean-Marie Sabatier, *Les classiques du cinéma fantastique* (Les Plans sur Bex: Balland, 1973), 166.
12. Renaud Walter and Guy Braucourt, "Fredda [sic] and Bory Sans Honte," *Cinéma 66* #106, May 1966, 32.
13. Freda, *Divoratori di celluloide*, 85.
14. Emanuela Martini and Stefano Della Casa, *Riccardo Freda* (Bergamo: Bergamo Film Meeting, 1993), 16.
15. Leo Longanesi, *Parliamo dell'elefante. Frammenti di un diario* (Milan: Longanesi (1947) 2005).
16. Lourcelles and Mizrahi, "Entretien avec Riccardo Freda," 18–19.
17. According to Luigi Cozzi, an unpublished piece of his 1970 interview with Freda (which came out in the magazine *Horror* the following year) dealt with the ending of the director's tormented relationship with Canale. "Then, one day, Freda told me with a look that suddenly became hallucinated, he said goodbye to her and went out to work. When he came home in the evening, Freda put the key in the lock to open the door and come in, and … the key did not work. During his absence, the lock had been replaced, and that evening, after he repeatedly knocked and rang the bell, he finally heard Gianna Maria Canale's voice from behind the door, as the woman, without even opening, abruptly dismissed him by simply saying, 'Go away, this is not your house anymore. Go away or I call the police!' So, they split up, and when in 1970 he told me this story and many other details, Freda was still upset … Freda also told me about all the works of art he had passionately collected during his life, which got lost on that occasion: they had been left in the house he gave to Gianna Maria Canale. I remember clearly what he said to me: 'In the morning I came out of my home a quiet, happy man, with a wife I loved [author's note: Canale and Freda were *not* married] and a beautiful house which I put together over the course of decades, whereas in the evening, when I got back … suddenly I found myself desperate, without nothing, without even a bed to sleep in…'" Luigi Cozzi, "Riccardo Freda, un ricordo personale," in Antonio Fabio Familiari, *Riccardo Freda. L'esteta dell'emozione* (Rome: Profondo Rosso, 2004). However, Cozzi's words have to be taken with a grain (or more…) of salt, considering the biographical details that this author collected from other sources, including Freda's daughters. On his part, Yves Boisset confirmed the director's grudge after the end of his love story with Canale. "He had been deeply in love with the actress Gianna Maria Canale, one of Italian cinema's most seducing bosoms. And she had left him for a hairdresser. From that day on, hairdressers were forbidden on the sets of Freda's films, and the actresses merely tolerated. Especially when they were young and pretty." Yves Boisset, *La vie est un choix* (Paris: Plon, 2011), 104.
18. Freda, *Divoratori di celluloide*, 3–4.
19. Ibid., 85.
20. Lourcelles, *Dictionnaire du cinéma. Les films*, 1440.
21. Christophe Champclaux, Linda Tahir Meriau, *Le Peplum* (Paris: Le Courriere du livre, 2016), 111.
22. Freda, *Divoratori di celluloide*, 83.
23. Ibid., 131.
24. Ibid., 85.
25. Lourcelles and Mizrahi, "Entretien avec Riccardo Freda," 18.
26. Always very frugal when it came to praising other directors, in his later years Freda was still capable

of the enthusiasm of his youth when going to the movies. His daughter Jacqueline recalls, "One day he came back from France and was as excited as a young kid: 'I've seen a wonderful film! As soon as it comes out in Italy we must watch it again together!' And it was *Raiders of the Lost Ark*." (Jacqueline Freda, interview with the author, May 2015). Besides Spielberg, he admired Clint Eastwood, Emir Kusturica's *Dom za vesanje* (a.k.a. *Time of the Gypsies*, 1988), and very few others. He considered Ettore Scola the best living Italian director, and in a 1987 interview he had words of appreciation for the Taviani brothers and Francesco Rosi. See Fabrice Branca and Gerard Stüm, "Entretien avec Riccardo Freda," *Monster Bis Collector*, 1999, 62.

27. Freda, *Divoratori di celluloide*, 83.
28. Lourcelles and Mizrahi, "Entretien avec Riccardo Freda," 20.
29. Jacques Lourcelles, "Un homme seul," *Présence du cinéma* #17, Spring 1963, 6.
30. Freda, *Divoratori di celluloide*, 84.
31. *Ibid.*, 92.
32. Champclaux, Meriau, *Le Peplum*, 111.
33. On the other hand, this approach has led to comments as the following, as misinformed as they are misleading: "Many of Freda's films seem static, and many of their praised moments of grandeur owe more to the technicians that supported him and, in some cases, finished the productions that he abandoned in midstream." Louis Paul, *Italian Horror Film Directors* (Jefferson NC: McFarland 2010), 275.
34. Freda, *Divoratori di celluloide*, 95.
35. Sabatier, *Les classiques du cinéma fantastique*, 168.
36. Freda, *Divoratori di celluloide*, 136–137.
37. Jacqueline Freda, interview with the author, May 2015.

Chapter 1

1. Poindron, *Riccardo Freda*, 29.
2. Freda, *Divoratori di celluloide*, 5.
3. Lourcelles and Mizrahi, "Entretien avec Riccardo Freda," 11.
4. Poindron, *Riccardo Freda*, 22–23.
5. *Ibid.*, 26. See also Lourcelles and Mizrahi, "Entretien avec Riccardo Freda," 12, and Giovanna Grassi, "Freda: come ho vissuto mezzo secolo di cinema," *Corriere della Sera*, June 7, 1981.
6. Poindron, *Riccardo Freda*, 40.
7. Riccardo Freda, interviewed by Roberto Torelli circa 1989. The complete video interview was broadcast during the TV show "Fuori Orario," circa 1996.
8. Poindron, *Riccardo Freda*, 39.
9. *Ibid.*, 51.
10. *Ibid.*, 72.
11. *Ibid.*, 81.
12. *Ibid.*
13. Boisset, *La vie est un choix*, 106.
14. The error—which Freda pointed out when speaking with Éric Poindron (Poindron, *Riccardo Freda*, 81)—generated from the interview with Lourcelles and Mizrahi, where, most likely due to a misunderstanding, Freda is wrongly quoted as follows: "J'avais un ami avec qui j'ai fait *les statues* du Centre" [italics by the author]. The same mistake can still be found in later books: see Stefano Della Casa, *Riccardo Freda* (Rome: Bulzoni, 1999), 20.

15. Guido Aristarco, *Il cinema fascista: il prima e il dopo* (Rome: Edizioni Dedalo, 1996) 77.
16. Mussolini's men also exerted a strict surveillance over the importing of foreign films: eventually, only those produced in the nations that were part of the Axis were released from 1938 onwards.
17. Poindron, *Riccardo Freda*, 82.
18. This error as well generates from the 1963 issue of *Présence du cinéma*, which states that "A l'âge de 24 ans, il est appelé a Rome pour travailler au 'Centro Sperimentale di Cinematografia'"; anyway, Freda's name is nowhere to be found in the CSC's official papers, and not surprisingly since his apprenticeship in Rome started by helping Freddi, Pratelli and Usellini write the statute of the Direzione Generale per la Cinematografia—that is, a purely administrative matter. What is more, the CSC did not even exist in 1933: it was founded two years later, in 1935, when Freda was 26. The error has been reprised several times ever since: see, for instance, Tim Lucas, *Mario Bava. All the Colors of the Dark* (Cincinnati, OH: Video Watchdog 2007), 120.

Chapter 2

1. Giuseppe Tornatore, *Il quarto moschettiere. Quattro chiacchiere con Riccardo Freda* (Taormina: TaorminaFilmFest, 2007), 13.
2. Poindron, *Riccardo Freda*, 86. On other occasions, Freda claimed that he had worked, uncredited, on a larger number of screenplays than those on which he is officially listed, whose number oscillated according to his whims. "I must have written forty or fifty screenplays … I don't know, I can't remember, but loads with Antonelli, Edoardo Antonelli, who called himself Edoardo Anton. We always worked together and they were the first films made for Cinecittà." Tornatore, *Il quarto moschettiere*, 8.
3. Denis, who had moved to Italy at 16, was one of the most popular divas of the late 1930s. During the war, to save the life of her lover Luchino Visconti, she became the mistress of the sinister Pietro Koch, a Fascist official who after the 1943 armistice became the head of a notorious secret special branch of the police of Mussolini's short-lived Italian Social Republic: the so-called "banda Koch" was responsible for many horrendous killings and tortures. Thanks to Denis' efforts, Visconti (then an active member of the Italian resistance) was released from prison, but broke all ties with the actress. In 1946, due to her frequentation with Koch (who had been sentenced to death in June 1945; the execution was filmed by Visconti), Denis was arrested and briefly detained with the accusation of

having been a collaborationist. The experience left her embittered and she gradually detached from the movie business, which she abandoned for good in the mid–1950s.

4. Della Casa, *Riccardo Freda*, 21.
5. Filippo Sacchi, "Fuochi d'artificio," *Corriere della Sera*, March 18, 1939.
6. *Telefoni bianchi* (White telephones) was the common appellations of the Italian comedies made in the 1930s, in imitation of U.S. screwball comedies. The name came from the luminous, expensive *art déco* sets featuring white telephones, then an uncommon occurrence in people's homes and thus a symbol of bourgeois wealth.
7. *Vieni avanti cretino* later became the title of a cult comic film directed in 1982 by Luciano Salce and starring Lino Banfi, and intended as a homage to the classic vaudeville comedy.
8. Freda, *Divoratori di celluloide*, 116.
9. Giuseppina Setti, "Voce senza volto," *Il lavoro*, May 16, 1939.
10. Tornatore, *Il quarto moschettiere*, 20.
11. Poindron, *Riccardo Freda*, 209.
12. Della Casa, *Riccardo Freda*, 20.
13. Freda, *Divoratori di celluloide*, 14.
14. Poindron, *Riccardo Freda*, 84.
15. Aldo Tonti, *Odore di cinema* (Florence: Vallecchi, 1964), 66–67.
16. Freda, *Divoratori di celluloide*, 81.
17. Lourcelles and Mizrahi, "Entretien avec Riccardo Freda," 12. Duranti was one of the Fascist regime's most popular divas (as well as the lover of the Minister of Popular Culture, Alessandro Pavolini). On the other hand, despite what some sources (including the IMDb) state, Freda did *not* appear in an uncredited role as a pilot in Henry Hathaway's *Sundown* (1941), filmed in New Mexico in 1941. Putting aside for a minute the fact that there is actually no trace of anyone resembling Freda in the movie, the idea that he would take a trip to the U.S. and end up acting in a small role in Hathaway's film, and all this while Italy was already at war, is beyond ridiculous.
18. Adolfo Franci, "Il cavaliere di San Marco," *Illustrazione Italiana*, April 16, 1939.
19. Filippo Sacchi, "In campagna è caduta una stella," *Corriere della Sera*, April 4, 1940.
20. The Fascist regime suggested the use of *voi* (second person plural pronoun) as a formal way to address people as opposed to the informal *tu* (second person singular), instead of *lei* (third person singular feminine) which was considered a sign of bourgeois behavior. As the writer Luigi Cicognani claimed, "The Fascist revolution intends to bring back the spirit of our race to its authentic origins, freeing it from any pollution. Then, let us bring forth this purification. Also in this, let us go back to the use of Rome, to the Christian and Roman *tu* which expresses the universal value of Rome and Christianity. Let the *voi* be a sign of respect and hierarchical recognition." *Corriere della Sera*, January 15, 1938.

21. Monicelli had fond words for Gentilomo, who helped him move his first steps in the movie business. See Mario Monicelli, "Gentilomo e la scuola del montaggio," in Luciano De Giusti, ed., *Giacomo Gentilomo, cineasta popolare* (Trieste: Kaplan, 2008), 143.
22. Poindron, *Riccardo Freda*, 88.
23. Filippo Sacchi, "Notte di fortuna," *Corriere della Sera*, June 1, 1941.
24. Freda, *Divoratori di celluloide*, 20.
25. Della Casa, *Riccardo Freda*, 22.
26. Mario Gromo, "Caravaggio, il pittore maledetto," *La Stampa*, February 7, 1941.
27. Lourcelles and Mizrahi, "Entretien avec Riccardo Freda," 12.
28. Della Casa, *Riccardo Freda*, 22.

Chapter 3

1. Poindron, *Riccardo Freda*, 98.
2. Earlier versions dated 1909 (*Ruy Blas*), 1912 (*Don Caesar de Bazan*, by Theo Frenkel, starring Irvin Cummings) and 1915 (*Don Caesar de Bazan* by Robert G. Vignola, starring Lawson Butt), while Ernst Lubitsch's *Rosita* (1923) also drew from the play, which was reshaped into a vehicle for Mary Pickford. Around the same time, the story was also filmed as *The Spanish Dancer* (1923, Herbert Brenon), starring Pola Negri, Antonio Moreno and Wallace Beery as the King. In the years following Freda's film, there were a French adaptation of Hugo's original play (Pierre Billon's *Ruy Blas*, 1948, scripted by Jean Cocteau and starring Jean Marais) and a little-seen 1957 Russian TV movie, *Don Sezar de Bazan*. More recent made-for-TV versions came from France (1972's *Ruy Blas* and a 2002 film of the same name by Jacques Weber, from a script by Jean-Claude Carrière) and Russia (*Don Sezar de Bazan*, 1989, by Yan Frid, this time a musical adaptation).
3. Riccardo Freda, "Fuori Orario."
4. Francesco Savio, *Cinecittà anni Trenta* (Rome: Bulzoni 1979), 60.
5. Poindron, *Riccardo Freda*, 99.
6. In order to support domestic production, the Royal Decree n. 1389 of 4 September 1938 (the so-called "Alfieri law" after the Minister of Popular Culture) introduced among other measures the monopoly on the part of ENIC (the National Agency for Cinematographic Industries, founded in 1935) regarding "the purchase, import and distribution of cinematographic films [sic]," thus imposing autocratic distribution. The effects were immediate: the four major Hollywood studios (20th Century Fox, Metro-Goldwyn-Mayer, Paramount and Warner Bros.) responded by withdrawing from the Italian market as of 1 January 1939.
7. Poindron, *Riccardo Freda*, 97.
8. Savio, *Cinecittà anni Trenta*, 566.
9. Vice, "Don Cesare di Bazan," *Cinema*, October 25, 1942; the reviewer gives the film three out of four stars.
10. Savio, *Cinecittà anni Trenta*, 568.

11. Poindron, *Riccardo Freda*, 103.
12. Savio, *Cinecittà anni Trenta*, 545.
13. *Ibid.*, 1147.
14. Fabrizio Sarazani, "L'abito nero da sposa," *Il Tempo*, May 23, 1945.
15. Freda, *Divoratori di celluloide*, 128.
16. *Ibid.*, 128–129. Freda's judgment on Fellini's work is even harsher. "Jumped to secure fame with *I Vitelloni*, the kind of film Mario Camerini used to make with much more modest means some decades earlier, he bumped into [Peppino] Amato, who ... let him make *La dolce vita*, a squalid landscape of Roman life that turned Fellini into a universal genius. But then, except for the parenthesis of *Amarcord*, the umpteenth autobiographical recollection..., what a squalor and bore in that crazy regurgitation of billions that are his films! To make a movie, Fellini shoots for months and months, wasting trainloads of negative ... it happens that from such an avalanche of celluloid, and under the scissors of a masterly editor, a number of sequences can be saved, but to what price of bore and conceit! Then, when the genius attempts a raid in the type of cinema that is the dearest to me, with the *Casanova*, then the disaster is total. ... Perhaps his best work is *Toby Dammit*, the horror featurette that was part of a trilogy, but Bava and I reached far better results, among other things, on a budget that equals what Fellini spends in catering and mineral water." *Ibid.*, 132.
17. *Ibid.*, 128.
18. The restored copy screened at the 2010 Venice festival, however, carries the on-screen title *6 × 8 / 48 (Tutta la città canta)*.
19. Savio, *Cinecittà anni Trenta*, 1064–1065.
20. *Ibid*. The score was co-written by Oscar De Mejo, a painter and jazz composer, husband of Alida Valli from 1944 to 1952 and father of Lorenzo and Carlo De Mejo.
21. Aldo Bernardini, "Il cinema interrotto," in Ernesto G. Laura and Alfredo Baldi, *Storia del cinema italiano 1940/1944* (Venice: Marsilio-Edizioni di Bianco & Nero 2010) 486.
22. G. Prosperi, "07 ... tassì," *Il Giornale d'Italia*, April 13, 1946.

Chapter 4

1. Freda, *Divoratori di celluloide*, 79.
2. Lourcelles and Mizrahi, "Entretien avec Riccardo Freda," 13.
3. Franca Faldini and Goffredo Fofi, eds. *L'avventurosa storia del cinema italiano raccontata dai suoi protagonisti 1935–1959* (Milan: Feltrinelli, 1979), 104.
4. Poindron, *Riccardo Freda*, 146
5. Lourcelles, *Dictionnaire du cinéma*, 24.
6. Poindron, *Riccardo Freda*, 148. Brazzi's first Hollywood film was actually MGM'S *Little Women* (1949, Mervyn LeRoy).
7. Contrary to what stated in some sources (such as IMDb and Tim Lucas' *Mario Bava*, 121), Gianna Maria Canale does *not* appear in the film.
8. Poindron, *Riccardo Freda*, 152–153.
9. *Ibid.*, 143.
10. Sergio Toffetti, "Dai telefoni bianchi alle bandiere rosse: generi, filoni, luoghi narrativi," in Cosulich, Callisto, ed. *Storia del cinema italiano 1945–1948* (Venice: Marsilio, Edizioni di Bianco e Nero, 2003), 284. Toffetti discusses the climactic duel, but mistakenly mentions Gino Cervi instead of Harry Feist as Rossano Brazzi's opponent.
11. Freda, *Divoratori di celluloide*, 79. Peppino (Giuseppe) Amato (real name Giuseppe Vasaturo, 1899–1964) was an important Italian producer, who had financed *La cena delle beffe* and would produce *La dolce vita*. The corpulent Aldo Fabrizi (1905–1990) was a very popular actor and director, equally versed in comedies and in dramas—he was unforgettable as the parish priest in *Rome Open City*—who often teamed up with Totò in a number of lively comedies.
12. "Last night, a friend who wrote a monumental history of cinema taught me that in *Aquila nera* there is a sequence that I was not aware of, which I never shot! There is a girl who takes a bath, completely naked. And I ignored its existence! Well, that's what they did back then! On Sunday, the producer would secretly shoot his own little stuff which he inserted into the movies. To me, that sequence is completely news, I learned about it last night." Fabrice Branca and Gerard Stüm, "Entretien avec Riccardo Freda," *Monster Bis Collector*, 1999, 59.
13. Alberto Farassino, "Roma, Via Po. Storia e sistema della Lux Film," in Alberto Farassino, ed., *Lux Film* (Milan: Il Castoro, 2000), 24.
14. Faldini and Fofi, *L'avventurosa storia del cinema italiano 1935–1959*, 184.
15. Poindron, *Riccardo Freda*, 162.
16. lan. [Arturo Lanocita], "Per fare un film il denaro si trova," *Corriere d'informazione*, February 20–21, 1947.
17. Bertrand Tavernier, "Riccardo Freda," *Cinéma 63* #81, December 1963, 70.
18. Novarese would win two Academy Awards for Best Costume Design, in 1964 (*Cleopatra*) and 1971 (*Cromwell*). He was the father of Leticia Román (real name Letizia Novarese), the lead actress in Mario Bava's *The Girl Who Knew Too Much*. Novarese is credited only on the second part, *Tempesta su Parigi*.
19. Lourcelles, *Dictionnaire du cinéma*, 956.
20. Poindron, *Riccardo Freda*, 163.
21. Tavernier, "Riccardo Freda," 70.
22. Lourcelles, *Dictionnaire du cinéma*, 955.
23. Tavernier, "Riccardo Freda," 70.
24. Tatti Sanguineti, "Le grandezze della Lux," in Farassino, ed., *Lux Film*, 86.
25. Carlo Testa, *Italian Cinema and Modern European Literatures, 1945–2000* (Santa Barbara, CA: Greenwood Publishing Group, 2002), 8–9.
26. Poindron, *Riccardo Freda*, 165.
27. Emanuela Martini, "Una vocazione romantica," in Emanuela Martini and Stefano Della Casa, *Riccardo Freda* (Bergamo: Bergamo Film Meeting, 1993), 10.

28. Valentina Cortese, *Quanti sono i domani passati* (Milan: Mondadori, 2012), 47.

29. In his later years, Freda would rant about the actor's ungratefulness toward him. "Two students who ran after me introduced him to me. They insisted, and since I was in debt with them ... I accepted to cast him in my film. At that time, he was very respectful and very grateful. Then, he forgot that he had worked with me. Mastroianni is permanently acting. He is the embodiment of the Italian: hammy and hypocrite. About 20 years ago, in Paris, we organized a little party among us Italians. There were my friend Simon Mizrahi, Mario Monicelli, Monica Vitti and others. Mastroianni showed up and pretended not to recognize me. All the guests reproached him, starting with Monicelli ... Monicelli told him, 'Are you kidding or what, you started making movies with Freda...'" Poindron, *Riccardo Freda*, 169.

30. Tornatore, *Il quarto moschettiere*, 10–11. True or not, the anecdote predates a similar one which occurred during the filming of *L'orribile segreto del Dr. Hichcock*, recalled by the latter film's a.d. Marcello Avallone.

31. Freda claimed that the whole film was screened at a cinema in Milan in its entirety before being split into two parts, but this is highly unlikely, as *Caccia all'uomo* and *Tempesta su Parigi* were submitted separately to the censors and obtained two different visas. On the other hand, it might be that the two parts were programmed and screened in sequence on that occasion.

32. Joe Pihodna, "Les Miserables," *New York Herald Tribune*, March 25, 1952. The film was shown at NYC's World Theater.

33. A.W., "Film Version No. 7 of 'Les Miserables,'" *New York Times*, March 25, 1952.

34. M.L.A., "Italian 'Miserables' Featured at Kenmore," *Daily Boston Globe*, May 31, 1952.

35. G.L., "Hugo Tale at Laurel," *Los Angeles Times*, May 17, 1952.

36. The other films on Casanova were the following: *Casanova* (1918, Alfréd Deésy); the German *Das Herz des Casanova* (1919, Erik Lund); the Austrian *Casanovas erste und letzte Liebe* (1920, Julius Szoreghi), *Casanova* (1927, Alexandre Volkoff) and the French *Les amours de Casanova* (1934, René Barberis).

37. Lourcelles, *Dictionnaire du cinéma*, 274.

38. Martini and Della Casa, *Riccardo Freda*, 74.

39. Riccardo Freda, "Quando eravamo alla Lux," in Farassino, ed., *Lux Film*, 110.

40. Poindron, *Riccardo Freda*, 174.

41. *Ibid.*, 177. Such a scene would be impossible to film today, and rightly so, because of the harm that the animals might undergo: however, Freda claimed that neither the riders nor the horses were wounded.

42. *Ibid.*, 176.

43. Giacomo Gambetti, *Vittorio Gassman* (Rome: Gremese, 1999), 91.

44. Other contenders that year were Eleonora Rossi Drago, who was disqualified because she was married; Silvana Mangano, who won the Miss Rome title; and Sophia Loren, eliminated because "not photogenic enough."

45. Faldini and Fofi, *L'avventurosa storia del cinema italiano 1935–1959*, 149.

46. Poindron, *Riccardo Freda*, 181.

Chapter 5

1. Faldini and Fofi, *L'avventurosa storia del cinema italiano 1935–1959*, 193.

2. Poindron, *Riccardo Freda*, 183.

3. According to Stefano Della Casa, Elio Pandolfi, who made his film debut at 22 in *Guarany* and whose role ended up in the cutting room floor, waited almost 50 years to approach Freda in 1997, invite him to dinner and ask him why he cut his part out of the film. Della Casa, *Riccardo Freda*, 90.

4. Maria Pia Fusco, "Repubblica," July 3, 1981. When speaking with Poindron, Freda embellished the anecdote, explaining that the machinists who were working on Henry Koster's *The Naked Maja* even stole props from Koster's set to help him, much to Koster's desperation. Too bad *The Naked Maja* was made in 1958, ten years after *Guarany*. *Ibid.*, 185.

5. Renato Morazzani Pietri, "Guarany," *Hollywood* #284, February 24, 1951.

6. Poindron, *Riccardo Freda*, 189.

7. *Ibid.*

8. Della Casa, *Riccardo Freda*, 34.

9. Lisa Shaw, "The Brazilian *Chanchada* and Hollywood Paradigms (1930–1959)," in *Framework: The Journal of Cinema and Media*, Vol. 44, No. 1, Spring 2003, 70.

10. "Caçula" means the youngest child, and "*do barulho*" means troublemaker in the slang of the forties.

11. João Carlos Rodrigues, "O caçula do barulho. Riccardo Freda no Brasil." *Filmecultura* #53, January 2011, 79.

12. *Ibid.*

13. Duarte recalled an anecdote, no doubt with some exaggeration, about his final scene with Gianna Maria Canale, in which he had to kiss the Italian actress: "We started filming: I gave a kiss to the miss and didn't stop kissing until I heard the word 'cut,' although the camera was far. And I kept kissing, and kissing. The shooting of the scene started locking my lips on her and did not stop until the director called 'Cut!,' really making out with her ... as until there was basically no more mouth left to kiss on the actress, and I ended up all red. And she responded in equal measure.... Only then Freda saw that my face was red from all the lipstick she smudged on me! He then said 'Cut!' and gave me a sermon before everyone on the set, raising his voice: 'Mr. Duarte, you will never make it in European cinema. You're not a professional, because professionals don't kiss for real. All cinema is interpretation!'" *Ibid.*, 80.

14. Lisa Shaw, Stephanie Dennison, *Brazilian National Cinema* (London: Routledge, 2014), 139.

15. Rodrigues, "O caçula do barulho. Riccardo Freda no Brasil," 79.
16. Ibid., 80.
17. Ibid., 79.
18. Ibid., 80.
19. Poindron, 188.
20. Ibid., 186.
21. In Middle Ages, *Podestà* (literally: the one holding power) was the chief magistrate of a city state, whereas the *Capitano del popolo* (Captain of the People) was a key administrative figure, as he controlled the *Podestà*, who usually represented the nobles, and represented the increasing wealthy classes of merchants and professionals of non-noble origins.
22. Besides Dante, Ugolino's case fascinated another writer, many centuries later: Jorge Luis Borges evoked the story of Ugolino and Ruggiero in the short story *The Wait*, included in his 1949 collection *The Aleph*.
23. Poindron, *Riccardo Freda*, 56.
24. Ibid., 196
25. Ibid.
26. Ibid., 100.
27. Freda, *Divoratori di celluloide*, 105.
28. Poindron, *Riccardo Freda*, 198.
29. Ibid.
30. Alberto Albertazzi, "Il figlio di d'Artagnan," *Intermezzo#* 13, April 15, 1950
31. Edwin Schallert, "Maxwell Much in Line for Lead in 'Road'; Don Taylor in 'Leathernecks,'" *Los Angeles Times*, November 16, 1950.
32. *The Gay Swordsman* was screened at RKO's 81st Street theater in New York, paired with the Swiss/UK war drama *The Tempest* (1953, Leopold Lindtberg), and at the St. George in Boston, paired with the John Derek vehicle *Sea of Lost Ships* (1953, Joseph Kane), in December 1953. See respectively *The New York Times*, November 16, 1953, and *The Daily Boston Globe*, December 20, 1953.
33. Anonymous, "Weill Eyes Europe for Prod. Deal," *Billboard*, January 30, 1954. The article states that Weill also picked up Freda's *La vendetta di Aquila Nera* (*The Vengeance of the Black Eagle*).
34. Poindron, *Riccardo Freda*, 248.
35. Ibid.
36. Ibid.

Chapter 6

1. Various, "Raffaello Matarazzo. Materiali, vol. I," in *Quaderni del Movie Club*, #1, 1976, 92.
2. Emiliano Morreale, *Così piangevano. Il cinema mélo nell'Italia degli anni cinquanta* (Rome: Donzelli 2011), 207.
3. Poindron, *Riccardo Freda*, 200–201.
4. Gambetti, *Vittorio Gassman*, 91.
5. *The Washington Post and Times Herald*, June 26, 1955.
6. Poindron, *Riccardo Freda*, 202.
7. Gian Piero Brunetta, *Storia del cinema italiano. Dal neorealismo al miracolo economico—1945-1959* (Rome: Editori Riuniti, 1982–2001), 298.
8. Giordano, *Giganti buoni*, 96.
9. Jacqueline Freda, interview with the author, May 2015.
10. Tornatore, *Il quarto moschettiere*, 31.
11. Poindron, *Riccardo Freda*, 64.
12. Fabrizio Gabella, "La vendetta di Aquila Nera," *Intermezzo* #16, August 31, 1952.
13. Vice, "La vendetta di Aquila Nera," *L'Unità*, August 2, 1952.
14. The film was even released in India, through a company named Noronha Pictures: the *Times of India*'s reviewer called it "well photographed and lavishly produced" (a testament to Freda's ability for concealing low-budgets) but found that "the film loses on the direction, editing, acting and the dubbing, which is mediocre." Anonymous, "Tale of Vengeance at Excelsior," *The Times of India*, July 30, 1953.
15. Villa sings the following songs: *Vedi Napoli e poi muori*; *Ho pianto per te*; *'A voce 'e mamma*; *Mattinata d'oro*; *Marechiaro*; plus the celebrated song written by Totò, *Malafemmena*.
16. Poindron, *Riccardo Freda*, 77.
17. Ferraniacolor was the color system used within the Italian industry until 1958, when Ferrania closed down. Production companies then resorted to Eastmancolor and Technicolor.
18. Freda's film is one of three to use this phrase as a title, the others being made in 1924 (by Eugenio Perego) and in 2007 (by Enrico Caria), signaling a shift in meaning: by 2007, "see Naples and die" means that you are unlikely to survive a visit to Naples, because of its widespread violence and Camorra wars, as depicted also in Matteo Garrone's outstanding *Gomorra* (2008).
19. Alberto Albertazzi, "Vedi Napoli e poi muori," *Intermezzo* # 11/12, June 30, 1952.
20. A. H. Weiler, "The Screen: *See Naples and Die* Opens at the Rialto," *New York Times*, August 31, 1959.
21. Poindron, *Riccardo Freda*, 210.
22. Lourcelles, *Dictionnaire du cinéma*, 838.
23. Freda, *Divoratori di celluloide*, 121.
24. Poindron, *Riccardo Freda*, 212.
25. Ibid., 211.

Chapter 7

1. Faldini and Fofi, *L'avventurosa storia del cinema italiano 1935-1959*, 171.
2. Poindron, *Riccardo Freda*, 217.
3. Tavernier, "Riccardo Freda," 71.
4. Flavia Brizio-Skov, *Popular Italian Cinema: Culture and Politics in a Postwar Society* (London: I.B. Tauris, 2011), 24–25.
5. Ibid.
6. Derek Elley, *The Epic Film. Myth and History* (London/Boston, Routledge & Kegan Paul, 1984), 114.
7. Freda recalled Girotti's obsessive care for the way he looked on screen, with amusing anecdotes.

"Prior to shooting one of the most important scenes in *Spartaco*, I noticed that Massimo Girotti was displaying clear signs of nervousness and preoccupation. He repeatedly asked his wife to come over and confabulated excitedly with her. I thought he was worried because of the long and difficult line he had to deliver, and I got close to comfort him. The actor looked right into my eyes and, obviously irritated, whispered: "The thighs ... the thighs!" I stood there, dumbfounded. Impatiently, he transfixed me with these exact words: "I'm afraid that Pogány's light makes my thighs look bigger!" Freda, *Divoratori di celluloide*, 109.

8. Elley, *The Epic Film*, 114.

9. Poindron, *Riccardo Freda*, 78. In view of Freda's words, and especially of Pogány's body of work as a director of photography, Tim Lucas' assumptions that "certain scenes—Rufus' visit to Sabina in her room, the gladiator school and dungeon scenes, Sabina's veiled visit to the rebels' encampment, Amitys walking through the spear-studded battlefield with a torch looking for her dead lover, and several glamorous close-ups of Gianna Maria Canale—more strongly resemble the work of Bava" seem questionable. See Lucas, *Mario Bava*, 125.

10. *Ibid.*, 219.

11. *Ibid.* A slightly different version of the anecdote, told by Bava's friend, actor Goffredo "Freddy" Unger, can be found in Lucas, *Mario Bava*, 123.

12. Ettore Fecchi, "Spartaco," *Intermezzo #5*, March 15, 1953.

13. Óscar Lapeña Marchena, "The Stolen Seduction: The Image of Spartacus in Riccardo Freda's *Spartaco, gladiatore della Tracia*," in Knippschild, Silke and Morcillo, Marta García, eds., *Seduction & Power: Antiquity in the Visual and Performing Arts* (London: A&C Black, 2013), 177.

14. Marjory Adams, "'Susan Slept Here' at Keith Memorial," *Daily Boston Globe*, August 23, 1954.

15. Anonymous, "'Bullet Is Waiting' Presented Today on Three Screens," *Los Angeles Times*, September 17, 1954.

16. M.O.S., "New Films. 'Passion' At Strand Theater," *The Hartford Courant*, October 7, 1954. All three reviewers declared themselves unfamiliar with the cast of Freda's film, save for Ludmilla Tchérina.

17. In Italy, however, Kubrick's film did generate a couple of spurious sequels: Sergio Corbucci's *Il figlio di Spartacus* and Michele Lupo's *La vendetta di Spartacus* (*The Revenge of Spartacus*, 1964), plus a number of films about gladiators fighting against the Roman empire, even with a comedy twist as was the case with Gianfranco Parolini's *I dieci gladiatori* (*The Ten Gladiators*, 1963) which was also marketed abroad with Spartacus' name in the title, as *Spartacus and the Ten Gladiators*.

18. The characters of Justinian and Theodora were featured again in Robert Siodmak's *Kampf um Rom* (*Battle for Rome/The Last Roman*, 1968), played respectively by Orson Welles and Sylva Koscina and reduced, to quote Derek Elley, to "shadows of their real selves." Elley, *The Epic Film*, 137.

19. Poindron, *Riccardo Freda*, 225.

20. Farassino, "Roma, Via Po. Storia e sistema della Lux Film," in Farassino, ed., *Lux Film*, 40.

21. Angelo Nizza, "Teodora imperatrice riveduta e corretta," *La Stampa*, September 3, 1953.

22. Poindron, *Riccardo Freda*, 229.

23. Lucas, *Mario Bava*, 126.

24. Tornatore, *Il quarto moschettiere*, 32–33. In Poindron's book, Freda had offered a more scathing version about his turn as cameraman, claiming that Lombardi's brother "did not understand a thing." Poindron, *Riccardo Freda*, 151.

25. Freda, "Quando eravamo alla Lux," in Farassino, *Lux Film*, 111.

26. The TV movie *Una domanda di matrimonio* (1966), with Lombardi as d.o.p., was Italy's very first TV program in color. Again, considering Rodolfo Lombardi's skills, Lucas' suspicion that Bava "substituted for Lombardi for the shooting of the horrific climax, in which the empress ... is surrounded by the spears of the guards and exposed to the revenge of a man earlier blinded with hot pokers for inadvertedly allowing her to escape" is unconvincing. Lucas, *Mario Bava*, 126.

27. Lourcelles, *Dictionnaire du cinéma*, 1440.

28. Faldini and Fofi, *L'avventurosa storia del cinema italiano 1935–1959*, 149.

29. Not that the filming went always smoothly for the director and his female lead. As Civirani recalled, "between her and Freda there was yet another working and personal relationship, and the same old story between the lead actress and the director: too many four-letter words on the set." Osvaldo Civirani, *Un fotografo a Cinecittà* (Rome: Gremese, 1995), 116–117.

30. Poindron, *Riccardo Freda*, 228.

31. Faldini and Fofi, *L'avventurosa storia del cinema italiano 1935–1959*, 224. See also Fabrice Branca and Gerard Stüm, "Entretien avec Riccardo Freda," *Monster Bis Collector*, 1999, 59.

32. Tavernier, "Riccardo Freda," 71.

33. Umberto Tani, "Teodora," *Intermezzo #19/20*, October 31, 1954.

34. Joe Hyams, "Miss Monroe Back at Fox But Firm on Own Company," *New York Herald Tribune*, January 11, 1955.

35. A.W., "'Theodora, Slave Princess' Seen at Globe," *New York Times*, January 12, 1955.

36. Freda, "Quando eravamo alla Lux," in Farassino, Lux Film, 110. Freda claims the documentary was 600 metres long, about 36 minutes, whereas the version submitted to the board of censors runs approximately 11 minutes.

37. Poindron, *Riccardo Freda*, 226.

38. *Ibid.*, 232. A reference to the ad can be found in *L'Unità*, 13 December 1954.

39. Riccardo Freda, in *Enciclopedia del cinema in Piemonte* (http://www.torinocittadelcinema.it/)

40. Poindron, *Riccardo Freda*, 233–236.

41. *Ibid.*, 190

42. "Subsequently, he wanted us to work together

agan. Let me explain, Totò often worked with his son-in-law ... Bragaglia, who is now a hundred years old.... When Totò made a movie, most of the times he wanted him as the director. One day he was shooting in Rome, and I paid him visit with Gianna Maria Canale. We were on good terms despite the breach of the contract. I already knew his future wife, Franca Faldini. She wanted to work in the show business and I took photographs of her. When I saw her in Totò's arms, she had forgotten about that... So Bragaglia sees me, gets in my way, a way of saying, 'What the fuck is Freda doing here? ...' Totò and I started a friendly conversation ... After some thinking, I asked him to shoot again with me... He was interested but he was moving from one film to another ... I asked him: 'But wouldn't you have just a couple of days?' 'Why not?' And I see Bragaglia leave his director's spot. He jumps from a trestle and heads toward us like a demon! 'Do not listen to that character, he is capable of doing it!' And it was true, I had everything prepared beforehand, in two days, I wanted to make a film with Totò again." *Ibid.*, 191.

43. It was possibly this scene that featured an uncredited contribution on the part of Mario Bava, which Freda mentioned without going into specifics. See Lucas, *Mario Bava*, 126.

44. Mario Caiano, *Mario Caiano. Autobiografia di un regista di B-Movies* (Piombino: Il Foglio Letterario 2014), 62.

45. Fulci's film—originally entitled *La vera storia di Beatrice Cenci* and starring Adrienne La Russa (as Beatrice), Tomas Milian (as Olimpio) and Georges Wilson (as Francesco Cenci)—chose to portray for the first time the more gruesome parts of the story, whereas Tavernier's film—which originally came to life as Freda's own project to remake his 1956 film (*see* "Epilogue")—was a looser adaptation set in 14th century France.

46. Sandra A. Waters, *Narrating the Italian Historical Novel* (Ann Arbor, MI: ProQuest, 2009), 40.

47. Martini and Della Casa, *Riccardo Freda*, 80.

48. Tavernier, "Riccardo Freda," 70.

49. Poindron, *Riccardo Freda*, 243.

50. Riccardo Freda, interviewed by Roberto Torelli, "Fuori Orario."

51. Morreale, *Così piangevano*, 208.

52. Guy Allombert, "Riccardo Freda: jouer avec le couleur," *Image et son* #207, June/July 1967, 6.

53. Poindron, *Riccardo Freda*, 65.

54. *Ibid.*

55. *Ibid.*, 247.

56. Even though a number of sources list the English title *Castle of the Banned Lovers*, the film was not released theatrically in the United States, and as of this writing no English language copies are available.

57. Jean A. Gili, ed., *Riccardo Freda* (Rome: Quaderni di Cinecittà International #5, 1993).

58. Lourcelles, *Dictionnaire du cinéma*, 264.

59. Boisset, *La vie est un choix*, 103.

60. Tavernier, "Riccardo Freda," 72.

Chapter 8

1. Poindron, *Riccardo Freda*, 258. A slightly different version of the anecdote is included in a March 1993 interview with Stefano Della Casa, included in the booklet of the Italian DVD *Caltiki il mostro immortale*. Tim Lucas suggests the possibility that "the subject came up as early as Freda's initial visit to Bava's home in 1953," perhaps prompted by the success of André De Toth's *House of Wax* (1953) and Eugenio Bava's sculptures, but this is highly unlikely, considering Freda's words. What is more, *House of Wax* came out in the States in April 1953 and in Italy in November 1953, after being initially rejected by the censors, whereas the filming of *Spartaco* took place in late 1952 and the film was submitted to the board of censors in January 1953. In addition to that, Lucas adds that Freda suggested the very fast shooting (two weeks) "knowing how quickly Bava worked with lighting and cinematography," not taking into account that Freda had always liked to work very quickly, no matter who was the d.o.p.: consider the time-saving tricks with shots/counter shots he had employed in *The Iron Swordsman*, for instance. Lucas, *Mario Bava*, 172.

2. *Ibid.*, 260. Since on other occasions Freda (in *Divoratori di celluloide*) or Bava mentioned Scalera Studios as the film's location, some confusion ensued on the incorrect assumption that these were two distinct studios: in fact, the Titanus Appia studios, sited in Circonvallazione Appia 180, were formerly Scalera Film Studios. Lombardo's company purchased the premises after Scalera became insolvent and was put under liquidation in 1952. The studios were demolished in 1967.

3. Oreste De Fornari, *Tutti i film di Sergio Leone* (Milan: Ubulibri, 1984, 1997), 158. Interestingly, Donati mentions the French title of the film, *Faites-moi confiance*—actually Chase's novel was published in France as *Fais-moi confiance*, in 1956, by Gallimard, which might hint at the fact that Freda got hold of a copy *before* it was published in Italy two years later, under the title *Sei tu che pagherai* (It'll Be You Who'll Pay; *I Gialli del Secolo Casini* #301, 1958). The other option, of course, is that Donati's recollections are confused and the scriptwriting sessions took place in 1958, *after* the Italian release of Chase's novel.

4. Sergio Donati, *C'era una volta il West (ma c'ero anch'io)* (Rome: Omero, 2007), 13.

5. *Ibid.*, 332.

6. Freda, *Divoratori di celluloide*, 6.

7. Poindron, *Riccardo Freda*, 258.

8. Freda, *Divoratori di celluloide*, 88–89.

9. Poindron, *Riccardo Freda*, 259.

10. Teo Mora, "*Elegia per una donna vampiro. Il cinema fantastico in Italia 1957–1966*," in Teo Mora, *Storia del cinema dell'orrore*, vol. 2 (Rome: Fanucci, 1978–2002), 166.

11. The Venetian-born Montresor (1926–2001) moved to the United States in 1960, and started working as an art director and costume designer in theaters

throughout the world: New York's Metropolitan, London's Covent Garden, the Paris Opera. He also directed two films, *Pilgrimage* (1972) and *La Messe dorée* (*The Golden Mass*, 1975): the latter was rejected by the Italian censorship commission due to its erotic content, and came out in Montresor's native country in a heavily manipulated version. *I vampiri* is widely regarded as one of his most remarkable efforts, and Mario Bava's astonishing black-and-white cinematography had a vital role in emphasizing it.

12. Freda, *Divoratori di celluloide*, 6.
13. Lucas, *Mario Bava*, 180.
14. "I wrote the script for *I vampiri* in a hurry, and shot it in twelve days. Then I left the movie, after an argument with the producers, and they finished that little that was left in two days." Luigi Cozzi, *Il cinema dei mostri* (Rome: Fanucci, 1987), 250.
15. Poindron, *Riccardo Freda*, p 262.
16. As Freda claimed, "It was the producers that made me take it out of the film: they were afraid that … the film would be too weird, too unusual … and that people would be too shocked." Antonio Tentori and Luigi Cozzi, *Guida al cinema Horror Made in Italy* (Rome: Profondo Rosso, 2007), p 325.
17. The comparison is discussed also in Simone Venturini, *Horror italiano* (Rome: Donzelli, 2014), 106.
18. Lucas, *Mario Bava*, 173.
19. Anonymous, "I vampiri," *La Stampa*, May 30, 1957.
20. Poindron, *Riccardo Freda*, 263.
21. *Ibid.*
22. Cinematographer Karl Struss had first achieved the effect in Fred Niblo's *Ben-Hur: A Tale of the Christ* (1925), in the scene where Ben Hur's leprous mother and sister are miraculously cured by Jesus. Bava's achievement in reproducing and simplifying Struss' technique is discussed at length in Lucas, *Mario Bava*, 179.
23. Carlo Piazza, "Gianna Maria Canale. La reine du peplum," *Monster Bis*, 1999, 40. Canale had actually been involved in a car accident a decade earlier, on the night of June 2, 1952, in Florence, when the car driven by Freda crashed against a wall to avoid three kids riding recklessly on a bike. Canale suffered a cranial concussion with a hematoma on her forehead, and broke her left hand's metacarpus. Nothing serious, of course, but perhaps the news was the source that years later had all the rumors spread. *See* Anonymous, "Ferita in un incidente d'auto un'attrice cinematografica," *Corriere della Sera*, June 3, 1952.
24. Faldini and Fofi, *L'avventurosa storia del cinema italiano 1960-1969*, 200.
25. "Get More Out of Life … Go Out to a Movie," *The Hartford Courant*, December 23, 1960. Freda's film was paired with *Mark of the Devil* (*Doña diabla*, 1951, Tito Davison), a lurid melodrama starring María Félix.
26. Lucas, *Mario Bava*, 189.
27. Tim Lucas, "Is There Life After *Suspiria*?" in Tim Lucas, *The Video Watchdog Book* (Cincinnati, OH: Video Watchdog, 1992), 181.

28. Freda, *Divoratori di celluloide*, 96.
29. *Ibid.*, 97.
30. The other names involved were Vittoriano Petrilli and Paolo Spinola: Petrilli co-wrote several interesting pictures in the 1960s, such as Damiano Damiani's *La rimpatriata* (*The Reunion*, 1963), Brunello Rondi's *Più tardi, Claire, più tardi…* (*Run, Psycho, Run*, 1968), Sergio Corbucci's *Il grande silenzio* (*The Great Silence*, 1968) and Alberto Lattuada's *Fräulein Doktor* (1969). Spinola would later become a director on his own, with four little-seen films (*La fuga*, 1964; *L'estate*, 1966; *La donna invisibile*, 1969; *Un giorno alla fine di ottobre*, 1977).
31. The dubbing is careless too: Cervi's character is alternatively referred to as "Bovelasco" and "Bolevasco."
32. Lourcelles and Mizrahi, "Entretien avec Riccardo Freda," 23.
33. Diego López and David Pizarro, *Silencios de pánico* (Madrid: Tyrannosaurus Books, 2014), 465–467.
34. *Ibid.*
35. *Variety*, July 6, 1960. The film played bottom of double bills with John Huston's *The Misfits* (in Atlanta: *Atlanta Daily World*, March 17, 1961) and Byron Haskin's *September Storm* (in Boston: Marjory Adams, "Majorca Looks Great, But Shark Is Silly," *Boston Globe*, October 26, 1960).
36. Della Casa, *Riccardo Freda*, 57.
37. Poindron, *Riccardo Freda*, 276.
38. Della Casa, *Riccardo Freda*, 58.
39. *Ibid.*
40. Jacqueline Freda recalls her amusing meeting with Branko Lustig in 2004, while shooting Ridley Scott's *Kingdom of Heaven* (where she acted as stunt double) in Morocco, at Ouarzazate. "After a week's shooting an assistant called me. 'You're wanted by Mr. Lustig.' Uh-oh, I thought, did I do anything wrong? So, I show up at his office: Branko is sitting behind a huge desk, his sleeves rolled up so that the numbers tattooed on his arm in Auschwitz are in plain sight—a way to say, 'Don't fuck up with me, I've seen too many things in life.' He greets me and says, 'So, what's your name?' 'Jacqueline Freda' 'What kinship do you have with Riccardo?' 'He was my father.' He gets up from the desk, looks at my feet and, speaking in Italian, 'And where's the dog?' I had brought my two dogs with me in Morocco, but left them at the hotel, since the assistant director would have fired me on the spot if I dared bring them on the set. 'Home,' I said. 'You're not Riccardo Freda's daughter if you don't bring your dogs on the set!' We laughed and started talking about dad. Branko told me they worked on *Agi Murad—Il diavolo bianco* together, and he did his driving exam on the American car that dad had lent him. He was one of those people my father had been really affectionate to, and the feeling was mutual, even after all those years. And when we parted ways, he said: 'And remember, tomorrow I want to see your dog on the set!' Of course, I obliged. And Branko took the dogs to the catering

tent with me, in front of the whole crew. He told the a.d. who I was, and that I could keep the dogs with me, since I was Riccardo Freda's daughter." Jacqueline Freda, interview with the author, May 2015.

41. Freda, *Divoratori di celluloide*, 90.
42. Poindron, *Riccardo Freda*, 276.
43. Tavernier, "Riccardo Freda," 72.
44. Chris LeClaire, *Worlds to Conquer: An Authorized Biography of Steve Reeves* (South Chatham MA: Monomoy Books, 1999), 190.
45. Alberto Farassino and Tatti Sanguineti, *Gli uomini forti* (Milan: Mazzotta, 1983), 101.
46. Moll (real name Giorgia Molinella) was an Italian singer of German origin. Even though she is credited as Georgia Moll, she more often used the alias *Giorgia* Moll.
47. The voices were the same as other *Hercules* pictures released by Joseph E. Levine: Reeves and Herter were dubbed by George Gonneau, Renato Baldini and Nikola Popiovic (Kin Shamyl) were dubbed by Brett Morrison, whereas Haji's son Yusep was dubbed by June Foray. The narrator's voice was provided by Marvin Miller.
48. Marjory Adams, "Mighty Muscle Man Reeves Wins Over Late Leo Tolstoy," *Boston Globe*, April 12, 1961. *The White Warrior* played in Boston with *Up Periscope* (1959, Gordon Douglas), and in Los Angeles with *Tormented* (1960, Bert I. Gordon).
49. Charles Stinson, "Tolstoy Novel Given Over to Steve Reeves," *Los Angeles Times*, March 31, 1961. Stinson only had kind words for Gérard Herter's acting.
50. Marco Giusti, "E di Agi Murad sulla via della critica," *Il falcone maltese: rivista di cinema* #5, 1974.
51. Cozzi, *Il cinema dei mostri*, 251.
52. Cozzi, "Riccardo Freda: un ricordo personale," in Familiari, *Riccardo Freda*, 203.
53. *Ibid.*, 204.
54. Poindron, *Riccardo Freda*, 279.
55. Lucas, *Mario Bava*, 257. As Lucas points out, there seems to be a bit of a confusion regarding the film's chronology: Bava recalled working on some special effects during summertime, whereas in the climax John Merivale's breath is visible, likely the sign of a chilly winter night. This might indicate a halt in the production, from early to mid-1959. *Ibid.*, 258.
56. (Not signed) "Caltiki la trippa immortale" in Aa. Vv. "Genealogia del delitto. Il cinema di Mario & Lamberto Bava," *Nocturno Dossier* #24, July 2004, 25.
57. Simone Venturini, *Galatea S.p.A. (1952–1965). Storia di una casa di produzione cinematografica* (Rome: Associazione italiana per le ricerche di storia del cinema, 2001), 205.
58. For a detailed analysis of the special effects, see Lucas, *Mario Bava*, 263–265.
59. Gozlino (1929–1992) was a well-known dancer and choreographer in Italy, due to his appearances in many TV shows. He would later embark on a marginal acting career, mostly in supporting roles: his main claim to fame is perhaps as the titular superhero (under the a.k.a. Paul Stevens) in *Flashman* (1967, Mino Loy, Luciano Martino). That same year he popped up as Mandrake in an episode of *Le streghe* (*The Witches*, 1967) directed by Vittorio De Sica and starring Silvana Mangano and Clint Eastwood. Gozlino used the same pseudonym in a number of Westerns in the early Seventies before gradually giving up on acting.

60. Lucas, *Mario Bava*, 263.
61. Poindron, *Riccardo Freda*, 280.

Chapter 9

1. Della Casa, *Riccardo Freda*, 65.
2. Besides *Le fatiche di Ercole*, *I giganti della Tessaglia* and *Jason and the Argonauts*, the myth of Jason and the Golden Fleece was brought to the screen in the 2000 miniseries *Jason and the Argonauts*, by Nick Willing, starring Jason London as the titular hero. Yet another version of the story, albeit a *sui generis* one, was *Das goldene Ding* (1972, Edgar Reitz, Ula Stöckl, Alf Brustellin, Nikos Perakis), where Jason and the Argonauts are all played by 11-year-old kids.
3. The subplot involving Aglaia and Euristeo's trial is yet another infraction to the myth: whereas in the film the young man is put to trial as he dared bring a woman onto the ship, several sources of the story include a female figure, Atalanta, in the crew.
4. The same casual approach to Greek mythology can be seen in the set designs: the Thessalian palace features a weird mixture of Doric columns and unlikely totemic statues, while Gaia's palace features classic bas-reliefs hanging on the walls and other kitschy details.
5. Michel Mardore, "Le Géant de Thessalie," *Cahiers du cinéma* #122, August 1961.
6. Bertrand Tavernier, "Le Géant de Thessalie," *Cinéma 61* #59, August 1961, 115.
7. Lucas, *Mario Bava*, 348–349.
8. Poindron, *Riccardo Freda*, 284.
9. Tavernier praised the scene's plastic quality, with "that statue which looks like it leans over marble and which is in fact surrounded by water." *Ibid.*, 116.
10. Poindron, *Riccardo Freda*, 65.
11. *Ibid.*, 284–285. Contrary to what Derek Elley states, Freda did not actually disown the film. Elley, *The Epic Film*, 60.
12. Lucas, *Mario Bava*, 348–350. Lucas debatably attributes various scenes to Bava—such as the fight with the cyclops, Nadine Duca's aging, the trial of Eurystheus, and even the storm scene (incidentally, the only moment Freda admitted to liking, together with Jason's ascent of the Colossus)—basing solely on the recurrence of the same lighting scheme, and on the aforementioned *Présence du Cinéma* footnote.
13. Tavernier, "Riccardo Freda," 72.
14. See *Newsday*, October 4, 1963; and *Boston Globe*, November 10, 1963.
15. Giordano, *Giganti buoni*, 132.
16. Riccardo Freda, "Fuori Orario."
17. Domenico Cammarota Jr., *Il cinema peplum* (Rome: Fanucci, 1987).

18. Faldini and Fofi, *L'avventurosa storia del cinema italiano 1960–1969*, 392.
19. Antonio José Navarro, "En la corte del gran Khan," *Dirigido por* #354, March 2006, 56.
20. Ibid.
21. Lucas, *Mario Bava*, 380. Again, Lucas hypothizes Bava taking over Pallottini as d.o.p. on a couple of scenes, on the basis that they "stand out strikingly from the rest of the film's photography."
22. Freda, *Divoratori di celluloide*, 116. The episode is reported with an absurd error (according to the authors, it was the tiger that soiled itself!) in Steve [Stefano] Della Casa and Marco Giusti, *Il grande libro di Ercole. Il cinema mitologico in Italia* (Rome: Edizioni Sabinae, 2013), 200. However, the anecdote, although amusing, has no correspondence in the film: in all the shots featuring the real tiger, a dummy can be glimpsed in the place of the actor who plays the prince.
23. Lucas, *Mario Bava*, 380.
24. Manlio Gomarasca and Davide Pulici, eds., *99 donne. Stelle e stelline del cinema italiano* (Milan: Media World, 1999), 107.
25. Margaret Harford, "Scott Flexes Muscles as Samson of Orient," *Los Angeles Times*, March 22, 1963.
26. Freda, *Divoratori di celluloide*, 84.
27. In 1975 writer Cyta Vacanti published *Dox il detective*, an account of Dox's extraordinary career. The book is still in print today.
28. Poindron, *Riccardo Freda*, 286.
29. Martini and Della Casa, *Riccardo Freda*, 85.
30. Lourcelles and Mizrahi, "Entretien avec Riccardo Freda," *Présence du cinéma* #17, Spring 1963 25.
31. Ibid., 23.
32. Poindron, *Riccardo Freda*, 295. Freda's low opinion of his lead was shared by art director Andrea Crisanti, who recalled that Bellini "was as a strong as a girl" and could not even move the tree. To achieve the effect of the flames of hell below the eradicated tree, Crisanti put some colored lamps in the hole. Antonio Fabio Familiari, "Maciste all'inferno. Intervista allo scenografo Andrea Crisanti," in Familiari, *Riccardo Freda. L'estetu dell'emozione*, 153.
33. "The script asked for the hero to stop these ferocious bulls, so I built a huge polystyrene trunk, which was held by the actor, only that at the moment of shooting, many of these cows fell into a valley [sic] and some died ... back then, I don't think there was animal protection around ... we are speaking of 1962, even though the movie was made in 1961." Ibid., 154.
34. Della Casa, *Riccardo Freda*, 68.
35. Giordano, *Giganti buoni*, 133.
36. Faldini and Fofi, *L'avventurosa storia del cinema italiano 1935–1959*, 392.
37. Giordano, *Giganti buoni*, 107.
38. Familiari, "Maciste all'inferno. Intervista allo scenografo Andrea Crisanti," 152.
39. Lucas, *Mario Bava*, 436.
40. "He was a huge fan of race horses, owned some horses himself, and was also a gentlemen rider. I often went to the race track, and sometimes enjoyed running the horses, and Freda appreciated the way I trained them. He had a horse called Zignago, so one day he told me, 'If you will train Zignago every morning I will make you my assistant director.' So, every morning, I woke up at 6, went to the race course and trained his horse. It was a big pain in the ass because it was very cold, but whenever he was about to make a film, he always called me. At the beginning, I worked as a volunteer, and step by step, I became a professional." Upchurch, Lucas and Boscaino, "Raptus. The Making of The Horrible Dr. Hichcock," 35. Avallone tells a similar anecdote (but maintains that the horse's name was Zimbala) in Eugenio Ercolani, "Tra cinema e cavalli: Intervista a Marcello Avallone," *Fascination Cinema*, 27 January 2014.
41. Ercolani, "Tra cinema e cavalli."
42. The IMDb website indicates November 1963, whereas the American Film Institute Catalog indicates December 4, 1963 (at Providence, Rhode Island). Richard Krafsur (Ex. Ed.), *The American Film Institute Catalog of Motion Pictures. Feature Films 1961–1970* (New York / London: R.R. Bowker, 1976), 1235.
43. Marjory Adams, "Lovely Italian Star Heroine at Paramount," *Boston Globe*, December 14, 1963.

Chapter 10

1. Riccardo Freda, "Fuori Orario."
2. Della Casa, *Riccardo Freda*, 54.
3. Ibid., 53.
4. Della Casa and Giusti, *Il grande libro di Ercole*, 236.
5. Giordano, *Giganti buoni*, 99.
6. Ibid., 100–101.
7. The English adaptation and dubbing was provided by the New York–based Titra Sound, and featured voice actors George Gonneau, Peggy Lobbin and Norman Rose.
8. As Kevin Heffernan noted, even though the *Motion Picture Herald* announced that the film marked AIP's "entry into the big-budget single-feature field," the advertising stressed the cinema of attractions "four SEEs" approach characteristics of its early genre pictures. Kevin Heffernan, *Ghouls, Gimmicks, and Gold: Horror Films and the American Movie Business, 1953-1968* (Durham, NC: Duke University Press, 2004), 137.
9. Tom Weaver, *Return of the B Science Fiction and Horror Heroes: The Mutant Melding of Two Volumes of Classic Interviews* (Jefferson, NC: McFarland, 2000), 31.
10. The song was released as a single, and the B-side *(Jungle) Slave Dance* was credited to the "Al Simms Sextet" (Simms being a senior exec in charge of the music department at AIP and the producer on the record).
11. Giordano, *Giganti buoni*, 39.
12. Poindron, *Riccardo Freda*, 270.
13. Lourcelles and Mizrahi, "Entretien avec Riccardo Freda," 25.

14. Freda, *Divoratori di celluloide*, 110–111.
15. According to Amilcare A. Iannucci and John Tulk, the film shares with the earlier version the "forced dichotomy between the West as good and the East as scheming and bad, a dichotomy fueled historically by post-war developments in China and the onset of the Cold War." Amilcare A. Iannucci and John Tulk, "From Alterity to Holism," in Suzanne Colklin, Amilcare A. Iannucci and John Tulk, eds., *Marco Polo and the Encounter of East and West* (Toronto: University of Toronto, 2008), 215.
16. Della Casa, *Riccardo Freda*, 54.
17. Poindron, *Riccardo Freda*, 273.
18. Della Casa and Giusti, *Il grande libro di Ercole*, 288.
19. *See also* Curti, *Italian Gothic Horror Films, 1957–1969*, 115–116.
20. Poindron, *Riccardo Freda*, 268.
21. *Ibid.*, 272.
22. Alvin Easter, *Lash!: The Hundred Great Scenes of Men Being Whipped in the Movies* (Bloomington, IN: Xlibris Corporation, 2004), 306–308.
23. For its part, *Alone Against Rome* also recycles bits from Vicario's earlier production *La schiava di Roma* (a.k.a. *Slave of Rome*, 1961, Sergio Grieco). Della Casa mistakenly refers to *La schiava di Roma* when speaking of the arena scenes shot by Freda in Pola. Della Casa, *Riccardo Freda*, 54.
24. Marjory Adams, "Lovely Italian Star Heroine at Paramount," *Boston Globe*, December 14, 1963.
25. Della Casa, *Riccardo Freda*, 56, 132.
26. Poindron, *Riccardo Freda*, 273.
27. Gary Allen Smith, *Epic Films: Casts, Credits and Commentary on More Than 350 Historical Spectacle Movies* (Jefferson, NC: McFarland, 2004), 97.
28. Jeffrey Hunter had traveled to Rome on August 24, 1962, to begin shooting on the film. See Paul Green, *Jeffrey Hunter: The Film, Television, Radio and Stage Performances* (Jefferson, NC: McFarland, 2014), 108.
29. Poindron, *Riccardo Freda*, 272.
30. Mylène Demongeot, *Tiroirs secrets* (Paris: Le Pré aux Clercs), 2001. The actress confirmed the version when discussing *Oro per i Cesari* on her website: "At the beginning, I was happy to work with André de Toth ... but I saw him so rarely on the set. Obviously, he went to Rome to play golf. We just did our jobs. A disappointment." (http://www.mylene-demongeot.fr/lordes-cesars/) The same had happened with *La battaglia di Maratona*, also starring Demongeot, where co-director Bruno Vailati took care of most of the directing: "It was Vailati who practically shot three quarters of the film, the battle scenes on the water. Once he did the Persians, then he did the Greeks. It was him who shot the arrow, it was him who received it.... Bruno Vailati was very skilled, it was he who made all the action scenes. In fact, I realized that all these directors, that is Jacques Tourneur, André De Toth, came over because they were very well paid, and to me it was the same." Champclaux, Meriau, *Le Peplum*, 101. In the same interview, Demongeot added an interesting recollection about both Bava and Freda: "...back then they were very much in love with that beautiful black-haired girl who played in many of their films, very vamp, very mysterious, very S&M. She did plenty of films for them. Then she was with Mario Bava, it seems to me. A sulphureous girl.... Barbara Steele, yes! My very young appearance with long blonde hair did not make an impression on those men. They wanted the *peplum* to be something different. In these films, there are always the gentle one and the malicious one. And they clearly preferred the latter." *Ibid.*, 103.
31. "Gold for the Caesars," *Variety*, June 17, 1964.

Chapter 11

1. Ugo Naldi, "Si dà al cinema il fratello della Cardinale," *Corriere d'informazione*, July 12–13, 1962.
2. Tim Lucas, "What Are Those Strange Drops of Blood in the Scripts of Ernesto Gastaldi?," *Video Watchdog* #39, May/June 1997, 34.
3. Poindron, *Riccardo Freda*, 299.
4. Ernesto Gastaldi, email interview with the author, March 2015.
5. Michel Caen and Jean-Claude Romer, "Entretien avec Riccardo Freda," *Midi-Minuit fantastique* #7, September 1963, 2
6. Poindron, *Riccardo Freda*, 58.
7. "The producers ... showed me an Italian print of *Pit and the Pendulum* before I started writing it: 'Give us something like this,' they said." Lucas, "What Are Those Strange Drops of Blood...," 38.
8. "Donati and Carpentieri were afraid that Alfred Hitchcock would be upset if they used the same spelling, so they decided to change a letter. Almost nobody in Italy noticed the difference!" *Ibid.*, 35.
9. Misha Kavka, "The Gothic on Screen," in Jerrold E. Hogle, ed., *The Cambridge Companion to Gothic Fiction* (Cambridge: Cambridge University Press, 2002), 219.
10. "The story seems fantastic, but I put on scene a fake terror, a fake *fantastique* because all the explanations are human" Poindron, *Riccardo Freda*, 299.
11. *Ibid.*, 304.
12. Glenn Erickson, "Women on the Verge of a Gothic Breakdown: Sex, Drugs and Corpses in *The Horrible Dr. Hichcock*," in Alain Silver and James Ursini, eds., *Horror Film Reader*, Limelight Editions, Pompton Plains NJ 2000, 278, note 8.
13. Freda, *Divoratori di celluloide*, 87.
14. Faldini and Fofi, *L'avventurosa storia del cinema italiano 1960–1969*, 203. Given Santoli's words, Mario Bava's alleged involvement in the scene (hypothized in Lucas, *Mario Bava*, 442) can be ruled out. The preparation for the nightmare scene was also the first thing Robert Flemyng was involved in after his arrival in Rome. "I was taken to the make-up department where a young man put rubber all over my face, with a sort of ... pipe thing to breathe through.... It was tight fitting. And then there was a long tube hanging down my back, so that off-camera, someone blew into the

tube, so that my face blew up ... it was extraordinary." Alan Upchurch, Tim Lucas and Luigi Boscaino, "Raptus. The Making of *The Horrible Dr. Hichcock*," *Video Watchdog* #49, January/February 1999, 36.

15. Caen and Romer, "Entretien avec Riccardo Freda," 5.

16. As for the gimmicks that Donati and Carpentieri employed during its theatrical run, Freda recalled an amusing one with Giuseppe Tornatore: "When they screened the film, I mean publicly ... they hired two old bit part actresses, specialized in just this sort of thing to scream out at a certain point of the film and faint. Well, to pretend to faint..." Tornatore, *Il quarto moschettiere*, 17.

17. Upchurch, Lucas and Boscaino, "Raptus. The Making of *The Horrible Dr. Hichcock*," 35.

18. Tim Lucas, "Harriet White Medin. Reflections of a Golden Age," *Video Watchdog* #22, March/April 1994, 44–45.

19. On the paternity of *The Murder Clinic*, see Roberto Curti, *Italian Gothic Horror Films 1957–1969* (Jefferson NC: McFarland, 2015), 168.

20. Barbara Steele, "Préface," in Michel Caen, Nicolas Stanzick, eds., *Midi-Minuit Fantastique Vol. 2*, Aix-en-Provence: Rouge Profond, 2015, 8.

21. Faldini and Fofi, *L'avventurosa storia del cinema italiano 1960–1969*, 203. Interestingly, Santoli labels Hichcock as "some sort of Dr. Jekyll."

22. Fago is credited as "John Farquhar." He debuted as a director in 1968, with the Western *Per 100.000 dollari t'ammazzo* (a.k.a. *Vengeance is Mine / $ 100,000 for a Killing*), signed as "Sidney Lean." Among his works as a director are the Western *O Cangaceiro* (1968) starring Tomas Milian, and the TV movie *Morte a passo di valzer* (1978), inspired by John Dickson Carr's novel *Fire, Burn!*

23. Ercolani, "Tra cinema e cavalli."

24. Lucas, "What Are Those Strange Drops of Blood...," 34.

25. Upchurch, Lucas and Boscaino, "Raptus. The Making of *The Horrible Dr. Hichcock*," 41.

26. Ibid., 40–41.

27. Ibid., 35.

28. Ercolani, "Tra cinema e cavalli."

29. Lucas, "What Are Those Strange Drops of Blood...," 34. There have been speculations on the missing pages (eight, according to Gastaldi). Commenting the Blu-ray American release of *The Horrible Dr. Hichcock* (the 76-minute long U.S. cut), Erickson proposed a fascinating theory in his "guest blog" column on the "Trailers From Hell" website. "During the entire second half of the movie, we only see housekeeper Martha ... and Margaretha together in the same frame once, seen through a window into the basement apartment. That shot is yet another echo of *Psycho*, in that we only see the back of Margaretha's head, sitting in a chair facing away from us. When Martha touches her, Margaretha doesn't even look alive.... If it weren't for the resurrected Margaretha telling Cynthia her story of premature burial, I'd believe that the 'ghost Margaretha' was Martha dressed up to impersonate the dead woman. It's also somewhat telling that Martha just disappears from the story before the events of the last day. Where'd she go? Even Mrs. Danvers was given the courtesy of a flaming farewell, in *Rebecca* ... what if, after Freda jettisoned a fistful of script pages during filming, the film's ending had to be hastily simplified? What if, originally, we discover that Margaretha really did die, and that the woman in the cellar is her shriveled corpse, pickled and preserved like Mrs. Bates? The prowling woman in the wedding dress is really Martha dressed up, assuming Margaretha's identity to both haunt Cynthia and provoke Bernard. Note that the 'ghost' Margaretha's cackling explanation to Cynthia is all handled without synch dialogue; it could have been rewritten. And Bernard's promise to rejuvenate Margaretha with Cynthia's blood is just the raving of a madman—improvised on the spot, perhaps. That's a whole lot of 'perhaps,' of course, even if it explains some of the movie's inconsistencies. The whole construction sounds far too complicated, as it would make Martha an equal partner in the macabre proceedings, and reduce Bernard to a pawn. It's also like one of Gastaldi's 'twisty,' overly talky giallos written ten years later." Glenn Erickson, *The Horrible Dr. Hichcock*, TFH Guest Blogs, September 12, 2016 (http://trailersfromhell.com/the-horrible-dr-hichcock/#.V9eryztqN7N). However, the original synopsis for *Raptus* deposited at the Archive of State prior to filming (with Hichcock still named Bernard Stoltz) is identical to the finished film, including Margaretha's premature burial and Stoltz's plan to rejuvenate her with Cynthia's blood.

30. Ercolani, "Tra cinema e cavalli."

31. Ibid.

32. Upchurch, Lucas and Boscaino, "Raptus. The Making of *The Horrible Dr. Hichcock*," 35.

33. Lucas, "Harriet White Medin," 45.

34. Upchurch, Lucas and Boscaino, "Raptus. The Making of *The Horrible Dr. Hichcock*," 31–39.

35. Christopher S. Dietrich and Peter Beckman, "Karma, Catsup, & Caskets. The Barbara Steele Interview," *Video Watchdog* #7, September/October 1991, 50. In the same interview, the actress maintains that *L'orribile segreto del Dr. Hichcock* "was made on a $10,000 bet between Riccardo Freda and two of his friends! They didn't believe he could get a script written and financed in a week. He did it—in fact, he had a script written in two days! He was an incredible gambler, Freda. That's really all he cared about." (*Ibid.*, 49). Steele's version fits more with *I vampiri*.

36. Upchurch, Lucas and Boscaino, "Raptus. The Making of *The Horrible Dr. Hichcock*," 43.

37. Caen and Romer, "Entretien avec Riccardo Freda," 1.

38. Freda, *Divoratori di celluloide*, 99.

39. Ibid., 100. In the book, Freda mistakenly refers to the film as *Operazione paura* (a.k.a. *Kill, Baby ... Kill!*, 1966).

40. Caen and Romer, "Entretien avec Riccardo Freda," 2.

41. Gérard Legrand, "L'Effroyable secret du Dr. Hichcock," *Positif* #53, June 1963, 88.
42. Tim Lucas, "Some Like It Cold. The Strange Case of Two Dr. Hichcocks," *Video Watchdog* #49, January/February 1999, 45.
43. Anonymous, "Blood Flows Freely in "Horrible Dr.": "The Awful Dr. Orlof," *The New York Amsterdam News*, December 12, 1964.
44. See Erickson, "Women on the Verge of a Gothic Breakdown," 277–78 n. 4. An even more detailed analysis of the differences between the two versions can be found in Lucas, "Some Like It Cold," 45–49.
45. Poindron, *Riccardo Freda*, 305.
46. Ibid., 308
47. Tavernier, "Riccardo Freda," 73.
48. Lourcelles, *Dictionnaire du cinéma*, 1350.
49. Steve Fenton and Dennis Capicik, "Brett Halsey," *Giallo Pages* #1, May 1999.
50. Brett Halsey, email interview with the author, April 2015.
51. In his later career Halsey starred in a couple of Lucio Fulci films, namely the downbeat erotic drama *Il miele del diavolo* (a.k.a. *The Devil's Honey*, 1986) and the TV movie *Quando Alice ruppe lo specchio* (a.k.a. *Touch of Death*, 1988).
52. Brett Halsey, email interview with the author, April 2015. However, claiming that *Le sette spade del vendicatore* "has the consistent and unmistakable feel of a film *painted* by Bava," as Lucas does, seems hazardous, given that, in Halsey's words, Bava's involvement in the picture was as a temporary replacement—not to mention Freda's acknowledgment of Masciocchi's work in Poindron's book—especially in the torture chamber sequences, which, according to Lucas, would be those where "Bava's command over the film's lighting and atmosphere" is more apparent. See Lucas, *Mario Bava*, 443.
53. A broadcasting is listed as early as October 1963. See *Newsday*, October 26, 1963.
54. Caen and Romer, "Entretien avec Riccardo Freda," 3.
55. Ibid., 6.
56. Ibid., 3.
57. Despite what some writers have claimed (see Sergio Bissoli, *Gli scrittori dell'orrore*, Ferrara Editore, Collegno 2007, 15), the similarities between *Lo spettro* and the pulp novel *La vecchia poltrona* ("The Old Armchair," "I racconti di Dracula" n. 20, June 1961, by Max Dave, a.k.a. Pino Belli) are actually minimal.
58. Freda, *Divoratori di celluloide*, 85.
59. Poindron, *Riccardo Freda*, 48.
60. Carlo Bocci, "Lo spettro," *Il falcone maltese: rivista di cinema* #1, June 1974, 40.
61. The outdoor scenes appear to have been filmed in the same locations as other Italian Gothic horror films of the period, such as *La jena di Londra* (a.k.a. *The Hyena of London*, 1964, Gino Mangini).
62. Lourcelles, *Dictionnaire du cinéma*, 1397.
63. Jacqueline Freda maintains that the two Gothic films were shot back-to-back, within the space of a month. "It was all born out of a challenge with a producer: 'How could you make a movie in twelve days,' he said. And my father: 'Then I'm shooting *two* in one month. If I don't manage to, you won't pay me, otherwise you're giving me the sum I'm asking." And he shot the two movies in twenty-four days!' Jacqueline Freda, interview with the author, May 2015. The statement, however, is contradicted by the official production data deposited at the Archive of State. The way it basically recycles the genesis of *I vampiri* shows how Freda's reputation at quick filmmaking became the stuff of legend.
64. Cozzi, *Il cinema dei mostri*, 251.
65. Jacqueline Freda is adamant that her mother was extraneous to the cinema industry (Jacqueline Freda, interview with the author, May 2015), so this might have been just a trick on the director's part to have Silvana by his side and have her earn some money. On the other hand, in an article that appeared in the newspaper *La Stampa* in 1990, Merli was described as a former script supervisor. Alessandra Pieracci, "Freda, lo Spielberg italiano degli Anni 50," *La Stampa*, April 26, 1990.
66. Caen and Romer, "Entretien avec Riccardo Freda," 4.
67. Bocci, "*Lo spettro*."
68. Filippo De Masi, email interview with the author, January 2016.
69. Caen and Romer, "Entretien avec Riccardo Freda," 6.
70. Ibid., 3.
71. According to the American Film Institute Catalog it opened in February 18, 1965, in Cincinnati. Krafsur, *The American Film Institute Catalog of Motion Pictures*, 396.
72. Poindron, *Riccardo Freda*, 315
73. Fenton and Capicik, "Brett Halsey."
74. Ibid.
75. J. Z. [Jacques Zimmer], "L'Aventurier Magnifique (L'Aigle de Florence)," *Image et Son* #190–191, January-February 1966, 67.
76. Tavernier, "Riccardo Freda," 74.
77. Della Casa, *Riccardo Freda*, 75.
78. Tavernier, "Riccardo Freda," 74.

Chapter 12

1. Namely, in Madrid and Ávila.
2. The source of this information bit is credited as being Stefano Della Casa in Vincenza Minutella, *Reclaiming Romeo and Juliet: Italian Translations for Page, Stage and Screen* (Amsterdam: Rodopi 2013), 176.
3. Ibid., 177.
4. Benedetto Croce, *Ariosto, Shakespeare e Corneille* (Bari: Laterza, 1968), 104.
5. Minutella, *Reclaiming Romeo and Juliet*, 177.
6. Ibid.
7. Brett Halsey, email interview with the author, April 2015. See also Tom Weaver, *Eye on Science Fiction:*

20 Interviews with Classic SF and Horror Filmmakers (Jefferson, NC: McFarland, 2003), 126–127.

8. Manlio Gomarasca, "Monsieur Cannibal. Il cinema di Ruggero Deodato," *Nocturno Dossier* #73, August 2008, 12. Deodato's words seem to imply that Freda took care of the editing, credited to Anna Amedei (Antonio Gimeno, in the Spanish version).

9. Riccardo Freda, "Fuori Orario."

10. According to the American Film Institute Catalog, it was released theatrically in September 1968, only one month earlier than Zeffirelli's version, with actor Geronimo Meynier and art director Tadeo Villalba credited respectively as Gerald Meynier and Teddy Villalba. Krafsur, *The American Film Institute Catalog of Motion Pictures*, 917.

11. Faldini and Fofi, *L'avventurosa storia del cinema italiano 1960–1969*, 210

12. Poindron, *Riccardo Freda*, 321.

13. According to Stephen Forsyth, from the start of costuming to the wrap—including a break between the filming of the indoor scenes and the exteriors and more interiors shot in Spain—there was a passage of time of around 6 to 8 weeks.

14. Stephen Forsyth, email interview with the author, September 2015.

15. *Ibid.*
16. *Ibid.*
17. *Ibid.*
18. Poindron, *Riccardo Freda*, 324.

19. The opening credits in the Italian version state "*Una produzione Imprecine realizzata da Riccardo Freda … regia di J. L. Monter*" (an Imprecine production carried out by Riccardo Freda … direction: J. L. Monter).

20. Poindron, *Riccardo Freda*, 330.

21. Interestingly, the French filmmaker would helm his own personal reinterpretation of the theme in a horrific key with *Les deux orphelines vampires* (1997), based on Rollin's own novel of the same name.

22. Boisset, *La vie est un choix*, 103.
23. Poindron, *Riccardo Freda*, 331.
24. Robert Monell, "Richard Wyler interview: A Conversation with FX-18," in Robert Monell, "Riccardo Freda," *European Trash Cinema Special* #2, 1997, 34.
25. *Ibid.*, 35.
26. *Ibid.*
27. *Ibid.*
28. Rémy Julienne, *Ma vie en cascades* (Paris: Editions 1, 2009), 33.
29. Monell, "Richard Wyler interview," 35.
30. F.C. [François Chevassu], "Coplan FX 18 casse tout," *Image et son* #197–198, September–October 1966, 42.
31. *Los Angeles Times*, December 29, 1968.
32. Walter and Braucourt, "Fredda and Bory Sans Honte," 34.
33. Boisset, *La vie est un choix*, 105.
34. Walter and Braucourt, "Fredda and Bory Sans Honte," 31.
35. Poindron, *Riccardo Freda*, 334

36. Walter and Braucourt, "Fredda and Bory Sans Honte," 35.
37. Tavernier, *Le cinéma dans le sang*, 126.
38. P. Br. [Pierre Bretigny], "Roger la Honte," *Image et son* #197/198, September–October 1966, 166.
39. Gilles Jacob, "Roger-la-Honte," *Cinéma 66* #108, July 1966, 115.
40. Boisset, *La vie est un choix*, 105.
41. Jacob, "Roger-la-Honte," 115.
42. The title of the Italian language translation of the script kept at Rome's CSC was actually *L'assassino è in trappola* (The Assassin is Trapped).
43. Tavernier, *Le cinéma dans le sang*, 126.
44. According to author Stephen Hay, however, Tavernier only wrote a few scenes and some of the dialogue, whereas most of the script was the work of Christian Plume. Stephen Hay, *Bertrand Tavernier: The Filmmaker of Lyon* (London: I.B. Tauris, 2000), 161.
45. Tavernier, *Le cinéma dans le sang*, 126.
46. Poindron, *Riccardo Freda*, 379.
47. *Ibid.*, 377.
48. Boisset, *La vie est un choix*, 104.
49. The anecdote is included in Marco Giusti, *007 all'italiana* (Milan: Isbn Edizioni 2010), 174–175. However, Giusti quotes Tavernier's alleged words from a book titled *Carte a l'autour* [sic], published in Paris in 1994, whose existence this author has not been able to verify.
50. Tavernier, *Le cinéma dans le sang*, 126.
51. Boisset recalled that the project of an action film shot in Turkey—which became his feature film debut—was actually an excuse on the part of De Nesle to smuggle to Europe some Turkish books blocked in Istanbul. Interestingly, *Coplan sauve sa peau* wasn't initially conceived as part of the Coplan series: it was titled *Les Jardins du diable*, and paid homage to *The Most Dangerous Game* (1932) and to other films that Boisset liked: for instance, the name of Claudio Brook's character was Stark, in a nod to John Boorman's *Point Blank* (1967). It was De Nesle, who, believing the film was too arthouse-oriented, decided to turn it into part of the Coplan franchise; therefore Brook had to be renamed Coplan, which resulted in some awkward redubbing work. Boisset, *La vie est un choix*, 108–119.
52. Giusti, *007 all'italiana*, 175.
53. Davide Pulici, "Intervista a Evelyn Stewart," August 2011, www.nocturno.it.
54. Poindron, *Riccardo Freda*, 340.

Chapter 13

1. The convoluted storyline is no excuse, however, for the following synopsis, which gets the facts and characters wrong: "A gunfighter named Lawrence (Mark Damon) arrives in Owell Rock to find out who killed his father. The witnesses are afraid to talk. They've all been threatened by town boss Harry Boyd (Stephen Forsyte [sic]). Eventually, Doc Lester (Giovanni Passafini [sic]) befriends Lawrence and together they confront and conquer the evil Boyd." Thomas

Weisser, *Spaghetti Westerns—The Good, the Bad and the Violent: A Comprehensive, Illustrated Filmography of 558 Eurowesterns and their Personnel, 1961–1977* (Jefferson, NC: McFarland & Company, 2005) 79–80.

2. See Bert Fridlund, *The Spaghetti Western. A Thematic Analysis* (Jefferson, NC: McFarland & Company, 2006) 170–71.

3. For instance, the main question remains unexplained: which one of the two heroes is the mysterious avenger who dispatches one by one all those involved in the murder of Major White? We never get to know, even though it is not very important once we have discovered they are in cahoots. Another unbelievable bit has White and his acolytes staging an attack on Owell Rock with horses launched at full gallop and mounted by straw puppets.

4. Poindron, *Riccardo Freda*, 378.

5. Ibid.

6. Stephen Forsyth, email interview with the author, September 2015.

7. Ibid.

8. Poindron, *Riccardo Freda*, 378.

9. Boisset, *La vie est un choix*, 107.

10. Stephen Forsyth, email interview with the author, September 2015.

11. Jacqueline Freda, interview with the author, May 2015.

12. Boisset, *La vie est un choix*, 108.

13. See, for instance, a similar episode as told by stuntman Giovanni Cianfriglia: "I remember that once a horseman died. He ended up on a bomb, one of those fake bombs which just made noise. The director was Riccardo Freda, I don't remember the film. 'Look, doctor, there has been a deadly accident,' we told Freda. 'Well, I'm sorry but who's next? I just can't stop.' He was crazy." (Giordano, *Giganti buoni*, 120). Could it be a urban legend, given Freda's notorious bad temper? Speaking of cynicism, Sergio Donati recalled a similar, notorious episode, told him by Sergio Leone's production manager Claudio Mancini, that happened during the shooting of *C'era una volta il West* following the suicide of actor Al Mulock, who threw himself from the window of his hotel room, still with the dust coat he wore in the film. Mancini ran to provide assistance to the actor: while leaning on the dying man, he heard a voice whispering in his ear: "Cla,' the costume! Retrieve the costume!" It was Leone, worried because the actor still had one day's worth of shooting: the next day he would use a double, wearing Mulock's dust coat. Months later, at the moviola, looking for a missing close-up of the actor he needed in the opening sequence, Leone would repeatedly curse him: "That asshole… Couldn't he kill himself twenty-four hours later?" Donati's comment: "It's not that he was particularly arid or ruthless. He was simply a director. The good ones I know are all like this: first of all, the movie." Donati, *C'era una volta il West (ma c'ero anch'io)*, 47.

14. Poindron, *Riccardo Freda*, 342.

15. Ibid.

16. According to a short article published in a 1972 issue of the magazine *Cinema d'Oggi*, Freda was still trying to make the movie five years later. (Information collected by Alessio Di Rocco.) He probably gave up for good when news of Rosi preparing his own movie on Lucky Luciano came out.

17. Garigliano distributed in Italy, on a regional basis, such titles as *Rangers: attacco ora X* (1970, Roberto Bianchi Montero), Corrado Farina's offbeat political vampire movie *…hanno cambiato faccia* (a.k.a. *They Have Changed Faces*, 1971) and José Maria Elorrieta's *Las amantes del diablo* (a.k.a. *Feast of Satan*, 1971).

18. The crew list included: Luigi Peratoner and Federico Canudas (assistant directors), Antonio Morelli (General manager), Genis Rodriguez (production manager), Valentino Trevisanato and Luis Arquero (Production supervisors), Otello Colangeli (editor), Juan Gelpí (director of photography), José Climent and Antonio Iannutti (cameramen), Juan Alberto Soler (production designer), Nora Orlandi (music).

19. The producers were asking access to the benefits provided by the State in accordance to Article 28 of the 1965 "Corona law," which provided a significant contribution to films being financed or co-financed by the personnel concerned, and "of particular artistic and cultural interest." Films which benefitted from Article 28 could receive up to 80 percent of their budget on loan.

20. Marcello Garofalo, "Uno, nessuno, centofulci," *Segnocinema* #65, January/February 1994, 15.

21. Poindron, *Riccardo Freda*, 344.

22. Ibid., 344–345.

23. Joachim Kramp, *Hallo! Hier spricht Edgar Wallace. Die Geschichte der Kriminalfilmserie von 1959 bis 1972. Dritte, überarbeitete und erweiterte Auflage* (Berlin: Schwarzkopf & Schwarzkopf, 2005), 391.

24. Joachim Kramp and Jürgen Wehnert, *Das Edgar Wallace Lexikon. Leben–Werk–Filme* (Berlin: Schwarzkopf & Schwarzkopf, 2004), 172–173.

25. Antonio José Navarro, "Riccardo Freda. Abismos de pasión," in Antonio José Navarro, ed., *El giallo italiano. La oscuridad y la sangre* (Madrid: Nuer, 2001), 171.

26. See Alessandro Tordini, *Così nuda così violenta. Enciclopedia della musica nei mondi neri del cinema italiano* (Rome: Arcana, 2012), 139.

27. Cozzi, *Il cinema dei mostri*, 250.

28. Branca and Stüm, "Entretien avec Riccardo Freda," 59–60.

29. Poindron, *Riccardo Freda*, 379.

30. Cozzi, *Il cinema dei mostri*, 250. Incidentally, Bava did *not* disown the film as Freda stated.

31. Poindron, *Riccardo Freda*, 354.

32. Ibid., 347.

33. Manlio Gomarasca and Davide Pulici, *Bruno Mattei*, «Nocturno Cinema» III, October 1998, 66.

34. Poindron, *Riccardo Freda*, 347.

35. Michael Maien, email interview with the author, March 2016.

36. Jacqueline Freda, interview with the author, May 2015.

37. Michael Maien, email interview with the author, March 2016.

38. Poindron, *Riccardo Freda*, 348.

39. Michael Maien, email interview with the author, March 2016.

40. The cuts demanded by the 7th section were as follows: 1) The scene of Dina's rape, from the part when Sachem rips Dina's dress off, uncovering her breasts, to the part when the man lies over the woman (10 seconds); 2) The lovemaking scene between Judas and Tamar "when the woman clings to Judas, giving the idea she is scratching him" (20 seconds); 3) In the same scene, "from the moment where Tamar's breast is glimpsed to the end of the scene" (49 seconds).

41. S.W., "At the Cinema: Biblical B Picture," *The Jerusalem Post*, December 13, 1972.

42. Navarro, "Riccardo Freda. Abismos de pasión," 174. The special effects are uncredited, but there is the possibility that they were the work of Carlo Rambaldi. In an interview with Luigi Cozzi, published in June 1970, Rambaldi recalled: "The movie I'm working on at the moment is directed by Riccardo Freda; I don't know the title yet, but it must be a horror or sci-fi story. We have to create the effect of a woman's face which gets old in a few seconds. First we make a mold of the actress' face, then work on it until it's identical to the original; then we insert a mechanical device which makes it move as if it was a real human face. With the pressure of air in a vacuum space, we obtain the effect of decomposing. And that's what you will see in the finished film." Luigi Cozzi, "Il fabbricante di mostri. Intervista con Carlo Rambaldi," *Horror* #7, June 1970, 21. It is not clear whether Rambaldi was actually discussing one of the "acid in the face" effects for *L'iguana dalla lingua di fuoco*, which was made around the same period, or another unmade (and unidentified) project.

43. Poindron, *Riccardo Freda*, 345.

44. *Ibid.*, 49.

45. Navarro, "Riccardo Freda. Abismos de pasión," 174.

46. For further details on Calabresi's figure and his depiction in Italian crime films of the era, see Roberto Curti, *Italian Crime Filmography 1968–1980* (Jefferson NC: McFarland & Co., 2013).

47. Spoiler alert: throughout the film, in fact, we are led to believe that the ambassador's son Marc is the young man whom we are seeing with Werner Pochath, whereas it is actually the other way round (the other man is implied to be Marc's lover, and possibly accomplice).

48. Poindron, *Riccardo Freda*, 345.

49. Igor Molino Padovan, Giorgio Navarro, and Luca Rea, "Dagmar Lassander. Il rosso segno della bellezza…," *Amarcord* #13, May-June 1998, 18.

50. *Ibid.*

51. Interestingly, said member objected that "within the concept of common morality should be included also the scenes of brutal violence and unbridled cruelty," in opposition to the widespread notion of the offense to morality being caused only by obscenity.

52. Poindron, *Riccardo Freda*, 346.

53. There are two scripts for the movie kept at the CSC library in Rome, titled respectively *Quella maledetta sera* and *Estratto dagli archivi segreti della polizia di una capitale europea*. They are identical save for the title: both are 166 pages long, and are dated June 6, 1972.

54. Stefano Ippoliti and Matteo Norcini, "Mario Bianchi. Il mio cinema pizza e fichi," in *Cine 70 e dintorni* #5, Summer 2004, 22.

55. Alessio Di Rocco, "*Estratto dagli archivi segreti della polizia di una capitale europea*," in Riccardo Fassone, ed., "La stagione delle streghe. Guida al gotico italiano," *Nocturno Dossier* #80, March 2009, 65.

56. Giordano, *Giganti buoni*, 128.

57. Jacqueline Freda, interview with the author, May 2015.

58. *Ibid.*

59. Alfredo Leone, phone interview with the author, August 2016.

60. The script also features the gory flashbacks from the "tragic ceremony"—over-the-top, in slow-motion and very similar to the ones in the film—starting from the very first scenes; Bill and friends do not travel on a dune buggy but (more realistically) on motorbikes, and their initial bet does not center on nautical terms, but on the non-existent "flying fish" that Bill's companions bet they can spot on the sea (a much more convincing idea, incidentally); during the massacre, the cultists—who are described as naked, save for their black cloaks and leather belts with Rosicrucian symbols that cover their pubic area—see each other as monsters ("they cannot see the real, natural faces, but horrible furry monsters, devilish, unreal-looking"), and the gory bits are slightly different: there is no mention of the bisected head, and Lord Alexander ends up impaled on a dagger "that almost cuts him in half." Also missing is a brief scene set in a church, where a beat combo is rehearsing: Bill seems to recognize the parish priest as Lord Alexander. The deaths of the three hippies are also different, and decidedly less gory: Bill is found in the bathroom, a mask of terror, a green foam coming out from his mouth, eyes wide open (but not that ugly blue-colored face); Fred hangs himself; Joe runs away from a horrible sight (which is implied to be Jane, whose monstrous alter ego is not mentioned in the script) and falls to his death into the sea.

Chapter 14

1. In his memoir the director sets the bar at twelve years—as if *L'iguana dalla lingua di fuoco*, *Tamar Wife of Er* and *Estratto dagli archivi segreti della polizia di una capitale europea* had never existed. Freda, *Divoratori di celluloide*, 80.

2. *Ibid.*, 80–81.

3. The details of Freda's private life, never before

discussed in print, were told to the author by his two daughters Jacqueline and Guislaine, who agreed to make them public.

4. Jacqueline Freda, interview with the author, May 2015.

5. Guislaine Freda, email interview with the author, October 2015.

6. Jacqueline Freda, interview with the author, May 2015.

7. *Ibid.*

8. Poindron, *Riccardo Freda*, 359.

9. Freda, *Divoratori di celluloide*, 80.

10. Giovanna Grassi, "L'eroe alato ritorna dalla guerra," *Corriere della Sera*, April 27, 1986.

11. Jacqueline Freda, interview with the author, May 2015.

12. Marginal differences involve character names (Nellina's first incarnation is called Silvia, a.k.a. Trillino; the Countess is called Angela Maria Zanardi) and depiction of events: Francesco's ride home with Nellina/Trillino is shown later on in the film in the form of flashback, as are the scenes at Reims. Incidentally, speaking of famous aviators of the era, a scene features the appearance of a young Fiorello La Guardia. The major difference between the 1973 script and the scenario as published in *L'avant scène cinéma* is the character of Baracca's adversary: in his earlier incarnation, Von Kleist (here called Brumovsky) is less present in the film (whereas mention is made of the legendary "Red Baron"), and the pilots' rivalry culminates in a duel where Baracca does not bring Brumovsky's plane down, but spares him. In the end, Brumovsky—now converted to Baracca's chivalry ways—is one of the pilots that drop flowers down their planes to mourn the death of the hero. A 48-page continuity treatment titled *Francesco Baracca: L'homme au trente cinq coups*, signed solely by Freda and not dated, is included in the Simon Mizrahi fund at the BiFi.

13. Poindron, *Riccardo Freda*, 363.

14. Jacqueline Freda, interview with the author, May 2015. The 1973 script does feature a similar ending, with the rampaging horse on the back of Baracca's plane dissolving into the horse on the back of a present-day jet, in a final shot conceived as a celebration of the Italian air force.

15. Poindron, *Riccardo Freda*, 357.

16. Tentori and Cozzi, *Guida al cinema Horror Made in Italy*, p, 321.

17. Luigi Cozzi, email interview with the author, October 2015.

18. The other crew members listed in the papers: Sante Romitelli (music), Carlo Carlini (director of photography), Sergio Rubini (cameraman), Silvio Laurenzi (costumes), Franco Cuppini (art director), Massimo Carlini (assistant cameraman), Roberto Petrozzi (sound), Salvatore Scarfone (production manager).

19. Alfredo Leone, phone interview with the author, August 2016.

20. The episode (mistakenly set in Spain during Leone's visit and under the incorrect assumption that Jacqueline was Canale's daughter) is discussed in Lucas, *Mario Bava*, 210.

21. *Ibid.*

22. Jacqueline Freda, interview with the author, May 2015.

23. The remaining crew: Mario Sbrenna (cameraman), Spartaco Pizzi (production manager), Giuseppe Ferrante (make-up), Palenzona (production designer), M. Mari (costumes), Giovanni Fratarcangeli (sound), Carlo Reali (assistant director), A. Buzzanca (production supervisor), G. Muzi (production secretary).

24. "It is a basic scheme, in which, from time to time, you can put everything," Piccioni commented. See Davide Pulici, "Il grido del capricorno," *Nocturno Cinema* #147, January 2015, 95.

25. Jacqueline Freda, interview with the author, May 2015.

26. Enzo Boetani, interview with the author, August 2016. As of this writing, *Superhuman* is still listed as completed in Freda's filmography (!) on the IMDb.

27. *Ibid.*

28. Manlio Gomarasca and Davide Pulici, *Io Emanuelle. Le passioni, gli amori e il cinema di Laura Gemser* (Milan: Media Word Publications 1997).

29. Stefano Ippoliti and Matteo Norcini, "Una favola chiamata cinema," *Cine 70 e dintorni* #6, 2004, 36.

30. *Ibid.*

31. Stefano Patrizi, phone interview with the author, February 2016. Patrizi did one more acting appearance in 2006, in the movie *Quale amore*, whereas he denies having worked on 2008's *Chi nasce tondo…* which nevertheless is listed in his IMDb filmography.

32. Enzo Boetani, interview with the author, August 2016.

33. Jacqueline Freda, interview with the author, May 2015.

34. When the interviewer asked him why such a severe judgment, Freda curtly answered, "It's not a good film. The actors were poor and so was the budget. I'd rather not talk about it." Gian Luca Castoldi, "Riccardo Freda o del decadentismo dell'orrore," *Amarcord* #8–9, May-August 1997, 109. Freda was less tranchent, but equally critical toward *Murder Obsession*, when discussing it with Giuseppe Tornatore: "Unfortunately it didn't turn out as I had wanted, also because there just weren't the necessary means, because it's strange how people are convinced that horror films are easy to make, even though they're some of the most difficult because you're always trying to balance, like a tightrope walker, right? It just takes one wrong footing and you fall, you can't save yourself by doing another sequence like in other films… Here, there's nothing you can do, either you fall into the ridiculous, or it gets boring, or you achieve the desired effect." Tornatore, *Il quarto moschettiere*, 24–25.

35. "'Is it true that your first film was *Murder Obsession* (1981) by Riccardo Freda?' 'Yes, I have been attributed this paternity [sic], but it is not a film that I can say I signed. I collaborated with Angelo Mattei

who did the effects, I was in his workshop but I only did a few things, working on some tricks. Nothing special.'" Pierpaolo De Sanctis, "Intervista a Sergio Stivaletti," www.nocturno.it, May 13, 2015.

36. Enzo Boetani, interview with the author, August 2016.

37. Cristiano Pogany was married to actress Pamela Villoresi, whom he had met in 1978, and they had three children. He died of cancer in February 1999, at only 51.

38. Jacqueline Freda, interview with the author, May 2015.

39. Freda, *Divoratori di celluloide*, 80. In Poindron's interview book, however, he claimed differently: "I never thought of Bava. It is a gory and perverse story like those he loved, but when I made it, I did not think of anyone. I tried to put myself in the criminal's skin…" Poindron, *Riccardo Freda*, 350.

40. *Ibid.*, 88.

41. On the other hand, at least one cut is welcomed, as the English language version did not feature one of the film's most awkward attempts at a red herring: in the scene following Shirley's chainsaw murder, Oliver is serving dinner, when out of the blue he passingly mentions to Glenda that the chainsaw is missing.

42. Poindron, *Riccardo Freda*, 349.

43. Lourcelles, *Dictionnaire du cinéma*, 1440.

44. Patrizia Pistagnesi, "Omaggio a Riccardo Freda," in Freda, *Divoratori di celluloide*, xiv.

45. Jacqueline Freda, interview with the author, May 2015.

Epilogue

1. Freda, *Divoratori di celluloide*, 134.
2. Tavernier, "Riccardo Freda," 69–70.
3. Stefano Della Casa, *Riccardo Freda, un homme seul* (Paris, Yellow Now 1993), 80.
4. Enzo Boetani, interview with the author, August 2016.
5. Della Casa, *Riccardo Freda*, 90.
6. Ed Senior, "Witchmaster. Forty Years in Another Town," *Shock Xpress* vol. 2 No. 2, Winter 1987, 11.
7. Tavernier, *Le cinéma dans le sang*, 191.
8. Poindron, *Riccardo Freda*, 358. According to Tavernier, he and Freda used to make long walks on the mountains, where the octagenarian mentor picked thyme to prepare herbal teas that prevented them from catching cold or flu.
9. Gianni Vitale, phone interview with the author, January 2016.
10. Ezzelino III da Romano (1194–1259) was an Italian feudal lord, a Ghibelline conductor, and ally of Frederick II of Hohenstaufen: he ruled the cities of Verona, Vicenza and Padua and was notorious for his cruelty, and his merciless use of torture against the enemies.
11. Pietro Reggiani, email interview with the author, January 2016.
12. A report from the 1990 Pesaro Festival brought the news that "Ettore Scola is collecting signatures to help the old master Riccardo Freda, evicted from his house in Rome and temporarily staying with friends in Paris." Sauro Borelli, "Age & Scarpelli e gli altri. Commedia all'italiana in festa," *L'Unità*, June 8, 1990.
13. Not signed, "La 'legge Bacchelli' per Freda?," *L'Unità*, July 11, 1993.
14. Franco Montini, "Per Riccardo Freda un film alla Disney," *La Repubblica*, 13 July 1991.
15. The 130-page long script is copyrighted Lucky International Film, Corso Trieste 90, Roma. According to the stamp on the cover, it was "delivered by hand by the concerned party," that is Freda himself.
16. Poindron, *Riccardo Freda*, 236.
17. During this period, Torelli shot several hours' worth of interviews, that were edited into a full 3-hour-long compendium, broadcast in the 1990s on RaiTre's night program "Fuori Orario."
18. Roberto Torelli, phone interview with Stefano Raffaele, January 2016.
19. According to Torelli, the new script was by Freda, Patrizia Pistagnesi and Torelli himself, although his name and Pistagnesi's were there only for merely productive reasons. However, according to Éric Poindron, the script for *Animal's gang* was signed by Freda, Dominique Bourboulon, Jean-Philippe Steffani and Poindron himself. Poindron, *Riccardo Freda*, 369, note.* When contacted by this author about the matter, Poindron did not reply to this and other questions.
20. Aldo Tassone, "Dumas, nostalgia per l'avventura," *La Repubblica*, July 20, 1994. On another occasion, Tavernier told the press: "Marceau had immediately lots of trouble communicating with Riccardo; he didn't do anything to settle disagreements and Sophie left the set. At that point my only other choice would have been to pay everybody back and cancel the movie." Goffredo De Pascale, "Io, nipotino di Dumas," *L'Unità*, August 4, 1994.
21. See Poindron, *Riccardo Freda*, 370. The version was confirmed by Tavernier's biographer Stephen Hay: "Marceau had little faith in Freda's direction, and eventually threatened to quit the project unless he was replaced, until Tavernier reluctantly agreed to come and co-direct the film with Freda. Ultimately, Marceau refused to continue with Freda, who left Tavernier to direct the project on his own." Hay, *Bertrand Tavernier*, 162. For his part, the French director added, "Even if I collaborated to the scenario with Jean Cosmos, it wasn't a personal project…" Tavernier, *Le cinema dans le sang*, 187.
22. Della Casa, *Riccardo Freda*, 91.
23. Jacqueline Freda, interview with the author, May 2015.
24. Filippo D'Angelo, "Dopo D'Artagnan e Neruda farò l'immigrato," *L'Unità*, December 16, 1994.
25. Tassone, "Dumas, nostalgia per l'avventura."
26. Jacqueline Freda, interview with the author, May 2015.
27. Tentori and Cozzi, *Guida al cinema Horror*

Made in Italy, 324. "I took that idea from him for my latest film, *Blood on Melies' Moon*, as many scenes are set inside inside the 'Museum of Horror.' Freda was right: it is a perfect set for a movie!" Luigi Cozzi, email interview, October 2015.

28. Jacqueline Freda, interview with the author, May 2015.

29. Luigi Cozzi, email interview with the author, October 2015.

30. Jacqueline Freda, interview with the author, May 2015.

31. Unfortunately the small booklet is saddled with a very badly done, error-ridden bio-filmography: for instance, *Estratto dagli archivi segreti della polizia di una capitale europea* is missing, whereas *Murder Obsession* (renamed *Follia omicida*) is dated 1983.

32. Della Casa, *Riccardo Freda*, 91.

33. Tornatore, *Il quarto moschettiere*, 25.

34. Jacqueline Freda, interview with the author, May 2015.

35. *Ibid.*

Essential Bibliography

Books by Riccardo Freda

Freda, Riccardo. *Divoratori di celluloide*. Milan: Edizioni del Mystfest, Il Formichiere, 1981.

Books on Riccardo Freda

Della Casa, Stefano. *Riccardo Freda: Un homme seul*. Paris: Yellow Now, 1993.
Della Casa, Stefano. *Riccardo Freda*. Rome: Bulzoni, 1999.
Familiari, Antonio Fabio. *Riccardo Freda: L'esteta dell'emozione*. Rome: Profondo Rosso, 2004.
Gili, Jean A., ed. *Riccardo Freda*. Rome: Quaderni di Cinecittà International #5, 1993.
Martini, Emanuela, and Stefano Della Casa, eds. *Riccardo Freda*. Bergamo: Bergamo Film Meeting, 1993.
Poindron, Éric. *Riccardo Freda: Un pirate à la camera*. Lyon-Arles: Institute Lumière/Actes Sud, 1994.
Tornatore, Giuseppe. *Il quarto moschettiere: Quattro chiacchiere con Riccardo Freda*. Taormina: TaorminaFilmFest, 2007.

Cinema Books with Notable References to Freda's Work

Brizio-Skov, Flavia. *Popular Italian Cinema: Culture and Politics in a Postwar Society*. London: I.B. Tauris, 2011.
Brunetta, Gian Piero. *Storia del cinema italiano dal neorealismo al miracolo economico 1945–1959*. Rome: Editori Riuniti, 1979–2001.
Brunetta, Gian Piero. *Storia del cinema italiano: Il cinema del regime 1929–1945*. Rome: Editori Riuniti, 1979–2001.
Bruschini, Antonio, and Antonio Tentori. *Operazione paura: i registi del gotico italiano*. Bologna: Puntozero, 1997.
Cozzi, Luigi. *Il cinema dei mostri*. Rome: Fanucci, 1987.
Curti, Roberto. *Fantasmi d'amore: Il gotico italiano tra cinema, letteratura e tv*. Turin: Lindau, 2011.
Curti, Roberto. *Italian Gothic Horror Films 1957–1969*. Jefferson NC: McFarland, 2015.
Di Chiara, Francesco. *I tre volti della paura: il cinema horror italiano (1957–1965)*. Ferrara: UniPress, 2009.
Elley, Derek. *The Epic Film: Myth and History*. London/Boston, Routledge & Kegan Paul, 1984.
Faldini, Franca, and Goffredo Fofi, eds. *L'avventurosa storia del cinema italiano raccontata dai suoi protagonisti 1935–1959* (Milan: Feltrinelli, 1979.
Faldini, Franca, and Goffredo Fofi, eds. *L'avventurosa storia del cinema italiano raccontata dai suoi protagonisti 1960–1969*. Milan: Feltrinelli, 1981.
Farassino, Alberto, ed. *Lux Film*. Milan: Il Castoro, 2000.
Fazzini, Paolo. *Gli artigiani dell'orrore. Mezzo secolo di brividi dagli anni '50 ad oggi*. Rome: Un mondo a parte, 2004.
Gambetti, Giacomo. *Vittorio Gassman*. Rome: Gremese, 1999.
Giordano, Michele. *Giganti buoni: Da Ercole a Piedone (e oltre) il mito dell'uomo forte nel cinema italiano*. Rome: Gremese 1998.
Hughes, Howard. *Cinema italiano: The Complete Guide from Classics to Cult*. London: I.B. Tauris, 2011.
Lafond, Frank, ed. *Cauchemars italiens*. Paris: L'Harmattan, 2011. 2 vol.
Lenne, Gérard. *Le cinéma "fantastique" et ses mythologies*. Saint-Ouen: Henri Veyrier, 1990.
Lourcelles, Jacques. *Dictionnaire du cinema: Les films*. Paris: Robert Laffont, 1992.
Lucas, Tim. *Mario Bava: All the Colors of the Dark*. Cincinnati OH: Video Watchdog, 2007.
Mora, Teo. *Storia del cinema dell'orrore, vol. 2*. Rome: Fanucci, 1978–2002.
Morreale, Emiliano. *Così piangevano. Il cinema mélo nell'Italia degli anni cinquanta*. Rome: Donzelli 2011.
Palmerini, Luca M., and Gaetano Mistretta. *Spaghetti Nightmares*. Rome: M&P Edizioni, 1994. The Italian "extended uncut edition" includes much more material than the English language version, as well as an interview with Freda, which seems to be actually made up with bits

and pieces from various interviews and excerpts from Freda's memoir.

Piselli, Stefano, and Riccardo Morlocchi, and Antonio Bruschini. *Bizarre sinema! Wildest sexiest weirdest sleaziest films: Horror all'italiana 1957–1979*. Florence: Glittering, 1996.

Prédal, René. *Le cinéma fantastique*. Paris: Éditions Seghers, 1970.

Sabatier, Jean-Marie. *Les classiques du cinéma fantastique*. Les Plans sur Bex: Balland, 1973.

Savio, Francesco. *Cinecittà anni Trenta*. Rome: Bulzoni 1979.

Tentori, Antonio, and Luigi Cozzi. *Horror Made In Italy*. Rome: Profondo Rosso, 2007.

Testa, Carlo. *Italian Cinema and Modern European Literatures, 1945–2000*. Santa Barbara, CA: Greenwood Publishing Group, 2002.

Venturini, Simone. *Galatea Spa (1952–1965): storia di una casa di produzione cinematografica*. Rome: Associazione italiana per le ricerche di storia del cinema, 2001.

Venturini, Simone. *Horror italiano*. Rome: Donzelli, 2014.

Memoirs with Notable References to Freda

Boisset, Yves. *La vie est un choix*. Paris: Plon, 2011.

Caiano, Mario. *Mario Caiano: Autobiografia di un regista di B-Movies*. Piombino: Il Foglio Letterario 2014.

Civirani, Osvaldo. *Un fotografo a Cinecittà*. Rome: Gremese, 1995.

Cortese, Valentina. *Quanti sono i domani passati*. Milan: Mondadori, 2012.

Julienne, Rémy. *Ma vie en cascades*. Paris: Editions 1, 2009.

Longanesi, Leo. *Parliamo dell'elefante (frammenti di un diario)*. Milan: Longanesi (1945) 2005.

Tavernier, Bertrand. *Le cinéma dans le sang*. Paris: Archipoche, 2011.

Essays on Freda or His Films

Erickson, Glenn. "Women on the Verge of a Gothic Breakdown: Sex, Drugs and Corpses in *The Horrible Dr. Hichcock*," in Silver, Alain, and James Ursini, eds. *Horror Film Reader*. Pompton Plains NJ: Limelight Editions, 2000.

Lapeña Marchena, Óscar. "The Stolen Seduction: The Image of Spartacus in Riccardo Freda's *Spartaco, gladiatore della Tracia*," in Knippschild, Silke, and Marta García Morcillo, eds. *Seduction and Power: Antiquity in the Visual and Performing Arts*. London: A&C Black, 2013.

Navarro, Antonio José. "Riccardo Freda: Abismos de pasión," in Navarro, Antonio José, ed. *El giallo italiano. La oscuridad y la sangre*. Madrid: Nuer, 2001.

Paniceres, Rubén. "El gotico italiano: Fantastico y ciencia ficción," in Palacios, Jesús, and Rubén Paniceres, eds. *Cara a cara. Una mirada al cine de género italiano*. Gijon: Semana Negra, 2004.

Pitassio, Francesco. "L'orribile segreto dell'horror italiano," in Manzoli, Giacomo, and Guglielmo Pescatore, eds. *L'arte del risparmio: stile e tecnologia. Il cinema a basso costo in Italia negli anni Sessanta*. Rome: Carocci, 2005.

Senior, Ed. "Witchmaster: Forty Years in Another Town." *Shock Xpress*, Winter 1987.

Special Magazine Issues, Articles with Notable References to Freda's Work

Bocci, Carlo. "Lo spettro." *Il falcone maltese: rivista di cinema* #1, June 1974.

Della Casa, Stefano, ed. "Speciale fantastico italiano." *Cineforum* #299, November 1990.

Fassone, Riccardo, ed. "La stagione delle streghe. Guida al gotico italiano." *Nocturno Dossier* #80, March 2009.

Garofalo, Marcello, ed. "Sangue, amore e fantasy." *Segnocinema* #85, May-June 1997.

Giusti, Marco. "E di Agi Murad sulla via della critica." *Il falcone maltese: rivista di cinema* #5, 1974.

Fofi, Goffredo. "Terreur in Italie." *Midi-Minuit Fantastique* #7, September 1963.

Legrand, Gérard. "L'effroyable secret du Dr. Hichcock." *Positif* #53, June 1963.

Lourcelles, Jacques. "Un homme seul." *Présence du cinéma* #17, Spring 1963.

Monell, Robert. "Riccardo Freda." *European Trash Cinema Special* #2, 1997.

Moutier, Norbert. "Riccardo Freda." *Monster Bis Collector*, 1999.

Magazine Interviews with Freda

Allombert, Guy. "Entretien avec Riccardo Freda." *Image et son* #207, June/July 1967.

Branca, Fabrice, and Gerard Stüm. "Entretien avec Riccardo Freda." *Monster Bis Collector*, 1999. (Note: The interview is dated April 24, 1987).

Caen, Michel, and Jean-Claude Romer. "Entretien avec Riccardo Freda." *Midi-Minuit fantastique* #7, September 1963.

Cozzi, Luigi. "L'orribile segreto del dottor Hampton." *Horror* #15, April 1971.

Lourcelles, Jacques, and Simon Mizrahi. "Entretien avec Riccardo Freda." *Présence du cinéma* #17, Spring 1963.

Tavernier, Bertrand. "Riccardo Freda." *Cinéma 63* #81, December 1963.

Walter, Renaud, and Guy Braucourt. "Fredda [sic] and Bory Sans Honte." *Cinéma 66* #106, May 1966.

Index

Abismos de pasión (1954) 50
L'Abito nero da sposa (1945) 39, 93, 295
Abuna Messias (1942) 28
Accattone (1961) 172
Achtung! Banditi! (1951) 96
Action immédiate (1957) 217
Addio Kira! (1942) 48
An Adventure of Salvator Rosa see *Un'Avventura di Salvator Rosa*
The Adventures of Huckleberry Finn (novel) 23, 201
The Adventures of Marco Polo (1938) 173
Agent Secret FX 18 (1964) 217
Agente 777 missione Summergame see *Coplan FX 18 casse tout*
Agguato a Tangeri (1957) 8, 134–137, 160, 168, 314
Agi Murad—Il diavolo bianco (1959) 14, 90, 124, 137–141, 150, 172, 181, 202, 211, 262, 314–315, 339
Agren, Janet 271
Agrippina (1910) 99
Akkad, Moustapha 271
Al diavolo la celebrità (1949) 37
Albertini, Giampiero 267
Aldrich, Robert 206
Aleksandr Nevskij (1938) 76
Alert in the South see *Alerte au sud*
Alerte au sud (1953) 16
Alessandrini, Goffredo 28, 48, 294
Alfonso, María José 213, 215, 321
Alfred Hitchcock Presents (TV series) 180
Alighieri, Dante 73
All the Colors of the Dark see *Tutti i colori del buio*
Allégret, Marc 210, 211
L'Allegro cantante (1938) 21, 22, 289
Alone Against Rome see *Solo contro Roma*
Alonso, Chelo 157, 169, 296
Altariba, Béatrice 193, 319
Altman, Robert 248
Amado, Jorge 70
L'Amante del vampire (1960) 178, 271

Amanti d'oltretomba (1965) 115
Amanti senza amore (1948) 50
Amato, Giuseppe "Peppino" [Giuseppe Vasaturo] 50, 334
Amauli, Giulio 211
American Guerrilla in Philippines (1950) 121
Le Amiche (1955) 161
Amidei, Sergio 32, 302
Ammar, Tarak Ben 279
Anderson, Michael 185
André, Carole 267
Andreotti, Giulio 77, 82, 101, 113
Andress, Ursula 266
Angels & Demons (2009) 91
Angioletti, Nino 275, 303
Angiolillo, Renato 27
Animal's Gang (unfilmed Freda project) 159, 283–284
Anita Garibaldi (unfilmed Freda project) 72–73
Anni difficili (1948) 32
Anton, Edoardo see Antonelli, Edoardo
Antonelli, Edoardo [a.k.a. Edoardo Anton] 20, 23, 25, 29, 289, 290, 291, 294, 332
Antonelli, Luigi 23, 292
Antonioni, Michelangelo 1, 9, 120, 161, 168, 169, 247, 279
Antropophagus (1980) 144
Os Apavorados (1962) 73
Aquila nera (1946) 5, 8, 14, 39, 45–50, 52, 55, 61, 62, 63, 69, 76, 77, 79, 80, 83, 87, 91, 127, 135, 138, 202, 208, 213, 224, 230, 237, 238, 257, 262, 275, 295, 303, 334
Arata, Ubaldo 48
L'Arca di Noé (Il diluvio universale) (unfilmed Freda project) 169–170, 246
Argento, Dario 3, 28, 77, 145, 161, 188, 193, 200, 201, 240, 248, 250, 251, 253, 265, 269, 281, 329, 330
Argento, Salvatore 269
Ariosto, Ludovico 32, 113, 344
Arkoff, Samuel 158, 169, 189
Armstrong, Louis 39, 40
Armstrong, Michael 248
Arno, Alice 244
Arnold, Jack 199

Arrivano i titani (1962) 154
Artaud, Antonin 119
Ascanio (novel) 16, 201, 204, 279
Ascanio (unfilmed Freda project) 201, 279–280
L'Assedio dell'Alcazar (1940) 93
L'Astuto barone (ovvero L'eredità contesa) (1950) 68, 308
El Ataúd del vampiro (1958) 128
Atlas in the Land of the Cyclops see *Maciste nella terra dei ciclopi*
L'Atleta di cristallo (unfilmed Freda project) 36
Attila (1954) 108, 112
Audiard, Michel 225, 261
Audin, Maurice 205
Aulin, Ewa 126
Autant-Lara, Claude 121
Autopsia de un criminal (1963) 189
Autopsy of a Criminal see *Autopsia de un criminal*
Avallone, Marcello 167, 185, 186, 187, 281, 319, 329, 335, 341
Les Aventures de Casanova (1947) 59
L'Avventura di Giacomo Casanova (1937) 59
Un'Avventura di Salvator Rosa (1939) 28, 35, 93, 202
L'Avventura (1960) 1
Le Avventure di Giacomo Casanova (1954) 59
L'Avventuriera del piano di sopra (1941) 28, 29, 30, 294
The Awful Dr. Orlof see *Gritos en la noche*
Azevedo, Alinor 71, 72, 305

Babe (1995) 284
Badoglio, Pietro 39
Baker, Roy Ward 142
Balcázar, Alfonso 226, 228, 324
Balcázar, Jaime Jesús 236, 237
Baldanello, Gianfranco 193, 245
Baldini, Renato 92, 96, 309, 310, 311, 314, 340
Balducci, Franco 212, 304, 321
Baldwin, Peter 77, 199, 320
Ballerini, Piero 37
Balpêtré, Antoine 131, 313

Balzac, Honoré de 60, 201, 221
La Bambola di Satana (1969) 151
La Banda Casaroli (1962) 193
Bánky, Vilma 48
Baracca e burattini (1954) 142
Barbed Wire Dolls see *Frauengefängnis*
Barbey d'Aurevilly, Jules Amédée 221
The Barefoot Contessa (1954) 48, 57
Barilli, Francesco 192
Il Barone di Corbò (1939) 22, 23, 292
Bassoli, Carlo 59
Battaglia, Rik 113
La Battaglia di Maratona (1959) 147, 171, 342
Battleship Potemkin (1925) 149
Batzella, Luigi 276
Baumgartner, Peter 247
Bava, Mario 3, 8, 10, 57, 87, 103, 104, 109, 110, 114, 121, 128, 130, 131, 132, 133, 138, 139, 140, 141, 142, 143, 144, 145, 146, 150, 151, 156, 161, 162, 163, 167, 168, 171, 179, 185, 188, 193, 200, 201, 212, 213, 215, 226, 239, 244, 248, 250, 252, 255, 256, 257, 266, 273, 274, 275, 276, 287, 296, 310, 312, 313, 314, 315, 318, 332, 334, 337, 338, 339, 340, 341, 342, 344, 346, 349
Baxter, Les 158, 169, 173, 297, 316
Bay of Blood see *Reazione a catena*
Bazzoni, Camillo 140
Bazzoni, Luigi 199, 230
Beat the Devil (1953) 184
Beatrice Cenci (1956) 5, 6, 8, 14, 75, 93, 109, 117–125, 126, 130, 133, 135, 168, 173, 182, 183, 200, 204, 208, 213, 246, 247, 275, 277, 282, 287, 312–313
Beatrice Cenci (1941) 37, 93, 119
Beatrice Cenci (1909) 119
Beatrice Cenci (1969) 119, 338
Beatrice Cenci (1926) 119
Béatrix Cenci (1908) 119
La Beauté du diable (1950) 68
Beautiful Antonio see *Il Bell'Antonio*
Beauty and the Devil see *La Beauté du diable*
Becker, Jacques 161
Becky Sharp (1935) 94
Beery, Wallace 333
Beethoven, Ludwig van 122
Bellalta, José María 268
Il Bell'Antonio (1959) 31
Belle de Jour (1967) 111
Belli, Agostina 267
Bellini, Adriano [Kirk Morris] 164, 165, 166, 318, 341
Bellini, Vincenzo 65, 292
Bellucci, Monica 157
Ben-Hur: A Tale of the Christ (1925) 339
Ben-Hur (1959) 109
Benjamin, Walter 156
Beresford, Bruce 281
Bergman, Ingmar 3, 9, 197

Bergman, Ingrid 37
Bergman, Vera 38, 293, 302
Bergonzelli, Sergio 161
Bernard, Raymond 58
Bernardi, Nerio 80, 89, 307, 308, 309, 311, 312
Bernardini, Aldo 44
Bernhardt, Sarah 106
Bernoudy, Edmond F. 70
Berry, Julian *see* Gastaldi, Ernesto
Bertini, Francesca 16
Best, George 1
La Bestia uccide a sangue freddo (1971) 250
The Betrothed (novel) 35
Bianchi, Giorgio 30, 94
Bianchi, Mario 254, 256, 267, 327, 347
Biancoli, Oreste 94, 154, 162, 195, 297, 316, 318, 319
Bibesco, Marthe 106
The Big Bluff (1957) 121
Big Deal on Madonna Street see *I Soliti ignoti*
The Big Parade (1925) 16
The Big Shave (1968) 257
Biliotti, Enzo 35, 293, 302
Billon, Jacques 333
Binoche, Juliette 282, 300
The Bird with the Crystal Plumage see *L'Uccello dalle piume di cristallo*
Bitter Rice see *Riso amaro*
Black Jack (1968) 245
Black Sabbath see *I Tre volti della paura*
Black Sunday see *La Maschera del demonio*
Blasco, Ricardo 189
Blasetti, Alessandro 25, 28, 35, 68, 93, 99, 100, 193, 204
Blier, Bernard 203, 320
The Blind Woman of Sorrento see *La Cieca di Sorrento*
The Blob (1958) 142
Blood and Black Lace see *Sei donne per l'assassino*
Blood and Sand (1940) 94
The Blood Beast Terror (1968) 185
Blood of Dracula (1957) 127
Blood on Melies' Moon (2016) 350
Blow Out (1981) 273
Blow-up (1966) 274
Bocci, Carlo 197, 200, 344
Boetani, Enzo 255, 266, 271, 272, 273, 280, 328, 348, 349
Bogarde, Dirk 234
Bogart, Humphrey 132
Boileau, Pierre 241
Boisset, Yves 1, 18, 124, 216, 221, 222, 225, 227, 228, 232, 233, 244, 245, 323, 324, 325, 331, 332, 338, 345, 346
Boito, Arrigo 67
Bolaños, José 185
Boleslawski, Richard 50
Bonnard, Mario 32, 144, 168, 204
Bonnie and Clyde (1967) 236
Bonos, Gianni 40, 42, 43, 303

Bonos, Luigi 40, 42, 43, 303
Bonos, Vittorio 40, 42, 43, 303
Boorman, John 345
Boratto, Caterina 87, 308
Borboni, Paola 37, 38, 302
Borderie, Bernard 174, 299
Borelli, Lyda 16
Borghesio, Carlo 22
Bory, Jean-Louis 79, 221, 223, 224, 225, 310, 323, 331, 345, 352
Bosch, Hieronymus 165
Bosé, Lucia 63
Bosetti, Giulio 176, 299, 319
Bosic, Andrea 203, 318, 320, 321
Il Boss (1973) 265
The Bounty Killer (1967) 217
Bourboulon, Dominique 349
Bourboulon, Frédéric 285, 300
Boy on a Dolphin (1957) 140
Boyer, Jean 59
Boyer, Marie-France 224, 225, 323
The Boys of via Paal (novel) 23
Bradbury, Ray 141
The Brady Bunch (TV series) 199
Bragaglia, Anton Giulio 38
Bragaglia, Arturo 38, 302
Bragaglia, Carlo Ludovico 38, 48, 271, 338
Brancati, Vitaliano 31, 113, 302
Brancucci, Ernesto 255, 327
Brass, Tinto 126, 156, 260
Il Bravo di Venezia (1941) 28
Brazzi, Rossano 46, 48, 50, 57, 62, 89, 137, 211, 224, 303, 309, 334
Brenon, Herbert 333
Bresson, Robert 287
Brignone, Guido 37, 119, 152, 162, 168, 169, 296
Brochard, Martine 271, 272, 273, 328
Brochero, Eduardo Manzanos 234, 236
Brook, Claudio 228, 345
Brother Sun, Sister Moon see *Fratello sole, sorella luna*
Brown, Clarence 46, 48
Brown, Fredric 141
Browning, Tod 129
Brunetta, Gian Piero 89, 336
Buazzelli, Tino 68, 305, 306, 308
Bubbio, Teodoro 111
A Bullet Is Waiting (1954) 105
Bulwer-Lytton, Edward 99
Buñuel, Luis 50, 111, 268
Buonanotte ... avvocato! (1955) 30
Buonarroti, Michelangelo 17, 27, 203, 227, 245, 277
Buongiorno, Madrid! (1942) 28
Burle, José Carlos 70
The Burning of Rome see *Il Magnifico avventuriero*
Butt, Lawson 333
The Bycicle Thief see *Ladri di biciclette*
Byleth (Il demone dell'incesto) (1972) 172

Das Cabinet des Dr. Caligari (1920) 130

Cabiria (1914) 16, 19, 99, 152, 164
Caccia all'uomo (1948) see *I Miserabili*
Caccia all'uomo (1961) 8, 140, 151, 158–162, 250, 283, 317–318
Cacoyannis, Michael 222
Um Caçula do barulho (1949) 68–73, 305–306, 335, 336
Cadorna, Luigi 94
La Caduta degli dei (1969) 245
Caen, Michel 194, 342, 343, 344
Caffarel, José María 226, 324
Caiano, Carlo 87, 91, 309, 311
Caiano, Mario 87, 117, 312, 338
Caiçará (1950) 70
Il Caimano del Piave (1950) 94
Calabresi, Luigi 251, 347
Calamai, Clara 28, 29, 269, 294
Calhoun, Rory 173, 297
Caligula (1979) 156, 260, 265
Callas, Maria 148
Calò, Carla 77, 306, 320
Calopresti, Mimmo 287, 329
Caltiki il mostro immortale (1959) 8, 131, 140, 141–146, 184, 275, 315, 338
Calvo, José "Pepe" 256, 327
Calzavara, Flavio 23, 24, 35, 93, 291
Camerini, Mario 21, 35, 50, 108, 152, 334
Camicie rosse (1952) 28
Camille 2000 (1969) 161
Il Camorrista (1986) 287
Campanini, Carlo 21, 29, 294, 295
Campogalliani, Carlo 28, 166, 204
Canale, Gianna Maria 5, 16, 40, 63, 64, 66, 67, 69, 70, 71, 73, 77, 79, 81, 82, 87, 89, 92, 94, 100, 103, 106, 108, 109, 110, 111, 112, 113, 115, 116, 129, 132, 134, 136, 157, 168, 182, 205, 266, 275, 305, 306, 307, 308, 309, 310, 311, 313, 331, 334, 335, 337, 338, 339, 348
Candy (1968) 244
Cannibal Holocaust (1980) 145
Cantafora, Antonio [a.k.a. Michael Coby] 248
Canti, Aldo 213, 321
Canutt, Yakima 156, 232
Capellani, Albert 119
Capitan Fracassa (1958) 140
Capitan Tempesta (1942) 22, 33
Il Cappello da prete (1944) 24, 172
Capra, Frank 192
Capriccio all'italiana (1968) 117
The Captain's Daughter (film) see *La Figlia del capitano*
The Captain's Daughter (novel) 137
Capuano, Luigi 151
Caravaggio, il pittore maledetto (1941) 27–28, 29, 65, 86, 202, 294
Caravaggio see Merisi da Caravaggio, Michelangelo
The Cardinal (play) 39, 295
Cardinale, Claudia 70, 177
Carey, Roland 151, 316

Carica eroica (1952) 94
Carlucci, Leopoldo 106
Carmen (novella) 230
Carmet, Jean 215, 322, 323
Carnaval no Fogo (1949) 72
Carnimeo, Giuliano 268
Carpentieri, Luigi 126, 131, 154, 173, 178, 184, 188, 189, 297, 318, 320, 342
The Carpet of Horror see *Der Teppich des Grauens*
Carradine, John 232
Carrière, Jean-Claude 333
La Casa dell'esorcismo (1975) 188
La Casa nel tempo (1990) 239
Casablanca (1942) 132
Casanova, Giacomo 5, 7, 53, 59–64, 135, 192, 202, 335
Il Casanova di Federico Fellini (1976) 334
Casapinta, Ferruccio 151
The Case of the Scorpion's Tail see *La Coda dello scorpione*
Caserini, Mario 119
Casorati, Felice 18
Cassandra Crossing (1976) 271
Cassinelli, Claudio 265
Castellani, Renato 25, 52, 206
Il Castello dei morti vivi (1964) 173, 192
Castle Keep (1969) 87
Castle of Blood see *Danza macabra*
Castle of the Living Dead see *Il Castello dei morti vivi*
Cat O'Nine Tails see *Il Gatto a nove code*
Catene (1949) 27, 48, 84
Cavalcanti, Alberto 70
Il Cavaliere di San Marco (1939) 25, 291–292, 333
Il Cavaliere misterioso (1948) 5, 7, 54, 55, 59–64, 65, 68, 78, 79, 80, 89, 132, 135, 202, 204, 208, 230, 247, 305
I Cavalieri dell'illusione (1954) 211
Cavalleria (1936) 28
Cavallone, Alberto 248
Cayatte, André 221, 225
Cela s'appelle l'aurore (1956) 111
Celi, Adolfo 70
Céline, Louis-Ferdinand 221
Cellini, Benvenuto 5, 6, 10, 201, 202, 203, 204, 279, 280, 320, 321
La Cena delle beffe (1942) 28, 334
Cenerentola e il signor Bonaventura (1941) 35
Cento lettere d'amore (1940) 26, 293
C'era una volta il West (1968) 346
Cerchio, Fernando 111
Cervi, Antonio "Tonino" 134, 193, 314
Cervi, Gino 34, 35, 46, 47, 48, 56, 57, 58, 115, 121, 134, 135, 136, 170, 192, 296, 302, 303, 304, 312, 314, 334, 339
Chaffey, Don 147, 150
Chaleur et jouissance (*A doppia faccia* re-edit) 244, 326

Chanel, Hélène 157, 166, 316, 318
Chaplin, Charles 16, 21, 54, 116, 240
Chaplin, Sydney 240, 241, 325
Chardin, Jean-Baptiste-Siméon 61
The Charge of the Light Brigade (1936) 264
Chase, James Hadley [René Brabazon Raymond] 126
Chasse à la drogue see *Caccia all'uomo* (1961)
Checchi, Andrea 161
Chiarelli, Luigi 21, 290, 291
Chiari, Walter 21
Christian-Jacque [Christian Maudet] 220
Christie, Agatha 10, 250
Cianfriglia, Giovanni 346
Ciangottini, Valeria 215, 219, 322, 323
Ciani, Sergio 139, 318
Ciano, Galeazzo 18
Cicognini, Alessandro 55, 60, 304, 306
El Cid (1961) 30
La Cieca di Sorrento (1952) 26
Il Cinema della paura (TV show) 281, 328
Cinema Paradiso see *Nuovo Cinema Paradiso*
5 bambole per la luna d'agosto (1970) 10, 257
5 tombe per un medium (1965) 144
Cipriani, Stelvio 250, 255, 266, 268, 326, 327
The Circus (1928) 21
Citizen Kane (1941) 34
La Città delle donne (1980) 247
City of Women see *La Città delle donne*
Ciuffini, Sabatino 174, 299
Civirani, Osvaldo 111
Clair, René 68
Clark, Ken 217
Cloche, Maurice 217, 225
The Clockmaker see *L'Horlogier de Saint-Paul*
Clouzot, Henri-Georges 131, 196, 241
Cluzet, François 282
Cochran, Steve 168
Cocteau, Jean 333
La Coda dello scorpione (1971) 272
Coedel, Lucien 221
Col cuore in gola (1967) 126
Colamonici, Raffaele 20, 78, 95, 113, 290, 291, 292, 306, 307
Colangeli, Otello 268, 296, 303, 304, 305, 308, 309, 312, 316, 346
Colasanti, Arduino 29
Colasanti, Veniero 29, 294, 311
Colbert, Claudette 164
Coletti, Duilio 94
Collodi, Carlo 23
Colman, Ronald 60
Il Colosso di Rodi (1961) 111
The Colossus of Rhodes see *Il Colosso di Rodi*
Un Colpo di pistola (1942) 52

Coltellacci, Oreste 238, 240, 325
Comas Gil, Jaime 267, 268
Comencini, Luigi 3, 60, 117
Cominetti, Gian Maria 28
Conan the Barbarian (1982) 157
Concerto per pistola solista (1970) 199
A Connecticut Yankee in King Arthur's Court (novel) 201
The Conqueror (1956) 172
Consolini, Giorgio 95, 310
Constantine, Eddie 121
Il Conte Ugolino (1949) 5, 7, 20, 36, 60, 67, 73–78, 80, 86, 124, 164, 165, 198, 209, 224, 277, 306
La Contessa Castiglione (1942) 35
Continenza, Alessandro "Sandro" 135, 249, 250, 251, 260, 301, 314, 326
Conversation Piece see Gruppo di famiglia in un interno
Cooper, Gary 37, 173
Coplan FX 18 casse tout (1965) 9, 217–221, 226, 227, 228, 229, 322–323, 345
Coplan III see Coplan ouvre le feu à Mexico
Coplan ouvre le feu à Mexico (1967) 9, 43, 225–229, 232, 242, 275, 324
Coplan prend des risques (1964) 217
Coplan sauve sa peau (1968) 228, 232, 345
Coplan Saves His Sin see Coplan sauve sa peau
Il Coraggio (1955) 115
Corbucci, Sergio 105, 142, 157, 232, 337, 339
Corman, Roger 38, 128, 164, 179, 232, 236
Cormon, Eugène 215
La Corona di ferro (1941) 35, 100
Il Corriere del re (1947) 50
Cortese, Valentina 57, 59, 252, 253, 304, 327, 335
Corti, Antonio Cesare 270, 271, 328
Cosa avete fatto a Solange? (1972) 239, 244, 257
Cosmatos, George Pan 271
Costa, Mario 65
Costa, Romolo 22, 290, 291, 293
Cottafavi, Vittorio 6, 8, 111, 154
Cotten, Joseph 117
Count of Bragelonne see Le Vicomte de Bragelonne
The Count of Monte Cristo (novel) 16, 80, 221, 223, 279
The Countess of Castiglione see La Contessa Castiglione
Cozzi, Luigi 142, 143, 244, 245, 264, 265, 286, 329, 331, 347
Crash (novel) 242
Craveri, Mario 34, 302
Crazy Desires of a Murderer see I Vizi segreti di una governante
Cries and Shadows see Un Urlo dalle tenebre

The Crimes of the Black Cat see Sette scialli di seta gialla
I Criminali della galassia (1965) 81
The Crimson Pirate (1952) 139
Crisanti, Andrea 163, 167, 318, 341
Croce, Benedetto 84, 298, 344
Il Crollo di Roma (1963) 173
Crossed Swords (1954) 139
Cry Chicago see La Vera storia di Frank Mannata
Cry of the Hunted (1953) 63
Cukor, George 182, 206
Curato, Francesco 27, 294
Curtiz, Michael 130, 132, 264
Cyrano de Bergerac (play) 80

Da qui all'eredità (1955) 68, 114–117, 151, 312
Da Roma, Giancarlo 236
Da Vinci, Leonardo 5, 6, 122
Dafauce, Félix 236, 314, 320
Dalla Torre, Giuseppe 65
Dallamano, Massimo 161, 239, 257
Damiani, Damiano 169, 170, 254
The Damned see La Caduta degli dei
Damon, Mark 230, 232, 233, 325, 345
D'Angelo, Carlo 210, 321
D'Angelo, Salvo 65, 292, 294, 307
Danger: Diabolik see Diabolik
D'Annunzio, Gabriele 154
D'Anza, Daniele 114
Danza macabra (1964) 155, 181, 185
Dapporto, Carlo 21, 114, 296
Darès, Sophie 215, 322
Dassin, Jules 57
D'Aversa, Alberto 44, 295
Daves, Delmer 104
David e Golia (1960) 161
Davis, Bette 117
Day for Night see La Nuit américaine
Day of the Outlaw (1959) 171
Day of the Woman see I Spit on Your Grave
Day of Wrath see Vredens dag
The Day the Sky Exploded see La Morte viene dallo spazio
De' Medici, Giuliano 39
Dead of Night (1945) 70
The Deadly Affair (1966) 185
Deadly Sweet see Col cuore in gola
De Alencar, José 65
Death in the Garden see La Mort en ce jardin
Death Smiles on a Murderer see La morte ha sorriso all'assassino
De Baroncelli, Jacques 221
De Blasi, Virginio 151
De Caro, Enzo 261
De Castro Alves, Antônio 70
De Chirico, Giorgio 199
La Decima vittima (1965) 114
De Concini, Ennio 91, 114, 147, 148, 163, 171, 297, 308, 309, 315

Deep Red see Profondo rosso
De Filippo, Eduardo 20, 25, 26, 292
De Filippo, Peppino 25, 26, 27, 292, 293
De Funès, Luis 221, 225
Degli Ubaldini, Ruggieri 73
Delamare, Gil 151, 220, 227, 316, 323
De la Loma, José Antonio 227
De Laurentiis, Luigi 62
De Laurentiis, Dino 52, 59, 61, 62, 108, 171, 305
De Liguoro, Giuseppe 74
Il Delitto di Giovanni Episcopo (1947) 53, 172
Della Casa, Stefano 3, 68, 138, 139, 155, 166, 169, 173, 174, 279, 281, 285, 287, 329, 338, 341, 342, 344
Della Gherardesca, Ugolino 5, 73
Delon, Alain 216
Delpy, Julie 124, 299
De Martino, Alberto 162
De Masi, Filippo 200, 344
De Masi, Francesco 200, 230
Demick, Irina 255, 327
DeMille, Cecil Blount 112, 199
Demongeot, Mylène 176, 342
Demoniac see Exorcismes
De Nesle, Robert 9, 189, 192, 215, 217, 219, 226, 227, 228, 244, 319, 322, 323, 324, 345
Denis, María 20, 289, 332
D'Ennery, Adolphe 31, 172, 215, 302, 322
Deodato, Ruggero 145, 210, 272, 321, 345
De Palma, Brian 252, 273
De Pirro, Nicola 4, 101, 102
De Rege, Guido 21, 289, 290
De Rege, Giorgio 21, 22, 289, 290
De Rita, Massimo 143, 144
La Dernière Momie d'Egypte (unfilmed Freda project) 267, 279–280
De Robertis, Francesco 94
D'Errico, Corrado 22, 33, 290
De Santis, Giuseppe 55, 63, 172
De Sica, Vittorio 25, 28, 29, 32, 38, 45, 63, 227, 294, 340
De Stefani, Alessandro 25, 291, 293
De Teffé, Antonio 121, 312
De Toth, André 157, 171, 172, 174, 176, 296, 299, 329, 338
Les Deux orphelines (1965) 9, 215–217, 219, 322
Les Deux orphelines vampires (1997) 345
D'Eva, Alessandro "Sandro" 151, 317
Devaivre, Jean 16
The Devil Is a Woman see La Lupa
Devilman Story (1967) 236
The Devil's Commandment see I Vampiri
Dexter, Rosemarie 210, 231
Di Leo, Fernando 250, 265, 271

Di Rocco, Alessio 237, 265, 266, 268, 346
Diable au corps (1947) 121
Diabolik (1968) 87
Diabolique see *Les Diaboliques*
Les Diaboliques (1955) 156, 241
Dial M for Murder (1954) 161
Diamante, Julio 236
Il Diavolo bianco (1947) 137
Diaz, Armando 95
Dick, Philip K. 141
Dick Smart 2007 (1967) 217
Dickens, Charles 23
I Dieci gladiatori (1963) 337
Dieterle, William 91
Dietrich, Erwin C. 245, 247, 248, 326
Diffring, Anton 252, 327
Dilián, Irasema 48, 50, 303
Il Dio chiamato Dorian (1970) 161
Dionisio, Silvia 77, 268, 271, 272, 275, 328
DiPaolo, Dante 157
Il Dito di Dio (unfilmed Freda project) 38, 114
Divorce Italian Style see *Divorzio all'italiana*
Divorzio all'italiana (1961) 120, 142, 160
Dr. Jekyll and Mr. Hyde (1931) 132
Dr. Mabuse, Der Spieler (1922) 129
Il Dolce corpo di Deborah (1968) 239
La Dolce vita (1960) 39, 40, 120, 167, 184, 185, 215, 334
Il Dominatore dei sette mari (Sir Francis Drake) (1962) 174, 298
Dominici, Arturo 144, 298
Don Caesar de Bazan (1915) 333
Don César de Bazan (comic opera) 31
Don Cesare di Bazan (1942) 25, 31–36, 37, 39, 48, 49, 67, 69, 75, 76, 80, 89, 127, 136, 142, 188, 190, 192, 295, 302, 329
El Don del mar (1957) 136
Don Giovanni in Sicilia (1967) 31
Don Juan in Sicily see *Don Giovanni in Sicilia*
Don Sezar de Bazan (1957) 333
Don Sezar de Bazan (1989) 333
Donati, Ermanno 3, 34, 126, 131, 152, 154, 156, 162, 166, 167, 173, 178, 186, 188, 189, 297, 313, 316, 318, 320, 342, 343
Donati, Piero 166, 313, 318
Donati, Sergio 126, 338, 346
Donatone, Mario 236
Dondina, Angiola 5, 17
La Donna del lago (1965) 199
La Donna invisibile (1969) 339
A doppia faccia (1969) 6, 238–245, 248, 252, 256, 325
Dora Nelson (1940) 22
Doré, Gustave 75, 165
Double Cross see *Il Tradimento (Passato che uccide)*
Douglas, Kirk 105, 139
Dove andiamo signora? (1942) 28

Dove si spara di più (1967) 207
Dressed To Kill (1980) 252
Dreyer, Carl Theodor 80, 130, 163
Duarte, Anselmo 69, 71, 72, 306, 335
Dubrovskiy (1936 film) 46
Dubrovsky (novel) 46, 303
Dubrowsky (1959) 91
Duca, Nadine [Nadine Ducasse] 151, 316
Due milioni per un sorriso (1939) 22
Due notti con Cleopatra (1953) 99
Le Due orfanelle (1977) 172
Dumanoir, Philippe 31, 302
Dumas, Alexandre, *père* 16, 31, 60, 78, 79, 190, 201, 204, 279, 280, 284
Dune (1984) 248
Dupuis, Claudine 120, 312
Duranti, Doris 24, 333
Dwan, Allan 105

The Eagle (1925 film) 16, 46
The Easy Life see *Il Sorpasso*
Ebert, Gunther 249
L'Ebreo errante (1947) 28
Eclipse see *L'Eclisse*
L'Eclisse (1962) 1, 120
The Edgar Wallace Mystery Theatre (TV series) 238
The Eerie Midnight Horror Show see *L'Ossessa*
8½ (1963) 87, 152, 167, 184
1860 (1934) 25
Eisenstein, Sergei 76, 149
Ekberg, Anita 120, 168, 169, 171, 172, 296, 297
El ángel exterminador (1962) 268
Elley, Derek 102, 104, 340
Equini, Arrigo 122, 266, 303, 312
Ercole al centro della terra (1961) 151, 162, 163
Ercole alla conquista di Atlantide (1961) 154
Ercole e la regina di Lidia (1959) 139
Ercoli, Luciano 182, 252
Erickson, Glenn 181, 343
Esorcisti, Gli (unfilmed Freda project) 265
L'Estate (1966) 339
Estate violenta (1959) 161
Estrada, Carlos 210, 321
Estratto dagli archivi segreti della polizia di una capitale europea (1972) 5, 9, 21, 93, 250, 253–258, 259, 260, 265, 267, 273, 276, 286, 327–328, 347, 350
Ettore Fieramosca (1938) 93
Evil Eye see *Malocchio*
Exodus (1960) 248
Exorcismes (1974) 244
Exstase (1933) 93
The Exterminating Angel see *El Ángel exterminador* (1962)
The Eye in the Labyrinth see *L'Occhio nel labirinto*
Eyeball see *Gatti rossi in un labirinto di vetro*

Eyes Without a Face see *Les Yeux sans visage*

Fabian, Françoise 203, 320
Fabiola and the Fighting Gladiator see *Fabiola* (1949)
Fabiola (1918) 99
Fabiola (1949) 68, 99
Fabrizi, Aldo 50, 334
Faccenna, Maria Luce 272, 328
The Face in the Night (novel) 238
Face of the Frog see *Der Frosch mit der Maske*
Fago, Giovanni 170, 185, 318, 343
Fairbanks, Douglas, Sr. 16, 60, 78, 263
Falk, Lee 164
Falk, Rossella 68, 306, 308
The Fall of Rome see *Il Crollo di Roma*
The Fall of the House of Usher (short story) 129
Fame and the Devil see *Al diavolo la celebrità*
Family Solicitor (TV series) 184
Farassino, Alberto 108
Farnese, Alberto 151, 296, 316, 317
Farrow, John 105
Fascino (1939) 23, 187, 292
Fast, Howard 100, 102
Le Fatiche di Ercole (1958) 112, 142, 147, 340
Fatigati, Giuseppe 112, 292, 312
Feist, Harry 48, 262, 303, 334
Felicità perduta (1946) 84
Fellini, Federico 37, 39, 40, 42, 57, 60, 79, 87, 120, 152, 161, 184, 240, 247, 334
Femina Ridens (1969) 252
Fenech, Edwige 91
Ferida, Luisa 41
Ferrara, Luigi 266
Ferrer, José 193
Ferroni, Giorgio 3, 41, 162, 250
Ferzetti, Gabriele 57, 59, 304
Fescourt, Henri 58
Feuillade, Louis 128, 223
Fiermonte, Enzo 37, 38, 41, 79, 114, 295, 302
I Figli di nessuno (1951) 84, 87
La Figlia del capitano (1947) 50
La Figlia del Corsaro Verde (1940) 33
Il Figlio di Aquila Nera (1968) 91
Il Figlio di d'Artagnan (1950) 5, 20, 77, 78–82, 284, 307
Il Figlio di Spartacus (1963) 105, 337
La Fille de d'Artagnan (1994) 10, 79, 284–286, 289, 300–301
Fiorini, Guido 54
A Fistful of Dollars see *Per un pugno di dollari*
Fitzcarraldo (1982) 70
Five Dolls for an August Moon see *5 bambole per la luna d'agosto*
Flaiano, Ennio 39, 295
Flashman (1967) 340
Flemyng, Robert 184, 185, 187, 189, 318, 342

Floradas na serra (1954) 70
Flynn, Errol 60, 139, 263, 264
Fofi, Goffredo 273
For a Few Dollars More see *Per qualche dollaro in più*
The Forbidden Photos of a Lady Above Suspicion see *Le Foto proibite di una signora per bene*
Ford, John 6, 33, 34, 42, 49, 54, 56, 67, 81, 138, 155, 174, 230, 232, 233
Foreign Correspondent (1940) 70, 80, 180
Forest, Mark 166
La Fornarina (1944) 28
Forsyth, Stephen 213, 214, 232, 233, 234, 321, 325, 345
La Fortuna si diverte (play) 20
Forty Guns (1957) 151
Foster, Norman 63
Le Foto proibite di una signora per bene (1970) 182, 252
Four Times That Night see *Quante volte... quella notte*
Fowler, Gene, Jr. 127
Fra' Diavolo (1942) 37
Fraile, Francisco 257, 327
Francesco Baracca (unfilmed Freda project) 10, 237, 254, 260–264, 270, 348
Franci, Carlo 164, 318
Franciolini, Gianni 50
Francisci, Pietro 99, 108, 112, 113, 143, 147, 152, 166
Franco, Francisco 32
Franco, Jesús "Jess" 189, 219, 244, 247, 252
Franju, Georges 193, 223
Frankenstein (1931) 164
Fratello sole, sorella luna (1972) 253
Frauengefängnis (1975) 252
Freda, Angela see Dondina, Angiola
Freda, Emma 13, 14, 15, 16
Freda, Federico 15
Freda, Guislaine 5, 15, 216, 259, 284, 286, 348
Freda, Jacqueline 5, 11, 66, 67, 90, 194, 216, 233, 246, 255, 259, 260, 261, 264, 266, 270, 272, 277, 283, 285, 286, 287, 328, 332, 339, 344, 348
Freda, Riccardo: on actors 21, 56, 57–58, 62, 78, 86–87, 111, 114, 115, 137, 139–140, 151, 156–157, 159, 164, 172–173, 176, 199, 215, 240, 252, 335; appearances as actor 24, 83, 253, 273, 333; apprenticeship as scriptwriter 20–30, 332; on censorship 36, 101, 111, 201, 234, 244–245;critical rediscovery: 2–3, 9–10, 62, 140–141, 158, 194, 204, 215–216, 225, 259, 281, 283, 286–287; *Divoratori di celluloide* (memoir) 1, 5, 11, 41, 156, 273, 338; family and childhood 13–16; on film directors 1, 3, 21, 26, 27, 29,
40, 143, 146, 154, 169, 171, 188, 197, 210, 245, 250, 331–332, 334; on filmmaking 1, 4–5, 6–8, 10, 14, 16, 34, 49, 76, 97, 104, 109, 113, 121, 124, 127, 130, 135, 156, 182, 187, 188, 194, 215, 229, 232, 250–251, 259, 289; interest in the occult 20, 82–83, 145, 198, 266–267, 275–277; on literature 16, 23, 53, 74, 78, 137, 230, 279; on Neorealism 32, 45, 49, 50; political views 4, 17–18, 19, 47, 102, 138; private life 5, 17; 63–64, 73, 110, 132, 136, 167, 194, 203, 216, 255, 259–260, 266, 283, 286, 287, 331, 337, 339, 344, 347–348; on producers 3–4, 37, 101, 46, 52, 61, 62, 97, 109, 126, 134–135, 151, 166, 172, 173, 184, 245, 259; pseudonyms 10, 141, 184, 197, 234, 244, 253; on television 260, 264; unfilmed projects 10, 32, 36, 38, 72–73, 113–114, 126, 169–170, 201, 204–205, 234–238, 260–271, 279–280, 283–284; work as sculptor 17–18, 66, 143, 150, 156, 276, 278
Freda, Vittorio 13, 14, 15
Freddi, Luigi 18, 19, 93, 332
Fregonese, Hugo 173, 297
Frenzy (1972) 217
Frid, Yan 333
The Frightened Woman see *Femina Ridens*
Frine, cortigiana d'Oriente (1953) 99
From Here to Eternity (1953) 114–115
Der Frosch mit der Maske (1959) 238
La Frusta e il corpo (1963) 179, 276
Fruttero, Carlo 141
Fryd, Joseph 174, 299
La Fuga (1964) 339
Fulci, Lucio 119, 120, 238, 239, 240, 268, 272, 287, 325, 338, 344
Fuller, Samuel 6, 151
Fumagalli, Franco 184, 297, 318, 320, 327
Funi, Achille 18
Fuochi d'artificio (1938) 21, 290
Furia a Marrakech (1966) 213
Furneaux, Yvonne 161, 317
Fury in Marrakech see *Furia a Marrakech*
Fury of Johnny Kid see *Dove si spara di più*
FX 18, Secret Agent see *Agent Secret FX 18*
FX 18 Superspy see *Coplan FX 18 casse tout*

Gabel, Scilla 138, 140, 314
Gaido, Domenico 204
Galassi, Angelo 131, 134, 297, 313
Gallea, Arturo 24, 291
Galli, Ida [a.k.a. Evelyn Stewart] 228
Gallone, Carmine 19, 21, 41, 50, 63, 65, 77, 99, 111, 163, 215
Gandusio, Antonio 20, 289
Garbo, Greta 37, 63
Garcin, Henri 272, 328
Gardner, Ava 108
Garibaldi, Anita [Ana Ribeiro da Silva] 73
Garibaldi, Giuseppe 72, 73
Garinei & Giovannini [Pietro Garinei, Sandro Giovannini] 114, 296
Garrone, Matteo 336
Garrone, Riccardo 161, 317
Gaslight (1944) 182
Gassman, Vittorio 28, 44, 62, 63, 78, 87, 119, 120, 161, 305, 305, 308
Gastaldi, Ernesto 173, 177, 178, 179, 180, 181, 182, 183, 185, 186, 189, 296, 318, 319, 343
Gatti, Guido 52
Gatti rossi in un labirinto di vetro (1975) 272
Il Gatto a nove code (1971) 161, 253
Il Gattopardo (1963) 2
The Gay Swordsman see *Il Figlio di d'Artagnan*
Gelosia (1942) 24
Gemser, Laura 193, 268, 271, 272, 328
Genoveffa di Brabante (1947) 62, 211
Genoveffa di Brabante (1964) 206, 211–215, 232, 237
Genoveffa—Il figlio della foresta (1933) 211
Gentile, Panfilo 4
Gentilomo, Giacomo 26, 157, 293, 333
Gerard, Henriette 130
Géret, Georges 221, *222*, 224, 225, 323
Germi, Pietro 120, 142, 160, 172
Das Gesicht im Dunkeln see *A doppia faccia*
Gherardi, Gherardo 25, 291, 294, 295
Ghezzi, Enrico 141
The Ghost see *Lo Spettro*
Giacci, Vittorio 286
Giachetti, Fosco 39, 295
Giacomo Casanova: Childhood and Adolescence see *Infanzia, vocazione e prime esperienze di Giacomo Casanova, veneziano*
The Giant of Marathon see *La Battaglia di Maratona*
The Giants of Thessaly see *I Giganti della Tessaglia—Gli Argonauti*
I Giganti della Tessaglia—Gli Argonauti (1960) 5, 17, 147–152, 165, 166, 200, 211, 220, 280, 315–316
Gigli, Beniamino 37
Gioi, Vivi 40, 41, 293, 303
Giombini, Marcello 160, 317
Un Giorno alla fine di ottobre (1977) 339

Giovagnoli, Raffaello 102
Giove in doppiopetto (1955) 114, 295
Giraldi, Duccia 57, 304
The Girl from Rio (1969) 217
The Girl Who Knew Too Much see *La Ragazza che sapeva troppo*
Girotti, Mario [a.k.a. Terence Hill] 174, 298
Girotti, Massimo 28, 100, 103, 149, 151, 170, 176, 299, 310, 316, 336–337
Gish, Lillian 16, 215
Giuliano, Salvatore 159
Giulietta degli spiriti (1965) 57, 87
Giusti, Marco 140, 141, 345
Glen or Glenda (1953) 162
Glori, Enrico 35, 292, 302
Go for Broke! (1951) 89
Godard, Jean-Luc 6, 21
The Godfather (1972) 97
Goebbels, Joseph 19
Gold for the Caesars see *Oro per i Cesari*
The Gold of Naples see *L'Oro di Napoli*
Der Golem (1920) 130
Goliath Against the Vampires see *Maciste contro il vampiro*
Goliath and the Vampires see *Maciste contro il vampiro*
Gomes, Antônio Carlos 65, 67, 68, 86, 307
Gomorra (2008) 336
Goodman, Benny 40
Gozlino, Paolo 145, 151, 316, 340
Graf, Dominik 240
Gramsci, Vittorio 102
La Grande guerra (1959) 47, 63, 140
Grande Otelo [Sebastião Bernardes de Souza Prata] 69, 70, 71, 72, 306
La Granduchessa si diverte (1940) 26, 293
Granelli, Mireille 121, 312
The Grapes of Wrath (1940) 155
Grassilli, Raoul 267
Grau, Jorge 136, 249, 314, 330
The Great War see *La Grande guerra*
Gregoretti, Ugo 210
Il Grido (1957) 168
Grieco, Sergio 342
Griffith, David Wark 16, 19, 33, 215
The Grim Reaper see *Antropophagus* (1980)
Grimaldi, Giovanni 30
Gritos en la noche (1961) 189
Gruault, Jean 261
Gruppo di famiglia in un interno (1974) 271
Gualino, Riccardo 3, 4, 9, 51, 52, 55, 57, 108, 109, 111, 112, 113, 169, 259
Guarany (1950) 65–68, 70, 81, 86, 90, 237, 306–307
Guardi, Francesco 61
Guazzoni, Enrico 22, 28, 33, 99

Guerra, Ugo 178, 296
Guerrazzi, Francesco Domenico 119
Guerrieri, Romolo 232, 239, 271
Guerrini, Mino 201
Guest, Val 142, 145
Guida, Wandisa 131, 134, 188, 313
The Guns of Navarone (1961) 222

Hacohen, Alexander 245
Hadji Murad (novelette) 137
Halsey, Brett 192, 193, 203, 205, 210, 319, 320, 344
Hamlet (1992) 210
Hampton, Robert see Freda, Riccardo (pseudonyms)
Hardy, Oliver 25, 190
Harryhausen, Ray 150
Hatchet for the Honeymoon see *Il Rosso segno della follia*
Hathaway, Henry 140, 196, 333
The Haunted Palace (1963) 164
Hawks, Howard 206
Hawthorne, Nathaniel 201
Hayers, Sidney 238
Hellström, Gunnar 270
Hengge, Paul 238, 325
Her Grace Commands see *Ihre Hoheit befiehit*
Hercules see *Le Fatiche di Ercole*
Hercules and the Captive Women see *Ercole alla conquista di Atlantide*
Hercules and the Treasure of the Incas see *Sansone e il tesoro degli Incas*
Hercules in the Haunted World see *Ercole al centro della terra*
Die Herrin von Atlantis (1932) 130
Herter, Gérard 140, 142, 314, 315, 340
Herzog, Werner 70
Heusch, Paolo 142, 177
Highway Racer see *Poliziotto Sprint*
Hill, Terence see Girotti, Mario
Hinrich, Hans 57, 61, 304, 305
Hintermann, Carlo 236
Hitchcock, Alfred 60, 70, 78, 80, 86, 161, 180, 217, 220, 224, 226, 241, 342
Holden, Lansing G. 130
Holiday, Joy 133, 313
Holiday, Ronny 133, 313
The Hollywood Revue of 1929 (1929) 192
Un Hombre vino a matar (1967) 217
Honthauer, Ronald 133
Hooper (1978) 286
Hope, Anthony 26
L'Horlogier de Saint-Paul (1973) 226
The Horrible Dr. Hichcock see *L'Orribile segreto del Dr. Hichcock*
Hoskins, Bob 79
House of Clocks see *La Casa nel tempo*

House of Usher (1960) 232
Hudson, Michael R. 189
Hudson, Rock 113
Hugo, Victor 16, 31, 50, 53, 55, 58, 221, 304, 333
Huston, John 142, 339
Hypnosis see *Ipnosi*

I Am a Fugitive from a Chain Gang (1932) 54
I Spit on Your Grave (1978) 258
I Was a Teenage Frankenstein (1957) 127
I Was a Teenage Werewolf (1957) 127
L'Idea fissa (1964) 214
L'Iguana dalla lingua di fuoco (1971) 9, 10, 135, 248–253, 257, 273, 326–327, 347
Ihre Hoheit befiehit (1931) 26
L'Imperatore di New York (unfilmed Freda project) 234–236
In campagna è caduta una stella (1939) 25–26, 292
In der Glut des Mittags see *Tamar wife of Er*
In the Country Fell a Star see *In campagna è caduta una stella*
In the Folds of the Flesh see *Nelle pieghe della carne*
Incontrera, Annabella 240, 325
Indiana Jones and the Temple of Doom (1984) 282
Infanzia, vocazione e prime esperienze di Giacomo Casanova, veneziano (1969) 60
Inferno (1980) 145
Inferno (poem) 20, 73, 74, 77, 165
Innocenzi, Carlo 158, 308, 309, 316
Interlude (1957) 48
Invasion of the Body Snatchers (1956) 142
Inventiamo l'amore (1938) 22
Ipnosi (1962) 161
The Iron Swordsman see *Il Conte Ugolino*
Isbert, Tony 255, 257, 258, 327
La Isla de la muerte (1967) 167
Island of the Doomed see *La Isla de la muerte*
It Happened One Night (1934) 192
It's All True (1942–1993) 70
Ivanovsky, Alexsandr 46

Jacob, Gilles 225
Jason and the Argonauts (1963) 147, 150, 340
Jeffries, Lang 173, 174, 226, 324
La Jena di Londra (1964) 344
The Jester's Supper see *La Cena delle beffe*
Johnny Hamlet, a.k.a. *Quella sporca storia nel West* 206
Johnny Oro (1966) 232
Johnny Yuma (1966) 232
Johnson, Van 89
Jotta, Elio 194, 195 196, 199, 320

Index

Judex (1963) 223
Julienne, Rémy 220
Juliet of the Spirits see *Giulietta degli spiriti*

Kampf um Rom (1968) 337
Kapò (1960) 142
Kardos, László 128
Karlatos, Olga 268
Karlsen, John 165, 318, 319
Kavka, Misha 180
Kaze tachinu (2013) 263
Kean—Genio e, sre golatezza (1957) 119, 161
Keaton, Buster 16, 116
Keaton, Camille 256, 257, 258, 327
Kelly, Gene 78
Kenny, Paul [Gaston Van den Panhuyse and Jean Libert] 217, 226, 322, 324
Kiefer, Warren 173, 192
Kier, Udo 248
Kieslowski, Krzystof 151
Kill, Baby ... Kill! see *Operazione paura*
Kill Johnny Ringo see *Uccidete Johnny Ringo*
King David (1985) 281
King of Kings (1961) 174, 176
Kinski, Klaus 6, 228, 230, 232, 240, 242, 243, 244, 245, 325
Kiss of Death (1947) 196
Klimovsky, León 217
Kneale, Nigel 145
The Knight of San Marco see *Il Cavaliere di San Marco*
Kommissar Rex (1994 TV series) 159
Koscina, Sylva 337
Krafft-Ebing, Richard von 179, 195
The Kreutzer Sonata (novella) 50
Kriminal (1966) 39
Krüger, Christiane 240, 325
Krüger, Hardy 267
Kubrick, Stanley 97, 102, 104, 105, 337

La Marca, Franco 267
La Russa, Adrienne 338
Labro, Maurice 217
Ladri di biciclette (1948) 32
Lady Frankenstein (1971) 167
The Lady from Shanghai (1947) 93
Lamarr, Hedy 211
Lancaster, Burt 139
Landres, Paul 128
Lane, John Francis 167, 318
Lang, Fritz 16, 33, 97, 121, 129, 197
Lasciate ogni speranza (1937) 20, 21, 289
Lassander, Dagmar 252, 253, 327
The Last Days of Pompeii see *Gli Ultimi giorni di Pompei*
The Last Musketeer see *Le Vicomte de Bragelonne*
Last Train from Gun Hill (1959) 151
Lastretti, Adolfo 265
Lattuada, Alberto 31, 53, 172, 247, 339

Laudadio, Francesco 157
Laurel, Stan 25, 190
Lavagnino, Angelo Francesco 169, 173, 296, 297
Lavant, Denis 282, 300
Lavia, Gabriele 269
Lawrence, Rosina 25, 292
Lee, Bill 169
Lee, Christopher 141, 162, 330
Lee, Margaret 240, 242, 325
Lee, Rowland V. 182
Legend of the Lost (1957) 140
La Leggenda del Piave (1952) 20, 47, 94–98, 150, 257, 262, 264, 310
La Leggenda di Genoveffa (1952) 20, 47, 94–98, 150, 257, 262, 264, 310
Legrand, Gérard 189
Leitão de Barros, José 70
Lelouch, Claude 221
Lenzi, Umberto 39, 178, 240, 241, 272
Leone, Alfredo 255, 265, 266
Leone, Sergio 106, 111, 127, 139, 168, 190, 200, 202, 206, 209, 230, 296, 346
Il Leone di Damasco (1942) 22
Leonviola, Antonio 166, 204
The Leopard see *Il Gattopardo*
Leroux, Xavier 106
LeRoy, Mervyn 54, 99, 334
Leroy, Philippe 161, 298, 317
Let Sleeping Corpses Lie see *Non si deve profanare il sonno dei morti*
Lévi, Eliphas 275
Léviant, Michel 285, 300
Lewis, Al 134, 313
Lewis, Herschell Gordon 247
Lewis, Joseph H. 63
Lewton, Val 83
L'Herbier, Marcel 68
Liberi, armati, pericolosi (1976) 271
Libido (1965) 182
Lincoln, George see Freda, Riccardo (pseudonyms)
Lion of the Desert (1980) 271, 272
Lisa and the Devil see *Lisa e il diavolo*
Lisa e il diavolo (1973) 188, 256, 274
The List of Adrian Messenger (1963) 142
Little Women (1949) 334
Livanov, Boris 46
Liz et Helen see *A doppia faccia*
A Lizard in a Woman's Skin see *Una Lucertola con la pelle di donna*
Lizzani, Carlo 96, 102
Lloyd, Frank 164
Lollobrigida, Gina 48, 63, 184
Lollobrigida, Guido 226, 324
Lombardi, Guglielmo 109, 304, 305, 306
Lombardi, Rodolfo 48, 49, 109, 110, 303, 304, 305, 306, 308, 311

Lombardi, Ugo 27, 70, 71, 293, 305, 306
Lombardo, Goffredo 2, 126, 206, 211, 338
A Long Ride from Hell see *Vivo per la tua morte*
Longanesi, Leo 4, 37, 39, 41, 59, 102
Loren, Sophia 99, 140, 335
Lotti, Mariella 66, 306
Lourcelles, Jacques 2, 6, 7, 48, 53, 54, 60, 62, 96, 109, 110, 124, 158, 172, 192, 198, 277, 279
Love from a Stranger (1937) 182
Lovecraft, Howard Phillips 145, 164
Loy, Mino 213, 340
Lualdi, Antonella 172, 297
Lubitsch, Ernst 26, 263
Lucas, Tim 134, 143, 145, 150, 157, 186, 332, 334, 337, 338, 339, 340, 341, 344
Lucentini, Franco 141
Una Lucertola con la pelle di donna (1971) 272
Luciano Serra Pilota (1938) 28
Lucky Luciano (1973) 236, 271, 346
Ludwig (1973) 140, 271
Lumet, Sidney 185
Luna Rossa (1951) 93
La Lupa (1953) 247
Lupi, Roldano 172, 297
Lupo, Alberto 213, 321
Lupo, Michele 109, 199, 296, 312, 337
Lustig, Branko 139, 314, 339
Luttazzi, Lelio 135, 314
Lycanthropus (1961) 177, 178
Lynch, David 248

M (1931) 97
Maccari, Giuseppe 186, 318
Maccari, Ruggero 30
Macedo, Watson 72
Machado, Paulo 72
Mácháty, Gustav 93
Maciste alla corte del Gran Khan (1961) 5, 17, 152–158, 164, 166, 167, 173, 316–317
Maciste all'inferno (1962) 5, 121, 151, 157, 162–167, 189, 192, 318
Maciste all'inferno (1926) 152, 168
Maciste alpino (1916) 152
Maciste contro il vampiro (1961) 26, 157, 162, 163
Maciste contro lo sceicco (1926) 152
Maciste L'uomo più forte del mondo (1961) 109
Maciste nella terra dei ciclopi (1961) 166
Maciste nella valle dei re (1960) 152, 164, 166
Maciste poliziotto (1918) 152
Maddalena ... zero in condotta (1940) 38, 48
Maddalena, Zero for Conduct see *Maddalena ... zero in condotta*
Madeleine, anatomia di un incubo (1974) 258

Mademoiselle (1966) 247
Madrid de mis sueños see *Buongiorno, Madrid!*
Maesso, José Gutiérrez 254, 327
Maggi, Giuseppe "Peppino" 245, 246, 326
Maggio, Beniamino 116, 312
Maggio, Dante 63, 66, 305, 306
Magia a prezzi modici (1951) 82–83, 275, 307–308
Magnani, Anna 28, 48
The Magnificent Adventurer see *Il Magnifico avventuriero*
Il Magnifico avventuriero (1963) 5, 6, 131, 176, 197, 201–205, 279, 280, 320–321
Maid of Salem (1937) 164
Maien, Michael 245, 246, 247, 248, 326
Maimone, Giovanni 160
Maiuri, Arduino "Dino" 50
Malasomma, Nunzio 137
Malatesta, Guido 91
Malocchio (1975) 257
Malombra (1942) 48, 52
Mambo (1954) 63
Mamoulian, Rouben 63, 94, 132
Man From Interpol (TV series) 217
The Man Who Turned to Stone (1957) 128
Mancini, Claudio 346
Mancori, Sandro 268
Manfredi, Nino 68, 308
Mangano, Silvana 117, 335, 340
Mangini, Gino 344
Mankiewicz, Joseph L. 48, 57
Mann, Anthony 104
Manni, Ettore 176, 246, 247, 248, 267, 268, 326
Mannino, Franco 176, 193, 200, 201, 276, 298, 299, 308, 312, 319, 328
Manuel, Robert 219, 323
Manurita, Giovanni 21, 22, 290
The Manuscript Found in Saragossa (novel) 19
Manzoni, Alessandro 35
Manzù, Giacomo 17
Marais, Jean 220, 225, 333
Marcantonio e Cleopatra (1913) 99
Marceau, Sophie 10, 285, 301, 349
March, Fredric 50, 132
Marchal, Georges 106 111, 168, 169, 296, 311
Marchesi, Marcello 37, 43, 303
Marco Polo—L'avventura di un italiano in Cina (1962) 152, 173, 297
Mardore, Michel 149
Margheriti, Antonio 3, 81, 155, 173, 181, 265, 330
Marielle, Jean-Pierre 222, 323
Mark of the Devil (1970) 248
The Mark of Zorro (1920 film) 16
Marnie (1964) 277
Marotta, Giuseppe 58
Marquand, Richard 244
Marshall, Mike 215, 216, 322
Martín, Eugenio 161, 217

Martínez Román, María del Carmen 246
Martini, Arturo 17, 18
Martino, Sergio 182, 241, 257, 267, 272
The Marx Brothers 40
Mary, Jules 221, 223, 323
Marzi, Franca 79, 81, 307, 309
La Maschera del demonio (1960) 103, 104, 144, 146, 161, 162, 163, 177, 183, 201, 256, 272
Masciocchi, Raffaele 176, 191, 192, 193, 203, 298, 299, 315, 318, 319, 320, 344
Masina, Giulietta 40, 79
Masini, Giuseppe 147, 230, 260, 261, 315, 324
Massaccesi, Aristide 144, 151, 201, 256
Massi, Stelvio 160, 213, 316, 321
Mastrocinque, Camillo 22, 172, 193
Mastroianni, Barbara 271
Mastroianni, Marcello 57, 60, 215, 271, 304, 335
Mastroianni, Ruggero 271
Matarazzo, Raffaello 26, 27, 28, 29, 30, 48, 57, 75, 77, 84, 87, 92, 247, 293, 294
Maté, Rudolph 174, 298
Mater Dei (1950) 93
Mattei, Angelo 273, 348
Mattei, Bruno 245
Mattoli, Mario 99
Mauri, Roberto 258
Mayo, Archie 173
Medea (1969) 148
Medin, Gastone 34, 184, 302
Medusa Against the Son of Hercules see *Perseo L'invincibile*
Men and Wolves see *Uomini e lupi* (1957)
Méndez, Fernando 128
Meniconi, Furio 79, 176, 299, 307
Mercader, María 63, 305
Mercanti, Pino 92
Mérimée, Prosper 230
Merisi da Caravaggio, Michelangelo 27, 28, 121, 122
Merivale, John 142, 145, 315, 340
Merli, Maurizio 160
Merli, Silvana 5, 194, 199, 203, 237, 259, 287, 320, 344
Messalina (1951) 99, 111
Messalina (1922) 99
Messaline see *Messalina* (1951)
La Messe dorée (1975) 339
Metz, Vittorio 37, 40, 42, 302, 303
Metzger, Radley 161, 242
Meurtre en 45 tours (1960) 241
Mexican Slayride see *Coplan ouvre le feu à Mexico*
Meynier, Geronimo 210, 321, 345
Michelangelo see Buonarroti, Michelangelo
Midnight Express (1978) 248
Midnight Lace (1960) 182
Migliari, Armando 23, 292
Migliorini, Romano 238, 325

Milian, Tomas 217, 338, 343
The Milky Way see *La Voie lactée*
Mill of the Stone Women see *Il Mulino delle donne di pietra*
Miller, David 182
Miller, Marvin 340
Minutella, Vincenza 207, 208, 209
Mio caro assassino (1972) 219
Mio figlio Nerone (1956) 99
Mioni, Fabrizio 148
Miracle in Milan see *Miracolo a Milano*
Miracolo a Milano (1951) 32
Miraglia, Emilio P. 253
Miranda, Carmen 71
I Miserabili (1948) 5, 7, 50–59, 61, 65, 69, 74, 75, 86, 89, 121, 132, 136, 155, 158, 213, 224, 252, 282, 287, 304–305
Les Misérables (novel) 16, 50, 53, 54, 58, 216, 221
Misiano, Fortunato 91
Mission: Impossible III (2006) 91
Mr. Arkadin (1955) 135
Mitchell, Gordon 166
Miyazaki, Hayao 263
Mizrahi, Simon 158, 271, 328, 335, 348
Modigliani, Amedeo 17, 209
Modugno, Domenico 116, 312
Moffa, Paolo 68
Molè, Franco 271
Mole Men Against the Son of Hercules see *Maciste L'uomo più forte del mondo*
Moll, Georgia 140, 160, 314, 317, 340
Molnar, Ferenc 23
Momi, Umberto 74, 91, 306, 309
Mondadori, Alberto 23
Monell, Robert 217
I Mongoli (1961) 157, 171–173, 174, 296–297
Monicelli, Mario 23, 26, 37, 47, 53, 63, 75, 79, 84, 85, 89, 167, 239, 282, 292, 293, 303, 305, 306, 307, 308, 333, 335
Monroe, Marilyn 185
La Montagna del dio cannibale (1978) 267
Monter, José Luis 215, 321, 345
Montero, Roberto 267, 268, 346
Montresor, Beni 129, 313, 338, 339
Moonraker (1979) 215
Moore, Roger 252
Mora, Teo 141
Moravia, Alberto 119
Morelli, Rina 49, 303
Moreno, Antonio 333
Moresque: obiettivo allucinante see *Coplan ouvre le feu à Mexico*
Morgan, Michèle 215
Morgan il pirata (1960) 171
Morgan the Pirate see *Morgan il pirata*
Mori, Claudia 203, 320
Morreale, Emiliano 85, 86, 121
Morris, Kirk see Bellini, Adriano
La Mort en ce jardin (1956) 111

Morte di un amico (1959) 142
La Morte ha sorriso all'assassino (1973) 201, 256
Morte in Indonesia (unfilmed Freda project) 236–238
La Morte non conta i dollari (1967) 213, 214, 230–234, 235, 240, 253, 260, 324–325
La Morte scende leggera (1972) 172
La Morte viene dallo spazio (1958) 142
La Morte vivante (1982) 215
I Mosaici di Ravenna (1954) 112–113, 312
Mosjoukine, Ivan 137
Mossinson, Yigal 246, 326
The Most Dangerous Game (1932) 345
Il Mostro dell'opera (1964) 178
Una Mujer entre los brazos (1945) 30
Mulargia, Edoardo 268
Il Mulino delle donne di pietra (1960) 140, 162, 183
Muller, Paul 129, 131, 133, 224, 255, 256, 276, 296, 313, 323, 327
Müller, Friedrich 211
Mulock, Al 346
The Munsters (TV series) 134
Murder at 45 R.P.M. see *Meurtre en 45 tours*
Murder Obsession (follia omicida) (1981) 5, 9, 10, 36, 77, 132, 145, 148, 198, 245, 250, 257, 268–278, 279, 280, 328, 348
Murnau, Friedrich Wilhelm 16, 33, 54, 127, 183
Musica proibita (1942) 28
Mussetto, Giambattista 238, 325
Mussolini, Benito 4, 18, 19, 27, 30, 38, 41, 101, 102, 108, 149, 332
Mussolini, Romano 39
Mussolini and I (1985) 79
Musumeci Greco, Enzo 139, 294, 314
My Darling Clementine (1946) 6
My Dear Killer see *Mio caro assassino*
My Son, the Hero see *Arrivano i titani*
Mystery of the Wax Museum (1933) 130

The Naked Maja (1958) 335
Naldi, Ugo 177
The Name of the Game Is Kill! (1968) 270
Napoli milionaria (1950) 25
Narcejac, Thomas 241
Navarro, Antonio José 156, 241, 250
La Nave delle donne maledette (1953) 247
The Navigator (1924) 116
Nazzari, Amedeo 28, 50, 84, 86, 87, 173, 290, 294, 308
Negri, Pola 16, 333
Negroni, Baldassarre 119
Negulesco, Jean 48, 140

Nel segno di Roma (1959) 136, 168–169, 171, 296
Nelle pieghe della carne (1970) 161
Nelli, Barbara 240, 244, 245, 325
Nero, Franco 201, 230, 330
Nero's Big Weekend see *Mio figlio Nerone*
Neufeld, Max 26, 28, 293
Nicholson, James H. 158, 189
Nicodemi, Aldo 57, 84, 304, 305
Nicolodi, Daria 77, 329
The Night Evelyn Came Out of the Grave see *La Notte che Evelyn uscì dalla tomba*
Night of the Devils see *La Notte dei diavoli*
A Night to Remember (1958) 142
Nightmare Castle see *Amanti d'oltretomba*
The Nights of Cabiria see *Le Notti di Cabiria*
Ninchi, Annibale 77
Ninchi, Carlo 77, 79, 170, 306, 307, 311
Noi vivi (1942) 48
Non canto più (1945) 22, 36–39, 71, 302–303
Non c'è pace tra gli ulivi (1950) 172
Non si deve profanare il sonno dei morti (1974) 249
Noonan, Chris 284
Nosferatu, eine Symphonie des Grauens (1922) 130, 183
Nostro, Nick 126
Notorious (1946) 180
Notre Dame de Paris (novel) 16
La Notte che Evelyn uscì dalla tomba (1971) 253
La Notte dei dannati (1971) 255
La Notte dei diavoli (1972) 250, 257
Notte di fortuna (1941) 26–27, 293–294
Le Notti di Cabiria (1957) 79
Novarese, Vittorio Nino 53, 296, 304, 305, 334
Nuda per Satana (1974) 276
Nude for Satan see *Nuda per Satana*
La Nuit américaine (1973) 57, 253
Nuovo Cinema Paradiso (1988) 286

Obsession see *Ossessione*
L'Occhio nel labirinto (1972) 115
Odissea nuda (1961) 161
Odissea (1968 TV series) 140
Oggi a me... domani a te! (1968) 193
O'Hagan, Colo 282, 299
O.K. Nero see *O.K. Nerone*
O.K. Nerone (1952) 99
Oliveras, Frank 227, 236, 324
Olivier, Laurence 210
Omicron (1963) 210
Once Upon a Time in the West see *C'era una volta il West*
Operazione paura (1966) 163, 343
Ophüls, Max 22, 26, 261

L'Orfèvre du roi, ou Ascanio (novel) 16, 201, 204, 279
Orgasmo (1969) 241
Orlandi, Nora 241, 325, 326, 346
Orlando e i Paladini di Francia (1956) 113
Orlando furioso (unfilmed Freda project) 32, 113
Orlando il paladino (unfilmed Freda project) 113
L'Oro di Napoli (1954) 25, 58
Oro per i Cesari (1963) 174–176, 193, 299, 342
L'Orribile segreto del Dr. Hichcock (1962) 8, 9, 77, 94, 122, 130, 131, 132, 149, 177–189, 195, 197, 198, 199, 200, 201, 209, 241, 273, 275, 277, 318–319, 335, 343
Orsini, Umberto 160, 161, 317
Ortas, Julio 203, 213, 320, 321
Oscarito [Oscar Lorenzo Jacinto de la Imaculada Concepción Teresa Diaz] 69, 70, 71, 305
L'Ossessa (1974) 265
Ossessione (1943) 28, 36, 100
Otto, Natalino 40, 43, 303

Pabst, Georg Wilhelm 130
Pacetti, Iva 23, 292
O Pagador de promessas (1962) 71
Pagano, Bartolomeo 152
Page, Géneviève 135, 136, 314
Pagliero, Marcello 44, 295
Pagnani, Andreina 58, 304
Paisà (1946) 184
Palance, Jack 171, 172, 173, 297
Palermi, Amleto 93
Palermini, Piero 78, 306, 307
Pallottini, Riccardo 155, 297, 298, 316, 318, 341
Palmara, Mimmo 169, 296
Palmer, Renzo 267
Paluzzi, Luciana 193, 257, 327
Pandolfi, Elio 335
Pane, amore e fantasia (1953) 3
Panelli, Paolo 68, 306, 308
Pannacciò, Angelo "Elo" 258, 265
Pannunzio, Mario 37, 39
Paolella, Domenico 115, 178
Paolieri, Germana 44, 290, 295
Paolo e Francesca (1950) 75
Paolo il caldo (1973) 31
Paolo Unbound see *Paolo il caldo*
Papas, Irene 111, 222, 225, 311, 323
Paranoia see *Orgasmo*
Pareto, Vilfredo 253
Pareto, Willy see Freda, Riccardo (pseudonyms)
Parker, Alan 248
Parker, Louis N. 39
Pasolini, Pier Paolo 87, 117, 148, 172
Pasquali, Ernesto Maria 106
La Passion Béatrice (1987) 119, 124, 282, 299–300
La Passion de Jeanne d'Arc (1928) 163
Passion (1954) 105
Pastore, Sergio 249

Index

Pastrone, Giovanni 16, 19, 99, 152
Paths of Glory (1957) 97
Patrizi, Stefano 271, 272, 274, 328, 348
Pavese, Luigi 58, 303, 304, 306
Payne, Tom 70
La Peau du chagrin (novel) 201
Penn, Arthur 236
Penne nere (1952) 94, 195
Per qualche dollaro in più (1965) 200
Per un pugno di dollari (1964) 139, 202, 209, 230
Pereg, Eugenio 336
Perego, Didi 142, 315
The Perfume of the Lady in Black see *Il Profumo della signora in nero*
Périer, Etienne 241
Perseo L'invincibile (1963) 162
Perversion Story see *Una sull'altra*
Pesce, Sergio 76, 81, 306, 307, 310
Petrolini, Ettore 101
Philipsen, Preben 238, 325
Pia de' Tolomei (1941) 75
Pica, Tina 116, 312
Piccioni, Fabio 268, 269, 270, 271, 328, 348
Piccoli naufraghi (1939) 23-24, 291
Piccolis, Giovanni 54, 113, 150, 304
Pichel, Irving 130
Pickford, Mary 16, 333
Pierotti, Piero 162, 164, 173, 205, 297, 318
Pierrot le Fou (1965) 6
Pignatelli, Valerio 17
Pihodna, Joe 58
Pilgrimage (1972) 339
Piranesi, Giovanni Battista 34, 104, 191
Pirosh, Robert 89
Pistagnesi, Patrizia 273, 281, 329, 349
Pistilli, Luigi 250, 252, 253, 257, 327
Pitfall (1948) 171
Planet of the Vampires see *Terrore nello spazio*
Platt, Louise 232
Play Dirty (1968) 176
The Playgirls and the Vampire see *L'Ultima preda del vampiro*
Plume, Christian 227, 324, 345
Podestà, Rossana 173, 174, 298
Poe, Edgar Allan 23, 129, 179, 180, 182, 185, 191, 195, 196, 241
Pogany, Cristiano 266, 275, 328, 349
Pogány, Gábor 93, 104, 122, 134, 135, 170, 209, 233, 241, 242, 243, 245, 266, 295, 309, 310, 312, 314, 321, 325, 337
Poggioli, Ferdinando Maria 24, 172, 291
Poindron, Éric 15, 24, 43, 68, 72, 113, 115, 143, 150, 173, 174, 202, 253, 284, 285, 300, 332, 335, 337, 344, 349

Point Blank (1967) 345
Poitevin, Robby 241, 325
Polanski, Roman 201
Poliziotto Sprint (1977) 160
Pollack, Sydney 87
Polselli, Renato 178, 215, 271
I Pompieri di Viggiù (1949) 116
Ponchielli, Amilcare 67
Il Ponte dei sospiri (1940) 204
Pontecorvo, Gillo 142
Ponti, Carlo 52, 57, 108, 169, 170, 304
Ponti, Giò 18
Popeye (1980) 248
Porto, Ismael 73
Potocki, Jan 19
Pouctal, Henri 106
Powell, Dick 172
Powell, Michael 100
Pratelli, Esodo 18, 75, 307, 332
Prelude to Madness see *Amanti senza amore*
Preminger, Otto 248
Prendoni, Attilio 17, 26
Presle, Micheline 121, 312
Pressburger, Emeric 100
Preti, Luigi 271
Pride and Vengeance see *L'Uomo, l'orgoglio, la vendetta*
Prima della lunga notte (l'ebreo fascista) (1980) 271
The Prince and the Pauper (novel) 26, 201
Princess Cinderella see *Cenerentola e il signor Bonaventura*
Il Principe dalla maschera rossa (1955) 172
La Principessa sul pisello (1976) 266
The Prisoner of Shark Island (1936) 54
The Prisoner of Zenda (novel) 26
The Professor see *Il Camorrista*
Profondo rosso (1975) 28, 188, 200, 250, 269
Il Profumo della signora in nero (1974) 192
Profumo di donna (1974) 63
I Promessi sposi (1941) 35
Prosperi, Franco 217
The Psychic see *Sette note in nero*
Puccini, Gianni 206, 214
Uma Pulga na balança (1953) 70
Pupillo, Massimo 144
Purdom, Edmund 135, 136, 314
Pushkin, Alexander 16, 46, 87, 89, 90, 91, 137, 261

Qualcosa penetra in noi (Le notti di Satana) (unfilmed Freda project) 267-268, 271
Quante volte... quella notte (1969-1972) 193, 244
Quatermass and the Pit (1958) 145
Quatermass 2 / Enemy From Space (1956) 142
The Quatermass Xperiment (1955) 142
Queen Christina (1933) 63

The Queen of Sheba see *La Regina di Saba*
Quei due (1935) 26
Quella sporca storia nel West (1968) 207
Questi fantasmi (1954) 25
The Quiller Memorandum (1966) 185
Quinn, Anthony 271
Quo Vadis? (novel) 152
Quo Vadis? (1951) 99, 108, 112
Quo vadis? (1912) 99

Rabenalt, Arthur Maria 211
Rachmaninoff, Sergei 208
Radici, Luigi 217
Raffaele, Stefano 237, 265, 266, 268
La Ragazza che sapeva troppo (1963) 57
Raho, Umberto 75, 197, 209, 210, 273, 298, 320, 321
Rains, Claude 132, 180
Rambaldi, Carlo 150, 162, 255, 257, 316, 327, 347
Randall, Mónica 228
Randell, Ron 176, 299
Randone, Salvo 267
Rashomon (1950) 277
Raskin, Milton 169
Ratti, Filippo Walter 21, 85, 255, 258, 290, 292, 327
Rattler Kid see *Un Hombre vino a matar*
Ray, Nicholas 157, 174
Reali, Carlo 266, 348
Rear Window (1954) 224
Reazione a catena (1971) 250, 257
Rebecca (1940) 70, 180, 343
Red see *Trois Couleurs: Rouge* (1994)
The Red and the Black (novel) 50
Red River (1948) 206
The Red Shoes (1948) 103
Reed, Oliver 271
Reeve, Christopher 261
Reeves, Steve 137, 139, 140, 141, 147, 152, 171, 314, 340
Reggiani, Pietro 282
La Regina di Saba (1952) 99
Regnoli, Piero 65, 126, 266, 267, 268, 313
Reisner, Charles F. 39
Rémy, Jacques 120, 312
Repulsion (1965) 201
The Return of Dracula (1958) 127
Return to Peyton Place (1961) 193
La Revanche de Roger la Honte (1946) 221
Revenge of the Crusader see *Genoveffa di Brabante* (1964)
The Revenge of the Fly (1959) 193
Revenge of the Musketeers see *La Fille de d'Artagnan*
Reynolds, Burt 286
Rhems, J.V. 133
Ribeiro, Luiz Severiano, Jr. 69, 70, 71, 72, 73
Ricci, Luciano 173

Riccio, Attilio 68, 82, 174, 298, 299, 307, 308
Richard, Claude-Marcel 219
Richardson, John 272, 328
Richardson, Tony 247
Riento, Virgilio 38, 302
La Riffa (1991) 157
Righelli, Gennaro 20, 21, 22, 23, 25, 26, 50, 289, 290, 291, 292
Rigoletto (1947) 25, 50, 63
La Rimpatriata (1963) 339
Risi, Dino 47, 63, 120, 167
Riso amaro (1949) 55, 63, 78, 87
Ritratti d'autore (TV series) 287, 329
La Rivolta dei gladiatori (1958) 111
Roach, Hal 25
Roberti, Roberto 106
Robin Hood (1922 film) 16
Rocca, Daniela 142, 315
Rocco and His Brothers see *Rocco e i suoi fratelli*
Rocco e i suoi fratelli (1960) 2
Rodann, Ziva 151, 316
Rodrigues, João Carlos 71, 72
Roger la Honte (1946) 221
Roger la Honte (1966) 5, 9, 86, 111, 124, 221–229, 323–324
Roger-la-Honte (novel) 221
Rojo, Alfredo Molino 136
Roland the Mighty see *Orlando e i Paladini di Francia*
Rollin, Jean 215, 345
Roma città aperta (1945) 48, 52
Roma contro Roma (1964) 162
Romano, Carlo 22
Romano, Renato 250
Rome Against Rome see *Roma contro Roma*
Rome Open City see *Roma città aperta*
Romeo and Juliet (tragedy) 31, 121, 206, 207, 210, 321
Romeo e Giulietta (1964) 9, 206–210, 217, 321
Romer, Jean-Claude 194
Una Rosa per tutti (1967) 70
Rosi, Francesco 119, 236, 271, 332
Rosita (1923) 333
Rossellini, Franco 199
Rossellini, Renzo 91, 291, 309 310, 311, 312
Rossellini, Roberto 45, 48, 50, 52, 184, 210, 216
Rossen, Robert 63
Rossetti, Mario 147, 315
Rossi, Franco 70, 142, 161
Rossi Drago, Eleonora 161, 250, 317, 335
Rossini, Gioachino 65
Il Rosso segno della follia (1970) 213, 252
Roudés, Gaston 221
Rovere, Luigi 52
Roy Colt e Winchester Jack (1970) 193
Running Out of Luck (1987) 70
Rustichelli, Carlo 150, 241, 310, 315, 321

Ruy Blas (drama) 31
Ruy Blas (1948) 333
Ruy Blas (1972) 333

Sabatier, Jean-Marie 3, 10, 172
The Saint Lies in Wait see *Le Saint prend l'affût*
Le Saint prend l'affût (1966) 220
The St. Valentine's Day Massacre (1967) 236
Saint-Just, Guido see Colamonici, Raffaele
La Salamandra del deserto see *Tamar wife of Er*
Le Salamandre (1969) 248
Salce, Luciano 68, 70, 308, 333
Salgari, Emilio 16, 22
Salice, Ermanno Gurgo 169
Salò o le 120 giornate di Sodoma (1975) 87
Salò, or the 120 Days of Sodom see *Salò o le 120 giornate di Sodoma*
Salvi, Domenico "Emimmo" 134, 135, 314
Samson and the 7 Miracles of the World see *Maciste alla corte del Gran Khan*
Sangue chiama sangue (1968) 236
Sanguineti, Tatti 55
Sanipoli, Vittorio 89, 92, 100, 297, 309, 311
Sanjust, Filippo 119, 122, 144, 145, 191, 202, 203, 298, 314, 315, 320
Sanson, Yvonne 48, 63, 84, 303, 305
Sansone e il tesoro degli Incas (1964) 164
Santi, Lionello "Nello" 142, 144, 315
Santilli, Antonia 265
Santoli, Euclide 184, 185, 297, 318, 342, 343
Sapritch, Alice 216, 217, 322
Sardou, Victorien 106
Sartre, Jean-Paul 198
Sassu, Aligi 17
The Savage Innocents (1960) 157
Savalas, Telly 256
Savio, Francesco 32
Savona, Leopoldo 138, 171, 172, 296, 314, 315
Scaccia, Mario 192, 319
Scalfaro, Oscar Luigi 60, 112
The Scarecrow (1920) 116
Scarpelli, Umberto 22, 294
Scent of a Woman see *Profumo di donna*
Lo Sceriffo che non spara (1965) 215
Schiaffino, Rosanna 114
La Schiava di Roma (1961) 342
Schivazappa, Piero 252
Schneider, Samuel 146
Schurer, Erna [Emma Costantino] 151
Schwarz, Hanns 26
Scicluna Sorge, Annibale 81, 97
The Scientific Cardplayer see *Lo Scopone scientifico*

Scipio Africanus: The Defeat of Hannibal see *Scipione l'Africano*
Scipione l'Africano (1937) 19, 77, 99
Sciuscià (1946) 32
Scola, Ettore 30, 60, 282, 284, 332, 349
La Sconosciuta (1982) 272
Lo Scopone scientifico (1972) 117
Scott, Gordon 156, 157, 166, 316
Scott, Ridley 339
The Searchers (1956) 56, 155, 174
La Seconda volta (1995) 287
The Secret Invasion (1964) 38
See Naples and Die see *Vedi Napoli e poi muori*
Il Segno del comando (1971) 114
Sei donne per l'assassino (1964) 185, 274
Sennett, Mack 15, 116
Senso (1954) 108, 122
Serafin, Enzo 86, 296, 307, 308
Serenata amara (1952) 92
Sergeant Rutledge (1960) 174
Sernas, Jacques 169, 296
Il Sesso della strega (1973) 257
Sette baschi rossi (1969) 166
I Sette dell'Orsa Maggiore (1953) 94
Sette note in nero (1977) 239
Sette orchidee macchiate di rosso (1972) 239
Sette scialli di seta gialla (1972) 249
Le Sette spade del vendicatore (1962) 35, 146, 155, 176, 189–193, 198, 202, 203, 319, 344
07... tassì (1945) 43–44, 295, 334
Seven Bloodstained Orchids see *Sette orchidee macchiate di rosso*
The Seven Red Berets see *Sette baschi rossi*
Seven Seas to Calais see *Il Dominatore dei sette mari (Sir Francis Drake)*
The Seventh Sword see *Le Sette spade del vendicatore*
Severini, Leonardo 157, 316
Seward, Florence A. 174, 299
Sewell, Vernon 185
Seyn, Seyna 236
Shakespeare, William 6, 9, 31, 121, 196, 206, 207, 208, 209, 210, 321
Shane (1953) 166
Sharoff, Pietro 48, 303, 306
Shaw, Lisa 70
She (1935) 130
Sheckley, Robert 141
Shelley, Percy Bysshe 119
Sheriff Won't Shoot see *Lo Sceriffo che non spara*
The Ship of Condemned Women see *La Nave delle donne maledette*
Shoeshine see *Sciuscià*
Siciliano, Mario 166, 257
Sidney, George 78, 80, 217
Siegel, Don 142

Sienkiewicz, Henryk 152
Sievert, Johannes 240
Sign of the Gladiator see *Nel segno di Roma*
La Signora di tutti (1934) 22
Signoret, Gabriel 221
Silenti, Vira 167, 318
Silva, Franco 172, 297
Simon, François 268
Singin' in the Rain (1952) 22
Sins of Pompeii (novel) 99
Sins of Rome see *Spartaco*
Sirk, Douglas 48, 182
Sironi, Mario 18
Sissia, Duccio 90, 97, 309, 310
6 × 8 / 48 see *Tutta la città canta*
Slattery's Hurricane (1949) 171
Slaughter Hotel see *La Bestia uccide a sangue freddo*
Slave of Rome see *La Schiava di Roma*
Slave of the Cannibal God see *La Montagna del dio cannibale*
Sleep, My Love (1948) 182
Slide, Anthony 174
Smith, Paul 248, 326
Sodom and Gomorrah (1962) 140, 206
Sogno di una notte di mezza sbornia (1959) 20
Solar, Silvia 227, 228, 324
Soldati, Mario 4, 22, 29, 41, 48, 52, 99
Soler, Toni 210, 321
I Soliti ignoti (1958) 63
Solo contro Roma (1962) 173–174, 298
Solomon and Sheba (1959) 184
Sombrero (1953) 63
The Son of D'Artagnan see *Il Figlio di d'Artagnan*
Son of Samson see *Maciste nella valle dei re*
Son of Spartacus see *Il Figlio di Spartacus*
Sordi, Alberto 30, 117
Il Sorpasso (1962) 63, 87, 120, 167
Sorrentino, Alberto 116, 117, 151, 193, 312, 316, 319
Spadoni, Luciano 239, 242, 243, 318, 325
The Spanish Dancer (1923) 333
Spartaco (1953) 5, 8, 14, 91, 99–105, 109, 110, 151, 165, 211, 223 282, 284, 310–311, 337, 338
Spartacus, il gladiatore della Tracia (1913) 100
Spartacus the Gladiator see *Spartaco*
Spartacus (novel) 100
Spartacus (1960 film) 102, 105
Spatafora, Armando 160
Spencer, Bud [Carlo Pedersoli] 248, 330
Spettri (1987) 281
Lo Spettro (1963) 8, 9, 10, 61, 645, 77, 141, 182, 183, 185, 191, 194–201, 203, 209, 241, 247, 250, 251, 256, 273, 277, 278, 319–320, 344

The Spirit and the Flesh see *I Promessi sposi*
The Spy I Love see *Coplan prend des risques*
Stagecoach (1939) 34, 49, 75, 138, 156, 232
Stajano, Giò 162, 317
Stallich, Jan 93
Star Pilot see *2+5: Missione Hydra*
Star Wars Episode I: The Phantom Menace (2001) 91
Steele, Barbara 77, 122, 130, 181, 184, 185, 187, 189, *194*, 199, 201, 241, 256, 275, 318, 320, 342, 343
Stendhal [Marie-Henri Beyle] 50, 119, 120
Steno see Vanzina, Stefano
Stevens, George 166
Stevens, Paul see Gozlino, Paolo
Stevenson, Robert Louis 23, 24, 129, 179, 183, 195
Stille di sangue e lacrime di rospo (1987) 282–283, 329
Stivaletti, Sergio 273, 328
Stoll, Günther 240, 243, 325
Stoppa, Paolo 35, 48, 79, 80, 302, 303, 307
The Strange Case of Dr. Jekyll and Mr. Hyde (novelette) 129, 179
The Strange Vice of Mrs. Wardh see *Lo Strano vizio della signora Wardh*
Lo Strano vizio della signora Wardh (1970) 241
Stravinsky, Igor 7
Le Streghe (1967) 340
Strindberg, Anita 148, 271, 272, 27, 328
Strock, Herbert L. 127
Sturges, John 151
Sue, Eugène 28, 128, 221
Sul ponte dei sospiri (1953) 204
Sun, Sabine 228, 323, 324
Sundown (1941) 333
Sunset Blvd. (1950) 132
Superhuman (unfilmed Freda project) 271, 348
Susan Slept Here (1954) 105
Suspicion (1941) 180
Sutherland, Donald 60
Swanson, Gloria 132
The Sweet Body of Deborah see *Il Dolce corpo di Deborah*
The System of Doctor Tarr and Professor Feather (short story) 23

The Tales of Hoffmann (1951) 100, 103
Tamar Wife of Er (1970) 170, 245–248, 252, 254, 326, 347
Também somos irmãos (1949) 71
Tani, Umberto 112
Tani, Yōko 157, 297
Taranto, Nino 40, 42, 43, 303
Tarchetti, Iginio Ugo 255
Tashlin, Frank 105
Tate, Sharon 256

Tati, Jacques 261
Tavernier, Bertrand 1, 53, 79, 119, 120, 124, 150, 151, 191, 204, 205, 216, 223, 225, 226, 227, 228, 234, 244, 279, 282, 283, 284, 285, 299, 300, 301, 324, 329
Taylor, Robert 99
Tchaikovsky, Pyotr Ilyich 121, 122
Tchérina, Ludmilla 100, 104, 310, 337
Tempesta su Parigi (1948) see *I Miserabili*
Temple, Julien 70
Tempo di Charleston (1969) 236
Tenebre (1982) 77
Tenori per forza (1951) 68, 308–309
Teodora imperatrice di Bisanzio (1909) 106
Teodora (1954) 5, 6, 8, 83, 91, 105–113, 114, 121, 132, 139, 147, 150, 156, 164, 165, 168, 170, 211, 247, 284, 311–312
Teodora (1914) 106
Teodora (1921) 106
Der Teppich des Grauens (1962) 161
La Terra trema (1948) 68
Terra Violenta (1948) 70, 72
The Terror of Dr. Hichcock see *L'Orribile segreto del Dr. Hichcock*
Terror-Creatures From the Grave see *5 tombe per un medium* (1965)
Il Terrore con gli occhi storti (1972) 256
Terrore nello spazio (1965) 151
Il Terzo occhio (1966) 201
Tessari, Duccio 154, 155, 297, 316
Testa, Carlo 55
Testi, Fabio 260
Il Testimone (1945) 172
Thanat 82 (unfilmed Freda project) 266–267
That Is the Dawn see *Cela s'appelle L'aurore*
Theodora, le cadeau de Dieu (novel) 106
Theodora, Slave Empress see *Teodora* (1954)
Theodora (1884 stage play) 106
Théodora (1912) 106
They Paid with Bullets: Chicago 1929 see *Tempo di Charleston* (1969)
Thieves' Highway (1949) 57
The Third Eye see *Il Terzo occhio*
Thompson, J. Lee 222
Three Coins in the Fountain (1954) 48
The Three Musketeers (novel) 16, 78, 279
The Three Musketeers (1948 film) 78, 217
Tichy, Gérard 237
Tinti, Gabriele 193, 225, 268, 298, 319, 323
To Catch a Spy see *Action immédiate*

Today We Kill... Tomorrow We Die! see *Oggi a me... domani a te!*
Tofano, Sergio 35, 293
Togni, Darix 104, 311
Tolnay, Ákos 93, 294, 314
Tolstoy, Leo 16, 50, 137, 140, 314, 340
Tonti, Aldo 24, 291, 294, 295
Torelli, Roberto 284, 349
Tormento (1950) 81
Torna! (1953) 84
Tornatore, Giuseppe 23, 57, 286, 287, 329, 343, 348
Torrisi, Pietro 157
Die Tote aus der Themse (1971) 243
Totò a colori (1952) 94, 115
Totò cerca casa (1950) 74
Totò e Carolina (1955) 85
Totò le Moko (1949) 74
Totò nella luna (1958) 142
Totò [Antonio De Curtis] 25, 38, 40, 42, 79, 116, 142, 152, 249, 334, 336, 338
Un Tour de manège (1989) 282, 300
The Tower of Nesle (novel) 16
Tozzi, Fausto 121, 312
Il Tradimento (Passato che uccide) (1951) 8, 28, 84–87, 91, 124, 164, 173, 224, 308
Tragic Ceremony see *Estratto dagli archivi segreti della polizia di una capitale europea*
Trágica ceremonia en villa Alexander see *Estratto dagli archivi segreti della polizia di una capitale europea*
Tranché, André 249
Tranquilli, Silvano 181, 185, 186, 187, 318
Trapeze (1956) 151
Trapped in Tangiers see *Agguato a Tangeri*
Trappola per l'assassino see *Roger la Honte* (1966)
Trasatti, Luciano 168, 296
Travolta, John 273
Tre notti violente (1966) 126
I Tre volti della paura (1963) 141, 200, 226
Treasure Island (novel) 24
Trent, Peter 77, 79, 89, 306, 307, 309
Trintignant, Jean-Louis 120, 126
Tristezas Não Pagam Dívidas (1944) 70
Trois Couleurs: Rouge (1994) 151
Le Trou (1960) 161
Il Trovatore (1949) 163
Truffaut, François 57, 221
Trumbo, Dalton 102
Il Tuo vizio è una stanza chiusa e solo io ne ho la chiave (1972) 182
Tutta la città canta (1945) 20, 21, 39–44, 71, 303, 334
Tutti i colori del buio (1972) 257
Twain, Mark 23, 26, 201

2+5: Missione Hydra (1966) 166
Two Nights with Cleopatra see *Due notti con Cleopatra*

L'Uccello dalle piume di cristallo (1970) 240, 248, 269
Uccidete Johnny Ringo (1966) 193
Uhlig, Anneliese 35, 302
Ulisse (1954) 108, 112
L'Ultima preda del vampiro (1960) 266
Gli Ultimi giorni di Pompei (1950) 68, 81
Gli Ultimi giorni di Pompei (1959) 144, 159
L'Ultimo combattimento (1941) 37
Umberto D. (1952) 50
Una sull'altra (1969) 240, 245
Under Capricorn (1949) 180
Under the Olive Tree see *Non c'è pace tra gli ulivi* (1950)
Uomini e lupi (1957) 172
L'Uomo di Toledo (1965) 214
L'Uomo, l'orgoglio, la vendetta (1967) 210
Un Uomo solo—Incontro con Riccardo Freda (1998) 287, 329
Upchurch, Alan 186
Un Urlo dalle tenebre (1975) 265
Usellini, Guglielmo 18, 332

Vadim, Roger 216
Vajda, László 93
Valenti, Osvaldo 41
Valentino, Rudolph 16, 46, 48
Valerii, Tonino 219, 330
Valori, Bice 68, 308
Der Vampir von Notre Dame see *I Vampiri*
The Vampire and the Ballerina see *L'Amante del vampiro*
The Vampire of the Opera see *Il Mostro dell'opera*
The Vampire see *El Vampiro*
The Vampire's Coffin see *El Ataúd del vampiro*
Les Vampires (1915) 128
I Vampiri (1957) 3, 5, 8, 10, 77, 80, 103, 123, 126–134, 141, 142, 144, 149, 165, 166, 183, 184, 188, 189, 201, 217, 241, 250, 256, 257, 266, 275, 277, 287, 313–314, 339, 343, 344
El Vampiro (1957) 128
Vampyr (1932) 80, 130, 182
Vancini, Florestano 193
Van Cleef, Lee 234
Van Vogt, Alfred Elton 141
Vanzina, Stefano [a.k.a. Steno] 4, 37 41, 43, 47, 53, 59, 75, 79, 89, 99, 142, 192, 256, 261, 302, 303, 305, 306
Varelli, Alfredo 236, 296, 316
Vargas, Daniele 144, 145, 315
Vari, Giuseppe 162
Vecchietti, Alberto 91, 309
Vedi Napoli e poi muori (1952) 7, 74, 79, 85, 91–94, 97, 109, 114, 116, 309–310

Velázquez, Diego 34
Vendaval maravilhoso (1949) 70, 72
La Vendetta di Aquila Nera (1951) 5, 74, 77, 79, 87–91, 97, 124, 135, 138, 202, 213, 309, 336
La Vendetta di Spartacus (1964) 337
La Vendetta di Ursus (1961) 151
The Vengeance of the Black Eagle see *La Vendetta di Aquila Nera*
La Vengeance of Ursus see *La Vendetta di Ursus*
Venturini, Simone 144, 339
La Vera storia di Frank Mannata (1969, Javier Setó) 236
Verdi, Giuseppe 65, 67, 307
Verfluchte Liebe deutscher Film (2016) 240
Verga, Giovanni 262
La Vergine di Norimberga (1963) 173
Verneuil, Henri 221
Veronese, Paolo 28, 121
Vertigo (1958) 241
Véry, Pierre 261
Vianello, Maria Teresa 152, 185, 316, 318
Vicario, Marco 31, 173, 298, 342
Vicario, Renato [Gastad Green] 173
Vích, Václav 27, 93, 293, 315
Le Vicomte de Bragelonne (1954) 111
Vidal, Henri 217
Vidali, Enrico 100
Vidor, King 16, 171
Vigezzi, Silvio 17
Vignola, Robert G. 333
Vilar, António 66, 67, 68, 306, 308
Villa, Claudio 92, 93, 309, 336
Villiers, Gérard de 217
Violent Summer see *Estate violenta*
The Virgin of Nuremberg see *La Vergine di Norimberga*
Visconti, Luchino 2, 28, 36, 53, 68, 100, 108, 122, 124, 140, 208, 245, 271, 332
Vitale, Gianni 282, 329
Vittorio Emanuele III of Savoia 41
Vivo per la tua morte (1968) 140
I Vizi morbosi di una governante (1977) 255
Vlad, Roman 188, 200, 313, 318
Una Voce nel tuo cuore (1949) 44
La Voce senza volto (1939) 22, 290–291
Vohrer, Alfred 238
La Voie lactée (1969) 111
Volonté, Gian Maria 236
Von Stroheim, Erich 16
Vredens dag (1943) 163
Vulcan Son of Jupiter see *Vulcano figlio di Giove*
Vulcano figlio di Giove (1962) 134

Wallace, Edgar 238, 239, 240, 243
Walsh, Raoul 3

War and Peace (novel) 137
War and Peace (1956) 171
The Warrior and the Slave Girl see *La Rivolta dei gladiatori*
The Wasp Woman (1959) 128
Waters, Sandra A. 119
Way Out West (1937) 25
Wayne, John 172, 232
Weber, Jacques 333
The Weekend Murders see *Concerto per pistola solista*
Welles, Mel 167
Welles, Orson 34, 70, 135, 337
Wells, Herbert George 141
Wendlandt, Horst 238, 240, 243
Werewolf in a Girls' Dormitory see *Lycanthropus*
West Side Story (1961) 206
What Have You Done to Solange? see *Cosa avete fatto a Solange?*
Wheeler, René 106, 311
The Whip and the Body see *La Frusta e il corpo*
White, Harriet 34, 184, 185, 186, 187, 196, 211, 318, 320
White, Pearl 14
The White Warrior see *Agi Murad—Il diavolo bianco*
The Whole Town's Talking (1935) 42
Whorf, Richard 182
Wiene, Robert 130
The Wild, Wild Planet see *I Criminali della galassia*
Wilder, Billy 26, 199
Wildt, Adolfo 17, 278
Wilson, Georges 338
Wiseman, Nicholas 99
The Witch's Curse see *Maciste all'inferno* (1962)
The Wonder Years (TV series) 199
Woods, Robert 245
Wordsworth, Richard 142
The Wrong Man (1956) 224
Wuthering Heights (novel) 50, 180
Wyler, Richard [Richard Staples] 217, 219, 200, 323
Wyler, William 109

Yeaworth, Irvin S., Jr. 142
Les Yeux sans visage (1960) 193
Young and Innocent (1937) 80
Young, Violent, Dangerous see *Liberi, armati, pericolosi*
Your Vice Is a Closed Room and Only I Have the Key see *Il Tuo vizio è una stanza chiusa e solo io ne ho la chiave*

Zampa, Luigi 32, 37, 39, 172, 193, 295
Zampari, Franco 69, 70
Zanolli, Angelo 164, 318
Zanuck, Darryl 48
Zappulla, Felice 30
Zarchi, Meir 258
Zavattini, Cesare 31, 32, 42, 113, 307
Zeffirelli, Franco 210, 253, 345
Zeglio, Primo 62
Zévaco, Michel 204
Zinneman, Fred 114
Zorba the Greek (1964) 222

www.ingramcontent.com/pod-product-compliance
Lightning Source LLC
Chambersburg PA
CBHW081535300426
44116CB00015B/2642